The hills and glens and wild coastline of Scotland's Highlands and Islands offer the ultimate escape – one of the last corners of Europe where you can discover genuine solitude.

(left) Loch Erisort, Lewis
(below) Highland Games

D0418398

coast rides, complemented by Britain's best purpose-built MTB (mountain bike) centres offering everything from beginners' zones to funparks to nerve-shredding downhill courses. For sea-kayaking enthusiasts, the turbulent tidal waters around the Outer Hebrides, Orkney and Shetland provide the ultimate test of paddling mettle.

And then there's a treasure trove of unparallelled wildlife experiences to be discovered. Where else can you watch an osprey swoop and snatch a trout from a loch, witness a minke whale breach through a shoal of mackerel, and make eye contact with an otter – all in one day?

Legend & Tradition

Legend and tradition run deep in the Highlands. Crumbling forts and monastic cells were once home to Gaelic chieftains and Irish saints; lonely beaches and mountain passes once echoed to the clash of clan battles and Viking raids; and empty glens are still haunted by the ghosts of the Clearances.

History is everywhere – in the tumbled stones and vague outlines of township and field preserved on a hillside like a fossil fragment; in the proud profile of broch and castle silhouetted against a Highland sunset; in the Gaelic lilt of Hebridean speech and the Nordic twang of Shetland dialect.

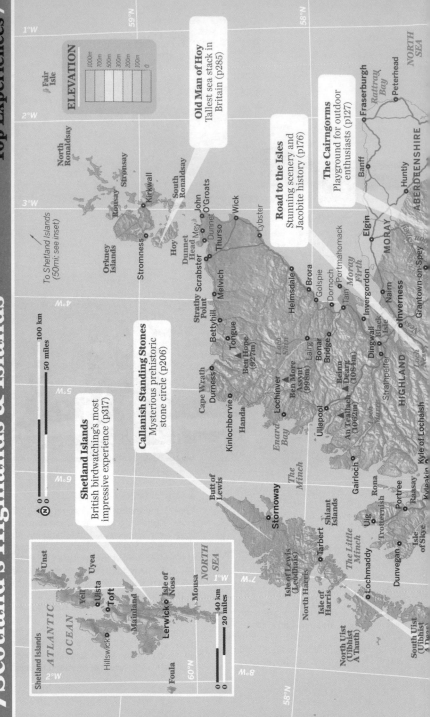

ELEVATION

1000m
700m
500m
300m
200m
100m
0

Old Man of Hoy
Tallest sea stack in Britain (p285)

The Cairngorms
Playground for outdoor enthusiasts (p127)

Road to the Isles
Stunning scenery and Jacobite history (p176)

Callanish Standing Stones
Mysterious prehistoric stone circle (p206)

Shetland Islands
British birdwatching's most impressive experience (p317)

To Shetland Islands (50mi; see inset)

Shetland Islands

ATLANTIC OCEAN

NORTH SEA

Unst
Uyea
Yell
Ulsta
Toft
Mainland
Hillswick
Lerwick
Isle of Noss
Mousa
Foula

100 km
50 miles
40 km
20 miles

North Ronaldsay
Stronsay
Sanday
Rousay
Kirkwall
South Ronaldsay
Orkney Islands
Stromness
Hoy
Dunnet Head
Mey
Dunnet
John O'Groats
Wick
Lybster
Scrabster
Thurso
Strathy Point
Melvich
Bettyhill
Tongue
Cape Wrath
Durness
Handa
Kinlochbervie
Lochinver
Ben Hope (927m)
Ben More Assynt (998m)
Ben Klibreck
Loch Shin
Lairg
Bonar Bridge
Helmsdale
Brora
Golspie
Dornoch
Tain
Portmahomack
Moray Firth
Invergordon
Nairn
Dingwall
Black Isle
Strathpeffer
Inverness
Grantown-on-Spey
Elgin
MORAY
Nairn
Loch Ness
HIGHLAND
An Teallach (1062m)
Beinn Dearg (1084m)
Ullapool
Enard Bay
Gairloch
Rona
Raasay
Portree
Trotternish
Isle of Skye
Uig
Dunvegan
Kyleakin
Kyle of Lochalsh
Lochmaddy
North Uist (Uibhist A Tuath)
Isle of Harris
North Harris
Tarbert
Isle of Lewis (Leodhais)
Stornoway
Butt of Lewis
The Minch
The Little Minch
Shiant Islands
South Uist (Uibhist A Deas)
Peterhead
Rattray Bay
Fraserburgh
Banff
Huntly
ABERDEENSHIRE
NORTH SEA

Fair Isle

Ben Nevis
Climb the highest Munro of them all (p169)

Glen Coe
Dramatic scenery meets deep history (p171)

South Harris
Spectacular white-sand beaches (p209)

Cuillin Hills
Craggy peaks and inaccessible pinnacles (p188)

Iona
Scotland's most sacred island (p97)

West Highland Way
The best Highland hiking (p106)

ROAD DISTANCES (mi)
Note: Distances are approximate

	Fort William	Inverness	Kyle of Lochalsh	Mallaig	Oban	Scrabster
Inverness	66					
Kyle of Lochalsh	76	82				
Mallaig	44	106	34			
Oban	45	110	120	85		
Scrabster	185	119	214	238	230	
Ullapool	90	135	88	166	161	125

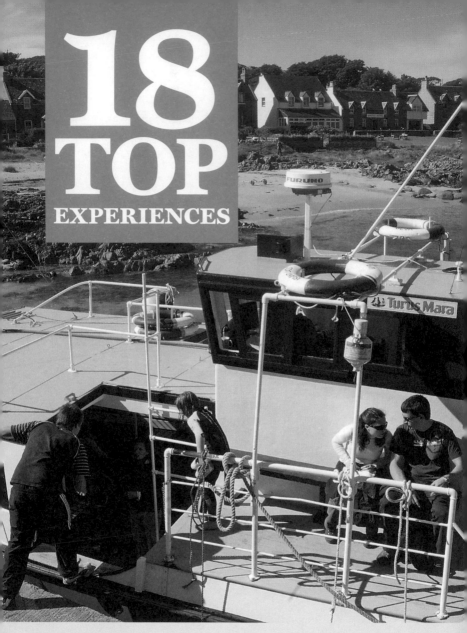

Island-hopping

1 Much of the unique character of western and northern Scotland is down to the expansive vistas of sea and islands – there are more than 700 islands off Scotland's coast, of which almost 100 are inhabited. A network of ferry services links these islands to the mainland and each other, and buying an Island Rover ticket (unlimited ferry travel for 15 days; see p36) provides a fascinating way to explore. It's possible to hop all the way from Arran or Bute to the Outer Hebrides, touching the mainland only at Kintyre and Oban.

Walking the West Highland Way

2 The best way to appreciate the scale and grandeur of Scotland's landscapes is to walk them. Despite the wind and midges and drizzle, walking here is a pleasure, with numerous short- and long-distance trails, coastal paths and mountains begging to be trekked. Top of the wish list for many hikers is the 95-mile West Highland Way (p106) from Milngavie (near Glasgow) to Fort William, a challenging, week-long walk through some of the country's finest scenery, finishing in the shadow of its highest peak, Ben Nevis. Glen Coe (p171)

ROCCO FASANO/LONELY PLANET IMAGES ©

Whisky

3 Scotland's national drink – from the Gaelic *uisge bagh*, meaning 'water of life' – has been distilled here for more than 500 years. More than 100 distilleries are still in operation, producing hundreds of varieties of single malt. Learning to distinguish the smoky, peaty whiskies of Islay, say, from the flowery, sherried malts of Speyside has become a hugely popular pastime. Many distilleries offer guided tours, rounded off with a tasting session, and ticking off the local varieties is a great way to explore the whisky-making regions. Glenfiddich Distillery (p136)

Cuillin Hills

4 In a country famous for its stunning scenery, the Cuillin Hills (p188) take top prize. This range of craggy peaks inspired the 19th-century poets and painters of the Romantic movement, and provided the ultimate training ground for British Alpinists. Its rocky summits are out of bounds to all except experienced walkers, but there are easy trails through the glens and into the corries, where hikers can soak up the views and share the landscape with red deer and golden eagles.

JONATHAN SMITH/LONELY PLANET IMAGES ©

Seafood

5 One of the great pleasures of a visit to Scotland is the opportunity to indulge in the rich harvest of the sea. The cold, clear waters around the Scottish coast provide some of the most sought-after seafood in Europe, with much of it being whisked straight from the quayside to waiting restaurant tables from London to Lisbon. Fortunately there are plenty of places to sample this bounty right here, with Oban (p75) topping the list of towns with more than their fair share of seafood restaurants.

Whale-watching

6 Scotland is one of the best places in Europe for seeing marine wildlife. In high season (July and August) many cruise operators on the west coast can almost guarantee sightings of Minke whales and porpoises, and the Moray Firth (p149) is famous for its resident population of bottlenose dolphins. Basking sharks – at up to 12m, the biggest fish to be found in British waters – are also commonly seen. And it's not just the wildlife that makes a boat trip a must – don't miss the chance to visit the Corryvreckan whirlpool (p86).

Castles

7 Whether you're looking for grim, desolate stone fortresses looming in the mist; noble royal castles towering over historic towns; or luxurious palaces built in expansive grounds by lairds more concerned with status and show than with military might – the Highlands sport the full range of castles, reflecting the region's turbulent history. Most castles have a story or 10 to tell of plots, intrigues, imprisonments and treachery, and a worryingly high percentage have a phantom rumoured to stalk their parapets. But for that perfect picture, none can beat Eilean Donan Castle (p163; above).

Sea Kayaking

8 The convoluted coastline and countless islands of Scotland's western seaboard are widely recognised as one of the finest sea kayaking areas in the world. Paddling your own canoe allows you to explore remote islands, inlets, creeks and beaches that are inaccessible on foot, and also provides an opportunity to get close to wildlife such as seals, otters, dolphins and seabirds. There are dozens of outfits offering guided kayaking tours for beginners, from a half day to a week, either camping on wild beaches or staying in comfortable B&Bs (see p34).

EOIN CLARKE/LONELY PLANET IMAGES ©

Glen Coe

9 Scotland's most famous glen combines those two essential qualities of the Highland landscape – dramatic scenery and deep history. The peacefulness and beauty of this valley today belie the fact that it was the scene of a ruthless 17th-century massacre that saw the local MacDonalds murdered by soldiers of the Campbell clan. Some of the glen's finest walks, for example to the Lost Valley (p171), follow the routes used by clansmen and women trying to flee their attackers, routes where many perished in the snow.

Ceilidhs

10 The traditional evening of Scottish dancing (*céilidh*, pronounced kay-ley, is Gaelic for a social gathering), with music provided by fiddles, bodhrans (handheld drums) and other instruments, has evolved into something of a tourist spectacle, but there are still plenty of places in the Highlands and Islands where *ceilidhs* are staged for the locals rather than tourists – and visitors are always welcome (see p339). Don't worry if you don't know the steps; there's usually a 'caller' to lead dancers through their paces, and no one cares if you get it wrong as long as you're enjoying yourself!

Callanish Standing Stones

11 Few sights conjure up the mystery and romance of the Highlands and Islands like the prehistoric monuments that punctuate the landscape from Orkney to the Western Isles. The 5000-year-old Callanish stones (p206) on the Isle of Lewis – contemporaries of the pyramids of Egypt – are the archetypal stone circle, with beautifully weathered slabs of banded gneiss arranged as if in worship around a central monolith. To experience the stones at dawn, before the crowds arrive, is to step back in time and sense something deep and truly ancient.

Picturesque Iona

12 Legend has it that when St Columba left Ireland in 563 to found a missionary outpost on Scotland's west coast, he kept sailing until he found a spot where he could no longer see his homeland on the southern horizon. That place was the little jewel of Iona (p97) – Scotland's most sacred island and one of its most beautiful, with lush green pastures bordered by pink granite rocks, white shell-sand beaches and shallow turquoise waters. The Iona Community continues the island's spiritual calling in an abbey on the site of Columba's first chapel. Baile Mor village

RICHARD BOOT / ALAMY ©

The Road to the Isles

13 Immortalised in song and story, the Road to the Isles (p176) is the route from Fort William to Mallaig – jumping off point for the Isle of Skye, the Small Isles and beyond to the Outer Hebrides. Steeped in Jacobite history – Bonnie Prince Charlie passed this way several times around 1745 – the route (followed by both road and railway) passes through some of Scotland's finest scenery, with views over dazzling white-sand beaches and emerald waters to a horizon pricked by the sharp peaks of Eigg, Rum and Skye.

Climbing Ben Nevis

14 The allure of Britain's highest peak is strong – around 100,000 people a year set off up the summit trail, though not all will make it to the top. Nevertheless, the highest Munro of them all is within the ability of anyone who's reasonably fit – treat Ben Nevis (p169) with respect and your reward (weather permitting) will be a truly magnificent view and a great sense of achievement. Real walking enthusiasts can warm up by hiking the 95-mile West Highland Way (p106) first.

Birdlife in Shetland

15 Sparsely populated, and with large areas of wild land, Scotland is an important sanctuary for all sorts of wildlife. Amazing birdwatching is on offer throughout the country, but the seabird cities of the Shetland Islands (p317) take first prize for spectacle. From their first arrival on the sea cliffs in late spring to the raucous feeding frenzies of high summer, the vast colonies of gannets, guillemots, puffins and kittiwakes at Hermaness, Noss and Sumburgh Head provide one of British bird-watching's most impressive experiences. Puffin, Shetland Islands

Old Man of Hoy

16 From the Mull of Kintyre to Duncansby Head, the patient craftsmanship of the sea has whittled the Scottish coastline into a profusion of sea stacks, chasms and natural arches. Many stacks are nicknamed 'old man', but none compare to the grandest old man of them all. At 137m tall (a third taller than London's Big Ben), the Old Man of Hoy (p285) is the tallest sea stack in Britain (excluding St Kilda). Hike from Rackwick Bay (p298) for a spectacular view of the stack and, if you're lucky, rock climbers in action on its sheer faces.

The Cairngorms

17 In the bare, boulder-strewn, 4000ft-high plateau of the Cairngorms (p127), Scotland harbours its own little haven of subarctic tundra. The haunt of ptarmigan and snow bunting, red deer and reindeer, these austerely beautiful granite mountains provide a year-round playground for outdoors enthusiasts, from summer hiking and mountain biking along winding trails through the ancient Caledonian pine forest to skiing, snowboarding and full-on mountaineering on the snowy summits in the midst of winter.

Beaches of South Harris

18 Scotland's Highlands and Islands are never going to be famous for bucket-and-spade seaside holidays, but when it comes to scenically spectacular beaches, the region is up there with the best. And the vast stretches of blinding white shell-sand that line the west coast of Harris (p209) in the Outer Hebrides are among the most beautiful in Europe – grass-covered dunes sprinkled with pink and yellow wild flowers, clear sparkling waters that range in hue from turquoise to emerald, and sunset views that take your breath away.

need to know

Currency
» Pound Sterling (£)

Language
» English
» Gaelic and Lallans

When to Go

Cool to mild summers, cold winters

Lerwick
GO mid-May–mid-July

Kirkwall
GO May–Aug

Stornoway
GO May

Inverness
• GO May–Sep

Fort William
• GO May or Sep

High Season
(Jul & Aug)

» Accommodation prices 10%–20% higher (book in advance if possible)

» Warmest time of year, but often wet, too

» Midges at their worst

Shoulder Season
(May, Jun & Sep)

» Wildflowers and rhododendrons bloom in May and June

» Best chance for dry weather; fewer midges

» June evenings have daylight till 11pm

Low Season
(Oct–Apr)

» Rural attractions and accommodation often closed

» Snow on hills November to March

» In December it gets dark at 4pm

» Can be very cold and wet November to March

Your Daily Budget

Less than
£30

» Dorm beds: £10–£20

» Wild camping is free

» Cheap supermarkets for self-caterers

» Lots of free museums and galleries

Midrange
£30–£100

» Double room in midrange B&B: £50–£90

» B&Bs often better value than midrange hotels

» Bar lunch: £10; dinner in midrange restaurant: £25

» Car hire: £30 a day

» Petrol costs: around 12p per mile

Top End over
£100

» Double room in high-end hotel: £120–£250

» Dinner at high-end restaurant: £40–£60

» Flights to islands: £60–£120 each

Money
» ATMs widely available. Credit cards widely accepted.

Visas
» Generally not needed for stays of up to six months. Not a member of the Schengen Zone.

Mobile Phones
» Uses the GSM 900/1800 network. Local SIM cards can be used in European and Australian phones. Patchy coverage in remote areas.

Driving
» Drive on the left; steering wheel on right side of car.

Websites
» **Lonely Planet** (www.lonelyplanet.com/Scotland) Destination information, forums, hotel bookings, shop.

» **VisitScotland** (www.visitscotland.com) Official tourism site; booking services.

» **Internet Guide to Scotland** (www.scotland-info.co.uk) Best online tourist guide to Scotland.

» **Traveline** (www.travelinescotland.com) Public transport timetables.

» **WalkHighlands** (www.walkhighlands.co.uk) Detailed walking guide with maps.

Exchange Rates

Australia	A$1	£0.63
Canada	C$1	£0.61
Euro zone	€1	£0.87
Japan	¥100	£0.79
New Zealand	NZ$1	£0.50
USA	US$1	£0.60

For current exchange rates, see www.xe.com.

Important Numbers

Country code	☏+44
International access code	☏00
Ambulance	☏112 or 999
Fire	☏112 or 999
Police	☏112 or 999

Arriving in Scotland
» **Edinburgh Airport**
Buses – to Edinburgh city centre every 10 to 15 minutes from 4.30am to midnight
Night buses – every 30 minutes from 12.30am to 4am
Taxis – £15–20; about 20 minutes to the city centre

» **Glasgow Airport**
Buses – to Glasgow city centre every 10 to 15 minutes from 6am to 11pm
Night buses – hourly 11pm to 4am, half-hourly 4am to 6am
Taxis – £20–25; about 30 minutes to city centre

Midges
If you've never been to the Scottish Highlands and Islands before, be prepared for an encounter with the dreaded midge. These tiny, 2mm-long blood-sucking flies appear in huge swarms in summer, and can completely ruin a holiday if you're not prepared to deal with them.

They proliferate from late May to mid-September, but especially mid-June to mid-August – which unfortunately coincides with the main tourist season – and are most common in the western and northern Highlands. Midges are at their worst during the twilight hours, and on still, overcast days; strong winds and bright sunshine tend to discourage them.

The only way to combat them is to cover up, particularly in the evening. Wear long-sleeved, light-coloured clothing (midges are attracted to dark colours) and, most importantly, use a reliable insect repellent (see also p33).

if you like...

Outdoor Adventures

Scotland is one of Europe's finest outdoor adventure playgrounds. The rugged mountain terrain and convoluted coastline of the Highlands and Islands offer unlimited opportunities for physical activities.

Fort William The self-styled 'Outdoor Capital of the UK'; a centre for hiking, climbing, mountain biking and winter sports (p165)

Shetland One of Scotland's top coastlines for sea kayaking, with an abundance of bird and sea life to observe from close quarters (p300)

Laggan Wolftrax Mountain biking for all abilities, from easy forest trails to black-diamond down hilling (p133)

Cairngorms Winter skiing and summer walking amid the epic beauty of this high, subarctic plateau (p130)

Thurso At the top of Scotland, this is an unlikely surfing mecca, but once you've got the drysuit on the waves are world-class (p237)

Scapa Flow The scuttling of the German High Seas Fleet at the end of WWI has made this one of Europe's top diving sites (p283)

Prehistoric Sites

The Highlands and Islands are home to some of the most impressive prehistoric remains in Europe, from perfectly preserved neolithic villages to entire ancient landscapes of stone circles and passage tombs.

Skara Brae Most famous of all is Orkney's neolithic village, where circular houses uncovered by eroding sand dunes preserve Stone Age furniture and fittings (p272)

Maes Howe This enormous passage tomb, with a corbelled roof skillfully constructed from stone slabs, has the added intrigue of Viking graffiti (p274)

Ring of Brodgar One of Scotland's most evocative prehistoric sites, this vast circle of weathered sandstone slabs impresses with sheer scale (p274)

Callanish Standing Stones Gnarled fingers of gneiss shaggy with lichen, the stones of Callanish are contemporary with the pyramids of Egypt (p206)

Kilmartin Glen With hill forts, chambered cairns, standing stones and rock carvings, this is Scotland's biggest concentration of prehistoric sites (p70)

Old Scatness This Shetland site is still being investigated, offering the chance to see archaeologists at work (p314)

Rural Museums

Every bit as interesting and worthy of study as 'big-picture' history such as Mary Queen of Scots and Bonnie Prince Charlie – and especially if you're investigating your Scottish ancestry – the history of rural communties is preserved in a wide range of fascinating museums, often in original farm buildings and historic houses.

Arnol Blackhouse Preserved in peat smoke since its last inhabitant left in the 1960s, a genuine slice of 'living history' (p206)

Highland Folk Museum Fascinating outdoor museum populated with real historic buildings that have been reassembled here on site (p133)

Scottish Crannog Centre Head back to the Bronze Age in this excellent archaeological reconstruction of a fortified loch house (p118)

Tain Through Time Very entertaining local museum with comprehensive display on Scottish history and Tain's silversmithing tradition (p225)

Stromness Museum Delightful small-town museum with exhibits on the Orkney fishing industry, the World Wars, and local marine wildlife (p271)

DAVID WALL/LONELY PLANET IMAGES ©

» Entrance to Fingal's Cave (p97).

Coastal Scenery

Scotland's 7000 miles of coastline conjures up a magical combination of mountain, sea and island that conspires with the low northern sunlight to create some of Europe's most beautiful coastal scenery.

Ardnamurchan The most westerly point on the British mainland is also one of the most scenic, with superb sunset views north and south to the islands of Skye and Mull (p174)

Achiltibuie This remote village enjoys a gorgeous coastal setting, looking out across the jewel-like Summer Isles to the distant mountains of Wester Ross (p250)

Applecross Majestic views of the hills of Skye and magical sunset moments at this isolated village (p261)

Tongue Wild sea lochs penetrate the rocky coast like steely blades on this lonely stretch of the north coast (p240)

Arisaig & Morar Long strands of silver sands and stunning panoramas to the isles of Eigg and Rum (p177)

Unst The most northerly point of the British Isles boasts seabird cities ranged on ragged cliffs, and the lighthouse-topped stack of Muckle Flugga (p318)

Classic Hikes

Scotland's wild, dramatic scenery and varied landscape has made hiking a hugely popular pastime. There's something for all levels of fitness and enthusiasm, but the really keen hiker will want to tick off some (or all) of these classic walks.

West Highland Way The grandaddy of Scottish long-distance walks, the one everyone wants to do (p106)

Glen Affric to Shiel Bridge A classic two-day cross-country hike, with a night in a remote hostel (p158)

Great Glen Way The easiest of Scotland's long-distance paths, linking Fort William to Inverness. It can be done as an extension of the West Highland Way (p159)

Speyside Way Follow the mighty River Spey through the heart of whisky country to the mountain resort of Aviemore (p31)

Cape Wrath Trail From Fort William to Scotland's northwest corner through some of the country's remotest landscapes (p244)

Machair Way A peaceful and leisurely path along the beaches and wildflower-strewn dunes of the Uists (p212)

Remote Islands

Scotland has more than 700 islands scattered around its shore. Most visitors stick to the larger ones, such as Arran, Skye, Mull and Lewis, but the highlights of Scottish island hopping can often be found on the more remote, lesser-known isles.

Iona Beautiful, peaceful (once the daytrippers have left) and of huge historic and cultural importance, Iona is the jewel of the Hebrides (p97)

Eigg The most intriguing of the Small Isles, with its miniature mountain, massacre cave and singing sands (p107)

Jura Wild and untamed, with more deer than people, and a dangerous whirlpool at its northern end (p86)

Handa Huge cliffs, raucous seabird colonies, and a view of the Great Stack of Handa are your reward for a hike to the western edge of this small but beautiful island (p247)

Westray & Papa Westray These magical islands at Orkney's northern end have great accommodation and eating options, coastal scenery, birdwatching, and historic sights (p294)

St Kilda Remote, spectacular and difficult to get to, the soaring stacks of St Kilda are the ultimate tick for island collectors (p214)

If you like... downhill mountain biking
Hit the trails at Nevis Range (p170) and Highland Wildcat (p230)

If you like... mystical islands
Head out to the Orkneys where shipwrecks and standing stones add ancient tales to its spectacular scenery (p267)

Natural Wonders

Scotland's stunning landscapes harbour many awe-inspiring natural features: spectacular sea stacks and rock formations, thundering waterfalls, impressive gorges and swirling tidal whirlpools.

Old Man of Hoy While most of the Orkneys is fairly flat, Hoy is rugged and rocky; its spectacular west coast includes Britain's tallest sea stack (p285)

Corryvreckan Whirlpool One of the world's three most powerful tidal whirlpools, squeezed between Jura and Scarba (p86)

Falls of Measach A trembling suspension bridge provides a scary viewpoint for one of Scotland's most impressive waterfalls (p257)

Quiraing Skye has many impressive rock formations, but the weird world of the Quiraing takes first place for strangeness (p194)

Fingal's Cave Accessible only by boat, this columnar sea cave inspired Mendelssohn's Hebrides Overture (p97)

Falls of Lora The surge of the sea through the narrow mouth of Loch Etive creates the country's most impressive tidal whitewater rapids (p79)

Historic Castles

The clash and conflict of Scotland's colourful history has left a legacy of military strongholds scattered across the Highlands and Islands, from clan strongholds perched on defensive crags to the island fortresses that controlled the seaways for the Lords of the Isles.

Dunvegan Castle The ancient seat of Clan Macleod is home to fascinating relics, including the legendary Fairy Flag (p193)

Duart Castle Commanding the entrance to the Sound of Mull, this Maclean stronghold is one of the oldest inhabited castles in Scotland (p92)

Dunrobin Castle The largest country house in the Highlands offers a peek at the opulent lifestyle enjoyed by the Duke of Sutherland (p229)

Kisimul Castle Seat of Clan MacNeil, this archetypal Highland castle is perched on a Hebridean islet, accessible only by boat (p213)

Craigievar Castle The epitome of the Scottish Baronial style, all towers and turrets (p137)

Eilean Donan Castle Perfect lochside location conveniently located by the main road to Skye makes this the Highlands' most photographed fortress (p163)

Wild Beaches

Nothing clears a whisky hangover like a walk along a wind-whipped shoreline, and Scotland is blessed with a profusion of wild beaches. The west coast in particular has many fine strands of blinding white sands and turquoise waters that could pass for Caribbean beaches if it wasn't for the weather.

Sandwood Bay A sea stack, a ghost story, and two miles of windblown sand – who could ask for more? (p264)

Kiloran Bay A perfect curve of deep golden sand, the ideal vantage point for stunning sunsets (p88)

Bosta A beautiful and remote cove filled with white sand beside an Iron Age house (p207)

Durness A series of pristine sandy coves and duney headlands surround this northwestern village (p242)

Scousburgh Sands Shetland's finest beach is a top spot for birdwatching, as well as for a bracing walk (p313)

Sanday This aptly named member of Orkney's North Isles is one giant sand dune, with many spectacular stretches of white sand beach (p293)

month by month

January

The nation shakes off its Hogmanay hangover and gets back to work, but only until Burns Night comes along. It's still cold and dark, but if there's snow on the hills the skiing can be good.

Burns Night

Suppers all over Scotland (and the world, for that matter) are held on 25 January to celebrate the anniversary of national poet Robert Burns, with much eating of haggis, drinking of whisky and reciting of poetry.

Up Helly Aa

Half of Shetland dresses up with horned helmets and battle-axes in this spectacular reenactment of a Viking fire festival, with a torchlit procession leading the burning of a full-size Viking longship. Held in Lerwick on the last Tuesday in January.

February

The coldest month of the year is usually the best for winter hillwalking, ice-climbing and skiing. The days are getting noticeably longer now, and snowdrops begin to bloom.

Fort William Mountain Festival

The UK's 'Outdoor Capital' celebrates the peak of the winter season with skiing and snowboarding workshops, talks by famous climbers, kids' events and a festival of mountaineering films.

April

The bluebell woods on the shores of Loch Lomond come into flower and ospreys arrive at their Loch Garten nest. Weather is improving, though heavy showers are still common.

Shetland Folk Festival

The end of April sees this engagingly eccentric music festival, with performances of traditional music from around the world staged everywhere from Lerwick pubs to remote island village halls.

May

Wildflowers bloom on the Hebridean machair and puffins arrive at their Orkney and Shetland nesting colonies – May is when the Scottish weather is often at its best.

Spirit of Speyside

Based in Dufftown, this festival of whisky, food and music involves five days of distillery tours, cooking, art and outdoor activities – and plenty of knocking back the 'water of life'. Held late April to early May in Moray and Speyside.

Scottish Series Yacht Races

The scenic harbour at the West Highland fishing village of Tarbert fills with hundreds of visiting yachts for five days of racing, drinking and partying.

Fèis Ìle

B&Bs in Islay are booked out for this week-long celebration of traditional Scottish music and whisky. Events include ceilidhs, pipe-band performances, distillery tours and whisky tastings.

June

Argyllshire is ablaze with pink rhododendron blooms. The long summer evenings (known in Orkney and Shetland as the *simmer dim*) stretch on till 11pm.

RockNess
The 'world's most beautiful rock festival' gathers on the shores of Loch Ness for three days of live music, chilling out and monster-watching.

UCI Mountain Bike World Cup
More than 18,000 mountain biking fans gather at Nevis Range near Fort William for the spectacular World Cup downhill and 4X finals.

St Magnus Festival
It barely gets dark at all at midsummer in Orkney, a magical setting for this celebration of music, poetry, literature and the visual arts. Held late June in Orkney.

July

School holidays begin at the start of July; the busiest time of year for campsites and B&Bs begins. It's high season for Shetland birdwatchers, with sea cliffs loud with nesting guillemots, razorbills and puffins.

Hebridean Celtic Festival
The gardens of Lews Castle in Stornoway provide the scenic setting for this four-day extravaganza of folk, rock, and Celtic music.

August

Highland games are taking place all over the region, but the midges are at their worst. On the west coast, this is the peak month for sighting minke whales and basking sharks.

Plockton Regatta
Plockton Bay fills with sails as a fortnight of yacht and small-boat racing culminates in Regatta Weekend with a street party, concert and ceilidh.

Argyllshire Gathering
Oban is the setting for one of the most important events on the Scottish Highland Games calendar, which includes a prestigious pipe-band competition.

September

School holidays are over, midges are dying off, wild brambles are ripe for picking in the hedgerows, and the weather is often dry and mild – an excellent time of year for outdoor pursuits.

Mull & Iona Food Festival
The beautiful islands of Mull and Iona host five days of food and drink tastings, cooking demonstrations, farm tours, produce markets and restaurant visits.

Braemar Gathering
The biggest and most famous Highland Games in the Scottish calendar, traditionally attended by members of the Royal Family, feature Highland dancing, caber-tossing and bagpipe-playing. Held early September in Braemar, Royal Deeside.

October

Autumn brings a blaze of colour to the forests of Perthshire and the Trossachs, as the tourist season winds down and thoughts turn to log fires and malt whisky in country house hotels.

Cowalfest
Dunoon and the lovely Cowal peninsula play host to this 10-day walking festival, As well as a huge range of guided walks, there are mountain bike rides, horse rides, orienteering, exhibitions, art, theatre and concerts.

Enchanted Forest
Crowds gather in the Explorers Garden at Pitlochry to experience this spectacular sound-and-light show. Three weeks of events occasionally spill into November.

December

Darkness falls mid-afternoon as the shortest day approaches. The often cold and wet weather is relieved by Christmas and New Year festivities, and the chance of seeing the Northern Lights in Orkney and Shetland.

itineraries

Whether you've got six days or 60, these itineraries provide a starting point for the trip of a lifetime. Want more inspiration? Head online to lonelyplanet. com/thorntree to chat with other travellers.

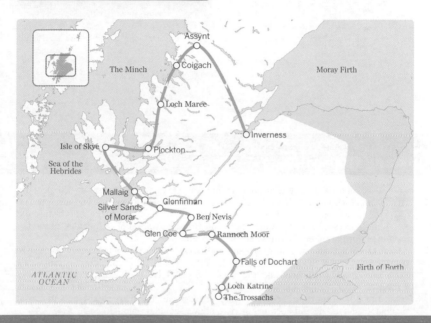

Two Weeks
A Highland Fling

Begin this tour with a visit to the **Trossachs** for your first taste of Highland scenery; take a cruise on **Loch Katrine** and spend the night in Callander. Continue north via the **Falls of Dochart** at Killin and the fringes of **Rannoch Moor.**

The mountain scenery becomes more impressive, culminating in the grandeur of **Glen Coe**. Keen hill walkers will pause for a day at Fort William to climb **Ben Nevis** (plus another day to recover!) before taking the Road to the Isles past glorious **Glenfinnan** and the **Silver Sands of Morar**, to **Mallaig**. Overnight here and dine at one of its seafood restaurants.

Take the ferry to the **Isle of Skye**, spending a day or two exploring Scotland's most famous island before crossing the Skye Bridge back to the mainland, then head north via the pretty village of **Plockton** to the magnificent mountain scenery of **Glen Torridon**. Spend a day or two hiking here, then follow the A832 alongside lovely **Loch Maree** and continue north into the big-sky wilderness of **Coigach** and **Assynt**, before making your way back south with an overnight in **Inverness**.

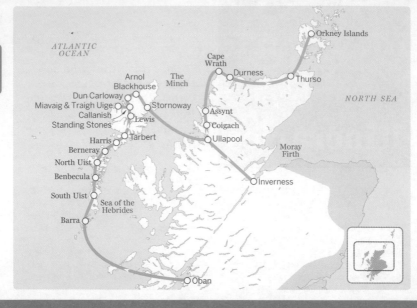

Two Weeks
Island Hopscotch

This route is usually done by car, but the Oban–Barra–Stornoway–Ullapool–Inverness loop also makes a brilliant cycle tour (around 270 miles, including the 60 miles from Ullapool ferry terminal to Inverness train station, making both start and finish accessible by rail). CalMac's Island Hopscotch ticket No 8 includes all the ferries needed for the Outer Hebrides part of this route.

From **Oban** it's a five-hour ferry crossing to **Barra**; you'll arrive in the evening so plan to spend the night there (book ahead). In the morning, after a visit to romantic Kisimul Castle and a tour around the island, take the ferry to **South Uist**. Walk along the wild beaches of the west coast, sample the local seafood and, if you've brought your fishing rod, look forward to a bit of sport on the island's many trout lochs. There are good places to stay at Polochar, Lochboisdale and Lochmaddy (two nights should be enough).

Keep your binoculars handy as you follow the road north through **Benbecula** and **North Uist**, as this is prime birdwatching country. If you're camping or hostelling, a night at **Berneray** is a must before taking the ferry to **Harris**. Pray for sun, as the road along Harris' west coast has some of the most spectacular beaches in Scotland. The main road continues north from **Tarbert** (good hotels) through the rugged Harris hills to **Lewis**.

Don't go directly to Stornoway, but take a turn west to the **Callanish Standing Stones**, **Dun Carloway** broch and **Arnol Blackhouse** museum – the highlights of the Western Isles. If you have time (two days is ideal), detour west to the beautiful beaches around **Miavaig** and **Traigh Uige**; there's plenty of wild and semiwild camping, or an unusual overnight option in the Gallan Head Hotel.

Spend your final night in the Hebrides in **Stornoway** (eat at Digby Chick), then take the ferry to **Ullapool**, where you have the choice of heading straight to **Inverness**, or continuing north around the mainland coast through the jaw-dropping wilderness of **Coigach** and **Assynt**, **Cape Wrath** and **Durness** to **Thurso**, where the ferry to the **Orkney Islands** awaits.

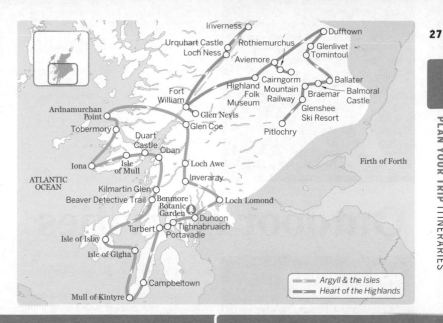

Map legend:
- Argyll & the Isles
- Heart of the Highlands

10 Days
Argyll & The Isles

Begin with a scenic drive across the Cowal peninsula from **Dunoon** to **Portavadie**, via **Benmore Botanic Garden** and **Tighnabruaich**, then take the ferry to the pretty fishing village of **Tarbert**. Devote a day to exploring the Kintyre peninsula, taking in **Campbeltown**, the **Mull of Kintyre** and a trip to the **Isle of Gigha**. Then allow at least two days for touring **Islay** and its famous distilleries.

Back on the mainland, head north through Knapdale – visit the **Beaver Detective Trail** near the Crinan Canal – to the prehistoric sites of **Kilmartin Glen** and then on to the bustling ferry port of **Oban**.

Take the ferry to Craignure for a tour of the **Isle of Mull**, making sure to visit **Duart Castle** and **Iona**, before spending a night at **Tobermory**. From here you can take another ferry to Kilchoan, allowing a trip to **Ardnamurchan Point**, the most westerly point of the British mainland, before the scenic drive along the shores of Loch Sunart to Corran Ferry.

Head back south via the scenic splendour of **Glen Coe** and the minor road through Glen Orchy to reach **Loch Awe**. From here you can return to your starting point by way of **Inveraray** and **Loch Lomond**.

One Week
Heart of the Highlands

Beginning in **Pitlochry**, abandon the main A9 road to the north and enjoy a day's scenic drive east across the hills on the A924, and then north on the A93 through the ski area of **Glenshee** to the remote Highland outpost of **Braemar**. Spend a night here, and the following day either hike in the Cairngorm hills nearby or visit **Balmoral Castle** before spending your second night at **Ballater**.

From here the rollercoaster A939 takes you north to **Tomintoul**; then it's back roads via **Glenlivet** to **Dufftown**, the capital of Speyside whisky. Next day, take your time visiting distilleries as you amble west along the Spey valley to **Aviemore**, in the heart of Cairngorm National Park. You'll need at least two nights here for time to explore the ancient pine forests of **Rothiemurchus** and to take a trip on the **Cairngorm Mountain Railway**.

Then head west, stopping to discover the **Highland Folk Museum** at Newtonmore before continuing to **Fort William**. Overnight here, then spend a morning exploring **Glen Nevis** and head north along the Great Glen to see **Urquhart Castle** and **Loch Ness** – leave time for a monster-spotting cruise – and finish up in **Inverness**.

Outdoor Activities

Best Time to Go
May, June and September are the best months for hiking and biking – best chance of dry weather and less chance of midges

Best Outdoor Experiences
Hike the West Highland Way
Climb Ben Nevis
Cycle-tour the Outer Hebrides
Mountain-bike a black trail at Laggan Wolftrax
Sea kayak in Shetland

Essential Hill Walking Gear
Good waterproofs
Spare warm clothing
Map and compass
Mobile phone (but don't rely on it)
First-aid kit
Head torch
Whistle (for emergencies)
Spare food and drink

Safety Checklist
Check the weather forecast first
Let someone know your plans
Set pace and objective to suit slowest member of party
Don't be afraid to turn back if it's too difficult

Scotland is a brilliant place for outdoor recreation and has something to offer everyone, from those who enjoy a short stroll to full-on adrenaline junkies. Although hiking, biking, fishing and golf are the most popular activities, there is an astonishing variety of things to do.

Most activities are well organised and have clubs and associations that can give visitors invaluable information and, sometimes, substantial discounts. **VisitScotland** (www.visitscotland.com) has brochures and dedicated websites covering the most popular activities.

Walking

Scotland's wild, dramatic scenery and varied landscape has made walking a hugely popular pastime for locals and tourists alike. There really is something for everyone, from after-breakfast strolls to the popular sport of Munro bagging.

The best time of year for hill walking is usually May to September, although snow can fall on the highest summits even in midsummer. Winter walking on the higher hills of Scotland is for experienced mountaineers only, requiring the use of ice axe and crampons.

There is a tradition of relatively free access to open country in Scotland, especially on mountains and moorlands. You should, however, avoid areas where you might disrupt or disturb **lambing** (generally mid-April to the end of May), **grouse shooting** (from 12 August to the third week in Octo-

THE RIGHT TO ROAM

Access to the countryside has been a thorny issue in Scotland for many years. In Victorian times, belligerent landowners attempted to prevent walkers from using well-established trails. Moves to counter this led to successful legislation for the walkers and the formation of what later became the **Scottish Rights of Way & Access Society** (www.scotways.com).

In January 2003 the Scottish parliament formalised access to the countryside and passed the *Land Reform (Scotland) Bill*, creating statutory rights of access to land in Scotland for the first time (popularly known as 'the right to roam'). Basically, the **Scottish Outdoor Access Code** (www.outdooraccess-scotland.com) states that everyone has the right to be on most land and inland waters, providing they act responsibly.

As far as wild camping goes, this means that you can pitch a tent almost anywhere that doesn't cause inconvenience to others or damage to property, as long as you stay no longer than two or three nights in any one spot, take all litter away with you, and keep well away from houses and roads.

ber) or **deer stalking** (1 July to 15 February, but the peak period is August to October). You can get up-to-date information on deer stalking in various areas through the **Hillphone** (www.hillphones.info) service.

Rights of way exist but local authorities aren't required to list and map them so they're not shown on Ordnance Survey (OS) maps of Scotland, as they are in England and Wales. However, the Scottish Rights of Way & Access Society keeps records of these routes, provides and maintains signposting, and publicises them in its guidebook, *Scottish Hill Tracks*.

What to Bring

Highland hikers should be properly equipped and cautious, as the weather can become vicious at any time of year. After rain, peaty soil can become boggy, so always wear stout shoes or boots and carry extra food and drink – many unsuspecting walkers have had to survive an unplanned night in the open. Don't depend on mobile phones (although carrying one with you is a good idea, and can be a life-saver if you can get a signal). If necessary, leave a note with your route and expected time of return in the windscreen of your car.

Maps

Britain's national mapping agency, the Ordnance Survey (OS), caters to walkers with a wide range of maps at different scales. The **Landranger** series at 1:50,000 (2cm to 1km, 1¼ inches to 1 mile; £5.99 per sheet) is the standard hiker's map. If you want more detail, the **Explorer** series at 1:25,000 (4cm to 1km, 2½ inches to 1 mile; £7.99 per sheet)

shows features such as field boundaries and fences. Both series are also available as 'Active' versions (£12.99 and £13.99), which are completely waterproof. Tourist offices and bookshops usually stock a selection, or you can buy them online.

Alternatively, look out for the excellent, weatherproof walkers' maps published by **Harveys** at scales of 1:40,000 and 1:25,000. These are tailored to particular walking and climbing areas such as Ben Nevis or the Cairngorms, and there are also maps dedicated to long-distance footpaths.

Walks in this Guide

We have included descriptions of more than a dozen walks in this guide, ranging from short strolls of a mile or so to day-long hill walks. The times and distances given are provided only as a guide. Times are based on the actual walking time and do not include stops for snacks, taking photos, rests or side trips; be sure to factor these in when planning your walk. Distances should be read in conjunction with altitudes – significant elevation can make a greater difference to your walking time than lateral distance, so please make sure to check the route on a proper hiking map before setting off.

Further Information

Every tourist office has leaflets (free or for a nominal charge) of suggested walks that take in local points of interest. Lonely Planet's *Walking in Scotland* is a comprehensive resource, covering short walks and long-distance paths; its *Walking in Britain* guide covers Scottish walks, too. For general advice, VisitScotland produces a

DISCLAIMER

Although the authors and publisher have done their utmost to ensure the accuracy of all information in this guide, they cannot accept any responsibility for any loss, injury or inconvenience sustained by people using this book. They cannot guarantee that paths and routes described here have not become impassable for any reason in the interval between research and publication.

The fact that a walk is described in this guidebook does not mean that it is safe for you and your walking party. You are ultimately responsible for judging your own capabilities in the conditions you encounter.

Walking Scotland (http://walking.visitscotland .com) website that describes numerous routes in various parts of the country, and also offers safety tips and other useful information.

Other useful sources:

» **Mountaineering Council of Scotland** (www.mcofs.org.uk)

» **Scottish Mountaineering Club** (www.smc.org.uk)

» **Ordnance Survey** (www.ordnancesurvey.co.uk)

» **Ramblers' Association Scotland** (www.ramblers.org.uk/scotland)

Mountain Biking

A combination of challenging, rugged terrain, a network of old drove roads, military roads and stalkers' paths, and legislation that enshrines free access to the countryside has earned Scotland a reputation as one of the world's top mountain-biking destinations. Fort William has hosted the UCI Mountain Bike World Championships every year since 2007.

The Highlands and Islands offer everything from custom-built forest trails with berms, jumps and skinnies to world-class downhill courses such as those at Laggan Wolftrax and Nevis Range. But perhaps the region's greatest appeal is its almost unlimited potential for adventurous, off-road riding. Areas such as the Angus Glens, the Cairngorms, Lochaber, Skye and most of the Northwest Highlands have large roadless regions where you can explore to your heart's content. The **10 Glens MTB Project** (www.10glens.co.uk) aims to develop mountain bike trails in the Highland glens to the west of Inverness, including the Great Glen, Glen Urquhart, Glen Affric, Glen Cannich and Glen Strathfarrar.

Top trails include Glen Feshie and Rothiemurchus Forest in the Cairngorms, Spean Bridge to Kinlochleven via the Lairig Leacach and Loch Eilde Mor, and the stretch of the West Highland Way between Bridge of Orchy and Kinlochleven. The 37-mile loop from Sligachan on Skye (south through Glen Sligachan to Camasunary, over to Kilmarie, and back north via Strath Mor) was voted by Mountain Bike Rider magazine as the best off-road trail in Britain.

OFFICIAL LONG DISTANCE FOOTPATHS

WALK	DISTANCE	FEATURES	DURATION	DIFFICULTY
Fife Coastal Path	78 miles	Firth of Forth, undulating country	5–6 days	easy
Great Glen Way	73 miles	Loch Ness, canal paths, forest tracks	4 days	easy
Pilgrims Way	25 miles	Machars peninsula, standing stones, burial mounds	2–3 days	easy
St Cuthbert's Way	62 miles	follows life of famous saint	6–7 days	medium
Southern Upland Way	212 miles	remote hills & moorlands	9–14 days	medium–hard
Speyside Way	66 miles	follows river, whisky distilleries	3–4 days	easy–medium
West Highland Way	95 miles	spectacular scenery, mountains & lochs	6–8 days	medium

This long-distance footpath follows the course of the River Spey, one of Scotland's most famous salmon-fishing rivers. It starts at Buckie and first follows the coast to Spey Bay, east of Elgin, then runs inland along the river to Aviemore in the Cairngorms (with branches to Tomintoul and Dufftown). At only 66 miles, the main walk can be done in three or four days, although including the branch trails to Dufftown and Tomintoul will push the total walking distance to 102 miles (allow seven days).

This route has also been dubbed the **Whisky Trail** as it passes near a number of distilleries, including Glenlivet and Glenfiddich, which are open to the public. If you stop at them all, the walk may take considerably longer than the usual three or four days.

The *Speyside Way* guidebook by Jacquetta Megarry and Jim Strachan describes the route in detail. Or check out the route at www.speysideway.org.

But the ultimate off-road experience is a **coast-to-coast ride**. There is no set route and no waymarking, so it's as much a planning and navigational challenge as a physical one. A coast-to-coast can be as short as the 36 miles from Ullapool to Bonar Bridge via Glen Achall and Glen Einig, or as long as the 250 miles from Aberdeen to Ardnamurchan (90% off-road).

The most popular route, though, is from Fort William to Montrose (starting and finishing at a railway station) via Fort Augustus, Aviemore, Tomintoul, Ballater and Edzell, taking in the Corrieyairack Pass, the Ryvoan Pass, Glen Builg, Glen Tanar and Glen Esk (195 miles). You can camp wild along the way or book accommodation at B&Bs and hostels, or join a guided expedition with an organisation such as Wilderness Scotland (p252) or Scottish Mountain Bike Guides (p131).

Mountain Biking Centres

» Nevis Range (p170) – Ski resort offering summer sport in the form of a world-championship downhill course, and a 6km red-grade cross-country trail from the top station of the gondola.

» Witch's Trails (p169) – Has 35km of forest road and single-track in the shadow of Ben Nevis. Hosts the annual cross-country world championships, and the annual 10 Under The Ben endurance event.

» Laggan Wolftrax (p133) – Forest centre near Newtonmore with everything from novice trails and a bike park to hard cross-country and a challenging black route with drop-offs, boulder fields and rock slabs.

» Highland Wildcat (p230) – The hills above Golspie harbour have the biggest single-track descent in the country (390m drop over 7km, from the top of Ben Bhraggie almost to sea level). Plenty for beginners and families, too.

» Learnie Red Rock (p219) – Just north of Rosemarkie; 16km of forest trails plus fun park, for all levels of skill and experience.

» Kyle of Sutherland Trails (p227) – Rocks and boardwalks add some technical challenges to 17km of blue-, red- and black-graded forest trails with great views.

Cycling

Cycling is an excellent way to explore Scotland. There are hundreds of miles of forest trails and quiet minor roads, and dedicated cycle routes along canal towpaths and disused railway tracks. Depending on your energy and enthusiasm, you can take a leisurely trip through idyllic glens, stopping at pubs along the way, or head off on a long and arduous road tour.

The network of signposted cycle routes maintained by **Sustrans** (www.sustrans.org.uk) makes a good introduction. Much of the network is on minor roads or cycle lanes, but there are long stretches of surfaced, traffic-free trails between Callander and Killin, between Oban and Ballachulish, and on Royal Deeside.

But it's the minor roads of the Northwest Highlands, the Outer Hebrides, Orkney and Shetland that are the real attraction for cycle tourers, offering hundreds of miles of peaceful pedalling through breathtaking landscapes. The classic Scottish cycle tour is a trip around the islands of the west coast, from Islay and Jura north via Mull, Coll and Tiree to Skye and the Outer Hebrides (bikes travel for free on Calmac car ferries).

Further Information

VisitScotland publishes a useful free bro-chure, *Active Scotland,* and has a website with more information (http://active.visit scotland.com). Many regional tourist offices have information on local cycling routes and places to hire bikes. They also stock cycling guides and books.

For up-to-date, detailed information on Scotland's cycle-route network contact Sus-trans. The **Cyclists' Touring Club** (www.ctc .org.uk) is a membership organisation offer-ing comprehensive information about cy-cling in Britain.

Birdwatching

Scotland is the best place in the British Isles (and in some cases, the only place) to spot bird species such as the golden eagle, white-tailed eagle, osprey, corncrake, capercaillie, crested tit, Scottish crossbill and ptarmigan, and the country's coast and islands are some of Europe's most important seabird nesting grounds.

There are more than 80 ornithologically important nature reserves managed by **Scottish Natural Heritage** (www.snh.gov .uk), the **Royal Society for the Protection of Birds** (www.rspb.org.uk) and the **Scottish Wildlife Trust** (www.swt.org.uk).

Further information can be obtained from the **Scottish Ornithologists Club** (www.the-soc.org.uk).

Whale Watching

The North Atlantic Drift – a swirling tendril of the Gulf Stream – carries warm water into the cold, nutrient-rich seas off the Scottish coast, resulting in huge blooms of plankton. Small fish feed on the plankton, and bigger fish feed on the smaller fish. And this huge seafood smorgasbord attracts large numbers of marine mammals, from harbour porpois-es and dolphins to minke whales and even – though sightings are rare – humpback and sperm whales.

In contrast to Iceland and Norway, Scot-land has cashed in on the abundance of min-ke whales off its coast by embracing whale watching rather than whaling. There are now dozens of operators around the coast offer-ing whale-watching boat trips lasting from a couple of hours to all day; some have whale-sighting success rates of 95% in summer.

The best places to base yourself for whale watching include Oban, the Isle of Mull,

Skye and the Outer Hebrides. Orkney and Shetland offer the best chance of spotting orcas (killer whales) while the Moray Firth has a resident population of bottle-nosed dolphins. While seals, porpoises and dol-phins can be seen year-round, minke whales are most commonly spotted from June to August, with August being the peak month for sightings.

The website of the **Hebridean Whale & Dolphin Trust** (www.whaledolphintrust.co.uk) has lots of information on the species you are likely to see, and how to identify them. A booklet titled *Is It a Whale?* is available from tourist offices and bookshops, and provides tips on identifying the various spe-cies of marine mammal that you're likely to see.

Outfits operating whale-watching cruises include:

» Sea Life Surveys (p78)
» Sea.fari Adventures (p78)
» Aquaxplore (p188)
» Gairloch Marine Cruises (p258)
» MV Volante (p98)

Golf

Scotland is the home of golf. The game has been played in Scotland for centuries and there are more courses per head of popula-tion here than in any other country. Most clubs are open to visitors; details can be found on the web at www.scotlands-golf -courses.com.

St Andrews is the headquarters of the game's governing body, the Royal and An-cient Golf Club, and the location of the world's most famous golf course, the Old Course. Although the major champion-ship courses, including those at Carnoustie, Royal Troon and Turnberry, are in the south of the country, there are some superb courses in the Highlands, such as Royal Dornoch, Tain and Nairn. Many visiting golfers enjoy the challenge of the wild and some eccentric golf courses can be found dotted among the islands, such as Mach-rie on Islay, Askernish on South Uist and Whalsay in Shetland.

VisitScotland publishes the *Official Guide to Golf in Scotland,* a free annual brochure listing course details, costs and clubs, as well as information on where to stay.

Forget Nessie. The Highlands have a real monster in their midst: a voracious, blood-sucking female fully 2mm long, known as *Culicoides impunctatus* – the Highland midge. (The male midge is an innocent vegetarian.) The bane of campers and as much a symbol of Scotland as the kilt or the thistle, they can drive sane folk to distraction as they descend in swarms of biting misery. Though mostly vegetarian too, the female midge needs a dose of blood in order to lay her eggs. And like it or not, if you're in the Highlands in summer, you've just volunteered as a donor.

The midge season lasts from late May to early September, with June to August being the worst months. Climate change has seen warmer, damper springs and summers that seem to suit the midges just fine – in recent years they've increased both in numbers and in range. They're at their worst in the morning and evening, especially in calm, overcast weather; strong winds and strong sunshine help keep them away.

You can get an idea of how bad they are going to be in your area by checking the **midge forecast** (www.midgeforecast.co.uk).

Be Prepared

Cover up by wearing long trousers and long-sleeved shirts, and (if they're really bad) a head net (available in most outdoor shops for £3 to £5) worn over a brimmed hat. Also be sure to use a repellent.

Many kinds of repellents have been formulated over the decades, some based on natural ingredients such citronella and bog myrtle, but until recently there was only one that worked reliably – DEET, which is a nasty, industrial chemical that smells bad, stings your eyes and seems to be capable of melting plastic. Today, a new repellent called Saltidin claims to be both effective and pleasant to use (marketed under the brand name Smidge).

However, there's another substance that has shot to prominence since 2005 despite not being marketed as an insect repellent. Avon's 'Skin So Soft' moisturiser spray is so effective that it is regularly used as a midge repellent by professionals including the Royal Marines, forestry workers and water engineers, as well as thousands of outdoor enthusiasts. You can find it in most outdoor stores in the west of Scotland. Not only does it keep the midges away, but it leaves your skin feeling 'velvety soft'.

Fishing

Fishing – coarse, sea and game – is enormously popular in Scotland; the lochs and rivers of the Highlands and Islands are filled with salmon, sea trout, brown trout and Arctic char. Fly-fishing in particular is a joy – it's a tricky but rewarding form of angling, closer to an art form than a sport.

Fishing rights to most waters are privately owned and you must obtain a permit to fish in them – these are often readily available at the local fishing-tackle shop or hotel. Permits cost from around £15 per day, but some salmon rivers – notably the Tay and the Spey – can be much more expensive.

There are numerous places throughout Scotland with stocked ponds where you can hire equipment and have a couple of lessons; they're a particularly good option for the kids. Examples include the Rothiemurchus Trout Fishery near Aviemore.

For wild brown trout the close season is early October to mid-March. The close season for salmon and sea trout varies between districts; it's generally from early November to early February.

The VisitScotland booklet *Fish in Scotland* (www.fishpal.com/VisitScotland) is a good introduction and is also available from tourist offices. Other organisations that can provide information include:

» **Scottish Anglers National Association** (www.sana.org.uk)

» **Scottish Federation of Sea Anglers** (www.fishsea.co.uk)

Kayaking & Canoeing

The islands, sea lochs and indented coastline of Scotland's Highlands and Islands provide some of the finest sea kayaking in the world. There are sheltered lochs and inlets ideal for beginners, long and exciting coastal and island tours, and gnarly tidal passages that will challenge even the most expert paddler, all amid spectacular scenery and wildlife – encounters with seals, dolphins and even whales are relatively common.

The inland lochs and rivers offer excellent Canadian and white-water canoeing. Lochs Lomond, Awe and Maree all have uninhabited islands where canoeists can set up camp, while a study of the map will suggest plenty of cross-country expeditions involving only minor portages. Classic routes include Fort William to Inverness along the Great Glen; Glen Affric; Loch Shiel; and Loch Veyatie–Fionn Loch–Loch Sionascaig in Assynt.

There are dozens of companies offering sea kayaking and canoeing courses and guided holidays, including:

» Arran Adventure Company (p61)

» Norwest Sea Kayaking (p252)

» Ridgway Adventure (p244)

» Rockhopper Sea Kayaking (p178)

» Sea Kayak Shetland (p313)

» Skyak Adventures (p185)

» Wilderness Scotland (p252)

Further Information

» **Scottish Canoe Association** (www.canoescotland.org) Publishes coastal navigation sheets and organises tours, including introductory ones for beginners.

» *The Northern Isles* (by Tom Smith & Chris Jex) A detailed guide to sea kayaking the waters around Orkney and Shetland.

» *The Outer Hebrides* (by Mike Sullivan, Robert Emmott & Tim Pickering) A detailed guide to sea kayaking around the Western Isles.

» *Scottish Sea Kayak Trail* (www.scottishseakayaktrail.com; by Simon Willis) Covers the Scottish west coast from the Isle of Gigha to the Summer Isles.

Winter Sports

There are five ski centres in Scotland, offering downhill skiing and snowboarding:

» Cairngorm Mountain (1097m; p130) Has almost 30 runs spread over an extensive area.

» Glencoe Mountain Resort (1108m; p172) Has only five tows and two chairlifts.

» Glenshee Ski Resort (920m; p144) Situated on the A93 road between Perth and Braemar; offers the largest network of lifts and the widest range of runs in all of Scotland.

» Lecht 2090 (793m; p138) The smallest and most remote centre, on the A939 between Ballater and Grantown-on-Spey.

» Nevis Range (1221m; p170) Near Fort William; offers the highest ski runs, the grandest setting and some of the best off-piste potential in Scotland.

The high season is from January to April but it's sometimes possible to ski from as early as November to as late as May. It's easy to turn up at the slopes, hire some equipment, buy a day pass and head right off.

VisitScotland's *Ski Scotland* brochure is useful and includes a list of accommodation options. General information, and weather and snow reports, can be obtained from:

» **Ski Scotland** (www.ski-scotland.com)

» **Snowsport Scotland** (www.snowsportscotland.org)

» **WinterHighland** (www.winterhighland.info)

Rock Climbing

Scotland has a long history of rock climbing and mountaineering, with many of the classic routes on Ben Nevis and Glen Coe having been pioneered in the 19th century. The country's main rock-climbing areas include Ben Nevis (with routes up to 400m in length), Glen Coe, the Cairngorms, the Cuillin Hills of Skye, Arrochar and the Isle of Arran, but there are also hundreds of smaller crags situated all over the country. One unusual feature of Scotland's rock-climbing scene is the sea stacks found around the coastlines, the most famous of these being the 140m-high Old Man of Hoy.

Rock Climbing in Scotland, by Kevin Howett, and the Scottish Mountaineering Club's regional Rock & Ice Climbs guides are excellent guidebooks that cover the whole country.

Further information:

» **Mountaineering Council of Scotland** (www.mountaineering-scotland.org.uk)

» **Scottish Mountaineering Club** (www.smc.org.uk)

Horse Riding

There are hundreds of miles of beautiful woodland, riverside and coastal trails to be ridden in the Highlands, and seeing the country from the saddle is a wonderful experience even if you're not an experienced rider.

At the end of the 19th century an eager hill walker, Sir Hugh Munro, published a list of 545 Scottish mountains measuring over 3000ft (914m) – a height at which he believed they gained a special significance. Of these summits, he classified 277 as mountains in their own right (new surveys have since revised this to a total of 283), the rest being satellites of lesser consequence (known as 'tops'). Sir Hugh couldn't have realised that his name would one day be used to describe any Scottish mountain over the magical 3000ft mark. Many keen hill walkers now set themselves the target of reaching the summit of (or 'bagging') all 283 Munros.

The peculiar practice of Munro bagging started soon after the list was published; by 1901 the Reverend AE Robertson had become the first person to bag the lot. Between 1901 and 1981, only 250 people managed to climb all of the Munros, but the huge increase in the popularity of hill walking from the 1980s onward saw the number of officially declared 'Munroists' soar to 4500 (see www.smc.org.uk/Munros) by 2010. Many people have completed the round more than once; the record for single-handed Munro bagging is held by Edinburgh's Steven Fallon, who completed his 14th round in 2010 (see p180).

To the uninitiated it may seem odd that Munro baggers think of a day (or longer) spent plodding around in mist, cloud and driving rain to the point of exhaustion as time well spent. However, for those who can add one or more ticks to their list, the vagaries of the weather are part of the enjoyment, at least in retrospect. And Munro bagging is, of course, much more than merely ticking names on a list – it takes you to some of the wildest, most beautiful parts of Scotland.

Once you've bagged all the Munros you can move onto the Corbetts, which are hills over 2500ft (700m) with a drop of at least 500ft (150m) on all sides, and the Donalds, lowland hills over 2000ft (610m). And for connoisseurs of the diminutive, there are the McPhies, so-called 'eminences in excess of 300ft (90m)', on the Isle of Colonsay.

There are riding schools catering to all levels of proficiency; a half-day's pony trekking should cost around £20, riding hat included. Many pony trekkers are novice riders so most rides are at walking speed, with the occasional trot. If you're an experienced horse rider there are numerous riding schools with horses for hire – tourist offices will have details.

VisitScotland publishes the *Riding in Scotland* brochure (http://riding.visit scotland.com), which lists riding centres around Scotland.

The **Trekking & Riding Society of Scotland** (www.ridinginscotland.com) can provide information on horse-riding courses and approved riding centres.

Sailing

The west coast of Scotland, with its myriad islands, superb scenery and challenging winds and tides, is widely acknowledged to be one of the finest yachting areas in the world.

Experienced skippers with suitable qualifications can charter a yacht from one of dozens of agencies; prices for bare-boat charter start at around £1800 a week in high season for a six-berth yacht; hiring a skipper to sail the boat for you will cost £135 a day or £850 a week. Sailing dinghies can be rented from many places for around £60 a day.

Beginners can take a **Royal Yachting Association** (www.rya.org.uk) training course in yachting or dinghy sailing at many sailing schools around the coast; for details of charter agencies, sailing schools and watersports centres, get hold of VisitScotland's *Sail Scotland* brochure, or check out their website http://sail.visitscotland.com.

Scuba Diving

It may lack coral reefs and warm waters but Scotland offers some of the most spectacular and challenging scuba diving in Europe. There are spectacular drop-offs, challenging drift dives (the Falls of Lora is a classic) and fascinating wildlife ranging from colourful jewel anemones and soft corals to giant conger eels, monkfish and inquisitive seals. There are also hundreds of fascinating shipwrecks.

Dive sites such as Scapa Flow in the Orkney Islands, where the seven remaining hulks of the WWI German High Seas Fleet, scuttled in 1919, lie on the sea bed, and the oceanic arches, tunnels and caves of St Kilda rank among the best in the world.

For more information on the country's diving options contact the **Scottish Sub Aqua Club** (www.scotsac.com).

Surfing

Even with a wetsuit on you definitely have to be hardy to enjoy surfing in Scottish waters. That said, the country does have some of the best surfing breaks in Europe.

The tidal range is large, which means there is often a completely different set of breaks at low and high tides. It's the north and west coasts, particularly around Thurso and in the Outer Hebrides, which have outstanding, world-class surf. Indeed, Lewis has the best and most consistent surf in Britain, with around 120 recorded breaks and waves up to 5m.

For more information contact **Hebridean Surf** (www.hebrideansurf.co.uk).

regions at a glance

Which parts of the Highlands and Islands you choose to visit will naturally depend on how much time you have, and whether you've been here before. First-time visitors will want to squeeze in as many highlights as possible, so could try following the well-trodden route through the Trossachs, Pitlochry, Inverness, Loch Ness and Skye.

It takes considerably more time to explore the further-flung corners of the country, but the jaw-dropping scenery of the northwest Highlands and the gorgeous white-sand beaches of the Outer Hebrides are less crowded and ultimately more rewarding. The long journey to Orkney or Shetland means that you'll want to devote more than just a day or two to these regions.

Southern Highlands & Islands

Wildlife ✓✓✓
Islands ✓✓
Food ✓✓✓

Wildlife
This region is home to some of Scotland's most spectacular wildlife, including magnificent white-tailed sea eagles, majestic Minke whales and 12m-long basking sharks. It's also where the beaver – extinct in Britain for hundreds of years – has been reintroduced into the wild.

Island-hopping
Island-hopping is one of the most enjoyable ways to explore Scotland's western seaboard. The cluster of islands within this region – Islay, with its whisky distilleries; wild and mountainous Jura; scenic Mull and the little jewel of Iona; and the gorgeous beaches of Colonsay, Coll and Tiree – provide a brilliant introduction.

Seafood
Whether you sit down to dine in one of Oban's or Tobermory's top restaurants or lounge by the harbourside and eat with your fingers, the rich harvest of the sea is one of the region's biggest drawcards.

p42

Central Highlands

Activities ✓✓✓
Whisky ✓✓✓
Royalty ✓✓

Outdoor Adventures
The Cairngorms National Park offers enough outdoor adventure to keep you busy for a year. Be it climbing Ben Macdui, walking the Lairig Ghru, biking the trails around Loch Morlich or skiing the slopes of Cairngorm, there's something here for every activity-lover.

Whisky Trail
No trip to Scotland is complete without a visit to a whisky distillery, and the Speyside region, around Dufftown and Glenlivet, is the epicentre of the industry. More than 50 distilleries open during Spirit of Speyside festivals, and many open all year long.

Royal-Watching
The valley of River Dee – often called Royal Deeside – has been associated with the royal family since Queen Victoria acquired a holiday home at Balmoral Castle in the 1850s. The nearby village of Ballater was once the terminus for the royal train and is filled with shops bearing the royal warrant.

p114

The Great Glen & Lochaber

Activities ✓✓✓
Legends ✓✓
Scenery ✓✓

The Ben
Fort William, the self-styled 'Outdoor Capital of the UK', offers everything from rock climbing and paragliding to skiing and snowboarding. The biggest draw is Ben Nevis, Britain's highest summit, which attracts would-be ascensionists from all over.

Myths & History
Scotland's most iconic legend, the Loch Ness monster, lurks in the heart of the Great Glen. You might not spot Nessie, but the magnificent scenery of Loch Ness makes a visit well worthwhile. Not far is Culloden battlefield, the nemesis of another Scottish legend, Bonnie Prince Charlie.

Mountain Panoramas
Landscape photographers are spoilt for choice here with classic views: from the rugged mountain beauty of Glen Coe and snowpatched summits of Ben Nevis and Aonach Mor to the Caledonian pine forests around Loch Affric and golden beach and island panoramas of Arisaig and Morar.

p148

Skye & the Western Isles

History ✓✓
Scenery ✓✓✓
Handicrafts ✓✓

Highland History
Abandoned rural communities of Skye and the Western Isles are ideal to learn about the Clearances – places such as Arnol Blackhouse and Skye Museum of Island Life. The region is also rich in prehistoric sites, including the famous Standing Stones of Callanish.

Photographer's Paradise
The quality of light in the Outer Hebrides – caused by sunlight reflecting up from the sea and lochs to the undersides of the clouds – that lends a special magic to its landscapes. Skye's scenery is sublime: from almost any angle, the jagged peaks of the Cuillin attract the photographer's lens.

The Crafts Trail
At times it seems as if every other house in Skye and the Western Isles has an artisan's studio. Colourful pottery, hand-dyed wool, silver jewellery, carved driftwood and moody watercolour landscapes – you'll find them all here.

p182

Northwest Highlands

Scenery ✓✓✓
Activities ✓✓✓
Drives ✓✓

Unspoilt Wilderness

From shapely peaks of Assynt and Torridon to wild seacliffs of Handa and Cape Wrath and gorgeous beaches of Sandwood and Durness, the big skies and lonely landscapes of the northwest Highlands are the essence of Scotland, a wilderness of sea and mountains that is one of Europe's unspoilt regions.

Adventure Playground

The vast spaces of the northwest are one huge adventure playground, offering challenges to hikers, bikers, climbers and kayakers, and the chance to see some of the UK's most spectacular wildlife.

Wee Mad Roads

The distances may not seem that long, but on the scenic, single-track back roads of the northwest, you'll be lucky to average 20mph. It's not just the narrow, steep and twisting roads, or having to give way to sheep – or even deer – but the fact that you'll keep having to stop and gawp at the scenery.

p218

Orkney Islands

History ✓✓
Wildlife ✓✓✓
Walking ✓✓

Prehistoric Sites

These treeless, cliff-bound islands have a fascinating Viking heritage and unique prehistoric villages, tombs and stone circles. Predating Stonehenge and the pyramids of Egypt, Skara Brae is the best-preserved neolithic village in northern Europe, while Maes Howe is one of Britain's finest prehistoric tombs.

Owls, Otters & Orcas

Every day brings a different wildlife experience: you can spot hen harriers and short-eared owls without even leaving your car. Otters are a common sight (often while you're waiting at a ferry pier), and orcas can be spotted from the headlands of Marwick Head, Hoxa Head and Deerness.

Old Man of Hoy

Orkney offers countless opportunities for coastal walking, often with spectacular cliff and stack scenery. But don't miss the rewarding walk to the daddy of them all – Britain's biggest sea stack, the Old Man of Hoy.

p267

Shetland Islands

Wildlife ✓✓✓
Music ✓✓
Solitude ✓✓✓

Seabird Central

Shetland is a paradise for birdwatchers, its cliffs teeming with nesting seabirds in summer: gannets, fulmars, kittiwakes, guillemots, razorbills and puffins, and Europe's largest colony of arctic terns. There are several nature reserves here, including Hermaness on Unst, Scotland's northernmost inhabited island.

Blazing Fiddles

The pubs of Lerwick are fertile ground for exploring the Scottish traditional music scene, with plenty of impromptu sessions of fiddle, *bodhrann* and guitar music. Shetland hosts an annual festival of folk music in April, and a fiddle and accordion festival in October.

Wild Islands

Shetland is the most remote part of the British Isles, and its outer islands are more remote still. Windswept spots such as Foula, Fair Isle and the Out Skerries offer the chance to really get away from it all.

p300

Look out for these icons:

TOP CHOICE Our author's recommendation

A green or sustainable option

FREE No payment required

On the Road

Southern Highlands & Islands

Includes »

Why Go?

From the rasping spout of a minke whale as it breaks the surface, to the 'krek-krek-krek' of a corncrake, Scotland's southern Highlands and Islands are filled with unusual wildlife experiences. You can spot otters tumbling in the kelp, watch sea eagles snatch fish from a lonely loch, and thrill to the sight of dolphins riding the bow wave of your boat. Here sea travel is as important as road and rail – dozens of ferries allow you to island-hop your way from the Firth of Clyde to Oban and beyond, via the whisky distilleries of Islay, the wild mountains of Jura and the scenic delights of diminutive Colonsay. The bustling town of Oban is the gateway to the isles – from the peaceful backwaters of Kerrera and Lismore to the dramatic coastal scenery of Mull and the wild, windswept beaches of Coll and Tiree.

Best Places to Eat

» Café Fish (p93)
» Colonsay Hotel (p89)
» Argyll Hotel (p99)
» Inver Cottage (p57)

Best Places to Stay

» Highland Cottage Hotel (p93)
» Achnadrish House (p94)
» George Hotel (p68)
» Roman Camp Hotel (p50)
» Lochranza SYHA (p63)

When to Go

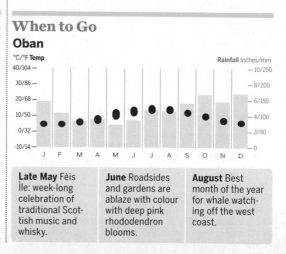

Oban

Late May Fèis Ìle: week-long celebration of traditional Scottish music and whisky.

June Roadsides and gardens are ablaze with colour with deep pink rhododendron blooms.

August Best month of the year for whale watching off the west coast.

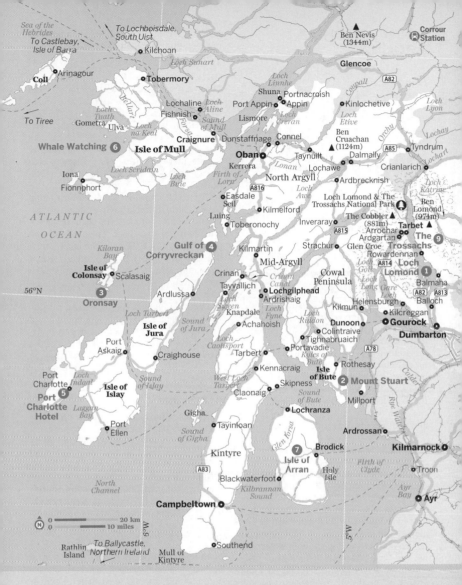

Southern Highlands & Islands Highlights

1 Hike through the bluebell woods on the bonnie banks of **Loch Lomond** (p44).

2 Stare in wonder at the magnificent marble-clad halls of **Mount Stuart** (p57).

3 Walk barefoot across the strand from Colonsay to Oronsay to visit the **medieval priory** (p88).

4 Ride a high-speed boat through surging water in the **Gulf of Corryvreckan** (p87).

5 Sit by a log fire in the **Port Charlotte Hotel** (p84), sampling some of Islay's finest single-malt whiskies.

6 Head out to watch the whales in the waters off the west coast of **Mull** (p90).

7 Blow away the cobwebs on the scenic, activity-packed **Isle of Arran** (p60).

8 Sample some of Europe's finest **seafood** in a waterside restaurant.

9 Marvel at the autumn colours reflected in the scenic lochs of **The Trossachs** (p44).

LOCH LOMOND & AROUND

The 'bonnie banks' and 'bonnie braes' of Loch Lomond have long been Glasgow's rural retreat – a scenic region of hills, lochs and healthy fresh air within easy reach of Scotland's largest city. Since the 1930s Glaswegians have made a regular weekend exodus to the hills, by car, by bike and on foot, and today the loch's popularity shows no sign of decreasing (Loch Lomond is within an hour's drive of 70% of Scotland's population).

The region's importance was recognised when it became the heart of **Loch Lomond & the Trossachs National Park** (www .lochlomond-trossachs.org) – Scotland's first national park, created in 2002.

Loch Lomond

Loch Lomond is the largest lake in mainland Britain and, after Loch Ness, perhaps the most famous of Scotland's lochs. Its proximity to Glasgow (20 miles away) means that the tourist honeypots of Balloch, Loch Lomond Shores and Luss get pretty crowded in summer. The main tourist focus is on the loch's western shore, along the A82, and at the southern end, around Balloch, which can occasionally be a nightmare of jet skis and motorboats. The eastern shore, which is followed by the West Highland Way long-distance footpath, is a little quieter.

The loch fills a trough that was gouged by a glacier flowing south from the ice sheet that covered Rannoch Moor during the last Ice Age, and straddles the boundary between the Highlands and the lowlands, so that two distinct environments can be seen along its shores.

The northern end of the loch is deep and narrow (at its deepest, just south of Inversnaid, the water depth is 190m), generally less than 1 mile wide, and enclosed by steep mountains rising to 900m. The slopes at the loch shore are covered by Scotland's largest remnant of native oak woodland, mixed with newer conifer plantations. Botanical studies have found that 25% of all known British flowering plants and ferns can be found along the eastern shore.

The southern part of the loch is broad, shallow and dotted with 38 islands, and bordered by relatively flat, low-lying arable land. This part of the loch freezes over during severe winters, and it has been possible to reach the islands on foot on several occasions over the last 50 years.

ORIENTATION

The town of **Balloch**, which straddles the River Leven where it flows from the southern end of Loch Lomond, is the loch's main population centre and transport hub. A Victorian resort once thronged by day-trippers transferring between the train station and the steamer quay, it is now a 'gateway centre' for Loch Lomond and the Trossachs National Park.

The road along the loch's eastern shore passes through the attractive village of **Balmaha**, where you can hire boats or take a cruise on the mail boat. There are several picnic areas along the loch; the most attractive is at Millarochy Bay (1.5 miles north of Balmaha), which has a nice gravel beach and superb views across the loch to the Luss hills.

The road ends at Rowardennan, but the West Highland Way continues north along the shore of the loch. It's 7 miles to Inversnaid, which can be reached by road from the Trossachs, and 15 miles to Inverarnan on the main A82 road at the northern end of the loch.

◉ Sights

Unless it's raining, give Loch Lomond Shores a miss and head for the little picture-postcard village of Luss. Stroll among the pretty cottages with roses around their doors (the cottages were built by the local laird in the 19th century for the workers on his estate), then pop into the **Clan Colquhoun tourist office** (☎01436-671469; Luss; adult/child £1/ free; ☺10.30am-6pm Easter-Oct) for some background history before enjoying a cup of tea at the Coach House Coffee Shop.

Loch Lomond Shores LEISURE COMPLEX (www.lochlomondshores.com; Balloch) Loch Lomond Shores, a major tourism development situated a half-mile north of Balloch, sports a national-park information centre plus various visitor attractions, outdoor activities and boat trips. In keeping with the times, the heart of the development is a large shopping mall.

Loch Lomond Aquarium AQUARIUM (www.sealife.co.uk; Loch Lomond Shores; adult/child £12/9; ☺10am-5pm) The centrepiece of Loch Lomond Shores (p44) is the Loch

Lomond Aquarium, which has displays on the wildlife of Loch Lomond, an otter enclosure (housing short-clawed Asian otters, not Scottish ones), and a host of sea-life exhibits ranging from sharks to stingrays to sea turtles.

Maid of the Loch   HISTORIC SHIP
(www.maidoftheloch.com; Balloch; admission free; ⊙11am-4pm daily May-Oct, Sat & Sun only Nov-Apr) The vintage paddle steamer *Maid of the Loch*, built in 1953, is moored at Loch Lomond Shores while awaiting full restoration – you can nip aboard for a look around.

🏃 Activities
Walking
The big walk around here is the **West Highland Way** (www.west-highland-way.co.uk), which runs along the eastern shore of the loch. There are shorter lochside walks at Firkin Point on the western shore and at several other places around the loch. You can get further information on local walks from the national-park information centres at Loch Lomond Shores and Balmaha.

Rowardennan is the starting point for an ascent of Ben Lomond (974m), a popular and relatively easy round trip of about five hours (p110). The route starts at the car park just past the Rowardennan Hotel.

Boat Tours
Sweeney's Cruises   BOAT TOURS
(www.sweeney.uk.com; Balloch Rd, Balloch) The main centre for boat trips is Balloch, where Sweeney's Cruises offers a range of trips including a one-hour cruise to Inchmurrin and back (adult/child £7/4, departs hourly), and a two-hour cruise (£12.50/6, departs 1pm and 3pm) around the islands.

The quay is directly opposite Balloch train station, beside the tourist office. Sweeney's also runs hourly cruises from the Maid of the Loch jetty at Loch Lomond Shores.

Cruise Loch Lomond   BOAT TOUR
(www.cruiselochlomondltd.com; Tarbet) Cruise Loch Lomond is based in Tarbet and offers trips to Inversnaid and Rob Roy MacGregor's Cave. You can also be dropped off at Rowardennan and picked up at Inversnaid after a 9-mile hike along the West Highland Way.

Balmaha Boatyard   ISLAND TOUR
(www.balmahaboatyard.co.uk; Balmaha) The mail boat, run by Balmaha Boatyard, cruises from Balmaha to the loch's four inhabited islands, departing at 11.30am and returning at 2pm, with a one-hour stop on Inchmurrin. Trips depart daily in July and August, and Monday, Thursday and Saturday in May, June and September, and cost £9/4.50 per adult/child.

Other Activities
The mostly traffic-free **Clyde and Loch Lomond Cycle Way** links Glasgow to Balloch (20 miles), where it links with the **West Loch Lomond Cycle Path**, which continues along the loch shore to Tarbet (10 miles).

You can rent rowing boats at Balmaha Boatyard for £10/30 per hour/day (or £20/50 for a boat with outboard motor). **Lomond Adventure** (☑01360-870218), also in Balmaha, rents out Canadian canoes (£30 per day) and sea kayaks (£25).

At Loch Lomond Shores you can hire canoes (£12/17 per half-hour/hour) and bicycles (£12/17 per three hours/full day), take a guided canoe trip on the loch (£30 for two hours) or try power kiting (£30 for 2½ hours).

🛏 Sleeping & Eating
Western Shore
Loch Lomond SYHA   HOSTEL £
(☑01389-850226; www.syha.org.uk; Arden; dm £18; ⊙Mar-Oct; P@ ⓢ) Forget about roughing it, this is one of the most impressive hostels in the country – an imposing 19th-century country house set in beautiful grounds overlooking the loch. It's 2 miles north of Balloch and very popular, so book in advance in summer. And yes, it *is* haunted.

Ardlui Hotel   HOTEL ££
(☑01301-704243; www.ardlui.co.uk; Ardlui; s/d £60/95; P) This plush and comfy country-house hotel has a great lochside location, and a view of Ben Lomond from the breakfast room.

TOP CHOICE **Drover's Inn**   PUB GRUB ££
(☑01301-704234; www.thedroversinn.co.uk; Inverarnan; s/d from £40/78; bar meals £8-10, steaks £15-17; ⊙lunch & dinner) This is one howff (drinking den) you shouldn't miss – a low-ceilinged place with smoke-blackened stone, bare wooden floors spotted with candle wax, barmen in kilts, and walls festooned with moth-eaten stags' heads and stuffed birds. There's even a stuffed bear and the desiccated husk of a basking shark.

The bar serves hearty hill-walking fuel such as steak-and-Guinness pie with mustard mash, and hosts live folk music on Friday and Saturday nights. We recommend this inn more as a place to eat and drink than to stay – accommodation varies from eccentric, old-fashioned and rather run-down rooms in the old building (including a ghost in room 6), to more comfortable rooms (with en suite bathrooms) in the modern annexe across the road. Ask to see your room before taking it.

Coach House Coffee Shop
SANDWICHES, SCOTTISH £

(Luss; mains £5-11; ☺10am-5pm) With its chunky pine furniture and deep, deep sofa in front of a rustic fireplace, the Coach House is one of the cosiest places to eat on Loch Lomond. The menu includes coffee and tea, home-baked cakes, scones, ciabattas and more substantial offerings such as haggis.

Eastern Shore

Oak Tree Inn
INN ££

(☎01360-870357; www.oak-tree-inn.co.uk; Balmaha; dm/s/d £30/60/75; ℙ▥) An attractive traditional inn built in slate and timber, the child-friendly Oak Tree offers luxurious guest bedrooms for pampered hikers, and two four-bed bunkrooms for hardier souls.

The rustic restaurant dishes up hearty lunches and dinners (meals £8 to £15) such as steak-and-mushroom pie, and roast Arctic char with lime and chive butter, and cooks up an excellent bowl of Cullen skink (soup made with smoked haddock, potato, onion and milk).

Passfoot Cottage
B&B ££

(☎01360-870324; www.passfoot.com; Balmaha; s/d from £55/64; ☺Apr-Sep) Passfoot is a pretty little whitewashed cottage decked out with colourful flower baskets, with a lovely location overlooking Balmaha Bay. The bright bedrooms have a homely feel, and there's a large lounge with a wood-burning stove and loch view.

Rowardennan Hotel
HOTEL ££

(☎01360-870273; www.rowardennanhotel.co.uk; Rowardennan; s/d £65/90; bar meals £7-11; ☺lunch & dinner; ℙ) Originally an 18th-century drovers' inn, the Rowardennan has two big bars (often crowded with rain-sodden hikers) and a good beer garden (often crowded with midges). It had just been taken over by new owners at the time of research, and refurbishment has made it a pleasant place to stay, with a choice of traditional hotel rooms and luxury self-catering lodges.

Rowardennan SYHA
HOSTEL £

(☎01360-870259; www.syha.org.uk; Rowardennan; dm £17; ☺Mar-Oct) Housed in an attractive Victorian lodge, this hostel has a superb setting right on the loch shore, beside the West Highland Way.

Cashel Campsite
CAMPGROUND £

(☎01360-870234; www.forestholidays.co.uk; Rowardennan; dm £6.50, tent sites per 2 people incl car £15-17; ☺Mar-Oct; ▥) This is the most attractive campsite in the area. It's 3 miles north of Balmaha, on the loch shore.

ⓘ Information

Balloch tourist office (☎0870 720 0607; Balloch Rd; ☺9.30am-6pm Jun-Aug, 10am-6pm Apr & Sep)

Balmaha National Park Centre (☎01389-722100; ☺9.30am-4.15pm Apr-Sep)

National Park Gateway Centre (☎01389-751035; www.lochlomondshores.com; ☺10am-6pm Apr-Sep, to 5pm Oct-Mar; @☎)

Tarbet tourist office (☎0870-720 0623; ☺10am-6pm Jul & Aug, to 5pm Easter-Jun, Sep & Oct) At the junction of the A82 and the A83.

ⓘ Getting There & Away

BUS First (☎0871 200 2233; www.firstgroup.com) Glasgow buses 204 and 215 run from Argyle St in central Glasgow to Balloch and Loch Lomond Shores (1½ hours, at least two per hour).

Scottish Citylink (www.citylink.co.uk) Coaches from Glasgow to Oban and Fort William stop at Luss (£8, 55 minutes, six daily), Tarbet (£8, one hour) and Ardlui (£14, 1¼ hours).

TRAIN There are frequent trains from Glasgow to Balloch (£4.15, 45 minutes, every 30 minutes) and a less-frequent service on the West Highland line from Glasgow to Arrochar & Tarbet station (£10, 1¼ hours, three or four daily), halfway between the two villages, and Ardlui (£13, 1½ hours), continuing to Oban and Fort William.

ⓘ Getting Around

Pick up the useful public transport booklet (free), which lists timetables for all bus, train and ferry services in Loch Lomond and the Trossachs National Park, available from any tourist office or park information centre.

BOAT There are several passenger ferries on Loch Lomond, with fares ranging from £3 to £7 per person; bicycles are carried free. Except for the ferries out of Loch Lomond Shores, these are mostly small motorboats that operate on demand, rather than to a set timetable – telephone or visit for more information.

MOVING ON?

For in-depth information, reviews and recommendations, head to the Apple App Store to buy Lonely Planet's *Glasgow City Guide* iPhone app, or to shop. lonelyplanet.com to purchase a downloadable PDF of the Glasgow chapter from Lonely Planet's *Scotland* guide.

Ardlui to Ardleish Ferry (☎01307-704243; Ardlui Hotel; ⊙9am-7pm May-Sep, to 6pm Apr & Oct) On demand.

Balmaha to Inchcailloch Ferry (☎01360-870214; ⊙9am-8pm) On demand.

Balmaha to Luss Ferry (www.cruiseloch lomondltd.com; ⊙Jul-Sep) Four daily.

Inveruglas to Inversnaid Ferry (☎01877-386223) On demand. No fixed timetable.

Loch Lomond Shores to Balmaha Ferry (www.clydecruises.com; ⊙late Jul-early Sep) Five daily.

Rowardennan to Luss Ferry (www.cruiseloch lomondltd.com; ⊙Jul-Sep) One daily. Departs Rowardennan at 9.30am; Luss at 4.15pm.

Tarbet to Inversnaid Ferry (www.cruiseloch lomondltd.com; ⊙Apr-Oct) Three daily.

Tarbet to Rowardennan (www.cruiseloch lomondltd.com; ⊙Apr-Oct) Twice daily. Departs Tarbet 10am and 4pm; Rowardennan at 10.45am and 4.45pm.

BUS McColl's Coaches (www.mccolls.org.uk) Bus 309 runs from Balloch to Balmaha (25 minutes, every two hours). An **SPT Daytripper** ticket gives a family group unlimited travel for a day on most bus and train services in the Glasgow, Loch Lomond and Helensburgh area. Buy the ticket (£9.80 for one adult and one or two children, £17.50 for two adults and up to four children) from any train station or the main Glasgow bus station.

Crianlarich & Tyndrum

POP 350

Surrounded by spectacular hillscapes begging to be walked, and situated on the West Highland Way, these villages are well-visited service junctions on the main A82 road, just north of the Loch Lomond & the Trossachs National Park. Crianlarich has a train station and more community atmosphere than Tyndrum (*tyne*-drum). But Tyndrum, 5 miles up the road, has two stations, a bus interchange, a petrol station, late-opening motorists' cafes and a flash tourist office (p48).

🛏 Sleeping & Eating

Crianlarich makes a more appealing base than Tyndrum: vehicles slow down through town and the views and food choice are better.

Crianlarich SYHA   HOSTEL **£**
(☎01838-300260; www.syha.org.uk; Station Rd, Crianlarich; dm £18.75; P@🛜♿) Well-run and comfortable, with spacious kitchen, dining area and lounge, this is a real haven for walkers or anyone passing through Crianlarich. Dorms vary in size – there are some great en suite family rooms that should be prebooked – but all are clean and roomy.

Strathfillan Wigwams   CAMPGROUND, CABINS **£**
(☎01838-400251; www.wigwamholidays.com/strathfillan; sites per adult/child £6/3, wigwam d small/large £28/33, lodge d from £45; P@) This charismatic place, 3 miles from Crianlarich and 2 miles from Tyndrum, is off the A82 and has 16 heated 'wigwams' – essentially wooden A-frame cabins with fridge and foam mattresses that can sleep four at a pinch. More upmarket are the self-contained lodges with their own bathroom and kitchen facilities. There's also camping with access to all facilities.

Crianlarich Hotel   HOTEL **££**
(☎01838-300272; www.crianlarich-hotel.co.uk; Crianlarich; budget/standard d £90/105; P🛜) At the junction in the middle of the village, this hotel has large rooms with appealingly comfortable beds, compact bathrooms and a we feel that they spent more on the reception area than the carpet. It's good value in the low season.

The bar meals (mains £8 to £13) are pricey, but served in a most elegant space, with venison, lamb hotpot and salmon available. The restaurant serves classier dinners (two courses £28).

Tyndrum Lodge Hotel   HOTEL **££**
(☎01838-400219; www.glhotels.co.uk; Tyndrum; s without bathroom £28, s/d £33/66; P🛜) This cheerily run pitstop is the heart of Tyndrum. It features decent-value rooms and two convivial bars. Walkers should head for rooms 1 to 12, which are towards the back and a bit quieter, ensuring a decent night's shut-eye. Shared bathrooms have baths not showers; breakfast is a buffet affair; and bar meals (£7 to £9) are supplemented by weekend all-you-can-eat curry nights.

BOOTS, BOATS, BIKES & BUSES

A new service called **Loch Lomond 4Bs** (www.lochlomond4bs.co.uk) allows you to explore Loch Lomond's hiking and biking trails by using ferry services and buses with bike trailers to deliver you to the start and finish of your chosen route.

For example, if you don't have time for the full 95 miles of the West Highland Way, you can spend just a day on one of its most scenic sections. Starting from Balloch train station, you can take a bus to Tarbet, then travel by boat to Rowardennan to start the 7-mile hike along the eastern shore of Loch Lomond to Inversnaid. From Inversnaid you can then get a boat back to Tarbet and the bus back to Balloch (bus £5, ferry £14.50).

The service operates daily from July to September, and on holiday weekends from Easter to June. See the website for full details of timetables and possible walking and cycling itineraries.

Real Food Café   FISH & CHIPS £
(www.therealfoodcafe.com; Tyndrum; meals £6-9; ⊙10am-10pm; 🖝) Don't be put off by the decor of this former chain eatery – concentrate on the food. The menu looks familiar – with fish and chips, soups, salads and sausages – but the owners make an effort to source sustainably and locally, and the quality shines through.

ⓘ Information

Tyndrum tourist office (☎01838-400246; ⊙10am-5pm Apr-Oct) This flash tourist office is a good spot for route information and maps for walking and ascents of popular An Caisteal (995m), Ben More (1174m) and magnificent Ben Lui (1130m).

ⓘ Getting There & Away

BUS Scottish Citylink (www.citylink.co.uk) Several buses daily to Edinburgh, Glasgow, Oban and Skye from Crianlarich and Tyndrum.
Royal Mail Postbus (☎08457 740 740; www.postbus.royalmail.com) Links Crianlarich, Tyndrum and Killin twice on each weekday and once on Saturday.

TRAIN Trains run from Tyndrum and Crianlarich to Fort William (£15, 1¾ hours, four daily Monday to Saturday, two on Sunday), Oban (£8.90, one hour, three or four daily) and Glasgow (£16.10, two hours, three or four daily).

Helensburgh

POP 16,500

With the coming of the railway in the mid-19th century, Helensburgh – named in the 18th century after the wife of Sir James Colquhoun of Luss – became a popular seaside retreat for wealthy Glaswegian families. Their spacious Victorian villas now populate the neat grid of streets that covers the hillside above the Firth of Clyde, but none can compare with the splendour of **Hill House** (NTS; ☎01436-673900; www.nts.org.uk; Upper Colquhoun St; adult/child £8.50/5.50; ⊙1.30-5.30pm Apr-Oct). Built in 1902 for the Glasgow publisher Walter Blackie, Hill House is perhaps architect **Charles Rennie Mackintosh's** finest creation – its timeless elegance feels as chic today as it no doubt did when the Blackies moved in a century ago.

Helensburgh has a ferry connection with Gourock via Kilcreggan, and a frequent train service to Glasgow (No 5, 50 minutes, two per hour).

Arrochar

POP 650

The village of Arrochar has a wonderful location, looking across the head of Loch Long to the jagged peaks of the **Cobbler** (881m). The mountain takes its name from the shape of its north peak (the one on the right, seen from Arrochar), which looks like a cobbler hunched over his bench. The village has several hotels and shops, a bank and a post office.

If you want to climb the Cobbler, start from the roadside car park at Succoth near the head of Loch Long. A steep uphill hike through the woods is followed by an easier section as you head into the valley below the triple peaks. Then it's steeply uphill again to the saddle between the north and central peaks. The central peak (to the left; south) is the highest point, but it's awkward to get to – scramble through the hole and along the ledge to reach the airy summit. The north peak (to the right) is an easy walk. Allow five to six hours for the 5-mile round trip.

🛏 Sleeping & Eating

**Ardgartan Caravan &
Campsite**   CAMPGROUND £

(📞01301-702293; www.forestholidays.co.uk; tent site plus car & 2 people £15-17; ☺Apr-Oct) There's good camping at Ardgartan Caravan & Campsite at the foot of Glen Croe. Bike hire is also available.

Village Inn   PUB GRUB ££

(📞01301-702279; www.villageinnarrochar.co.uk; s/d from £50/75, mains £8-18; ☺lunch & dinner; 🛜) The black-and-white, 19th-century Village Inn is a lovely spot for lunch, or just a pint of real ale – the beer garden has a great view of the Cobbler. There are 14 en suite bedrooms; the ones at the top end of the price range have four-poster beds and a view over the loch.

ℹ Getting There & Away

Citylink (www.citylink.co.uk) Buses from Glasgow to Inveraray and Campbeltown call at Arrochar and Ardgartan (£8, 1¼ hours, three daily).

THE TROSSACHS & AROUND

The Trossachs region has long been a favourite weekend getaway, offering outstanding natural beauty and excellent walking and cycling routes within easy reach of the southern population centres. With thickly forested hills, romantic lochs and an increasingly interesting selection of places to stay and eat, its popularity is sure to continue, protected by its national-park status.

The Trossachs first gained popularity as a tourist destination in the early 19th century, when curious visitors came from all over Britain drawn by the romantic language of Walter Scott's poem *Lady of the Lake*, inspired by Loch Katrine, and *Rob Roy*, about the derring-do of the region's most famous son.

In summer the Trossachs can be overburdened with coach tours, but many of these are day-trippers – peaceful, long evenings gazing at the reflections in the nearest loch are still possible. It's worth timing your visit not to coincide with a weekend.

Aberfoyle & Around

POP 580

Crawling with visitors on most weekends and dominated by a huge car park, little Aberfoyle is a fairly uninteresting place, easily overwhelmed by day-trippers. Instead of staying here, we recommend Callander or other Trossachs towns.

☉ Sights & Activities

Queen Elizabeth Forest Park
**David Marshall Lodge Visitor
Centre**   VISITOR CENTRE

(www.forestry.gov.uk/qefp; admission free, car park £2; ☺10am-4pm Nov-Mar, 10am-5pm Apr-Oct, to 6pm Jul & Aug) Half a mile north of Aberfoyle on the A821, this place offers info about the many walks and cycle routes in and around the Queen Elizabeth Forest Park. The Royal Society for the Protection of Birds (RSPB) has a display on local bird life, the highlight being a live video link to the resident osprey family.

The centre is worth visiting solely for the views; plus several picturesque but busy waymarked trails start from here, ranging from a light 20-minute stroll to a nearby waterfall to a hilly 4-mile circuit.

Go Ape!   AMUSEMENT PARK

(www.goape.co.uk; adult/child £30/20; ☺daily Apr-Oct, Sat & Sun Mar & Nov) Discover your inner monkey on this exhilarating adventure course of long ziplines, swings and rope bridges through the forest.

Lake of Menteith

Three miles east of the forest park is the Lake of Menteith (called lake not loch due to a mistranslation from Gaelic). A ferry takes visitors to the substantial ruins of **Inchmahome Priory** (HS; www.historic-scotland.gov.uk; adult/child incl ferry £4.70/2.80; ☺9.30am-5.30pm Apr-Sep, last return ferry 4.30pm). Mary, Queen of Scots, was kept safe here as a child during Henry VIII's 'Rough Wooing'. Henry attacked Stirling trying to force Mary to marry his son in order to unite the kingdoms.

Cycling

An excellent 20-mile circular cycle route links with the boat at Loch Katrine: from Aberfoyle, join the **Lochs & Glens Cycle Way** on the forest trail, or take the A821 over Duke's Pass. Following the southern shore of Loch Achray, you reach the pier on Loch Katrine. The ferry can take you to Stronachlachar (one way with bike £14) on the western shore, from where you can follow the beautiful B829 via Loch Ard back to Aberfoyle.

🛏 Sleeping & Eating

Lake of Menteith Hotel
HOTEL £££

(☎01877-385258; www.lake-hotel.com; Port of Menteith; d £130-190; P🖘) Soothingly situated on a lake (yes, it's the only non-loch in Scotland) 3 miles east of Aberfoyle, this makes a great romantic getaway. Rooms vary substantially in size, and are being upgraded, so it's worth shelling out a little extra for views and modernity. The **restaurant** serves sumptuous dinners (£40) with excellent service. Check the website for packages.

Mayfield Guest House
B&B ££

(☎01877-382962; www.mayfield-aberfoyle.co.uk; Main St, Aberfoyle; s/d £35/55; P) Nothing is too much trouble for the friendly hosts at this guesthouse. It has a double and two twin rooms, all very well kept, and a garage at the back for bikes. Pets welcome.

Forth Inn
PUB GRUB ££

(☎01877-382372; www.forthinn.com; Main St, Aberfoyle; mains £6-9; ⊘breakfast, lunch & dinner; 🖭) In the middle of the village, the solid Forth Inn seems to be the lifeblood of the town, with locals and visitors alike queuing up for good, honest pub fare. It also provides **accommodation** and beer, with drinkers spilling outside into the sunny courtyard. Single/double rooms are available for £50/80, but they can be noisy at weekends.

ℹ️ Information

Aberfoyle tourist office (☎01877-382352; aberfoyle@visitscotland.com; Main St; ⊘10am-5pm Apr-Oct, to-4pm Sat & Sun Nov-Mar) This office details a history of the Trossachs and provides currency exchange and a soft play area.

ℹ️ Getting There & Away

First (☎0871 200 2233; www.firstgroup.com) Up to four daily buses travel from Stirling to Aberfoyle (40 minutes); you'll have to connect at Balfron on Sundays.

Callander

POP 2754

Callander has been pulling in the tourists for over 150 years, and has a laid-back ambience along its main thoroughfare. It's a far better place than Aberfoyle to spend time in, quickly lulling visitors into lazy pottering. There's also an excellent array of accommodation options here.

◉ Sights & Activities

The **Hamilton Toy Collection** (www.the hamiltontoycollection.co.uk; 111 Main St; adult/child £2/50p; ⊘10am-4.30pm Apr-Oct) is a powerhouse of 20th-century juvenile memorabilia, chock-full of dolls houses, puppets and toy soldiers. It's a guaranteed nostalgia trip.

The impressive **Bracklinn Falls** are reached by track and footpath from Bracklinn Rd (30 minutes each way from the car park). Also off Bracklinn Rd, a woodland trail leads up to **Callander Crags**, with great views over the surroundings; a return trip is about 4 miles from the car park.

The Trossachs is a lovely area to cycle around. On a cycle route and based at Trossachs Tryst hostel, the excellent **Wheels Cycling Centre** (☎01877-331100; www.wheels cyclingcentre.com) has a wide range of hire bikes starting from £10/15 per half-/full day.

🛏 Sleeping

TOP CHOICE **Roman Camp Hotel**
HOTEL £££

(☎01877-330003; www.roman-camp-hotel.co.uk; d £95, s/d/superior £145/185; P🖘) Callander's best hotel is centrally located but feels rural, set by the river, off Main St, in its own beautiful grounds with birdsong the only sound. Its endearing features include a lounge with blazing fire and a library with a tiny secret chapel. Reassuringly, the name refers not to toga parties but to a ruin in the adjacent fields.

There are three grades of room; the standards are certainly luxurious, but the superior ones are even more appealing, with period furniture, armchairs and a fireplace. The upmarket restaurant is open to the public.

Trossachs Tryst
HOSTEL £

(☎01877-331200; www.scottish-hostel.co.uk; Invertrossachs Rd; dm/tw £17.50/45; P@🖘) Set up to be the perfect hostel for outdoorsy people, this cracking spot is in fresh-aired surroundings a mile from Callander. To get there, take Bridge St off Main St, then turn right onto Invertrossachs Rd and continue for a mile. Facilities and accommodation are excellent, with dorms offering heaps of space and their own bathrooms.

Help yourself to a continental breakfast in the morning, and enjoy the great feel that pervades this helpful place. Cycle hire is available, with plenty of route advice.

TROSSACHS TRANSPORT

In a bid to cut public transport costs, 'Demand Responsive Transport' (DRT) has recently been brought to the Trossachs. Sounds complex, but basically it means you get a taxi to where you want to go, for the price of a bus (eg 10 miles for £3.30). Taxis run Monday to Saturday and need to be booked in advance; call or text 0844-567 5670 between 7am and 7pm Monday to Saturday, or book online at www.aberfoylecoaches.com.

Abbotsford Lodge   B&B ££

(☎01877-330066;   www.abbotsfordlodge.com; Stirling Rd; s/d £50/75; Ⓟ@) This friendly Victorian house (on the main road on the eastern side of town; look for the monkey puzzle tree) offers something different to the norm, with tartan and florals consigned to the bonfire, replaced by stylish comfortable contemporary design that enhances the building's original features. Ruffled fabrics and ceramic vases with flower arrangements characterise the renovated rooms.

The top-floor rooms (doubles £55) share a bathroom, but their offbeat under-roof shapes are lovable.

Arden House   B&B ££

(☎01877-330235; www.ardenhouse.org.uk; Bracklinn Rd; s/d £35/70; ☀Apr-Oct; Ⓟ☎) A redoubt of peaceful good taste, this elegant home features faultlessly welcoming hospitality and a woodsy, hillside location close to the centre but far from the crowds. The commodious rooms have flatscreen TV and plenty of little extras, including a suite (£80) with great views. Homebaked banana bread and a rotating dish-of-the-day keep breakfast well ahead of the competition.

Callander Meadows   B&B ££

(☎01877-330181; www.callandermeadows.co.uk; 24 Main St; s £45, d £70-80) Upstairs at this restaurant (p51) are three very appealing rooms, elegantly kitted-out with dark-varnished furnishings and striped wallpaper (one has a four-poster bed).

White Shutters   B&B £

(☎01877-330442; 6 South Church St; s/d £22/39) A cute little house just off the main street, White Shutters offers pleasing rooms with shared bathroom and a friendly welcome.

The mattresses aren't exactly new, but it's comfortable and offers great value for this part of the world.

Linley Guest House   B&B ££

(☎01877-330087; www.linleyguesthouse.co.uk; 139 Main St; s/d incl breakfast £36/52) A spick-and-span B&B with bright rooms and helpful owners. The double en suite is worth the extra: it's beautifully appointed with a large window drawing in lots of natural light. Room-only rate available.

✗ Eating & Drinking

TOP CHOICE Mhor Fish   FISH & CHIPS £

(☎01877-330213; www.mhor.net; 75 Main St; fish supper £5.50, mains £8-12; ☀lunch & dinner Tue-Sun) Both chip shop and fish restaurant, but wholly different, this endearing black-and-white-tiled cafe displays the day's fresh catch. You can choose how you want it cooked, whether pan-seared and accompanied by one of many good wines, or fried and wrapped in paper with chips to take away. The fish comes from sustainable stock, and includes oysters and other goodies.

If they run out of fresh fish, they shut, so opening hours can be a bit variable.

Callander Meadows   RESTAURANT ££

(☎01877-330181; www.callandermeadows.co.uk; 24 Main St; lunch £7.95, mains £11-17; ☀lunch & dinner Thu-Sun) Informal but smart, this well-loved restaurant in the centre of Callander occupies the two front rooms of a house on the main street. There's a contemporary flair for presentation and unusual flavour combinations, but a solidly British base underpins the cuisine, with things like mackerel, red cabbage, salmon and duck making regular and welcome appearances.

It's also open on Mondays from April to September, and Wednesdays too in high summer.

Lade Inn   PUB GRUB £

(www.theladeinn.com; bar meals £8-11; ☀lunch & dinner; 🚗) Callander's best pub isn't in Callander – it's a mile north of town. It serves hearty bar meals, doesn't mind kids, and pulls a good pint (the real ales here are brewed to a house recipe). Next door, the owners run a shop with a dazzling selection of Scottish beers.

There's low-key live music here at weekends too, but it shuts early if it's quiet midweek.

ℹ Information

Loch Lomond & the Trossachs National Park tourist office (☎01389-722600; www.loch lomond-trossachs.org; 52 Main St; ◷9.30am-4.30pm Mon-Fri, 9.30am-12.30pm Sat) This place is a useful centre for specific information on the park.

Rob Roy & Trossachs tourist office (☎01877-330342; callander@visitscotland.com; Ancaster Sq; ◷10am-5pm daily Apr-Oct, 10am-4pm Mon-Sat Nov-Mar) This centre has heaps of info on the area.

ℹ Getting There & Away

First (☎0871 200 2233; www.firstgroup.com) Operates buses from Stirling (45 minutes, hourly Monday to Saturday).

Kingshouse (www.kingshousetravel.co.uk) Buses run from Killin (45 minutes, three to six daily Monday to Saturday).

Citylink (www.citylink.co.uk) Operates buses from Edinburgh to Oban or Fort William via Callander (£15.10, 1¾ hours, daily).

Aberfoyle Coaches (www.aberfoylecoaches .com) Runs between Callander and Aberfoyle (30 minutes, four times daily Monday to Saturday).

Lochs Katrine & Achray

This rugged area, 6 miles north of Aberfoyle and 10 miles west of Callander, is the heart of the Trossachs. From April to October two **boats** (☎01877-332000; www.lochkatrine.com; Trossachs Pier; 1hr cruise adult/child £10/7) run cruises from Trossachs Pier at the eastern tip of Loch Katrine. At 10.30am there's a departure to Stronachlachar at the other end of the loch before returning (single/return adult £12/14, child £8/9). From Stronachlachar (also accessible by car via Aberfoyle), you can reach the eastern shore of Loch Lomond at isolated Inversnaid.

A tarmac path links Trossachs Pier with Stronachlachar, so you can also take the boat out and walk/cycle back (12 miles). At Trossachs Pier, you can hire good bikes from **Katrinewheelz** (www.wheelscyclingcentre.com; hire per half-/full day from £10/15; ◷daily Apr-Oct). It even has electric buggies for the less mobile or inclined (£40 for two hours).

There are two good walks starting from nearby Loch Achray. The path to the rocky cone called **Ben A'an** (460m) begins at a car park near the old Trossachs Hotel. It's easy to follow, and the return trip is just under 4 miles (allow 2½ hours).

A tougher walk is up rugged **Ben Venue** (727m) – there is a path all the way to the summit. Start walking from Loch Achray Hotel, follow the Achray Water westwards to Loch Katrine, then turn left and ascend the steep flanks of Ben Venue. There are great views of the Highlands and the Lowlands from the top. The return trip is about 5.5 miles – allow around four to five hours.

Balquhidder & Around

Steeped in clan history, this mountainous and sparsely populated area is the wildest part of the Trossachs; get off the busy A84 for some tranquil lochscapes and great walking. North of Callander, you'll skirt past the shores of gorgeous Loch Lubnaig. Not as famous as some of its cousins, it's still well worth a stop for its sublime views of forested hills. In the small village of **Balquhidder** (ball-whidder), 9 miles north of Callander off the A84, there's a churchyard with Rob Roy's grave. It's an appropriately beautiful spot in a deep, winding glen in big-sky country. Rob Roy's wife and two of his sons are also interred here. In the church is the 8th-century St Angus' stone, probably a marker to the original tomb of St Angus, an 8th-century monk who built the first church here.

The minor road at the A84 junction continues along pretty **Loch Voil** to Inverlochlarig, where you can climb **Stob Binnein** (1165m) by its southern ridge. Stob Binnein is one of the highest mountains in the area, and it has a most unusual shape, like a cone with its top chopped off.

Local buses between Callander and Killin stop at the Kings House Hotel, as do daily **Citylink** (www.citylink.co.uk) buses between Edinburgh and Oban/Fort William.

🛏 Sleeping & Eating

[TOP CHOICE] **Monachyle Mhor** HOTEL £££
(☎01877-384622; www.mhor.net; dinner, bed & breakfast s/d from £166/220) Monachyle Mhor is a luxury hideaway with a fantastically peaceful location overlooking two lochs. It's a great fusion of country Scotland and contemporary attitudes to design and food. The rooms and suites are superb and feature quirkily original decor. The restaurant offers set lunch (£20 for two courses) and dinner (£46) menus which are high in quality, sustainably sourced, and deliciously innovative.

Nicknamed 'Red' ('ruadh' in Gaelic, anglicised to 'roy') for his ginger locks, Robert Mac-Gregor (1671–1734) was the wild leader of the wildest of Scotland's clans. Although the MacGregor's had rights to the lands they occupied, these estates stood between powerful neighbours who had the MacGregors outlawed, hence their sobriquet 'Children of the Mist'. Incognito, Rob became a prosperous livestock trader, before a dodgy deal led to a warrant for his arrest.

A legendary swordsman, the fugitive from justice then became notorious for his daring raids into the Lowlands to carry off cattle and sheep. He was forever hiding from potential captors; he was twice imprisoned, but escaped dramatically on both occasions. He finally turned himself in, and received his liberty and a pardon from the King. He lies buried in the churchyard at Balquhidder; his uncompromising epitaph reads 'MacGregor despite them'.

His life has been glorified over the years due to Walter Scott's novel and the 1995 film. Many Scots see his life as a symbol of the struggle of the common folk against the inequitable ownership of vast tracts of the country by landed aristocrats.

Enchantment lies in its successful combination of top-class hospitality with a relaxed rural atmosphere; dogs and kids happily romp on the lawns, and no-one looks askance if you come in flushed and muddy after a day's fishing or walking.

Kings House Hotel　　　　　HOTEL **££**
(☎01877-384646; www.kingshouse-scotland.co.uk; s/d £45/70) At the A84 junction, Kings House Hotel is a classic inn built in 1779 for £40 at the request of passing drovers. Nowadays it offers B&B in more salubrious surroundings. The upstairs rooms are lovely, with fine views, and there's an ancient, narrow, sloping passageway that reminds visitors they're treading in the 200-year-old-plus footsteps of many a passing traveller.

The cosy bar provides food and shelter from the elements.

Killin

POP 670

A fine base for the Trossachs or Perthshire, this lovely village sits at the western end of Loch Tay and has a spread-out, relaxed sort of a feel, particularly around the scenic **Falls of Dochart**, which tumble through the centre. On a sunny day people sprawl over the rocks by the bridge, pint or picnic in hand. Killin offers some fine walking around the town, and mighty mountains and glens close at hand.

The helpful, informative **tourist office** (☎01567 820254; killin@visitscotland.com) is in the **Breadalbane Folklore Centre** (www.breadalbanefolklorecentre.com; adult/child

£2.95/1.95; ◉10am-4pm Wed-Mon Apr-Oct), in an old water mill overlooking the falls. The centre has an audiovisual presentation about St Fillan – a local saint whose religious teachings are said to have helped unite the ancient kingdoms of the Scots and the Picts in the 8th century – as well as displays about local and clan history, including the Mac-Gregors and MacNabs. The **Clan MacNab burial ground** lies on an island in the river by the falls; ask at the tourist office for the gate key.

🏃 Activities

Five miles northeast of Killin, **Ben Lawers** (1214m) rises above Loch Tay; in addition to its ascent, other routes abound here. One rewarding circular walk heads up into the Acharn forest south of town, emerging above the tree line to great views of Loch Tay and Ben Lawers. The tourist office has walking leaflets and maps covering the area.

Glen Lochay runs westwards from Killin into the hills of Mamlorn; you can take a mountain bike for about 11 miles up the glen to just beyond Batavaime. The scenery is impressive and the hills aren't too difficult to climb. It's possible, on a nice summer day, to climb over the top of **Ben Challum** (1025m) and descend to Crianlarich, but it's hard work. A potholed road also connects this glen with Glen Lyon.

Killin is on the **Lochs & Glens Cycle Way** from Glasgow to Inverness. Hire bikes at **Killin Outdoor Centre** (☎01567-820652; www.killinoutdoor.co.uk; Main St; ◉daily), which also hires out canoes and kayaks.

BAG A MUNRO: BEN LAWERS

The trip to the top of Ben Lawers and back can take up to five hours: pack wet weather gear, water and food. From the now-closed visitor centre, take the nature trail that heads northeast. After the boardwalk protecting a bog, cross a stile, then fork left and ascend along the Edramucky burn (to the right). At the next rise, fork right and cross the burn. A few minutes later ignore the nature trail's right turn and continue ascending parallel to the burn's left bank for just over half a mile. Leave the protected zone by another stile and steeply ascend Beinn Ghlas's shoulder. Reaching a couple of large rocks, ignore a northbound footpath and continue zigzagging uphill. The rest of the ascent is a straight-forward succession of three false summits. The last and steepest section alternates between erosion-sculpted rock and a meticulously crafted cobbled trail. Long views of majestic hillscape, and even the North Sea and Atlantic, are your reward on a clear day.

🛏 Sleeping & Eating

There are numerous good guesthouses strung along the road through town, and a couple of supermarkets for trail supplies.

Falls of Dochart Inn   PUB ££
(☎01567-820270; www.falls-of-dochart-inn.co.uk; s/d from £60/80; P 🐾 🛜) In a prime position overlooking the falls, this is an excellent place to stay and eat. Handsome renovated rooms are comfortable, with slate bathrooms; it's worth the investment for one overlooking the falls themselves (double £95), but visitors warn they can be chilly in winter.

Downstairs is a very snug, atmospheric space with a roaring fire, personable service and really satisfying pub food, ranging from light meals to tasty, tender steaks and a couple of more advanced creations.

High Creagan   CAMPGROUND £
(☎01567-820449; Aberfeldy Rd; sites per person £6; ☺Mar-Oct) This place has a well-kept, sheltered campground with plenty of grass set high on the slopes overlooking sparkling Loch Tay, just outside Killin. Kids under five years of age aren't allowed in the tent area as there's a stream running through it.

Braveheart Backpackers   HOSTEL £
(☎07796-886899; info@cyclescotland.co.uk; dm/ s/d £17.50/20/40) Tucked away alongside the Killin Hotel (on the main road through town), these two adjoining cottages offer several types of room, all wood-clad with comfortable beds and bunks including sheets. The comfy kitchen and lounge area won't appeal to hygiene nuts, but make the place feel like a home rather than a hostel.

There's a rather negotiable attitude to prices and bookings: in short, it's not for everyone, but we like it.

❶ Getting There & Away

Citylink (www.citylink.co.uk) Two daily buses between Edinburgh and Oban/Fort William stop at Killin.

Royal Mail Postbus (☎08457 740 740; www .postbus.royalmail.com) There's a postbus to Crianlarich and Tyndrum twice on weekdays and once on Saturday.

Kingshouse Travel (www.kingshousetravel .co.uk) Runs buses to Callander, where you can change to a Stirling service.

COWAL PENINSULA

The remote Cowal peninsula is cut off from the rest of the country by the lengthy fjords of Loch Long and Loch Fyne – it's an area more accessible by boat than by car. It comprises rugged hills and narrow lochs, with only a few small villages; the scenery around Loch Riddon is particularly enchanting. The only town on the mainland is the old-fashioned holiday resort of Dunoon.

From Arrochar, the A83 to Inveraray loops around the head of Loch Long and climbs up Glen Croe. The pass at the head of the glen is called the **Rest and Be Thankful** – when the original military road through the glen was repaired in the 18th century, a stone was erected at the top inscribed 'Rest, and be thankful. This road was made, in 1748, by the 24th Regt...repaired by the 93rd Regt. 1786'. A copy of the stone can be seen at the far end of the parking area at the top of the pass.

There's a Forest Enterprise **Visitor Centre** (☎01301-702432; admission free; ☺10am-5pm Apr-Oct) at the foot of the glen, with information on various walks on the Cowal peninsula.

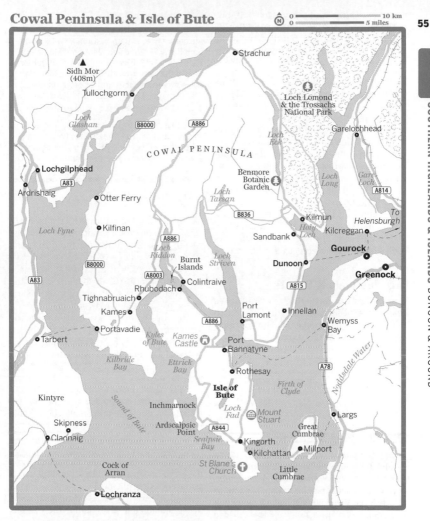

As you descend Glen Kinglas on the far side of the Rest and be Thankful, the A815 forks to the left just before Cairndow; this is the main overland route into Cowal. From Glasgow, the most direct route is by ferry from Gourock to Dunoon.

Dunoon & Around

Like Rothesay on the Isle of Bute, Dunoon (population 9100) is a Victorian seaside resort that owes its existence to the steamers that once carried thousands of Glaswegians on pleasure trips 'doon the watter' (down

the water) in the 19th and 20th centuries. As with Rothesay, Dunoon's fortunes declined in recent decades when cheap foreign holidays stole its market – however, while the Bute resort appears to be recovering, Dunoon is still a bit down in the dumps.

◉ Sights & Activities

The town's main attraction is still, as it was in the 1950s, strolling along the **promenade**, licking an ice-cream cone and watching the yachts at play in the Firth of Clyde. On a small hill above the seafront is a **statue of Highland Mary** (1763–86), one of the great loves of Robert Burns' life. She was born near Dunoon, but died tragically young; her statue gazes longingly across the firth to Burns' home territory in Ayrshire.

Benmore Botanic Garden   GARDEN
(www.rbge.org.uk; adult/child £5/1; ⊙10am-6pm Apr-Sep, to 5pm Mar & Oct) This garden, 7 miles north of Dunoon, was originally planted in the 19th and early 20th centuries. It contains the country's finest collection of flowering trees and shrubs, including impressive displays of rhododendrons and azaleas, and is entered along a spectacular avenue of giant Californian redwoods planted in 1863.

A highlight is the recently restored Victorian fernery, which is nestled in an unlikely fold in the crags. The cafe here (which stays open all year) is a nice place for lunch or a coffee.

✯ Festivals & Events

Cowal Highland Gathering   HIGHLAND GAMES
(www.cowalgathering.com) Held in Dunoon in mid-August. The spectacular finale traditionally features 3000 bagpipers playing en masse.

Cowalfest   ARTS, OUTDOORS
(www.cowalfest.org) A 10-day arts and walking festival featuring art exhibitions, film screenings, guided walks and bicycle rides throughout the Cowal peninsula.

⊨ Sleeping & Eating

Dhailling Lodge   B&B ££
(☑01369-701253; www.dhaillinglodge.com; 155 Alexandra Pde; s/d £40/76; ℗@⊛) You can experience some of Dunoon's former elegance at this large Victorian villa overlooking the bay about 0.75 miles north of the CalMac ferry pier. The owners are the essence of Scottish hospitality, and can provide excellent evening meals (£20 per person) if you wish.

Chatters   SCOTTISH ££
(☑01369-706402; 58 John St; mains lunch £5-9, dinner £15-22; ⊙lunch & dinner Wed-Sat) This pretty little cottage restaurant has tartan sofas in the sitting room and a few tables in the tiny garden. It serves a mix of lunchtime snacks and brasserie dishes, and is famous for its open sandwiches and tempting homemade puddings. Booking recommended.

❶ Information

Dunoon tourist office (☑0870 720 0629; 7 Alexandra Pde; ⊙9am-5.30pm Mon-Fri, 10am-5pm Sat & Sun Apr-Sep, 9am-5pm Mon-Thu, 10am-5pm Fri & 10am-4pm Sat & Sun Oct-Mar; @) On the waterfront 100m north of the pier; there's internet access for £1 per 12 minutes.

❶ Getting There & Away

Dunoon is served by two competing ferry services from Gourock – the **CalMac** (www.calmac .co.uk) ferry is better if you are travelling on foot and want to arrive in the town centre.

Tighnabruaich

POP 200

Sleepy little Tighnabruaich (tinna-*broo*-ach), a colony of seaside villas built by wealthy Glasgow families at the turn of the 20th century, is one of the most attractive villages on the Firth of Clyde. It was once a regular stop for Clyde steamers, and the old wooden pier is still occasionally visited by the paddle steamer *Waverley*.

The link with the sea continues in the **Tighnabruaich Sailing School** (www .tssargyll.co.uk; Carry Farm; ⊙May-Sep), 2 miles south of Tighnabruaich. A five-day dinghy-sailing course costs £230, excluding your accommodation.

The village is home to **An Lochan** (☑01700-811239; www.anlochan-argyll.co.uk; r £110-180; ℗), a luxurious boutique hotel that's comfortable but, in our opinion, a tad over-priced. The food (mains £10 to £22), made with fresh, locally sourced produce, is exquisite – from summer-vegetable risotto with basil dressing to seared scallops with black pudding, apple puree and curry oil.

If all you want to do is fill up with good, hearty homemade grub, go for the mussels and chips at the **Burnside Bistro** (mains £6-15; ⊙breakfast, lunch & dinner) in the village centre, or a bar meal at the **Kames Hotel** (☑01700-811489; http://kames-hotel.com; s/d from £45/75; mains £8-15; ⊙lunch & dinner), a mile to the south.

Cowal's West Coast

In Cowal, the tour buses and weekend crowds tend to stick to the scenic route along the Kyles of Bute between Colintraive and Tighnabruaich. If you're in search of tranquillity, head for the peninsula's much more peaceful west coast.

⊙ Sights

From the village of **Strachur**, where you'll find the fascinating **Smiddy Museum** (www .strachursmiddy.org.uk; adult/child £1/0.50; ⊙1-4pm Easter-Sep), a perfectly preserved blacksmith's forge, a minor road runs south to Portavadie through the tiny hamlets of Otter Ferry and Kilfinan.

Otter Ferry, once linked to Lochgilphead via a ferry, has nothing to do with the aquatic mammal, though sea life abounds. The name comes from *an oitir*, the Gaelic for 'gravel spit' – a gravel bank extends almost a mile into Loch Fyne here.

At **Kilfinan**, there's an ancient churchyard to explore, while **Kilbride Bay**, south of Portavadie, is Cowal's 'secret beach' – to get there park at the entrance to Kilbride Farm and walk along the farm road for half a mile to reach the broad, sandy bay with panoramic views of Arran's peaks.

⌸ Sleeping & Eating

Kilfinan Hotel   HOTEL **££**
(☑01700-821201; www.kilfinan.com; Kilfinan; d from £106; ℗) Cosy and romantic, the Kilfinan is a small, peaceful and luxurious hotel with just ten rooms, a snug wee bar with a log fire, and no mobile phone reception. The restaurant serves local seafood, steak and venison, and there are plenty of nearby walks to explore.

⌁ Inver Cottage   RESTAURANT **££**
(☑01369-860537; www.invercottage.com; Strathlachlan, Strachur; mains £9-18; ⊙10.30am-10pm Wed-Sat & 10.30am-5.30pm Sun Jan-Oct, open daily Jul-Aug, shorter hours Nov-Dec) Operating as both cafe and restaurant, Inver Cottage enjoys a scenic setting with views over Castle Lachlan and Loch Fyne from its outdoor terrace tables. Indoors is bright and contemporary, with local arts and crafts on display. The menu focuses on local produce, including scallops, lobster and langoustines. Try the venison burger with melted Arran cheddar and redcurrant relish.

Oystercatcher   PUB GRUB **££**
(www.theoystercatcher.co.uk; Otter Ferry; mains £9-18; ⊙11am-11pm Mon-Sat, from 12.30pm Sun, closed Tue-Wed low season; ☏⌂) A convivial pub with a sea view – the kids can run wild on the grass overlooking the beach outside – the Oystercatcher pulls in visiting yachties with its free moorings, foaming pints of real ale and a menu of posh pub grub that runs from homemade burgers to local mussels and langoustines.

ISLE OF BUTE

POP 7350

The island of Bute lies pinched between the thumb and forefinger of the Cowal peninsula, separated from the mainland by a narrow, scenic strait known as the Kyles of Bute. The Highland Boundary Fault cuts through the middle of the island so that, geologically speaking, the northern half is in the Highlands and the southern half is in the central Lowlands – a metal arch on Rothesay's Esplanade marks the fault line.

From the mid-19th century until the 1960s, **Rothesay** – once dubbed the Margate of the Clyde – was one of the most popular holiday resorts in Scotland. Its Esplanade was bustling with day-trippers disembarking from the numerous steamers crowded around the pier, and its hotels were filled with elderly holidaymakers and convalescents taking advantage of the town's famously mild climate.

The fashion for foreign holidays, which took off in the 1970s, saw Rothesay's fortunes decline, and by the late 1990s it had become dilapidated and despondent. But in the last few years a nostalgia-fuelled resurgence of interest in Rothesay's holiday heyday has seen many of its Victorian buildings restored, the ferry terminal and harbour rebuilt and marinas constructed at Rothesay and Port Bannatyne. There's a new feeling of optimism in the air.

The five-day **Isle of Bute Jazz Festival** (www.butejazz.com) is held over the first weekend of May.

⊙ Sights

Mount Stuart   HISTORIC BUILDING
(☑01700-503877; www.mountstuart.com; Mount Stuart; adult/child £8/4; ⊙11am-5pm May-Sep) The Stuart Earls of Bute are direct descendants of Robert the Bruce, and have lived on the island for 700 years. Their family seat, Mount Stuart, is the finest neo-Gothic palace in Scotland, and one of the most magnificent stately homes in Britain, and the first to have electric lighting, central heating and a heated swimming pool.

When a large part of the original house was destroyed by fire in 1877, the third Marquess of Bute, John Patrick Crichton-Stuart (1847–1900) – the builder of Cardiff Castle and Castell Coch in Wales and one of the greatest architecture patrons of his day – commissioned Sir Robert Rowand Anderson to create a new one. The result, built in the 1880s and 1890s, and restored a hundred years later, is a byword for flamboyance.

The heart of the house is the stunning **Marble Hall**, a three-storey extravaganza of Italian marble that soars 25m to a dark-blue vault spangled with constellations of golden stars. Twelve stained-glass windows represent the seasons and the signs of the zodiac, with crystal stars casting rainbow-hued highlights across the marble when the sun is shining.

The design and decoration reflect the third marquess' fascination with astrology, mythology and religion, a theme carried over into the grand **Marble Staircase** beyond (where wall panels depict the six days of the Creation), and the lavishly decorated **Horoscope Bedroom**. Here the central ceiling panel records the positions of the stars and planets at the time of the marquess' birth on 12 September 1847.

Yet another highlight is the **Marble Chapel**, built entirely out of dazzling white Carrara marble. It has a dome lit to spectacular effect by a ring of ruby-red stained-glass windows – at noon on midsummer's day a shaft of blood-red sunlight shines directly onto the altar. It was here that Stella McCartney – daughter of ex-Beatle Sir Paul, and friend of the present marquess, former racing driver Johnny Dumfries – was married in 2003.

Mount Stuart is 5 miles south of Rothesay. Bus 90 runs from the bus stop outside the ferry terminal at Rothesay to Mount Stuart (15 minutes, hourly May to September). You can buy a special Mount Stuart day-trip ticket (adult/child £16/8) that includes return ferry and bus travel from Wemyss Bay ferry terminal to Mount Stuart, as well as admission.

Rothesay Castle CASTLE
(HS; www.historic-scotland.gov.uk; King St, Rothesay; adult/child £4.20/2.50; 9.30am-5.30pm Apr-Sep, to 4.30pm Sat-Wed Oct-Mar) The splendid ruins of 13th-century Rothesay Castle, with seagulls and jackdaws nesting in the walls, was once a favourite residence of the Stuart kings. It is unique in Scotland in having a circular plan, with four massive round towers. The landscaped moat, with its manicured turf, flower gardens and lazily cruising ducks, makes a picturesque setting.

Bute Museum MUSEUM
(www.butemuseum.org; 7 Stuart St, Rothesay; adult/child £2/1; 10.30am-4.30pm Mon-Sat & from 2.30pm Sun Apr-Sep, 2.30-4.30pm Tue-Sat Oct-Mar) The most interesting displays in Bute Museum are those recounting the history of the famous Clyde steamers. Other galleries cover natural history, archaeology and geology; the prize exhibit is a stunning jet necklace found in a Bronze Age burial on the island.

Victorian Toilets HISTORIC BUILDING
(Rothesay Pier, Rothesay; adult/child 10p/free) There aren't too many places where a public toilet would count as a tourist attraction, but Rothesay's Victorian toilets, dating from 1899, are a monument to lavatorial luxury – a disinfectant-scented temple of green marble, glistening white enamel, glass-sided cisterns and gleaming copper pipes.

The attendant will escort ladies into the hallowed confines of the gents for a look around when the facilities are unoccupied.

South & West Coast
In the southern part of the island you'll find the haunting 12th-century ruin of **St Blane's Chapel**, set in a beautiful wooded grove, and a sandy beach at **Kilchattan Bay**.

There are more good beaches on the west coast. **Scalpsie Bay** is a 400m walk across a field from the parking area, and has a fantastic outlook to the peaks of Arran. You can often spot seals basking at low tide off Ardscalpsie Point, to the west.

Ettrick Bay is bigger, easier to reach, and has a tearoom (not the most attractive building on the island), but it's not as pretty as Scalpsie.

Activities
There are lots of easy walks on Bute, including **West Island Way**, a waymarked, 30-mile walking route from Kilchattan Bay to Port Bannatyne; map and details are available from the Isle of Bute Discovery Centre.

Cycling on Bute is excellent – the roads are well surfaced and fairly quiet. You can hire a bike from the **Bike Shed** (07718-023571; www.thebikeshed.org.uk; 23-25 East Princes St) for £10/15 per half-/full day.

Kingarth Trekking Centre HORSE RIDING
(01700-831673; www.kingarthtrekkingcentre.co.uk; Kilchattan Bay) Paddock rides for kids (£5; minimum age eight years), riding lessons (£20 per hour), and pony treks (£35 for two hours).

🛌 Sleeping

Boat House
B&B ££

(☎01700-502696; www.theboathouse-bute.co.uk; 15 Battery Pl, Rothesay; s/d from £45/65; 🛜) The Boat House brings a touch of class to Rothesay's guesthouse scene, with quality fabrics and furnishings and an eye for design that makes it feel a bit like a boutique hotel without the expensive price tag. Other features include sea views, a central location and a ground-floor room kitted out for wheelchair users.

Glendale Guest House
B&B ££

(☎01700-502329; www.glendale-guest-house.com; 20 Battery Pl, Rothesay; s/d/f from £35/60/90; P🛜) Look out for the ornate, flower-bedecked facade on this beautiful Victorian villa, complete with pinnacled turret. All those windows mean superb sea views from the front-facing bedrooms, the elegant, 1st-floor lounge and the breakfast room, where you'll find homemade smoked haddock fish-cakes on the menu as well as the traditional fry-up.

Moorings
B&B ££

(☎01700-502277; www.themoorings-bute.co.uk; 7 Mountstuart Rd, Rothesay; s/d from £37/55; P) The family-friendly Moorings is a delightful Victorian lodge with good sea views. It has an outdoor play area for kids and a high chair in the breakfast room. Vegetarian breakfasts are not a problem.

Roseland Caravan Park
CAMPGROUND £

(☎01700-504529; www.roselandcaravanpark.co.uk; Roslin Rd, Canada Hill; tent site & 2 people £8) The island's only official campsite is a steep climb up the winding Serpentine Rd from the ferry terminal. There's a small but pleasant grassy area for tents amid the static caravans, and a handful of pitches for campervans.

🍴 Eating

Waterfront Bistro
SCOTTISH ££

(www.thewaterfrontbistro.co.uk; 16 East Princes St, Rothesay; mains £8-16; ⊙dinner Thu-Mon) Cheerful and informal, the wood-panelled Waterfront has a bistro menu that ranges from haddock and chips to venison in red-wine sauce, and grilled langoustines with garlic butter. Bottled real ale from the Arran Brewery complements the wine list.

Brechin's Brasserie
INTERNATIONAL ££

(☎01700-502922; 2 Bridgend St, Rothesay; mains £9-16; ⊙lunch Tue-Sat, dinner Fri & Sat) A friendly neighbourhood brasserie owned by jazz fan Tim (check out the sheet music and posters on the wall), Brechin's serves unpretentious but delicious dishes such as homemade lasagne, local lamb chops with redcurrant and red-wine sauce, and grilled salmon with savoury herb butter.

Pier at Craigmore
SCOTTISH, SEAFOOD ££

(Mount Stuart Rd, Rothesay; mains £7-13; ⊙lunch daily, dinner Sat) Housed in the former waiting room of a Victorian pier on the eastern edge of town, the Craigmore is a neat little bistro with fantastic views. The lunch menu offers sandwiches, salads, homemade burgers and quiche, while Saturday dinner is more sophisticated, with seafood, steak and roast lamb. No credit cards.

Musicker
SANDWICHES £

(11 High St, Rothesay; mains £3-5; ⊙breakfast & lunch) This cool little cafe, decked out in pale minty green, serves the best coffee on the island, alongside a range of sandwiches with imaginative fillings (haggis and cranberry, anyone?). It also sells music CDs (folk, world and country) and sports an old-fashioned jukebox.

THE MAIDS OF BUTE

One of the best walks on Bute is from the ferry pier at Rhubodach to the northern tip of the island (1.5 miles), where you can watch yachts negotiate the rocky narrows at the Burnt Islands. Just around the point are the Maids of Bute, two rocks painted to look like old women. The story goes that the distinctively shaped (but then unpainted) rocks were first noticed by the skipper of a pleasure steamer in the early 20th century, who always pointed them out to the passengers on his boat. Frustrated that the tourists could never see the resemblance, he sent a deckhand ashore with a couple of tins of paint to give them some clothes and recognisable faces. No one is quite sure who now maintains the maids, but every time the paint begins to peel, it's not long before a fresh coat brightens them up.

ℹ Information

Isle of Bute Discovery Centre (☎01700-505156; www.bestofbute.co.uk; Esplanade; ⏰10am-6pm Mon-Fri, 9.30am-5pm Sat & Sun Jul & Aug, 10am-5pm daily Apr-Jun & Sep, shorter hours Oct-Mar; @) In Rothesay's restored Winter Gardens.

ℹ Getting There & Away

BOAT CalMac (www.calmac.co.uk) Ferries travel between Wemyss Bay and Rothesay (passenger/car £4.25/16.85, 35 minutes, hourly). Another crosses the short stretch of water between Rhubodach in the north of the island and Colintraive (passenger/car £1.35/8.50, five minutes, every 15 to 20 minutes) in Cowal.

BUS West Coast Motors (www.westcoast motors.co.uk) Buses run four or five times a week from Rothesay to Tighnabruaich and Dunoon via the ferry at Colintraive. On Monday and Thursday a bus goes from Rothesay to Portavadie (via the Rhubodach–Colintraive ferry), where there's a ferry to Tarbert in Kintyre (passenger/car £3.60/16.25, 25 minutes, hourly).

ISLE OF ARRAN

POP 4800

Enchanting Arran is a jewel in Scotland's tourism crown. Strangely undiscovered by foreign tourists, the island is a visual feast, and boasts culinary delights, cosy pubs (including its own brewery) and stacks of accommodation. The variations in Scotland's dramatic landscape can all be experienced on this one small island, best explored by pulling on the hiking boots or jumping on a bicycle.

The ferry from Ardrossan docks at Brodick, the island's main town. To the south, Lamlash is actually the capital and, like nearby Whiting Bay, a popular seaside resort. From the pretty village of Lochranza in the north there's a ferry link to Claonaig on the Kintyre peninsula.

🏃 Activities

Arran offers some challenging walks in the mountainous north, often compared to the Highlands. There are also many walking trails clearly signposted around the island. Several leave from Lochranza, including the spectacular walk to the island's northeast tip, **Cock of Arran**, which finishes in the village of Sannox (8 miles one way).

The island's 50-mile coastal road circuit is very popular with cyclists and has few serious hills – more in the south than the north.

Drop into the tourist office in Brodick for excellent walking and cycling suggestions; there are plenty of walking booklets and maps available.

🛏 Sleeping

Camping isn't allowed without permission from the landowner, but there are several camping grounds. Good sleeping options are dotted all around the island, although especially in Brodick and the south. Accommodation is a good deal more expensive on Arran than on the mainland.

ℹ Information

Arran Library (☎01770-302835; Brodick Hall; ⏰10am-5pm Tue, to 7.30pm Thu & Fri, to 1pm Sat) Free internet access.

Hospital (☎600777; Lamlash)

Brodick tourist office (☎01770-303774; www .ayrshire-arran.com; Brodick; ⏰9am-5pm Mon-Sat) Efficient. Located by Brodick pier; also open Sunday in July and August.

ℹ Getting There & Away

CalMac (www.calmac.co.uk) Car ferries run between Ardrossan and Brodick (passenger/car return £9.70/59, 55 minutes, four to eight daily); from April to late October services also run between Claonaig and Lochranza (passenger/car return £8.75/39.10, 30 minutes, seven to nine daily).

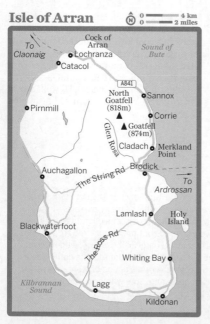

Isle of Arran

Getting Around

BICYCLE Several places hire out bicycles in Brodick.

CAR Arran Transport (☑01770-700345; Brodick; car rental half-/full day from £25/32) At the service station near the ferry pier.

PUBLIC TRANSPORT Four to seven buses daily go from Brodick pier to Lochranza (45 minutes), and many daily go from Brodick to Lamlash and Whiting Bay (30 minutes), then on to Kildonan and Blackwaterfoot. Pick up a timetable from the tourist office. An Arran Rural Rover ticket costs £4.75 and permits travel anywhere on the island for a day (buy it from the driver). For a taxi, call ☑01770-302274 in Brodick or ☑01770-600903 in Lamlash.

Brodick & Around

Most visitors arrive in Brodick, the heartbeat of the island, and congregate along the coastal road to admire the town's long curving bay.

As you follow the coast along Brodick Bay, look out for seals, often seen on the rocks around **Merkland Point**. Two types live in these waters, the Atlantic grey seal and the common seal. The common seal has a face like a dog; the Atlantic grey seal has a Roman nose.

◎ Sights

Many of Brodick's attractions are just out of town, off the main road that runs north to Lochranza.

Brodick Castle & Park   CASTLE
NTS; (☑01770-302202; www.nts.org.uk; adult/child castle & park £10.50/7.50, park only £5.50/4.50; ⊙castle 11am-4pm Sat-Wed Apr-Oct, open daily late Jun–early Sep, park 9.30am-sunset) The first impression of this estate 2.5 miles north of Brodick is that of an animal morgue – as you enter via the hunting gallery, which is wallpapered with prized deer heads. On your way to the formal dining room (with its peculiar table furnishings), note the intricacy of the fireplace in the library.

The castle has more of a lived-in feel than some NTS properties. Only a small portion is open to visitors. The extensive grounds, now a country park with various trails among the rhododendrons, justify the steep entry fee.

Arran Aromatics   SOAP FACTORY
(☑01770-302595; www.arranaromatics.com; Duchess Court; ⊙9.30am-5pm) Here you can purchase any number of scented items

and watch the production line at work. Free factory tours run on Thursdays in summer at 6pm. While you're here, check out **Soapworks** (soapmaking from £7.50; 10am-4pm), a fun little place where kids (and adults!) can experiment by making their own soaps, combining colours and moulds to make weird and wonderful creations.

Isle of Arran Brewery   BREWERY
(☑01770-302353; www.arranbrewery.com; ⊙10am-5pm Mon-Sat & from 12.30pm Sun Apr-Sep, 10am-3.30pm Mon & Wed-Sat Oct-Mar) Offers an excellent self-guided brewery tour for £2.50, which includes tastings in the shop. Arran beers are pure quality; warning: Arran Dark is highly addictive. There's a good outdoors shop here too, if you're heading up Goatfell.

Marvin Elliott   GALLERY
Just beyond the Cladach Centre, local artist Marvin Elliott creates impressive wooden sculptures in his workshop.

✴ Activities

Arran Adventure Company OUTDOOR ACTIVITIES
(☑01770-302244; www.arranadventure.com; Shore Rd; ⊙Easter-Oct) Offers loads of activities (such as gorge walking, sea kayaking, climbing, abseiling and mountain biking), running a different one each day. All activities run for about three hours and cost around £48/28 for adults/kids. Lower age limits apply for some activities. Drop in to see what's available while you're around.

Auchrannie Resort   RESORT, SPA
(☑01770-302234; www.auchrannie.co.uk) This resort offers a bit of everything and can make a good destination if you're looking for something to do in Brodick. As well as tennis courts and a gym, it has a pool and spa complex that nonguests can access for £4.60.

NTS Countryside Rangers   WALKING
(☑01770-302462; Brodick Country Park) The NTS countryside rangers, located about 2 miles (3km) north of Brodick, organise a program of walks from May to October, ranging from afternoon wildlife strolls through low-level forests to days out on Goatfell (see p61).

✦ Festivals & Events

There are annual local festivals at villages around the area from June to September

Arran Folk Festival   FOLK MUSIC
(☎01770-302623; www.arranfolkfestival.org) A
week-long festival in early June.

Arran Wildlife Festival   WILDLIFE
(www.arranwildlife.co.uk) This celebration of local fauna is held mid-May.

🛏 Sleeping

TOP CHOICE Kilmichael Country House Hotel
                                        HOTEL £££
(☎01770-302219; www.kilmichael.com; s £95, d
£160-199; P🛜) The island's best hotel, the
Kilmichael is also the oldest building – it has
a glass window dating from 1650. The hotel
is a luxurious, tastefully decorated spot, a
mile outside Brodick, with eight rooms and
an excellent **restaurant** (3-course dinner
£42). It's an ideal, utterly relaxing hideaway,
and feels very classy without being overly
formal.

🏄 Glenartney   B&B ££
(☎01770-302220;   www.glenartney-arran.co.uk;
Mayish Rd; s/d £56/78; ⊙late Mar–Sep; P🛜) Uplifting bay views and genuine, helpful hosts
make this a cracking option. Airy, stylish
rooms make the most of the natural light
available here at the top of the town. Cyclists
will appreciate the bike wash and storage facilities, while hikers can benefit from the drying rooms and expert trail advice. The owners make big efforts to be sustainable too.

Fellview   B&B ££
(☎01770-302153; fellviewarran@yahoo.co.uk; 6
Strathwhillan Rd; r per person £30) This lovely
house near the ferry is an excellent place to
stay. The two rooms – which share a good
bathroom – are full of thoughtful personal
touches, such as bathrobes, and breakfast is
in a pretty garden conservatory. The owner
is warm, friendly and encapsulates Scottish
hospitality; she doesn't charge a supplement
for singles (because, in her words, 'it's not
their fault').

To get here, head south out of Brodick
and take the left-hand turn to Strathwhillan.
Fellview is just up on the right.

Rosaburn Lodge   B&B ££
(☎01770-302383; www.rosaburnlodge.co.uk; s
£70-80, ste £90-100; P) By the River Rosa,
800m from the centre of Brodick, this very
friendly lodge gets heaps of natural light.
There are three excellent rooms (and a
chairlift to them). The Rosa suite overlooks
the river via its bay window and is closer to
an apartment than a bedroom. Note that
there are no singles.

Belvedere Guest House   B&B ££
(☎01770-302397;   www.vision-unlimited.co.uk;
Alma Rd; s £35, d £60-80; P🛜) Imperiously
overlooking the town, bay and surrounding
mountains, Belvedere has well-presented
rooms and very welcoming hosts, who also
offer reiki, healing and de-stressing packages. They provide very good island information and good breakfasts with vegetarian
choices.

Glen Rosa Farm   CAMPGROUND £
(☎01770-302380; Glen Rosa; sites per person £4;
P) In a lush glen by a river, 2 miles north
of Brodick, this large place has plenty of
nooks and crannies to pitch a tent. It's remote camping with cold water and toilets
only.

To get there from Brodick head north,
take String Rd, then turn right almost immediately on the road signed to Glen Rosa.
After 400m, on the left is a white house
where you book in; the campground is further down the road.

🍴 Eating & Drinking

Creelers   SEAFOOD ££
(☎01770-302810; www.creelers.co.uk; Duchess Ct;
mains £11-21; ⊙lunch & dinner Tue-Sun Easter-Oct)
Creelers is likely to close in the near future,
but if it's still going when you read this, get
on the phone and book a table. Situated
1.5 miles north of Brodick, it's Arran's top
choice for fresh seafood. It's not licensed, so
bring a bottle.

Eilean Mòr   PIZZA, PASTA ££
(www.eileanmorarran.com; Shore Rd; mains £8-
10; ⊙food 10am-9pm, bar 11am-midnight; 🛜)
Upbeat and modern, this likeable little
cafe-bar does tasty meals through the day.
Pizzas and pastas feature, and it's not afraid
to give them a Scottish twist; try the haggis
ravioli.

Arran on a Plate   SCOTTISH, SEAFOOD ££
(☎01770-303886;   www.arranonaplate.com;
Shore Rd; 2-course lunch/dinner £10/20; ⊙lunch
& dinner) Unprepossessing from the outside, this new restaurant makes up for it
inside, with solicitous service, a striking
mural, and great sunset views over the
bay. Dishes focus on fresh seafood and are
attractively presented, if a little short on
quantity.

Ormidale Hotel
PUB GRUB **£**

(✆01770-302293; Glen Cloy; mains £8-10; ⊙lunch & dinner; ✦) This hotel has decent bar food. Dishes change regularly, but there are always some good vegetarian options, and daily specials. Quantities and value-for-money are high, and Arran beers are on tap.

Wineport
CAFE **££**

(✆01770-302101; Cladach Centre; lunch mains £7-11, dinner mains £12-19; ⊙lunch daily, dinner Fri & Sat Apr-Oct) This cafe-bar has a fine sunny terrace and does a nice line in sophisticated bistro fare in the summer months.

Island Cheese Co
CHEESE

(www.islandcheese.co.uk; Duchess Ct) Anyone with a fetish for cheese should stop by this place where you can stock up on the famed local varieties. There are free samples.

Corrie to Lochranza

The coast road continues north to the small, pretty village of Corrie, where there's a shop and hotel. One of the tracks up **Goatfell** (the island's tallest peak) starts here. After **Sannox**, which has a sandy beach and great views of the mountains, the road cuts inland. Heading to the very north, on the island's main road, visitors weave through lush glens flanked by Arran's towering mountain splendour.

Moderate walks here include the trail through **Glen Sannox**, which goes from the village of Sannox up the burn and is a two-hour return trip.

The traditional stone **Corrie Hotel** (✆01770-810273; www.corriehotel.co.uk; r per person £34, without bathroom £28; P🐾) offers simple but comfortable rooms, several with great views, above a pub with a wonderful beer garden that scrapes the water's edge. Groups of four or more can reserve a bunkroom (£15 per head, bed only).

Lochranza

The village of Lochranza is in a stunning location in a small bay at the north of the island. The area bristles with red deer, who wander into the village without concern to crop the grass on the golf course.

⊙ Sights

Lochranza Castle
CASTLE

(HS; www.historic-scotland.gov.uk; admission free; ⊙24hr) The 13th-century Lochranza Castle is said to have been the inspiration for the castle in *The Black Island,* Hergé's Tintin adventure. Standing on a promontory, it's now basically a draughty shell inside, with interpretative signs to help you decipher the layout.

Isle of Arran Distillery
DISTILLERY

(✆01770-830264; www.arranwhisky.com; tours adult/child £5/free; ⊙10am-6pm Mon-Sat, from 11am Sun mid-Mar–Oct) The Isle of Arran Distillery produces a light, aromatic single malt. The tour is a good one; it's a small distillery and the whisky-making process is thoroughly explained. Opening hours are reduced in winter.

🛏 Sleeping & Eating

Lochranza SYHA
HOSTEL **£**

(✆01770-830631; www.syha.org.uk; dm/f £17.50/72; ⊙mid-Feb–Oct; P@🐾) A recent refurbishment has made a really excellent hostel of what was always a charming place, with lovely views. The rooms are great, with chunky wooden furniture, keycards, and lockers. Rainwater toilets, a heat exchange system, and an excellent disabled room shows the thought that's gone into the redesign.

Plush lounging areas, a kitchen you could run a restaurant out of, laundry, drying room, red deer in the garden, and welcoming management make this a top option.

Apple Lodge
B&B **££**

(✆01770-830229; s/d/ste £54/78/90; P) Once the village manse, this rewarding choice, with courteous hosts, is the most dignified and hospitable in town. Rooms are individually furnished and very commodious. One has a four-poster bed, while another is a self-contained suite in the garden. The guest lounge is perfect for curling up with a good book; you should book well ahead in summer.

Catacol Bay Hotel
PUB **££**

(✆01770-830231; www.catacol.co.uk; r per person £30; ⊙lunch & dinner; P@🐾✦) Genially run, and with a memorable position overlooking the water, this no-frills pub two miles south of Lochranza offers comfortable-enough rooms with shared bathroom and views to lift the heaviest of hearts.

No-frills bar food comes out in generous portions, there's a Sunday lunch buffet (£10.50), and the beer garden is worth a contemplative pint or two as you gaze off across the water into the west.

Lochranza Hotel
HOTEL ££

(☎01770-830223; www.lochranza.co.uk; s/d £58/94; P) The focus of the village, being the only place you can get an evening meal, this bastion of Arran hospitality has comfortable rooms decked out in pink. The showers are pleasingly powerful, and the double and twin rooms at the front have super views. Rooms are a bit overpriced, but they get cheaper if you stay more than one night.

West Coast

On the western side of the island, reached by String Rd across the centre (or the coast road), is the **Machrie Moor Stone Circle** (String Rd), upright sandstone slabs erected around 6000 years ago. It's an eerie place, and these are the most impressive of the six stone circles on the island. There's another group at nearby **Auchagallon**, surrounding a Bronze Age burial cairn.

Blackwaterfoot is the largest village on the west coast; it has a shop and hotel. You can walk to **King's Cave** from here, via Drumadoon Farm – Arran is one of several islands that lay claim to a cave where Robert the Bruce had his famous arachnid encounter. This walk could be combined with a visit to the Machrie stones.

South Coast

The landscape in the southern part of the island is much gentler; the road drops into little wooded valleys, and it's particularly lovely around **Lagg**. There's a 10-minute walk from Lagg Hotel to **Torrylinn Cairn**, a chambered tomb over 4000 years old where at least eight bodies were found. **Kildonan** has pleasant sandy beaches, a gorgeous water outlook, a hotel, a campground and an ivy-clad ruined castle.

In **Whiting Bay** you'll find some small sandy beaches, a village shop, a post office and **Arran Art Gallery** (☎01770-700250; www .arranartgallery.com; Shore Rd), which has exquisite landscape portraits of Arran. From Whiting Bay there are easy one-hour walks through the forest to the **Giant's Graves** and **Glenashdale Falls**, and back – keep an eye out for golden eagles and other birds of prey.

🛏 Sleeping & Eating

TOP CHOICE Kildonan Hotel
HOTEL ££

(☎01770-820207; www.kildonanhotel.com; Kildonan; s/d/ste £70/95/125; P🅿🐕) Luxurious rooms and a grounded attitude – dogs and kids are made very welcome – combine to make this one of Arran's best options. Oh, and it's right by the water, with fabulous views and seals basking on the rocks. The standard rooms are beautifully furnished and spotless, but the suites – with private terrace or small balcony – are superb.

Other amenities include great staff, a bar serving good bar meals, a restaurant doing succulent seafood, an ATM, book exchange, and laptops lent to guests if you didn't bring one. Applause.

Royal Arran Hotel
B&B ££

(☎01770-700286; www.royalarran.co.uk; Whiting Bay; s £50, d £90-105; P🅿) This personalised, intimate spot has just four rooms. The double upstairs is our idea of accommodation heaven – four-poster bed, big heavy linen, a huge room and gorgeous water views. Room No 1 downstairs is a great size and has a private patio. The hosts couldn't be more welcoming (except to kids under 12, who aren't allowed).

Lagg Hotel
HOTEL ££

(☎01770-870255; www.lagghotel.com; Lagg; s/d £45/80; P🅿) An 18th-century coach house, this inn has a beautiful location and is the perfect place for a romantic weekend away from the cares of modern life. Rooms have been recently refurbished; grab a superior one (£90) with garden views. There's also a cracking beer garden, a fine bar with log fire, and an elegant restaurant (dinner mains £11 to £16).

Viewbank House
B&B ££

(☎01770-700326; www.viewbank-arran.co.uk; Whiting Bay; s £35, d £60-79; P🅿) Appropriately named, this friendly place does indeed have tremendous views from its vantage point high above Whiting Bay. Rooms, of which there are a variety with and without bathroom, are tastefully furnished and well kept. It's well signposted from the main road.

Sealshore Campsite
CAMPGROUND £

(☎01770-820320; www.campingarran.com; Kildonan; sites per person £6, per tent £1-3; P)

Living up to its name, this small campsite is right by the sea, with one of Arran's finest views from its grassy camping area. There's a good washroom area with heaps of showers, and the breeze keeps the midges away.

Isle of Arran Brewery Guesthouse   B&B ££
(☏01770-700662; guesthouse@arranbrewery.co.uk; Shore Rd, Whiting Bay; s/d from £55/80; P☎) Newly refurbished, this bright, light place offers five rooms named after Arran beers. The best of them have sea views, and cost slightly more.

Kilmory Lodge Bunkhouse   HOSTEL £
(☏01770-870345; www.kilmoryhall.com; Kilmory; dm £20; P) This new bunkhouse in Kilmory normally only opens for groups, but you may be able to grab a spare bed.

Coast   SEAFOOD, GRILLS £
(☏01770-700308; Shore Rd, Whiting Bay; mains £9-10; ⊙lunch Wed-Mon, dinner Thu-Sat) This funky place decked out in suave red tones and with a sun-drenched conservatory on the water's edge serves grills, seafood and salads in the evening, with lighter offerings during the day.

Lamlash

Lamlash is an upmarket town (even the streets feel wider here) in a dazzling setting, strung along the beachfront. The bay was used as a safe anchorage by the navy during WWI and WWII.

Just off the coast is **Holy Island** It's owned by the Samye Ling Tibetan Centre and used as a retreat, but day visits are allowed. Depending on tides, the **ferry** makes around seven trips a day (adult/child return £10/5, 15 minutes) from Lamlash between May and September. The same folk also run fun **mackerel-fishing** expeditions (£20 per person).

No dogs, bikes, alcohol or fires are allowed on Holy Island. There's a good walk to the top of the hill (314m), taking two or three hours return. It is possible to stay on the island in accommodation belonging to the grandiose-named **Holy Island Centre for World Peace & Health** (☏01770-601100; www.holyisle.org; dm/s/d £25/45/65). Prices include full (vegetarian) board. Although designed more for groups doing yoga and meditation courses at the centre, individuals are welcome.

🛏 Sleeping & Eating

Lilybank Guest House   B&B ££
(☏01770-600230; www.lilybank-arran.co.uk; Shore Rd; s/d £50/70; P☎) Built in the 17th century, Lilybank retains its heritage but has been refurbished for 21st-century needs. Rooms are clean and comfortable, with one adapted for disabled use. The front ones have great views over Holy Island. Breakfast includes oak-smoked kippers and Arran goodies.

Drift Inn   PUB GRUB £
(☏01770-600656; Shore Rd; mains £8-9; ⊙lunch & dinner; 🚺) There are few better places to be on the island on a sunny day than the beer garden at this child-friendly hotel, ploughing your way through an excellent bar meal while gazing over to Holy Island. There are pub faves and genuine Angus beef burgers, with generous portions all round.

Glenisle Hotel   PUB GRUB ££
(☏01770-600559; www.glenislehotel.com; Shore Rd; mains £9-12; ⊙lunch & dinner; ☎) Excellent pub food; serves Scottish classics such as Cullen skink (soup made with smoked haddock, potato, onion and milk). Good wine list, too.

Lamlash Bay Hotel   PUB GRUB ££
(www.lamlashbayhotel.co.uk; Shore Rd; mains £10-16, pizzas £7-8; ⊙lunch & dinner) Locals love a big meal out here; known for its toothsome pizza and filling Italian-style dishes.

KINTYRE

The Kintyre peninsula – 40 miles long and 8 miles wide – is almost an island, with only a narrow isthmus at Tarbert connecting it to the wooded hills of Knapdale. During the Norse occupation of the Western Isles, the Scottish king decreed that the Vikings could claim as their own any island they could circumnavigate in a longship. So in 1098 the wily Magnus Barefoot stood at the helm while his men dragged their boat across this neck of land, thus validating his claim to Kintyre.

Tarbert

POP 1500

The attractive fishing village and yachting centre of Tarbert is the gateway to Kintyre, and well worth a stopover for a bite to eat. There's a **tourist office** (☏01880-820429; Harbour St; ⊙9am-5pm Mon-Sat Apr-Oct) here.

Sights & Activities

The picturesque harbour is overlooked by the crumbling, ivy-covered ruins of **Tarbert Castle**, built by Robert the Bruce in the 14th century. You can hike up to it via a signposted footpath beside the **Loch Fyne Gallery** (www.lochfynegallery.com; Harbour St; ⏲10am-5pm), which showcases the work of local artists.

Kintyre Way WALKING
(www.kintyreway.com) Tarbert is the starting point for the 103-mile Kintyre Way, a walking route that runs the length of the peninsula to Southend at the southern tip. The first section, from Tarbert to Skipness (9 miles), makes a pleasant day-hike, climbing through forestry plantations to a high moorland plateau where you can soak up superb views to the Isle of Arran.

Highland Horse Riding HORSE RIDING
(☎01880-820333; www.highlandhorseriding.com; An Tairbeart; per person per hr £25-30; ⏲Apr-Oct) Offers sightseeing and wildlife-spotting pony treks into the hills of Knapdale.

Festivals & Events

Scottish Series Yacht Races SAILING
(www.scottishseries.com) Held over five days around the last weekend in May. The harbour is crammed with visiting yachts.

Tarbert Seafood Festival FOOD & DRINK
(www.seafood-festival.co.uk) First weekend in July; food stalls, cooking demonstrations, music, family entertainment.

Tarbert Music Festival MUSIC
(www.tarbertmusicfestival.com) On the third weekend in September: live folk, blues, beer, jazz, rock, ceilidhs (evening of traditional Scottish entertainment), more beer...

Sleeping

There are plenty of B&Bs and hotels here, but be sure to book ahead during major events.

Springside B&B B&B **££**
(☎01880-820413; www.scotland-info.co.uk/springside; Pier Rd; s/d £35/60; Ⓟ) You can sit in front of this attractive fisherman's cottage, which overlooks the entrance to the harbour, and watch the yachts and fishing boats come and go. There are four comfy rooms, three with en suite, and the house is just five minutes' walk from the village centre in one direction, and a short stroll from the Portavadie ferry in the other.

Getting There & Away

BOAT **CalMac** (www.calmac.co.uk) Operates a car ferry from Tarbert to Portavadie on the Cowal peninsula (passenger/car £3.60/16.25, 25 minutes, hourly). Ferries to the islands of Islay and Colonsay depart from Kennacraig ferry terminal on West Loch Tarbert, 5 miles southwest of Tarbert.

BUS **Scottish Citylink** (www.citylink.co.uk) Tarbert is served by five coaches a day between Campbeltown and Glasgow (Glasgow to Tarbert £14, 3¼ hours; Tarbert to Campbeltown £7, 1¼ hours).

Skipness

POP 100

Tiny Skipness is on the east coast of Kintyre, about 13 miles south of Tarbert, in a pleasant and quiet setting with great views of Arran. It has a post office and general store.

Beyond the village rise the substantial remains of 13th-century **Skipness Castle** (admission free; ⏲24hr), a former possession of the Lords of the Isles. It's a striking building, composed of dark-green local stone trimmed with contrasting red-brown sandstone from Arran. The tower house was added in the 16th century and was occupied until the 19th century. From the top you can see the roofless, 13th-century **St Brendan's Chapel** down by the shore. The kirkyard contains some excellent carved grave slabs.

Skipness Seafood Cabin (sandwiches £3, mains £5-9; ⏲11am-6pm Sun-Fri late May-Sep), in the grounds of nearby Skipness House, serves tea, coffee and home baking, as well as local fish and shellfish dishes. In fine weather you can scoff the house special – crab sandwiches – at outdoor picnic tables with grand views of Arran.

Local bus 448 runs between Tarbert and Skipness (35 minutes, two daily Monday to Saturday).

At Claonaig, 2 miles southwest of Skipness, there's a daily car ferry to Lochranza on the Isle of Arran (passenger/car £5.20/23, 30 minutes, seven to nine daily).

Isle of Gigha

POP 120

Gigha (*ghee*-ah; www.gigha.org.uk) is a low-lying island 6 miles long by about a mile wide. It's famous for sandy beaches and mild climate – subtropical plants thrive here in the island's **Achamore Gardens** (☎01583-505254; www.gigha.org.uk/gardens; Achamore House; admission free, donation requested; ⏲9am-dusk).

Locally made Gigha cheese is sold in many parts of Argyll – there are several varieties produced on the island, including pasteurised goats cheese and oak-smoked cheddar.

The island's limited accommodation includes **Post Office House** (☎01583-505251; www.gighastores.co.uk; d £45; **P**), a Victorian house at the top of the hill above the ferry slip with two self-catering cottages (it houses the island post office and shop as well). There's also the **Gigha Hotel** (☎01583-505254; www.gigha.org.uk/accom; r per person £50), 100m south of the post office, which serves up bar meals, or if you're feeling peckish, four-course dinners. You can also eat at the **Boat House Café Bar** (☎01583-505123; www.boathouse-bar.com; mains £7-12; ⊙lunch & dinner) near the ferry slip.

There's a range of self-catering cottages available as well. Camping is allowed on a grassy area beside the Boat House near the ferry slip – there's no charge but space is limited, so call the Boat House in advance to check availability.

CalMac (www.calmac.co.uk) runs a ferry from Tayinloan in Kintyre to Gigha (passenger/car return £6.20/22.80, 20 minutes, hourly Monday to Saturday, six on Sunday). Bicycles travel free.

You can rent bikes from Post Office House for £12 per day.

Campbeltown

POP 6000

Campbeltown, with its ranks of gloomy, grey council houses, feels a bit like an Ayrshire mining town that's been placed incongruously on the shores of a beautiful Argyllshire harbour. It was once a thriving fishing port and whisky-making centre, but industrial decline and the closure of the former airforce base at nearby Machrihanish saw Campbeltown's fortunes decline.

The town feels a very long way from anywhere else, a feeling intensified by the continuing failure to reopen the ferry link from Campbeltown to Ballycastle in Northern Ireland (every year the message from the government is, 'something will be done *next* year'). But renewal is in the air – the spruced-up seafront, with its flower beds, smart Victorian buildings and restored art-deco cinema, lends the town a distinctly optimistic air.

☉ Sights & Activities

Springbank Distillery DISTILLERY
(☎01586-552085; www.springbankwhisky.com; tours £4; ⊙tours by arrangement 10am & 2pm Mon-Fri, 2pm only Oct-Apr) There were once no fewer than 32 distilleries in the Campbeltown area, but most closed down in the 1920s. Today Springbank Distillery is one of only three that now operate in town. It is also one of the very few distilleries in Scotland that distils, matures and bottles all its whisky on the one site.

Davaar Cave CAVE
One of the most unusual sights in Argyll is in this cave on the southern side of the island of Davaar, at the mouth of Campbeltown Loch. On the wall of the cave is an eerie painting of the Crucifixion by local artist Archibald MacKinnon, dating from 1887. You can walk to the island at low tide.

The approach leads across a shingle bar called the Dhorlinn (allow at least 1½ hours for the round trip), but make sure you're not caught by a rising tide – check tide times with the tourist office before you set off.

Mull of Kintyre Seatours WILDLIFE TRIP
(☎0870 720 0609; www.mull-of-kintyre.co.uk; adult/child from £30/£20) This outfit operates two-hour high-speed boat trips out of Campbeltown harbour to look for wildlife – seals, porpoises, minke whales, golden eagles and peregrine falcons – in the turbulent tidal waters beneath the spectacular sea cliffs of the Mull of Kintyre. Book in advance by phone or at the tourist office (p67).

✯ Festivals & Events

Mull of Kintyre Music Festival FESTIVAL
(☎01586-551053; www.mokfest.com) Held in Campbeltown in late August, this is a popular event featuring traditional Scottish and Irish music.

❶ Information

The **tourist office** (☎01586-552056; The Pier; ⊙9am-5.30pm Mon-Sat) is beside the harbour.

❶ Getting There & Away

AIR **Loganair/FlyBe** (www.loganair.co.uk) Operates two flights daily, Monday to Friday, from Glasgow to Campbeltown (£50, 35 minutes).

BOAT **Kintyre Express** (☎01294-270160; www.kintyreexpress.com) From April to September a small, high-speed passenger ferry travels from Troon to Campbeltown (£50 one way, 1¼ hours, once daily Wednesday, Friday and Sunday). Tickets must be booked in advance.

BUS Scottish Citylink (www.citylink.co.uk) Buses run from Campbeltown to Glasgow (£17, four hours, three daily) via Tarbert, Inveraray, Arrochar and Loch Lomond. There is also a bus to Oban (£15, four hours, three daily), changing at Inveraray.

Mull of Kintyre

A narrow winding road, about 18 miles long, leads south from Campbeltown to the Mull of Kintyre, passing some good sandy beaches near Southend. The name of this remote headland was immortalised in Paul McCartney's famous song – the former Beatle owns a farmhouse in the area. A lighthouse marks the spot closest to Northern Ireland, the coastline of which, only 12 miles away, is visible across the North Channel.

MID-ARGYLL

Inveraray
POP 700

You can spot Inveraray long before you get here – its neat, whitewashed buildings stand out from a distance on the shores of Loch Fyne. It's a planned town, built by the Duke of Argyll in Georgian style when he revamped his nearby castle in the 18th century.

◉ Sights

Inveraray Castle CASTLE
(☑01499-302203; www.inveraray-castle.com; adult/child £9/6.10; ☉10am-5.45pm Apr-Oct) Inveraray Castle has been the seat of the Dukes of Argyll – chiefs of Clan Campbell – since the 15th century. The 18th-century building, with its fairytale turrets and fake battlements, houses an impressive armoury hall, its walls patterned with a collection of more than 1000 pole arms, dirks, muskets and Lochaber axes.

The castle is 500m north of town, entered from the A819 Dalmally road.

Inveraray Jail MUSEUM
(☑01499-302381; www.inverarayjail.co.uk; Church Sq; adult/child £8.25/5.50; ☉9.30am-6pm Apr-Oct, 10am-5pm Nov-Mar) At this award-winning, interactive tourist attraction you can sit in on a trial, try out a cell and discover what harsh tortures were meted out to unfortunate prisoners. The attention to detail – including a life-sized model of an inmate squatting on a 19th-century toilet – more than makes up for the sometimes tedious commentary.

Inveraray Maritime Museum MUSEUM
(☑01499-302213; www.inverarypier.com; The Pier; adult/child £5/2.50; ☉10am-4pm) The *Arctic Penguin*, a three-masted schooner built in 1911 and one of the world's last surviving iron sailing ships, is permanently moored in Inveraray harbour, and houses a museum with interesting photos and models of the old Clyde steamers and puffers. Kids will love exploring below the decks – there's a special play area in the bowels of the ship.

There's also a display about Para Handy, the fictional sea captain created by local novelist Neil Munro (and celebrated in two successful TV series in the 1960s and 1990s).

🛏 Sleeping & Eating

George Hotel HOTEL ££
(☑01499-302111; www.thegeorgehotel.co.uk; Main St E; s/d from £35/70; Ⓟ) The George Hotel boasts a magnificent choice of opulent rooms complete with four-poster beds, period furniture, Victorian roll-top baths and private jacuzzis (superior rooms cost £130 to £165 per double). The cosy wood-panelled bar, with its rough stone walls, flagstone floor and peat fires, is a delightful place for a bar meal (mains £7 to £10, open for lunch and dinner).

Claonairigh House B&B ££
(☑01499-302160; s/d from £45/90; Ⓟ@🛜) This grand 18th-century house, built for the Duke of Argyll in 1745, is set in 3 hectares of grounds on the bank of a river (salmon-fishing available). There are three homely en suite rooms, one with a four-poster bed, and a resident menagerie of dogs, ducks, chickens and goats. It's 4 miles south of town on the A83.

Inveraray SYHA HOSTEL £
(☑01499-302454; www.syha.org.uk; Dalmally Rd; dm £16; ☉Apr-Oct; @) To get to this hostel, housed in a comfortable, modern bungalow, go through the arched entrance on the seafront – it's set back on the left of the road about 100m further on.

🍴 Loch Fyne Oyster Bar SEAFOOD ££
(☑01499 600236; www.lochfyne.com; mains £10-22; ☉breakfast, lunch & dinner) Six miles northeast of Inveraray is this rustic-themed restaurant that serves excellent seafood, though the service can be a bit hit and miss.

It's housed in a converted byre, and the menu includes locally farmed oysters, mussels and salmon. The neighbouring shop sells packaged seafood and other deli goods to take away, as well as bottled beer from the nearby Fyne Ales microbrewery.

ℹ Information

Inveraray tourist office (☎0845 225 5121; Front St; ⊙9am-6pm Jul & Aug, 10am-5pm Mon-Sat Apr-Jun, Sep & Oct, 10am-3pm Mon-Sat Nov-Mar; @) On the seafront.

ℹ Getting There & Away

Scottish Citylink (www.citylink.co.uk) Scottish Citylink buses run from Glasgow to Inveraray (£10, 1¾ hours, six daily Monday to Saturday, two Sunday). Three of these buses continue to Lochgilphead and Campbeltown (£11, 2½ hours); the others continue to Oban (£9, 1¼ hours).

Knapdale

Stretching southwards from the Crinan Canal to West Loch Tarbert and Kintyre is Knapdale, with its gently rolling hills and three distinct 'fingers' jutting into the Sound of Jura. There are plenty of walking trails here and more head-spinning views, west to Jura and east to the hills of Cowal. The **Knapdale Forest**, planted during the 1920s Depression, is dotted with tiny lochs and walking trails. A remote corner of the forest

was chosen in 2009 for a trial reintroduction of beavers into the wild.

The single-track B8025 road leads south from Bellanoch, past the Forestry Commission's Barnluasgan car park (start of the Beaver Detective Trail) and on to the picture-postcard harbour village of **Tayvallich**. From here it's another 7 miles to the end of the road at **Keills Chapel**. This tiny 12th-century church contains a remarkable collection of carved Celtic crosses and grave slabs, including the 9th-century High Cross of Keills. Today this spot feels very remote, but in times past it was the main landing place for the ferry from Jura, where hundreds of cattle were brought to the mainland on their way to market.

Across Loch Sween to the east lies **Castle Sween**, a sprawling ruin surrounded by a grim caravan park, and a few miles south is yet another venerable old church, the 13th-century **Kilmory Knap Chapel**, housing another collection of medieval carved stones. Nearby is the impressive 15th-century **MacMillan's Cross**, a 3m-high carving that depicts the crucifixion on one side and a hunting scene on the other.

On the isolated southern tip of the third 'finger' of Knapdale is the **Kilberry Inn** (☎01880-770223; www.kilberryinn.com; mains £16-20, ⊙lunch & dinner Tue-Sun). Housed in a pretty whitewashed cottage with a red tin roof, the inn has a well-earned reputation for championing local produce that includes

---

CRINAN CANAL

Completed in 1801, the picturesque Crinan Canal runs for 9 miles from Ardrishaig to Crinan. It allows seagoing vessels – mostly yachts, these days – to take a short cut from the Firth of Clyde and Loch Fyne to the west coast of Scotland, avoiding the long and sometimes dangerous passage around the Mull of Kintyre. You can easily walk or cycle the full length of the canal towpath in an afternoon.

The canal basin at Crinan is the focus for the annual **Crinan Classic Boat Festival** (www.crinanclassic.com), held over the first weekend in July, when traditional wooden yachts, motor boats and dinghies gather for a few days of racing, drinking and music.

The basin is overlooked by the **Crinan Hotel** (☎01546-830261; www.crinanhotel.com; s/d incl dinner from £145/260 ; ℙ), which boasts one of the west coast's most spectacular sunset views and one of Scotland's top seafood restaurants. You're paying for that view, and for the olde-worlde atmosphere – don't expect five-star luxury. You can also eat in the hotel's **Crinan Seafood Bar** (mains £9-12, 4-course dinner £65; ⊙lunch & dinner) – the menu includes excellent local mussels with lemon, thyme and garlic.

The **coffee shop** (snacks £2-5; ⊙10am-5:30pm) on the western side of the canal basin at Crinan has great homebaked cakes and scones.

If you want to walk along the canal and take the bus back, bus 425 from Lochgilphead to Tayvallich stops at Cairnbaan, Bellanoch and Crinan Cottages (20 minutes, three or four daily Monday to Saturday).

fresh scallops, crab and langoustine supplied by a Tarbert fisherman, beef and lamb from the nearby Ormsary Estate, and honey from the beekeeper at Kilberry Castle. It's a long drive from anywhere, but if you want to stay the night the inn also offers accommodation in five comfortable and stylish double bedrooms, all with en-suite facilities (dinner, bed and breakfast £195).

Kilmartin Glen

In the 6th century, Irish settlers arrived in this part of Argyll and founded the kingdom of Dalriada, which eventually united with the Picts in 843 to create the first Scottish kingdom. Their capital was the hill fort of Dunadd, on the plain to the south of Kilmartin Glen.

This magical glen is the focus of one of the biggest concentrations of prehistoric sites in Scotland. Burial cairns, standing stones, stone circles, hill forts and cup-and-ring-marked rocks litter the countryside. Within a 6-mile radius of Kilmartin village there are 25 sites with standing stones and over 100 rock carvings.

◎ Sights

Kilmartin House Museum   MUSEUM
(☑01546-510278; www.kilmartin.org; adult/child £5/2; ⊙10am-5.30pm Mar-Oct, 11am-4pm Nov-23 Dec) This museum, in Kilmartin village, is a fascinating interpretive centre that provides a context for the ancient monuments you can go on to explore, alongside displays of artefacts recovered from various sites. The project was partly funded by midges – the curator exposed his body in Temple Wood on a warm summer's evening and was sponsored per midge bite!

Kilmartin Prehistoric Sites   PREHISTORIC SITE
The oldest monuments at Kilmartin date from 5000 years ago and comprise a linear cemetery of burial cairns that runs south from Kilmartin village for 1.5 miles. There are also ritual monuments (two stone circles) at **Temple Wood**, three-quarters of a mile southwest of Kilmartin. The museum bookshop sells maps and guides.

Kilmartin Churchyard   HISTORIC SITE
Kilmartin Churchyard contains some 10th-century Celtic crosses and lots of medieval grave slabs with carved effigies of knights. Some researchers have surmised that these were the tombs of Knights Templar who fled persecution in France in the 14th century.

Dunadd   HISTORIC SITE
The hill fort of Dunadd, 3.5 miles south of Kilmartin village, was the seat of power of the first kings of Dalriada, and may have been where the Stone of Destiny was originally located. The faint rock carvings of a wild boar and two footprints with an Ogham inscription may have been used in some kind of inauguration ceremony. The prominent little hill rises straight out of the boggy plain of the **Moine Mhor Nature Reserve**. A slippery path leads to the summit where you can gaze out on much the same view that the kings of Dalriada enjoyed 1300 years ago.

🛏 Sleeping & Eating

Burndale B&B   B&B ££
(☑01546-510235; www.burndale.net; s/d from £35/54; 🅿🛜) Set in a lovely Victorian manse (minister's house), this homely and hospitable B&B is just a short walk north from the Kilmartin House Museum. Expect a warm welcome and Loch Fyne kippers for breakfast. Credit cards not accepted.

Kilmartin Hotel   INN ££
(☑01546-510250; www.kilmartin-hotel.com; s/d £40/65; 🅿) Though the rooms here are a bit on the small side, this attractively old-

---

RETURN OF THE BEAVER

Beavers have been extinct in Britain since the 16th century. But in 2009 they returned to Scotland, when a population of Norwegian beavers was released into the hill lochs of Knapdale in Argyllshire. The five-year **Scottish Beaver Trial** (www.scottishbeavers.org. uk) hopes to reveal whether the animals have a positive effect on habitat and biodiversity. If so, they could be introduced to other parts of the country.

Meanwhile, you can try and get a glimpse of them on the **Beaver Detective Trail**. It starts from the Loch Coille-Bharr forestry car park on the B8025 road to Tayvallich, about 1.5 miles south of the Crinan Canal.

fashioned hotel is full of atmosphere. There's a **restaurant** (mains £8-15) here too, and a whisky bar with real ale on tap where you can enjoy live folk music at weekends.

TOP CHOICE Glebe Cairn Café   CAFE £
(📞01546-510278; mains £5-8; ⊗breakfast & lunch, dinner Thu-Sat Jun-Aug) The cafe in the Kilmartin House Museum has a lovely conservatory with a view across fields to a prehistoric cairn. Dishes include homemade Cullen skink, a Celtic cheese platter and hummus with sweet-and-sour beetroot relish. The drinks menu ranges from espresso to elderflower wine by way of Fraoch heather-scented ale.

ℹ️ Getting There & Away
You can walk or cycle along the Crinan Canal from Ardrishaig, then turn north at Bellanoch on the minor B8025 road to reach Kilmartin (12 miles one way).

BUS Bus 423 between Oban and Ardrishaig (four daily Monday to Friday, two on Saturday) stops at Kilmartin (£4.50, one hour 20 minutes).

OBAN & AROUND

POP 8120

Oban is a peaceful waterfront town on a delightful bay, with sweeping views to Kerrera and Mull. OK, that first bit about peaceful is true only in winter; in summer the town centre is a heaving mass of humanity, its streets jammed with traffic and crowded with holidaymakers, day-trippers and travellers headed for the islands. But the setting is still lovely.

There's not a huge amount to see in the town itself, but it's an appealing place with some excellent restaurants and lively pubs, and it's the main gateway to the islands of Mull, Iona, Colonsay, Barra, Coll and Tiree.

◉ Sights
McCaig's Tower   HISTORIC BUILDING
(cnr Laurel & Duncraggan Rds; admission free; ⊗24hr) Crowning the hill above the town centre is the Victorian folly known as McCaig's Tower. Its construction was commissioned in 1890 by local worthy John Stuart McCaig, an art critic, philosophical essayist and banker, with the philanthropic intention of providing work for unemployed stonemasons.

To reach it on foot, make the steep climb up Jacob's Ladder (a flight of stairs) from Argyll St and then follow the signs. The views over the bay are worth the effort.

Oban Distillery   DISTILLERY
(📞01631-572004; www.discovering-distilleries.com; Stafford St; tour £7; ⊗9.30am-5pm Mon-Sat Easter-Oct, plus noon-5pm Sun Jul-Sep, closed Sat & Sun Nov-Dec & Feb-Easter, closed Jan) This distillery has been producing Oban single-malt whisky since 1794. There are guided tours available (last tour begins one hour before closing time), but even without a tour, it's still worth a look at the small exhibition in the foyer.

War & Peace Museum   MUSEUM
(📞01631-570007; www.obanmuseum.org.uk; Corran Esplanade; admission free; ⊗10am-6pm Mon-Sat & to 4pm Sun May-Sep, to 4pm daily Mar, Apr, Oct & Nov) Military buffs will enjoy the little War & Peace Museum, which chronicles Oban's role in WWII as a base for Catalina seaplanes and as a marshalling area for Atlantic convoys.

Dunollie Castle   CASTLE
(Dunollie Rd; ⊗24hr) A pleasant 1-mile stroll north along the coast road beyond Corran Esplanade leads to Dunollie Castle, built by the MacDougalls of Lorn in the 13th century and unsuccessfully besieged for a year during the 1715 Jacobite rebellion. It's always open but very much a ruin.

Pulpit Hill   VIEWPOINT
An excellent viewpoint south of Oban Bay; the footpath to the summit starts to the right of Maridon House B&B on Dunuaran Rd.

Ganavan Sands   BEACH
A sandy, bucket-and-spade beach only 2.5 miles north of Oban along Corran Esplanade.

🏃 Activities
A tourist-office leaflet lists local bike rides, which include a 7-mile Gallanach circular tour, a 16-mile route to the Isle of Seil and routes to Connel, Glenlonan and Kilmore.

Various operators offer boat trips to spot seals and other marine wildlife, departing from the North Pier slipway (adult/child £8/5.50); ask for details at the tourist office.

Evo Bikes   BICYCLE HIRE
(📞01631-566996; 29 Lochside St; mountain bike hire per day from £15-30; ⊗9am-5.30pm Mon-Sat) Opposite Tesco supermarket.

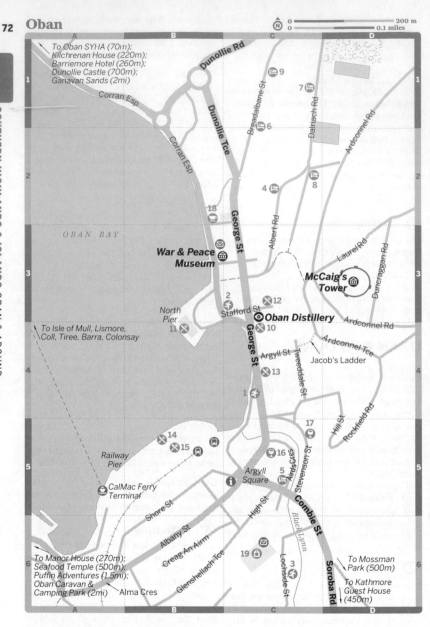

N 0 ——— 200 m
0 ——— 0.1 miles

To Oban SYHA (70m);
Kilchrenan House (220m);
Barriemore Hotel (260m);
Dunollie Castle (700m);
Ganavan Sands (2mi)

Corran Esp

Dunollie Rd

Dunollie Tce

Breadalbane St

Dalriach Rd

Ardconnel Rd

Corran Esp

OBAN BAY

George St

Albert Rd

Laurel Rd

Duncraggan Rd

War & Peace
Museum

McCaig's
Tower

North
Pier

2
Stafford St

12

Oban Distillery

10

Ardconnel Rd

To Isle of Mull, Lismore,
Coll, Tiree, Barra, Colonsay

11

George St

Argyll St

Tweedale St

Ardconnel Tce

Jacob's Ladder

13

1

17

Hill St

Rockfield Rd

Railway
Pier

14

15

CalMac Ferry
Terminal

16

Argyll
Square

Airds Cres

Stevenson St

Shore St

Albany St

Creag An Airm

High St

Glenshellach Tce

Combie St

Black Lynn

Lochside St

19

3

Soroba Rd

To Mossman
Park (500m)

To Kathmore
Guest House
(450m)

To Manor House (270m);
Seafood Temple (500m);
Puffin Adventures (1.5mi);
Oban Caravan &
Camping Park (2mi)

Alma Cres

Rowland Woollven   SEA KAYAKING
(☎01631-710417; www.rwoollven.co.uk) Based at
North Connel, sea-kayaking coach Rowland
Woollven offers instruction for beginners
and guided tours (£100 for a full day for
one person, £60 per person for two or three
people), for more experienced paddlers, in
the waters around Oban.

Puffin Adventures   DIVING
(☎01631-566088; www.puffin.org.uk; Port Gallanach) If you fancy exploring the underwater

Oban

◎ Top Sights

◉ Activities, Courses & Tours

◎ Sleeping

⊗ Eating

◎ Drinking

◎ Shopping

world, Puffin Adventures offers a 1½-hour Try-a-Dive package (£87) for complete beginners.

☞ Tours

Bowman's Tours   COACH TOUR
(☑01631-566809; www.bowmanstours.co.uk; 1 Queens Park Pl) From April to October, Bowman's offers a Three Isles day-trip (adult/child £49/24.50, 10 hours, daily) from Oban that visits Mull, Iona and Staffa. Note that the crossing to Staffa is weather dependent. Bowman's also runs a wildlife tour (adult/child £49/24.50) departing from Oban at 9.50am Sunday to Friday from May to July, and returning to Oban at 8pm.

The trip takes in a ferry crossing to Craignure on Mull, travel by coach to Fionnphort, and a cruise around Staffa and the Treshnish Isles, plus two hours ashore on Lunga to visit a puffin colony. There's also a branch (☑01631-563221, 01631-566809; www.bowmanstours.co.uk; 3 Stafford St) in Stafford St.

✹✺ Festivals & Events

West Highland Yachting Week   SAILING
(☑01631-563309; www.whyw.co.uk) At the end of July/beginning of August, Oban becomes the focus of one of Scotland's biggest yachting events. Hundreds of yachts cram into the harbour and the town's bars are jammed with thirsty sailors.

Argyllshire Gathering   HIGHLAND GAMES
(☑01631-562671; www.obangames.com; adult/child £8/4) Held over two days in late August, this is one of the most important events on the Scottish highland-games calendar and includes a prestigious pipeband competition. The main games are held at Mossfield Park on the eastern edge of town.

🛏 Sleeping

Despite having lots of B&B accommodation, Oban's beds can still fill up quickly in July and August so try to book ahead. If you can't find a bed in Oban, consider staying at Connel, 4 miles to the north.

Barriemore Hotel   B&B ££
(☑01631-566356; www.barriemore-hotel.co.uk; Corran Esplanade; s/d from £65/92; ℗) The Barriemore enjoys a grand location, overlooking the entrance to Oban Bay. There are 13 spacious rooms (ask for one with a sea view), plus a guest lounge with magazines and newspapers, and plump Loch Fyne kippers on the breakfast menu.

Heatherfield House   B&B ££
(☑01631-562681; www.heatherfieldhouse.co.uk; Albert Rd; s/d from £35/70; ℗@⊚) The welcoming Heatherfield House occupies a converted 1870s rectory set in extensive grounds and has six spacious rooms. If possible, ask for room 1, which comes complete with fireplace, sofa and a view over the garden to the harbour.

Kilchrenan House   B&B ££
(☑01631-562663; www.kilchrenanhouse.co.uk; Corran Esplanade; s/d £50/90; ℗) You'll get a warm welcome at the Kilchrenan, an elegant Victorian villa built for a textile magnate in 1883. Most of the rooms have views across Oban Bay, but rooms 5 and 9 are the best: room 5 has a huge freestanding bath tub, perfect for soaking weary bones.

GAELIC & NORSE PLACE NAMES

Throughout the Highlands and Islands of Scotland the indigenous Gaelic language has left a rich legacy of place names. They're often intermixed with Old Norse names left behind by the Viking invaders who occupied the western and northern islands between the 8th and 13th centuries. The spelling is now anglicised but the meaning is still clear once you know what to look for. Here are a few of the more common Gaelic and Norse names and their meanings.

Gaelic Place Names

» **ach**, **auch** – from achadh (field)
» **ard** – from ard or aird (height, hill)
» **avon** – from abhainn (river or stream)
» **bal** – from baile (village or homestead)
» **ban** – from ban (white, fair)
» **beg** – from beag (small)
» **ben** – from beinn (mountain)
» **buie** – from buidhe (yellow)
» **dal** – from dail (field or dale)
» **dow**, **dhu** – from dubh (black)
» **drum** – from druim (ridge or back)
» **dun** – from dun or duin (fort or castle)
» **glen** – from gleann (narrow valley)
» **gorm** – from gorm (blue)
» **gower, gour** – from gabhar (goat), eg Ardgour (height of the goats)
» **inch, insh** – from inis (island, water-meadow or resting place for cattle)
» **inver** – from inbhir (river mouth or meeting of two rivers)
» **kil** – from cille (church), as in Kilmartin (Church of St Martin)
» **kin, ken** – from ceann (head), eg Kinlochleven (head of Loch Leven)
» **kyle, kyles** – from caol or caolas (narrow sea channel)
» **more**, **vore** – from mor or mhor (big), eg Ardmore (big height), Skerryvore (big reef)
» **strath** – from srath (broad valley)
» **tarbert, tarbet** – from tairbeart (portage), meaning a narrow neck of land between two bodies of water, across which a boat can be dragged
» **tay, ty** – from tigh (house), eg Tyndrum (house on the ridge)
» **tober** – from tobar (well), eg Tobermory (Mary's well)

Norse Place Names

» **a, ay, ey** – from ey (island)
» **bister**, **buster**, **bster** – from bolstaor (dwelling place, homestead)
» **geo** – from gja (chasm)
» **holm** – from holmr (small island)
» **kirk** – from kirkja (church)
» **pol**, **poll**, **bol** – from bol (farm)
» **quoy** – from kvi (sheep fold, cattle enclosure)
» **sker, skier, skerry** – from sker (rocky reef)
» **ster, sett** – from setr (house)
» **vig, vaig, wick** – from vik (bay, creek)
» **voe, way** – from vagr (bay, creek)

Old Manse Guest House B&B ££
(☎01631-564886; www.obanguesthouse.co.uk; Dalriach Rd; s/d from £62/74; P 📶 👪) Set on a hillside above the town, the Old Manse commands great views over to Kerrera and Mull. The sunny, brightly decorated bedrooms have some nice touches (a couple of wine glasses and a corkscrew), and kids are made welcome with Balamory books, toys and DVDs.

Manor House HOTEL £££
(☎01631-562087; www.manorhouseoban.com; Gallanach Rd; r £154-199; P) Built in 1780 for the Duke of Argyll as part of his Oban estates, the Manor House is now one of Oban's finest hotels. It has small but elegant Georgian-style rooms, a posh bar frequented by local and visiting yachties, and a fine restaurant serving Scottish and French cuisine. Children under 12 years are not welcome.

Oban Backpackers Lodge HOSTEL £
(☎01631-562107; www.obanbackpackers.com; Breadalbane St; dm £12.50-13.50; @ 📶) This is a friendly place with a good vibe and a large and attractive communal lounge with lots of sofas and armchairs. Breakfast is included in the price, plus there's free tea and coffee, a laundry service (£2.50) and powerful showers.

Oban Caravan & Camping Park CAMPGROUND £
(☎01631-562425; www.obancaravanpark.com; Gallanachmore Farm; tent & campervan sites £17; ⊙Apr-Oct) This spacious campground has a superb location overlooking the Sound of Kerrera, 2.5 miles south of Oban (bus twice a day). The quoted rate includes up to two people and a car; extra people stay for £2 each. A one-person tent with no car is £8. No prebooking – it's first-come, first-served.

Oban SYHA HOSTEL £
(☎01631-562025; www.syha.org.uk; Corran Esplanade; dm £17, r per person £17-20; P @ 📶) Oban's SYHA hostel is set in a grand Victorian villa on the Esplanade, 0.75 miles north of the train station. The metal bunks are a bit creaky, but there are good showers and the lounge has great views across Oban Bay. The neighbouring lodge has three- and four-bedded rooms with en suite bathrooms.

Jeremy Inglis Hostel HOSTEL £
(☎01631-565065; jeremyinglis@mctavishs.freeserve.co.uk; 21 Airds Cres; dm/s £15/22; 📶) This bargain place is more of an eccentric B&B than a hostel – most 'dorms' have only two or three beds, and are decorated with original artwork, books, flowers and cuddly toys. The kitchen is a little cramped, but the owner is friendly and knowledgeable (and makes delicious home-made jam). The price includes a continental breakfast.

Sand Villa Guest House B&B ££
(☎01631-562803; www.holidayoban.co.uk; Breadalbane St; r per person £28-33; P 📶) Ground floor room with wheelchair access. No credit cards.

Roseneath Guest House B&B ££
(☎01631-562929; www.roseneathoban.com; Dalriach Rd; s/d from £40/60; P) Peaceful location with sea views.

Kathmore Guest House B&B ££
(☎01631-562104; www.kathmore.co.uk; Soroba Rd; s £45-65, d £55-75; P) Good value, homey and welcoming.

Eating

TOP CHOICE **Waterfront Restaurant** SEAFOOD ££
(☎01631-563110; www.waterfrontoban.co.uk; Railway Pier; mains £10-18; ⊙lunch & dinner) Housed on the top floor of a converted seamen's mission, the Waterfront's stylish, unfussy decor – dusky pink and carmine with pine tables and local art on the walls – does little to distract from the superb seafood freshly landed at the quay just a few metres away.

The menu ranges from crispy-battered haddock and chips to pan-fried scallops with lime, chilli and coriander pickle. There's an early evening menu (5.30pm to 6.45pm) offering two courses for £11.50, or soup followed by fish and chips for £9.75. Best to book for dinner.

TOP CHOICE **Shellfish Bar** SEAFOOD £
(Railway Pier; mains £2-7; ⊙breakfast & lunch) If you want to savour superb Scottish seafood without the expense of an upmarket restaurant, head for Oban's famous seafood stall – it's the green shack on the quayside near the ferry terminal. Here you can buy fresh and cooked seafood to take away – excellent prawn sandwiches (£2.75), dressed crab (£4.75), and fresh oysters for only 65p each.

Seafood Temple SEAFOOD £££
(☎01631-566000; Gallanach Rd; mains £15-25; ⊙dinner Thu-Sun) Locally sourced seafood is the god that's worshipped at this tiny temple – a former park pavilion with glorious views over the bay. Owned by a former fisherman

who smokes his own salmon, what must be Oban's smallest restaurant serves up whole lobster cooked to order, scallops in garlic butter, plump langoustines, and the 'platter magnifique' (£60 for two persons), which offers a taste of everything. Booking essential.

Cuan Mor INTERNATIONAL ££
(📞01631-565078; www.cuanmor.co.uk; 60 George St; mains £8-16; ⊙lunch & dinner) This always-busy bar and bistro sports a no-nonsense menu of old favourites – from haddock and chips to sausage and mash with onion gravy – spiced with a few more-sophisticated dishes such as scallops with black pudding, and a decent range of vegetarian dishes. And the sticky toffee pudding is not to be missed!

Ee'usk SEAFOOD ££
(📞01631-565666; www.eeusk.com; North Pier; mains £12-20; ⊙lunch & dinner) Bright and modern Ee'usk (it's how you pronounce *iasg*, the Gaelic word for fish) occupies Oban's prime location on the North Pier. Floor-to-ceiling windows allow diners on two levels to enjoy views over the harbour to Kerrera and Mull, while sampling a seafood menu ranging from fragrant Thai fish cakes to langoustines with chilli and ginger.

A little pricey, perhaps, but both food and location are first class.

Kitchen Garden CAFE £
(📞01631-566332; www.kitchengardenoban.co.uk; 14 George St; mains £3-8; ⊙9am-5pm Mon-Sat, 10.30am-5pm Sun, plus 6-9pm Thu-Sat) A deli packed with delicious picnic food. It also has a great little cafe above the shop – good coffee, scones, cakes, homemade soups and sandwiches.

Julie's Tearooms CAFE £
(📞01631-565952; 37 Stafford St; mains £4-10; ⊙breakfast & lunch Tue-Sat) Tea and scones, delicious Luca's ice-cream and homemade soup with crusty bread.

Tesco SUPERMARKET
(Lochside St; ⊙8am-10pm Mon-Sat, 9am-6pm Sun) Self-caterers and campers can stock up here.

🍷 Drinking

Oban Chocolate Company CAFE
(📞01631-566099; www.obanchocolate.co.uk; 34 Corran Esplanade; ⊙10am-5pm Mon-Sat, 12.30-4pm Sun Easter-Sep, shorter hours in winter, closed Jan) This shop specialises in hand-crafted chocolates (you can watch them being made) and also has a cafe serving excellent coffee

and hot chocolate (try the chilli chocolate for a kick in the tastebuds), with big leather sofas in a window with a view of the bay.

Lorne Bar PUB
(www.thelornebar.co.uk; Stevenson St; 📶) A traditional pub with a lovely old island bar, the Lorne serves Deuchars IPA and local Oban Brewery real ales, as well as above-average pub grub. Food is served from noon to 9pm, and there's a trad music session every Wednesday from 10pm.

Aulay's Bar PUB
(📞01631-562596; 8 Airds Cres) An authentic Scottish pub, Aulay's is cosy and low-ceilinged, its walls covered with old photographs of Oban ferries and other ships. It pulls in a mixed crowd of locals and visitors with its warm atmosphere and wide range of malt whiskies.

🛈 Information

Fancy That (📞01631-562996; 112 George St; internet per hr £3; ⊙10am-5pm; @)

Lorn & Islands District General Hospital (📞01631-567500; Glengallan Rd) Southern end of town.

Main Post Office (📞01631-510450; Lochside St; ⊙8am-6pm Mon-Sat, 10am-1pm Sun) Inside Tesco supermarket.

Oban tourist office (📞01631-563122; www .oban.org.uk; Argyll Sq; ⊙9am-7pm daily Jul & Aug, 9am-5.30pm Mon-Sat, 10am-5pm Sun May, Jun & Sep, 9am-5.30pm Mon-Sat Oct-Apr; @) Internet access available.

🛈 Getting There & Away

The bus, train and ferry terminals are all grouped conveniently together next to the harbour on the southern edge of the bay.

BOAT CalMac (www.calmac.co.uk) Links Oban with the islands of Kerrera, Mull, Coll, Tiree, Lismore, Colonsay, Barra and Lochboisdale. See the relevant island entries for details of ferry services. Information and reservations for all CalMac ferry services are available at the ferry terminal on Oban's West Pier.

Ferries to the Isle of Kerrera (p77) depart from a separate jetty (p77), about 2 miles southwest of Oban town centre.

BUS Scottish Citylink (www.citylink.co.uk) Buses run to Oban from Glasgow (£17, three hours, four daily) via Inveraray; and from Perth (£12, three hours, twice daily Friday to Monday) via Tyndrum and Killin.

West Coast Motors (www.westcoastmotors .co.uk) West Coast Motors bus 423 runs from Oban to Lochgilphead (£5, 1¾ hours, four daily

Monday to Friday, two on Saturday) via Kilmartin. Bus 918 goes to Fort William via Appin and Ballachulish (£9, 1½ hours, three daily Monday to Saturday).

TRAIN Oban is at the terminus of a scenic route that branches off the West Highland line at Crianlarich. There are up to three trains daily from Glasgow to Oban (£19, three hours).

The train isn't much use going north from Oban – to reach Fort William requires a detour via Crianlarich (3¾ hours). Take the bus instead.

ℹ Getting Around

BUS The main bus stop is outside the train station. West Coast Motors (p76) bus 417 runs from here to Ganavan Sands via Oban Youth Hostel (five minutes, two per hour Monday to Saturday). Bus 431 connects the train station with the Kerrera ferry and Oban Caravan & Camping Park (15 minutes, two or three daily Monday to Saturday from late May to September).

CAR Hazelbank Motors (☑01631-566476; www.obancarhire.co.uk; Lynn Rd; ⊙8.30am-5.30pm Mon-Sat) Hires out small cars per day/week from £40/225 including VAT, insurance and CDW (Collision Damage Waiver).

TAXI There's a taxi rank outside the train station. Otherwise, call **Oban Taxis** (☑01631-564666).

Isle of Kerrera

POP 40

Some of the best walking in the area is on Kerrera, which faces Oban across the bay. There's a 6-mile circuit of the island (allow three hours), which follows tracks or paths (use Ordnance Survey map 49) and offers the chance to spot wildlife such as sheep, wild goats, otters, golden eagles, peregrine falcons, seals and porpoises. At **Lower Gylen**, at the southern end of the island, there's a ruined castle.

Kerrera Bunkhouse (☑01631-570223; www.kerrerabunkhouse.co.uk; dm £14) is a charming seven-bed bothy (hut or mountain shelter) in a converted 18th-century stable near **Gylen Castle**, a 2-mile walk south from the ferry (keep left at the fork just past the telephone box). Booking ahead is recommended. You can get snacks and light meals at the neighbouring **Tea Garden** (☑01631-570223; ⊙lunch Wed-Sun Apr-Oct), which also has B&B (£20 per person).

ℹ Getting There & Away

A daily **passenger ferry** (www.kerrera-ferry .co.uk; adult/child return £5/2.50, bicycle free)

runs to Kerrera from Gallanach (10 minutes), 2 miles southwest of Oban town centre, along Gallanach Rd. Easter to October it runs half-hourly from 10.30am to 12.30pm and 2pm to 6pm daily, plus 8.45am Monday to Saturday. November to Easter there are five or six crossings a day.

Isle of Seil

POP 500

The small island of Seil, 10 miles southwest of Oban, is best known for its connection to the mainland – the so-called **Bridge over the Atlantic**, designed by Thomas Telford and opened in 1793. The graceful bridge has a single stone arch and spans the narrowest part of the tidal Clachan Sound.

Anyone who fancies their hand at ducks and drakes should try to attend the **World Stone-Skimming Championships** (www .stoneskimming.com), held each year in Easdale on the last Sunday in September.

⊙ Sights & Activities

Ellanbeich   VILLAGE

On the west coast of the island is the pretty conservation village of Ellanbeich, with its whitewashed cottages. It was built to house workers at the local slate quarries, but the industry collapsed in 1881 when the sea broke into the main quarry pit – the flooded pit can still be seen. The **Scottish Slate Islands Heritage Trust** (☑01852 300449; www.slateislands.org.uk; Ellanbeich; admission free; ⊙10.30am-1pm & 2-5pm Apr-Oct) displays fascinating old photographs illustrating life in the village in the 19th and early 20th centuries.

Highland Arts Studio   ARTS & CRAFTS

(☑01852-300273; www.highlandarts.co.uk; Ellanbeich; admission free; ⊙9am-7pm Apr-Sep, to 5pm Oct-Mar) Coach tours flock to this crafts and gift shop, which is a shrine to the eccentric output of the late 'poet, artist and composer' C John Taylor. Please, try to keep a straight face.

Easdale Island Folk Museum   MUSEUM

(☑01852-300370; www.easdalemuseum.org; Easdale; adult/child £2.25/50p; ⊙11am-4.30pm Apr-Oct, to 5pm Jul & Aug) This interesting museum, on the small island of **Easdale** just offshore from Ellanbeich, has displays about the slate industry and life on the islands in the 18th and 19th centuries. Climb to the top of the island (a 38m peak!) for a great view of the surrounding area.

Boat Trips

Sea.fari Adventures   BOAT TRIP
(☎01852-300003; www.seafari.co.uk; Easdale Harbour; ☺Apr-Oct) This operator runs a series of exciting boat trips in high-speed rigid inflatable boats (RIBs) to the Corryvreckan Whirlpool (adult/child £35/27; call for the dates of 'Whirlpool Specials', when the tide is at its strongest), as well as three-hour whale-watching trips (£44/34), mostly in July and August.

There are also cruises to Iona and Staffa (£70/55), and a weekly day-trip to Colonsay (£44/34), plus trips to the remote Garvellach Islands (£44/34).

Sea Life Adventures   BOAT TRIP
(☎01631-571010; www.sealife-adventures.co.uk; Clachan Seil) Exciting boat trips, based on the eastern side of the island. It has a large, comfortable boat offering wildlife cruises and trips to the Corryvreckan whirlpool.

ℹ Getting There & Around
BOAT Argyll & Bute Council (☎01631-562125) Operates the daily passenger-only ferry service from Ellanbeich to Easdale island (£1.55 return, bicycles free, five minutes, every 30 minutes).
BUS West Coast Motors (www.westcoast motors.co.uk) Bus 418 runs four times a day, except Sunday, from Oban to Ellanbeich (45 minutes) and on to North Cuan (one hour) for the ferry to Luing.

Isle of Luing

Luing (pronounced ling), about 6 miles long and 1.5 miles wide, is separated from the southern end of Seil by the narrow Cuan Sound. There are two attractive villages – **Cullipool** at the northern end and Toberonochy in the east – but Luing's main pleasures are scenic.

The **slate quarries** of Cullipool were abandoned in 1965. About 1.5 miles out to sea you can see the remains of the extensively quarried slate island of **Belnahua** – workers used to live on this remote and desolate rock. You can get a closer look on a boat trip from Easdale with Sea.fari Adventures (p78).

There are two Iron Age forts on the island, the better being Dun Leccamore, about a mile north of Toberonochy. In Toberonochy itself are the ruins of the late medieval **Kilchatton Church** and a graveyard with unusual slate gravestones.

You can visit both villages, the fort, ruined chapel and the scenic west coast on a pleasant 8-mile circular **walk**.

ℹ Getting There & Around
BOAT Argyll & Bute Council (☎01631-569160; www.argyll-bute.gov.uk) Operates a small car ferry from Cuan (on Seil) to Luing (passenger/car return £1.50/6, bicycles free, five minutes, every 30 minutes).
BUS Royal Mail Postbus (☎01631-314243; www.postbus.royalmail.com) Operates a Monday to Saturday postbus service from the ferry at Cuan to Cullipool (four daily) and Toberonochy (twice daily).

NORTH ARGYLL

Loch Awe

Loch Awe is one of Scotland's most beautiful lochs, with rolling forested hills around its southern end and spectacular mountains in the north. It lies between Oban and Inveraray and is the longest loch in Scotland – about 24 miles long – but is less than a mile wide for most of its length. See www.loch-awe .com for more information.

At its northern end, Loch Awe escapes to the sea through the narrow **Pass of Brander**, where Robert the Bruce defeated the MacDougalls in battle in 1309.

◉ Sights

Cruachan Power Station   POWER STATION
(☎01866-822618; www.visitcruachan.co.uk; adult/child £6/2.50; ☺9.30am-4.45pm Easter-Oct, tours every 30min) In the Pass of Brander, by the A85, you can visit Cruachan power station. Electric buses take you more than half a mile inside Ben Cruachan, allowing you to see the pump-storage hydroelectric scheme which occupies a vast cavern hollowed out of the mountain.

St Conan's Kirk   CHURCH
(☺9am-5pm daily) St Conan's Kirk is a contemplative if somewhat bizarre place that shouldn't be missed if you're passing through Loch Awe. Situated at the northern end of the loch, the original building, completed in 1886, was a tiny affair, but when eccentric architect Walter Campbell got his hands on it he turned it into one of Scotland's most unusual churches, a heady mix of Norman mini-grandeur and Saxon strangeness.

He began transforming the existing church in 1907 and, on his death in 1914, his sister Helen carried out the remaining plans. The best parts of the church are definitely the views over Loch Awe through its clouded glass, and the cloisters in the northwestern corner.

Kilchurn Castle
CASTLE

(HS; admission free; ⊙9am-5pm Apr-Sep) At the northern end of Loch Awe are the scenic ruins of the strategically situated and much-photographed Kilchurn Castle. Built in 1440, it enjoys one of Scotland's finest settings. You can climb to the top of the four-storey castle tower for impressive views of Loch Awe and the surrounding hills. It's a half-mile walk from the A85 road, just east of the bridge over the River Orchy.

The castle is situated on a tiny peninsula guarding the northern tip of the loch. Long held by the Campbell clan, it was enlarged in 1693 to garrison government troops during the Jacobite uprising; it was then abandoned in the 1750s after a fire ran through most of it. Nowadays it's just a shell, although a very picturesque one.

❶ Getting There & Away

Scottish Citylink (www.citylink.co.uk) Buses from Glasgow to Oban go via Dalmally, Lochawe village and Cruachan power station.
Trains from Glasgow to Oban stop at Dalmally and Lochawe village.

Connel & Taynuilt

Hemmed in by dramatic mountain scenery, **Loch Etive** stretches for 17 miles from Connel to Kinlochetive (accessible by road from Glencoe). At Connel Bridge, 5 miles north of Oban, the loch is joined to the sea by a narrow channel partly blocked by an underwater rock ledge. When the tide flows in and out – as it does twice a day – millions of tons of water pours through this bottleneck, creating spectacular white-water rapids known as the **Falls of Lora**. You can park near the north end of the bridge and walk back to the middle to have a look.

◉ Sights & Activities

Dunstaffnage Castle
CASTLE

(HS; ☑562465; www.historic-scotland.gov.uk; adult/child £3.70/2.20; ⊙9.30am-5.30pm Apr-Sep, to 4.30pm Oct, closed Thu & Fri Nov-Mar) Dunstaffnage, 2 miles west of Connel, looks like

a child's drawing of what a castle should be – square and massive, with towers at the corners, and perched on top of a rocky outcrop. It was built around 1260 and was captured by Robert the Bruce during the Wars of Independence in 1309. The haunted ruins of the nearby 13th-century **chapel** contain lots of Campbell tombs decorated with skull-and-crossbone carvings.

Bonawe Iron Furnace
HISTORIC SITE

(HS; ☑822432; www.historic-scotland.gov.uk; adult/child £4.20/2.50; ⊙9.30am-5.30pm Apr-Sep) Bonawe Iron Furnace is one of the region's most unusual historical sights. Near Taynuilt, and dating from 1753, it was built by an iron-smelting company from the English Lake District because of the abundance of birchwood in the area. The wood was made into the charcoal that was needed for smelting the iron.

It took 10,000 acres of woodland to produce Bonawe's annual output of 700 tons of pig iron. A fascinating self-guided tour leads you around the various parts of the site.

Loch Etive Cruises
BOAT TOUR

(☑07721-732703, 01866-822430; ⊙Mar-Nov) From the jetty opposite the entrance to the Bonawe Iron Furnace, Loch Etive Cruises runs boat trips to the head of Loch Etive and back. You might spot eagles, otters, seals and deer, and at the head of the loch you can see the famous Etive slabs – dotted with rock climbers in dry weather. Bookings are essential.

Cruises depart one to three times daily, except Saturday, from March to November. There are two-hour cruises (adult/child £10/8, departing 10am and noon) and three-hour cruises (£15/12, departing 2pm).

❶ Getting There & Away

Buses between Oban and Fort William or Glasgow, and trains between Oban and Glasgow, all stop in Connel and Taynuilt.

Appin & Around

The Appin region, once ruled over by the Stewarts of Appin from their stronghold at Castle Stalker, stretches north from the rocky shores of Loch Creran to the hills of Glencoe.

Port Appin, a couple of miles off the main road north of Loch Creran, is a pleasant spot, from where you can catch a passenger ferry to the island of **Lismore**.

Sights & Activities

Scottish Sea Life Sanctuary AQUARIUM
(☎720386; www.sealsanctuary.co.uk; adult/child £12.50/10; ⏰10am-5pm Mar-Oct) The Scottish Sea Life Sanctuary, 8 miles north of Oban on the shores of Loch Creran, provides a haven for orphaned seal pups. As well as the seal pools there are tanks housing herrings, rays and flatfish, touch pools for children, an otter sanctuary and displays on Scotland's marine environment.

Castle Stalker CASTLE
North of Loch Creran, at Portnacroish, there's a wonderful view of this castle perched on a tiny offshore island – Monty Python buffs will recognise it as the castle that appears in the final scenes of the film *Monty Python and the Holy Grail*.

Port Appin Bike BICYCLE RENTAL
(☎01631-730391; half-/full day £8/12) You can hire bikes at the entrance to the village.

Sleeping & Eating

Ecopod Boutique Retreat SELF-CATERING £££
(☎07725 409003; www.domesweetdome.co.uk; Lettershuna; 2-person pod per week £1100 ; P wifi) 'Glamping' (glamorous camping) has been all the rage these last few years, but the Ecopod Retreat takes things to a new level of luxury. Technically they're tents, but these geodesic structures cover 70 sq ft and include designer furniture, handmade kitchens, sheepskin rugs, gourmet hampers and private wooden decks complete with cedar hot tubs. Meantime, the sylvan setting is superb, nestled among rhododendrons and native birch woodland, with a stunning outlook over Loch Linnhe and Castle Stalker.

Pierhouse Hotel HOTEL £££
(☎01631-730302; www.pierhousehotel.co.uk; Port Appin; s £70-120, d £120-175; mains £15-25; P wifi) The delightfully quaint Pierhouse Hotel sits on the waterfront above the pier for the Lismore ferry, and has stylish modern rooms, a sauna and an excellent **restaurant** (Port Appin; mains £15-25; ⏰lunch & dinner) that enjoys a view across the water to Lismore, and specialises in local seafood and game.

Getting There & Away

Scottish Citylink (www.citylink.co.uk) Buses between Oban and Fort William stop at the Sea Life Sanctuary (p80) and Appin village.

Isle of Lismore

POP 170

The first thing you notice about the island of Lismore is how green it is (the Gaelic name, Lios Mor, means 'Great Garden') – all lush grassland sprinkled with wildflowers, with grey blades of limestone breaking through the soil. And that's the secret – limestone is rare in the Highlands, but it weathers to a very fertile soil.

The island is long and narrow – 10 miles long and just over a mile wide – with a road running almost its full length. **Clachan**, a scattering of houses midway between Achnacroish and Point, is the nearest the island has to a village. **Lismore Stores** (⏰9am-5.30pm Mon, Tue, Thu & Fri, to 1pm Wed & Sat; @), between Achnacroish and Clachan, is a grocery store and post office, and has internet access.

St Moluag's Centre (☎01631-760300; www.celm.org.uk; adult/child £3.50/free; ⏰11am-4pm May-Sep, noon-3pm Apr, Oct & Nov) houses a fascinating exhibition on Lismore's history and culture; alongside stands a reconstruction of a crofter's cottage. The **Lismore Café** (☎01631-760020; mains £3-6; ⏰lunch daily, dinner Fri & Sat Apr-Oct) here has an outdoor deck with a stunning view of the mainland mountains (booking necessary for dinner). The centre is in the middle of the island – if you're walking, you can take a short cut by starting along the coastal path north of the pier at Achnacroish (2 miles by road, just over 1 mile by the path).

The romantic ruins of 13th-century **Castle Coeffin** have a lovely setting on the west coast, a mile from Clachan (follow the waymarked path). **Tirefour Broch**, a defensive tower with double walls reaching 4m in height, is directly opposite on the east coast.

There is very little short-stay accommodation on Lismore. However, there are several self-catering options that are advertised on www.isleoflismore.com.

Getting There & Around

BIKE **Lismore Bike Hire** (☎01631-760213) Will deliver your bike to the ferry slip; hire costs £6/10 per half-/full day.

BOAT **CalMac** (www.calmac.co.uk) Runs a car ferry from Oban to Achnacroish, with two to five sailings Monday to Saturday (passenger/car return £5.55/45.90, 50 minutes).

Argyll & Bute Council (www.argyll-bute.gov.uk) Operates the passenger ferry from Port

Robert Louis Stevenson's novel *Kidnapped* was based around the story of the Appin Murder, a killing which took place at Lettermore, just west of Ballachulish, in 1752. Colin Campbell, nicknamed the Red Fox, was the factor of several West Highland properties that had been confiscated from Jacobite clans in the aftermath of the 1746 Battle of Culloden. He was shot dead with a musket while on his way to collect rents at Ardsheal, and the murderer escaped into the hills.

A local man, James Stewart, known as James of the Glens, was arrested two days later and put on trial at Inveraray. Eleven of the 15 men in the jury were Campbells, and the judge was the Duke of Argyll, chief of Clan Campbell. James (not surprisingly) was found guilty and sentenced to death by hanging. But his family always maintained his innocence (the chief suspect was his half-brother Alan Breck Stewart, the swashbuckling antihero of *Kidnapped*).

James Stewart's execution ranks as one of the longest-standing potential miscarriages of justice in Scotland. Several books have been written on the subject, and as recently as 2008 a Glasgow lawyer asked the Scottish Criminal Cases Review Commission to reopen the case (he was unsuccessful).

A simple cairn on the hillside (now surrounded by conifer plantations) marks the site of the murder; it is signposted off the A828 a mile west of Ballachulish Bridge. Another memorial, at the south end of Ballachulish Bridge, marks the spot where James of the Glens was hanged.

Appin to Point (£1.35, 10 minutes, hourly). Bicycles are carried for free.

TAXI Mrs Livingstone (01631-760220)

SOUTHERN HEBRIDES

Isle of Islay

POP 3400

The most southerly island of the Inner Hebrides, Islay (*eye*-lah) is best known for its single-malt whiskies, which have a distinctive smoky flavour. There are eight working distilleries here, all of which welcome visitors and offer guided tours.

Islay's whisky industry contributes approximately £100 million a year to the government in excise duty and value-added tax (VAT); that's about £30,000 for every man, woman and child on the island. Little wonder that the islanders complain about the lack of government investment in the area.

With a list of over 250 recorded bird species, Islay also attracts birdwatchers. It's an important wintering ground for thousands of white-fronted and barnacle geese. As well as the whisky and wildfowl, there are miles of sandy beaches, pleasant walking trails, and good food and drink.

Hotels and B&Bs are scattered across the island. There's a campsite and bunkhouse at Kintra, near Port Ellen, and a campsite and youth hostel in Port Charlotte. If you want to camp elsewhere, ask permission first. Camping is prohibited on the Ardtalla and Dunlossit estates on the eastern side of Islay.

Tours

Islay Birding BIRDWATCHING
(www.islaybirding.co.uk) Birdwatching tours by bicycle (£30/60 per half-/full day). There are also 2½-hour wildlife walks (£30 per person) and family bushcraft courses (two adults plus children £60 per half day) teaching outdoor-survival skills.

Islay Sea Safaris BOAT TOURS
(07768-450000; www.islayseasafari.co.uk) Can arrange customised tours (£25 per person per hour) by sea from Port Ellen to visit some or all of Islay and Jura's distilleries in a single day, as well as bird-watching trips, coastal exploration, and trips to Jura's remote west coast and the Corryvreckan whirlpool.

Islay Stalking WILDLIFE WATCHING
(01496-850120; www.thegearach.co.uk) Here's your chance to stalk deer and other wildlife in the company of a gamekeeper, and shoot them – not with a gun but with a camera. Morning and evening photographic tours are £20/10 per adult/child.

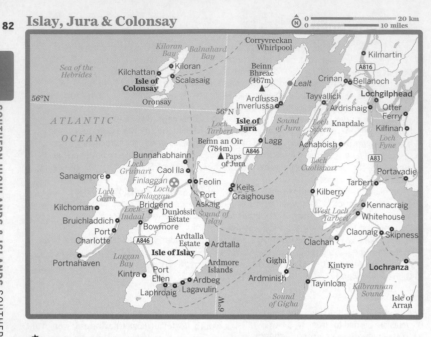

✦ Festivals & Events

Fèis Ìle   FOLK MUSIC, WHISKY
(Islay Festival; www.theislayfestival.co.uk)   A
week-long celebration of traditional Scottish music and whisky at the end of May.
Events include *ceilidhs*, pipe-band performances, distillery tours, barbecues and
whisky tastings.

Islay Jazz Festival   MUSIC
(☑01496-810262;   www.islayjazzfestival.co.uk)
This three-day festival takes place over the
second weekend in September. A varied line-
up of international talent plays at various
venues across the island.

❶ Information

Islay Service Point (☑01496-810332; Jamieson St, Bowmore; ⊙9am-12.30pm & 1.30-5pm
Mon-Fri; @) Free internet access.

MacTaggart Community CyberCafé
(☑01496-302693; www.islaycybercafe.co.uk;
30 Mansfield Pl, Port Ellen; per 30min £1;
⊙9am-10pm Mon & Wed-Sat, to 5pm Tue &
Sun; @☎) Internet access.

MacTaggart Leisure Centre (☑01496-810767;
School St, Bowmore; ⊙noon-9pm Mon-Fri,
10.30am-5.30pm Sat & Sun) Coin-operated
laundrette.

❶ Getting There & Away

AIR Islay airport lies midway between Port Ellen
and Bowmore.

Loganair/FlyBe (www.loganair.co.uk) Flies
from Glasgow to Islay (£70 one way, 45 minutes, two or three flights daily Monday to
Friday, one or two Saturday and Sunday).

Hebridean Air Services (☑0845 805 7465;
www.hebrideanair.co.uk) Operates flights (£65
one way, twice daily Tuesday and Thursday)
from Connel Airfield (near Oban) to Colonsay
(30 minutes) and Islay (40 minutes).

BOAT CalMac (www.calmac.co.uk) CalMac
runs ferries from Kennacraig in West Loch
Tarbert to Port Ellen (passenger/car £9.20/49,
2¼ hours, one to three daily) and Port Askaig
(£9.20/49, two hours, one to three daily). On
Wednesday only in summer the ferry continues
from Port Askaig to Colonsay (£4.85/24.70,
1¼ hours).

❶ Getting Around

BICYCLE You can hire bikes from Bowmore Post
Office, and from the house opposite the Port
Charlotte Hotel.

BUS A bus service links Ardbeg, Port Ellen,
Bowmore, Port Charlotte, Portnahaven and Port
Askaig (limited service on Sunday). Pick up a
copy of the *Islay & Jura Public Transport Guide*
from the tourist office.

CAR **D & N Mackenzie** (☏01496-302300; Port Ellen; from £30 a day) Hire cars.

TAXI **Bowmore** (☏01496-810449); **Port Ellen** (☏01496-302155)

PORT ELLEN & AROUND

Port Ellen is the main point of entry for Islay. It has a **Co-op Food minimarket** (⊗8am-8pm Mon-Sat, noon-7.30pm Sun), a pub and a bank (closed most afternoons and Wednesdays). There's an ATM in the Spar shop around the corner from the bank. While there's nothing to see in the town itself, the coast stretching northeast from Port Ellen is one of the loveliest parts of the island.

◎ Sights & Activities

Kildalton Chapel CHAPEL
A pleasant bike ride leads past the distilleries to the atmospheric, age-haunted Kildalton Chapel, 8 miles northeast of Port Ellen. In the kirkyard is the exceptional late-8th-century **Kildalton Cross**, the only remaining Celtic high cross in Scotland (most surviving high crosses are in Ireland). There are carvings of biblical scenes on one side and animals on the other. There are also several extraordinary grave slabs around the chapel, some carved with swords and Celtic interlace patterns.

Ardmore Islands WILDLIFE
The kelp-fringed skerries (small rocky islands or reefs) of the Ardmore Islands, off the southeastern corner of Islay near Kildalton, are a wildlife haven and home to the second-largest colony of common seals in Europe.

DISTILLERIES
There are three whisky distilleries in close succession.

Laphroaig Distillery DISTILLERY
(www.laphroaig.com; tours £3; ⊗9.30am-5.30pm Mon-Fri, also 10am-4pm Sat & Sun Mar-Dec)

Lagavulin Distillery DISTILLERY
(www.discovering-distilleries.com; tours £6; ⊗9am-5pm Mon-Fri Apr-Oct, to 12.30pm Nov-Mar, plus 9am-5pm Sat & 12.30-4pm Sun Jul & Aug)

Ardbeg Distillery DISTILLERY
(www.ardbeg.com; tours £5; ⊗10am-5pm Jun-Aug, 10am-4pm Mon-Fri Sep-May)

🛏 Sleeping & Eating

TOP CHOICE Kintra Farm CAMPGROUND, B&B ££
(☏01496-302051; www.kintrafarm.co.uk; Kintra; tent sites £4-10, plus per person £3, r per person £30-38; ⊗Apr-Sep) At the southern end of Laggan Bay, 3.5 miles northwest of Port Ellen, Kintra offers three bedrooms in a homely farmhouse B&B. There's also a basic but beautiful campsite on buttercup-sprinkled turf amid the dunes, with a sunset view across the beach.

Oystercatcher B&B B&B ££
(☏01496-300409; www.islay-bedandbreakfast.com; 63 Frederick Cres, Port Ellen; r per person £32; @�🌐) If you like your breakfasts fishy, then this welcoming waterfront house is the place for you – there's smoked haddock, smoked salmon and kippers on the menu, as well as the usual stuff. Bedrooms are small but comfortable and very nicely decorated.

TOP CHOICE Old Kiln Café SCOTTISH £
(☏01496-302244; Ardbeg; mains £4-10; ⊗10am-4pm daily Jun-Aug, Mon-Fri only Sep-Jun, lunch served from noon) Housed in the former malting kiln at Ardbeg Distillery, this well-run cafe serves hearty homemade soups, tasty light meals (try a panini sandwich with haggis and apple chutney, or a platter of smoked Islay beef, venison and pastrami); and a range of home-baked desserts, including traditional clootie dumpling (a rich steamed pudding filled with currants and raisins) with ice cream.

BOWMORE

The attractive Georgian village of Bowmore was built in 1768 to replace the village of Kilarrow, which just had to go – it was spoiling the view from the laird's house. Bowmore's centrepiece is the distinctive **Round Church** at the top of Main St, built in circular form to ensure that the devil had no corners to hide in.

◎ Sights & Activities

Bowmore Distillery DISTILLERY
(☏01496-810671; www.bowmore.co.uk; School St; tours adult/child £4/2; ⊗9am-5pm Mon-Fri, to noon Sat, plus 9am-5pm Sat Easter–mid-Sep & noon-4pm Sun Jul–mid-Sep) Bowmore is the only distillery on the island that still malts its own barley. The tour (check website for times), which begins with an overblown 10-minute marketing video, is redeemed by a look at (and taste of) the germinating grain laid out in golden billows on the floor of the malting shed, and a free dram at the end.

Islay Ales BREWERY
(www.islayales.com; ⌚10.30am-5pm Mon-Sat, plus noon-4pm Sun Jun-Aug) This microbrewery produces a range of real ales, all bottled by hand. After a complementary tour of the premises, you can taste the ales for free, and buy a bottle or two to drink outdoors or back home (the brewery doesn't have a bar licence). Our favourite is Saligo Ale, a refreshing, summery pale ale.

The brewery is located at Islay House Square, a collection of craft shops and studios 3 miles northeast of Bowmore at Bridgend.

Sleeping & Eating

Harbour Inn RESTAURANT £££
(☎01496-810330; www.harbour-inn.com; The Square; s/d from £95/130; @📶) The plush seven-room Harbour Inn, smartly decorated with a nautical theme, is the poshest place in town. The restaurant (mains £16 to £24, open for lunch and dinner) has harbour views and serves fresh local oysters, lobster and scallops, Islay lamb and Jura venison.

Lambeth House B&B ££
(☎01496-810597; lambethguesthouse@tiscali.co.uk; Jamieson St; s/d £60/90; @👪) A short stroll from the harbour, the Lambeth is a simple, good-value guesthouse with comfy en suite bedrooms. Breakfasts are excellent, and it also offers a two-course evening meal for £12.

Lochside Hotel HOTEL ££
(☎01496-810244; www.lochsidehotel.co.uk; 19 Shore St; r per person from £50; 📶) The 10 en suite bedrooms at the Lochside are kitted-out with chunky pine furniture, including one room adapted for wheelchair users. The conservatory dining room provides sweeping views over Loch Indaal, plus the bar boasts a range of more than 250 single-malts, including many rare bottlings.

PORT CHARLOTTE

Eleven miles from Bowmore, on the opposite shore of Loch Indaal, is the attractive village of Port Charlotte. It has a **general store** (⌚9am-12.30pm & 1.30-5.30pm Mon-Sat, 11.30am-1.30pm Sun) and post office.

Sights & Activities

Museum of Islay Life MUSEUM
(☎01496-850358; www.islaymuseum.org; adult/child £3/1; ⌚10am-5pm Mon-Sat, 2-5pm Sun Easter-Oct) Islay's long history is lovingly recorded in this museum, housed in the former Free Church. Prize exhibits include an illicit still, 19th-century crofters' furniture, and a set of leather boots once worn by the horse that pulled the lawnmower at Islay House (so it wouldn't leave hoof prints on the lawn!).

There are also touch-screen computers displaying archive photos of Islay in the 19th and early 20th centuries.

Islay Natural History Visitor Centre WILDLIFE EXHIBITION
(www.islaynaturalhistory.org; adult/child £3/1.50; ⌚10am-4pm Mon-Fri Apr-Oct, also Sat Jun-Aug) Next to the youth hostel, this centre has displays explaining the island's natural history, with advice on where to see wildlife and lots of interesting hands-on exhibits for kids.

Bruichladdich Distillery DISTILLERY
(☎01496-850190; www.bruichladdich.com; tours £5; ⌚9am-5pm Mon-Fri & 10am-4pm Sat) At the northern edge of Port Charlotte, this distillery reopened in 2001 with all its original Victorian equipment restored to working condition. Independently owned and independently minded, Bruichladdich (brook-*lah*-day) produces an intriguing range of distinctive, very peaty whiskies. Call ahead to book a tour.

Sleeping & Eating

Port Charlotte Hotel HOTEL £££
(☎01496-850360; www.portcharlottehotel.co.uk; s/d £95/160; ⌚restaurant 6.30-9pm, bar meals noon-2pm & 5-8pm; P📶👪) This lovely old Victorian hotel has stylish, individually decorated bedrooms with sea views, and a candlelit **restaurant** (mains £15 to £22, open for dinner) serving local seafood (such as seared scallops with braised leeks and truffle cream sauce), Islay beef, venison and duck.

The **bar** (bar meals £7 to £10, open for lunch and dinner) is well stocked with Islay malts and real ales, and has a nook at the back with a view over the loch towards the Paps of Jura.

Port Mor Campsite CAMPGROUND £
(☎01496-850441; www.islandofislay.co.uk; tent sites per person £8; @📶) The sports field to the south of the village doubles as a campground – there are toilets, showers, laundry and a children's play area in the main building. Open all year.

Islay SYHA HOSTEL £
(☎01496-850385; www.syha.org.uk; dm £15; ⌚Apr-Oct; @📶) This modern and comfortable hostel is housed in a former distillery building with views over the loch.

Debbie's Minimarket
DELI £

(☎01496-850319; ◷9am-5.30pm Mon-Sat) The village shop and post office at Bruichladdich doubles as a deli that stocks good wine and posh picnic grub, and also serves the best coffee on Islay – sit at one of the outdoor tables and enjoy an espresso with a sea view.

Croft Kitchen
RESTAURANT £

(☎01496-850230; mains lunch £4-7, dinner £11-15; ◷lunch & dinner) This laid-back little bistro serves as a cafe during the day and transforms into a restaurant serving quality meals in the evening.

PORTNAHAVEN

Six miles southwest of Port Charlotte the road ends at **Portnahaven**, another pretty village that was purpose-built as a fishing harbour in the 19th century. A mile north of the village is the pretty little shell-sand beach of Currie Sands, with a lovely view of Orsay island.

The next inlet to the north of the beach is occupied by the world's first commercially viable wave-powered electricity generating station, built on cliffs that are open to the Atlantic swell. The 500kW plant – known as the **Limpet** (Land-installed, marine-powered energy transformer) – provides enough electricity to power 200 island homes.

LOCH GRUINART

Seven miles north of Port Charlotte is **Loch Gruinart Nature Reserve**, where you can hear corncrakes in summer and see huge flocks of migrating ducks, geese and waders in spring and autumn; there's a hide with wheelchair access. The nearby **RSPB Visitor Centre** (admission free; ◷10am-5pm Apr-Oct, to 4pm Nov-Mar) offers two- to three-hour guided walks around the reserve (£3 per person, 10am Thursday April to October).

Kilchoman Distillery (☎01496-850011; www.kilchomandistillery.com; Rockfield Farm; tours £4; ◷10am-5pm Mon-Fri, plus Sat Apr-Oct), 5 miles southwest of Loch Gruinart, is Islay's newest, going into production in 2005. The distillery grows its own barley on Islay, and the tourist office explores the history of farmhouse distilling on the island. Its first single-malt was released in 2010, and was so popular it sold out within days.

The **cafe** (mains £5-10; ◷10am-5pm Mon-Fri Mar-Oct, plus Sat Apr-Sep, plus Sun Jul & Aug) at Kilchoman Distillery rustles up an excellent lunch – crusty brown rolls filled with hot-smoked salmon and dill mayo, and bowls of rich, smoky Cullen skink.

FINLAGGAN

Lush meadows scattered with buttercups and daisies slope down to reed-fringed Loch Finlaggan, the medieval capital of the Lords of the Isles. This bucolic setting, 3 miles southwest of Port Askaig, was once the most important settlement in the Hebrides, and the central seat of power of the Lords of the Isles from the 12th to the 16th centuries. From the little island at the northern end of the loch the descendants of Somerled administered their island territories and entertained visiting chieftains in their great hall. Little remains now except the tumbled ruins of houses and a chapel, but the setting is beautiful and the history fascinating. A wooden walkway leads over the reeds and water lilies to the island, where information boards describe the remains.

Finlaggan Visitor Centre (www.finlaggan .com; adult/child £3/1; ◷10.30am-4.30pm Mon-Sat & 1.30-4.30pm Sun Apr-Sep), in a cottage (plus modern extension) on the island, explains the site's history and archaeology.

Buses from Port Askaig stop at the road's end, from where it's a 15-minute walk to the loch.

PORT ASKAIG & AROUND

Port Askaig is little more than a hotel, a shop (with ATM), a petrol pump and a ferry pier, set in a picturesque nook halfway along the Sound of Islay, the strait that separates the islands of Islay and Jura.

There are two distilleries within easy reach: **Caol Ila Distillery** (☎01496-840207; www.discovering-distilleries.com; tours £6; ◷9.15am-5pm Mon-Fri & 1.30-4.30pm Sat Apr-Oct, shorter hours in winter), pronounced 'cull *ee*-lah', a mile to the north, and **Bunnahabhain Distillery** (☎01496-840646; www .bunnahabhain.com; tours £5; ◷9am-4.30pm Mon-Fri Mar-Oct, by appointment Nov-Feb), pronounced 'boo-na-*hah*-ven', 3 miles north. Both enjoy wonderful locations with great views across to Jura.

The rooms at the **Port Askaig Hotel** (☎01496-840245; www.portaskaig.co.uk; s/d from £40/90; [P]), beside the ferry pier, seem to be pleasantly stuck in the 1970s. But that's all okay because the staff are warm and friendly, the breakfast is good and there's a great view of the Paps of Jura from the residents' lounge. The beer garden is a popular spot to sit and watch the comings and goings at the quay.

Isle of Jura

POP 170

Jura lies off the coast of Argyll – long, dark and low like a vast Viking longship, its billowing sail the distinctive triple peaks of the Paps of Jura. A magnificently wild and lonely island, it's the perfect place to get away from it all – as George Orwell did in 1948. Orwell wrote his masterpiece *1984* while living at the remote farmhouse of Barnhill in the north of the island, describing it in a letter as 'a very un-get-at-able place'.

Jura takes its name from the Old Norse dyr-a (deer island) – an apt appellation, as the island supports a population of around 6000 red deer, outnumbering their human cohabitants by about 35 to one.

There are regular *ceilidhs* held throughout the year where visitors are made very welcome; check the notice board outside Jura Stores for announcements.

⊙ Sights

Apart from the superb wilderness walking and wildlife-watching, there's not a whole lot to do on the island except for visiting the **Isle of Jura Distillery** (www.isleofjura .com; admission free; ⊘by appointment Mon-Fri) or wandering around the beautiful walled gardens of **Jura House** (www.jurahouseandgardens .co.uk; adult/child £2.50/free; ⊘9am-5pm) at the southern end of the island. There's a lovely walk from the gardens down to a tiny white-sand beach where, if you're lucky, you might spot an otter. In summer a **tea tent** (⊘11am-5pm Mon-Fri, to 4pm Sun Jun-Aug) sells hot drinks, home baking, crafts and plants.

There's also the **Feolin Study Centre** (www.theisleofjura.co.uk; admission free; ⊘9am-5pm), just south of the ferry slip at Feolin, which has a small exhibition on Jura's history and provides information on all aspects of the island's history, culture and wildlife.

🏃 Activities

There are few proper footpaths on Jura, but any off-the-beaten-path exploration will involve rough-going through giant bracken, knee-deep bogs and thigh-high tussocks. Most of the island is occupied by deer-stalking estates, and access to the hills may be restricted during the stalking season (July to February); the Jura Hotel can provide details of areas to be avoided.

There are easier short walks (one or two hours) east along the coast from Jura House, and north along a 4WD track from

---

THE SCOTTISH MAELSTROM

It may look innocuous on the map, but the **Gulf of Corryvreckan** - the 1km-wide channel between the northern end of Jura and the island of Scarba - is home to one of the three most notorious tidal whirlpools in the world (the others are the Maelstrom in Norway's Lofoten Islands, and the Old Sow in Canada's New Brunswick).

The tide doesn't just rise and fall twice a day, it flows – dragged around the earth by the gravitational attraction of the moon. On the west coast of Scotland, the rising tide – known as the flood tide – flows northwards. As the flood moves up the Sound of Jura, to the east of the island, it is forced into a narrowing bottleneck jammed with islands, and builds up to a greater height than the open sea to the west of Jura. As a result, millions of gallons of sea water pour westwards through the Gulf of Corryvreckan at speeds of up to 8 knots – an average sailing yacht is going fast at 6 knots.

The **Corryvreckan whirlpool** forms where this mass of moving water hits an underwater pinnacle – which rises from the 200m-deep sea bed to within just 28m of the surface – and swirls over and around it. The turbulent waters create a magnificent spectacle, with white-capped breakers, standing waves, bulging boils and overfalls, and countless miniature maelstroms whirling around the main vortex.

Corryvreckan is at its most violent when a flooding spring tide, flowing west through the gulf, meets a westerly gale blowing in from the Atlantic. In these conditions, standing waves up to 5m high can form and dangerously rough seas extend more than 3 miles west of Corryvreckan, a phenomenon known as the Great Race.

You can see the whirlpool by making the long hike to the northern end of Jura (check tide times at the Jura Hotel), or by taking a boat trip from Easdale with Seafari Adventures (p78).

For more information, see www.whirlpool-scotland.co.uk.

Feolin. *Jura – A Guide for Walkers* by Gordon Wright (£2) is available from the tourist office in Bowmore, Islay.

Evans Walk
WALKING

The only real trail on the island is a stalkers' path that leads for 6 miles from the main road through a pass in the hills to a hunting lodge above the remote sandy beach at Glenbatrick Bay. The path leaves the road 4 miles north of Craighouse (just under a mile north of the bridge over the River Corran). The first 0.75 mile is hard-going along an interwoven braid of faint, squelchy trails through lumpy bog; aim at or just left of the cairn on the near horizon. The path firms up and is easier to follow after you cross a stream. On the descent on the far side of the pass, look out for wild orchids and sundew, and keep an eye out for adders basking in the sun. Allow six hours for the 12-mile round trip.

Corryvreckan Whirlpool Viewpoint Walk
WALKING

The walk to a viewpoint for the Corryvreckan Whirlpool, the great tidal race between the northern end of Jura and the island of Scarba, is a good one. From the northern end of the public road at Lealt you hike along a 4WD track past Barnhill to Kinuachdrachd Farm (6 miles). About 30m before the farm buildings a footpath forks left (there's an inconspicuous wooden signpost low down) and climbs up the hillside before traversing rough and boggy ground to a point 50m above the northern tip of the island. A rocky slab makes a natural grandstand for viewing the turbulent waters of the Gulf of Corryvreckan; if you have timed it right (check tide times at the Jura Hotel), you will see the whirlpool as a writhing mass of white water diagonally to your left and over by the Scarba shore. Allow five to six hours for the round trip (16 miles) from the road end.

Paps of Jura
CLIMBING

Climbing the Paps of Jura is a truly tough hill-walk over ankle-breaking scree that requires good fitness and navigational skills (you'll need eight hours for the 11 long, hard and weary miles). A good place to start is by the bridge over the River Corran, 3 miles north of Craighouse. The first peak you reach is **Beinn a'Chaolais** (734m), the second is **Beinn an Oir** (784m) and the third is **Beinn Shiantaidh** (755m). Most people also climb **Corra Bheinn** (569m), before joining Evans' Walk to return to the road. If you succeed in bagging all four, you can reflect on the fact that the record for the annual Paps of Jura fell race is just three hours!

🛏 Sleeping & Eating

Places to stay on the island are very limited, so book ahead – don't rely on just turning up and hoping to find a bed. Most of Jura's accommodation is in self-catering cottages that are let by the week (see www.jura development.co.uk). The only places to eat are Antlers and the Jura Hotel in Craighouse.

You can **camp** for free in the field below the Jura Hotel (p87) (ask at the bar first, and pop a donation in the bottle); there are toilets and hot showers (£1 coin) in the block behind the hotel.

Sealladh Na Mara
B&B £££

(☏01496-820349; www.isleofjura.net; Knockrome; per person from £25) A modern croft house about 4 miles north of Craighouse, this place offers B&B in two cosy, IKEA-furnished bedrooms and a lovely guest lounge with a patio overlooking the sea. Evening meals can be provided, and there's also a self-catering two-bedroom chalet (from £200 a week).

Jura Hotel
HOTEL £££

(☏01496-820243; www.jurahotel.co.uk; Craighouse; s/d from £50/84; P) The 18-room Jura is the most comfortable place to stay on the island; ask for a room at the front with a view of the bay. The hotel also serves decent bar meals (£7 to £12, open for lunch and dinner) and the bar itself is a very sociable place to spend the evening.

Food is served from noon to 2pm and 6.30pm to 9pm.

🍴 Antlers
SCOTTISH £££

(☏01496-820123; www.theantlers.co.uk; Craighouse; mains £5-9, 2-/3-course dinner £25/29; ⊙10.30am-4.30pm daily, plus 6.30-9.30pm Tue-Sun; 🐾) This bistro makes the most of locally sourced produce, offering soup, sandwiches and burgers during the day, and an unexpectedly classy menu at dinner time, with dishes such as grilled goats cheese on black pudding with onion marmalade, glazed loin of pork with a cider reduction, and Cajun-style pan-fried venison.

❶ Information

There's no bank or ATM in town, but you can get cash on a debit card at the Jura Hotel.

Jura Service Point (☏01496-820161; Craighouse; ⊙10am-1pm Mon-Fri; @) Community-run office, 400m north of the Jura Hotel; provides tourist information and free internet access.

SOUTHERN HIGHLANDS & ISLANDS ISLE OF JURA

Jura Stores (www.jurastores.co.uk; Craighouse; ◎9am-1pm & 2-5pm Mon-Fri, 9am-1pm & 2-4.30pm Sat) The island's only shop.

❶ Getting There & Away

Jura Passenger Ferry (☑07768-450000; www.jurapassengerferry.com) From April to September, a ferry runs from Tayvallich on the mainland to Craighouse on Jura (£17.50, one hour, one or two daily except Wednesday). Booking recommended.

A **car ferry** shuttles between Port Askaig on Islay and Feolin on Jura (passenger/car/bicycle £1.25/7.60/free, five minutes, hourly Monday to Saturday, every two hours Sunday). There is no direct car-ferry connection to the mainland.

❶ Getting Around

BICYCLE Jura Bike Hire (☑07092-180747; www.jurabikehire.com; Bramble Cottage; per day £12.50) A mile northeast of Craighouse.

BUS The island's only bus service runs between the ferry slip at Feolin and Craighouse (20 minutes), timed to coincide with ferry arrivals and departures. One or two of the runs continue north as far as Inverlussa.

TAXI Mike Richardson (☑07899-912116) A Landrover taxi service operates from the road's end at Lealt to Kinuachdrachd Farm for those wanting to shorten the hike to the Corryvreckan Whirlpool (minimum £20 per two people, plus £5 per extra person).

Isle of Colonsay

POP 100

Legend has it that when St Columba set out from Ireland in 563, his first landfall was Colonsay. But on climbing a hill he found he could still see the distant coast of his homeland, and pushed on further north to found his monastery in Iona, leaving behind only his name (Colonsay means 'Columba's Isle').

Colonsay is a connoisseur's island, a little jewel-box of varied delights, none exceptional but each exquisite – an ancient priory, a woodland garden, a golden beach – set amid a Highland landscape in miniature: rugged, rocky hills, cliffs and sandy strands, machair and birch woods, even a trout loch. Here, hill walkers bag McPhies – defined as 'eminences in excess of 300ft' – instead of Munros. There are 22 in all; the super-competitive will bag them all in one day.

◉ Sights & Activities

There are good sandy beaches at several points around the coast, but **Kiloran Bay** in the northwest, a scimitar-shaped strand of dark golden sand, is outstanding. If there are too many people here for you, walk the 3 miles north to beautiful **Balnahard Bay,** accessible only on foot or by boat.

Oronsay   ISLAND
If the tides are right, don't miss the chance to walk across the half-mile of cockleshell-strewn sand that links Colonsay to the smaller island of Oronsay. Here you can explore the 14th-century ruins of **Oronsay Priory,** one of the best-preserved medieval priories in Scotland. The island is accessible on foot for about 1½ hours either side of low tide, and it's a 45-minute walk from the road end on Colonsay to the priory. There are tide tables posted at the ferry terminal in Scalasaig.

There are two beautiful late-15th-century stone crosses in the kirkyard, but the highlight is the collection of superb 15th- and 16th-century carved grave slabs in the Prior's House; look for the ugly little devil trapped

---

GEORGE ORWELL ON JURA

George Orwell first stepped onto Jura's shores in 1945 as a tourist. Less than a year later, he was living at a remote farmhouse called Barnhill at the isolated far north of the island. Determined to escape being 'constantly smothered by journalism', Orwell came to Jura to recover from the death of his first wife, and 'to write another book'. That book was *1984* (working title: *The Last Man in Europe*), and it would be his last.

Having escaped London and the telephone that rang incessantly in his job at the *Observer*, Orwell was determined to write. He finished *1984* in 1948 (he named his book by simply reversing the last two digits), having spent countless nights alone in his bedroom furiously banging away at a typewriter balanced on his knees.

He was also determined to turn the remote farmhouse (even today the road to Barnhill remains untarred) into a dairy farm. It was a dream he would never realise; suffering from tuberculosis even before his arrival on Jura, Orwell's condition worsened steadily until he was forced to head to a London sanatorium. He died in January 1950.

beneath the sword-tip of the knight on the right hand side of the two horizontal slabs.

Woodland Garden
GARDEN

(☏01951-200211; Colonsay House, Kiloran; admission free; ☉garden dawn-dusk, cafe breakfast & lunch Wed & Fri Easter-Sep) Situated at Colonsay House, 1.5 miles north of Scalasaig, this garden is tucked in an unexpected fold of the landscape and is famous for its outstanding collection of hybrid rhododendrons and unusual trees. The formal walled garden around the mansion has a terrace cafe.

Colonsay Brewery
BREWERY

(☏01951-200190; www.colonsaybrewery.co.uk; Scalasaig; ☉shop 10.30am-1pm & 2.30-5.30pm Wed, 4-7pm Fri & Sun, 10am-1pm Sat) The Colonsay Brewery offers you the chance to have a look at how it produces its hand-crafted ales – the Colonsay IPA is a grand pint.

☞ Tours

Kevin & Christa Byrne
WALKING TOURS

(☏01951-200320; byrne@colonsay.org.uk) Kevin & Christa Byrne offer customised guided tours on foot (£25 per hour per tour for up to eight people), or by minibus (£50 per hour per tour for up to eight people). There's also a regular 'Hidden Colonsay' walking tour (adult/child £10/5) every Saturday in summer; booking essential.

🛏 Sleeping & Eating

Short-stay accommodation on Colonsay is limited and should be booked before coming to the island. Wild camping is allowed, as long as you abide by the provisions of the **Scottish Outdoor Access Code** (www .outdooraccess-scotland.com). See www.colon say.org.uk for self-catering accommodation options.

TOP CHOICE Colonsay Hotel
HOTEL £££

(☏01951-200316; www.colonsayestate.co.uk; Scalasaig; r £100-145; P🖂) This wonderfully laid-back hotel is set in an atmospheric old inn dating from 1750, a short walk uphill from the ferry pier. The stylish **restaurant** (mains £11-18, ☉lunch & dinner) offers down-to-earth cooking using local produce as much as possible, from Colonsay oysters and lobsters to herbs and salad leaves from the Colonsay House gardens.

The bar is a convivial melting pot of locals, guests, hikers, cyclists and visiting yachties.

Backpackers Lodge
HOSTEL £

(☏01951-200312; www.colonsayestate.co.uk; Kiloran; dm £14-16, tw £36) Set in a former game-keeper's house near Colonsay House, this lodge is about a 30-minute walk from the ferry terminal (you can arrange to be picked up at the pier). Advance bookings are essential. You can hire bikes here for £7 per day, and you can even use the tennis court at Colonsay House.

Island Lodges
SELF-CATERING ££

(☏01343-890752; www.colonsayislandlodges.co. uk; Scalasaig; chalets 2-night stay £150-250; 🖂) These comfortable and modern self-catering holiday chalets, sleeping from two to five people, are just a 10-minute walk from the ferry pier at Scalasaig. You can check last-minute availability on the website.

Pantry
CAFE £

(☏01951-200325; Scalasaig; ☉breakfast & lunch Mon-Sat, dinner Mon-Fri plus Sun Apr-Sep) This tearoom, close to the ferry pier, serves up light meals, snacks and ice creams. It also opens from October to March on the days that the ferry calls.

ℹ Information

The ferry pier is at **Scalasaig**, the main village, where you'll find a **general store** (☉9am-1pm & 2-5.30pm Mon & Wed-Fri, 9am 1pm Tue & Sat), post office, public telephone and free internet access at the **Service Point** (☉9.30am-12.30pm Mon-Fri; @). There isn't a tourist office, bank or ATM on the island. General information is available at the CalMac waiting room beside the ferry pier, and at www.colonsay.org.uk.

Colonsay Bookshop (☏01951-200232; Port Mor; ☉2-5pm Mon, Tue & Thu-Sat, 12.30-5pm Wed) This tiny bookshop at Kilchattan, on the west side of the island, has an excellent range of books on Hebridean history and culture.

ℹ Getting There & Around

AIR Hebridean Air Services (☏0845 805 7465; www.hebrideanair.co.uk) Operates flights from Connel Airfield (near Oban) to Colonsay and Islay (£65 one way, twice daily Tuesday and Thursday).

BOAT CalMac (www.calmac.co.uk) From April to October, CalMac operates a car ferry from Oban to Colonsay (passenger/car £13/65, 2¼ hours, one daily except Saturday). From November to March the ferry runs on Monday, Wednesday and Friday only.

From April to October, on Wednesday only, the ferry from Kennacraig on the Kintyre peninsula to Islay's Port Askaig continues to Colonsay.

A day-trip from Kennacraig or Port Askaig to Colonsay allows you six hours on the island; the day return fare from Port Askaig to Colonsay per passenger/car is £8.35/44.

BUS Minibus Tour (☑01951-200320; per person £10; ⊙11.30am Tue) A 90-minute minibus tour of the island departs from the Colonsay Hotel; bookings essential. On Wednesdays, the minibus service is aimed at day-trippers, and makes two circuits of the island – you can be dropped off/picked-up at any point (per person £7.50). See www.colonsay.org.uk/walks.html for details.

Isle of Mull

POP 2600

From the rugged ridges of Ben More and the black basalt crags of Burg to the blinding white sand, rose-pink granite and emerald waters that fringe the Ross, Mull can lay claim to some of the finest and most varied scenery in the Inner Hebrides. Add in two impressive castles, a narrow-gauge railway, the sacred island of Iona and easy access from Oban and you can see why it's sometimes impossible to find a spare bed on the island.

Despite the number of visitors who flock to the island, it seems to be large enough to absorb them all; many stick to the well-worn routes from Craignure to Iona or Tobermory, returning to Oban in the evening. Besides, there are plenty of hidden corners where you can get away from the crowds.

The waters to the west of Mull provide some of the best whale-spotting opportunities in Scotland, with several operators offering whale-watching cruises.

About two-thirds of Mull's population lives in and around Tobermory, the island's capital, in the north. Craignure, at the southeastern corner, has the main ferry terminal and is where most people arrive. Fionnphort is at the far-western end of the long Ross of Mull peninsula, and is where the ferry to Iona departs.

☞ Tours

Bowman's Tours (p73) in Oban operates day-trips from Oban to Mull, Staffa and Iona by ferry and bus.

Gordon Grant Marine   BOAT TOURS
(☑01681-700388; www.staffatours.com) Runs boat trips from Fionnphort to Staffa (adult/child £20/10, 2½ hours, daily April to October), and to Staffa and the Treshnish Isles (£40/20, five hours, Sunday to Friday May to July).

Isle of Mull

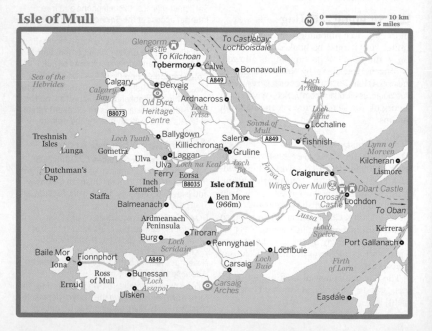

Mull Magic WALKING TOURS
(01688-301245; www.mullmagic.com) Offers guided walking tours in the Mull countryside (£32.50 per person), as well as customised tours and four-day walking holidays.

✦✦ Festivals & Events

Mishnish Music Festival MUSIC
(01688-302383; www.mishnish.co.uk) On the last weekend of April; three days of foot-stomping traditional Scottish and Irish folk music at Tobermory's favourite pub.

Mendelssohn on Mull MUSIC
(01688-301108; www.mullfest.org.uk) A week-long festival of classical music in early July.

Mull Highland Games HIGHLAND GAMES
(01688-302001; www.mishnish.co.uk) Third Thursday in July; piping, highland dancing etc.

Mull & Iona Food Festival FOOD & DRINK
(www.mict.co.uk) Five days of food and drink tastings in early September, with chef demonstrations, farm tours, produce markets, restaurant visits and a host of other events.

Tour of Mull Rally CAR RALLY
(01254-826564; www.2300club.org) Part of the Scottish Rally Championship, with around 150 cars involved. Public roads are closed for parts of the early-October weekend.

ℹ Information

Clydesdale Bank (Main St, Tobermory; ⊙9.15am-4.45pm Mon-Fri) The island's only bank and 24-hour ATM. You can get cash using a debit card from the post offices in Salen and Craignure, or get cash back with a purchase from Co-op food stores.

Craignure tourist office (01680-812377; Craignure; ⊙8.30am-5pm Mon-Sat, 10.30am-5pm Sun)

Dunaros Hospital (01680-300392; Salen) Has a minor injuries unit; the nearest casualty department is in Oban.

Post Office (Main St, Tobermory; ⊙9am-1pm & 2-5.30pm Mon, Tue, Thu & Fri, 9am-1pm Wed & Sat) There are also post office counters in Salen, Craignure and Fionnphort.

Tobermory tourist office (01688-302182; The Pier, Tobermory; ⊙9am-6pm Mon-Sat & 10am-5pm Sun Jul & Aug, 9am-5pm Mon-Sat & 11am-5pm Sun May & Jun, shorter hours rest of the year)

ℹ Getting There & Away

CalMac (www.calmac.co.uk) There are frequent car ferries from Oban to Craignure (passenger/car £4.65/41.50, 40 minutes, every two hours). There's another car-ferry link from Lochaline to Fishnish, on the east coast of Mull (£2.80/12.55, 15 minutes, at least hourly). A third car ferry links Tobermory to Kilchoan on the Ardnamurchan peninsula (£4.45/23, 35 minutes, seven daily Monday to Saturday). From June to August there are also five sailings on Sunday.

ℹ Getting Around

Public transport on Mull is fairly limited. (p91)

BICYCLE You can hire bikes for around £10 to £15 per day.

Brown's Hardware Shop (01688-302020; www.brownstobermory.co.uk; Main St)

On Yer Bike (01680-300501) Easter to October only. Also has an outlet by the ferry terminal at Craignure.

BUS Bowman's Tours (01680-812313; www.bowmanstours.co.uk) The main operator on Mull, connecting the ferry ports and the island's main villages. The routes useful for visitors are bus 495 from Craignure to Tobermory (£7 return, one hour, six daily Monday to Friday, four or five Saturday and Sunday) and bus 496 from Craignure to Fionnphort (£11 return, 1¼ hours, three or four daily Monday to Saturday, one Sunday). Bus 494 goes from Tobermory to Dervaig and Calgary (three daily Monday to Friday, two on Saturday).

CAR Almost all of Mull's road network consists of single-track roads. There are petrol stations at Craignure, Fionnphort, Salen and Tobermory.

TAXI Mull Taxi (07760-426351; www.mulltaxi.co.uk) Based in Tobermory; has a vehicle that is wheelchair accessible.

CRAIGNURE & AROUND

There's not much to see at Craignure other than the ferry terminal and the hotel, so turn left, walk 200m and hop onto the **Mull Railway** (www.mullrail.co.uk; Old Pier Station; adult/child return £5/3.50; ⊙Apr-Oct), a miniature steam train that will take you 1.5 miles south to Torosay Castle.

◉ Sights

Torosay Castle & Gardens CASTLE, GARDEN
(01680-812421; www.torosay.com; adult/child £7/4; ⊙house 10.30am-5pm Apr-Oct, gardens 9am-sunset year-round) Torosay Castle is a rambling Victorian mansion in the Scottish Baronial style, stuffed with antique furniture, family portraits and hunting trophies. You're left to wander at will: a sign advises, 'Take your time but not our spoons.'

Duart Castle
CASTLE

(☎01680-812309; www.duartcastle.com; adult/child £5.30/2.65; ⊙10.30am-5.30pm daily May–mid-Oct, 11am-4pm Sun-Thu Apr) Duart Castle is a formidable fortress dominating the Sound of Mull. The seat of the Clan Maclean, this is one of the oldest inhabited castles in Scotland – the central keep was built in 1360. It was bought and restored in 1911 by Sir Fitzroy Maclean and has damp dungeons, vast halls and bathrooms equipped with ancient fittings.

Duart is two miles beyond Torosay. A bus to the castle meets the 9.50am, 11.55am and 2pm ferries from Oban to Craignure.

🛏 Sleeping

Shieling Holidays
CAMPGROUND £

(☎01680-812496; www.shielingholidays.co.uk; tent site & 2 people £14, with car £16.50, dm £12.50; ⊙late Mar-Oct; 🚌from Oban-Craignure) To camp within walking distance of the Oban–Craignure ferry, turn left and walk south for five minutes to this well-equipped campground with great views. Most of the permanent accommodation, including the hostel dorms and toilet block (dribbly showers), consists of 'cottage tents' made from heavy-duty tarpaulin, which gives the place a bit of a PVC-fetish feel.

Recommended B&Bs within 10 minutes' walk of the ferry include **Pennygate Lodge** (☎01680-812333; www.pennygatelodge.com; s/d from £50/70; 🅿🛜), next to the Shieling Holidays entrance, and **Dee-Emm B&B** (☎01680-812440; www.dee-emm.co.uk; s/d from £50/60; 🅿), a half-mile south of Craignure on the road towards Fionnphort.

TOBERMORY
POP 750

Tobermory, the island's main town, is a picturesque little fishing port and yachting centre with brightly painted houses arranged around a sheltered harbour, with a grid-patterned 'upper town'. The village was the setting for the children's TV program *Balamory*, and while the series stopped filming in 2005 regular repeats mean that the town still swarms in summer with toddlers towing parents around looking for their favourite TV characters (frazzled parents can get a *Balamory* booklet from the tourist offices in Oban and Tobermory).

◉ Sights & Activities

Mull Museum
MUSEUM

(☎01688-302603; www.mullmuseum.org.uk; Main St; admission by donation; ⊙10am-4pm Mon-Fri Easter-Oct) Mull Museum, which re-

---

WALKING ON MULL

More information on the following walks can be obtained from the tourist offices in Oban, Craignure and Tobermory.

The highest peak on the island, **Ben More** (966m) offers spectacular views of the surrounding islands when the weather is clear. A trail leads up the mountain from Loch na Keal, by the bridge on the B8035 over the Abhainn na h-Uamha (the river is 8 miles southwest of Salen – see Ordnance Survey (OS) 1:50,000 map sheet 49, grid reference 507368). Return the same way or continue down the narrow ridge to the eastern top, A'Chioch, then descend to the road via Gleann na Beinn Fhada. The glen can be rather wet and there's not much of a path. The round trip is 6.5 miles; allow five to six hours.

One of the most adventurous walks on Mull is along the coast west of Carsaig Bay to the **Carsaig Arches** at Malcolm's Point. There's a good path below the cliffs most of the way from Carsaig, but it becomes a bit rough and exposed near the arches – the route climbs and then traverses a very steep slope above a vertical drop into the sea (not for the unfit or faint-hearted). You'll see spectacular rock formations on the way, culminating in the arches themselves. One, nicknamed the 'keyhole', is a freestanding rock stack; the other, the 'tunnel', is a huge natural arch. The western entrance is hung with curtains of columnar basalt – an impressive place. The round trip is 8 miles – allow three to four hours' walking time from Carsaig plus at least an hour at the arches.

At the tip of the remote Ardmeanach peninsula there is a remarkable 50-million-year-old fossil tree preserved in the basalt lava flows of the cliffs. A 4WD track leads from the car park at Tiroran to a house at **Burg**; the last 2.5 miles to the tree is on a very rough coastal path. About 500m before the tree, a metal ladder allows you to climb down to the foreshore, which is only accessible at low tide – check tide times at Tobermory tourist office before setting off. Allow six to seven hours for the strenuous 14-mile round trip.

cords the history of the island, is a good rainy day retreat. There are interesting exhibits on crofting, and on the *Tobermory Galleon*, a ship from the Spanish Armada that sank in Tobermory Bay in 1588 and has been the objective of treasure seekers ever since.

Marine Discovery Centre WILDLIFE EXHIBITION
(☑01688-302620; www.whaledolphintrust.co.uk; 28 Main St; admission free; ☉10am-5pm Mon-Fri, 11am-4pm Sun Apr-Oct, 11am-5pm Mon-Fri Nov-Mar) The Hebridean Whale & Dolphin Trust's Marine Discovery Centre has displays, videos and interactive exhibits on whale and dolphin biology and ecology, and is a great place for kids to learn about sea mammals. It also provides information about volunteering and reporting sightings of whales and dolphins.

There's also **An Tobar Arts Centre** (☑info 01688-302211; www.antobar.co.uk; Argyll Tce; admission free; ☉10am-5pm Mon-Sat May-Sep, plus 1-4pm Sun Jul & Aug, 10am-4pm Tue-Sat Oct-Apr), an art gallery and exhibition space with a good vegetarian-friendly cafe; and the tiny **Tobermory Distillery** (☑302645; www.tobermorymalt.com; tour £3; ☉10am-5pm Mon-Fri Easter-Oct), established in 1798.

Sea Life Surveys (p96), based in the new harbour building beside the main car park, runs whale-watching boat trips out of Tobermory harbour.

🛏 Sleeping

TOP CHOICE Highland Cottage

Hotel   BOUTIQUE HOTEL **£££**
(☑01688-302030; www.highlandcottage.co.uk; Breadalbane St; d £155-190; ☉mid-Mar–Oct; P🖰) Antique furniture, four-poster beds, embroidered bedspreads and fresh flowers and candlelight lend this small hotel (only six rooms) an appealingly old-fashioned cottage atmosphere, but with all mod cons including cable TV, full-size baths and room service. There's also an excellent fine-dining restaurant here.

Sonas House   B&B **£££**
(☑01688-302304; www.sonashouse.co.uk; The Fairways, Erray Rd; s/d £80/125; P🖰🏊) Here's a first – a B&B with a heated, indoor 10m swimming pool! Sonas is a large, modern house that offers luxury B&B in a beautiful setting with superb views over Tobermory Bay; ask for the 'Blue Poppy' bedroom, which has its own balcony.

Cuidhe Leathain   B&B **££**
(☑01688-302504; www.cuidhe-leathain.co.uk; Salen Rd; r per person £35; 🖰) A handsome 19th-century house in the upper town, Cuidhe Leathain (coo-lane), which means Maclean's Corner, exudes a cosily cluttered Victorian atmosphere. The breakfasts will set you up for the rest of the day, and the owners are a fount of knowledge about Mull and its wildlife.

2 Victoria St   B&B **£**
(☑01688-302263; 2 Victoria St; s/d £25/40; ☉Easter-Oct) Traditional, old-school B&B with simple, homely bedrooms (with shared bathroom) and a friendly and hospitable landlady.

Tobermory Campsite   CAMPGROUND **£**
(☑01688-302624; www.tobermorycampsite.co.uk; Newdale, Dervaig Rd; tent sites per adult/child £6/3; ☉Mar-Oct; 🖰) A quiet, family-friendly campground a mile west of town on the road to Dervaig.

Tobermory SYHA   HOSTEL **£**
(☑01688-302481; www.syha.org.uk; Main St; dm £15; ☉Mar-Oct; @) Great location in a Victorian house right on the waterfront. Bookings recommended.

🍴 Eating & Drinking

TOP CHOICE Café Fish   SEAFOOD **££**
(☑01688-301253; www.thecafefish.com; The Pier; mains £10-16; ☉lunch & dinner) Seafood doesn't come much fresher than the stuff served at this warm and welcoming little restaurant overlooking Tobermory harbour as their motto says, 'The only thing frozen here is the fisherman'! Langoustines and squat lobsters go straight from boat to kitchen to join rich shellfish bisque, fat scallops, seafood pie and catch-of-the-day on the daily-changing menu.

Also has freshly baked bread, homemade desserts and a range of Scottish cheeses on offer.

Fish & Chip Van   SEAFOOD **£**
(Main St; mains £4-7; ☉12.30-9pm Mon-Sat Apr-Dec) If it's a takeaway you're after, you can tuck into some of Scotland's best gourmet fish and chips down on the waterfront. And where else will you find a chip van selling freshly cooked prawns and scallops?

MacGochan's   PUB GRUB **££**
(☑01688-302350; Ledaig; mains £9-15; ☉lunch & dinner) A lively pub beside the car park at

the southern end of the waterfront, Mac-Gochan's does good bar meals (haddock and chips, steak pie, vegetable lasagne), and often has outdoor barbecues on summer evenings. There's a more formal restaurant upstairs, and live music in the bar on weekends.

Mishnish Hotel
PUB ££

(☑01688-302009; www.mishnish.co.uk; Main St; mains £11-20; ☺lunch & dinner; ☺) 'The Mish' is a favourite hang-out for visiting yachties and a good place for a bar meal, or dinner at the more formal restaurant upstairs. Wood-panelled and flag-draped, this is a good old traditional pub where you can listen to live folk music, toast your toes by the open fire, or challenge the locals to a game of pool.

Tobermory Chocolate Factory
CAFE £

(☑01688-302526; www.tobermorychocolate.co.uk; Main St; ☺9.30am-5pm Mon-Sat & 10.30am-3pm Sun) This tempting little shop not only sells exquisite handmade chocolates, but also has a cafe that serves excellent espresso, cappuccino and hot chocolate.

Campers can stock up on provisions at the **Co-op supermarket** (Main St; ☺8am-8pm Mon-Sat, 12.30-7pm Sun), and the **Tobermory Bakery** (Main St; ☺9am-5pm Mon-Sat), which sells delicious, locally baked wholegrain bread, cakes, biscuits and pastries, as well as having a great deli counter.

☆ Entertainment

Mull Theatre
THEATRE

(☑01688-302828; www.mulltheatre.com; Salen Rd) One of Scotland's best-known touring companies, putting on shows all over Scotland. It is based at Druimfin, about a mile south of Tobermory, which is the venue for most of its Mull-based performances; check the website for details of the latest shows.

NORTH MULL

The road from Tobermory west to Calgary cuts inland, leaving most of the north coast of Mull wild and inaccessible.

◉ Sights

FREE Glengorm Castle
GARDEN

(☑01688-302321; www.glengorm.com; ☺10am-5pm Easter–mid-Oct) Just outside Tobermory a long, single-track road leads north for 4 miles to majestic Glengorm Castle with views across the sea to Ardnamurchan, Rum and the Outer Hebrides. The castle outbuildings house an art gallery featuring the work of local artists, a farm shop selling local produce, and an excellent coffee shop.

The castle itself is not open to the public, but you're free to explore the beautiful castle grounds.

Old Byre Heritage Centre
HERITAGE CENTRE

(☑01688-400229; www.old-byre.co.uk; adult/child £4/2; ☺10.30am-6.30pm Wed-Sun Easter-Oct) The Old Byre Heritage Centre brings Mull's heritage and natural history to life through a series of tableaux and half-hour film shows. The prize for most bizarre exhibit goes to the 40cm-long model of a midge. The centre's tearoom serves good, inexpensive snacks, including homemade soup and clootie dumpling, and there's a kids' outdoor play area.

Calgary
BEACH

Mull's best (and busiest) silver-sand beach, flanked by cliffs and with views out to Coll and Tiree, is about 12 miles west of Tobermory. And yes – this is the place from which the more famous Calgary, in Alberta, Canada, takes its name.

🛏 Sleeping & Eating

TOP CHOICE Achnadrish House
B&B ££

(☑01688-400388; www.achnadrish.co.uk; Dervaig Rd; d from £85; P@☎) There aren't too many B&Bs where *pad Thai* noodles appear on the breakfast menu, but Achnadrish is one. The dish is a legacy of the owner's extensive Asian travels, as are many of the decorative touches in this wonderfully welcoming guesthouse.

A three-course dinner (£30 per person) based on fresh local produce is also available, as is a dram of Tobermory single-malt (complementary) beside the open fireplace while Mike tells you all about the local wildlife (and his three friendly Labradors).

🏄 Calgary Farmhouse
SELF-CATERING ££

(☑01688-400256; www.calgary.co.uk; 2-person apt per 2 nights from £120; P☎) This farmhouse complex offers eight fantastic self-catering properties (including apartments, cottages and a farmhouse; sleeping from two to eight people), beautifully designed and fitted out with timber furniture and wood-burning stoves. The Hayloft (sleeps eight, £850 a week in the high season) includes a spectacular lounge/dining room with curved oak frames and locally produced art work.

Bellachroy

HOTEL ££

(📞01688-400314; www.bellachroyhotel.co.uk; s/d from £65/90; P🛜🍴) The Bellachroy is an atmospheric 17th-century droving inn with six plain but comfortable bedrooms. The **bar** is a focus for local social life and serves excellent meals (mains £9 to £15, plus kids' menu) based on fresh local produce: pork from a local Dervaig farm, lamb from Ulva, mutton from Iona, mussels from Inverlussa and Mull-landed seafood.

Dervaig Hall Bunkhouse

HOSTEL £

(📞01688-400491; www.dervaigbunkroomsmull.co.uk; dm/q £14/50; P) Basic but very comfortable bunkhouse accommodation in Dervaig's village hall, with self-catering kitchen and sitting room.

FREE Calgary Bay Campsite

CAMPGROUND

You can camp for free at the southern end of the beach at Calgary Bay – keep to the area south of the stream. There are no facilities other than the public toilets across the road; water comes from the stream.

🍴 Glengorm Coffee Shop

SCOTTISH £

(www.glengorm.com; mains £5-8; ⏱10am-5pm) Set in a cottage courtyard in the grounds of Glengorm Castle, this cafe serves superb lunches (from noon to 4.30pm) – the menu changes daily, but includes sandwiches and salads (much of the salad veg is grown on the Glengorm estate), soups and specials such as curry-flavoured salmon fishcakes with mint and cucumber salad.

Calgary Farmhouse Tearoom

CAFE £

(www.calgary.co.uk; mains £5-8; ⏱10.30am-4.30pm; 🛜) Just a few minutes' walk from the sandy beach at Calgary Bay, this tearoom serves soups, sandwiches, coffee and cake using fresh local produce as much as possible. There's also an art gallery and craft shop here. Open till 5.30pm in July and August.

CENTRAL MULL

The central part of the island, between the Craignure–Fionnphort road and the narrow isthmus between Salen and Gruline, contains the island's highest peak, **Ben More** (966m) – with the exception of Skye's Cuillin Hills, the only island munro.

Surrounding Ben More is a dramatic landscape that feeds down into the Ardmeanach Peninsula. The B8035 road around the peninsula squeezes its way beneath spectacular cliffs, and has fantastic views over to the island of Inch Kenneth, which lies a few hundred metres off the coast.

The prominent Victorian shooting lodge on **Inch Kenneth** was where Unity Mitford, infamous supporter of Hitler and the Nazis, saw out her final years. Living in Germany from 1934 to 1939, Mitford was brought home by her parents after shooting herself in the head with a gun given to her by Hitler, soon after Britain declared war on Germany. Her suicide attempt was successful, in a way: the bullet lodged in her brain and she died 12 years later of a brain abscess. Her life was later satirically chronicled by her sister Nancy in her book *Love in a Cold Climate*.

The narrow B8035 road along the southern shore of Loch na Keal squeezes past some impressive cliffs before cutting south towards Loch Scridain. About a mile along the shore from Balmeanach, where the road climbs away from the coast, is **Mackinnon's Cave**, a deep and spooky fissure in the basalt cliffs that was once used as a refuge by Celtic monks. A big, flat rock inside, known as Fingal's Table, may have been their altar.

Balmeanach Park Caravan & Camping Site (📞01680-300342; per 2 people, tent & car £15; ⏱Mar-Oct) is a peaceful campground a 10-minute walk from the Fishnish–Lochaline ferry, on the main road between Craignure and Tobermory (booking advised).

There's a very basic **campsite** (per person £3) at Killiechronan, half a mile north of Gruline (toilets and water are a five-minute walk away), and plenty of wild camping on the south shore of Loch na Keal below Ben More.

ISLE OF ULVA

POP 16

Ulva, meaning 'Wolf's Island' in Norse, is a privately owned island on the west coast of Mull. A peaceful place to escape the crowds thronging Mull in the summer, it has good walking and off-road-biking, a 9th-century Viking fort, and an old chapel with a graveyard. It is linked by a bridge to the even more remote Isle of Gometra.

Once Scotland's main centre for kelp gathering, the island formerly had a population approaching 1000; kelp was an essential ingredient in soap production. Today the population has fallen to 16, with many removed from the area in the clearances in 1850. You can still see many of the derelict cottages used by crofters in centuries long past.

WATCHING WILDLIFE ON MULL

Mull's varied landscapes and habitats, from high mountains and wild moorland to wave-lashed sea cliffs, sandy beaches and seaweed-fringed skerries, offer the chance to spot some of Scotland's rarest and most dramatic wildlife, including eagles, otters, dolphins and whales.

Mull Wildlife Expeditions
WILDLIFE WATCHING

(☎01688-500121; www.torrbuan.com; null) This outfit offers full-day Land Rover tours of the island with the chance of spotting red deer, golden eagles, peregrine falcons, white-tailed sea eagles, hen harriers, otters and perhaps dolphins and porpoises. The cost (adult/child £43/40) includes pick-up from your accommodation or from any of the ferry terminals, a picnic lunch and use of binoculars.

The timing of this tour makes it possible as a day-trip from Oban, with pick-up and drop-off at the Craignure ferry.

Sea Life Surveys
WILDLIFE WATCHING

(☎01688-302916; www.sealifesurveys.com; Ledaig) Whale-watching trips head from Tobermory harbour to the waters north and west of Mull. An all-day whale-watch (£60 per person) gives up to seven hours at sea (not recommended for kids under 14), and has a 95% success rate for sightings. The four-hour family whale-watch is geared more towards children (£39/35 per adult/child).

Turus Mara
BOAT TOURS

(☎0800 085 8786; www.turusmara.com) Turus Mara runs boat trips from Ulva Ferry in central Mull to Staffa and the Treshnish Isles (adult/child £50/25, 6½ hours), with an hour ashore on Staffa and two hours on Lunga, where you can see seals, puffins, kittiwakes, razorbills and many other species of seabird.

Loch Frisa Sea Eagle Hide
BIRDWATCHING

(☎01680-812556; www.forestry.gov.uk/mullseaeagles) The RSPB runs escorted trips to a viewing hide on Loch Frisa where you can watch white-tailed sea eagles. Tours (£5/2 per adult/child) leave twice a day, Monday to Friday, from the Aros end of the Loch Frisa access trail (book in advance at the Craignure tourist office).

A short walk north of the ferry landing is **Sheila's Cottage** (☎01688-500264; www.isleofulva.com; admission included with ferry ticket; ⊙9am-5pm Mon-Fri Apr-late Sep, plus 9am-5pm Sun Jun-Aug), a reconstruction of a traditional thatched crofter's cottage, with displays about the history of the island.

Freerange and homemade are the watchwords at the **Boathouse tearoom** (☎01688-500241; www.theboathouseulva.co.uk; mains £5-16; ⊙9am-5pm Mon-Fri Apr-late Sep, also 9am-5pm Sun Jun-Aug) beside the ferry landing, where bread is freshly baked on the premises, the oysters are farmed in a nearby bay, and the prawns, crabs and squat lobsters come from the family fishing boat. Lunch is served from noon to 4pm, and tea, coffee and home baking is available all day.

There's no accommodation on the island, but you can **camp wild**; contact the **island manager** (☎01688-500264; enquiries@isleofulva.com) for permission.

The two-minute ferry crossing (adult/child/bicycle £5/2/50p return) runs on demand during Sheila's Cottage opening hours.

SOUTH MULL

The road from Craignure to Fionnphort climbs through some wild and desolate scenery before reaching the southwestern part of the island, which consists of a long peninsula called the **Ross of Mull**. The Ross has a spectacular south coast lined with black basalt cliffs that give way further west to white-sand beaches and pink granite crags. The cliffs are highest at Malcolm's Point, near the superb **Carsaig Arches**.

The little village of **Bunessan** has a hotel, tearoom, pub and some shops, and is home to the **Ross of Mull Historical Centre** (☎01681-700659; www.romhc.org.uk; admission £2; ⊙10am-4pm Mon-Fri Apr-Oct), a cottage museum that houses displays on local history, geology, archaeology, genealogy and wildlife.

A minor road leads south from here to the beautiful white-sand bay of **Uisken**, with views of the Paps of Jura. You can camp beside the beach here (£1 per person; ask for permission at Uisken Croft), but there are no facilities.

At the western end of the Ross, 38 miles from Craignure, is **Fionnphort** (*finn*-a-fort) and the ferry to Iona. The coast here is a beautiful blend of pink granite rocks, white sandy beaches and vivid turquoise sea.

Sleeping & Eating

TOP CHOICE **Seaview** B&B **££**
(01681-700235; www.iona-bed-breakfast-mull .com; Fionnphort; s/d £55/75; P 🛜) Barely a minute's walk from the Iona ferry, the Seaview has five beautifully decorated bedrooms and a breakfast conservatory with grand views across to Iona. The owner – a semiretired fisherman and his wife – offers tasty three-course dinners (£22 per person, September to April only), often based around local seafood. Bike hire available for guests only.

Staffa House B&B **££**
(01681 700677; www.staffahouse.co.uk; Fionnphort; s/d from £48/66; P) This charming and hospitable B&B is packed with antiques and period features, and offers breakfast in a conservatory with a view of Iona. Solar panels top up the hot-water supply, and the hearty breakfasts, packed lunches (£5.50 to £7) and evening meals (£25 per person) make use of local and organic produce where possible.

Fidden Farm CAMPGROUND **£**
(01681-700427; Fidden; tent sites per adult/ child £6/3; ☉Apr-Sep) A basic but beautifully situated campground, with views over pink granite reefs to Iona and Erraid. It's 1.25 miles south of Fionnphort.

Ninth Wave SEAFOOD **£££**
(01681-700757; www.ninthwaverestaurant.co .uk; Bruach Mhor; 4-course dinner £42; ☉dinner) A new venture based in a former croft a mile east of Fionnphort, this restaurant is owned and operated by a lobster fisherman and his Canadian wife. The daily menu makes use of locally landed shellfish and crustaceans, and vegetables and salad grown in the croft garden, served in a stylishly converted bothy. Advance booking essential.

Isle of Iona

POP 130

There are few more uplifting sights on Scotland's west coast than the view of Iona from Mull on a sunny day – an emerald island set in a sparkling turquoise sea. From the moment you step off the ferry you begin to appreciate the hushed, spiritual atmosphere that pervades this sacred island.

Not surprisingly, Iona attracts a lot of day-trippers, so if you want to experience the island's peace and quiet, the solution is to spend a night here. Once the crowds have gone for the day, you can wander in peace around the ancient graveyard where the early kings of Scotland are buried, attend an evening service at the abbey, or walk to the top of Dun I and gaze south towards

WORTH A TRIP

STAFFA & THE TRESHNISH ISLES

Felix Mendelssohn, who visited the uninhabited island of Staffa in 1829, was inspired to compose his 'Hebrides Overture' after hearing waves echoing in the impressive and cathedral-like **Fingal's Cave**. The cave walls and surrounding cliffs are composed of vertical, hexagonal basalt columns that look like pillars (Staffa is Norse for 'Pillar Island'). You can land on the island and walk into the cave via a causeway. Nearby Boat Cave can be seen from the causeway, but you can't reach it on foot. Staffa also has a sizable puffin colony, north of the landing place.

Northwest of Staffa lies a chain of uninhabited islands called the Treshnish Isles. The two main islands are the curiously shaped **Dutchman's Cap** and **Lunga**. You can land on Lunga, walk to the top of the hill, and visit the shag, puffin and guillemot colonies on the west coast at Harp Rock.

Unless you have your own boat, the only way to reach Staffa and the Treshnish Isles is on an organised boat trip with Turus Mara (p96) or MV Iolaire (p98).

Ireland, as St Columba must have done so many centuries ago.

History

St Columba sailed from Ireland and landed on Iona in 563 before setting out to spread Christianity throughout Scotland. He established a monastery on the island and it was here that the *Book of Kells* – the prize attraction of Dublin's Trinity College – is believed to have been transcribed. It was taken to Kells in Ireland when Viking raids drove the monks from Iona in 849.

The monks returned within a decade, and the monastery prospered until its destruction during the Reformation. The ruins were given to the Church of Scotland in 1899, and by 1910 a group of enthusiasts called the **Iona Community** (www.iona.org.uk) had reconstructed the abbey. It's still a flourishing spiritual community that holds regular courses and retreats.

◉ Sights & Activities

If you do only have a day on the island, you could cover the following in approximately three hours. Head uphill from the ferry pier and turn right through the grounds of a ruined 13th-century **nunnery** with fine cloistered gardens, and exit at the far end. Across the road is the **Iona Heritage Centre** (☎01681-700576; adult/child £2/free; ☺10.30am-4.30pm Mon-Fri Apr-Oct), which covers the history of Iona, crofting and lighthouses; the centre's coffee shop serves delicious home baking.

Turn right here and continue along the road to **Reilig Oran**, an ancient cemetery that holds the graves of 48 of Scotland's early kings, including Macbeth, and a tiny Romanesque chapel. Beyond rises the spiritual heart of the island – **Iona Abbey** (HS;

☎01681-700512; www.iona.org.uk; adult/child £4.70/2.80; ☺9.30am-5.30pm Apr-Sep, to 4.30pm Oct-Mar). The spectacular nave, dominated by Romanesque and early Gothic vaults and columns, contains the elaborate, white marble tombs of the 8th duke of Argyll and his wife. A door on the left leads to the beautiful Gothic cloister, where medieval grave slabs sit alongside modern religious sculptures. A replica of the intricately carved **St John's Cross** stands just outside the abbey – the massive 8th-century original is in the **Infirmary Museum** (around the far side of the abbey) along with many other fine examples of early Christian and medieval carved stones.

Continue past the abbey and look for a footpath on the left signposted **Dun I** (dunee). An easy walk of about 15 to 20 minutes leads to the highest point on Iona, with fantastic views in all directions.

Boat Trips

Alternative Boat Hire   BOAT TOURS
(☎01681-700537; www.boattripsiona.com) Offers cruises in a traditional wooden sailing boat for fishing, birdwatching, picnicking, or just drifting along admiring the scenery. One-/three-hour trips cost £9.50/18.50 per adult (child £5/8.50).

MV Iolaire   STAFFA TOURS
(☎01681-700358; www.staffatrips.co.uk) Three-hour boat trips to Staffa (£25/10), departing Iona pier at 9.45am and 1.45pm, and from Fionnphort at 10am and 2pm, with one hour ashore on Staffa.

MV Volante   WILDLIFE & FISHING TOURS
(☎01681-700362; www.volanteiona.com) Four-hour sea-angling trips (£35 per person including tackle and bait), as well as 1½-hour round-the-island wildlife cruises (adult/

ST COLUMBA

Born in County Donegal in AD 521, Columba was a descendant of a legendary 4th-century Irish king, Niall of the Nine Hostages.

Carefully groomed for the priesthood, Columba founded monasteries all over Ireland until, at age 40, he involved his clan in the bloody Battle of Cooldrevny, where many lost their lives. As penance for his role in their deaths, he vowed to never again set foot on his beloved Ireland; instead he would gain as many souls for Christ as those he had lost at Cooldrevny.

Twelve disciples followed him, and in May 563 Columba set out in a small boat made of wickerwork and covered with hides (a *curaich*). Days later, after first landing on Colonsay (whose name means 'Columba's Isle') they reached Iona, and here Columba's work really began. His 32 remaining years were spent spreading the Christian faith around Northern Scotland, with remarkable success.

child (£15/8) and 3½-hour whale-watching trips (£35 per person).

🛏 Sleeping & Eating

TOP CHOICE **Argyll Hotel**   HOTEL **££**
(☎01681-700334; www.argyllhoteliona.co.uk; Baile Mor; s/d from £61/97; ☻Mar-Oct; @🛉) This cute little hotel has 16 snug rooms (a sea view costs rather a bit more – £131 for a double) and a country-house **restaurant** (☎01681-700334; www.argyllhoteliona.co.uk; Baile Mor; mains £11-15; ☻8-10am, 12.30-1.20pm & 7-8pm) (mains £11 to £15) with wooden fireplace and antique tables and chairs. The kitchen is supplied by a huge organic garden around the back, and the menu includes Cullen skink, home-grown salads, and venison-and-rabbit hotpot.

TOP CHOICE **Iona Hostel**   HOSTEL **£**
(☎01681-700781; www.ionahostel.co.uk; Lagandorain; dm £19.50; ☻check-in 4-7pm) This hostel is set in an attractive, modern timber building on a working croft, with stunning views out to Staffa and the Treshnish Isles. Rooms are clean and functional, and the well-equipped lounge/kitchen area has an open fire.

It's at the northern end of the island – to get here, continue along the road past the abbey for 1.5 miles (a 20- to 30-minute walk).

Tigh na Tobrach   B&B **££**
(☎01861-700700; www.bandb-iona.co.uk; Baile Mor; per person £28) Comfortable B&B in modern house, with one family and one twin room. A short distance south of the ferry.

Cnocoran Campsite   CAMPGROUND **£**
(☎01681-700112; cnocoran@yahoo.co.uk; Cnocoran; tent sites per person £5) Basic campsite about a mile west of the ferry. Open year-round.

ℹ Information

There's a tiny post office on the right as you head uphill from the ferry.

Finlay Ross Ltd (Baile Mor; ☻9.30am-5pm Mon-Sat, 11.30am-4pm Sun) To the left of the ferry slip; sells gifts, books and maps, hires out bikes and provides a laundry service.

Iona Community Council (www.isle-of-iona .com) There's no tourist office on the island, but a Community Council notice board at the top of the ferry slip lists accommodation and services available on the island.

Spar (Baile Mor; ☻9am-5.15pm Mon-Sat, noon-4pm Sun) Grocery store above the ferry slip.

ℹ Getting There & Away

The passenger ferry from Fionnphort to Iona (£4.30 return, five minutes, hourly) runs daily. There are also various day-trips available from Oban to Iona.

Isle of Coll

POP 100

Rugged and low-lying, Coll is Tiree's less fertile and less populous neighbour. The northern part of the island is a mix of bare rock, bog and lochans (small lochs), while the south is swathed in golden shell-sand beaches and machair dunes up to 30m high.

⊙ Sights & Activities

The island's main attraction is the peace and quiet – empty beaches, bird-haunted coastlines, and long walks along the shore. The biggest and most beautiful sandy beaches are at **Crossapol** in the south, and Hogh Bay and **Cliad** on the west coast.

In summer you may be lucky enough to hear the 'krek-krek-krek' of the corncrake at the **RSPB Nature Reserve** at Totronald in the southwest of the island; there's a **tourist office** (admission free; ☻24hr) here.

From Totronald a sandy 4WD track runs north past the dunes backing Hogh Bay to the road at Totamore, allowing walkers and cyclists to make a circuit back to Arinagour rather than returning the way they came.

There are two ruined castles about 6 miles southwest of Arinagour, both known as **Breachachadh Castle**, built by the Macleans in medieval times.

🛏 Sleeping & Eating

Most accommodation on Coll is self-catering, but a few places offer B&B, including **Taigh-na-Mara** (☎01879-230354; www .taighnamara.info; Arinagour; r per person £30-35) in Arinagour. You can camp for free on the hill above the Coll Hotel (no facilities); ask at the hotel first.

Coll Hotel   HOTEL **££**
(☎01879-230334; www.collhotel.com; Arinagour; s/d £55/100; ℗) The island's only hotel is an atmospheric old place. Its quirkily shaped rooms have white-painted, wood-panelled walls, and many also have lovely views over the manicured hotel gardens and the harbour. The hotel also has a really good

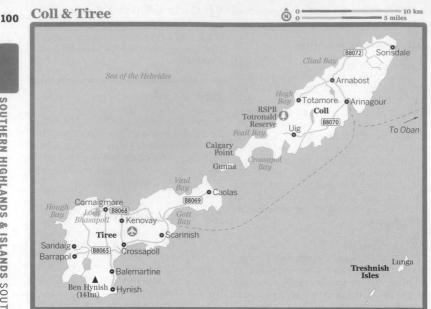

restaurant (mains £9 to £18) serving dishes ranging from crab chowder to lamb chops with herb-and-Parmesan crust.

Garden House Camping & Caravan Site
CAMPGROUND **£**

(☎01879-230374; Uig; per person £2, tent site £3-4; ⊙May-Sep) Basic campsite with toilets and cold water only, 4.5 miles southwest of Arinagour. Dogs are not allowed.

Island Café
CAFE **£**

(Arinagour; mains £5-8; ⊙11am-5.30pm Mon & Tue, to 7.30pm Fri & Sat, to 4pm Sun) This cheerful little cafe serves hearty, homemade meals such as sausage and mash with onion gravy, haddock and chips, and vegetarian cottage pie, accompanied by organic beer, wine and cider.

❶ Information

Arinagour, a half-mile from the ferry pier, is the only village on Coll, and is home to the **Island Stores** (⊙10am-5.30pm Mon & Fri, 10am-1pm Tue & Thu, 9am-5.30pm Wed, 9.30am-5pm Sat) grocery shop, a post office (with ATM), some craft shops and a petrol pump. There is no reliable mobile-phone signal on the island; there are payphones at the pier and in the hotel. For more info see www.visitcoll.co.uk.

❶ Getting There & Around

AIR Hebridean Air Services (☎0845 805 7465; www.hebrideanair.co.uk) Operates flights from Connel Airfield (near Oban) to Coll (£65 one way, twice daily Monday and Wednesday).

BIKE Mountain bikes can be hired from the post office in Arinagour for £10 per day.

BOAT CalMac (www.calmac.co.uk) A ferry runs from Oban to Coll (passenger/car £16.70/85.50 return, 2¾ hours, one daily) and continues to Tiree (one hour), except on Wednesday and Friday when the boat calls at Tiree first. The one-way fare from Coll to Tiree is £2.60/12.75 per passenger/car.

On Thursdays only, you can take a ferry from Coll and Tiree to Barra in the Outer Hebrides (£7.10/35.25 one way, four hours).

Isle of Tiree

POP 765

Low-lying Tiree (tye-*ree*; from the Gaelic *tiriodh,* meaning 'land of corn') is a fertile sward of lush, green machair liberally sprinkled with yellow buttercups, much of it so flat that, from a distance, the houses seem to rise out of the sea. It's one of the sunniest places in Scotland, but also one of the windiest – cyclists soon find that although it's flat, heading west usually feels like going uphill. One major benefit – the constant breeze keeps away the midges.

The surf-lashed coastline here is scalloped with broad, sweeping beaches of white sand, hugely popular with windsurfers and kite-surfers. Most visitors, however, come for the birdwatching, beachcombing and lonely coastal walks.

In the 19th century Tiree had a population of 4500, but poverty and overcrowding – plus food shortages following the potato famine of 1846 – led the landowner, the Duke of Argyll, to introduce a policy of assisted emigration. Between 1841 and 1881, more than 3600 people left the island, many of them emigrating to Canada, the USA, Australia and New Zealand.

◎ Sights

For the best view on the island, walk up nearby **Ben Hynish** (141m), which is capped by a conspicuous radar station known locally as the Golf Ball.

An Iodhlann   LIBRARY, EXHIBITION
(☑01879-220793; www.aniodhlann.org.uk; Scarinish; admission free; ☺9am-5pm Mon-Fri; 🖝) Many of the estimated 38,000 descendants of Tiree emigrants come to this historical and genealogical library and archive to trace their ancestry. The centre stages a **summer exhibition** (adult/child £3/free; ☺11am-5pm Tue-Fri Jul-Sep) on island life and history.

Island Life Museum   MUSEUM
(Sandaig; admission free; ☺2-4pm Mon-Fri Easter-Sep) At Sandaig, in the far west of the island, is a row of quaint thatched cottages, each restored as a 19th-century crofter's home.

Hynish   HAMLET
The picturesque harbour and hamlet of Hynish, near the southern tip of the island, was built in the 19th century to house workers and supplies for the construction of the Skerryvore Lighthouse, which stands 10 miles offshore. **Skerryvore Lighthouse Museum** (Hynish; admission free; ☺9am-5pm) occupies the signal tower above the harbour, which was once used to communicate by semaphore with the lighthouse site.

🏃 Activities

Reliable wind and big waves have made Tiree one of Scotland's top windsurfing venues. The annual **Tiree Wave Classic** (www.tireewaveclassic.com) competition is held here in October.

Wild Diamond Watersports   WINDSURFING
(☑01879-220399; www.wilddiamond.co.uk) Based at Loch Bhasapoll in the northwest of the island, this outfit runs courses in windsurfing, kitesurfing, sand-yachting and stand-up paddleboarding, and rents out equipment. Six hours' equipment hire costs from £50, and a beginners course (six hours over two days) costs £100 including gear. Sand-yachting on Gott Bay beach at low tide is £25 per hour.

🛏 Sleeping & Eating

Scarinish Hotel   HOTEL ££
(☑01879-220308; www.tireescarinishhotel.com; Scarinish; s/d £50/80; 🅿) There's hospitality on tap at the Scarinish, with enthusiastic owners who go out of their way to make you feel welcome. The refurbished rooms are crisp and clean, and the **restaurant** (mains £8 to £18) and traditional lean-to bar have a cosy atmosphere.

Ceabhar   B&B ££
(☑01879-220684; www.ceabhar.com; Sandaig; r per person from £35; 🅿🖝) This snug little cottage B&B has a fantastic location at the western end of the island, looking out over the Atlantic towards the sunset. The owners are outdoor enthusiasts and can advise on kite-surfing, power-kiting and scuba diving. There's also a **restaurant** (mains £8 to £14, open for dinner Wednesday to Saturday) in a sunny conservatory with sea views.

Kirkapol   B&B ££
(☑01879-220729; www.kirkapoltiree.co.uk; Gott Bay; s/d £35/66; 🅿) Set in a converted 19th-century church overlooking the island's biggest beach, the Kirkapol has six homely rooms and a big lounge with a leather sofa. It's 2 miles north of the ferry terminal.

Millhouse Hostel   HOSTEL £
(☑01879-220435; www.tireemillhouse.co.uk; Cornaigmore; dm/tw £15/35) Housed in a converted barn next to an old water mill, this small but comfortable hostel is 5 miles west from the ferry pier.

Balinoe Croft Campsite   CAMPGROUND £
(☑01879-220399; www.wilddiamond.co.uk; Balinoe; tent sites per person £12; 🖝) A sheltered site with full facilities in the southwest of the island, near Balemartine, with great views of Mull.

ℹ Information

There's a bank (without ATM), post office and **Co-op supermarket** (☺8am-8pm Mon-Fri, 8am-6pm Sat, noon-6pm Sun) in Scarinish, the main village, a half-mile south of the ferry pier. You can get cash back with debit-card purchases at the Co-op.

Tourist information and internet access are available at the **Rural Centre** (☎01879-220677; ☺11am-4pm Mon-Sat), and An Iodhlann, but there is no accommodation booking service. For more information see www.isleoftiree.com.

ℹ Getting There & Around

AIR Loganair/FlyBe (www.loganair.co.uk) Flies from Glasgow to Tiree once daily (£56, 50 minutes) from Monday to Saturday.

Hebridean Air Services (☎0845 805 7465; www.hebrideanair.co.uk) Operates flights from Connel Airfield (near Oban) to Tiree via Coll (one way from Oban/Coll £65/25, twice daily Monday and Wednesday).

BIKE You can rent bicycles from Millhouse Hostel and from **McLennan Motors** (☎01879-220555); the latter can also rent you a car.

BOAT Ferry connections and fares are the same as for Coll. Except on Wednesday and Friday the ferry goes to Coll first; journey time from Oban to Tiree is then four hours.

WALKING IN THE SOUTHERN HIGHLANDS & ISLANDS

Ben Lomond Walk

Standing guard over the eastern shore of Loch Lomond is Ben Lomond (974m), the most southerly Munro. It's thought that the name Lomond comes from an old Lowland Scots word *llumon,* or the Gaelic *laom,* meaning 'beacon' or 'light'. On fine weekends the droning of powerboats and jet skis on Loch Lomond is all too audible, even on the summit.

More than 30,000 people climb Ben Lomond each year. Most follow the 'tourist route' up and down, which starts at Rowardennan car park. It's a straightforward climb on a well-used and maintained path; allow about five hours for the 7-mile (11km) round trip. The scenic Ptarmigan Route, described here, is less crowded and follows a narrower, but clearly defined, path up the western flank of Ben Lomond, directly overlooking the loch, to a curving

BEN LOMOND WALK

Duration 4½–5 hours
Distance 7 miles
Difficulty moderate
Start/Finish Rowardennan
Transport ferry
Summary A circuit over one of the most popular 'hills' in central Scotland, via the quiet Ptarmigan Route; the views of 'the bonnie, bonnie banks of Loch Lomond' are magnificent.

ridge leading to the summit. You can then descend via the tourist route, making a satisfying circuit.

There are no easier alternative routes. Ben Lomond slopes very steeply down to the loch and tracks through the forest on the eastern side aren't particularly attractive. The West Highland Way passes between the loch and the Ben, and many Way walkers take a day off to do the climb.

PLANNING

Harvey's 1:25,000 map *Glasgow Popular Hills* includes Ben Lomond but isn't much help for identifying surrounding features. For this purpose, use either the OS Landranger 1:50,000 map *No 56 Loch*

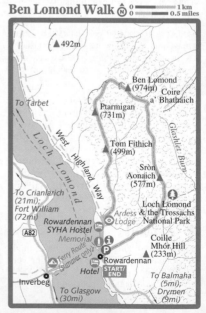

Lomond & Inveraray or the OS Explorer 1:25,000 map No 364 Loch Lomond North.

Loch Lomond, Trossachs, Stirling & Clackmannan by John Brooks is a useful guide covering a wide variety of walks.

THE WALK

With your back to the toilet block, walk towards Loch Lomond, where there's a view of the distinctive rounded knob of Ptarmigan, a couple of miles due north. Turn right (north) along the loch-side path; you'll soon pass a granite war-memorial sculpture. A few minutes past where the path becomes a gravel road, swing right through a gate in front of the youth hostel, then turn left, following the West Highland Way with its thistle-and-hexagon waymarker.

Pass Ardess Lodge National Trust for Scotland Ranger Centre and Ben Lomond Cottage on the right, cross the burn and immediately turn right along an unmarked path up through the trees. The path climbs beside the burn for a short distance to a small cascade then veers left up the bracken-covered hillside. As you climb steadily across the slope, you'll be treated to views of the loch and the hills on its western side. Further on, Ptarmigan summit comes into view. Higher up, above some rock outcrops, go through the kissing gate. The path gains more height on an open spur then zigzags steeply up a grassy bluff to the ridge and on to the summit of Ptarmigan (731m), near a small lochan (1½ to two hours from Rowardennan). The fine views from here include virtually the full length of the loch and its cluster of islands, and the Arrochar hills to the west.

The path leads on along the bumpy ridge, through a chain of grassy, rocky knobs, to a narrow gap where stepping stones keep you out of the mud. The final steep climb starts through formidable crags, but natural rock steps and the well-maintained path make it comparatively easy. From a grassy shelf there's one more straightforward rocky climb to the trig point on the summit of Ben Lomond, less than one hour from Ptarmigan summit. The all-round view includes Ben Nevis on the northern horizon, the islands of Arran and Jura in the southwest, the Firth of Clyde, the Arrochar hills immediately across the loch (notably the anvil-like profile of the Cobbler) and the Campsie Fells and Glasgow to the south.

The wide, well-trodden path starts to descend immediately, past the spectacular,

north-facing cliffs on the left. Soon it swings round to the right and makes a series of wide zigzags down the steep slope to the long ridge stretching ahead, which it follows south. Eventually the grade steepens over Sròn Aonaich (577m) and the path resumes zigzagging through open moorland. Cross a footbridge and continue into the pine forest, along an open clearing. The path steepens again, becoming rockier and more eroded, down through mixed woodland. Eventually it emerges at the toilet block at Rowardennan, two hours from the top.

Goatfell Walk

You can't really visit Arran and not climb Goatfell; it beckons you from Ardrossan and it's ever-present once you reach Brodick. Most walkers tramp up the eastern routes, from Cladach or from Brodick Castle. However, there's a less crowded and more satisfying approach from the west, via beautiful Glen Rosa, North Goatfell and along Stacach Ridge. The descent is via the steep, rocky eastern face to moorland and forest paths.

The National Trust for Scotland (NTS) has done a superb job of repairing and building paths; the descent is completely mud-free. The cliffs on both sides of the west ridge and Stacach Ridge are precipitous, so extra care is needed.

This route can be done in either direction but we recommend clockwise. The overall ascent is more gentle, with some steep bits, and the summit comes in the latter part of the route. There are signposts where paths leave the road, but not on Goatfell itself. The route includes at least 800m of ascent and some minor scrambling.

It can turn very cold, wet and windy on Goatfell very quickly, at any time of the year, and the mountain creates its own weather – Brodick can be basking in hot sunshine while Goatfell is mist-bound.

THE WALK

From Brodick tourist office, walk north beside the main road (A841) for about 1.5 miles (along a path for all but the last 200m) to a major junction. Turn left along the B880 towards Blackwaterfoot. About 100m along this road turn right down the narrow 'Glen Rosa Cart Track'. Follow this to the Glen Rosa Farm campsite, above which there's a small car park and the bitumen ends. Continue along a clear vehicle

GOATFELL WALK

Duration 6–7 hours
Distance 11 miles
Difficulty moderate to demanding
Start/Finish Brodick
Summary Take the connoisseur's route to Arran's highest peak, through superbly scenic Glen Rosa and along steep, rock-encrusted ridges to spectacular wrap-around views from the summit.

track into Glen Rosa itself. There are superb views of the precipitous peaks on the western side of the glen, culminating in Cir Mhòr (799m) at its head.

The track becomes a path at the crossing of Garbh Allt, the boundary of the NTS property. Aiming unerringly for the Saddle, the low point between Cir Mhòr and the massive, rock-encrusted bulk of Goatfell, the path climbs gently then quite steeply. From the Saddle (2½ to three hours from the start) there's a fine view among the granite boulders down Glen Sannox to the sea. Cir Mhòr's alarmingly steep crags rise immediately to the left. To the north are the castellated ridge of Caisteal Abhail (859m), Arran's second-highest peak, and the no-

torious cleft, Ceum na Caillich (Witch's Step). To the right the features of the next section of the walk are clearly visible: the bouldery west ridge, leading steeply up to North Goatfell; and Stacach Ridge, which is crowned by four small, rocky peaks.

From the Saddle, the path leads up the ridge towards North Goatfell. There are some narrow, exposed sections and a few near-vertical 'steps' where you'll need to use your hands. More tricky, though, are the patches of loose granite gravel. About an hour from the Saddle the route nears the summit of North Goatfell (818m). The final section is a scramble, but if this is too intimidating, pass below the top, keeping it on your left, then return to the ridge. Turn back to gain the summit from the east, over large slabs and boulders.

From North Goatfell you can keep to the crest of the ridge, scrambling over the rocky knobs. Alternatively, drop down to the less exposed eastern side of the ridge and follow paths below the knobs. The final section involves hopping over giant boulders to the summit of Goatfell (874m), 45 minutes from North Goatfell. The summit is topped by a trig point and a large viewpoint indicator, from which you can identify features in the panoramic view. On a good day, Ben Lomond and the coast of Northern Ireland

Goatfell Walk

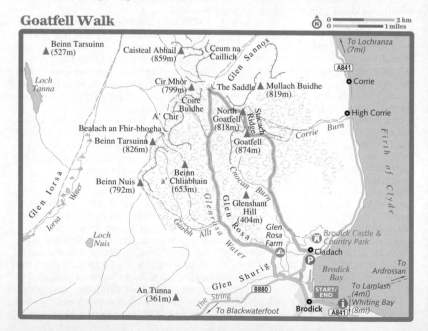

can be seen. The whole of Arran is spread out below, with the conical Holy Island rearing up from the sea in Lamlash Bay.

From the summit a path winds down the steep eastern face, then straightens out as the ridge takes shape. At a shallow saddle the path changes direction and leads southeast then south across moorland, down Cnocan Burn glen and into scattered woodland. At a junction in a conifer plantation, continue straight ahead then turn right at a T-junction. Descend through conifers, cross a road and go on to Cladach and Arran Brewery; the main road is a little further on.

The last leg starts along a footpath on the western side of the main road. Where the path ends, cross the road to a signposted path beside, and then briefly across, Brodick golf course, leading back to the main road beside Arran Heritage Museum. Follow the roadside path into town (2½ hours from Goatfell summit).

If you'd like to have a look around Brodick Castle and Country Park, turn left 30m after the T-junction in the conifer plantation mentioned above. Follow Cemetery Trail past the eponymous site (the resting place of the 11th and 12th Dukes of Hamilton and a wife), over bridges and into the castle grounds. The ranger service office is in the first building on the right; continue straight on to the NTS shop and tearoom.

Walking the West Highland Way

Includes »

Best Viewpoints

» Conic Hill (p110)

» Inversnaid (p110)

» Above Crianlarich (p111)

» Mam Carraigh (p112)

» Devil's Staircase (p112)

» Old military road above
Kinlochleven (p113)

Why Go?

From the outskirts of Glasgow, Scotland's biggest city, the West Highland Way leads through fertile, populous lowland countryside to the shores of Loch Lomond, on the threshold of the Highlands. From there it carries you north, through rugged glens, beside fast-flowing streams and past wild moorland where magnificent mountains are never out of sight. The very names have an alluring ring: Rannoch Moor, Glen Coe, Devil's Staircase.

Not only is the West Highland Way a rich sensory experience, it's also steeped in history. The route follows long stretches of drove roads, along which cattle were once taken to market; the flat beds of old railway lines; roads along which coach-and-horses once jolted; and the 18th-century military road built to subdue rebellious Highlanders.

This is the most popular long-distance path in Scotland (and Britain for that matter); something like 15,000 walkers go the full distance each year, so you'll rarely be short of like-minded company from around the world.

When to Go

Tyndrum

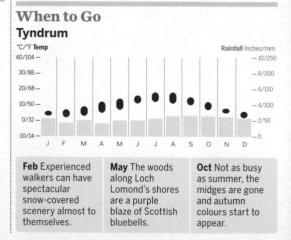

Feb Experienced walkers can have spectacular snow-covered scenery almost to themselves.

May The woods along Loch Lomond's shores are a purple blaze of Scottish bluebells.

Oct Not as busy as summer, the midges are gone and autumn colours start to appear.

PLANNING

The walk begins at Milngavie, easing you into things with the two least strenuous days before you hit the harder going north of Rowardennan. Spreading it over seven days means only one long day (between Tyndrum and Kings House) and a majority of comfortable days; don't overlook the fact that it's not only horizontal distance that matters – the Way involves a total of 3500m (11,500ft) of ascent.

Of course, you can take much longer, by doing shorter days, or by taking time out to knock off some of the nearby Munros – Ben Lomond and Ben Nevis are the two obvious candidates. Or you can do a one-day hike on a part of the way – recommended sections include Inversnaid to Inverarnan (7 miles), and Kings House to Glen Nevis (19 miles).

Navigation is generally straightforward: the Way is clearly waymarked with the official thistle-and-hexagon logo, and there's a shelf-full of guidebooks and maps

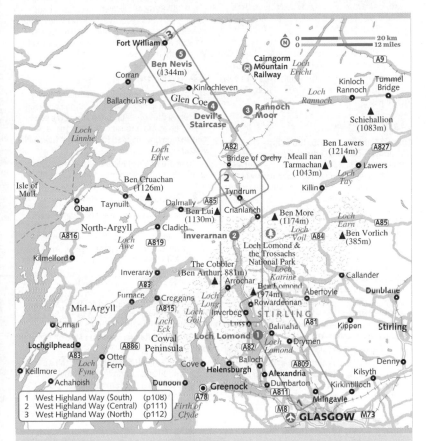

1 West Highland Way (South) (p108)
2 West Highland Way (Central) (p111)
3 West Highland Way (North) (p112)

WALKING THE WEST HIGHLAND WAY

107

West Highland Way Highlights

❶ Soak up the gorgeous scenery along the bonnie banks of lovely **Loch Lomond** (p46)

❷ Enjoy a well-earned pint of ale in the atmospheric **Drover's Inn** (p45) at Inverarnan

❸ Revel in the wild open spaces of bleak but beautiful **Rannoch Moor** (p121)

❹ Take in the dramatic views from the **Devil's Staircase** (p113), the highest point of the walk

❺ Round off your achievement with an ascent of **Ben Nevis** (p169), Britain's highest summit

PRACTICALITIES

Duration seven days
Distance 96 miles (154km)
Difficulty moderate
Start Milngavie
Finish Fort William
Transport train, bus
Summary Scotland's most popular long-distance path, passing through some of the country's finest land-scapes, from suburban Glasgow to the foot of the highest mountain in Britain.

to enlighten and entertain you along the way. By the time you reach Fort William you might even be supremely fit and ready to continue along the Great Glen Way to Inverness.

Maps & Books

Four OS Landranger 1:50,000 maps – No 64 *Glasgow*, No 56 *Loch Lomond & Inveraray*, No 50 *Glen Orchy & Loch Etive* and No 41 *Ben Nevis* – cover the Way, although it's much easier to use a purpose-designed, all-in-one route map. Both the excellent Harvey 1:40,000 Route map *West Highland Way* and the superbly designed Ruck-sack Readers guide *The West Highland Way* are more than adequate, and include lots of practical information for walkers.

Trailblazer's *West Highland Way*, by Charlie Loram, is the most comprehensive guidebook, with detailed trail maps and information on ac-commodation, places to eat and tourist attrac-tions in Glasgow, Fort William and all the villages along the way.

Accommodation

If you're planning to rely on serviced accommo-dation (hotels, B&Bs and hostels) it's essential to book rooms in advance; the official website lists accommodation along the route. Note that Kings House is an accommodation 'bottleneck' with just the one hotel. Public transport here is limited to one bus every two hours (last bus westbound 8.15pm) and taxis are expensive, so plan ahead and don't get caught out.

There are several fully serviced campgrounds along the way, as well as three official back-packer campgrounds (free, no facilities, one-night stay only) at Garadhban Forest, Ardess and Inversnaid Boathouse. Local bylaws forbid camping on the eastern shore of Loch Lomond between Drymen and Rowardennan, except at recognised campgrounds.

Guided Walk & Baggage Services

Rather than doing all the organising, you can take advantage of the services offered by a few small companies who can arrange all your ac-commodation and carry your luggage between overnight stops. Some outfits go a step further and provide you with sheafs of information about the Way and the places through which you pass, or can provide a guide to lead you on the walk.

Easyways (☎01324-714132; www.easyways .com) has years of experience organising accom-modation and baggage transfer; **Transcotland** (☎01887-820848 ; www.transcotland.com) also has a good track record and can provide reams of directions and background information. C-n-Do Scotland (p244) offer guided walks along the West Highland Way.

ℹ Information

The *West Highland Way Pocket Companion*, a free booklet listing accommodation and facili-ties along the route (updated annually), can be picked up at most tourist offices in the region; it can also be downloaded for free from the official website.

There are ATMs at Milngavie, Drymen, Crian-larich, Tyndrum, Kinlochleven and Fort William.

ℹ Getting There & Away

The official start of the West Highland Way is a granite obelisk (unveiled in 1992) beside the bridge over the Allander Water on Douglas St, Milngavie, but for most people the journey be-gins at Milngavie train station. Buses stop here and there's a car park near the station, just off Station Rd. To reach the obelisk from the sta-tion, go through the underpass and up a flight of steps to the pedestrianised centre of Milngavie. Bear left at the underpass exit to join Douglas St, passing through a shopping precinct before reaching the Allander Water and the official start point.

Fort William (p165), at the end of the walk, has frequent rail and bus connections to other parts of Scotland, including an overnight sleeper train to London.

ℹ The official **West Highland Way** (☎01389-722600; www.west-highland -way.co.uk) website is a comprehensive resource, covering pretty much every-thing you need to know: from the route itself, equipment and planning to weath-er, accommodation, food and public transport.

If you plan to walk just a section of the Way, Crianlarich, Tyndrum and Bridge of Orchy (p366) are well served by trains; contact **ScotRail** (☎08457 55 00 33; www.scotrail.co .uk) for details. Scottish Citylink (p365) buses on the Glasgow–Fort William route stop at Crianlarich, Tyndrum and Bridge of Orchy. Traveline Scotland (p366) provides a journey planner and timetable information for all public transport in Scotland.

In addition, a network of **passenger ferries** (p46) links the main A82 road on the west side of Loch Lomond with various destinations along the southern part of the West Highland Way on the eastern shore, including Rowardennan and Inversnaid. From 2010 a waterbus service has been undergoing trials, providing an on-demand ferry service for hikers; check out the National Park Gateway Centre (p46) and West Highland Way (p108) websites for the latest situation.

THE WALK

Day One: Milngavie to Drymen

» **Duration** 4½ to 5½ hours
» **Distance** 12 miles (19km)

From the obelisk on Douglas St, descend the ramp beneath the huge West Highland Way sign, pass through a small car park and follow a path along a disused railway, then upstream beside Allander Water, to **Mugdock Wood**. At the end of the wood, paths and a track take you past a couple of small lochs to the B821. Turn left and follow the road for about 300m to a stile giving onto a path to the right. As you skirt **Dumgoyach Hill** watch out for Bronze Age standing stones to your right, just before the hill. A mile past Dumgoyach Bridge you pass **Glengoyne Distillery**; 800m further on you reach the **Beech Tree Inn** (☎01360 550297; www.the beechtreeinn.co.uk; ☺food noon-9pm daily Apr-Sep, noon-9pm Thu-Sun, to 4pm Mon-Wed Oct-Mar) at Dumgoyne. In the village of **Killearn**, 1.5 miles to the right, there's accommodation, shops, pubs and a post office.

Follow the old railway track to **Gartness**, from where you're on a road most of the way to the edge of Drymen. A mile beyond Gartness there's camping available at **Easter Drumquhassle Farm** (Drymen Camping; ☎01360-660597; www.drymencamping.co.uk; Gartness Rd; sites per person £5, wigwams per person £7), from where a view of Loch Lomond

makes its first appearance. Pass a quarry and continue along the road; just past a sharp left bend, the Way leaves the road and follows a path to the right. If you're going to Drymen, continue along the road and cross the A811 to enter the village.

West Highland Way (South)

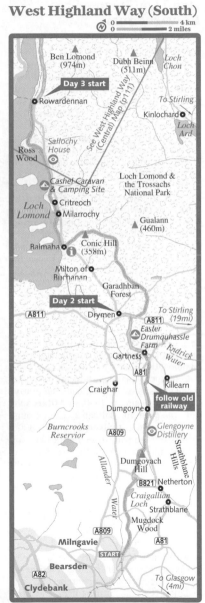

DRYMEN

Drymen is a pretty village with a central green and lots of character. There are plenty of accommodation and eating options, an excellent pub, several shops and a small supermarket.

Day Two: Drymen to Rowardennan

» **Duration** five to 6½ hours
» **Distance** 14 miles (22.5km)

From near the A811 just outside Drymen, a forest track gradually climbs to **Garadhban Forest** (backpacker campground, no facilities). Just over an hour from Drymen, a side path runs left to the village of **Milton of Buchanan**; it's also the alternative route when Conic Hill is closed to dog walkers during the lambing season (late April to early May). There are a couple of B&Bs in the village but no pubs or shops.

The Way climbs then contours north of the summit of **Conic Hill** (358m), but it's worth the short detour to the top for the wonderful panorama over **Loch Lomond**. This viewpoint also has a special, even unique significance: from the summit you can make out the unmistakeable line of the Highland Boundary Fault, separating the lowlands from the Highlands – so from this point on you really are in the Highlands.

Descend to **Balmaha**, a small lakeside village usually thronged with people messing about in boats. As well as the National Park Centre (p46) there's also a small shop and the Oak Tree Inn (p46), which offers accommodation, food and a bar.

Continue along the shore of Loch Lomond, passing a marker commemorating the Way's opening in 1980, to **Milarrochy** (one hour from Balmaha; campground available). From **Critreoch**, about 800m further on, the path dives into a dark forest and emerges to follow the road for about 1 mile. Just after you join the road is the Cashel Caravan and Camping Site (p46). A mile beyond Sallochy House, the Way climbs through **Ross Wood**, its magnificent oaks making it one of Scotland's finest natural woodlands, to Rowardennan.

ROWARDENNAN

Rowardennan is little more than a hamlet, but it has a hotel (p46) and a youth hostel (p46); Ardess backpacker campground (no facilities) is a mile north of here, and Rowchoish Bothy (free, no facilities) is 2.5 miles north. Rowardennan is also the starting point for the ascent of **Ben Lomond** (974m; p102).

Day Three: Rowardennan to Inverarnan

» **Duration** six to 7½ hours
» **Distance** 14 miles (22.5km)

From Rowardennan follow the unsealed road that parallels the loch shore. Just past private Ptarmigan Lodge an alternative path branches left and follows the shoreline; it's more interesting, but much rougher going (not recommended with a heavy backpack) than the upper route, which follows a track higher up the hillside. The lower path leads past a natural rock cell in a crag about 1.5 miles north of Ptarmigan Lodge; known as **Rob Roy's prison**, the famous outlaw is said to have kept kidnap victims here. From both routes you can reach **Rowchoish Bothy**, a simple stone shelter.

Not far beyond the bothy the forestry track gives way to a path, which dives down to the loch for a stretch of difficult walking to **Cailness**. From here the going improves to **Inversnaid**, shortly before which the path crosses Snaid Burn just above the impressive **Inversnaid Falls**. The huge Inversnaid Hotel could be a good place to stop for refreshments before you tackle the next and toughest section of all.

For a couple of miles north from Inversnaid, the path twists and turns around large boulders and tree roots, a good test of balance and agility. A mile or so into this, the Way passes close to **Rob Roy's cave**, where he is alleged to have hidden from the authorities, although it's little more than a gap beneath fallen blocks of rock. Further on, **Doune Bothy** provides basic accommodation (no facilities). Almost 1 mile beyond the bothy, at **Ardleish**, there's a landing stage used by the ferry across to the Ardlui Hotel (p45).

From Ardleish, you leave the loch and climb to a col below **Cnap Mór** (164m), where on a clear day there are good views north towards the Highlands and south over Loch Lomond. The path descends into **Glen Falloch**; a footbridge over **Ben Glas Burn** heralds your arrival at Inverarnan. Just upstream is the spectacular **Beinglas Falls**, a cascade of 300m (1000ft) – very impressive after heavy rain.

INVERARNAN

There's a choice of B&B and camping accommodation in Inverarnan, as well as an excellent country pub, the Drover's Inn (p45), which also offers food and lodging.

Day Four: Inverarnan to Tyndrum

» **Duration** 4½ to 5½ hours
» **Distance** 13 miles (21km)

From Inverarnan the route follows the attractive River Falloch most of the way to **Crianlarich**, the approximate halfway point of the Way. About 4 miles along, it crosses the river and joins an old military road. This track climbs out of Glen Falloch, and then at a stile into the forest, a path leads down to the right towards Crianlarich. There's no real need to go to Crianlarich, though there are B&Bs, a youth hostel, a bar and restaurant and a small shop with an ATM.

The Way climbs to the west from the stile, offering good views east to **Ben More** (1174m), and continues through the trees for about 2 miles. Next, it crosses under the railway line, goes over the road and crosses a wooden bridge over the River Fillan. Pass the remains of **St Fillan's Priory**, turn left and go on to Strathfillan Wigwams (p47) at Auchtertyre Farm. The route crosses the A82 once more and, in less than an hour, you make it to Tyndrum.

TYNDRUM

Tyndrum, originally a lead-mining settlement and now a popular staging point between Glasgow and Fort William, is strung out along the A82. It has a tourist office (p48), shops (including one selling outdoor equipment), hotels, B&Bs and campgrounds, and is well served by train and bus. Eating places include the Real Food Cafe (p48).

Day Five: Tyndrum to Kings House Hotel

» **Duration** 6½ to eight hours
» **Distance** 19 miles (30.5km)

From Tyndrum the route soon rejoins the old military road and crosses the railway line, affording easy walking with lovely views. Three miles from Tyndrum, you cross a burn at the foot of **Beinn Dòrain** (1074m), the 'hill' that dominates this section of the path.

The path climbs gradually to pass the entrance to Glen Orchy, crossing the railway again, heralding the beginning of the really mountainous scenery. The hamlet of **Bridge of Orchy** is dominated by the **Bridge of Orchy Hotel** (✆01838-400208; www.bridgeoforchy.co.uk; mains £9-19; ⊙food noon-9pm daily). Cross the old bridge (built in 1750) that gives the settlement its name and climb through the trees to the crest of **Mam Carraigh**, from where there are superb views across to **Rannoch Moor** (p121). The path then winds down to the secluded Inveroran Hotel. It's possible to camp wild (no facilities) beside a stone bridge 400m west of the hotel (caution: this area is subject to flooding after heavy rains).

The Way follows the minor road, which soon becomes a track, climbing gently past some plantations and out onto Rannoch Moor. There's no shelter for about 7 miles, and **Bà Bridge**, about 3 miles beyond the plantations, is the only real marker point. It can be very wild and windy up here, and there's a real sense of isolation. A cairn marks the summit at 445m and from here there's a wonderful view down into Glen Coe.

As the path descends from the moor to join the road again, you can see the chairlift of the Glencoe Mountain Resort (p172) to the left. There's a cafe at the base station, about 500m off the West Highland Way. Kings House Hotel is just over 1 mile ahead, across the A82.

KINGS HOUSE HOTEL

Dating from the 17th century, the **Kings House Hotel** (✆01855-851259; www.kingy.com; s/d £30/65; ℗) was originally used as barracks for George III's troops (hence the name). If you can't get a bed here you can catch a bus to Glencoe village, 11 miles west, where there's a wider selection of accommodation. It's possible to camp for free across the bridge behind the hotel.

Day Six: Kings House Hotel to Kinlochleven

» **Duration** three to four hours
» **Distance** 9 miles (14.5km)

From Kings House Hotel the route follows the old military road and then goes alongside the A82 to a parking area at **Altnafeadh**. This is a wonderful vantage point

West Highland Way (North)

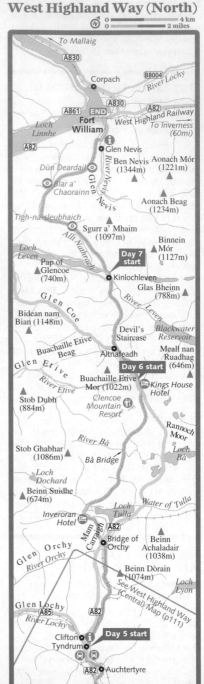

from which to appreciate all of the mountainous scenery of Glen Coe. The conical peak to your left is **Buachaille Etive Mór** (1022m).

From here the Way turns right, leaving the road to begin a steep, zigzagging climb up the **Devil's Staircase**. The cairn at the top is at 548m and marks the highest point of West Highland Way. The views from here are stunning, especially on a clear day, and you may even be able to see **Ben Nevis** (1344m).

The path now winds gradually down towards Kinlochleven, hidden below in the glen. As you descend you join the **Blackwater Reservoir** access track, and meet the pipes that carry water from there down to the town's hydroelectric power station. It's not a particularly pretty sight but was essential for the now-defunct aluminium smelter, the original reason for the town's establishment in 1907; the electricity generated is used these days to power Fort William's aluminium works.

KINLOCHLEVEN

Kinlochleven eases you back into 'civilisation' before you arrive at Fort William and experience the sensory onslaught that you always feel after the time in the wilderness. You'll find plenty of B&B, hostel and camping accommodation in Kinlovhleven, including the Blackwater Hostel (p174), as well as the village store and a small supermarket.

The Ice Factor (p174), housed in part of the former smelting plant, houses the world's largest indoor ice-climbing wall (plus a 'normal' climbing wall), so you can watch people performing amazing vertical feats while you tuck into a large pizza in the centre's cafe.

Day Seven: Kinlochleven to Fort William

» **Duration** six to 7½ hours
» **Distance** 15 miles (24km)

From Kinlochleven follow the road north out of town and turn off opposite the school. The path climbs through woodland to the **old military road**, from which you get a grand view along Loch Leven to the **Pap of Glencoe** (740m). Climb gradually to the crest, just beyond which are the ruins of several old farm buildings at **Tigh-na-sleubhaich**. From here the Way continues gently downhill and into conifer plantations 2 miles further on. You emerge at **Blar a' Chaorainn**, which is nothing more than a bench and an information board.

The Way leads on and up, through more plantations; occasional breaks in the trees provide fine views of Ben Nevis. After a few miles, a sign points to nearby **Dùn Deardail**, an Iron Age fort with walls that have been partly vitrified (turned to glass) by fire.

A little further on, cross another stile and follow the forest track down towards **Glen Nevis**. Across the valley the huge bulk of Ben Nevis fills the view. A side track leads down to Glen Nevis, which can make a good base for an ascent of 'the Ben'.

Stay on the path if you're heading for Fort William, passing a small graveyard just before you meet the road running through Glen Nevis. Turn left here; soon after, there's a visitor centre on the right. Continue into Fort William. The official end of the West Highland Way is in Gordon Square, at the far end of the pedestrianised main street, marked by a bronze sculpture of a hiker rubbing his feet. After a rest on one of the benches thoughtfully provided here, look forward to an end-of-walk celebration in one of the town's several restaurants and bars (p167).

Central Highlands

Includes »

Best Places to Eat

» Moulin Hotel (p125)

» Gathering Place (p140)

» The Cross (p133)

Best Places to Stay

» Moor of Rannoch Hotel (p120)

» Dalmunzie House (p144)

» Glen Clova Hotel (p143)

» Eagleview Guest House (p133)

» Auld Kirk (p139)

» Rucksacks (p140)

» Milton Eonan (p119)

Why Go?

The road from Perth to Inverness cuts through the heart of the Central Highlands, following the valleys of Scotland's two longest rivers: the Tay, whose headwaters lead to the picture-postcard scenery of Loch Tay and Loch Tummel, and the majestic desolation of Rannoch Moor; and the Spey, whose lower reaches are dotted with dozens of whisky distilleries.

The subarctic summits of the Cairngorm Mountains, which form the focus of Cairngorm National Park, rise close to the watershed. With its ice-sculpted glens, glittering lochs and ancient Caledonian pine forests, the park provides endless opportunities for outdoor adventures – hiking, hillwalking, mountain biking and wildlife watching are all on offer.

On the eastern side of the mountains, Royal Deeside stretches along the banks of one of Scotland's most famous salmon rivers, sporting the greatest concentration of Scottish Baronial castles anywhere in the country – including Balmoral, the Royal Family's Highland retreat.

When to Go

Aviemore

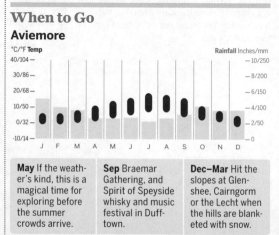

°C/°F Temp
Rainfall Inches/mm

May If the weather's kind, this is a magical time for exploring before the summer crowds arrive.

Sep Braemar Gathering, and Spirit of Speyside whisky and music festival in Dufftown.

Dec–Mar Hit the slopes at Glenshee, Cairngorm or the Lecht when the hills are blanketed with snow.

WEST PERTHSHIRE

The jewel in central Scotland's crown, West Perthshire achieves a Scottish ideal with rugged, noble hills reflected in some of the nation's most beautiful lochs. Bring your hiking boots and camera and prepare to stay a few days.

Aberfeldy

POP 1900

Aberfeldy is the gateway to west Perthshire, and a good base: adventure sports, walks (see p122), art and castles all feature on the menu. It's a peaceful, pretty place on the banks of the Tay, but if it's moody lochs and glens that steal your heart, you may want to push a little further on into the region.

◉ Sights & Activities

Castle Menzies   CASTLE
(www.menzies.org; adult/child £6/2.50; ◔10.30am-5pm Mon-Sat, 2-5pm Sun Apr–mid-Oct) About 1½ miles west of town by the B846, Castle Menzies is the impressive restored 16th-century seat of the chief of the clan Menzies (*ming-iss*). The Z-plan tower house is magnificently located against a backdrop of Scottish forest. And inside it doesn't disappoint: the place smells just like a castle should – musty and lived in.

It reeks of authenticity despite extensive restoration work and is a highly recommended ramble. Check out the fireplace in the dungeon-like kitchens and the gaudy great hall upstairs, with windows unfurling a ribbon of lush, green countryside extending into wooded hills beyond the estate. You'll get in for free if you share a surname with the castle.

Dewar's World of Whisky   DISTILLERY
(www.dewarsworldofwhisky.com; tour £6.50; ◔10am-6pm Mon-Sat & noon-4pm Sun Apr-Oct, 10am-4pm Mon-Sat Nov-Mar) Dewar's Distillery and their World of Whisky visitor centre is on the eastern outskirts of Aberfeldy. The tour is a good one, fully 90 minutes long; after the usual overblown film, there's a very entertaining interactive blending session as well as the tour of the whisky-making process.

Watermill   HISTORIC BUILDING
(✆01887-822896; www.aberfeldywatermill.com; Mill St; admission free; ◔10am-5pm Mon-Sat, from 11am Sun) The Watermill is an unusual attrac-

tion in the centre of town, incorporating a bookshop with a great Scottish collection, a gallery with contemporary works of art and a coffee shop. You could while away several hours in this old mill.

Highland Safaris   WILDLIFE TOURS
(✆01887-820071; www.highlandsafaris.net; ◔9am-5pm) This outfit, just past Castle Menzies, offers an ideal way to spot some wildlife or simply enjoy Perthshire's magnificent countryside. Standard trips include the 2½-hour Mountain Safari (per adult/child £37.50/15), which includes a dram in the wilderness; and the Safari Trek (adult/child £60/30), which includes a walk in the mountains and a picnic.

You can hire mountain bikes here (per day £15), and for another £15 they'll drive you up the top of the hill and you make your own way down (a good option for walkers too). Wildlife you may spot include golden eagles, osprey and red deer. There's also gold-panning for kids.

Splash   RAFTING
(✆01887-829706; www.rafting.co.uk; Dunkeld Rd, ◔9am-9pm; ⊕) Splash offers family-friendly whitewater rafting on the River Tay (per adult/child £25/40) and more advanced adult trips on the Tummel and the Orchy. It also runs canyoning trips and hires mountain bikes (per half-/full day £10/20).

▭ Sleeping

Guinach House   B&B ££
(✆01887-820251; www.guinachhouse.co.uk; Urlar Rd; d £95-125; ⓟ☜) More like a boutique hotel, Guinach House has modish rooms and a casual, relaxed ambience. Rooms are individually styled – our favourite is the zebra room, although the red room, with freestanding bathtub, runs a close second. The whole place is set on a large estate, so there are plenty of rambling options just beyond the front doorstep.

Tigh'n Eilean Guest House   B&B ££
(✆01887-820109; www.tighneilean.com; Taybridge Dr; s/d £52/66; ⓟ☜) Everything about this property screams comfort. It's a gorgeous place overlooking the Tay, with individually designed rooms all creating a unique sense of space. For couples our fave is the jacuzzi room – it's huge, and the same price as the others. The Tay riverbank here is delightful, with birdsong above and ducks paddling below.

Central Highlands Highlights

1 Hike through the hills around beautiful **Glen Clova** (p142)

2 Wander through the ancient Caledonian pine forest at **Rothiemurchus Estate** (p128)

3 Explore the hills, forests, castles and pretty villages of **Royal Deeside** (p138)

4 Be initiated into the mysteries of malt whisky on a **Speyside distillery tour** (p136)

5 Make eye contact with a wildcat at the **Highland Wildlife Park** (p131)

6 Improve your mountain biking skills at **Laggan Wolftrax** (p133)

7 Ride the **Cairngorm Mountain Railway** (p130) to the top of the Cairngorm plateau

8 Experience life at the end of the road amid the bleak landscapes of **Rannoch Moor** (p121)

9 Try to capture on camera the epic splendour of **Glen Lyon** (p119)

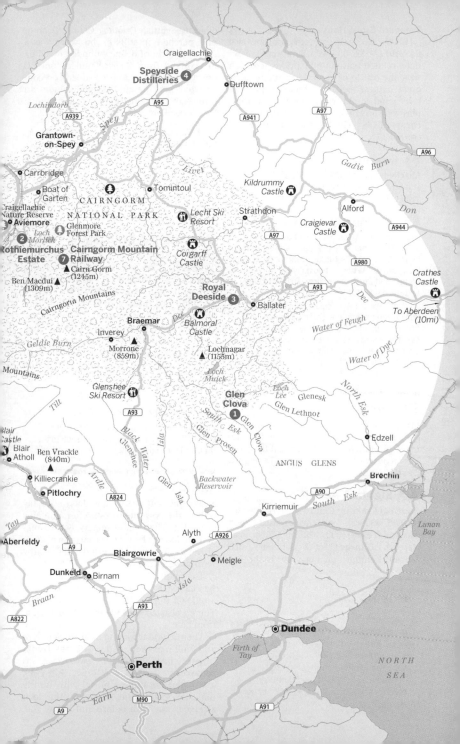

Balnearn Guest House
B&B ££

(☑01887-820431; www.balnearnhouse.com; Crieff Rd; s/d/f £40/65/95; P☎) Balnearn is a sedate, refined and quite luxurious mansion near the centre of town. Most rooms have great natural light, and there's a particularly good family room downstairs. Doubles with private but exterior bathroom are cheaper (£58). The hosts are attentive and cordial.

ℹ Information

Aberfeldy tourist office (☑01887-820276; The Square; ⊗Mon-Sat Nov-Mar, daily Apr-Oct) In an old church on the central square.

ℹ Getting There & Away

Stagecoach (www.stagecoachbus.com) Runs buses from Aberfeldy to Pitlochry (45 minutes, hourly Monday to Saturday, fewer on Sunday), Blairgowrie (1¼ hours, two daily Monday to Friday) and Perth (1¼ hours, 10 daily Monday to Saturday)!

Local buses run a circular route from Aberfeldy through Kenmore, Fortingall and back to Aberfeldy up to five times daily Monday to Friday. There's also a service through to Killin (one hour, up to five times daily Monday to Saturday, Saturday only June to September), connecting with an Oban service.

Kenmore

Pretty Kenmore lies at Loch Tay's eastern end, 6 miles west of Aberfeldy, and is dominated by church, clock tower, and the striking archway of privately owned **Taymouth Castle**.

⦿ Sights & Activities

Scottish Crannog Centre
PREHISTORIC SITE

(☑01887-830583; www.crannog.co.uk; tours adult/child £6.50/4.50; ⊗10am-5.30pm mid-Mar–Oct, 10am-4pm Sat & Sun Nov) Just outside Kenmore on Loch Tay is the fas-

cinating Scottish Crannog Centre. A crannog, perched on stilts in the water, was a favoured form of defence-minded dwelling in Scotland from the 3rd millennium BC onwards. This one has been superbly reconstructed, and the guided tour includes an impressive demonstration of firemaking. It's an excellent attraction.

Loch Tay Boating Centre
OUTDOOR ACTIVITIES

(☑01887-830291; www.loch-tay.co.uk; mountain bikes per half-/full day £12/20; ⊗daily) Kenmore is a good activity base, and Loch Tay Boating Centre can have you speeding off on a mountain bike or out on the loch itself, in anything from a canoe to a cabin cruiser that'll sleep a whole family.

✗ Eating & Drinking

Kenmore Hotel
HOTEL £££

(☑01887-830205; www.kenmorehotel.com; The Square; s/d £85/140; P@☎) The heart of Kenmore, this hotel has a bar with a roaring fire and some verses scribbled on the chimneypiece by Robert Burns in 1787, when the inn was already a couple of centuries old. There's also a riverbank beer garden and a wide variety of rooms that sport modern conveniences; the nicest have bay windows and river views. Prices plummet off-season and midweek.

ℹ Getting There & Away

Regular buses link Aberfeldy with Kenmore, some continuing to Killin via the turnoff to the trailhead for Ben Lawers.

Loch Tay

Serpentine and picturesque, long Loch Tay reflects the powerful forests and mountains around it. The bulk of mighty Ben Lawers (1214m) looms above and is part of a National Nature Reserve that includes the nearby **Tarmachan Range**.

The main access point for the ascent of Ben Lawers is the now-defunct tourist office, a mile off the A827 five miles east of Killin. There's also an easier nature trail leaving from here.

There's good accommodation in Kenmore and Killin, as well as the **Culdees Bunkhouse** (☑01887-830519; www.culdeesbunkhouse.co.uk; dm/tw/f £17/44/66; P@☎⟆), a wonderfully offbeat hostel with utterly majestic vistas: the whole of the loch stretches out both before and below you.

MOVING ON?

For in-depth information, reviews and recommendations, head to the Apple App Store to buy Lonely Planet's *Edinburgh City Guide* iPhone app, or to shop.lonelyplanet.com to purchase a downloadable PDF of the Edinburgh chapter from Lonely Planet's *Scotland* guide.

The trip to the top of Ben Lawers and back can take up to five hours: pack wet weather gear, water and food. From the now-closed visitor centre on the minor road leading from Loch Tay to glen Lyon, 4 miles northeast of Killin, take the nature trail that heads north-east. After the boardwalk protecting a bog, cross a stile, then fork left and ascend along the Edramucky burn (to the right). At the next rise, fork right and cross the burn. A few minutes later ignore the nature trail's right turn and continue ascending parallel to the burn's left bank for just over half a mile.

Leave the protected zone by another stile and steeply ascend Beinn Ghlas' shoulder. Reaching a couple of large rocks, ignore a northbound footpath and continue zigzagging uphill. The rest of the ascent is a straightforward succession of three false summits. The last and steepest section alternates between erosion-sculpted rock and a meticulously crafted cobbled trail. Long views of majestic hillscape, and even the North Sea and Atlantic, are your reward on a clear day.

It's a quirky place you could get lost in, with compact, spotless dorms, lovable family rooms with the best views in Perthshire, and a range of cluttered, homelike lounging areas. It's a top spot to relax but also a fine base for hill walking or for mucking-in with the volunteers who help run the sustainable farm here. It's half a mile above the village of Fearnan, 4 miles west of Kenmore.

Fortingall

Fortingall is one of the prettiest villages in Scotland, with 19th-century thatched cottages in a very tranquil setting. The church (⊘10am-4pm Apr-Oct) has impressive wooden beams and a 7th-century **monk's bell**. In the churchyard, there's a **2000-year-old yew**, probably the oldest tree in Europe. This tree was around when the Romans camped in the meadows by the River Lyon; popular if unlikely tradition says that Pontius Pilate was born here. Today the tree is a shell of its former self – at its zenith it had a girth of over 17m! But souvenir hunters have reduced it to two much smaller trunks.

Fortingall Hotel (☑01887-830367; www .fortingallhotel.com; s/d £110/160; P🛜), nearby, is a peaceful, old-fashioned country hotel with polite service and is furnished with quiet good taste. The bedrooms are spotless, with huge beds, modern bathrooms and little extras like bathrobes, whisky and DVD players. Rooms look out over green meadows; in all a perfect spot for doing very little except enjoying the clean air and excellent dinners.

Glen Lyon

At the end of a road that runs for some 34 unforgettable miles of rickety stone bridges is this remote and stunningly beautiful glen of Caledonian pine forest and sheer heather-splashed peaks poking through swirling clouds. It becomes wilder and more uninhabited as it snakes its way west, and is proof that hidden treasures still exist in Scotland. The ancients believed it to be a gateway to Faerieland, and even the most sceptical of people will be entranced by the valley's magic.

From Fortingall, a narrow road winds up the glen – another road from Loch Tay crosses the hills and reaches the glen halfway in, at **Bridge of Balgie**. The glen continues up to a dam (past a memorial to explorer Robert Campbell); bearing left here you can actually continue over a wild and remote road (unmarked on maps) to isolated **Glen Lochay** and down to Killin. Cycling through Glen Lyon is a wonderful way to experience this special place.

There's little in the way of attractions in the valley – the majestic and lonely scenery is the reason to be here – but at **Glenlyon Gallery** (www.glenlyongallery.co.uk; admission free; ⊘10am-5pm Thu-Tue), next to the Bridge of Balgie post office (which does more-than-decent lunches), a selection of fine handmade pieces are for sale.

There is no public transport in the glen.

🛏 Sleeping & Eating

TOP CHOICE **Milton Eonan**   B&B ££
(☑01887-866318; www.miltoneonan.com; d £70; P🛜) Milton Eonan is a must for those seek-

ing utter tranquillity in a glorious natural setting. On an effervescent stream where a historic watermill once stood, it's a working croft that offers a romantic one-bedroom cottage (breakfast available for a little extra) at the bottom of the garden. It can sleep three at a pinch.

The lively owners do packed lunches and evening meals (£18.50) using local and homegrown produce. After crossing the bridge at Bridge of Balgie, you'll see Milton Eonan signposted to the right.

Wester Camusvrachan B&B **££**
(☑01887-866320; www.glenlyonbb.co.uk; s/tw/d £24/48/60; P🖘) Between Fortingall and Bridge of Balgie about 8½ miles up the glen, Wester Camusvrachan offers cosy, good-value B&B; there's an en suite double room and a twin with bunks. Evening meals (BYO bottle) are £15 a head.

Lochs Tummel & Rannoch

The route along Lochs Tummel and Rannoch is worth doing any way you can – by foot, bicycle or car – just don't miss it!

◉ Sights

Tay Forest Park PARK
Hills of ancient birch and forests of spruce, pine and larch make up the Tay Forest Park – the king of Scotland's forests. It's the product of a brilliant bit of forward thinking: the replanting of Tay Forest 300 years ago. These wooded hills roll into the glittering waters of the lochs; a visit in autumn is recommended, when the birch trees are at their finest.

Queen's View Centre VIEWPOINT
(www.forestry.gov.uk; ⊙10am-6pm late-Mar–mid-Nov) Queen's View Centre is at the eastern end of Loch Tummel. Despite the signage, the shop here is a shop and not an exhibition, so if you pay the parking fee (£2) it's for the magnificent viewpoint over the water and towards Schiehallion (1083m).

Kinloch Rannoch VILLAGE
Waterfalls, towering mountains and a shimmering loch greet visitors to the hidden treasure of Kinloch Rannoch. It's a great base for cycle trips around Loch Rannoch and local walks, including the hike up Schiehallion (1083m), a relatively easy climb rewarded by spectacular views unobstructed by other hills, from Braes of Foss.

Rannoch Train Station TRAIN STATION
Sixteen miles west of Kinloch Rannoch, the road ends at romantic, isolated Rannoch train station, which is on the Glasgow–Fort William line. Beyond lies desolate, intriguing Rannoch Moor, a vast, vaguely menacing peat bog that stretches as far as the A82 and Glen Coe. There's a tearoom on the platform, and a welcoming small hotel situated alongside the station.

🛏 Sleeping & Eating

TOP CHOICE Moor of Rannoch Hotel HOTEL **££**
(☑01882-633238; www.moorofrannoch.co.uk; s/d £56/96; ⊙mid-Feb–Oct) At the end of the road beside Rannoch train station, it's all about you and the moorland. This is one of Scotland's most isolated places, but luckily this friendly hotel is here to keep your spirits up if the solitude gets too much. Great food, cosy rooms and great walks right from the doorstep – a magical getaway.

Bunrannoch House B&B **££**
(☑01882-632407; www.bunrannoch.co.uk; s/d £40/80, with dinner £65/130; P🖘) This historic former shooting lodge is a short way from town but feels utterly isolated and makes a great away-from-it-all destination. It has an ongoing renovation process and a friendly, 'can-do' attitude that's missing from other such country places. Walkers are most welcome, and there's a variety of rooms (including some great family ones upstairs).

Excellent meals (vegan/vegetarian diets catered for) feature the likes of pike fished from Loch Rannoch or locally stalked venison. Dinner for nonguests is £30.

Gardens B&B B&B **££**
(☑01882-632434; www.thegardensdunalastair .co.uk; s/d £40/70; P) Right off the beaten track between Kinloch Rannoch and Tummel Bridge, this place has just two rooms – a double and a twin. But what rooms they are: effectively suites, each with their own bathroom and sitting room. The conservatory space is great for soaking up the sun and contemplating the stunning view of Schiehallion.

If you're looking for solitude and a touch of eccentricity, this is the place.

Loch Tummel Inn SEAFOOD **££**
(☑01882-634272; bar meals £6-10, restaurant mains £10-14; ⊙lunch & dinner) This old coaching inn is a snug spot for a decent feed from a menu featuring seafood. The bar is open

all day for a leisurely pint in the beer garden overlooking Loch Tummel. The inn is about 3 miles from Queen's View.

ℹ️ Getting There & Away

Broons Buses (☑️01882-632331) Operates a service between Kinloch Rannoch and Pitlochry (50 minutes, up to five a day Monday to Saturday) via Queen's View and Loch Tummel Inn.

Royal Mail Postbus (☑️08457 740 740; www .postbus.royalmail.com) The Pitlochry–Rannoch Station postbus has a once-daily service (Monday to Saturday) via Kinloch Rannoch and both sides of the loch.

ScotRail (www.scotrail.co.uk) Runs two to four trains daily from Rannoch station north to Fort William (£8.40, one hour) and Mallaig, and south to Glasgow (£19.30, 2¾ hours).

Rannoch Moor

Beyond Rannoch Train Station, civilisation fades away and Rannoch Moor begins. This is the largest area of moorland in Britain, stretching west for eight barren, bleak and uninhabited miles to the A82 Glasgow–Fort William road. A triangular plateau of blanket bog occupying more than 50 sq miles, the moor is ringed by high mountains and puddled with countless lochs, ponds and peat hags. Water covers 10% of the moor, and it has been canoed across, swum across, and even skated across in winter.

The moor owes its present form – a huge, shallow basin – to the last Ice Age when it lay beneath a vast ice cap, perhaps 600m thick, from which glaciers flowed out radially, scouring the deep glacial valleys of Glen Coe, Strathtummel and Glen Orchy. Since the ice melted about 10,000 years ago, a combination of poorly drained granite bedrock, acid soils and high rainfall has resulted in the creation of blanket bog.

No roads cross the moor, but in the 1890s Victorian engineers drove the **West Highland Railway** across this huge expanse of bog. The peat is more than 10m deep in many places, and where the navvies could not find bedrock, the railway line was 'floated' over the boggier stretches on a 'mattress' composed of brushwood, turf and ashes. To this day, trains observe a speed limit of 30mph on the moor so as not to damage the track bed.

Despite the appearance of desolation, the moor is rich in wildlife, with curlew, golden plover and snipe darting among the tussocks; black-throated diver, goosander and merganser on the lochs; and – if you're lucky – osprey and golden eagle overhead. Herds of red deer forage alongside the railway, and otters patrol the loch shores. And keep an eye out for the sundew, a tiny, insect-eating plant with sticky-fingered leaves.

A couple of excellent (and challenging) **walks** start from Rannoch Train Station – north to Corrour Station (11 miles, four to five hours) from where you can return by train; and west along the northern edge of the moor to the Kings House Hotel (p112) at the eastern end of Glen Coe, (11 miles, four hours).

Corrour Station

Corrour Station (the next stop northbound after Rannoch Station) is the highest (408m) and most remote railway station in the UK, and the only mainline station with no road access (the nearest public road is 10 miles away). It was built in 1894 for Sir John Stirling Maxwell, an investor in the West Highland Railway. He allowed the line to cross his land on condition that a station was built to serve his shooting lodge at Corrour Estate.

Today, the station sports a modern Scandinavian-style building that houses a hikers' hostel and restaurant, and is the starting point for several wilderness walks and Munro ascents. The classic route is the **circuit of Loch Ossian** to the east (9 miles, around five hours), via the tiny Loch Ossian youth hostel (formerly the waiting room for guests travelling by steam yacht from Corrour Station to the shooting lodge at the far end of the loch).

Corrour Estate (www.corrour.co.uk) is now owned by an heir to the Rausing TetraPak empire, and the old shooting lodge - which burned down in 1942 - has been replaced by a controversial 21st-century 'castle' designed by architect Moshe Safdie (available to rent for upwards of £25,000 a week!). You can get a peek at this rather incongruous country retreat – regularly hired for parties by Russian billionaires – on the walk around the loch.

🛏️ Sleeping & Eating

Corrour Station House SYHA HOSTEL **££** (☑️01397-732236; www.syha.org.uk; per person £30; ☺daily Apr-Oct, Wed-Sun nights only Dec, Feb & Mar, closed Nov & Jan) This wonderfully remote lodging, set on the West Highland railway line 10 miles from the nearest public road, is more like an upmarket B&B than a hostel. There are only three rooms – a double, a triple and a quad – and no self-catering facilities – you eat at the hostel's licensed cafe (open 8.30am to 8pm, cooked breakfast £1.95).

📍**Loch Ossian SYHA** HOSTEL £
(☎01397-732207; www.syha.org.uk; dm £18; ⊙mid-Apr–mid-Oct) If Corrour Station House is too posh for your tastes, this more traditional hikers' hostel (opened in 1931) is just one mile to the east, in a lovely setting on the shore of Loch Ossian. Recently refurbished in pine panelling, the hostel is eco-friendly, making use of wind and solar power, composting toilets and recycled grey water.

PERTH TO BLAIR CASTLE

There are a number of major sights strung along the busy but scenic A9, the main route north to the Cairngorms and Inverness.

Dunkeld & Birnam
POP 1000
Ever been to a feel-good town? Well, Dunkeld and Birnam, with their enviable location nestled in the heart of Perthshire's big-tree country, await. The River Tay runs like a storybook river between the two. As well as Dunkeld's lovely cathedral, there's much walking to be done in this area of magnificent forested hills. These same walks inspired Beatrix Potter to create her children's tales.

⊙ Sights & Activities

Dunkeld Cathedral HISTORIC BUILDING
(HS; www.historic-scotland.gov.uk; High St; admission free; ⊙9.30am-6.30pm Mon-Sat & 2-6.30pm Sun Apr-Sep, 9.30am-4pm Mon-Sat & 2-4pm Sun Oct-Mar) Situated between open grassland and the River Tay on one side and rolling hills on the other, Dunkeld Cathedral is one of the most beautifully sited cathedrals in Scotland. It partly dates from the 14th century; the cathedral was damaged during the Reformation and burnt in the battle of Dunkeld (Jacobites vs government) in 1689.

The **Wolf of Badenoch** is buried – undeservedly – here in a fine medieval tomb behind the wooden screen in the church. Half the cathedral is still in use as a church; the rest is in ruins, and you can explore it all. Don't miss it on a sunny day, as there are few lovelier places to be.

Birnam VILLAGE
Across the bridge is Birnam, made famous by *Macbeth*. There's not much left of Birnam Wood, but there is a small, leafy **Beatrix Potter Park** (the children's author, who wrote the evergreen story of *Peter Rabbit*, spent childhood holidays in the area). Next to the park, in the **Birnam Arts Centre** (Station Rd; admission £1; ⊙10am-4.30pm), is a small exhibition on Potter and her characters.

Loch of the Lowes Wildlife Centre WILDLIFE
(☎01350-727337; www.swt.org.uk; adult/child £4/50p; ⊙10am-5pm Apr-Sep) Loch of the Lowes Wildlife Centre, 2 miles east of Dunkeld off the A923, has wildlife displays mostly devoted to the majestic osprey. There's also an excellent birdwatching hide (with binoculars provided), where you can see the birds nesting during the breeding season.

Going Pottie HANDICRAFTS
(www.goingpottie.com; Cathedral St; activities from £5; ⊙10am-5pm Mon-Sat, 11am-4pm Sun) If you're looking to entertain the kids for a few hours, drop by Going Pottie where kids can get a paintbrush in their hand and create colourful ceramics – and mayhem.

🛏 Sleeping & Eating

Birnam Hotel HOTEL ££
(☎01350-728030; www.birnamhotel.com; Perth Rd, Birnam; s/d/f £79/98/135; 🅿🛜) This grand-looking place with crow-stepped gables has tastefully fitted rooms – superiors (double £130) are substantially larger than the standards. Service is very welcoming. There's a fairly formal restaurant, as well as a livelier pub alongside serving creative bar meals.

TOP
CHOICE Taybank PUB GRUB £
(☎01350-727340; www.thetaybank.com; Tay Tce, Dunkeld; bar mains £5-8) Top choice for a sun-kissed pub lunch by the river is the Taybank, a regular meeting place and performance space for musicians of all creeds and a wonderfully open and welcoming bar. The menu includes a tasty selection of traditional and offbeat stews.

Of all the hardman figures of medieval Scotland, few inspired as much terror as Alexander Stewart, Earl of Buchan (1343–1405), illegitimate son of the king and better known as the Wolf of Badenoch. A cruel landowner with a number of castles in the Strathspey region, he was not a man to get on the wrong side of, as the Bishop of Moray found out in 1390.

When the earl ditched his wife in favour of his mistress, the bishop excommunicated him. The monk that bore the message of excommunication was thrown headfirst into a well, and the infuriated Wolf, accompanied by a band of 'wild wicked Highland men', embarked on an orgy of destruction, burning first Forres, then Elgin, to the ground, destroying the cathedral and nearby Pluscarden Abbey in the process.

Amazingly, Stewart still managed to end up being buried in Dunkeld cathedral. Legend says his death occurred on a dark, stormy night. The devil came calling on a black horse and challenged him to a game of chess. The Wolf was checkmated, and the devil took his life (and soul) as his prize.

ℹ Information

Dunkeld tourist office (☏01350-727688; dunkeld@visitscotland.com; The Cross; ⊙daily Apr-Oct, Fri-Sun Nov-Mar) Has information on local trails and paths.

ℹ Getting There & Away

Dunkeld is 15 miles north of Perth (p123).

BUS Citylink (www.citylink.co.uk) Buses between Glasgow/Edinburgh and Inverness stop at Birnam House Hotel. Birnam to Perth (£7.90) or Pitlochry (£7.60) takes 20 minutes.

Stagecoach (www.stagecoachbus.com) Bus runs between Blairgowrie (30 minutes) and Aberfeldy (40 minutes), via Dunkeld, twice daily Monday to Friday only.

TRAIN Trains run to Edinburgh (£12.90, 1½ hours, approximately hourly Monday to Saturday, four on Sunday), Glasgow (£12.90, 1½ hours, roughly hourly Monday to Saturday, four on Sunday) and Inverness (£21.50, two hours, eight daily Monday to Saturday, five on Sunday).

Pitlochry

POP 2570

Pitlochry, with its air already smelling of the Highlands, is a popular stop on the way north and a convenient base for exploring northern Central Scotland. On a quiet spring evening it's a pretty place, with salmon jumping in the Tummel and good things brewing at the Moulin Hotel. In summer the main street can be a conga-line of tour groups, but get away from that and it'll still charm you.

◉ Sights

One of Pitlochry's attractions is its beautiful riverside; the River Tummel is dammed here,

and you can watch salmon swimming (not jumping) up a **fish ladder** to the loch above.

Bell's Blair Athol Distillery   DISTILLERY (☏01796-482003; www.discovering-distilleries.com; Perth Rd; tour £5; ⊙Mon-Fri low season, plus Sat Apr-Oct, plus Sun Jun-Oct) One of two distilleries around Pitlochry, this one is at the southern end of town. Tours focus on whisky making and the blending of this well-known drop. The tour price is discountable off a bottle purchase.

Edradour Distillery   DISTILLERY (☏01796-472095; www.edradour.co.uk; free; ⊙daily) This is proudly Scotland's smallest distillery and a great one to visit: you can see the whole process, easily explained, in one room. It's 2.5 miles east of Pitlochry along the Moulin road, and it's a pleasant walk.

Explorers Garden   GARDEN (☏01796-484600; www.explorersgarden.com; Foss Rd; adult/child £3/1; ⊙10am-5pm Apr-Oct) At the Pitlochry Festival Theatre, this excellent garden commemorates 300 years of plant collecting and those who hunted down 'new' species. The whole collection is based on plants brought back to Scotland by Scottish explorers.

Heathergems   CRAFTS (☏01796-474391; www.heathergems.com; 22 Atholl Rd; ⊙9am-5.30pm May-Sep, to 5pm Mon-Sat Oct-Apr) Just behind the tourist office, Heathergems is a factory outlet of a most unusual and beautiful form of Scottish jewellery. The jewellery is made from natural heather stems, which are dyed and pressed to create colourful, original pieces. You can actually view the jewellery being made through windows into the workshop. Definitely worth a browse.

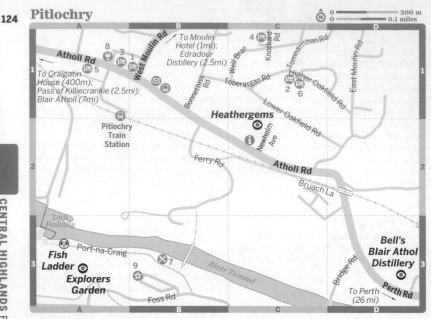

Pitlochry

⊙ Top Sights

🛏 Sleeping

⊗ Eating

⊖ Drinking

⊕ Entertainment

✯✯ Festivals & Events

Pitlochry Festival Theatre　　　THEATRE
(☎01796-484626; www.pitlochry.org.uk; Foss Rd; tickets £14-25) This well-known theatre stages a different mainstream play for six nights out of seven during its season from May to mid-October.

Étape　　　CYCLING EVENT
(www.etapecaledonia.co.uk) Étape, an 81-mile charity cycling event, brings competitors of all standards onto the beautiful highland roads around Pitlochry in mid-May. It's become a big deal; you'll have to prebook accommodation.

Enchanted Forest　　　LIGHT SHOW
(www.enchantedforest.org.uk; adult £11-14, child £6) This spectacular sound-and-light show in a forest near Pitlochry in the last week of October and first week of November is a major family hit.

🛏 Sleeping

Craigatin House　　　B&B ££
(☎01796-472478; www.craigatinhouse.co.uk; 165 Atholl Rd; d standard/deluxe £78/88; P⊙) Several times more tasteful than the average Pitlochry lodging, this noble house and garden is set back from the main road at the western end of town. Chic contemporary fabrics covering expansive beds offer a standard of comfort above and beyond the reasonable price; the rooms in the converted stable block are particularly inviting.

Breakfast choices include whisky-laced porridge, smoked-fish omelettes, and apple pancakes.

Pitlochry Backpackers Hotel
HOSTEL £
(☎01796-470044; www.scotlands-top-hostels.com; 134 Atholl Rd; dm/tw/d £15/38/40; P@🛜) Friendly, laid-back and very comfortable, this is a cracking hostel smack-bang in the middle of town, with three- to eight-bed dorms that are in mint condition. There are also good-value en suite twins and doubles, with beds, not bunks. Cheap breakfast and a pool table add to the convivial party atmosphere. No extra charge for linen.

Ashleigh
B&B £
(☎01796-470316; nancy.gray@btinternet.com; 120 Atholl Rd; s/d £25/50; P) Genuine welcomes don't come much better than Nancy's, and her place on the main street makes a top Pitlochry pitstop. Three comfortable rooms share an excellent bathroom, and there's an open kitchen stocked with goodies where you make your own breakfast in the morning. A home-away-from-home and standout budget choice.

Knockendarroch House
HOTEL ££
(☎01796-473473; www.knockendarroch.co.uk; Higher Oakfield; s/d dinner, bed & breakfast £120/170; P🛜) Top of the town and boasting the best views, this genteel, well-run hotel has a range of luxurious rooms with huge windows that take advantage of the Highland light. The standard rooms have better views than the larger, slightly pricier superior ones. A couple of rooms have great little balconies, perfect for a sundowner. Meals are highly commended here too.

Strathgarry
HOTEL ££
(☎01796-472469; www.strathgarryhotel.co.uk; 113 Atholl Rd; s/d £40/60, deluxe s/d £60/80; 🛜) With a top main-street location, Strathgarry is a hotel-bar-cafe-restaurant that's all done pretty well. En suite rooms are very snug and have some luxurious touches – we lost a researcher who sunk into one of the beds and was never seen again.

Tir Aluinn
B&B ££
(☎01796-473811; www.tiraluinn.co.uk; 10 Higher Oakfield Rd; s/d £32/64; P) Tucked away above the main street, this is a little gem of a place, with bright rooms with easy-on-the-eye furniture, and an excellent personal welcome.

Pitlochry SYHA
HOSTEL £
(☎01796-472308; www.syha.org.uk; Knockard Rd; dm £17.25; ⊙Feb-Oct; P@🛜) Great location overlooking the town centre. Popular with families and walkers.

🍴 Eating & Drinking

TOP CHOICE Moulin Hotel
SCOTTISH ££
(☎01796-472196; www.moulinhotel.co.uk; bar mains £7-11; ⊙lunch & dinner) A mile away but a world apart, this atmospheric hotel was trading centuries before the tartan tack came to Pitlochry. With its romantic low ceilings, ageing wood and booth seating, the inn is a wonderfully atmospheric spot for a house-brewed ale or a portion of Highland comfort food: try the filling haggis or venison stew.

A more formal restaurant (mains £13 to £16) serves equally delicious fare, and the hotel has a variety of rooms (single/double £60/75) as well as a self-catering annexe. The best way to get here from Pitlochry is walking: it's a pretty uphill stroll through green fields, and an easy roll down the slope afterwards.

Port-na-Craig Inn
PUB GRUB ££
(☎01796-472777; www.portnacraig.com; Port Na Craig; mains £13-17; ⊙lunch & dinner) Right on the river, this top little spot sits in what was once a separate hamlet. Delicious main meals are prepared with confidence and panache – scrumptious scallops or lamb steak bursting with flavour, but also simpler sandwiches, kids' meals and light lunches. Or you could just sit out by the river with a pint and watch the anglers.

McKay's Hotel
PUB
(☎01796 473885; www.mckayshotel.co.uk; 138 Atholl Rd; mains £9; ⊙lunch & dinner) This is the place to go to meet locals and have a big night out. Live music at weekends, weekly karaoke and DJs make this Pitlochry's most popular place. The action moves from the spacious front bar (which serves food) to the boisterous dancefloor out the back.

ℹ Information
Computer Services Centre (☎01796-473711; 67 Atholl Rd; per hr £3; ⊙9.30am-5.30pm Mon-Fri, to 12.30pm Sat; @) Internet access.
Pitlochry tourist office (☎01796-472215; pitlochry@visitscotland.com; 22 Atholl Rd; ⊙8.30am-7pm Mon-Sat & 9.30am-5.30pm Sun

Easter-Oct, 10am-4pm Mon-Sat Nov-Mar; @)
Good information on local walks.

ℹ Getting There & Away

BUS **Citylink** (www.citylink.co.uk) Services run roughly hourly to Inverness (£15.10, two hours), Perth (£9.40, 40 minutes), Edinburgh (£14.40, two hours) and Glasgow (£14.40, 2¼ hours).
Megabus (✆0871 266 3333; www.megabus .com) Offers discounted fares on the same routes as Citylink.
Stagecoach (www.stagecoachbus.com) Runs services to Aberfeldy (30 minutes, hourly Monday to Saturday, three Sunday), Dunkeld (25 minutes, up to 10 daily Monday to Saturday) and Perth (one hour, up to 10 daily Monday to Saturday).
TRAIN Pitlochry is on the main railway from Perth (£11, 30 minutes, nine daily Monday to Saturday, five on Sunday) to Inverness.

ℹ Getting Around

BICYCLE **Escape Route** (✆01796-473859; www.escape-route.biz; 3 Atholl Rd; bike hire per half-/full day from £10/18; ☉daily) Worth booking ahead at weekends.

TAXI **Broons** (✆01882-632331) A taxi to Blair Castle will cost you £15.

Pass of Killiecrankie

The **Killiecrankie Visitor Centre** (NTS; ✆01796-473233; www.nts.org.uk; admission free, parking £2; ☉10am-5.30pm Apr-Oct), set in a beautiful, rugged gorge 3.5 miles north of Pitlochry, has great interactive displays on the Jacobite rebellion. The **Battle of Killiecrankie**, fought here in 1689, was a famous victory for the Jacobites. There are also exhibits on local flora and fauna, with plenty to touch, pull and open – great for kids. There are some stunning walks into the wooded gorge, too; keep an eye out for red squirrels.

Almost halfway between Pitlochry and Blair Atholl, **Killiecrankie House Hotel** (✆01796-473220; www.killiecrankiehotel.co.uk; d standard/superior dinner, bed and breakfast £230/250; P☎) is brilliant for treating that someone special. Rates for bed-and-breakfast are also available.

Local buses run between Pitlochry and Blair Atholl via Killiecrankie (15 minutes, three to seven daily).

Blair Castle & Blair Atholl

One of the most popular tourist attractions in Scotland, magnificent **Blair Castle** (✆01796-481207; www.blair-castle.co.uk; adult/child/family £8.75/5.25/24; ☉9.30am-5.30pm Apr-Oct) – and the 108 square miles it sits on – is the seat of the Duke of Atholl, head of the Murray clan. It's an impressive white building set beneath forested slopes above the River Garry.

The original tower was built in 1269, but the castle has undergone significant remodelling since. Thirty rooms are open to the public and they present a wonderful picture of upper-class Highland life from the 16th century on. The dining room is sumptuous – check out the 9-pint wine glasses – and the ballroom is a vaulted chamber that's a virtual stag cemetery.

The current duke visits the castle every May to review the Atholl Highlanders, Britain's only private army.

For a great cycle, walk or drive, take the stunning road to **Glenfender** from Blair Atholl village. It's about 3 miles on a long, winding uphill track to a farmhouse; the views of snowcapped peaks along the way are spectacular.

🛏 Sleeping & Eating

Atholl Arms Hotel   HOTEL **££**
(✆01796-481205; www.athollarms.co.uk; s/d from £65/80; P☎) The Gothic Atholl Arms Hotel, a pub near the train station, is convenient for the castle and sometimes does special deals. The fussy rooms are of a high standard; book ahead on weekends. The **Bothy Bar** here is the sibling pub of the Moulin Hotel in Pitlochry, snug with booth seating, low-slung roof, bucketloads of character and an enormous fireplace. There's no better place to be when the rain is lashing outside

ℹ Getting There & Away

Blair Atholl is 6 miles northwest of Pitlochry, and the castle a further mile beyond it. Local buses run a service between Pitlochry and Blair Atholl (15 minutes, three to seven daily). Four buses a day (Monday to Saturday) go directly to the castle. There's a train station in the village, but not all trains stop here.

THE CAIRNGORMS

The **Cairngorms National Park** (www.cairn gorms.co.uk) encompasses the highest landmass in Britain – a broad mountain plateau, riven only by the deep valleys of the Lairig Ghru and Loch Avon, with an average altitude of over 1000m and including five of the six highest summits in the UK. This wild mountain landscape of granite and heather has a sub-Arctic climate and supports rare alpine tundra vegetation and high-altitude bird species, such as snow bunting, ptarmigan and dotterel.

The harsh mountain environment gives way lower down to scenic glens softened by beautiful open forests of native Caledonian pine, home to rare animals and birds such as the pine marten, wildcat, red squirrel, osprey, capercaillie and crossbill.

This is prime hill-walking territory, but even couch potatoes can enjoy a taste of the high life by taking the Cairngorm Mountain Railway (p130) up to the edge of the Cairngorm plateau.

Aviemore

POP 2400

Aviemore is the gateway to the Cairngorms, the region's main centre for transport, accommodation, restaurants and shopping. It's not the prettiest town in Scotland by a long stretch – the main attractions are in the surrounding area – but when bad weather puts the hills off limits, Aviemore fills up with hikers, cyclists and climbers (plus skiers and snowboarders in winter) cruising the outdoor-equipment shops or recounting their latest adventures in the cafes and bars. Add in tourists and locals and the eclectic mix makes for a lively little town.

The Cairngorm skiing area and mountain railway lie 9 miles east of Aviemore along the B970 (Ski Rd) and its continuation through Coylumbridge and Glenmore.

◎ Sights

Aviemore is on a loop off the A9 Perth–Inverness road; almost everything of note is to be found along the main drag, Grampian Rd.

Strathspey Steam Railway   HERITAGE RAILWAY
(☏01479-810725; www.strathspeyrailway.co.uk; Station Sq) Strathspey Steam Railway runs steam trains on a section of restored line

Aviemore

◉ Top Sights
Aviemore Highland Resort	A2
Strathspey Steam Railway	B3

🛏 Sleeping
1	Ardlogie Guest House	B3
2	Cairngorm Hotel	B3
3	Kinapol Guest House	B2

✕ Eating
4	Café Mambo	B2
5	Mountain Cafe	B1
6	Ski-ing Doo	B1

🍸 Drinking
7	Coffee Corner	B2

between Aviemore and Broomhill, 10 miles to the northeast, via Boat of Garten. There are four or five trains daily from June to September, and a more limited service in April, May, October and December; a return ticket from Aviemore to Broomhill is £9.50/4.75 per adult/child.

An extension to Grantown-on-Spey is planned; in the meantime, you can continue from Broomhill to Grantown-on-Spey by bus.

Rothiemurchus Estate FOREST
(www.rothiemurchus.net) The Rothiemurchus Estate, which extends from the River Spey at Aviemore to the Cairngorm summit plateau, is famous for having Scotland's largest remnant of the ancient **Caledonian forest**, the ancient forest of Scots pine that once covered most of the country. The forest is home to a large population of red squirrels, and is one of the last bastions of the Scottish wildcat.

The **Rothiemurchus Estate visitor centre** (admission free; ⊙9am-5.30pm), a mile southeast of Aviemore along the B970, sells an Explorer Map detailing more than 50 miles of **footpaths** and **cycling trails**, including the wheelchair-accessible 4-mile trail around **Loch an Eilein**, with its ruined castle and peaceful pine woods.

Craigellachie Nature Reserve NATURE RESERVE
(www.snh.org.uk/nnr-scotland; Grampian Rd) A trail leads west from Aviemore Youth Hostel and passes under the A9 into the Craigellachie Nature Reserve, a great place for short hikes across steep hillsides covered in natural birch forest. Look out for wildlife, including the peregrine falcons that nest on the crags from April to July. If you're very lucky, you may even spot a capercaillie.

Aviemore Highland Resort LEISURE COMPLEX
(☎0845 223 6217; www.aviemorehighlandresort.com) This complex of hotels, chalets and restaurants to the west of Grampian Rd includes a **swimming pool** (adult/child £10/5; ⊙8am-8pm), gym, spa, videogame arcade and a huge, shiny shopping mall. The swimming pool and other leisure facilities are open to nonresidents.

Activities

Bothy Bikes MOUNTAIN BIKING
(www.bothybikes.co.uk; ⊙9am-5.30pm) Located just outside Aviemore on the way to Cairngorm, this place rents out mountain bikes for £15/20 a half-/full day. Staff can also advise on routes and trails; a good choice for beginners is the **Old Logging Way**, which runs from the hire centre to Glenmore, where you can make a circuit of Loch Morlich before returning.

For experienced bikers, the whole of the Cairngorms is your playground.

Rothiemurchus Fishery FISHING
(☎01479-810703; www.rothiemurchus.net; Rothiemurchus Estate) Cast for rainbow trout at this loch at the southern end of the village; buy permits (from £10 to £30 per day, plus £3.50 for tackle hire) at the Fish Farm Shop. If you're a fly-fishing virgin, there's a beginner's package, including tackle hire, one hour's instruction and one hour's fishing, for £35.

For experienced anglers, there's also salmon and sea-trout fishing on the River Spey – a day permit costs around £20; numbers are limited, so it's best to book in advance.

Cairngorm Sled-Dog Centre DOG SLEDDING
(☎07767-270526; www.sled-dogs.co.uk; Ski Rd) This outfit will take you on a two- to three-hour sled tour of local forest trails in the wake of a team of huskies (adult/child £60/40). The sleds have wheels, so snow's not necessary. There are also one-hour guided tours of the kennels (adult/child £8/4). The centre is 3 miles east of Aviemore, signposted off the road to Loch Morlich.

Alvie & Dalraddy Estate QUAD BIKING
(☎01479-810330; www.alvie-estate.co.uk; Dalraddy Holiday Park; per person £39) Join a cross-country quad-bike trek at this estate, 3 miles south of Aviemore on the B9152 (call first).

Sleeping

Old Minister's House B&B ££
(☎01479-812181; www.theoldministershouse.co.uk; s/d £65/96; P🐕) This former manse dates from 1906 and has four rooms with a homey, country-farmhouse feel. It's in a lovely setting amid Scots pines on the banks of the River Druie, just 0.75 miles southeast of Aviemore.

Ardlogie Guest House B&B ££
(☎01479-810747; www.ardlogie.co.uk; Dalfaber Rd; s/d from £40/60; P🐕) Handy for the train station, the five-room Ardlogie has great views over the River Spey towards the Cairngorms. There's a boules pitch in the garden, and guests get free use of the local country club's pool, spa and sauna.

Aviemore Bunkhouse HOSTEL £
(☎01479-811181; www.aviemore-bunkhouse.com; Dalfaber Rd; dm/tw/f £15/50/60; P@🐕) This independent hostel, next door to the Old Bridge Inn, provides accommodation in bright, modern six- or eight-bed dorms, each with private bathroom, and one twin/family room. There's a drying room, secure bike storage and wheelchair-accessible dorms. From the train station, cross the pedestrian bridge over the tracks, turn right and walk south on Dalfaber Rd.

Ravenscraig Guest House
B&B ££

(☎01479-810278; www.aviemoreonline.com; Grampian Rd, r per person £30-40; P📶) Ravenscraig is a large, flower-bedecked Victorian villa which offers six spacious en-suite rooms, plus another six rooms in a modern annexe at the back (one wheelchair accessible). It serves traditional and veggie breakfasts in an attractive conservatory dining room.

Cairngorm Hotel
HOTEL ££

(☎01479-810233; www.cairngorm.com; Grampian Rd; s/d £55/88; P) Better known as 'the Cairn', this long-established hotel is set in the fine old granite building with the pointy turret opposite the train station. It's a welcoming place with comfortable rooms and a determinedly Scottish atmosphere, all tartan carpets and stags' antlers. There's live music on weekends, so it can get a bit noisy – not for early-to-bedders.

Hilton Coylumbridge
HOTEL ££

(☎01479-810661; www.coylumbridge.hilton.com; d from £98; P📶🐕🎿🏊) This modern, low-rise Hilton, set amid the pine woods just outside Aviemore, is a wonderfully child-friendly hotel, with bedrooms for up to two adults and two children, indoor and outdoor play areas, a crèche and a baby-sitting service. The hotel is 1.5 miles east of Aviemore, on the road to Loch Morlich.

Kinapol Guest House
B&B £

(☎01479-810513; Dalfaber Rd; s/d from £30/40; P📶) The Kinapol is a modern bungalow offering basic but comfortable B&B accommodation, across the tracks from the train station. All three rooms have shared bathrooms.

Aviemore SYHA
HOSTEL £

(☎01479-810345; www.syha.org.uk; 25 Grampian Rd; dm £17; P@📶) Upmarket hostelling in a spacious, well-equipped building, five minutes' walk south of the village centre. There are four- and six-bed rooms, and the doors stay open until 2am.

Rothiemurchus Camp &
Caravan Park
CAMPGROUND £

(☎014/9-812800; www.rothiemurchus.net; sites per person £7.50-8.50) The nearest camping ground to Aviemore is this year-round park set among Scots pines at Coylumbridge, 1.5 miles along the B970.

✗ Eating & Drinking

Old Bridge Inn
PUB

(☎01479-811137; www.oldbridgeinn.co.uk; 23 Dalfaber Rd; 📶) The Old Bridge has a snug bar, complete with roaring log fire in winter, and a cheerful, chalet-style **restaurant** (www.oldbridgeinn.co.uk; 23 Dalfaber Rd; mains £10-16; ⊗noon-3pm & 6-9pm Sun-Thu, to 10pm Fri & Sat) at the back serving quality Scottish cuisine.

Mountain Cafe
CAFE £

(www.mountaincafe-aviemore.co.uk; 111 Grampian Rd; mains £4-9; ⊗8.30am-5pm Tue-Thu, to 5.30pm Fri-Mon; 🍴) The Mountain Cafe offers fresh, healthy breakfasts of muesli, porridge and fresh fruit (till 11.30am), hearty lunches of seafood chowder, salads or burgers, and homebaked breads, cakes and biscuits. Vegan, coeliac and nut-allergic diets catered for.

Ski-ing Doo
INTERNATIONAL ££

(☎01479-810392; 9 Grampian Rd; mains £7-11, steaks £14-16; ⊗noon-2.30pm & 5-11pm; 🍴) A long-standing Aviemore institution, the child-friendly Ski-ing Doo (it's a pun...oh, ask the waiter!) is a favourite with family skiers and hikers. An informal place offering a range of hearty, homemade burgers, chilli dishes and juicy steaks; the Doo Below cafe bar is open all day from noon.

Café Mambo
TEX MEX £

(☎01479-811670; The Mall, Grampian Rd; mains £5-10; ⊗food noon-8.30pm Mon-Thu, noon-7.30pm Fri & Sat, 12.30-8.30pm Sun; 📶) This is a popular chill-out cafe in the afternoon, serving burgers, steaks and Tex-Mex grub. It turns into a clubbing and live band venue come evening.

Coffee Corner
CAFE £

(☎01479-810564; 85 Grampian Rd; snacks £3-5; ⊗9am-5pm) This cosy cafe is a good place to relax with newspapers and a steaming mug of coffee on a rainy day. It does hearty breakfasts, scones and ice-cream sundaes, too.

❶ Information

There are ATMs outside the Tesco supermarket, and currency exchange at the post office and the tourist office, all located on Grampian Rd.

Old Bridge Inn (23 Dalfaber Rd; per 30min £1; ⊗11am-11pm Sun-Thu, to midnight Fri & Sat; @) Has internet access.

Aviemore tourist office (☎01479-810363; www.visitaviemore.com; The Mall, Grampian Rd; ⊗9am-6pm Mon-Sat, 9.30am-5pm Sun Jul & Aug, 9am-5pm Mon-Sat, 10am-4pm Sun Easter-Jun, Sep & Oct) Hours are limited from October to Easter.

❶ Getting There & Away

BUS Buses stop on Grampian Rd opposite the train station; buy tickets at the tourist office.

Scottish Citylink services include Edinburgh (£23, 3¾ hours), Glasgow (£23, 3¾ hours), Inverness (£9, 45 minutes) and Perth (£18, 2¼ hours).

Bus 33 travels to Grantown-on-Spey (35 minutes, five daily weekdays, two Saturday) via Carrbridge (15 minutes); and Bus 34 travels to Grantown-on-Spey & Cairngorm car park (hourly, less frequent between Aviemore and Grantown-on-Spey on weekends).

TRAIN The train station is towards the southern end of town.

There are direct train services to Glasgow/Edinburgh (£40, three hours, three daily) and Inverness (£10, 40 minutes, nine daily).

❶ Getting Around

BIKE Several places in Aviemore, Rothiemur-chus Estate and Glenmore have mountain bikes for hire.

Bothy Bikes (☎01479-810111; www.bothybikes .co.uk; Ski Rd; ◷9am-5.30pm) Charges £20 a day for a quality bike with front suspension and disc brakes.

BUS Bus 34 links Aviemore to Cairngorm car park (20 to 30 minutes, hourly, no Sunday ser-vice late October to late December) via Coylum-bridge and Glenmore. A Strathspey Dayrider/Megarider ticket (£6/20) gives one/seven days unlimited bus travel from Aviemore as far as Cairngorm, Carrbridge and Kingussie (buy from the bus driver).

Cairngorm Mountain

Aviemore's most popular attraction is the **Cairngorm Mountain Railway** (☎01479-861261; www.cairngormmountain.co.uk; adult/child return £9.75/6.15; ◷10am-5pm May-Nov, 9am-4.30pm Dec-Apr), a funicular railway that whisks you to the Cairngorm summit pla-teau in eight minutes. At the top is an exhi-bition, a shop (of course) and a restaurant. Unfortunately, for environmental reasons, you're not allowed out of the top station in summer – you must return to the car park on the train.

However, a trial project launched in 2010 offers 90-minute guided walks to the sum-mit (adult/child £13/10) four times a day from mid-July to October. Check the website for details. The bottom station is at the Coire Cas car park at the end of Ski Rd.

Aspen or Val d'Isere it ain't, but with 19 runs and 23 miles of piste **Cairngorm** (www .cairngormmountain.co.uk) is Scotland's biggest ski area. A ski pass for one day is £30/18 for adults/under 16s. Ski or snowboard hire is around £20/14.50 per adult/child per day; there are lots of hire outlets at Coire Cas, Glenmore and Aviemore.

When the snow is at its best and the sun is shining you can close your eyes and imagine you're in the Alps; sadly, low cloud, high winds and horizontal sleet are more common. The season usually runs from December until the snow melts, which may be as late as the end of April, but snow-fall here is unpredictable – in some years the slopes can be open in November, but closed for lack of snow in February. Dur-ing the season the tourist office displays snow conditions and avalanche warnings. You can check the latest snow conditions on the Ski Hotline.

MOUNTAIN WALKS IN THE CAIRNGORMS

The Cairngorm plateau is a sub-Arctic environment where navigation is difficult and weather conditions can be severe, even in midsummer. Hikers must have proper hill-walking equipment, and know how to use a map and compass. In winter it is a place for experienced mountaineers only.

The climb from the car park at the Coire Cas ski area to the summit of **Cairn Gorm** (1245m) takes about two hours (one way). From there, you can continue south across the high-level plateau to Ben Macdui (1309m), Britain's second-highest peak. This takes eight to 10 hours return from the car park and is a serious undertaking; for experienced and well-equipped walkers only.

The **Lairig Ghru trail**, which can take eight to 10 hours, is a demanding 24-mile walk from Aviemore through the Lairig Ghru pass (840m) to Braemar. An alternative to doing the full route is to make the six-hour return hike up to the summit of the pass and back to Aviemore. The path starts from Ski Rd, a mile east of Coylumbridge, and involves some very rough going.

The hill paths and forest trails of Cairngorm National Park provide a playground for mountain bikers, with something for all levels of experience from beginner to expert. Recommended routes include the easy trails around **Loch Morlich**, a longer and more challenging circuit from **Loch an Eilein** to Glen Feshie, and the experts-only downhill trails at Laggan Wolftrax (p133). For more routes, see www.visitcairngorms.com/onabike.

If you want to learn the basics, or improve your intermediate skills, you can take a half- or full-day course at **Bike School Scotland** (☎01479-810676; www.bikeschoolscotland .co.uk; half-/one-day course from £50/80; ☉9am-5pm) or Glenmore Lodge (p131).

Loch Morlich

Six miles east of Aviemore, Loch Morlich is surrounded by some 8 sq miles of pine and spruce forest that make up the **Glenmore Forest Park**. Its attractions include a sandy beach (at the east end).

◎ Sights & Activities

Cairngorm Reindeer Centre   WILDLIFE PARK
(www.cairngormreindeer.co.uk; adult/child £9.50/5) The warden here will take you on a tour to see and feed Britain's only herd of reindeer, who are very tame and will even eat out of your hand. Walks take place at 11am, plus another at 2.30pm from May to September, and 3.30pm Monday to Friday in July and August.

Loch Morlich Watersports Centre   WATERSPORTS
(www.lochmorlich.com; ☉9am-5pm May-Oct) This popular outfit rents out Canadian canoes (£18 an hour), kayaks (£8.50), windsurfers (£16.50), sailing dinghies (£20) and rowing boats (£18).

Glenmore Lodge   ADVENTURE SPORTS
(www.glenmorelodge.org.uk) One of Britain's leading adventure sports training centres, offering courses in hill walking, rock climbing, ice climbing, canoeing, mountain biking and mountaineering. The centre's comfortable **B&B accommodation** (per person £25-33) is available to all, even if you're not taking a course, as is the indoor-climbing wall, gym and sauna.

🛏 Sleeping

Cairngorm Lodge SYHA   HOSTEL £
(☎01479-861238; dm £17; ☉closed Nov & Dec; @) Set in a former shooting lodge that enjoys a great location at the east end of Loch Morlich; prebooking is essential.

Glenmore Caravan & Camping Site   CAMPGROUND £
(☎01479-861271; www.forestholidays.co.uk; tents & campervans £19-20; ☉year-round) Campers can set up base at this attractive lochside site with pitches amid the Scots pines; rates include up to four people per tent/campervan.

Kincraig & Glen Feshie

The **Highland Wildlife Park** (☎01540-651270; www.highlandwildlifepark.org; adult/child £13.50/10; ☉10am-5pm Apr-Oct, to 6pm Jul & Aug, to 4pm Nov-Mar) near Kincraig, 6 miles southwest of Aviemore, features a drive-through safari park and animal enclosures offering the chance to view rarely-seen native wildlife, such as wildcats, capercaillies, pine martens, white-tailed sea eagles and red squirrels, as well as species that once roamed the Scottish hills but have long since disappeared, including the wolf, lynx, wild boar, beaver and European bison. Visitors without cars get driven around by staff (at no extra cost). Last entry is two hours before closing.

At Kincraig the Spey widens into Loch Insh, home of the **Loch Insh Watersports Centre** (☎01540-651272; www.lochinsh.com), which offers canoeing, windsurfing, sailing, bike hire and fishing, as well as B&B accommodation from £27 per person. The food here is good, especially after 6.30pm when the lochside cafe metamorphoses into a cosy restaurant.

Beautiful, tranquil **Glen Feshie** extends south from Kincraig, deep into the Cairngorms, with Scots pine woods in its upper reaches, which are surrounded by big, heathery hills. The 4WD track to the head of the glen makes a great mountain-bike excursion (25-mile round trip).

Glen Feshie Hostel (☑01540-651323; www .glenfeshiehostel.co.uk; Glen Feshie; dm £17; ☎), about 5 miles south of Kincraig, is a cosy, independent 16-bed hostel in a wonderfully remote setting halfway up the glen. It is generally block-booked at weekends and during school holidays, but you may be able to get a bed midweek or off-season by calling ahead (booking necessary).

Carrbridge

POP 540

Carrbridge, 7 miles northeast of Aviemore, is a good alternative base for exploring the region. It takes its name from the graceful old bridge (spotlit at night), built in 1717, over the thundering rapids of the Dulnain.

The **Landmark Forest Heritage Park** (☑01479-841613; www.landmarkpark.co.uk; adult/child £11.55/9.25; ⏱10am-7pm mid-Jul-Aug, to 6pm Apr–mid-Jul, to 5pm Sep-Mar), set in a forest of Scots pines, is a theme park with a difference; the theme is timber. The main attractions are the Ropeworx highwire adventure course, the Treetops Trail (a raised walkway through the forest canopy that allows you to view red squirrels, crossbills and crested tits), and the steam-powered sawmill.

Watching red squirrels from your bedroom window is just one of the things that makes **Pine Ridge B&B** (☑01479-841653; www.pineridgecarrbridge.com; Main St; per person from £26; ℗) such an enticing place to stay; big, bright bedrooms and bounteous breakfasts seal the deal.

Bus 15 runs from Inverness to Carrbridge (45 minutes, four daily Monday to Friday, two on Saturday) and onwards to Grantown-on-Spey (20 minutes).

Boat of Garten

Boat of Garten is known as Osprey Village because these rare and beautiful birds of prey nest nearby at the **RSPB Loch Garten Osprey Centre** (☑01479-831694; www.rspb.org .uk; Tulloch; adult/child £3/50p; ⏱10am-6pm Apr-Aug). The ospreys migrate here each spring from Africa and nest in a tall pine tree – you can watch from a hide as the birds feed their young. The centre is signposted about 2 miles east of the village.

There is good-quality hostel accommodation at **Fraoch Lodge** (☑01479-831331; www .scotmountain.co.uk; Deshar Rd; per person £20; ℗), while the **Boat Hotel** (☑01479-831258; www.boathotel.co.uk; s/d from £85/110; ℗☎) offers luxurious accommodation and has a superb restaurant.

Boat of Garten is 6 miles northeast of Aviemore. The most interesting way to get here is on the Strathspey Steam Railway (p127).

Grantown-on-Spey

POP 2170

Grantown (*gran*-ton) is an elegant Georgian town on the banks of the Spey, a favoured haunt of anglers and the tweed-cap-and-green-wellies brigade. Thronged with tourists in summer, it reverts to a quiet backwater in winter. Most hotels can kit you out for a day of fly-fishing or put you in touch with someone who can.

🛏 Sleeping & Eating

Brooklynn   B&B ££
(☑01479-873113; www.woodier.com; Grant Rd; r per person £35-40; ℗☎) This beautiful Victorian villa features original stained glass and wood panelling, and seven spacious, luxurious rooms (all doubles have en suites). The food – dinner is available as well as breakfast – is superb, too.

Craggan Mill   SCOTTISH ££
(☑01479-872288; www.cragganmill.co.uk; mains £13-23; ⏱noon-2.30pm & dinner Wed-Mon) Housed in a restored 18th-century meal mill just south of Grantown-on-Spey on the A95 towards Aviemore, the Craggan is strong on rustic atmosphere and friendly service. The menu doesn't disappoint either, with expertly prepared Scottish seafood, salmon, beef and venison, and desserts that include traditional clootie dumpling made to an old family recipe.

Glass House   SCOTTISH £££
(☑01479-872980; Grant Rd; mains £18-22; ⏱noon-1.45pm Wed-Sat, 7-9pm Tue-Sat, 12.30-2pm Sun) Elegant but unpretentious restaurant famous for fresh, seasonal menus that focus on local produce.

Chaplin's Coffee House &
Ice Cream Parlour   ICE CREAM £
(High St; ⏱9.30am-5pm Mon-Sat, 10am-4.30pm Sun) Traditional family cafe selling delicious homemade ice cream.

ℹ Getting There & Away

Bus services operate to and from Aviemore.

Kingussie & Newtonmore

The gracious old Speyside town of Kingussie (kin-*yew*-see) and the peaceful backwater Newtonmore sit at the foot of the great heather-clad humps known as the Monadhliath Mountains. The towns are best known as the home of the excellent Highland Folk Museum.

The Monadhliath Mountains attract fewer hikers than the nearby Cairngorms and make an ideal destination for walkers seeking peace and solitude. However, during the deer-stalking season (August to October), you'll need to check with the Aviemore tourist office (p129) before setting out.

⊙ Sights & Activities

The recommended six-hour circular walk to the 878m summit of **Carn an Fhreiceadain**, above Kingussie, begins north of the village. It continues to Pitmain Lodge and along the Allt Mor river before climbing to the cairn on the summit. You can then follow the ridge east to the twin summits of Beinn Bhreac before returning to Kingussie via a more easterly track.

Highland Folk Museum   MUSEUM
(☑01540-661307; www.highlandfolk.museum; Kingussie Rd, Newtonmore; free; ☉10.30am-5.30pm Apr-Aug, 11am-4.30pm Sep & Oct) The open-air Highland Folk Museum comprises a collection of historical buildings and relics revealing many aspects of Highland culture and lifestyle. Laid out like a farming township, it has a community of traditional thatch-roofed cottages, a sawmill, a schoolhouse, a shepherd's bothy (hut) and a rural post office. Actors in period costume give demonstrations of woodcarving, spinning and peat-fire baking.

You'll need two to three hours to make the most of a visit here.

Ruthven Barracks   HISTORIC BUILDING
(HS; Kingussie; admission free; ☉24hr) Ruthven Barracks was one of four garrisons built by the British government after the first Jacobite rebellion of 1715, as part of a Hanoverian scheme to take control of the Highlands. Ironically, the barracks were last occupied by Jacobite troops awaiting the return of Bonnie Prince Charlie after the Battle of Culloden.

Learning of his defeat and subsequent flight, they set fire to the barracks before taking to the glens (the building is still roof-

less). Perched dramatically on a river terrace and clearly visible from the main A9 road near Kingussie, the ruins are spectacularly floodlit at night.

Laggan Wolftrax   MOUNTAIN BIKING
(www.basecampmtb.com; Strathmashie Forest, Laggan; ☉10am-6pm Mon, 9.30am-5pm Tue, Thu & Fri, 9.30am-6pm Sat & Sun) Ten miles southwest of Newtonmore, on the A86 road towards Spean Bridge, this is one of Scotland's top mountain-biking centres with purpose-built trails ranging from open-country riding to black-diamond downhills. Bike hire is available on site, from £25 a day for a hardtail mountain bike to £40 for a full-suspension downhill rig.

🛌 Sleeping & Eating

TOP CHOICE》 Eagleview Guest House   B&B ££
(☑01540-673675; www.eagleviewguesthouse.co.uk; Perth Rd, Newtonmore; r per person £25-35; P） The family-friendly Eagleview is one of the nicest places to stay in the area, with beautifully decorated bedrooms, super-king-size beds, spacious bathrooms with power showers, and nice little touches like wall-mounted flatscreen TVs, cafetières with real coffee on your hospitality tray and real milk rather than that yucky UHT stuff.

Homewood Lodge   B&B ££
(☑01540-661507; www.homewood-lodge-kingussie .co.uk; Newtonmore Rd, Kingussie; r per person £25-30; P） This elegant Victorian lodge on the western outskirts of Kingussie offers double rooms with exquisite views of the Cairngorms – a nice way to wake up in the mornings! The owners are committed to recycling and energy efficiency, and have created a mini-nature reserve in the garden.

TOP CHOICE》 The Cross   MODERN SCOTTISH £££
(☑01540-661166; www.thecross.co.uk; Ardbroilach Rd, Kingussie; 3-course dinner £50; ☉7-9pm Tue-Sat, closed Jan) Housed in a converted water mill beside the Allt Mor burn, the Cross is one of the finest restaurants in the Highlands. The intimate, low-raftered dining room has an open fire and a patio overlooking the stream, and serves a daily-changing menu of fresh Scottish produce accompanied by a superb wine list.

If you want to stay the night, there are eight stylish rooms (double or twin £100 to £140) to choose from.

Blasta
MODERN SCOTTISH ££

(☎01540-673231; Main St, Newtonmore; mains £13-18; ☺dinner Tue-Sat) An unpretentious interior of polished wood, plain white walls and black leather chairs puts the focus on the food at this popular local bistro (the name is Gaelic for 'tasty'). Local produce is showcased in dishes such as venison steak with sweet potato and ginger puree, and smoked salmon with egg mimosa and watercress dressing.

❶ Getting There & Away

BUS There are Scottish Citylink buses from Kingussie to Perth (£14, 1¾ hours, five daily), Aviemore (£7, 25 minutes, five to seven daily) and Inverness (£11, one hour, six to eight Monday to Saturday, three Sunday).

TRAIN From the train station at the southern end of town there are trains to Edinburgh (£32, 2½ hours, seven a day Monday to Saturday, two Sunday) and Inverness (£10, one hour, eight a day Monday to Saturday, four Sunday).

Dalwhinnie

The remote village of Dalwhinnie, bypassed by the main A9 road, straggles along its single street in glorious isolation amid wild and windswept scenery. From a distance you can spot the distinctive twin pagoda-shaped roofs of the malt kiln at **Dalwhinnie Distillery** (☎01540-672219; www.discovering -distilleries.com; guided tour £6; ☺9.30am-5pm Mon-Sat & 10am-5pm Sun Apr-Oct, 11am-2pm Mon-Fri Nov-Mar), the highest in Scotland (326m above sea level) and one of the most remote. As well as the standard tour, the distillery offers a range of special tasting sessions (from £8 to £30) that give you the chance to sample some older and rarer single malts.

Three or four trains a day on the Glasgow/Edinburgh to Inverness line stop at Dalwhinnie's tiny station, 600m from the distillery.

MORAY

The old county of Moray (pronounced mur-ray), centred on the lower valley of the River Spey, lies at the heart of an ancient Celtic earldom and is famed for its mild climate and rich farmland. The barley fields of the 19th century once provided the raw material for the Speyside whisky distilleries, one of the region's main attractions for present-day visitors.

Famous brands include Glenfiddich and Glenlivet, but there are many other less well-known, but just as excellent, distilleries in the region, such as Cardhu, Cragganmore and Glenfarclas – in fact, more than half of Scotland's whisky distilleries are to be found in Speyside.

Dufftown

POP 1450

Rome may be built on seven hills, but Dufftown's built on seven stills, say the locals. Founded in 1817 by James Duff, 4th Earl of Fife, Dufftown is 17 miles south of Elgin and lies at the heart of the Speyside whisky-distilling region.

◉ Sights & Activities

Keith and Dufftown Railway
HERITAGE RAILWAY

(☎01340-821181; www.keith-dufftown-railway .co.uk; Dufftown Station) A line running for 11 miles from Dufftown to Keith is still used for trains hauled by 1950s diesel motor units that run on weekends from June to September, plus Fridays in July and August; a return ticket costs £9.50/4.50 for an adult/child. There are also two 1930s 'Brighton Belle' Pullman coaches, and a cafe housed in a 1957 British Railways cafeteria car.

Whisky Museum
MUSEUM

(☎01340-821097; www.dufftown.co.uk; 12 Conval St; ☺1-4pm Mon-Fri May-Sep) As well as housing a selection of distillery memorabilia (try saying that after a few drams), the Whisky Museum holds 'nosing and tasting evenings' where you can learn what to look for in a fine single malt (£8 per person; 8pm Wednesday in July and August).

You can then test your new-found skills at the nearby **Whisky Shop** (☎01340-821097; www.whiskyshopdufftown.co.uk; 1 Fife St), which stocks hundreds of single malts.

Malt Whisky Trail
SELF-GUIDED TOUR

(www.maltwhiskytrail.com) With seven working distilleries nearby, Dufftown has been dubbed Scotland's malt whisky capital. Ask at the tourist office for a Malt Whisky Trail booklet, a self-guided tour around the seven stills plus the Speyside Cooperage.

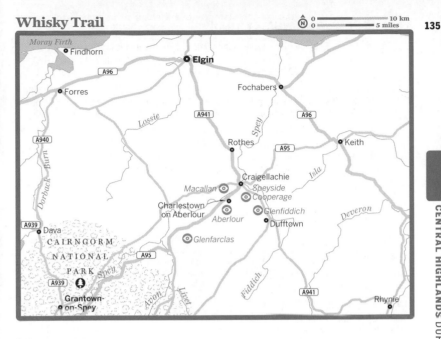

🛏 Sleeping & Eating

Davaar B&B   B&B ££
(☎01340-820464;   www.davaardufftown.co.uk;
17 Church St; s/d from £40/60) Just along the
street opposite the tourist office, Davaar is
a sturdy Victorian villa with three smallish
but comfy rooms; the breakfast menu is superb, offering the option of Portsoy kippers
instead of the traditional fry-up (which uses
eggs from the owners' own chickens).

Fife Arms Hotel   HOTEL ££
(☎01340-820220; www.fifearmsdufftown.co.uk; 2
The Square; s/d from £35/60; P) This welcoming hotel offers slightly cramped but comfortable accommodation in a modern block
around the back; its bar is stocked with a
wide range of single malts, and the restaurant (mains £9 to £16) dishes up sizzling
steaks, homemade steak pies and locally
farmed ostrich steaks.

🍴**La Faisanderie**   FRENCH, SCOTTISH £££
(☎01340-821273; The Square; mains £18-21;
☺noon-1.30pm & 5.30-8.30pm) This is a great
place to eat, run by a local chef who shoots
much of his own game. The interior is decorated in French *auberge* style with a cheerful mural and pheasants hiding in every
corner. The set menus (three-course lunch

£18.50, four-course dinner £32) won't disappoint, but you can order à la carte as well.

🍴**A Taste of Speyside**   SCOTTISH ££
(☎01340-820860; 10 Balvenie St; mains £16-20;
☺noon-9pm Tue-Sun Easter-Sep, noon-2pm &
6-9pm Tue-Sun Oct-Easter) This upmarket restaurant prepares traditional Scottish dishes
using fresh local produce, including a challenging platter of smoked salmon, smoked
venison, brandied chicken liver pâté, cured
herring, a selection of Scottish cheeses and
homemade bread (phew!). A two-course
lunch costs £13.50.

ℹ Information

Dufftown tourist office (☎01340-820501;
☺10am-1pm & 2-5.30pm Mon-Sat, 11am-3pm
Sun Easter-Oct) In the clock tower in the main
square; the adjoining museum contains some
interesting local items.

ℹ Getting There & Away

BUS Buses link Dufftown to Elgin (50 minutes,
hourly), Huntly, Aberdeen and Inverness.

TRAIN On summer weekends, you can take a
train from Aberdeen or Inverness to Keith, and
then ride the Keith and Dufftown Railway to
Dufftown.

Visiting a distillery can be memorable, but only hard-core malthounds will want to go to more than two or three. Some are great to visit; others are depressingly corporate. The following are some recommendations for Speyside distilleries.

Aberlour Distillery   DISTILLERY
(☑01340-881249; www.aberlour.com; tours £10; ☉10.30am & 2pm daily Easter-Oct, by appointment Mon-Fri Nov-Mar) Has an excellent, detailed tour with a proper tasting session. It's on the main street in Aberlour.

Glenfarclas Distillery   DISTILLERY
(☑01807-500257; www.glenfarclas.co.uk; admission £3.50; ☉10am-4pm Mon-Fri Oct-Mar, to 5pm Mon-Fri Apr-Sep, plus to 4pm Sat Jul-Sep) Small, friendly and independent, Glenfarclas is 5 miles south of Aberlour on the Grantown road. The last tour leaves 90 minutes before closing. The in-depth Ambassador's Tour (Fridays only) costs £15.

Glenfiddich Distillery Visitor Centre   DISTILLERY
(☑01340-820373; www.glenfiddich.co.uk; admission free; ☉9.30am-4.30pm Mon-Sat, from noon Sun Easter–mid-Oct, 9.30am-4.30pm Mon-Fri mid-Oct–Easter) The Glenfiddich distillery is big and busy, but the handiest for Dufftown, and foreign languages are available. The standard tour starts with an overblown video, but it's fun, informative and free. An in-depth Connoisseur's Tour (£20) must be prebooked. Glenfiddich kept single malt alive during the dark years.

Macallan Distillery   DISTILLERY
(☑01340-872280; www.themacallan.com; ☉9.30am-4.30pm Mon-Sat Easter-Oct, 11am-3pm Mon-Fri Nov-Mar) Macallan makes an excellent sherry-casked malt. Several small-group tours are available (last tour at 3.30pm), including an expert one (£15); all should be prebooked. Lovely location 2 miles northwest of Craigellachie.

Speyside Cooperage   HISTORIC BUILDING
(☑01340-871108; www.speysidecooperage.co.uk; admission £3.30; ☉9am-4pm Mon-Fri) Here you can see the fascinating art of barrel-making in action. It's a mile from Craigellachie on the Dufftown road.

Spirit of Speyside Whisky Festival   FOOD & DRINK
(www.spiritofspeyside.com) This biannual whisky festival in Dufftown has a number of great events. It takes place in early May and late September; both accommodation and events should be booked well ahead.

Tomintoul

POP 320

This high-altitude (345m) village was built by the Duke of Gordon in 1775 on the old military road that leads over the Lecht pass from Corgarff, a route now followed by the A939 (usually the first road in Scotland to be blocked by snow when winter closes in). The duke hoped that settling the dispersed population of his estates in a proper village would help to stamp out cattle stealing and illegal distilling.

Tomintoul (tom-in-*towel*) is a pretty, stone-built village with a grassy, tree-lined main square, where you'll find the **tourist office** (☑01807-580285; The Square; ☉9.30am-1pm & 2-5pm Mon-Sat Easter-Oct, plus 1-5pm Sun Aug).

Next door, the **Tomintoul Museum** (☑01807-673701; The Square; admission free; ☉9.30am-5pm Mon-Sat Apr-Oct, plus 1-5pm Sun Jul & Aug), which has displays on a range of local topics.

The surrounding **Glenlivet Estate** (now the property of the Crown) has lots of walking and cycling trails – the estate's **information centre** (☑01807-580283; www.crownestate.co.uk/glenlivet; Main St) distributes free maps of the area – and a spur of the Speyside Way long-distance footpath runs between Tomintoul and Ballindalloch, 15 miles to the north.

💤 Sleeping & Eating

Tomintoul SYHA   HOSTEL £
(☎01807-580364; www.syha.org.uk; Main St; dm £15; ⊗May-Sep) Housed in the old village school.

Argyle Guest House   B&B ££
(☎01807-580766; www.argyletomintoul.co.uk; 7 Main St; d/f £59/100) Comfortable accommodation for walkers.

Clockhouse Restaurant   SCOTTISH ££
(The Square; mains £10-12; ⊗lunch & dinner) Serves light lunches and bistro dinners made with fresh Highland lamb, venison and salmon.

ℹ Getting There & Away

There is a very limited bus service to Tomintoul from Elgin, Dufftown and Aberlour. Check with the tourist office in Elgin for the latest timetable.

STRATHDON

The valley of the River Don, home to many of Aberdeenshire's finest castles, stretches westward from Kintore, 13 miles northwest of Aberdeen, taking in the villages of Kemnay, Monymusk, Alford (ah-ford) and tiny Strathdon. The A944 parallels the lower valley; west of Alford, the A944, A97 and A939 follow the river's upper reaches.

Stagecoach bus 220 runs from Aberdeen to Alford (1½ hours, seven a day Monday to Saturday, four on Sunday); bus 219 continues from Alford to Strathdon village (50 minutes, two daily Tuesday and Thursday, one on Saturday) via Kildrummy

Alford

POP 1925

Alford has a **tourist office** (☎01975-562052; Old Station Yard, Main St; ⊗10am-5pm Mon-Sat, 12.45-5pm Sun Jun-Aug, 10am-1pm & 2-5pm Mon-Fri, 10am-noon & 1.45-5pm Sat, 12.45-5pm Sun Apr, May & Sep), banks, ATMs and a supermarket.

The **Grampian Transport Museum** (☎01975-562292; www.gtm.org.uk; adult/child £6/3; ⊗10am-5pm Apr-Sep, 10am-4pm Oct) houses a fascinating collection of vintage motorbikes, cars, buses and trams, including a Triumph Bonneville in excellent nick, a couple of Model T Fords (including one used by Drambuie), a Ferrari F40 and an Aston Martin V8 Mk II. Unusual exhibits include a 19th-century horse-drawn sleigh

from Russia, a 1942 Mack snowplough and the Craigievar Express, a steam-powered tricycle built in 1895 by a local postman.

Next to the museum is the terminus of the narrow-gauge **Alford Valley Steam Railway** (☎01975-562811; www.alfordvalleyrailway.org.uk; adult/child £2.50/1.50; ⊗11.30am-4pm May-Sep, Sat & Sun only Apr), a heritage line that runs from here to Haughton Country Park.

Craigievar Castle

The most spectacular of the Strathdon castles is **Craigievar** (NTS; adult/child £10/7; ⊗noon-5.30pm daily Jul & Aug & Fri-Tue Easter-Jun & Sep), located 9 miles south of Alford. A superb example of the original Scottish Baronial style, it has managed to survive pretty much unchanged since its completion in the 17th century (although the exterior has recently been restored to its original pink colour after a £500,000 facelift). The lower half is a plain tower house, the upper half sprouts corbelled turrets, cupolas and battlements – an extravagant statement of its builder's wealth and status.

Kildrummy Castle

Nine miles west of Alford lie the extensive remains of the 13th-century **Kildrummy Castle** (HS; ☎01975-571331; adult/child £3.70/2.20; ⊗9.30am-5.30pm Apr-Sep), former seat of the Earl of Mar and once one of Scotland's most impressive fortresses. After the 1715 Jacobite rebellion the earl was exiled to France and his castle fell into ruin.

If you're in the mood for a night of luxury, head for **Kildrummy Castle Hotel** (☎01975-571288; www.kildrummycastlehotel.co; s/d from £90/139; P🛈) – just along the road – a splendid Baronial hunting lodge complete with original oak panelling, log fires and four-poster beds.

Corgarff Castle

In the wild upper reaches of Strathdon, near the A939 from Corgarff to Tomintoul, is the impressive fortress of **Corgarff Castle** (HS; ☎01975-651460; adult/child £4.70/2.80; ⊗9.30am-5.30pm daily Apr-Sep, to 4.30pm Sat & Sun Oct-Mar). The tower house dates from the 16th century, but the star-shaped defensive curtain wall was added in 1748 when the castle was converted to a military barracks in the wake of the Jacobite rebellion.

Jenny's Bothy (☎01975-651449; www .jennysbothy.co.uk; dm £10) is a welcoming year-round bunkhouse that's set in a remote croft; look out for the sign by the main road, then follow the old military road (drivable) for 0.75 miles. Phone ahead before you arrive.

Lecht Ski Resort

At the head of Strathdon the A939 – a magnificent rollercoaster of a road, much loved by motorcyclists – crosses the Lecht pass (637m), where there's a small skiing area with lots of short easy and intermediate runs. **Lecht 2090** (www.lecht.co.uk) hires out skis, boots and poles for £17 a day; a one-day lift pass is £25. A two-day package, including ski hire, lift pass and instruction, costs £90.

The ski centre opens in summer, too, when you can rent mountain bikes (£20 for four hours) and quad bikes (£10 for a 12-minute session).

DEESIDE

The valley of the **River Dee** – often called Royal Deeside because of the royal family's long association with the area – stretches west from Aberdeen to Braemar, closely paralleled by the A93 road. From Deeside north to Strathdon is serious castle country – there are more examples of fanciful Scottish Baronial architecture here than anywhere else in Scotland.

The Dee, world-famous for its salmon fishing, has its source in the Cairngorm Mountains west of Braemar, the starting point for long walks into the hills. The **Fish Dee website** (www.fishdee.co.uk) has all you need to know about fishing on the river.

Crathes Castle

The atmospheric, 16th-century **Crathes Castle** (NTS; ☎01330-844525; adult/child £10.50/7.50; ⊙10.30am-5pm Jun-Aug, to 4.30pm Sat-Thu Apr, May, Sep & Oct, to 3.45pm Sat & Sun Nov-Mar; ⚑) is famous for its Jacobean painted ceilings, magnificently carved canopied beds, and the 'Horn of Leys', presented to the Burnett family by Robert the Bruce in the 14th century. The beautiful formal gardens include 300-year-old yew hedges and colourful herbaceous borders.

The castle is on the A93, 16 miles west of Aberdeen, on the main Aberdeen to Ballater bus route.

Ballater
POP 1450

The attractive little village of Ballater owes its 18th-century origins to the curative waters of nearby Pannanich Springs (now bottled commercially as Deeside Natural Mineral Water) and its prosperity to nearby Balmoral Castle.

Note the crests on the shop fronts along the main street proclaiming 'By Royal Appointment' – the village is a major supplier of provisions to Balmoral.

◉ Sights & Activities

Old Royal Station   MUSEUM
(☎01339 755306; Station Sq; admission £2; ⊙9am-6pm Jul & Aug, 10am-5pm Sep-Jun) When Queen Victoria travelled to Balmoral Castle she would alight from the royal train at Ballater's Old Royal Station. The station has been beautifully restored and now houses the tourist office, a cafe and a museum with a replica of Victoria's royal coach.

Dee Valley Confectioners   SWEET SHOP
(☎01339-755499; www.dee-valley.co.uk; Station Sq; admission free; ⊙9am-noon & 2-4.30pm Mon-Thu Apr-Oct) Drool over the manufacture of traditional Scottish sweeties at this confectioner on Station Sq.

Walking
As you approach Ballater from the east the hills start to close in, and there are many pleasant walks in the surrounding area. The steep woodland walk up **Craigendarroch** (400m) takes just over one hour. **Morven** (871m) is a more serious prospect, taking about six hours, but offers good views from the top; ask at the tourist office for more informatiion.

Cycling
Cycle Highlands   BICYCLE HIRE
(www.cyclehighlands.com; The Pavilion, Victoria Rd; bicycle hire per day £16; ⊙9am-6pm) Also offers guided bike rides and advice on local trails.

Cabin Fever   BICYCLE HIRE
(☎01339-54004; Station Sq; bicycle hire per 2hr £8; ⊙9am-6pm) Can also arrange pony trekking, quad-biking, clay-pigeon shooting or canoeing.

🛏 Sleeping & Eating

Accommodation here is fairly expensive and budget travellers usually continue on to Braemar.

TOP CHOICE **Auld Kirk** RESTAURANT ££
(☎01301-755762; www.theauldkirk.com; Braemar Rd; s/d from £73/110; 🐾) Here's something a little out of the ordinary – a six-bedroom 'restaurant with rooms' housed in a converted 19th-century church. The interior blends original features with sleek modern decor, and the stylish Scottish restaurant (two-/three-course dinner £29/35) serves local lamb, venison and seafood.

Green Inn RESTAURANT ££
(☎01339-755701; www.green-inn.com; 9 Victoria Rd; s/d from £58/76; P) A lovely old house with plush armchairs, this is a 'restaurant with rooms' – three comfortable en suite bedrooms, with the accent on fine dining. The menu includes French-influenced dishes such as roast quail with crayfish, truffle and wild mushrooms. A two-/three-course dinner costs £34/41 and meals are served from 7pm till 9pm Tuesday to Saturday.

Celicall B&B ££
(☎01339-755699; www.celicallguesthouse.co.uk; 3 Braemar Rd; d from £54; P) Celicall is a friendly, family-run B&B in a modern cottage right across the street from Station Sq, within easy walking distance of all attractions.

Old Station Cafe CAFE ££
(☎01339-755050; Station Sq; mains £9-15; ⊙10am-5pm daily, plus 6.30-8.30pm Thu-Sat) The former waiting room at Queen Victoria's train station is now an attractive dining area with black-and-white floor tiles, basketwork chairs, and marble fireplace and table tops. Daily specials make good use of local produce, from salmon to venison, and good coffee and home-baked goods are available all day.

ℹ Information

Ballater tourist office (☎01339-755306; Station Sq; ⊙9am-6pm Jul & Aug, 10am-5pm Sep-Jun) In the Old Royal Station.
Cybernaut (☎01339-755566; www.cybernaut .org.uk; 14 Bridge St; per 15min £1; ⊙9am-5pm Mon-Fri, 10am-4pm Sat; @) For internet access.

ℹ Getting There & Away

Bus 201 runs from Aberdeen to Ballater (£9, 1¾ hours, hourly Monday to Saturday, six on Sunday) via Crathes Castle, and continues to Braemar (30 minutes) every two hours.

Balmoral Castle

Eight miles west of Ballater lies **Balmoral Castle** (☎01339-742334; www.balmoralcastle .com; adult/child £8.70/4.60; ⊙10am-5pm Apr-Jul, last admission 4pm), the Queen's Highland holiday home, screened from the road by a thick curtain of trees. Built for Queen Victoria in 1855 as a private residence for the royal family, it kicked off the revival of the Scottish Baronial style of architecture that characterises so many of Scotland's 19th-century country houses.

The admission fee includes an interesting and well thought-out audioguide, but the tour is very much an outdoor one through garden and grounds; as for the castle itself, only the ballroom, which displays a collection of Landseer paintings and royal silver, is open to the public. Don't expect to see the Queen's private quarters! The main attraction is learning about Highland estate management, rather than royal revelations. Guided tours are available on Saturdays from October to December – check the website for details.

The massive pointy-topped mountain that looms to the south of Balmoral is **Lochnagar** (1155m), immortalised in verse by Lord Byron, who spent his childhood years in Aberdeenshire:

England, thy beauties are tame and domestic / To one who has roamed o'er the mountains afar. / O! for the crags that are wild and majestic / The steep frowning glories of dark Lochnagar.

Balmoral is beside the A93 at Crathie and can be reached on the Aberdeen–Braemar bus.

Braemar

POP 400

Braemar is a pretty little village with a grand location on a broad plain ringed by mountains where the Dee valley and Glen Clunie meet. In winter this is one of the coldest places in the country – temperatures as low as -29°C have been recorded – and during spells of severe cold hungry deer wander the streets looking for a bite to eat. Braemar is an excellent base for hill walking (see p146), and there's also skiing at nearby Glenshee.

⊙ Sights & Activities

Braemar Highland Heritage Centre
HERITAGE CENTRE

(☑01339-741944; Mar Rd; admission free; ☺9am-6.30pm Jul & Aug, 10am-6pm Jun & Sep, 10am-5.30pm Mon-Sat, noon-5pm Sun Mar-May, shorter hours low season) The Braemar Highland Heritage Centre, beside the tourist office, tells the story of the area with displays and videos.

Braemar Castle
CASTLE

(www.braemarcastle.co.uk; adult/child £5/3; ☺11am-6pm Sat & Sun, also Wed Jul & Aug) Just north of Braemar village, turreted Braemar Castle dates from 1628 and served as a government garrison after the 1745 Jacobite rebellion. It was taken over by the local community in 2007, which now offers guided tours of the historic castle apartments.

Creag Choinnich
WALKING

An easy walk from Braemar is up Creag Choinnich (538m), a hill to the east of the village above the A93. The route is waymarked and takes about 1½ hours. Ask at the tourist office for details of this and other walks.

Morrone
WALKING

For a longer walk (three hours) and superb views of the Cairngorms, head for the summit of Morrone (859m), southwest of Braemar. Ask at the tourist office for details of this and other walks.

🛏 Sleeping

⬛TOP CHOICE Rucksacks Bunkhouse
BUNKHOUSE £

(☑01339-741517; 15 Mar Rd; bothy £7, dm £12-15, tw £36; P@) An appealing cottage with a comfy dorm, and cheaper beds in an alpine-style bothy (shared sleeping platform for 10 people; bring your own sleeping bag). Extras include a drying room (for wet-weather gear), laundry and even a sauna (£10 an hour). Nonguests are welcome to use the internet (£3 per hour, 10.30am to 4.30pm), laundry and even the showers (£2).

The friendly owner is a fount of knowledge about the local area.

Craiglea
B&B ££

(☑01339-741641; www.craigleabraemar.com; Hillside Dr; r £70; P) Craiglea is a homey B&B set in a pretty stone cottage with three en suite bedrooms. Vegetarian breakfasts are available and the owners can give advice on local walks.

Clunie Lodge Guesthouse
B&B ££

(☑01339-741330; www.clunielodge.com; Cluniebank Rd; r per person from £30; P) A spacious Victorian villa set in beautiful gardens, the Clunie is a great place to relax after a hard day's hiking, with its comfortable residents lounge, bedrooms with views of the hills and red squirrels scampering through the neighbouring woods. There's a drying room and secure storage for bicycles.

Braemar Lodge Hotel
HOTEL, BUNKHOUSE ££

(☑01339-741627; www.braemarlodge.co.uk; Glenshee Rd; dm from £12, s/d £75/120; P) This Victorian shooting lodge on the southern outskirts of Braemar has bags of character, not least in the wood-panelled Malt Room bar, which is as well stocked with mounted deer heads as it is with single-malt whiskies. There's a good restaurant with views of the hills, plus a 12-berth hikers' bunkhouse in the hotel grounds.

Braemar SYHA
HOSTEL £

(☑01339-741659; www.syha.org.uk; 21 Glenshee Rd; dm £16-17; ☺Jan-Oct; @) This hostel is housed in a grand former shooting lodge just south of Braemar viilage centre on the A93 to Perth. It has a comfy lounge with pool table, and a barbecue in the garden.

St Margarets
B&B ££

(☑01339-741697; 13 School Rd; s/tw £32/54; ☏) Grab this place if you can, but there's only one room – a twin with a serious sunflower theme. The genuine warmth of the welcome is heart-warming.

Invercauld Caravan Club Site
CAMPGROUND £

(☑01339-741373; tent sites £10-15; ☺late Dec-Oct) There is good camping here, or you can camp wild (no facilities) along the minor road on the east bank of the Clunie Water, 3 miles south of Braemar.

✗ Eating

⬛TOP CHOICE Gathering Place
SCOTTISH ££

(☑01339-741234; www.the-gathering-place.co.uk; 9 Invercauld Rd; mains £15-18; ☺dinner Tue-Sun) This bright and breezy bistro is an unexpected corner of culinary excellence, with a welcoming dining room and sunny conservatory, tucked below the main road junction at the entrance to Braemar village.

Taste
CAFE £

(☑01339-741425; www.taste-braemar.co.uk; Airlie House, Mar Rd; mains £3-5; ☺10am-5pm Thu-Mon;

There are Highland games in many towns and villages throughout the summer, but the best known is the **Braemar Gathering** (☎01339-755377; www.braemargathering.org; adult/child £7/2), which takes place on the first Saturday in September. It's a major occasion, organised every year since 1817 by the Braemar Royal Highland Society. Events include Highland dancing, pipers, tug-of-war, a hill race up Morrone, tossing the caber, hammer- and stone-throwing and the long jump. International athletes are among those who take part.

These kinds of events took place informally in the Highlands for many centuries as tests of skill and strength, but they were formalised around 1820 as part of the rise of Highland romanticism initiated by Sir Walter Scott and King George IV. Queen Victoria attended the Braemar Gathering in 1848, starting a tradition of royal patronage that continues to this day.

🍴) Taste is a relaxed little cafe with armchairs in the window, serving soups, snacks, coffee and cakes.

Hungry Highlander   TAKEAWAY £
(14 Invercauld Rd; mains £3-7; ⊙10am-9pm Mon, Wed & Thu, to 10pm Fri & Sat, to 8pm Sun) Serves a range of takeaway meals and hot drinks.

ℹ Information

There's a bank with an ATM in the village centre, a couple of outdoor equipment shops and an **Alldays** (⊙7.30am-9pm Mon-Sat, 9am-6pm Sun) grocery store.
Braemar tourist office (☎01399-741600; The Mews, Mar Rd; ⊙9am-6pm Aug, 9am-5pm Jun, Jul, Sep & Oct, 10am-1.30pm & 2-5pm Mon-Sat, 2-5pm Sun Nov-May) Opposite the Fife Arms Hotel; has lots of useful info on walks in the area.

ℹ Getting There & Away

Bus 201 runs from Aberdeen to Braemar (£9, 2¼ hours, eight daily Monday to Saturday, five on Sunday). The 50-mile drive from Perth to Braemar is beautiful, but there's no public transport on this route.

Inverey

Five miles west of Braemar is the tiny settlement of Inverey. Numerous mountain walks start from here, including the adventurous walk through the **Lairig Ghru** pass to Aviemore. The Linn of Dee Circuit starts about 1.5 miles west of Inverey.

A good short walk (3 miles, 1½ hours) begins at the **Linn of Quoich** – a waterfall that thunders through a narrow slot in the rocks. Head uphill on a footpath on the east bank of the stream, past the impressive rock scenery of the **Punch Bowl** (a giant pothole), to a modern bridge that spans the narrow gorge, and return via an unsurfaced road on the far bank.

THE ANGUS GLENS

The northern part of Angus is bounded by the Grampian Mountains, where five scenic glens – Isla, Prosen, Clova, Lethnot and Esk – cut into the hills along the southern edge of the Cairngorms National Park. All have attractive scenery, though each glen has its own distinct personality: Glen Clova and Glenesk are the most beautiful, while Glen Lethnot is the least frequented. You can get detailed information on walks in the Angus Glens from the tourist office in Kirriemuir and from the Glen Clova Hotel in Glen Clova.

Since the withdrawal of the postbus service, there is no public transport to the Angus glens other than a limited school-bus service along Glen Clova; ask at the tourist office in Kirriemuir or Dundee for details and a timetable.

Kirriemuir

POP 6000

Known as the Wee Red Town because of its close-packed, red-sandstone houses, Kirriemuir is famed as the birthplace of JM Barrie (1860–1937), writer and creator of the much-loved *Peter Pan*. A bronze statue of the 'boy who wouldn't grow up' graces the intersection of Bank and High Sts.

The tourist office is in the Gateway to the Glens Museum.

142

☉ Sights

JM Barrie's Birthplace   MUSEUM
(☎01575-572646; 9 Brechin Rd; adult/child £5.50/
4.50; ☉11am-5pm Jul & Aug, from noon Sat-Wed
Apr-Jun, Sep & Oct) JM Barrie's Birthplace is
Kirriemuir's big attraction, a place of pilgrimage for Peter Pan fans from all over the
world. The two-storey house where Barrie
was born has been furnished in period style,
and preserves Barrie's writing desk and the
wash house at the back that served as his
first 'theatre'.

The ticket also gives admission to the
Camera Obscura (adult/child £3/2; ☉noon-
5pm Mon-Sat, 1-5pm Sun Jul-Sep, noon-5pm Sat &
1-5pm Sun Easter-Jun) on the hilltop northeast
of the town centre, given to the town by Barrie himself.

Gateway to the Glens Museum   MUSEUM
(☎01575-575479; 32 High St; admission free;
☉10am-5pm Mon-Sat Apr-Sep, closed Thu 10am-
noon Oct-Mar) The old Town House opposite
the Peter Pan statue dates from 1604 and
houses the Gateway to the Glens Museum, a
useful introduction to local history, geology
and wildlife for those planning to explore
the Angus Glens.

⊨ Sleeping & Eating

Airlie Arms Hotel   HOTEL ££
(☎01575-572847; www.theairliearms.co.uk; St
Malcolm's Wynd; s/d £45/75; ℗) This attractive
old coaching inn, just a few minutes' walk
from the tourist office, has been recently revamped with modern, stylish en suite rooms
and a candle-lit restaurant called the **Wynd**
(St Malcolm's Wynd; mains £8-14; ☉5-9pm Wed-Fri,
from noon Sat & Sun).

88 Degrees   CAFE £
(17 High St; mains £3-6; ☉9am-5pm) A new cafe
and deli that serves superb coffee (named
for the ideal temperature of an espresso),
delicious cakes and handmade chocolates.
Breakfast till 10.30am and light lunches till
2.30pm.

🛍 Shopping

Star Rock Shop   CONFECTIONERY
(☎01575-572579; 27-29 Roods) For generations
of local kids, the big treat when visiting Kirriemuir was a trip to the Star Rock Shop.
Established in 1833, it still specialises in traditional Scottish 'sweeties' (candy), arranged
in colourful jars along the walls – humbugs,
tablet, cola cubes, pear drops, and the original Star Rock, still made to an 1833 recipe.

ℹ Getting There & Away

Stagecoach bus 20 runs from Dundee to Kirriemuir (£5.30, one hour, hourly Monday to
Saturday, every two hours Sunday) via Glamis
(20 minutes, two daily Monday to Saturday) and
Forfar (25 minutes).

Glen Isla

At Bridge of Craigisla at the foot of the Glen
Isla is a spectacular 24m waterfall called
Reekie Linn; the name Reekie (Scottish for
'smoky') comes from the billowing spray
that rises from the falls.

A 5-mile walk beyond the road end at
Auchavan leads into the wild and mountainous upper reaches of the glen, where
the **Caenlochan National Nature Reserve** protects rare alpine flora on the high
plateau.

Glen Prosen

Near the foot of Glen Prosen, 6 miles north
of Kirriemuir, there's a good forest walk up
to the **Airlie monument** on Tulloch Hill
(380m); start from the eastern road, about a
mile beyond Dykehead.

From Glenprosen Lodge, at the head of
the glen, a 9-mile walk along the **Kilbo Path**
leads over a pass between Mayar (928m)
and Driesh (947m), and descends to Glen-
doll Lodge at the head of Glen Clova (allow
five hours).

Prosen Hostel (☎01575-540238; www.prosen
hostel.co.uk; per person £18; ☉year round; @) is
an 18-bed bunkhouse with excellent facilities (including a red-squirrel viewing area
in the lounge). It's 7 miles up the glen, just
beyond Prosen village, but there's no public
transport.

Glen Clova

The longest and loveliest of the Angus Glens
stretches north from Kirriemuir for 20
miles, broad and pastoral in its lower reaches but growing narrower and craggier as the
steep, heather-clad Highland hills close in
around its head.

The minor road beyond the Glen Clova
Hotel ends at a Forestry Commission car
park with toilets and a picnic area, which
is the trailhead for a number of strenuous
walks through the hills to the north.

Jock's Road is an ancient footpath that was much used by cattle drovers, soldiers, smugglers and shepherds in the 18th and 19th centuries; 700 Jacobite soldiers passed this way during their retreat in 1746, en route to final defeat at Culloden. From the car park the path strikes west along Glen Doll, then north across a high plateau (900m) before descending steeply into Glen Callater and on to Braemar (15 miles; allow five to seven hours). The route is hard going and should not be attempted in winter; you'll need OS 1:50,000 maps, numbers 43 and 44.

An easier, but still strenuous, circular walk starts from the Glen Clova Hotel, making a circuit of the scenic corrie (glacial hollow) that encloses **Loch Brandy** (6 miles, four hours).

Glen Clova Hotel (☎01575-550350; www .clova.com; s/d £60/90; P) is a lovely old drover's inn near the head of the glen and a great place to get away from it all. As well as 10 comfortable, country-style, en suite rooms (one with a four-poster bed), it has a bunkhouse out the back (£14 per person), a rustic, stonefloored climbers' bar with a roaring log fire, and a bay-windowed **restaurant** (mains £8-13; noon-8.15pm Sun-Thu, noon-8.45pm Fri & Sat) with views across the glen. The menu includes cock-a-leekie soup, venison in Drambuie sauce, and lamb and rosemary lasagne, and there are separate children's and vegetarian menus.

Glen Lethnot

This glen is noted for the **Brown & White Caterthuns** – two extraordinary Iron Age hill forts, defended by ramparts and ditches, perched on twin hilltops at its southern end. A minor road crosses the pass between the two summits, and it's an easy walk to either fort from the parking area in the pass; both are superb viewpoints. If you don't have a car, you can walk there from Brechin (6 miles) or from Edzell (5 miles).

Glenesk

The most easterly of the Angus Glens, Glenesk runs for 15 miles from Edzell to lovely **Loch Lee**, surrounded by beetling cliffs and waterfalls. Ten miles up the glen from Edzell is **Glenesk Folk Museum** (adult/child £2/1; ☻noon-6pm daily Jun–mid-Oct, noon-6pm Sat & Sun only Easter-May; @☎), an old shoot-

ing lodge that houses a fascinating collection of antiques and artefacts documenting the local culture of the 17th, 18th and 19th centuries. It also has a tearoom, restaurant and gift shop, and has public internet access.

Five miles further on, the public road ends at **Invermark Castle**, an impressive ruined tower guarding the southern approach to the Mounth, a hill track to Deeside.

Edzell

POP 785

The picturesque village of Edzell, with its broad main street and grandiose monumental arch, dates from the early 19th century when Lord Panmure decided that the original medieval village, a mile to the west, spoiled the view from Edzell Castle. The old village was razed and the villagers moved to this pretty, planned settlement.

◉ Sights & Activities

Edzell Castle   CASTLE
(HS; adult/child £4.70/2.80; ☻9.30am-5.30pm Apr-Sep, to 4.30pm Oct, 9.30am-4.30pm Sat-Wed Nov-Mar) Sir David Lindsay, a cultured and well-travelled man, laid out this castle's beautiful pleasance in 1604 as a place of contemplation and learning. Unique in all of Scotland, this Renaissance walled garden is lined with niches for nesting birds, and sculptured plaques illustrating the cardinal virtues, the arts and the planetary deities.

The Lindsay earls of Crawford, Lord Panmure's predecessors as owners of Edzell Castle, built the L plan tower house in the 16th century.

Rocks of Solitude   WALKING
Two miles north of Edzell, the B966 to Fettercairn crosses the River North Esk at Gannochy Bridge. From the lay-by just over the bridge, a blue-painted wooden door in the stone wall gives access to a delightful footpath that leads along the wooded river gorge for 1.5 miles to a scenic spot known as the Rocks of Solitude.

🛏 Sleeping & Eating

Alexandra Lodge   B&B ££
(☎01365-648266; www.alexandralodge.co.uk; Inveriscandye Rd; s/d £45/70) This attractive Edwardian villa has comfortable bedrooms and a lovely wood-panelled lounge.

Panmure Arms Hotel

HOTEL ££

(☑01365-648950; www.panmurearmshotel.co.uk; 52 High St; s/d from £55/80) This pretty, mock-Tudor place serves excellent bar meals (£11 to £15) from noon till 2pm Monday to Friday and fromnoon till 9pm Saturday and Sunday.

ℹ️ Getting There & Away

Bus 29 or 29A from Brechin to Laurencekirk stops at Edzell (15 minutes, seven a day Monday to Friday, five on Saturday).

BLAIRGOWRIE & GLENSHEE

The A93 road from Blairgowrie to Braemar via Glenshee is one of the most spectacular drives in the country. Meandering burns and soaring peaks splotched with blinding-white snow dwarf open-mouthed drivers – it's surprising that there aren't more accidents!

It's fantastic walking country in summer, and there's skiing in winter. **Blairgowrie** and **Braemar** are the main accommodation centres for the Glenshee resort, although there is a small settlement 5 miles south of the ski runs at **Spittal of Glenshee** with a couple of good sleeping options.

◉ Sights

About 5 miles east of Blairgowrie, **Alyth** is a charming little historic village with a small canal and some exquisite stone bridges. Ask at Blairgowrie's tourist office for the *Walk Old Alyth* leaflet. If you're looking to escape the rain, perusing the displays on local history at **Alyth Museum** (www.pkc.gov.uk; Commercial St; admission free; ◷1-5pm Wed-Sun May-Sep) is a fine way to pass an hour or so.

Off the A94 and 8 miles east of Blairgowrie, **Meigle** is worth the trip for those with a fascination for **Pictish stones**. The tiny **Meigle Museum** (HS; www.historic-scotland .gov.uk; adult/child £3.20/1.90; ◷9.30am-5.30pm Apr-Sep) has 26 such carved stones from the 7th to the 10th century, all found in the local area. The pieces range from the Nordic to the exotic – they include a Viking headstone and, bizarrely, a carving of a camel.

🏃 Activities

Glenshee Ski Resort

WINTER SPORTS

(☑01339-741320; www.ski-glenshee.co.uk; half-/full day lift pass £20/25) With 38 pistes Glenshee is one of Scotland's largest skiing areas.

When the sun burns through the clouds after a good fall of snow, you'll be in a unique position to drink in the beauty of the country; the skiing isn't half bad either. The chairlift can whisk you up to 910m, near the top of the **Cairnwell** (933m).

🛏️ Sleeping & Eating

TOP CHOICE **Dalmunzie House**

HOTEL £££

(☑01250-885224; www.dalmunzie.com; Glenshee; s £105-145, d £170-230, dinner £45; P@🛜) A noble estate with a dash of antipodean hospitality thrown into the mix, this classy retreat lives up to the best Highland stereotypes: roaring fires, leather armchairs, antlers and decanters of malt. There are four classes of room, offering plenty of comfort (some with four-poster beds), and a beautiful library set up to help research into Scottish forebears.

Dinners in the restaurant are opulent affairs with three courses broken by a cleansing sorbet. As well as wonderful walks hereabouts, the property offers golf, tennis, fishing and other activities; bikes can also be hired.

Spittal of Glenshee Hotel

HOTEL, HOSTEL ££

(☑01250-885215; www.spittalofglenshee.co.uk; Spittal of Glenshee; dm/s/d £16/55/65; P🛜) This hotel is a very 'Scottish experience' – it's a great old country lodge that has burnt down numerous times, but don't worry: the insurers have calculated that it is likely the next fire won't be until 2029. There's a good bar, and a bunkhouse, too (without cooking facilities).

Rosebank House

B&B ££

(☑01250-872912; colhotel@rosebank35.fsnet.co.uk; Balmoral Rd, Blairgowrie; s/d £28/56; ◷Jan-Nov; P) This fine Georgian property is a great deal. Good-sized rooms upstairs are well kept and have small but clean en suites, and there's a large front garden. The friendly owners take good care of guests, and no surcharge is levied on solo travellers. Try to get a room overlooking the garden.

Alyth Hotel

HOTEL ££

(☑01828-632447; www.alythhotel.com; 6 Commercial St, Alyth; s/d £50/75, mains £8-11; P) This classic town pub has had an excellent refurbishment. The old-style rooms upstairs are better than the renovated ones though, with a lot more space and a user-friendly design. Either way, try to get a room overlooking the Square; Room 1 is a good choice.

The downstairs bar and restaurant is cosy with low-slung roof, stone walls and all manner of clutter giving it a homey feel.

ℹ Information

Blairgowrie tourist office (☎01250-872960; blairgowrie@visitscotland.com; 26 Wellmeadow; ⏱daily Apr-Oct & Dec, Mon-Sat Nov & Jan-Mar) On the central square in Blairgowrie; has plenty of walking and skiing information.

ℹ Getting There & Away

Stagecoach (www.stagecoachbus.com) Operates from Perth to Blairgowrie (50 minutes, three to seven daily). Buses also run from Dundee to Blairgowrie (50 minutes, hourly, less frequent on Sunday). The only service from Blairgowrie to the Glenshee area, about 30 miles away, is Stagecoach bus 71, which runs twice on Wednesday and four times on Saturday to Spittal of Glenshee.

WALKING IN THE CENTRAL HIGHLANDS

Schiehallion Walk

Famed for its pointed, conical silhouette, especially when viewed from Loch Rannoch's birch-lined north shore, Schiehallion (1083m), Gaelic for 'the fairy hill of the Caledonians', is an isolated whale of a mountain. A distinctive landmark from many viewpoints, it even got a mention from the great chronicler Ptolemy in the 2nd century AD, in his pioneering work *Geography*.

The mountain played an important role in the history of science as the setting in

» **Duration** 4 hours
» **Distance** 7.6 miles (12km)
» **Difficulty** moderate
» **Start/Finish** Braes of Foss car park
» **Summary** Ascend the famous landmark in Scotland's centre, the hill that also sired the contour lines on topographical maps.

1774 for the 'Schiehallion Experiment', the first scientific attempt to measure the mean density of the earth. This was done by observing tiny deflections of a pendulum on either side of the hill, caused by its own gravitational attraction (Schiehallion's isolation and symmetry made it ideal for the purpose). While taking survey measurements to calculate the volume of the mountain, the scientists came up with the idea of contour lines, used to show elevation on topographical maps ever since.

Now designated a Site of Special Scientific Interest, there are areas of limestone pavement on Schiehallion's northern slopes (just above the road to the west of Lochan an Daim, 2 miles west of the Braes of Foss car park) that provide a habitat for lime-loving plants such as wild thyme, rock rose, bottle sedge and the rare astragalus and northern felwort. The summit ridge of shattered grey quartzite is frequented by ptarmigan and snow bunting.

The **John Muir Trust** (www.jmt.org) owns and manages the summit, path and eastern slopes and has re-routed the path to the sum-

Schiehallion Walk

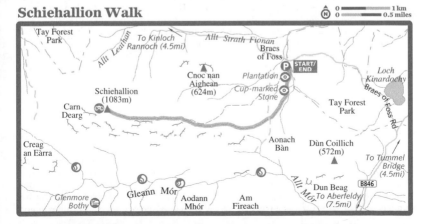

mit ridge, providing a narrow but firm walking surface. This has allowed restoration of vegetation along the former route, which was heavily eroded with deep, wet, peaty troughs. The all-encompassing views are especially fine in summer when the setting sun makes the Highlands glow in the west.

To reach the start of the walk, take the B846 and turn down Braes of Foss Rd between Coshieville and Tummel Bridge. Continue 2 miles on Braes of Foss Rd and turn left into the well-marked Braes of Foss car park, which has metered parking.

THE WALK

Leave the car park by the marked gate and follow the path climbing gently south between a small conifer plantation on the right (west) and a much larger expanse of commercial forest on the left (east). The narrow path is perfectly clear ahead, curving right past the wood to climb southwest past a prehistoric, cup-marked rock close to the path on the right (not easy to spot). Continue towards a rough hill track and cross it near a former sheep pen. From here the path begins to climb more steeply southwest, up onto Schiehallion's east ridge, swinging gradually to the right (west).

The trail disappears in places on the rocky ridge but cairns guide the way. You'll notice an abundance of rose and white quartz veining the rocks. The upper part of the ridge can be awkward as the rock strata dip away at an angle to the line of ascent. There's no real danger of a dramatic plunge, though it would be all too easy to twist an ankle here. The final rise to the Schiehallion summit is on bare, gently sloping rock. On sunny days the top is transformed into a high-level outdoor bistro, and you may have to wait a few minutes for the party ahead of you to finish taking photos at the cairn atop this popular hill.

Enjoy the 360-degree views from the numerous stone-built windbreaks. Return by the same route.

Linn of Dee Circuit Walk

This is a superbly scenic, comparatively low-level walk exploring Glen Dee and Glen Lui, west of Braemar, starting from the woodland car park 250m beyond the Linn of Dee, a narrow gorge at the road bridge about 1.5 miles west of Inverey. It's a good way to familiarise yourself with the area and its

LINN OF DEE CIRCUIT WALK

» **Duration** 6½–7 hours
» **Distance** 16 miles (26km)
» **Difficulty** moderate
» **Start/Finish** Linn of Dee
» **Summary** A generally low-level exploration of two beautiful glens and superb Scots pine woodlands, with awesome views of the Braeriach massif above the Lairig Ghru.

special feeling of remoteness and isolation. With a high point of 610m (only 250m of ascent), it is ideal for a misty day. A clockwise direction is recommended so you walk up the ever-narrowing Glen Dee towards spectacular Lairig Ghru, and the easiest going is concentrated in the second half. The walk can be extended further up Lairig Ghru as far as the Pools of Dee; this involves an extra 7 miles (11km) return.

During the walk you see plenty of evidence of the NTS's work to restore the magnificent pine woodlands, with fenced areas (exclosures) in Glen Luibeg where the native woodland, safe from hungry deer, is slowly making a comeback. In Glen Dee conifer plantations and their enclosing fences are being removed, to make way for native species and to give capercaillie and black grouse a better chance of thriving without the hazard of lethal fencing. Less obviously, the number of red deer has been greatly reduced.

PLANNING

The OS Landranger 1:50,000 map No 43 *Braemar & Blair Atholl* covers this walk. The Harvey Superwalker 1:25,000 *Cairn Gorm* map excludes the area northwest from Linn of Dee, between Glen Luibeg and the River Dee.

The SMC's guide *The Cairngorms* contains some relevant information. The NTS booklet about Mar Lodge Estate is available from the rangers' office at Mar Lodge or, more conveniently, from the tourist offices in Braemar and Ballater.

THE WALK

From the car park head west along the road and continue past a barrier, along a vehicular track. You soon leave a pine plantation behind, entering wide, steep-sided **Glen Dee**. Follow the track past many former settlements and scattered Scots pines almost to White Bridge (about 1¼ hours from the start). Just before the bridge, leave the track on the well-made path to the right (west). In about 250m you pass close to the picturesque clear pools and cascades of the **Chest of Dee**. The path, generally pretty rough but properly constructed in places and easy to follow, leads northwest up Glen Dee with the river in view.

About 0.75 miles beyond the Chest of Dee, the path fords a small burn, beside which are the remains of two small dwellings. After a couple of miles it drops down to the river bank where the glen narrows; views of the mighty cliffs of the **Devil's Point**, the gateway to Lairig Ghru, and Cairn Toul beyond begin to unfold. As the glen widens again, near cliff-lined Glen Geusachan to the west, the path rises across the heathery-peaty slope and leads to a junction, spectacularly overlooked by the Devil's Point and just about opposite **Corrour Bothy** (2½ hours from White Bridge).

To reach the bothy go down a narrow path on the left to a bridge across the river. Pick your way through the peat hags up to the bothy, standing more or less high and dry above the peaty morass. Built in 1877 to house an estate deer watcher on the lookout for poachers, it was renovated in 2006 by the Mountain Bothies Association. The outlook to Ben Macdui is most impressive.

From here it takes a good three hours to continue up through the magnificent depths of the **Lairig Ghru** to the Pools of Dee (source of the River Dee) and to return – well worth the effort if time is on your side.

The route back to Linn of Dee heads south from the path junction. The path rises steadily up the lower slopes of Carn a' Mhaim to the watershed between Glen Dee and Glen Luibeg. Around here the quality of the path improves dramatically, with sections of stone paving and beautifully built culverts. The path descends into **Glen Luibeg** to a fenced wood – go through the gate. There's a choice to be made here; the dry-feet option is to turn left (north), cross 300m of muddy ground to **Luibeg Bridge**, then go back downstream past a path junction (to Ben Macdui) on the left (1½ hours from Corrour Bothy). The alternative, when Luibeg Burn is low, is to go straight ahead and cross the stream on widely spaced stepping stones, then rejoin the main path.

From here, the path soon becomes wider and well made, winding east through Glen Luibeg where the scattered pine woodlands provide a dramatic contrast to the earlier moors and crags. After about 1.5 miles you reach the edge of a flat stretch of open grassland. Follow a rough path east from here to a bridge over Derry Burn, near boarded-up **Derry Lodge** (one hour from Luibeg Bridge). There is a telephone for public and emergency use in a red box on the side of a brown timber building near the lodge. It's coin-operated and maintained (at a loss) by the volunteer Braemar Mountain Rescue Team.

The last hour of walking is easy, down **Glen Lui** on a vehicular track past exclosures, areas cleared of non-native conifers, and the scattered remains of former settlements. After crossing the **Black Bridge** the track rises a little then falls, passing a fenced plantation on the left. On the downhill section, look out for the sign indicating the path to the right, which leads through a plantation to the car park.

The Great Glen & Lochaber

Includes »

Best Places to Eat

» Lime Tree (p168)

» Contrast Brasserie (p154)

» Lochleven Seafood
Cafe (p174)

» Old Forge (p179)

Best Places to Stay

» Rocpool Reserve (p153)

» Lime Tree (p167)

» Lovat Arms Hotel (p162)

» Trafford Bank (p152)

» Ben Nevis Inn (p169)

Why Go?

From the rugged, rocky crags of Glen Coe to the shapely, pointed peaks of Knoydart, Glenelg and Kintail, the mountain ranges of the Great Glen and Lochaber are testimony to the sculpting power of ice and weather. Here the Highland landscape is at its grandest, with soaring hills of rock and heather bounded by wooded glens and rushing waterfalls.

Not surprisingly, this part of the country is an adventure playground for outdoor sports enthusiasts. Glen Coe and Nevis Range draw hordes of hill walkers, climbers and mountain bikers in summer, and skiers, snowboarders and ice climbers in winter. Inverness, the Highland capital, provides urban rest and relaxation, while nearby Loch Ness and its elusive monster add a hint of mystery.

From Fort William, base camp for climbing Ben Nevis, the Road to the Isles leads past the gorgeous beaches along the coast from Arisaig to Morar and to Mallaig, jumping-off point for the islands of Skye, Eigg and Rum.

When to Go
Fort William

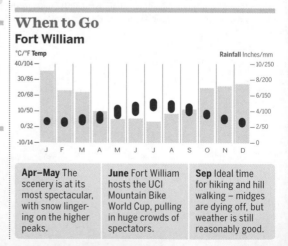

Apr–May The scenery is at its most spectacular, with snow lingering on the higher peaks.

June Fort William hosts the UCI Mountain Bike World Cup, pulling in huge crowds of spectators.

Sep Ideal time for hiking and hill walking – midges are dying off, but weather is still reasonably good.

INVERNESS

Inverness, the primary city and shopping centre of the Highlands, has a great location astride the River Ness at the northern end of the Great Glen. In summer it overflows with visitors intent on monster hunting at nearby Loch Ness, but it's worth a visit in its own right for a stroll along the picturesque River Ness and a cruise on the Moray Firth in search of its famous bottlenose dolphins.

The city was probably founded by King David in the 12th century, but thanks to its often violent history few buildings of real age or historical significance have survived. Much of the older part of the city dates from the period following the completion of the Caledonian Canal in 1822. The broad and shallow River Ness, which flows a short 6 miles from Loch Ness into the Moray Firth, runs through the heart of the city.

◎ Sights & Activities

Ness Islands   PARK
The main attraction in Inverness is a leisurely stroll along the river to the Ness Islands. Planted with mature Scots pine, fir, beech and sycamore, and linked to the river banks and each other by elegant Victorian footbridges, the islands make an appealing picnic spot.

They're a 20-minute walk south of the castle – head upstream on either side of the river (the start of the Great Glen Way), and return on the opposite bank. On the way you'll pass the red-sandstone towers of **St Andrew's Cathedral**, dating from 1869, and the modern **Eden Court Theatre**, which hosts regular art exhibits, both on the west bank.

Inverness Museum & Art Gallery   MUSEUM
(☑01463-237114; www.inverness.highland.museum; Castle Wynd; free; ☺10am-5pm Mon-Sat) Between the castle and the tourist office is Inverness Museum & Art Gallery, which has wildlife dioramas, geological displays, period rooms with historic weapons, Pictish stones and contemporary Highland arts and crafts.

Victorian Market   MARKET
If the rain comes down, you could opt for a spot of retail therapy in the Victorian Market, a shopping mall that dates from the 1890s and has rather more charm than its modern equivalents.

Inverness Castle   CASTLE
(Castle St) The hill above the city centre is topped by the picturesque Baronial turrets of Inverness Castle, a pink-sandstone confection dating from 1847 that replaced a medieval castle blown up by the Jacobites in 1746; it serves today as the Sheriff's Court. It's not open to the public, but there are good views from the surrounding gardens.

☞ Tours

Moray Firth Cruises   WILDLIFE CRUISES
(☑01463-717900; www.inverness-dolphin-cruises .co.uk; Shore St Quay; ☺10.30am-4.30pm Mar-Oct) Offers 1½-hour wildlife cruises (adult/child £14/10) to look for dolphins, seals and bird life. Sightings aren't guaranteed, but the commentaries are excellent, and on a fine day it's good just being out on the water.

Follow the signs to Shore St Quay from the far end of Chapel St or catch the free shuttle bus that leaves from the tourist office 15 minutes before sailings (which depart every 1½ hours). In July and August there are also departures at 6pm.

Jacobite Cruises   CRUISES
(☑01463-233999; www.jacobite.co.uk; Glenurquhart Rd) Cruise boats depart at 10.35am and 1.35pm from Tomnahurich Bridge for a 3½-hour trip along Loch Ness, including visits to Urquhart Castle and Loch Ness Exhibition Centre (adult/child £26/20 including admission fees). You can buy tickets at the tourist office and catch a free minibus to the boat. Other cruises, from one to 6½ hours, are also available.

Happy Tours   WALKING TOURS
(www.happy-tours.biz; adult/child £10/free) Offers 1¼-hour guided walks exploring the town's history and legends. Tours begin outside the tourist office at 11am, 1pm and 3pm daily.

Inverness Taxis   TAXI TOURS
(☑01463-222900; www.inverness-taxis.co.uk) Wide range of day tours to Urquhart Castle, Loch Ness, Culloden, and even Skye. Fares per car (up to four people) range from £50 (two hours) to £200 (all day).

John O'Groats Ferries   BUS/FERRY TOURS
(☑01955-611353; www.jogferry.co.uk; ☺departs 7.30am) From May to September, daily tours are run (lasting 13½ hours; adult/child £57/28.50) by bus and passenger ferry from Inverness bus station to Orkney.

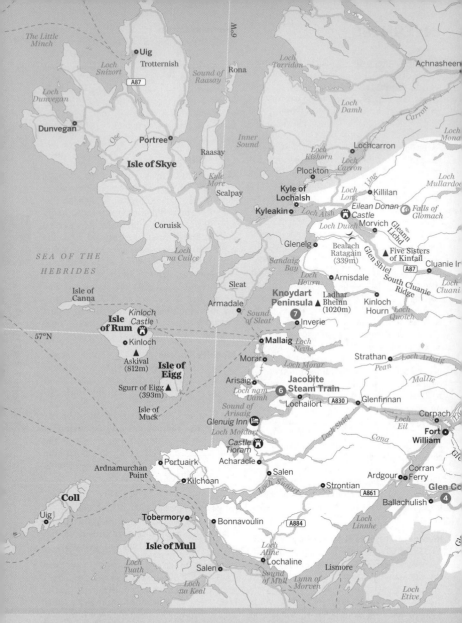

The Great Glen & Lochaber Highlights

❶ Hike among the hills, lochs and forests of beautiful **Glen Affric** (p158)

❷ Make it to the summit of **Ben Nevis** – and enjoy the view (p169)

❸ Rattle your teeth loose on the downhill mountain-bike course at **Nevis Range** (p170)

❹ Soak up the scenery (when you can see it!) in moody but magnificent **Glen Coe** (p171)

❺ Cruise **Loch Ness** (p159) in search of that elusive monster

❻ Ride the rails of the scenic West Highland Line aboard the **Jacobite Steam Train** (p166)

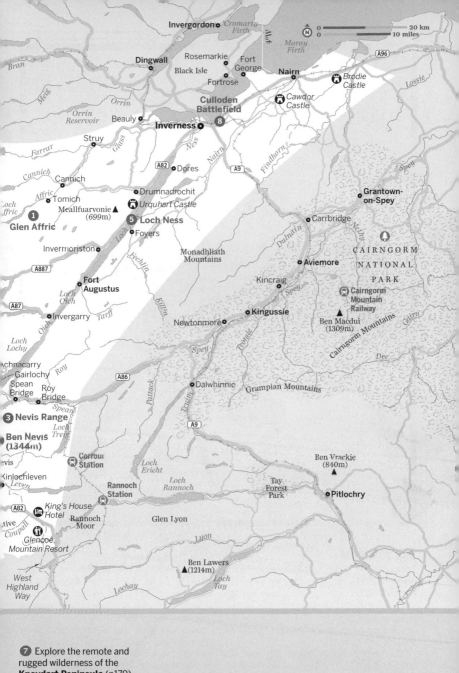

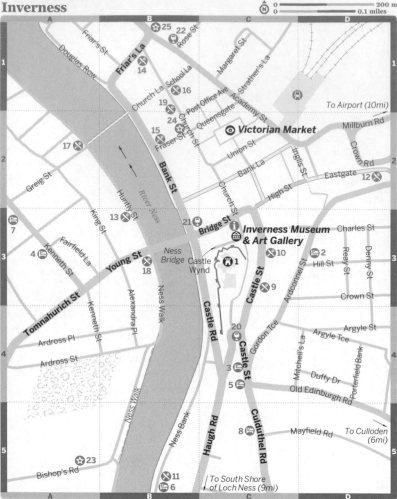

🛏 Sleeping

Inverness has a good range of backpacker accommodation, and there are lots of guesthouses and B&Bs along Old Edinburgh Rd and Ardconnel St on the east side of the river, and on Kenneth St and Fairfield Rd on the west bank; all are within 10 minutes' walk of the city centre.

The city fills up quickly in July and August, so you should either prebook your accommodation or get an early start looking for somewhere to stay.

TOP CHOICE Trafford Bank B&B ££

(☎01463-241414; www.traffordbankguesthouse .co.uk; 96 Fairfield Rd; s/d from £85/110) Lots of word-of-mouth rave reviews for this elegant Victorian villa that was once home to a bishop, just a mitre-toss from the Caledonian Canal and 10 minutes' walk west from the city centre. The luxurious rooms include fresh flowers and fruit, bathrobes and fluffy towels – ask for the Tartan Room, which has a wrought-iron king-size bed and Victorian roll-top bath.

Inverness

This ranges from iPod docks to balcony hot tubs with aquavision TV. A new restaurant by Albert Roux completes the package.

Ardconnel House B&B ££
(☎01463-240455; www.ardconnel-inverness.co.uk; 21 Ardconnel St; per person from £35; ☜) The six-room Ardconnel is one of our favourites – a terraced Victorian house with comfortable en suite rooms, a dining room with crisp white table linen, and a breakfast menu that includes Vegemite for homesick Antipodeans. Kids under 10 not allowed.

Ach Aluinn B&B ££
(☎01463-230127; www.achaluinn.com; 27 Fairfield Rd; r per person £25-35; ℗) This large, detached Victorian house is bright and homey, and offers all you might want from a guesthouse – private bathroom, TV, reading lights, comfy beds with two pillows each, and an excellent breakfast. Less than 10 minutes' walk west from the city centre.

Loch Ness Country House Hotel HOTEL £££
(☎01463-230512; www.lochnesscountryhousehotel.co.uk; d from £165; ℗☜) This sumptuous country-house hotel offers traditional decor, featuring Victorian four-poster beds, Georgian-style furniture and Italian marble bathrooms, all set in beautiful wooded grounds just five minutes' stroll from the Caledonian Canal and River Ness. The hotel is a mile southwest of Inverness on the A82 to Fort William.

Crown Hotel Guest House B&B ££
(☎01463-231135; www.inverness-guesthouse.info; 19 Ardconnel St; s/d from £36/56; ℗☗) Similar in its layout to the ever-popular Ardconnel next door, the Crown has kind and helpful owners and welcomes children. Two of the six bedrooms are family rooms (with a double, single, and folding bed in each), and there's a spacious lounge equipped with games consoles, DVDs and board games.

MacRae Guest House B&B ££
(☎01463-243658; joycemacrae@hotmail.com; 24 Ness Bank; s/d from £45/64; ℗) This pretty, flower-bedecked Victorian house on the eastern bank of the river has smart, tastefully decorated bedrooms (one is wheelchair accessible), and vegetarian breakfasts are available. Minimum two-night bookings in July and August.

TOP CHOICE ▸ Rocpool Reserve BOUTIQUE HOTEL £££
(☎01463-240089; www.rocpool.com; Culduthel Rd; s/d from £160/195; ℗☜) Boutique chic meets the Highlands in this slick and sophisticated little hotel, where an elegant Georgian exterior conceals an oasis of contemporary cool. A gleaming white entrance hall lined with contemporary art leads to designer rooms in shades of chocolate, cream and coffee; expect lots of high-tech gadgetry in the more expensive rooms.

Bazpackers Backpackers Hotel   HOSTEL £
(☎01463-717663; 4 Culduthel Rd; dm/tw £14/38;
@) This may be Inverness' smallest hostel (30
beds), but it's hugely popular – it's a friendly,
quiet place with a convivial lounge centred
on a wood-burning stove; it also has a small
garden and great views. The dorms can be a
bit cramped, but the showers are great.

Inverness Student Hotel   HOSTEL £
(☎01463-236556; www.scotlands-top-hostels.com;
8 Culduthel Rd; dm from £14) Set in a rambling
old house with comfy beds and views across
the River Ness, this hostel has a party atmosphere, and runs organised pub crawls in
town. It's a 10-minute walk from the train
station, just past the castle.

Inverness SYHA   HOSTEL £
(☎01463-231771; www.syha.org.uk; Victoria Dr; dm
£18.50; ☺Apr-Dec; P@🖅) Inverness' modern
166-bed hostel is 10 minutes' walk northeast
of the city centre. With its comfy beds and
flashy stainless-steel kitchen, some reckon
it's the best hostel in the country. Booking
is essential, especially at Easter, and in July
and August.

**Glenmoriston Town House
Hotel**   BOUTIQUE HOTEL £££
(☎01463-223777; www.glenmoristontownhouse
.com; 20 Ness Bank; s/d from £105/150; P🖅)
Luxurious boutique hotel on the banks of
the River Ness. Can organise golfing and
fishing for guests.

Mardon Guest House   B&B ££
(☎01463-231005; www.mardonguesthouse.co.uk;
37 Kenneth St; r per person £30-38; P🖅) Friendly
B&B with six cosy rooms (all en suite), just
five minutes' walk west from the city centre.

Moyness House Hotel   B&B ££
(☎01463-233836; www.moyness.co.uk; 6 Bruce
Gardens; r per person £40-50; P🖅) Elegant
Victorian villa with a beautiful garden and
peaceful setting, 10 minutes' walk southwest of the city centre.

Bluebell House   B&B ££
(☎01463-238201; www.bluebell-house.com; 31
Kenneth St; r per person £30-45; P🖅) Warm and
welcoming hosts, top breakfasts, close to city
centre.

Amulree   B&B ££
(☎01463-224822; amulree@btinternet.com; 40
Fairfield Rd; per person £30; P🖅) Comfortable,
four-bedroom Victorian B&B less than 10
minutes' walk west of the city centre.

**Bught Caravan Park &
Campsite**   CAMPGROUND £
(☎01463-236920;   www.invernesscaravanpark
.com; Bught Lane; tent site per person £7, campervan £15; ☺Easter–mid-Oct) A mile south-west
of the city centre near Tomnahurich Bridge,
this camping ground is hugely popular with
backpackers.

✖ Eating

TOP CHOICE Contrast Brasserie   INTERNATIONAL ££
(☎01463-227889; 22 Ness Bank; mains £10-19;
☺noon-2.30pm & 5-10pm) Book early for what
we think is the best restaurant in Inverness
– a dining room that drips designer style,
smiling professional staff, and truly delicious food. Try mussels with Thai red curry,
wild mushroom risotto, or pork belly with
glazed walnuts and watercress; 10 out of 10.
And at £10 for a two-course lunch, the value
is incredible.

TOP CHOICE Café 1   INTERNATIONAL ££
(☎01463-226200; www.cafe1.net; 75 Castle St;
mains £10-20; ☺noon-2pm & 5.30-9.30pm Mon-
Sat) Café 1 is a friendly and appealing bistro
with candlelit tables amid elegant blonde-
wood and wrought-iron decor. There is an
international menu based on quality Scottish produce, from Aberdeen Angus steaks
to crisp sea bass with chilli, lime and soy
sauce. Lunch and early-bird menu (two
courses for £9.50) is served noon to 6.45pm
weekdays, and noon to 3pm Saturday.

Rocpool   MEDITERRANEAN ££
(☎01463-717274; www.rocpoolrestaurant.com; 1
Ness Walk; mains £13-18; ☺noon-2.30pm & 5.45-
10pm) Lots of polished wood, navy-blue
leather and crisp white linen lend a nautical air to this relaxing bistro, which offers a
Mediterranean-influenced menu that makes
the most of quality Scottish produce, especially seafood. The two-course lunch (noon
to 2.30pm Monday to Saturday) is £12.

Mustard Seed   MODERN SCOTTISH ££
(☎01463-220220;   www.mustardseedrestaurant
.co.uk; 16 Fraser St; mains £12-16; ☺noon-10pm)
This bright and bustling bistro brings a
dash of big-city style to Inverness. The menu
changes weekly, but focuses on Scottish and
French cuisine with a modern twist. Grab a
table on the upstairs balcony – it's the best
outdoor lunch spot in Inverness, with a
great view across the river. And a two-course
lunch for £6 – yes, that's hard to beat.

Sam's Indian Cuisine
INDIAN ££

(77-79 Church St; mains £8-13; ☺noon-2.30pm & 6-11pm) The stylish decor in Sam's is a cut above your average curry shop, and so is the food – lots of fresh and flavoursome spices and herbs make dishes such as jeera chicken (cooked with cumin seed) really zing. Wash it down with Indian Cobra beer.

River House
MODERN SCOTTISH £££

(☎01463-222033; www.riverhouseinverness.co.uk; 1 Greig St; mains £16-22; ☺noon-2pm & 5.30-9.30pm Tue-Sat, 6-9.30pm Sun) This is an elegant restaurant of the polished-wood and crisp-white-linen variety, serving the best of British venison, beef, lamb, duck and seafood.

Délices de Bretagne
FRENCH £

(☎01463-712422; 6 Stephen's Brae; mains £3-7; ☺9am-5pm Mon-Sat, from 10am Sun) This cafe brings a little taste of France to the Highlands, with its art-nouveau decor and a menu of tasty *galettes* (savoury pancakes), crepes, Breton cider and excellent coffee.

Kitchen
MODERN SCOTTISH ££

(☎01463-259119; www.kitchenrestaurant.co.uk; 15 Huntly St; mains £12-16; ☺noon-3pm & 5.30-10pm) This spectacular glass-fronted restaurant is under the same management as the Mustard Seed, and offers a good menu and a view of the River Ness.

Leakey's
CAFE £

(Church St; mains £3-5; ☺10am-5.30pm Mon-Sat) Cafe in a secondhand bookshop.

Castle Restaurant
CAFE £

(☎01463-230925; 41-43 Castle St; mains £4-8; ☺9am-8.30pm) This is a classic old fashioned cafe.

Red Pepper
CAFE £

(☎01463-237111; 74 Church St; mains £3-4; ☺9am-5.30pm) Cool coffee and sandwich place.

🍷 Drinking

TOP CHOICE Clachnaharry Inn
PUB

(☎01463-239806; www.clachnaharryinn.co.uk; 17-19 High St) Just over a mile northwest of the city centre, on the bank of the Caledonian Canal just off the A862, this is a delightful old coaching inn (with beer garden out back) serving an excellent range of real ales and good pub grub.

Castle Tavern
PUB

(☎01463-718718; www.castletavern.net; 1-2 View Pl) Under the same management as the Clachnaharry Inn and with a tasty selection of

real ales, this pub has a wee suntrap of a terrace out the front. It's a great place for a pint on a summer afternoon.

Phoenix
PUB

(☎01463-233685; 108 Academy St) This is the best of the traditional pubs in the city centre, with a mahogany horseshoe bar, a comfortable, family friendly lounge, and good food at both lunchtime and in the evening. Real ales on tap include the rich and fruity Orkney Dark Island.

Johnny Foxes
BAR

(☎01463-236577; www.johnnyfoxes.co.uk; 26 Bank St) Stuck beneath the ugliest building on the riverfront, Johnny Foxes is a big and boisterous Irish bar with a wide range of food served all day and live music nightly. Part of the premises, The Den, is now a smart cocktail bar.

☆ Entertainment

Hootananny
LIVE MUSIC

(☎01463-233651; www.hootananny.com; 67 Church St) Hootananny is the city's best live-music venue, with traditional folk- and/or rock-music sessions nightly, including big-name bands from all over Scotland (and, indeed, the world). The bar is well stocked with a range of beers from the local Black Isle Brewery.

Eden Court Theatre
THEATRE

(☎01463-234234; www.eden-court.co.uk; Bishop's Rd) The Highlands' main cultural venue – with theatre, art-house cinema and conference centre – Eden Court stages a busy program of drama, dance, comedy, music, film and children's events, and has a good bar and restaurant. Pick up a program from the foyer or check the website.

Ironworks
LIVE MUSIC, COMEDY

(www.ironworksvenue.com; 122 Academy St) With live bands (rock, pop, tribute) and comedy shows two or three times a week, the Ironworks is the town's main venue for big-name acts.

Vue Cinema
CINEMA

(☎08712-240240; www.myvue.com; Eastfield Way) This is a seven-screen multiplex cinema way out on the eastern edge of the city, just south of the A96 to Nairn.

ℹ Information

ClanLAN (22 Baron Taylor's St; ☺10am-8pm Mon-Fri, 11am-8pm Sat, noon-5pm Sun; @) Internet access £1 per 20 minutes.

Inverness tourist office (☎01463-234353; www.visithighlands.com; Castle Wynd; internet access per 20 min £1 ; ◷9am-6pm Mon-Sat, 9.30am-5pm Sun Jul & Aug, 9am-5pm Mon-Sat, 10am-4pm Sun Jun, Sep & Oct, 9am-5pm Mon-Sat Apr & May; @) Bureau de change and accommodation booking service; also sells tickets for tours and cruises. Opening hours limited November to March.

New City Laundrette (☎01463-242507; 17 Young St; ◷8am-8pm Mon-Fri, to 6pm Sat, 10am-4pm Sun; @) Charges £3 per load and £1.40 to dry for laundry; internet access £1 per 20 minutes.

❶ Getting There & Away

AIR Inverness Airport (☎01667-464000; www.hial.co.uk/inverness-airport) At Dalcross, 10 miles east of the city on the A96 towards Aberdeen. There are scheduled flights to London, Bristol, Manchester, Belfast, Stornoway, Benbecula, Orkney, Shetland and several other British airports.

Stagecoach Jet (www.stagecoachbus.com) Buses run from the airport to Inverness bus station (£3, 20 minutes, every 30 minutes).
A taxi from the airport into town costs around £15.

BUS National Express (☎08717 81 81 78; www.gobycoach.com) Operates a direct overnight bus from London to Inverness (£45, 13 hours, one daily), with more frequent services requiring a change at Glasgow.

Scottish Citylink (www.citylink.co.uk) Has connections to Glasgow (£26, 3½ to 4½ hours, hourly), Edinburgh (£26, 3½ to 4½ hours, hourly), Fort William (£11, two hours, five daily), Ullapool (£9, 1½ hours, two daily except Sunday), Portree (£17, 3½ hours, five daily) on the Isle of Skye and Thurso (£18, 3½ hours, two daily).

Megabus (☎0871 266 3333; www.megabus.com) If you book far enough in advance, Megabus offers fares from as little as £5 for buses from Inverness to Glasgow and Edinburgh, and £15 to London.

TRAIN There is one direct train daily from London to Inverness (£99, eight hours); others require a change at Edinburgh (nine hours, five daily). There are several direct trains a day from Glasgow (£55, 3½ hours), Edinburgh (£55, 3¼ hours) and Aberdeen (£25, 2¼ hours), and three daily Monday to Saturday (one or two on Sunday) to Thurso and Wick (£16, four hours).

The line from Inverness to Kyle of Lochalsh (£18, 2½ hours, four daily Monday to Saturday, two Sunday) provides one of Britain's great scenic train journeys.

❶ Getting Around

BICYCLE Great Glen Cycle Hire (☎07752-102700; www.greatglencyclehire.com; 18

Harbour Rd) Hire mountain bikes for £20 per day. Will deliver bikes to local hotels and B&Bs.

BUS City services and buses to places around Inverness, including Nairn, Forres, the Culloden battlefield, Beauly, Dingwall and Lairg, are operated by Stagecoach. An Inverness City Dayrider ticket costs £3.20 and gives unlimited travel for a day on buses throughout the city.

CAR The tourist office has a handy Car Hire leaflet.

Sharp's Vehicle Rental (☎01463-236694; www.sharpsreliablewrecks.co.uk; Inverness train station) The big boys charge from around £40 per day, but Sharp's has cheaper rates starting at £23 per day.

TAXI Highland Taxis (☎01463-222222)

AROUND INVERNESS

Culloden Battlefield

The Battle of Culloden in 1746, the last pitched battle ever fought on British soil, saw the defeat of Bonnie Prince Charlie and the end of the Jacobite dream when 1200 Highlanders were slaughtered by government forces in a 68-minute rout. The duke of Cumberland, son of the reigning king, George II, and leader of the Hanoverian army, earned the nickname 'Butcher' for his brutal treatment of the defeated Scottish forces. The battle sounded the death knell for the old clan system, and the horrors of the Clearances soon followed. The sombre moor where the conflict took place has scarcely changed in the ensuing 260 years.

The impressive new **visitor centre** (NTS; www.nts.org.uk/culloden; adult/child £10/7.50; ◷9am-6pm Apr-Oct, 10am-4pm Nov-Mar) presents detailed information about the battle, including the lead-up and the aftermath, with perspectives from both sides. An innovative film puts you on the battlefield in the middle of the mayhem, and a wealth of other audio presentations must have kept Inverness' entire acting community in business for weeks. The admission fee includes an audioguide for a self-guided tour of the battlefield itself.

Culloden is 6 miles east of Inverness. Bus No 1 runs from Queensgate in Inverness to the Culloden battlefield (30 minutes, hourly).

Fort George

The headland guarding the narrows in the Moray Firth opposite Fortrose is occupied by the magnificent and virtually unaltered 18th-century artillery fortification of **Fort George** (HS; ☑01667-462777; adult/child £6.70/4; ☻9.30am-5.30pm Apr-Sep, to 4.30pm Oct-Mar). One of the finest examples of its kind in Europe, it was established in 1748 as a base for George II's army of occupation in the Highlands – by the time of its completion in 1769 it had cost the equivalent of around £1 billion in today's money. The mile-plus walk around the ramparts offers fine views out to sea and back to the Great Glen. Given its size, you'll need at least two hours to do the place justice. The fort is off the A96 about 11 miles northeast of Inverness.

Nairn
POP 11,000

Nairn is a popular golfing and seaside resort with a good sandy beach.

◉ Sights & Activities

The most interesting part of Nairn is the old fishing village of **Fishertown**, down by the harbour.

You can spend many pleasant hours wandering along the **East Beach**, one of the finest in Scotland.

Nairn Museum   MUSEUM
(☑01667-456791; www.nairnmuseum.co.uk; Viewfield House; adult/child £3/50p; ☻10am-4.30pm Mon-Fri, to 1pm Sat Apr-Oct) Nairn Museum, a few minutes' walk from the tourist office, has displays on the history of the harbour community of Fishertown, as well as on local archaeology, geology and natural history.

✯✯ Festivals & Events

Nairn Highland Games   HIGHLAND GAMES
(www.nairnhighlandgames.co.uk) The big event in Nairn's calendar is the annual Highland Games, held in mid-August.

Nairn International Jazz Festival   MUSIC
(www.nairnjazz.com) The week-long festival is held in August.

🛌 Sleeping & Eating

Glebe End   B&B ££
(☑01667-451659; www.glebe-end.co.uk; 1 Glebe Rd; r per person £25-40; P☻) It's people as much as place that make a good B&B, and the owners here are all you could wish for – helpful and welcoming. The house is lovely too, a spacious Victorian villa with home-away-from-home bedrooms and a sunny conservatory where breakfast is served.

Sunny Brae Hotel   HOTEL ££
(☑01667-452309;   www.sunnybraehotel.com; Marine Rd; s £92, d from £99; P☻) Beautifully decked out with fresh flowers and pot plants, the Sunny Brae enjoys an enviable location with great views across the Moray Firth. The hotel restaurant specialises in Scottish produce cooked with continental flair, with dishes such as rack of local lamb with ratatouille and garlic jus.

Boath House Hotel   HOTEL £££
(☑01667-454896;   www.boath-house.com; Auldearn; s/d from £180/220; P) This beautifully restored Regency mansion, set in private woodland gardens 2 miles east of Nairn on the A96, is one of Scotland's most luxurious country-house hotels, and includes a spa offering holistic treatments and a Michelin-starred restaurant (six-course dinner £65).

Classroom   SCOTTISH ££
(☑01667-455999; www.theclassroombistro.com; 1 Cawdor St; mains £13-20; ☻10am-midnight Mon-Sat, noon-10.30pm Sun) Recently revamped in an appealing mixture of modern and traditional styles – lots of richly glowing wood with designer detailing – the Classroom doubles as cocktail bar and gastropub with a tempting menu that goes from Cullen skink (soup made with smoked haddock, potato, onion and milk) to slow-roast pork belly with black pudding and scallops.

❶ Information

The town has a **tourist office** (☑01667-452763; 62 King St; ☻Apr-Oct), banks with ATMs and a post office.

❶ Getting There & Away

Buses run hourly (less frequently on Sunday) from Inverness to Aberdeen via Nairn. The town also lies on the Inverness–Aberdeen railway line; there are five to seven trains a day from Inverness (£6, 20 minutes).

Cawdor

Cawdor Castle (☑01667-404615; www.cawdorcastle.com; adult/child £8.30/5.20; ☻10am-5.30pm May–mid-Oct) was the 14th-century home of the Thanes of Cawdor, one of the titles prophesied by the three witches for the eponymous character of Shakespeare's *Macbeth*. Macbeth couldn't have moved in, though, since the central tower dates from the 14th century (the wings were 17th-century additions) and he died in 1057. The castle is 5 miles southwest of Nairn.

Cawdor Tavern (www.cawdortavern.co.uk; bar meals £8-15; ⊙lunch & dinner) in the nearby village is worth a visit, though it can be difficult deciding what to drink as it stocks over 100 varieties of whisky. There's also good pub food, with tempting daily specials.

Brodie Castle

Set in 70 hectares of parkland, **Brodie Castle** (NTS; ☑01309-641371; adult/child £8/5; ⊙10.30am-5pm daily Jul & Aug, 10.30am-4.30pm Sun-Wed Apr-Jun, Sep & Oct) has several highlights, including a library with more than 6000 peeling, dusty volumes. There are wonderful clocks, a huge Victorian kitchen and a 17th-century dining room with wildly extravagant moulded plaster ceilings depicting mythological scenes. The Brodies have been living here since 1160, but the present structure dates mostly from 1567, with many additions over the years.

The castle is 8 miles east of Nairn. Stagecoach bus 10A or 11 from Inverness to Elgin stops at Brodie (35 minutes, hourly Monday to Saturday).

WEST OF INVERNESS

Beauly

POP 1160

Mary, Queen of Scots is said to have given this village its name in 1564 when she exclaimed, in French: *'Quel beau lieu!'* (What a beautiful place!). Founded in 1230, the red-sandstone **Beauly Priory** is now an impressive ruin; a small information kiosk next door has information on the history of the priory.

The central **Priory Hotel** (☑01463-782309; www.priory-hotel.com; The Square; s/d £53/90; P🅟🛜) has bright, modern rooms and serves good bar meals. However, the best place for lunch is across the street at the **Corner on the Square** (www.corneronthesquare.co.uk; 1 High St; mains £5-7; ⊙9am-5pm Mon-Sat), a superb little delicatessen and cafe that serves breakfast (till 11.30am), daily lunch specials (noon to 4.30pm) and excellent coffee.

Buses 28 and 28A from Inverness run to Beauly (45 minutes, hourly Monday to Saturday, five on Sunday), and the town lies on the Inverness–Thurso railway line.

Strathglass & Glen Affric

The broad valley of Strathglass extends about 18 miles inland from Beauly, followed by the A831 road to **Cannich** (the only village in the area), where there's a grocery store and a post office.

Glen Affric (www.glenaffric.org), one of the most beautiful glens in Scotland, extends deep into the hills beyond Cannich. The upper reaches of the glen, now designated as **Glen Affric National Nature Reserve**, is a scenic wonderland of shimmering lochs, rugged mountains and native Scots pine, home to pine marten, wildcat, otter, red squirrel and golden eagle.

About 4 miles southwest of Cannich is **Dog Falls**, a scenic spot where the River Affric squeezes through a narrow, rocky gorge. A waymarked walking trail leads there easily from Dog Falls car park.

The road continues beyond Dog Falls to a parking area and picnic site at the eastern end of **Loch Affric** where there are several short walks along the river and the loch shore. The circuit of Loch Affric (10 miles, allow five hours) follows good paths right around the loch and takes you deep into the heart of some very wild scenery.

It's possible to walk all the way from Cannich to Glen Shiel on the west coast (35 miles) in two days, spending the night at the remote Glen Affric Youth Hostel.

The minor road on the east side of the River Glass leads to the pretty little conservation village of **Tomich**, 3 miles southwest of Cannich, built in Victorian times as accommodation for estate workers. The road continues (unsurfaced for the last 2 miles) to a forestry car park, the starting point for a short (800m) walk to **Plodda Falls**. A restored Victorian viewing platform extends above the top of the falls like a diving board, giving a dizzying view straight down the cascade into a remote and thickly forested river gorge. Keep your eyes peeled for red squirrels and crossbills.

🛏 Sleeping & Eating

Kerrow House B&B ££

(☑01456-415243; www.kerrow-house.co.uk; Cannich; per person £35-40; P) This wonderful Georgian hunting lodge has bags of old-fashioned character – it was once the home of Highland author Neil M Gunn – and has spacious grounds with 3.5 miles of private trout fishing. It's a mile south of Cannich on the minor road along the east side of the River Glass.

Tomich Hotel HOTEL ££
(☎01456-415399; www.tomichhotel.co.uk; Tomich; s/d from £74/117; P🛈☀) About 3 miles southwest of Cannich on the southern side of the river, this Victorian hunting lodge has a blazing log fire, a Victorian restaurant, eight comfortable en suite rooms and – a bit of a surprise out here in the wilds – a small, heated indoor swimming pool.

Glen Affric SYHA HOSTEL £
(☎bookings 0845 293 7373; www.syha.org.uk; Allt Beithe, Glen Affric; dm £18.50; ☺Apr–mid-Sep) This remote and rustic hostel is set amid magnificent scenery at the halfway point of the cross-country walk from Cannich to Glen Shiel, 8 miles from the nearest road. Facilities are basic and you'll need to take all supplies with you. Book in advance. There is no phone at the hostel.

Cannich Caravan Park CAMPGROUND £
(☎01456-415364; www.highlandcamping.co.uk; Cannich; tent sites per person £5.50, plus per car £1; 🛈) Good, sheltered site. Mountain bikes for hire at £15 a day.

Glen Affric Bar PUB
(info@glenaffrichostel.com; Cannich; ☺11am-11pm; 🛈) This is a friendly hill-walkers' pub (walking guides are scattered around the place) serving cappuccino and bar meals as well as An Teallach real ale; it also has the only ATM for miles around.

ⓘ Getting There & Away

Stagecoach bus 17 runs from Inverness to Cannich (one hour, three a day Monday to Saturday) via Drumnadrochit; there are also three buses a day (except Sunday) from Cannich to Tomich (10 minutes).

Ross's Minibuses (www.ross-minibuses.co.uk) Operates a service from Inverness to the Glen Affric car park via Beauly and Cannich (two hours, once daily Monday, Wednesday and Friday only, July to mid-September). Check the website for the latest timetables.

LOCH NESS

Deep, dark and narrow, Loch Ness stretches for 23 miles between Inverness and Fort Augustus. It is Britain's largest body of fresh water, holding more than all the lakes in England and Wales combined. Its bitterly cold waters, reaching depths of up to 330m, have been extensively explored in search of Nessie, the elusive Loch Ness monster, but most visitors see her only in cardboard-cutout form at the monster exhibitions.

The busy A82 road runs along the northwestern shore, while the more tranquil and picturesque B862 follows the southeastern shore. A complete circuit of the loch is about 70 miles – travel anticlockwise for the best views.

🏃 Activities

The 73-mile **Great Glen Way** (www.greatglenway.com) long-distance footpath stretches from Inverness to Fort William, where walkers can connect with the West Highland Way. It is described in detail in *The Great Glen Way*, a guide by Jacquetta Megarry and Sandra Bardwell.

The Great Glen Way footpath shares some sections with the 80-mile **Great Glen Mountain Bike Trail**, a waymarked mountain-bike route that follows canal towpaths and gravel tracks through forests, avoiding roads where possible.

The climb to the summit of **Meallfuarvonie** (699m), on the northwestern shore of Loch Ness, makes an excellent short hill walk: the views along the Great Glen from the top are superb. It's a 6-mile round trip, so allow about three hours. Start from the car park at the end of the minor road leading south from Drumnadrochit to Bunloit.

🎉 Festivals & Events

RockNess Music Festival MUSIC
(www.rockness.co.uk) A vast lochside field at the village of Dores hosts this annual festival, a three-day smorgasbord of the best in Scottish and international DJs and bands. Recent headliners include Fat Boy Slim, Leftfield and The Strokes.

🛏 Sleeping

Loch Ness Inn INN ££
(☎01456-450991; www.staylochness.co.uk; Lewiston; s/d/f £69/99/140; P🛈) The Loch Ness Inn ticks all the weary traveller's boxes, with comfortable bedrooms (the family suite sleeps two adults and two children), a cosy bar pouring real ales from the Cairngorm and Isle of Skye breweries, and a rustic restaurant serving hearty, wholesome fare such as smoked haddock chowder, and venison sausages with mash and onion gravy.

It's conveniently located in the quiet hamlet of Lewiston, between Drumnadrochit and Urquhart Castle.

STRANGE SPECTACLE ON LOCH NESS

Highland folklore is filled with tales of strange creatures living in lochs and rivers, notably the kelpie (water horse) that lures unwary travellers to their doom. The use of the term 'monster', however, is a relatively recent phenomenon, the origins of which lie in an article published in the *Inverness Courier* on 2 May 1933, entitled 'Strange Spectacle on Loch Ness'.

The article recounted the sighting by Mrs Aldie Mackay and her husband of a disturbance in the loch: 'The creature disported itself, rolling and plunging for fully a minute, its body resembling that of a whale, and the water cascading and churning like a simmering cauldron.'

The story was taken up by the London press and sparked off a rash of sightings that year, including a notorious on-land encounter with London tourists Mr and Mrs Spicer on 22 July 1933, again reported in the *Inverness Courier*:

'It was horrible, an abomination. About 50 yards ahead, we saw an undulating sort of neck, and quickly followed by a large, ponderous body. I estimated the length to be 25 to 30 feet, its colour was dark elephant grey. It crossed the road in a series of jerks, but because of the slope we could not see its limbs. Although I accelerated quickly towards it, it had disappeared into the loch by the time I reached the spot. There was no sign of it in the water. I am a temperate man, but I am willing to take any oath that we saw this Loch Ness beast. I am certain that this creature was of a prehistoric species.'

The London newspapers couldn't resist. In December 1933 the *Daily Mail* sent Marmaduke Wetherall, a film director and big-game hunter, to Loch Ness to track down the beast. Within days he found 'reptilian' footprints in the shoreline mud (soon revealed to have been made with a stuffed hippopotamus foot, possibly an umbrella stand). Then in April 1934 came the famous 'long-necked monster' photograph taken by the seemingly reputable Harley St surgeon Colonel Kenneth Wilson. The press went mad and the rest, as they say, is history.

In 1994, however, Christian Spurling – Wetherall's stepson, by then 90 years old – revealed that the most famous photo of Nessie ever taken was in fact a hoax, perpetrated by his stepfather with Wilson's help. Today, of course, there are those who claim that Spurling's confession is itself a hoax. And, ironically, the researcher who exposed the surgeon's photo as a fake still believes wholeheartedly in the monster's existence.

Hoax or not, there's no denying that the bizarre mini-industry that has grown up around Loch Ness and its mysterious monster since that eventful summer 75 years ago is the strangest spectacle of all.

Loch Ness Backpackers Lodge HOSTEL £
(☎01456-450807; www.lochness-backpackers .com; Coiltie Farmhouse, East Lewiston; dm/d/f £12.50/30/45; ℗) This snug, friendly hostel housed in a cottage and barn has six-bed dorms, one double and a large barbecue area. It's about 0.75 miles from Drumnadrochit, along the A82 towards Fort William; turn left where you see the sign for Loch Ness Inn, just before the bridge.

Loch Ness SYHA HOSTEL £
(☎01320-351274; www.syha.org.uk; Glenmoriston; dm £18; ☺Apr-Sep; @) This hostel is housed in a big lodge overlooking Loch Ness, and many dorms have loch views. It's located on the A82 road, 13 miles southwest of Drumnadrochit, and 4 miles northeast of Invermoriston. Buses from Inverness to Fort William stop nearby.

❶ Getting There & Away

Scottish Citylink and Stagecoach buses from Inverness to Fort William run along the shores of Loch Ness (six to eight daily, five on Sunday); those headed for Skye turn off at Invermoriston. There are bus stops at Drumnadrochit (£6.20, 30 minutes), Urquhart Castle car park (£6.60, 35 minutes) and Loch Ness Youth Hostel (£10, 45 minutes).

Drumnadrochit

POP 800

Seized by monster madness, its gift shops bulging with Nessie cuddly toys, Drumnadrochit is a hotbed of beastie fever, with two monster exhibitions battling it out for the tourist dollar.

⊙ Sights & Activities

Loch Ness Exhibition Centre EXHIBITION
(☎01456-450573; www.loch-ness-scotland.com;
adult/child £6.50/4.50; ⊙9am-6.30pm Jul & Aug,
to 6pm Jun & Sep, 9.30am-5pm Feb-May & Oct,
10am-3.30pm Nov-Jan) This Nessie-themed
attraction uses a scientific approach that allows you to weigh up the evidence for yourself. Especially helpful is the original footage
of monster sightings plus it features exhibits
of equipment used in the various underwater monster hunts.

**Nessieland Castle Monster
Centre** EXHIBITION
(www.lochness-hotel.com; adult/child £5.50/4;
⊙9am-8pm Jul & Aug, 10am-5.30pm Apr-Jun, Sep
& Oct, 10am-4pm Nov-Mar) More homely than
the nearby Loch Ness Exhibition Centre,
this attraction is a miniature theme park
aimed squarely at the kids, but its main
function is to sell you Loch Ness monster
souvenirs.

Nessie Hunter CRUISE
(☎01456-450395; www.lochness-cruises
.com; adult/child £10/8) One-hour monster-
hunting cruises, complete with sonar and
underwater cameras. Cruises depart from
Drumnadrochit hourly from 9am to 6pm
daily from Easter to December.

🛏 Sleeping & Eating

Drumbuie Farm B&B ££
(☎01456-450634; www.loch-ness-farm.co.uk;
person from £30; ⊙Mar-Oct; [P]) Drumbuie is a
B&B in a modern house on a working farm –
the surrounding fields are full of sheep and
highland cattle – with views over Urquhart
Castle and Loch Ness. Walkers and cyclists
are welcome.

Borlum Farm CAMPGROUND £
(☎01456-450220; www.borlum.co.uk; sites per
person £5.50; ⊙Mar-Oct) Beside the main road
800m southeast of Drumnadrochit.

**Fiddler's Coffee Shop &
Restaurant** SCOTTISH ££
(www.fiddledrum.co.uk; mains £8-16; ⊙11am-
11pm) The coffee shop does cappuccino
and croissants, while the restaurant serves
traditional Highland fare, such as venison
casserole, and a wide range of bottled Scottish beers. There's also a whisky bar with
huge range of single malts.

Urquhart Castle

Commanding a brilliant location 1.5 miles
east of Drumnadrochit, with outstanding
views (on a clear day), **Urquhart Castle**
(☎01456-450551; adult/child £7/4.20; ⊙9.30am-
6pm Apr-Sep, to 5pm Oct, to 4.30pm Nov-Mar) is
a popular Nessie-watching hotspot. A huge
visitor centre (most of which is beneath
ground level) includes a video theatre (with
a dramatic 'unveiling' of the castle at the end
of the film) and displays of medieval items
discovered in the castle.

The castle was repeatedly sacked and rebuilt (and sacked and rebuilt) over the centuries; in 1692 it was blown up to prevent
the Jacobites from using it. The five-storey
tower house at the northern point is the
most impressive remaining fragment and
offers wonderful views across the water. The
site includes a huge gift shop and a restaurant, and is often very crowded in summer.

Fort Augustus

POP 510
Fort Augustus, at the junction of four old
military roads, was originally a government
garrison and the headquarters of General
George Wade's road-building operations in
the early 18th century. Today it's a neat and
picturesque little place, often overrun by
tourists in summer.

⊙ Sights & Activities

Caledonian Canal CANAL
At Fort Augustus, boats using the Caledonian Canal are raised and lowered 13m by
a 'ladder' of five consecutive locks. It's fun
to watch, and the neatly landscaped canal
banks are a great place to soak up the sun
or compare accents with fellow tourists.
The **Caledonian Canal Heritage Centre**
(☎01320-366493; admission free; ⊙10am-5pm
Apr-Oct), beside the lowest lock, showcases
the history of the canal.

Clansman Centre MUSEUM
(www.scottish-swords.com; admission free; ⊙10am-
6pm Apr-Oct) This exhibition of 17th-century
Highland life has live demonstrations of how
to put on a plaid (the forerunner of the kilt)
and how the claymore (Highland sword) was
made and used. There is also a workshop
where you can purchase handcrafted repro-
duction swords, dirks and shields.

DORES INN

While tour coaches pour down the west side of Loch Ness to the hotspots of Drumnadrochit and Urquhart Castle, the narrow B862 road on the eastern shore is relatively peaceful. It leads to the village of Foyers, where you can enjoy a pleasant hike to the **Falls of Foyers**.

But it's worth making the trip just for the **Dores Inn** (☎01463-751203; www.thedoresinn.co.uk; mains £ 8-20; ⏱lunch & dinner; 🛜), a beautifully restored country pub furnished with old church seating, local landscape paintings and fresh flowers. The menu specialises in quality Scottish produce, from haggis, neeps and tatties, and haddock and chips, to steaks, scallops and seafood platters.

The pub garden enjoys a stunning view along the length of Loch Ness, and even has a dedicated monster-spotting vantage point. The nearby campervan, emblazoned with Nessie-Serry Independent Research, has been home to dedicated Nessie hunter Steve Feltham (www.haveyouseenityet.co.uk) since 1991; he sells clay models of the monster, and is a fund of fascinating stories about the loch.

Royal Scot CRUISES
(www.cruiselochness.com; adult/child £11/6.50; ⏱10am-4pm Mar-Oct, 2pm Sat & Sun only Nov & Dec) One-hour cruises on Loch Ness accompanied by the latest high-tech sonar equipment so you can keep an underwater eye open for Nessie.

🛏 Sleeping & Eating

TOP CHOICE **Lovat Arms Hotel** HOTEL ££
(☎01456-459250; www.thelovat.com; Main Rd; d from £110; P🛜♿) Recently given a luxurious but ecoconscious boutique-style makeover in shades of pink and grey, this former huntin'-and-shootin' hotel is set apart from the tourist crush around the canal. The bedrooms are spacious and stylishly furnished, while the lounge is equipped with a log fire, comfy armchairs and grand piano.

The **restaurant** (mains £10-17), which has a separate kids' menu, serves top quality cuisine, from posh fish and chips to roast venison, seared sea bass, and wild mushroom risotto.

Morag's Lodge HOSTEL £
(☎01320-366289; www.moragslodge.com; Bunnoich Brae; dm/tw/f from £18/46/59; P@🛜) This large and well-run hostel is based in a big Victorian house with great views of Fort Augustus' hilly surrounds, and has a convivial bar with open fire. It's hidden away in the trees up the steep side road just north of the tourist office car park.

Lorien House B&B ££
(☎01320-366736; www.lorien-house.co.uk; Station Rd; s/d £45/70) Lorien is a cut above your usual B&B – the bathrooms come with bidets and the breakfasts with smoked salmon, and there's a library of walking, cycling and climbing guides in the lounge.

FREE **Cumberland's Campsite** CAMPGROUND
(☎01320-366257; www.cumberlands-campsite.com; Glendoe Rd; sites per person £7-8; ⏱Apr-Sep) Southeast of the village on the B862 towards Whitebridge.

Lock Inn PUB GRUB ££
(Canal Side; mains £9-14; ⏱food served noon-8pm) A superb little pub right on the canal bank, the Lock Inn has a vast range of malt whiskies and a tempting menu of bar meals (served noon to 8pm), which includes Orkney salmon, Highland venison and daily seafood specials; the house speciality is beer-battered haddock and chips.

ⓘ Information

There's an ATM and bureau de change (in the post office) beside the canal.
Fort Augustus tourist office (☎01320-366367; ⏱9am-6pm Mon-Sat, to 5pm Sun Easter-Oct) In the central car park.

ⓘ Getting There & Away

Scottish Citylink and Stagecoach buses from Inverness to Fort William stop at Fort Augustus (£10, one hour, six to eight daily Monday to Saturday, five on Sunday).

THE ROAD TO SKYE

It's 55 miles northwest via the A87 from Invergarry in the Great Glen to Kyle of Lochalsh and the bridge to Skye. It's a very scenic drive, taking you past the picture-postcard **viewpoint** above Loch Garry and along the wild, rocky shores of **Loch Cluanie**, before descending lovely **Glen Shiel** to reach another classic postcard view of **Eilean Donan**, perhaps Scotland's most photographed castle.

Cluanie Inn

At the west end of Loch Cluanie, about halfway between the Great Glen and Kyle of Lochalsh, the A87 passes the remote Cluanie Inn. This is the heart of hill-walking country – there are no fewer than 21 Munros within striking distance, including the classic **South Cluanie Ridge** (also known as the South Glen Shiel Ridge), which alone boasts seven 3000-ft summits in its 8-mile length.

A few hundred metres west of the inn (to the north of the main road) you can see the **old military road**, built in the late 18th century to link Fort Augustus to Bernera barracks at Glenelg, as part of the campaign to pacify the Highlands after the Jacobite rebellion of 1745–46.

The **Cluanie Inn** (☎01320-340238; www .cluanieinn.com; s £70, d standard/luxury £110/135, mains £8-14; ☺lunch & dinner; P🐾) has a great lived-in feel to it, providing shelter and good cheer on a stormy day. The luxury room comes with a four-poster bed and sauna, while the compact adjacent 'clubhouse' provides cheaper accommodation (per person £37.50).

Eilean Donan Castle

Photogenically sited at the entrance to Loch Duich, near Dornie village, **Eilean Donan Castle** (☎01599-555202; www.eileandonan castle.com; adult/child £5.50/4.50; ☺9.30am-6pm mid-Mar–mid-Nov) is one of Scotland's most evocative castles, and must be represented in millions of photo albums. It's on an off-shore islet, magically linked to the mainland by an elegant, stone-arched bridge. It's very much a re-creation inside, with an excellent introductory exhibition. Keep an eye out for the photos of castle scenes from the movie *Highlander*; there's also a sword used at the battle of Culloden in 1746. The castle was bombarded into ruins by government ships in 1719 when Jacobite forces were defeated at the Battle of Glenshiel; it was rebuilt between 1912 and 1932.

Citylink buses from Fort William and Inverness to Portree, on the Isle of Skye, stop opposite the castle.

Glen Shiel & Kintail

West of Cluanie Inn the A87 descends through spectacular **Glen Shiel**, with 1000m-high peaks soaring up on either side of the road. Halfway down the glen, where the old military road bridges the river (just downstream of the modern highway), is the site of the **Battle of Glenshiel**. Here, in 1719, a Jacobite army based at Eilean Donan Castle was defeated by Hanoverian government forces. Among those fighting on the rebel side were clansmen led by the famous outlaw Rob Roy MacGregor, and 300 soldiers loaned by the king of Spain; the mountain above the battlefield is still called Sgurr nan Spainteach (Peak of the Spaniard).

✗ Activities

There are several good walks in the area, most of which falls under the National Trust for Scotland's **Kintail Estate**. These include the two-day, cross-country hike from Morvich to Cannich via scenic **Gleann Lichd** and Glen Affric Youth Hostel (p159) (35 miles), and the walk from Killilan, near the north end of Loch Long, to the **Falls of Glomach**, which at 113m is one of the highest – and definitely the most impressive of the – waterfalls in Britain (13 miles round trip, allow five or six hours).

A traverse of the **Five Sisters of Kintail** is a classic but seriously challenging hill-walking expedition, taking in three Munro summits; start at the parking area just east of the Glen Shiel battlefield and finish at Morvich (eight to 10 hours). Less experienced hikers can take a **guided walk** (booking essential) along the ridge with an **NTS Countryside Ranger** (NTS; ☎01599-511231; www.nts.org.uk; per person £45; ☺on request Apr-Oct). For more information on these walks and the surrounding area, visit the NTS's **Countryside Centre** (NTS; www.nts.org.uk; admission free; ☺9am-10pm Apr-Sep) at Morvich.

🛏 Sleeping & Eating

Ratagan SYHA HOSTEL £
(☎01599-511243; www.syha.org.uk; Ratagan; dm £16; ☺mid-Mar–Oct; P@) This hostel has excellent facilities and a to-die-for spot on the south shore of Loch Duich. If you want a break from Munro bagging, this is the

place. There's at least one local bus a day from Kyle of Lochalsh to the hostel (half an hour). Turn towards Glenelg from Shiel Bridge, then take the turning on the right to Ratagan.

Kintail Lodge Hotel
HOTEL ££

(☑01599-511275; www.kintaillodgehotel.co.uk; Shiel Bridge; dm/s/d £13.50/85/120; P🕿) With 10 of the 12 fine rooms at this hotel facing the loch, you'd be unlucky not to get a decent outlook. Tasty bar meals (£9 to £16), including local venison and seafood, are available at lunch and dinner. There are also two bunkhouses with self-catering facilities, sleeping six people each.

❶ Getting There & Away

BOAT At Shiel Bridge at the foot of the glen, home to a famous colony of wild goats, a narrow side road goes over the Bealach Ratagain (pass) to Glenelg, where a community-run ferry links to Skye (summer only).

BUS Citylink buses between Fort William or Inverness and Skye travel along the A87.

Glenelg

The Glenelg peninsula, to the south of Loch Duich, is one of the most remote parts of the Highlands, reached via a narrow, twisting road over the high pass of the **Bealach Ratagain** (339m). The summit of the pass provides a superb view back to the Five Sisters of Kintail.

The road descends to the peaceful backwater of **Glenelg village**, which hosts the annual **Glenelg Music Festival** (www.glenelg musicfestival.com), one of the Highlands' best local festivals, in September. Before the road and railway arrived at Kyle of Lochalsh (in

1816 and 1897 respectively), Glenelg had been for centuries the main crossing point to the Isle of Skye, just 0.3 miles away across Kyle Rhea. As such, it was where the government garrison of **Bernera Barracks** was built in 1722 to control the local clans after the Battle of Glenshiel; the massive, gloomy ruins still stand near the ferry slip.

From Glenelg village a minor road continues to a dead end at **Arnisdale**, where the scenery becomes even more spectacular, with great views across Loch Hourn to the remote Knoydart Peninsula. About halfway to Arnisdale is Upper Sandaig, where you can walk down to **Sandaig Bay**, the former home of *Ring of Bright Water* author, Gavin Maxwell.

Along the way to Upper Sandaig, a side road leads inland along Gleann Beag to the **Iron Age brochs** of Dun Telve and Dun Troddan. These are the best-preserved brochs in mainland Britain – part of Dun Telve still stands to a height of 10m, Dun Trodden to 7m.

One of the Highlands' most picturesque places for a pint or a romantic away-from-it-all stay (doubles £120), the **Glenelg Inn** (☑01599-522273; www.glenelg-inn.com; mains £11-19; ⏱lunch & dinner) has tables in a lovely garden with cracking views of Skye. The elegant dining room serves up excellent food, with the local catch always featuring.

A bus runs weekdays from Broadford on Skye to Arnisdale, via Kyle of Lochalsh, Ratagan hostel and Glenelg.

The **Skye ferry** (www.skyeferry.com) runs every 20 minutes between 10am and 6pm from Easter to mid-October. Passengers are free and cars cost £12/15 single/return; there's no need to book.

RING OF BRIGHT WATER

Ring of Bright Water (1960), Gavin Maxwell's classic account of sharing his life with pet otters, was set in a place he called **Camusfearna** in an (ultimately futile) attempt to keep its location a secret. The real Camusfearna, where Maxwell and his otters lived from 1949 until it burned down in January 1968, and where he wrote most of his books, was a remote farmhouse on Sandaig Bay, about 5 miles south of Glenelg village.

Although the house is long gone, you can still walk down to Sandaig Bay from a parking place at Upper Sandaig (3 miles round trip) to see Maxwell's **memorial stone** (his ashes are buried beneath it). Another memorial, on a cairn over by the burn, is to his pet otter **Edal** who died in the fire. The latter reads: 'Edal, the otter of Ring of Bright Water, 1958–1968. Whatever joy she gave to you, give back to nature'.

A full description of the walk can be found at www.eileanban.org/gavin-maxwell/san-daig-walk.html. For more on Gavin Maxwell, visit the Bright Water Visitor Centre (p186).

Kyle of Lochalsh

POP 739

Before the controversial bridge, Kyle of Lochalsh was Skye's main ferry-port. Visitors now tend to buzz through town, but Kyle has an intriguing attraction if you're interested in marine life.

⊙ Sights & Activities

Seaprobe Atlantis BOAT TOUR
(☑0800 980 4846; www.seaprobeatlantis.com; adult/child £9.50/4.75; ⊙Easter-Oct) A glass-hulled boat takes you on a spin around the kyle to spot seabirds, seals and maybe an otter or two. The basic trip includes an entertaining guided tour and plenty of beautiful jellyfish; longer trips also take in a WWII shipwreck. Book at the tourist office.

🛏 Sleeping & Eating

There's a string of B&Bs just outside of town on the road to Plockton.

Waverley RESTAURANT ££
(☑01599-534337; Main St; mains £12-20; ⊙dinner Fri-Wed) This superb restaurant is an intimate place with excellent service; try the Taste of Land and Sea, combining Aberdeen Angus fillet steak with fresh local prawns.

ⓘ Information

Kyle of Lochalsh tourist office (☑01599-534276; ⊙daily Easter-Oct) Beside the main seafront car park; stocks information on Skye. Next to it is one of Scotland's most lavishly decorated public toilets.

ⓘ Getting There & Away

BUS Citylink runs to Kyle a few times daily from Inverness (£18.60, 2¼ hours), and Glasgow (£34, 5¾ hours).

TRAIN The train route between Inverness and Kyle of Lochalsh (£18.20, 2½ hours, up to four daily) is one of Scotland's most scenic.

FORT WILLIAM

POP 9910

Basking on the shores of Loch Linnhe amid magnificent mountain scenery, Fort William has one of the most enviable settings in the whole of Scotland. If it wasn't for the busy dual carriageway crammed between the town centre and the loch, and one of the highest rainfall records in the country, it would be almost idyllic. Even so, the Fort has carved out a reputation as Outdoor Capital of the UK (www.outdoorcapital.co.uk), and its easy access by rail and bus makes it a good place to base yourself for exploring the surrounding mountains and glens.

Magical **Glen Nevis** begins near the northern end of the town and wraps itself around the southern flanks of Ben Nevis (1344m) – Britain's highest mountain and a magnet for hikers and climbers. The glen is also popular with movie makers – parts of *Braveheart, Rob Roy* and the *Harry Potter* movies were filmed there.

History

There is little left of the original fort from which the town derives its name – it was pulled down in the 19th century to make way for the railway. The first castle here was constructed by General Monk in 1654 and called Inverlochy, but the meagre ruins by the loch are those of the fort built in the 1690s by General Mackay and named after King William II/III. In the 18th century it became part of a chain of garrisons (along with Fort Augustus and Fort George) that controlled the Great Glen in the wake of the Jacobite rebellions.

Originally a tiny fishing village called Gordonsburgh, the town took its present name with the opening of the railway in 1901, which, along with the building of the Caledonian Canal, helped it grow into a tourist centre. This has been consolidated in the last three decades by the huge increase in popularity of climbing, skiing, mountain biking and other outdoor sports.

⊙ Sights & Activities

West Highland Museum MUSEUM
(☑01397-702169; www.westhighlandmuseum.org.uk; Cameron Sq; adult/child £4/1; ⊙10am-5pm Mon-Sat Jun-Sep, plus 2-5pm Sun Jul & Aug, 10am-4pm Mon-Sat Oct-May) This small but fascinating museum is packed with all manner of Highland memorabilia. Look out for the secret portrait of Bonnie Prince Charlie – after the Jacobite rebellions all things Highland were banned, including pictures of the exiled leader, and this tiny painting looks like nothing more than a smear of paint until viewed in a cylindrical mirror, which reflects a credible likeness of the prince.

West Highland Way Finishing Line MONUMENT
(Gordon Sq) In 2010, the official end-point of the West Highland Way long-distance trail

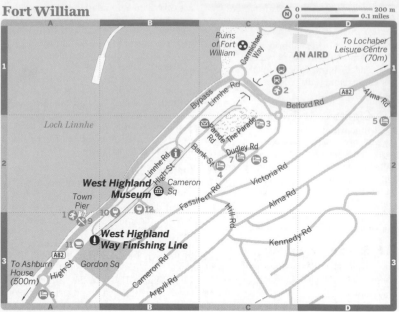

Fort William

was moved from Nevis Bridge on the outskirts of town to Gordon Square, adding a mile to the total length. There's a map of the route carved in Caithness flagstone, a bronze sculpture of a weary walker rubbing his feet, and benches for real walkers to rest on.

Ben Nevis Distillery　　　　　　DISTILLERY
(☑01397-702476; www.bennevisdistillery.com; guided tour adult/child £4/2; ◎9am-5pm Mon-Fri year-round, plus 10am-4pm Sat Easter-Sep & noon-4pm Sun Jul & Aug) A tour of this distillery makes for a warming rainy day alternative to exploring the hills.

Jacobite Steam Train　　　　　STEAM TRAIN
(☑0845 128 4681; www.steamtrain.info; day return adult/child £28/£16; ◎departs Fort William 10.20am and Mallaig 2.10pm Mon-Fri late May-early Oct, plus Sat & Sun Jul & Aug) From late May to early October, the Jacobite Steam Train makes the scenic two-hour run between Fort William and Mallaig, departing from Fort William train station in the morning and returning from Mallaig in the afternoon. There's a brief stop at Glenfinnan station, and you get 1½ hours in Mallaig.

Classed as one of the great railway journeys of the world, the route crosses the historic **Glenfinnan Viaduct**, made famous in the *Harry Potter* films – the Jacobite's owners supplied the steam locomotive and rolling stock used in the film.

Lochaber Leisure Centre
HEALTH & FITNESS

(☎01397-704359; Belford Rd; pool £2.30; ☺715am-9pm Mon-Fri, 12.30-4pm Sat & Sun) The Lochaber Leisure Centre has a 25m swimming pool, gym, sauna and other leisure facilities.

✦✦ Festivals & Events

UCI Mountain Bike World Cup
MOUNTAIN BIKING

(www.fortwilliamworldcup.co.uk) In June, Fort William pulls in crowds of more than 18,000 spectators for this World Cup downhill mountain-biking event. The gruelling downhill course is at nearby Nevis Range ski area.

☞ Tours

Al's Tours
TAXI TOUR

(☎01397-700700; www.alstours.com) Taxi tours with driver-guide around Lochaber and Glencoe cost £80/195 for a half-/full day.

Crannog Cruises
WILDLIFE CRUISE

(☎01397-700714) Operates 1½-hour wildlife cruises (adult/child £10/5, four daily) on Loch Linnhe, visiting a seal colony and a salmon farm.

🛏 Sleeping

It's best to book well ahead in summer, especially for hostels.

TOP CHOICE Lime Tree
HOTEL ££

(☎01397-701806; www.limetreefortwilliam.co.uk; Achintore Rd; s/d from £70/100; ℗) Much more interesting than your average guesthouse, this former Victorian manse overlooking Loch Linnhe is an 'art gallery with rooms', decorated throughout with the artist-owner's atmospheric Highland landscapes. Foodies rave about the restaurant, and the gallery space – a triumph of sensitive design – stages everything from serious exhibitions (David Hockney in summer 2010) to folk concerts.

Grange
B&B ££

(☎01397-705516; www.grangefortwilliam.com; Grange Rd; r per person £56-59; ℗) An exceptional 19th-century villa set in its own landscaped grounds, the Grange is crammed with antiques and fitted with log fires, chaise longues and Victorian roll-top baths. The Turret Room, with its window seat in the turret overlooking Loch Linnhe, is our favourite. It's 500m southwest of the town centre.

Crolinnhe
B&B £££

(☎01397-702709; www.crolinnhe.co.uk; Grange Rd; r per person £56-64; ℗) This grand 19th-century villa has a lochside location, beautiful gardens and sumptuous accommodation. A vegetarian breakfast is provided on request.

Calluna
APARTMENT £

(☎01397-700451; www.fortwilliamholiday.co.uk; Heathercroft, Connochie Rd; dm/tw £15/34; ℗☎) Run by well-known mountain guide Alan Kimber and wife Sue, the Calluna offers self-catering apartments geared to groups of hikers and climbers, but also takes individual travellers prepared to share; there's a fully equipped kitchen and an excellent drying room for your soggy hiking gear.

St Andrew's Guest House
B&B ££

(☎01397-703038; www.standrewsguesthouse.co.uk; Fassifern Rd; r per person £22-28; ℗☎) Set in a lovely 19th-century building that was once a rectory and choir school, St Andrew's retains period features, such as carved masonry, wood panelling and stained-glass windows. It has six spacious bedrooms, some with stunning views.

Glenlochy Guest House
B&B ££

(☎01397-702909; www.glenlochyguesthouse.co.uk; r per person £35-38; ℗) Convenient for Glen Nevis, Ben Nevis and the end of the West Highland Way, the Glenlochy is a sprawling modern place with 12 en-suite rooms set in a huge garden beside the River Nevis; a pleasant place to sit on summer evenings.

Fort William Backpackers
HOSTEL £

(☎01397-700711; www.scotlands-top-hostels.com; Alma Rd; dm/tw from £14/38; ⓐ) A 10-minute walk from the bus and train stations, this lively and welcoming hostel is set in a grand Victorian villa, perched on a hillside with great views over Loch Linnhe.

Bank Street Lodge
HOSTEL £

(☎01397-700070; www.bankstreetlodge.co.uk; Bank St; dm/tw £14.50/48) Part of a modern hotel and restaurant complex, the Bank Street Lodge offers the most central budget beds in town, only 250m from the train station. It has kitchen facilities and a drying room.

No 6 Caberfeidh
B&B ££

(☎01397-703756; www.6caberfeidh.com; Fassifern Rd; r per person £22-35; ☎) Friendly B&B; vegetarian breakfast on request.

Ashburn House
B&B ££

(☎01397-706000; www.highland5star.co.uk; Achintore Rd; r per person £45-55; ℗☎) Grand Victorian villa south of the centre; children under 12 not welcome.

Alexandra Hotel HOTEL ££££
(☎01397-702241; www.strathmorehotels.com; The
Parade; s/d from £69/109; 🅿🛜) Large, traditional, family-oriented hotel bang in the
middle of town.

✖ Eating & Drinking

Lime Tree MODERN SCOTTISH £££
(☎01397-701806; www.limetreefortwilliam.co.uk;
Achintore Rd; mains £19-25; ⏰dinner daily, noon-
3pm Sun) Fort William is not over-endowed
with great places to eat, but the restaurant
at this small hotel and art gallery has put
the UK's Outdoor Capital on the gastro-
nomic map. The chef won a Michelin star
in his previous restaurant, and turns out
technically accomplished dishes such as
beer-braised beef with shallot mousse, and
slow-roast pork belly with truffled honey.
The two-course Sunday lunch costs £13.

Crannog Seafood Restaurant SEAFOOD ££
(☎01397-705589; www.crannog.net; Town Pier;
mains £14-20; ⏰lunch & dinner) The Crannog
wins the prize for best location in town –
perched on the Town Pier, giving window-
table diners an uninterrupted view down
Loch Linnhe. Informal and unfussy, it specialises in fresh local seafood – there are
three or four daily fish specials plus the
main menu – though there are beef, poul-
try and vegetarian dishes, too. Two-course
lunch £10.

Grog & Gruel PUB
(☎01397-705078; www.grogandgruel.co.uk; 66
High St; ⏰bar meals noon-9pm) The Grog &
Gruel is a traditional-style, wood-panelled
pub with an excellent range of cask ales
from regional Scottish and English microbreweries.

Fired Art Cafe CAFE
(☎01397-705005; www.fired-art.co.uk; 147 High St;
mains £3-4; ⏰10am-5pm Mon-Sat; 🛜👶) Enjoy
what is probably the best coffee in town at
this colourful cafe, or go for a hot chocolate,
milkshake or smoothie; the kids can be kept
busy painting their own coffee mugs in the
pottery studio at the back.

Ben Nevis Bar PUB
(☎01397-702295; 105 High St) The lounge here
enjoys a good view over the loch, and the bar
exudes a relaxed, jovial atmosphere where
climbers and tourists can work off leftover
energy jigging to live music (Thursday and
Friday nights).

ℹ Information

Belford Hospital (☎01397-702481; Belford
Rd) Opposite the train station.
Post Office (☎0845 722 3344; 5 High St)
Fort William tourist office (☎01397-703781;
www.visithighlands.com; 15 High St; internet
per 20 min £1; ⏰9am-6pm Mon-Sat, 10am-
5pm Sun Apr-Sep, limited hours Oct-Mar)
Internet access.

ℹ Getting There & Away

BUS Scottish Citylink buses link Fort William
with Glasgow (£21, three hours, eight daily) and
Edinburgh (£30, 4½ hours, one daily direct,
seven with a change at Glasgow) via Glencoe and
Crianlarich, as well as Oban (£9, 1½ hours, three
daily), Inverness (£11, two hours, five daily) and
Portree (£28, three hours, four daily) on the Isle
of Skye.

Shiel Buses service No 500 runs to Mallaig
(1½ hours, three daily Monday to Friday only) via
Glenfinnan (30 minutes) and Arisaig (one hour).
CAR Fort William is 146 miles from Edinburgh,
104 miles from Glasgow and 66 miles from Inverness. The tourist office has listings of car-hire
companies.

Easydrive Car Hire (☎01397-701616; www
.easydrivescotland.co.uk; Unit 36a, Ben Nevis
Industrial Estate, Ben Nevis Dr) Hires out small
cars from £32/185 a day/week, including tax
and unlimited mileage, but not Collision Damage Waiver (CDW).
TRAIN The spectacular West Highland line runs
from Glasgow to Mallaig via Fort William. There
are three trains daily (two on Sunday) from
Glasgow to Fort William (£24, 3¾ hours), and
four daily (three on Sunday) between Fort William and Mallaig (£10, 1½ hours). Travelling from
Edinburgh (£40, five hours), you have to change
at Glasgow's Queen St station.

There's no direct rail connection between
Oban and Fort William – you have to change at
Crianlarich, so it's faster to use the bus.

The overnight *Caledonian Sleeper* service
connects Fort William and London Euston (£103
sharing a twin-berth cabin, 13 hours).

ℹ Getting Around

BIKE Off-Beat Bikes (☎01397-704008; 117
High St; ⏰9am-5.30pm) Off-Beat Bikes rents
out mountain bikes for £15/10 for a day/
half-day.

BUS The Fort Dayrider ticket (£2.60) gives
unlimited travel for one day on Stagecoach bus
services in the Fort William area. Buy from the
bus driver.

TAXI There's a taxi rank on the corner of High St
and The Parade.

AROUND FORT WILLIAM

the Achintee start of the path up Ben Nevis, and only a mile from the end of the West Highland Way. Food served noon to 9pm; closed Monday to Wednesday in winter.

Glen Nevis

You can walk the 3 miles from Fort William to Glen Nevis in about an hour or so.

From the car park at the far end of the road along Glen Nevis, there is an excellent 1.5-mile walk through the spectacular **Nevis Gorge** to **Steall Meadows**, a verdant valley dominated by a 100m-high bridal-veil waterfall. You can reach the foot of the falls by crossing the river on a wobbly, three-cable wire bridge – one cable for your feet and one for each hand – a real test of balance!

🛏 Sleeping & Eating

TOP CHOICE Ben Nevis Inn HOSTEL £
(☎01397-701227; www.ben-nevis-inn.co.uk; Achintee; dm £14) A good alternative to the youth hostel is this great barn of a pub (real ale and tasty bar meals available; mains £9 to £12), with a comfy 24-bed hostel downstairs. It's at

Achintee Farm HOSTEL, B&B £
(☎01397-702240; www.achinteefarm.com; Achintee; dm/tw £15/34) This attractive farmhouse offers excellent B&B accommodation and also has a small bunkhouse attached. It's just 100m from the Ben Nevis Inn, and ideally positioned for climbing Ben Nevis.

Glen Nevis Youth Hostel HOSTEL £
(SYHA; ☎01397-702336; www.glennevishostel.co.uk; Glen Nevis; dm £19; @🛜) Large, impersonal and reminiscent of a school camp, this hostel is 3 miles from Fort William, right beside one of the starting points for the tourist track up Ben Nevis.

Glen Nevis Caravan & Camping Park CAMPGROUND £
(☎01397-702191; www.glen-nevis.co.uk; tent site £6.50, tent & car £11, campervan £11, per person £3;

CLIMBING BEN NEVIS

As the highest peak in the British Isles, **Ben Nevis** (1344m) attracts many would-be ascensionists who would not normally think of climbing a Scottish mountain – a staggering (often literally) 100,000 people reach the summit each year.

Although anyone who is reasonably fit should have no problem climbing Ben Nevis on a fine summer's day, an ascent should not be undertaken lightly. Every year people have to be rescued from the mountain. You will need proper walking boots (the path is rough and stony, and there may be soft, wet snowfields on the summit), warm clothing, waterproofs, a map and compass, and plenty of food and water. And don't forget to check the weather forecast.

Here are a few facts to mull over before you go racing up the tourist track: the summit plateau is bounded by 700m-high cliffs and has a sub-Arctic climate; at the summit it can snow on any day of the year; the summit is wrapped in cloud nine days out of 10; in thick cloud, visibility at the summit can be 10m or less; and in such conditions the only safe way off the mountain requires careful use of a map and compass to avoid walking over those 700m cliffs.

The tourist track (the easiest route to the top) was originally called the Pony Track. It was built in the 19th century for the pack ponies that carried supplies to a meteorological observatory on the summit (now in ruins), which was manned continuously from 1883 to 1904.

There are three possible starting points for the tourist track ascent – Achintee Farm; the footbridge at Glen Nevis Youth Hostel; and, if you have a car, the car park at Glen Nevis Visitor Centre. The path climbs gradually to the shoulder at Lochan Meall an t-Suidhe (known as the Halfway Lochan), then zigzags steeply up beside the Red Burn to the summit plateau. The highest point is marked by a trig point on top of a huge cairn beside the ruins of the old observatory; the plateau is scattered with countless smaller cairns, stones arranged in the shape of people's names and, sadly, a fair bit of litter.

The total distance to the summit and back is 8 miles; allow at least four or five hours to reach the top, and another 2½ to three hours for the descent. Afterwards, as you celebrate in the pub with a pint, consider the fact that the record time for the annual Ben Nevis Hill Race is just under 1½ hours – up *and* down. Then have another pint.

Then have another pint.

⊘mid-Mar–Oct) This big, well-equipped site is a popular base camp for Ben Nevis and the surrounding mountains.

ℹ Information

Glen Nevis Visitor Centre (☑01397-705922; www.bennevisweather.co.uk; ⊘9am-5pm Apr-Oct) The Glen Nevis Visitor Centre is situated 1.5 miles up the glen, and provides information on walking as well as specific advice on climbing Ben Nevis.

ℹ Getting There & Away

Bus 41 runs from Fort William bus station up Glen Nevis to the youth hostel (10 minutes, five daily Monday to Saturday, three on Sunday, limited service October to April) and on to the Lower Falls 3 miles beyond the hostel (20 minutes). Check at the tourist office for the latest timetable, which is liable to alteration.

Nevis Range

The **Nevis Range ski area** (☑01397-705825; www.nevisrange.co.uk), 6 miles north of Fort William, spreads across the northern slopes of Aonach Mor (1221m). The **gondola** that gives access to the bottom of the ski area at 655m operates year-round from 10am to 5pm; a return trip costs £10.50/6 for an adult/child (15 minutes each way). At the top there's a restaurant and a couple of walking routes through nearby **Leanachan Forest**.

During the ski season a one-day lift pass costs £28/16.50 per adult/child; a one-day package, including equipment hire, lift pass and two hours' instruction, costs £62.

A world championship **downhill mountain-bike trail** (☑01397-705825; bike.nevisrange.co.uk; ⊘11am-3pm mid-May–mid-Sep) – for experienced riders only – runs from the Snowgoose restaurant to the base station; bikes are carried on a rack on the gondola cabin. A single trip with your own bike costs £12; full-suspension bike hire costs from £40/70 per half-/full day depending on the bike. There are also 25 miles of way-marked mountain-bike trails in the nearby forest.

Bus 41 runs from Fort William bus station to Nevis Range (15 minutes, five daily Monday to Saturday, three on Sunday, limited service October to April). Check at the tourist office for the latest timetable, which is liable to alteration.

Corpach to Loch Lochy

Corpach lies at the southern entrance to the **Caledonian Canal**, 3 miles north of Fort William; there's a classic picture-postcard view of Ben Nevis from the mouth of the canal. Nearby is the award-winning **Treasures of the Earth** (☑01397-772283; www.treasuresoftheearth.co.uk; adult/child £5/3; ⊘9.30am-7pm Jul-Sep, 10am-5pm Mar-Jun & Oct, shorter hours Nov-Feb) exhibition, a rainy-day diversion with a great collection of gemstones, minerals, fossils and other geological curiosities.

A mile east of Corpach, at **Banavie**, is **Neptune's Staircase**, an impressive flight of eight locks that allows boats to climb 20m to the main reach of the Caledonian Canal. The B8004 road runs along the west side of the canal to **Gairlochy** at the south end of Loch Lochy, offering superb views of Ben Nevis; the canal towpath on the east side makes a great walk or bike ride (6.5 miles).

From Gairlochy the B8005 continues along the west side of Loch Lochy to **Achnacarry** and the **Clan Cameron Museum** (☑01397-712480; www.clan-cameron.org; adult/child £3.50/free; ⊘11am-5pm Jul & Aug, 1.30-5pm Easter-Jun & Sep–mid-Oct), which records the history of the clan and its involvement with the Jacobite rebellions, including items of clothing that once belonged to Bonnie Prince Charlie.

From Achnacarry the Great Glen Way (p159) heads north along the roadless western shore of Loch Lochy, while a minor road leads west through the **Mile Dorcha** (Dark Mile), a dim, wooded defile draped in moss, to the lovely waterfalls of **Eas Chia-aig**. Beyond the falls, the road continues along the northern shore of lovely **Loch Arkaig** to end at the tiny settlement of Strathan.

Strathan is the starting point for an epic **cross-country hike** via Glen Dessary to Inverie in Knoydart (17 miles), where you can take the ferry to Mallaig – for the fit and experienced only! It's possible to begin at Glenfinnan and hike north to Strathan (12 miles), breaking the journey by camping out or spending the night in the bothy at A'Chuil in Glen Dessary. That way you can reach the start and finish points by train.

There are a couple of backpacker hostels in Corpach: **Farr Cottage Lodge** (☑01397-772315; www.farrcottage.com; dm/tw £15/36; ℗@) and **Blacksmiths Hostel** (☑01397-772467; www.highland-mountain-guides.co.uk; dm £15; ℗) – the latter is part of an outdoor activities centre and can organise courses in climbing, kayaking and other sports.

Glen Spean & Glen Roy

Near Spean Bridge, at the junction of the B8004 and A82, 2.5 miles east of Gairlochy, stands the **Commando Memorial**, which commemorates the WWII special forces soldiers who trained in this area.

Four miles further east, at Roy Bridge, a minor road leads north up Glen Roy, which is noted for its intriguing, so-called **parallel roads**. These prominent horizontal terraces contouring around the hill side are actually ancient shorelines formed during the last ice age by the waters of an ice-dammed glacial lake. The best viewpoint is 3 miles up Glen Roy.

GLEN COE

Scotland's most famous glen is also one of the grandest and, in bad weather, the grimmest. The approach to the glen from the east, watched over by the rocky pyramid of **Buachaille Etive Mor** – the Great Shepherd of Etive – leads over the Pass of Glencoe and into the narrow upper valley. The southern side is dominated by three massive, brooding spurs, known as the **Three Sisters**, while the northern side is enclosed by the continuous steep wall of the knife-edged **Aonach Eagach** ridge. The main road threads its lonely way through the middle of all this mountain grandeur, past deep gorges and crashing waterfalls, to the more pastoral lower reaches of the glen around Loch Achtriochtan and Glencoe village.

Glen Coe was written into the history books in 1692 when the resident MacDonalds were murdered by Campbell soldiers in what became known as the Glencoe Massacre.

🏃 Activities

There are several short, pleasant walks around **Glencoe Lochan**, near the village. To get there, turn left off the minor road to the youth hostel, just beyond the bridge over the River Coe. There are three **walks** (40 minutes to an hour), all detailed on a signboard at the car park. The artificial lochan was created by Lord Strathcona in 1895 for his homesick Canadian wife Isabella and is surrounded by a North American–style forest.

A more strenuous hike, but well worth the effort on a fine day, is the climb to the **Lost Valley** (p180), a magical mountain sanctuary still haunted by the ghosts of the murdered MacDonalds (only 2.5 miles round trip, but allow three hours). A rough path from the car park at Allt na Reigh (on the A82, 6 miles east of Glencoe village) bears left down to a footbridge over the river, then climbs up the wooded valley

THE CALEDONIAN CANAL

Running for 59 miles from Corpach, near Fort William, to Inverness via lochs Lochy, Oich and Ness, the Caledonian Canal links the east and west coasts of Scotland, avoiding the long and dangerous sea passage around Cape Wrath and through the turbulent Pentland Firth. Designed by Thomas Telford and completed in 1822 at a cost of £900,000 – a staggering sum then – the canal took 20 years to build, including 29 locks, four aqueducts and 10 bridges.

Conceived as a project to ease unemployment and bring prosperity to the Highlands in the aftermath of the Jacobite rebellions and the Clearances, the canal proved to be a commercial failure – the locks were too small for the new breed of steamships which came into use soon after its completion. But it proved to be a success in terms of tourism, especially after it was popularised by Queen Victoria's cruise along the canal in 1873. Today the canal is used mainly by yachts and pleasure cruisers, though in late 2010 a pilot scheme was introduced to assess the viability of using it to transport timber from local forestry plantations.

Much of the Great Glen Way (p159) follows the line of the canal, and it can be followed on foot, by mountain bike, on horseback, or by canoe, and 80% of the route has even been done on mobility scooters. An easy half-day hike or bike ride is to follow the canal towpath from Corpach to Gairlochy (10 miles), which takes you past the impressive flight of eight locks known as Neptune's Staircase, and through beautiful countryside with grand views to the north face of Ben Nevis.

between Beinn Fhada and Gearr Aonach (the first and second of the Three Sisters). The route leads steeply up through a maze of giant, jumbled, moss-coated boulders before emerging – quite unexpectedly – into a broad, open valley with an 800m-long meadow as flat as a football pitch. Back in the days of clan warfare, the valley – invisible from below – was used for hiding stolen cattle; its Gaelic name, Coire Gabhail, means 'corrie of capture'.

The summits of Glen Coe's mountains are for experienced mountaineers only; but there are other walks around the area that will give you a good taste of the scenery without having to tackle the serious terrain (p180). Details of **hill-walking** routes can be found in the Scottish Mountaineering Club's guidebook *Central Highlands* by Peter Hodgkiss.

East of Glencoe

A few miles east of Glencoe proper, on the south side of the A82, is the car park and base station for the **Glencoe Mountain Resort** (www.glencoemountain.com), where commercial skiing in Scotland first began back in 1956. The **Lodge Café-Bar** has comfy sofas where you can soak up the view through the floor-to-ceiling windows.

The **chairlift** (adult/child £10/5; ⊙9.30am-4.30pm Thu-Mon) continues to operate in summer – there's a grand view over the Moor of Rannoch from the top station – and provides access to a downhill mountain-biking track. In winter a lift pass costs £30 a day and equipment hire is £25 a day.

Two miles west of the ski centre, a minor road leads along peaceful and beautiful **Glen Etive**, which runs southwest for 12 miles to the head of Loch Etive. On a hot summer's day the River Etive contains many tempting pools for swimming in, and there are lots of good picnic sites.

The remote **Kings House Hotel** (p112) claims to be one of Scotland's oldest licensed inns, dating from the 17th century. It lies on the old military road from Stirling to Fort William (now followed by the **West Highland Way**), and after the Battle of Culloden it was used as a Hanoverian garrison – hence the name. The hotel serves good pub grub (bar meals £8 to £12) and has long been a meeting place for climbers, skiers and hill walkers – the rustic **Climbers Bar** (⊙11am-11pm) is round the back. There's free

wild camping across the wee bridge behind the hotel – no facilities, but you're allowed to use the toilets in the Climbers Bar.

Glencoe Village

POP 360

The little village of Glencoe stands prettily on the south shore of Loch Leven at the western end of the glen, 16 miles south of Fort William.

◉ Sights & Activities

Glencoe Folk Museum   MUSEUM
(☑01855-811664; adult/child £2/free; ⊙10am-5.30pm Mon-Sat Apr-Oct) This small, thatched museum houses a varied collection of military memorabilia, farm equipment, and tools of the woodworking, blacksmithing and slate-quarrying trades.

Glencoe Visitor Centre   VISITOR CENTRE
(NTS; ☑01855-811307; www.glencoe-nts.org.uk; adult/child £5.50/4.50; ⊙9.30am-5.30pm Apr-Aug, 10am-5pm Sep & Oct, 10am-4pm Thu-Sun Nov-Mar) About 1.5 miles east of Glencoe village is this modern facility with an ecotourism angle. The centre provides comprehensive information on the geological, environmental and cultural history of Glencoe via high-tech interactive and audiovisual displays, and tells the story of the Glencoe Massacre in all its gory detail.

Lochaber Watersports   WATER SPORTS
(☑01855-821391; www.lochaberwatersports.co.uk; ⊙9.30am-5pm Apr-Oct) You can hire kayaks (£12 an hour), rowing boats (£15 an hour), sailing dinghies (£12 an hour), and even a 10m sailing yacht complete with skipper (£150 for three hours, up to five people) here.

⌂ Sleeping & Eating

TOP
CHOICE **Clachaig Inn**   HOTEL, PUB ££
(☑01855-811252; www.clachaig.com; Clachaig; s/d £70/88; P🖃) The Clachaig has long been a favourite haunt of hill walkers and climbers. As well as comfortable en-suite accommodation, there's a smart, wood-panelled lounge bar, with lots of sofas and armchairs, mountaineering photos and climbing magazines to leaf through.

Climbers usually head for the lively **Boots Bar** on the other side of the hotel – it has log fires, serves real ale and good pub grub (mains £8 to £12), and has live Scottish, Irish and blues music every Saturday night.

Glen Coe – Gleann Comhann in Gaelic – is sometimes (wrongly) said to mean 'the glen of weeping', a romantic mistranslation that gained popularity in the wake of the brutal murders that took place here in 1692.

Following the Glorious Revolution of 1688, in which the Catholic King James VII/II (VII of Scotland, II of England) was replaced on the British throne by the Protestant King William II/III, supporters of the exiled James – known as Jacobites, most of them Highlanders – rose up against William in a series of battles. In an attempt to quash Jacobite loyalties, King William offered the Highland clans an amnesty on the condition that all clan chiefs take an oath of loyalty to him before 1 January 1692.

Maclain, the elderly chief of the MacDonalds of Glencoe, had long been a thorn in the side of the authorities. Not only was he late in setting out to fulfil the king's demand, but he mistakenly went first to Fort William before travelling slowly through winter mud and rain to Inveraray, where he was three days late in taking the oath before the Sheriff of Argyll.

The secretary of state for Scotland, Sir John Dalrymple, decided to use the fact that Maclain had missed the deadline to punish the troublesome MacDonalds, and at the same time set an example to other Highland clans, some of whom had not bothered to take the oath.

A company of 120 soldiers, mainly from the Campbell territory of Argyll, were sent to the glen under cover of collecting taxes. It was a long-standing tradition for clans to provide hospitality to travellers and, since their commanding officer was related to Maclain by marriage, the troops were billeted in MacDonald homes.

After they'd been guests for 12 days, the government order came for the soldiers to 'fall upon the rebels the MacDonalds of Glencoe and put all to the sword under 70. You are to have a special care that the Old Fox and his sons do upon no account escape'. The soldiers turned on their hosts at 5am on 13 February, killing Maclain and 37 other men, women and children. Some of the soldiers alerted the MacDonalds to their intended fate, allowing them to escape; many fled into the snow-covered hills, where another 40 people died of exposure.

The ruthless brutality of the incident caused a public uproar, and after an inquiry several years later Dalrymple lost his job. There's a monument to Maclain in Glencoe village, and members of the MacDonald clan still gather here on 13 February each year to lay a wreath.

THE GREAT GLEN & LOCHABER GLENCOE VILLAGE

Glencoe Independent Hostel HOSTEL £
(☎01855-811906; www.glencoehostel.co.uk; Glencoe; dm £12-15, bunkhouse £11-12; P) This handily located hostel, just 10 minutes' walk from the Clachaig Inn, is set in an old farmhouse with six- and eight-bed dorms, and a bunkhouse with another 16 bed spaces in communal, Alpine-style bunks. There's also a cute little wooden cabin that sleeps up to three (£48 to £54 per night).

Glencoe SYHA HOSTEL £
(☎08155-811219; www.syha.org.uk; Glencoe; dm £18.50; P@🛜) Very popular with hikers, though the atmosphere is a little institutional. It's a 1.5-mile walk from the village along the minor road on the northern side of the river.

Invercoe Caravan & Camping Park CAMPGROUND £
(☎01855-811210; www.invercoe.co.uk; Glencoe; tent sites per person £8, campervan £20) Our favourite official campground in Glencoe, this place has great views of the surrounding mountains and a covered area for campers to cook in.

Crafts & Things CAFE £
(☎01855-811325; www.craftsandthings.co.uk; Annat; mains £3-6; ⏰9.30am-5pm Mon-Fri, to 5.30pm Sat & Sun; 🅿) Just off the main road between Glencoe village and Ballachulish, the coffee shop in this craft shop is a good spot for a lunch of homemade lentil soup with crusty rolls, ciabatta sandwiches, or just coffee and carrot cake. There are tables outdoors, and a box of toys to keep the little ones occupied.

❶ Getting There & Away

Scottish Citylink buses run between Fort William and Glencoe (£7, 30 minutes, eight daily) and from Glencoe to Glasgow (£19, 2½ hours, eight daily). Buses stop at Glencoe village, Glencoe Visitor Centre and Glencoe Mountain Resort.

Stagecoach bus 44 links Glencoe village with Fort William (35 minutes, hourly Monday to Saturday, three on Sunday) and Kinlochleven (25 minutes).

Kinlochleven

POP 900

Kinlochleven is hemmed in by high mountains at the head of the beautiful Loch Leven, about 7 miles east of Glencoe village. The aluminium smelter that led to the town's development in the early 20th century has long since closed, and the opening of the Ballachulish Bridge in the 1970s allowed the main road to bypass it completely. Hope was provided by the opening of the West Highland Way, which now brings a steady stream of hikers through the village.

The final section of the **West Highland Way** stretches for 14 miles from Kinlochleven to Fort William. The village is also the starting point for easier walks up the glen of the River Leven, through pleasant woods to the **Grey Mare's Tail waterfall**, and harder mountain hikes into the Mamores.

Activities

Ice Factor CLIMBING
(01855-831100; www.ice-factor.co.uk; Leven Rd; 9am-10pm Tue & Thu, to 7pm Mon, Wed & Fri) If you fancy trying your hand at ice-climbing, even in the middle of summer, head for the Ice Factor, the world's biggest indoor ice-climbing wall; a one-hour beginner's 'taster' session costs £30. There's also a rock-climbing wall, sauna and steam room, and a cafe and bar-bistro.

Sleeping & Eating

Blackwater Hostel HOSTEL, CAMPGROUND £
(01855-831253; www.blackwaterhostel.co.uk; Lab Rd, Kinlochleven; sites per person £6, dm/tw £14/32) This 40-bed hostel has spotless dorms with en suite bathrooms and TV, and a level, well-sheltered camping ground.

TOP CHOICE Lochleven Seafood Cafe SEAFOOD ££
(01855-821048; www.lochlevenseafoodcafe.co.uk; Loch Leven; mains £8-18; noon-9pm Wed-Sun) This outstanding place serves superb shellfish freshly plucked live from tanks – oysters on the half shell, razor clams, scallops, lobster and crab – plus a daily fish special and some nonseafood dishes. For warm days, there's an outdoor terrace with a view across the loch to the Pap of Glencoe, a distinctive conical-shaped mountain.

Getting There & Away

Stagecoach bus 44 runs from Fort William to Kinlochleven (50 minutes, hourly Monday to Saturday, three on Sunday) via Ballachulish and Glencoe village.

LOCHABER

Ardgour & Ardnamurchan

The drive from Corran Ferry, 8 miles south of Fort William, to **Ardnamurchan Point** (www.ardnamurchan.com), the most westerly point on the British mainland, is one of the most beautiful in the western Highlands, especially in late spring and early summer when much of the narrow, twisting road is lined with the bright pink and purple blooms of rhododendrons.

The road clings to the northern shore of Loch Sunart, going through the pretty villages of **Strontian** – which gave its name to the element strontium, first discovered in ore from nearby lead mines in 1790 – and **Salen**.

The mostly single-track road from Salen to Ardnamurchan Point is only 25 miles long, but it'll take you 1½ hours each way. It's a dipping, twisting, low-speed roller coaster of a ride through sun-dappled native woodlands draped with lichen and fern. Just when you're getting used to the views of Morvern and Mull to the south, it makes a quick detour to the north for a panorama over the islands of Rum and Eigg.

The scattered crofting village of **Kilchoan**, the only village of any size west of Salen, is best known for the scenic ruins of 13th-century **Mingary Castle**. The village has a tourist office, a shop and a hotel, and there's a ferry (p91) to Tobermory on the Isle of Mull.

Sights

Ardnamurchan Lighthouse HISTORIC BUILDING
(www.nlb.org.uk; Ardnamurchan Point; adult/child £3/1.70; 10am-5pm Apr-Oct) The final 6 miles of road from Kilchoan end at the 36m-high, grey granite tower of Ardnamurchan Lighthouse, built in 1849 by the 'Lighthouse Stevensons', family of Robert Louis, to guard the westernmost point of the British mainland. There's a good tearoom, and the visitor centre will tell you more than you'll ever

need to know about lighthouses, with lots of hands-on stuff for kids.

The guided tour (£6) includes a trip to the top of the lighthouse. But the main attraction here is the expansive view over the ocean – this is a superb sunset viewpoint, provided you don't mind driving back in the dark.

Ardnamurchan Natural History Centre
WILDLIFE CENTRE

(Glenmore; adult/child £4/2; ☺10.30am-5.30pm Mon-Sat, noon-5.30pm Sun Easter-Oct) This fascinating centre, devised by local photographer Michael MacGregor, tries to bring you face to face with the flora and fauna of the Ardnamurchan peninsula. The Living Building exhibit is designed to attract local wildlife, with a mammal den that is occasionally occupied by hedgehogs or pine martens, an owl nest-box, a mouse nest and a pond.

If the beasties are not in residence, you can watch recorded video footage of the animals. There's also live CCTV coverage of a golden eagle feeding site. The centre is midway between Salen and Kilchoan.

🛏 Sleeping & Eating

Salen Hotel
INN **££**

(☎01967-431661; www.salenhotel.co.uk; Salen; r £60; 🅿) A traditional Highland inn with views over Loch Sunart, the Salen Hotel has three rooms above the pub (with sea views) and another three rooms (each with en suite) in a modern chalet out the back. The cosy lounge has a roaring fire and comfy sofa, and the bar meals, including seafood, venison and other game dishes, are very good.

Inn at Ardgour
INN **££**

(☎01855-841225; www.ardgour.biz; Ardgour; d/t £90/120; 🅿) This pretty, whitewashed coaching inn, draped in colourful flower baskets, makes a great place for a lunch break or overnight stop. The restaurant (mains £8 to £13) is set in the row of cottages once occupied by the Corran ferrymen, and serves traditional, homemade Scottish dishes.

Resipole Caravan Park
CAMPGROUND **£**

(☎01967-431235; www.resipole.co.uk; Resipole; tent sites £8, with car £13) An attractive coastal caravan park, 3 miles east of Salen.

Ardnamurchan Campsite
CAMPGROUND **£**

(☎01972-510766; www.ardnamurchanstudycentre .co.uk; tent site & 1 person £7, extra person £6; ☺May-Sep; 🅿) Just west of Kilchoan village.

Ardnamurchan Natural History Centre
CAFE **£**   **175**

(Glenmore; mains £4-8; ☺10.30am-5.30pm Mon-Sat, noon-5.30pm Sun Easter-Oct) The cafe at this wildlife centre serves delicious lunches, ranging from fresh salads and sandwiches to daily specials such as prawns and crayfish tails.

❶ Information

Kilchoan tourist office (☎01972-510222; Pier Rd, Kilchoan; ☺8.30am-5pm Easter-Oct) Near the pier; has information and leaflets on walking and wildlife.

❶ Getting There & Away

BOAT Corran Ferry (www.highland.gov.uk; car/bicycle & foot passenger £6.70/free; ☺every half hour) A 10 minute crossing by car ferry from the Fort William–Glencoe road to Ardgour.

BUS Shiel Buses bus 502 runs from Fort William to Glenuig and Acharacle, continuing to Salen and Kilchoan on request (3¼ hours, one daily Monday to Saturday).

Salen to Lochailort

The A861 road from Salen to Lochailort passes through the low, wooded hills of Moidart.

A minor road (signposted Dorlin) leads west from the A861 at Shiel Bridge to a picnic area looking across to the picturesque roofless ruin of 13th-century **Castle Tioram**. The castle sits on a tiny island in Loch Moidart, connected to the mainland by a narrow strand that is submerged at high tide (the castle's name, pronounced *chee* -ram, means 'dry'). It was the ancient seat of the Clanranald Macdonalds, but the Clanranald chief ordered it to be burned (to prevent it falling into the hands of Hanoverian troops) when he set off to fight for the Jacobite side in the 1715 rebellion. A proposal by the owner to restore the castle was turned down by Historic Scotland; it is now closed to the public due to its unsafe condition.

As the A861 curls around the north shore of Loch Moidart you will see a line of three huge beech trees (and two obvious stumps) between the road and the shore. Known as the **Seven Men of Moidart** (four have been blown down by gales and replaced with saplings), they were planted in the late 18th century to commemorate the seven local men who accompanied Bonnie Prince Charlie from France and acted as his bodyguards at the start of the 1745 rebellion.

ROAD TO THE ISLES

The 46-mile A830 from Fort William to Mallaig is traditionally known as the Road to the Isles, as it leads to the jumping-off point for ferries to the Small Isles and Skye, itself a stepping stone to the Outer Hebrides. This is a region steeped in Jacobite history, having witnessed both the beginning and the end of Bonnie Prince Charlie's doomed attempt to regain the British throne.

The final section of this scenic route, between Arisaig and Mallaig, has recently been upgraded to a fast straight road. Unless you're in a hurry, instead opt for the old coastal road (signposted Alternative Coastal Route).

Between the A830 and the A87 far to the north lies Scotland's 'Empty Quarter', a rugged landscape of wild mountains and lonely sea lochs roughly 20 miles by 30 miles in size, mostly uninhabited and penetrated only by two minor roads (along Lochs Arkaig and Quoich). If you want to get away from it all, this is the place to go.

❶ Getting Around

BUS Shiel Buses bus 500 runs to Mallaig (1½ hours, three daily Monday to Friday only) via Glenfinnan (30 minutes) and Arisaig (one hour).

TRAIN The Fort William–Mallaig railway line has four trains a day (three on Sunday), with stops at many points along the way, including Corpach, Glenfinnan, Lochailort, Arisaig and Morar.

Glenfinnan

POP 100

Glenfinnan is hallowed ground for fans of Bonnie Prince Charlie, and its central shrine is the **Glenfinnan Monument**.

◉ Sights & Activities

Glenfinnan Monument   MONUMENT
This tall column, topped by a statue of a kilted Highlander, was erected in 1815 on the spot where the Young Pretender first raised his standard and rallied the clans on 19 August 1745, marking the start of the ill-fated campaign that would end in disaster 14 months later. The setting, at the north end of Loch Shiel, is hauntingly beautiful.

Glenfinnan Visitor Centre   VISITOR CENTRE
(NTS; adult/child £3/2; ⊙9.30am-5.30pm Jul & Aug, 10am-5pm Easter-Jun, Sep & Oct) This centre recounts the story of the '45, as the Jacobite rebellion of 1745 is known, when the prince's

loyal clansmen marched and fought from Glenfinnan south to Derby, then back north to final defeat at Culloden.

Glenfinnan Station Museum   MUSEUM
(www.glenfinnanstationmuseum.co.uk; adult/child £1/50p; ⊙9am-5pm Jun–mid-Oct) A half-mile west of the Glenfinnan visitor centre, this museum is a shrine of a different kind whose object of veneration is the great days of steam on the West Highland line. The famous 21-arch-Glenfinnan Viaduct, just east of the station, was built in 1901, and featured in the movie *Harry Potter & the Chamber of Secrets*.

A pleasant walk of around 0.75 miles leads to a viewpoint for the viaduct and the loch.

Loch Shiel Cruises   BOAT TRIPS
(☎07801-537617; www.highlandcruises.co.uk; ⊙Apr-Sep) Offers boat trips along Loch Shiel. There are one- to 2½-hour cruises (£8 to £16 per person) daily except Saturday and Wednesday. On Wednesday the boat goes the full length of the loch to **Acharacle** (£15/22 one way/return), calling at Polloch and Dalilea, allowing for a range of walks and bike rides using the forestry track on the eastern shore.

The boat departs from a jetty near Glenfinnan House Hotel

🛏 Sleeping & Eating

Sleeping Car Bunkhouse   BUNKHOUSE £
(☎01397-722295; www.glenfinnanstationmuseum.co.uk; dm £14; ⊙Jun–mid-Oct) Two converted railway carriages at Glenfinnan Station house this 10-berth bunkhouse and the atmospheric **Dining Car Tearoom** (snacks £2-4; ⊙9am-4.30pm Jun–mid-Oct), which serves scones with cream and jam and pots of tea. There are superb views of the mountains above Loch Shiel.

Prince's House Hotel   INN ££
(☎01397-722246; www.glenfinnan.co.uk; s/d £69/100; ℗) A delightful old coaching inn dating back to 1658, the Prince's House is a good place to pamper yourself and your nearest and dearest – ask for the spacious, tartan-clad Stuart Room if you want to stay in the oldest part of the hotel. Note that only dinner, bed and breakfast rates (£160 to £190 a double) are available on weekends from Easter to October.

There's no documentary evidence that Bonnie Prince Charlie actually stayed here in 1745, but it was the only sizable house in Glenfinnan at that time, so...

Many visitors to Scotland are captivated by the romanticised legend of Bonnie Prince Charlie, who in 1745 tried to recapture the British throne for the Stuart dynasty. The Young Pretender first set foot on Scottish soil at **Prince's Strand** on the island of Eriskay (23 July 1745), before making his way to the mainland at **Loch nan Uamh** in Arisaig (11 August 1745). He raised his standard at Glenfinnan (p176; 19 August 1745) before leading his army of Highlanders south as far as Derby in England (4 December 1745).

But his advisers made the fatal decision not to press on to London, and the Prince's army was harried in retreat all the way to final defeat at Culloden (p156; 16 April 1746). After the battle he was on the run for five months in the West Highlands, the **Isle of Skye** and the **Outer Hebrides**, famously escaping the redcoats while disguised as Flora MacDonald's maid (16 June 1746). He finally escaped to France, departing Scotland for the last time from a point in Arisaig marked by the **Prince's Cairn** (19 September 1746). He died in Rome in 1788, lonely, embittered and alcoholic.

Museums and other places associated with Bonnie Prince Charlie and his campaign include:

» Ruthven Barracks (p133)
» West Highland Museum (p165)
» The Seven Men of Moidart (p175)
» Clan Cameron Museum (p170)
» Museum of the Isles (p187)
» Dunvegan Castle (p193)

Arisaig & Morar

The 5 miles of coast between Arisaig and Morar is a fretwork of rocky islets, inlets and gorgeous silver-sand beaches backed by dunes and machair, with stunning sunset views across the sea to the silhouetted peaks of Eigg and Rum. The **Silver Sands of Morar**, as they are known, draw crowds of bucket-and-spade holidaymakers in July and August, when the many camping grounds scattered along the coast are filled to overflowing.

The waters of **Loch nan Uamh** (loch nan oo-ah; 'the loch of the caves') lap at the southern shores of Arisaig; this was where Bonnie Prince Charlie first set foot on Scottish mainland on 11 August 1745, on the shingle beach at the mouth of the Borrodale burn. Just 2 miles to the east of this bay, on a rocky point near a parking area, the **Prince's Cairn** marks the spot where he finally departed Scottish soil, never to return, on 19 September 1746.

⊙ Sights

Camusdarach Beach   BEACH
Fans of the movie *Local Hero* still make pilgrimages to Camusdarach Beach, just south of Morar, which starred in the film as Ben's beach. To find it, look for the car park 800m north of Camusdarach campsite; from here, a wooden footbridge and a 400m walk through the dunes lead to the beach.

(The village that featured in the film is on the other side of the country, at Pennan.)

Land, Sea & Islands Visitor Centre   VISITOR CENTRE
(www.arisaigcentre.co.uk; adult/child £2/free; ⊙10am-4pm Mon-Fri, 1-4pm Sun) This centre in Arisaig village houses a small but fascinating exhibition on the part played by the local area as a base for training spies for the Special Operations Executive (SOE, forerunner of MI6) during WWII.

🛏 Sleeping & Eating

There are at least a half-dozen camping grounds between Arisaig and Morar; all are open in summer only, and are often full in July and August, so book ahead. Some are listed on www.road-to-the-isles.org.uk.

Garramore House   B&B **££**
(✆01687-450268; South Morar; r per person £25-35; ⓟ🐾) Built as a hunting lodge in 1840, this house served as a Special Operations Executive HQ during WWII. Today it's a wonderfully atmospheric, child- and pet-friendly guesthouse set in lovely woodland gardens with great views to the Small Isles and Skye.

Camusdarach Campsite CAMPGROUND £
(☑01687-450221; www.camusdarach.com; South Morar; tent sites £14; ☉Mar-Oct) A small and beautiful site with good facilities, only three minutes' walk from the *Local Hero* beach.

Old Library Lodge & Restaurant RESTAURANT ££
(☑01687-450651; www.oldlibrary.co.uk; Arisaig; mains £10-15; ☉food served noon-2.30pm & 6.30-9.30pm) The Old Library is a charming restaurant with rooms (B&B per person £45 to £55) set in converted 200-year-old stables overlooking the waterfront in Arisaig village. The lunch menu concentrates on soups and freshly made sandwiches, while dinner is a more sophisticated affair offering local freshly prepared seafood, game and lamb.

Mallaig

POP 800

If you're travelling between Fort William and Skye, you may find yourself overnighting in the bustling fishing and ferry port of Mallaig. Indeed, it makes a good base for a series of day trips by ferry to the Small Isles and Knoydart.

◉ Sights & Activities

Mallaig Heritage Centre HERITAGE CENTRE
(☑01687-462085; www.mallaigheritage.org.uk; Station Rd; adult/child £2/free; ☉9.30am-4.30pm Mon-Sat, noon-4pm Sun) The village's rainy-day attractions are limited to this centre, which covers the archaeology and history of the region, including the heartrending tale of the Highland Clearances in Knoydart.

MV Grimsay Isle BOAT TRIPS
(☑07780-815158) The MV Grimsay Isle provides entertaining, customised sea-fishing

trips and seal-watching tours (book at the tourist office).

🛏 Sleeping & Eating

Seaview Guest House B&B ££
(☑01687-462059; www.seaviewguesthousemallaig.com; Main St; r per person £28-35; ☉Mar-Nov; ℗) Just beyond the tourist office, this comfortable three-bedroom B&B has grand views over the harbour, not only from the upstairs bedrooms but also from the breakfast room. There's also a cute little cottage next door that offers self-catering accommodation (www.selfcateringmallaig.com; one double and one twin room) for £350 to £450 a week.

Springbank Guest House B&B ££
(☑01687-462459; www.springbank-mallaig.co.uk; East Bay; r per person £25; ℗🛜) The Springbank is a traditional West Highland house with seven homey guest bedrooms, with superb views across the harbour to the Cuillin of Skye.

Mallaig Backpacker's Lodge HOSTEL £
(☑01687-462764; www.mallaigbackpackers.co.uk; Harbour View; dm £14.50) The Lodge is a friendly, 12-bed hostel in a lovely old house overlooking the harbour. On a sunny day the hostel's Tea Garden **terrace cafe** (mains £5 to £10), with its flowers, greenery and cosmopolitan backpacker staff, feels more like the Mediterranean than Mallaig. The speciality of the house is a pintglass full of Mallaig prawns with dipping sauce (£10). From late May to September the cafe opens in the evening with a bistro menu.

Fish Market Restaurant (TOP CHOICE) SEAFOOD ££
(☑01687-462299; Station Rd; mains £9-20; ☉lunch & dinner) At least half-a-dozen signs in Mallaig advertise 'seafood restaurant', but this bright, modern, bistro-style place next to the harbour is our favourite, serv-

---

WORTH A TRIP

GLENUIG INN

Set on a peaceful bay on the Arisaig coast, halfway between Lochailort and Acharacle on the A830 road, the recently renovated **Glenuig Inn** (☑01687-470219; www.glenuig.com; B&B s/d/q £60/90/120, bunkhouse per person £25; ℗🛜) is a great place to get away from it all. As well as offering comfortable accommodation, good food (mains £9 to £19), and real ale on tap, it's a great base for exploring Arisaig, Morar and the Loch Shiel area.

Apart from the countless hiking and biking options, **Rockhopper Sea Kayaking** (www.rockhopperscotland.co.uk; half-/full day £40/70) can take you on a guided tour along the wild and beautiful coastline, starting and finishing at the inn.

ing simply prepared scallops with smoked salmon and savoy cabbage, grilled langoustines with garlic butter, and Mallaig haddock in breadcrumbs, as well as the tastiest Cullen skink on the west coast.

Upstairs is a **coffee shop** (mains £4-5; ⊙11am-5pm) that serves delicious hot roast-beef rolls with horseradish sauce, and scones with clotted cream and jam.

❶ Information

Mallaig has a post office and bank with ATM.
Mallaig tourist office (☑01687-462170; ⊙10am-5.30pm Mon-Fri, 10.15am-3.45pm Sat, noon-3.30pm Sun)
Co-op Supermarket (⊙8.00am-10pm Mon-Sat, 9am-9pm Sun)

❶ Getting There & Away

BOAT Ferries run from Mallaig to the Small Isles, the Isle of Skye and Knoydart; see the transport information for these areas for more details.

BUS Shiel Buses bus 500 runs from Fort William to Mallaig (1½ hours, three daily Monday to Friday only) via Glenfinnan (30 minutes) and Arisaig (one hour).

TRAIN The West Highland line runs between Fort William and Mallaig (£10, 1½ hours) four times a day (three on Sunday).

KNOYDART PENINSULA

POP 70

The Knoydart peninsula is the only sizable area in Britain that remains inaccessible to the motor car, cut off by miles of rough country and the embracing arms of Lochs Nevis and Hourn – Gaelic for the lochs of Heaven and Hell. No road penetrates this wilderness of rugged hills. **Inverie**, its sole village, can only be reached by ferry from Mallaig, or on foot from the remote road's end at Kinloch Hourn (a tough 16-mile hike).

The main reasons for visiting are to climb the remote 1020m peak of **Ladhar Bheinn** (*laar* -ven), which affords some of the west coast's finest views, or just to enjoy the feeling of being cut off from the rest of the world. There are no shops, no TV and there is no mobile-phone reception (although there is internet access); electricity is provided by a private hydroelectric scheme – truly 'off the grid' living! For more information and full accommodation listings, see www.knoydart.org.

🛏 Sleeping & Eating

Knoydart Lodge   B&B ££
(☑01687-460129; www.knoydartlodge.co.uk; Inverie; s/d £55/80; ⌾) This must be some of the most spacious and luxurious B&B accommodation on the whole west coast, let alone in Knoydart. On offer are large, stylish bedrooms in a fantastic, modern timber-built lodge reminiscent of an Alpine chalet. Gourmet evening meals are available on Wednesday and Saturday (£30 per person).

Knoydart Foundation
Bunkhouse   BUNKHOUSE £
(☑01687-462163; www.knoydart.org; Inverie; £14; ⌨) A 15-minute walk east of the ferry pier.

Torrie Shieling   BUNKHOUSE £
(☑01687-462669; torrie@knoydart.org; Inverie; dm £15) A 20-minute walk to the west of the ferry pier.

Barisdale Bothy   BUNKHOUSE £
(☑01764-684946; www.barisdale.com; Barisdale; dm £3, tent sites per person £1) The Barisdale Bothy, six miles west of Kinloch Hourn on the footpath to Inverie, has sleeping platforms without mattresses – you'll need your own sleeping bag and foam mat.

Long Beach   CAMPGROUND £
(Long Beach; per tent £4) Basic but beautiful campsite, a 10-minute walk east of the ferry; water supply and composting toilet, but no showers.

🔝 **Old Forge**   PUB/RESTAURANT ££
(☑01687-462267; www.theoldforge.co.uk; Inverie; mains £10-20; ☷) The Old Forge is listed in the *Guinness Book of Records* as Britain's most remote pub. It's surprisingly sophisticated – as well as having real ale on tap, there's an Italian coffee machine for those wilderness lattes and cappuccinos, and the house special is a platter of langoustines with Marie Rose dipping sauce.

In the evening you can sit by the fire, pint of beer in hand and join the impromptu *ceilidh* (an evening of traditional Scottish entertainment including music, song and dance) that seems to take place just about nightly.

❶ Getting There & Away

Bruce Watt Cruises (☑01687-462320; www .knoydart-ferry.co.uk) Passenger ferry linking Mallaig to Inverie (£9/12 single/return, 45 minutes) twice daily Monday to Friday from

STEVEN FALLON: CHAMPION MUNRO BAGGER

Steven Fallon, a hill walker, fell runner and qualified Mountain Leader who lives in Edinburgh, is the world's most prolific Munro bagger, having climbed all of Scotland's 283 Munros (peaks of 3000ft and higher) no fewer than 14 times.

Do you have a favourite, and/or least favourite Munro? As to my favourites, practically anything in the northwest Highlands could feature – they tend to be pointy with great views. I'd single out Slioch by Loch Maree; Beinn Alligin, Liathach and Beinn Eighe in Torridon; the Five Sisters of Kintail and all of the mountains in the Cuillin on Skye. However, my most-most-favourite has to be Ladhar Bheinn on the Knoydart Peninsula. It's pretty remote and to reach it requires a long walk-in along the southern shore of Loch Hourn. It's just so beautiful there. The mountain itself is complex with corries and ridges, and the summit has great views over Eigg to Skye and beyond.

Which is the easiest Munro, and which is the hardest? With only 430m of ascent over 5km, the easiest Munros have to be the Cairnwell and Carn Aosda from the Glenshee ski resort. Good paths and ski-tows make for simple navigation over these two peaks, and if you time it right, you'll be back at the cafe in time for something to eat. Check out my website (www.stevenfallon.co.uk) for the 10 easiest Munro walks (click on Hill Lists and Maps/Munros/Easiest Munros).

The most difficult technically has to be the aptly named Inaccessible Pinnacle in the Cuillin Hills on Skye. It's a clamber up a long fin of rock with sensational, tremble-inducing exposure, followed by an abseil down a short but vertical drop. Most Munro baggers will have to enlist the help of their rock-climbing friends or hire a guide.

mid-May to mid-September, and on Monday, Wednesday and Friday only the rest of the year (no weekend ferries). Taking the morning boat gives you four hours ashore in Knoydart before the afternoon return trip.

WALKING IN THE GREAT GLEN & LOCHABER

Glen Coe & Glen Etive Walk

This walk circumnavigates the base of Buachaille Etive Beag, the 'little shepherd of Etive', passing through Lairig Eilde and Lairig Gartain, two classic U-shaped glacial valleys. It offers a taste of the wilder reaches of Glen Coe's dramatic mountain scenery without tackling any really serious terrain. There's a catch though – the paths are mostly rough and rocky or, beside the River Coupall, very muddy. The route is described here in an anticlockwise direction for aesthetic reasons (the views are better), but there's no reason why it can't be walked in the opposite direction. The walk includes more than 600m of ascent.

THE WALK

Start at the large car park on the south side of the road near the Pass of Glen Coe, op-

posite a rounded memorial cairn (OS grid reference 187563), where a signpost points to 'Glen Etive by the Lairig Eilde'. The path first leads southwest and crosses the Allt Lairig Eilde – if the river is in spate it is dangerous to ford so, if in doubt, continue along the east bank until you can rejoin the main path higher up. The well-defined path on the west bank of the stream continues for around 1 mile then crosses back to the east side. The way, marked by a few cairns, now leads uphill and bends round to the south, with views of increasingly wild country – you might see red deer here. When you eventually reach the top of the pass known as the **Lairig Eilde** (489m)

ℹ️ **GLEN COE & GLEN ETIVE WALK**

» **Duration** 5 hours

» **Distance** 10 miles (16km)

» **Difficulty** moderate

» **Start/Finish** Pass of Glencoe

» **Summary** A low-level walk across two dramatic passes in magnificent glaciated valleys overlooked by rugged peaks and ridges.

the views open up across Glen Etive to the mountains beyond.

Descend and cross a small stream. The path continues steeply down towards **Dalness** in Glen Etive. After about 0.6 miles go through a gate in a high fence and cross the stream on rock slabs. Bear left, uphill, and go through another gate. Traverse the spur briefly then pick up a formed path leading northeast across the lower slopes of Stob Dubh. A few hundred metres further on, join a path coming up from the right. Continue up the steep and fairly narrow valley, with Allt Gartain tumbling down in a series of small waterfalls. The route involves some easy scrambling and on a fine day there are many opportunities to stop by the waterfalls and enjoy the views back to Loch Etive.

Soon you crest the **Lairig Gartain** (489m), with extensive views ahead to the mountains around Loch Treig. The next stage, down another classic, U-shaped, glaciated valley, is boggy and wet. Walk down the glen, between Buachaille Etive Beag on the left and Buachaille Etive Mór on the right, to a car park beside the A82. Cross the road and follow a path that leads to an old road; turn left to follow it west for about 1 mile to where it meets the A82. Then you've little choice but to walk beside the road for several hundred metres, back to the start of the walk.

Skye & the Western Isles

Includes »

Best Places to Eat

» Three Chimneys (p194)
» Digby Chick (p205)
» Café Arriba (p192)
» Lochbay Seafood
Restaurant (p194)
» Bistro at the Bosville
(p192)

Best Places to Stay

» Garenin Crofters' Hostel
(p206)
» Toravaig House Hotel
(p187)
» Ben Tianavaig B&B (p190)
» Polochar Inn (p213)
» Langass Lodge Hotel (p212)

Why Go?

The Isle of Skye is the distilled essence of the Highlands and Islands, where the jagged peaks of the Cuillin Hills tear at the mist and the ghosts of Bonnie Prince Charlie and Flora MacDonald haunt the hallways of Dunvegan Castle. This rugged island is a paradise for walkers, climbers and wildlife enthusiasts, with its dramatic mountains and lonely lochs, home to golden eagles, peregrine falcons, otters, deer and seals.

Skye points the way to the Western Isles – the 'isles at the edge of the sea' – with their landscapes of peat bog, lochan and bare, glaciated gneiss. These harsh landscapes are softened by glittering shell-sand beaches, wildflower-strewn machair, and buttercup meadows where the outlines of ruined crofts are visible in the turf like fossils in a stone. This necklace of remote islands is a last bastion of Gaelic culture, where the hardships of life in the old 'blackhouses' still remain within living memory.

When to Go

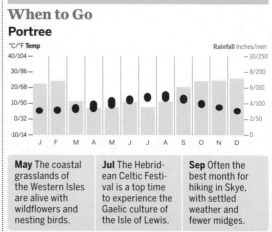

Portree

May The coastal grasslands of the Western Isles are alive with wildflowers and nesting birds.

Jul The Hebridean Celtic Festival is a top time to experience the Gaelic culture of the Isle of Lewis.

Sep Often the best month for hiking in Skye, with settled weather and fewer midges.

Skye & the Western Isles Highlights

1 Leave footprints in the sand along the beautiful beaches of **South Harris** (p209)

2 Take on the challenge of the **Cuillin Hills** (p188), whose rugged ridges attract climbers from all over Britain

3 Launch yourself in a **sea-kayak** to explore the wildlife-rich waters of the Western Isles (p212)

4 Soak up the stunning panorama from the summit of the **Sgurr of Eigg** (p197)

5 Explore the weird and wonderful landscape features of the **Quiraing** (p194)

6 Marvel at the self-indulgence that furnished the fabled halls of **Kinloch Castle** (p197)

7 Ponder the mysteries of the ancient stones at **Callanish** (p206)

8 Make the once-in-lifetime sea crossing to remote **St Kilda** (p214)

ISLE OF SKYE

POP 9900

The Isle of Skye (an t-Eilean Sgiathanach in Gaelic) takes its name from the old Norse *sky-a,* meaning 'cloud island', a Viking reference to the often-mist-enshrouded Cuillin Hills. It's the biggest of Scotland's islands, a 50-mile-long smorgasbord of velvet moors, jagged mountains, sparkling lochs and towering sea cliffs. The stunning scenery is the main attraction, but when the mist closes in there are plenty of castles, crofting museums and cosy pubs and restaurants to retire to.

Along with Edinburgh and Loch Ness, Skye is one of Scotland's top three tourist destinations. However, the hordes tend to stick to Portree, Dunvegan and Trotternish – it's almost always possible to find peace and quiet in the island's further-flung corners. Come prepared for changeable weather: when it's fine it's very fine indeed, but all too often it isn't.

🏃 Activities

Walking

Skye offers some of the finest – and in places the roughest and most difficult – walking in Scotland. There are many detailed guidebooks available, including a series of four walking guides by Charles Rhodes, available from the Aros Experience (p190) and the tourist office in Portree. You'll need Ordnance Survey (OS) 1:50,000 maps 23 and 32. Don't attempt the longer walks in bad weather or in winter.

Easy, low-level routes include: through **Strath Mor** from Luib (on the Broadford–Sligachan road) and on to Torrin (on the Broadford–Elgol road, allow 1½ hours, 4 miles); from **Sligachan to Kilmarie** via Camasunary (four hours, 11 miles); and from **Elgol to Kilmarie** via Camasunary (2½ hours, 6.5 miles). The walk from **Kilmarie to Coruisk** via Camasunary and the 'Bad Step' is superb but slightly harder.

Isle of Skye

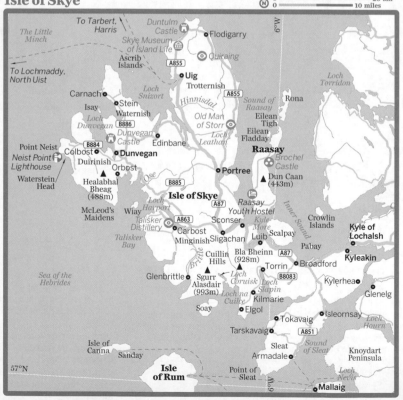

Skye Walking Holidays WALKING
(☎01470-552213; www.skyewalks.co.uk; Duntulm Castle Hotel) Organises three-day guided walking holidays for £400 per person, including four nights of hotel accommodation.

Climbing
The Cuillin Hills is a veritable playground for rock climbers, and the two-day traverse of the Cuillin Ridge is the finest mountaineering expedition in the British Isles. There are several mountain guides in the area who can provide instruction and safely introduce inexperienced climbers to the harder routes.

Skye Guides ROCK CLIMBING
(☎01471-822116; www.skyeguides.co.uk) A five-day basic rock-climbing course costs around £800 and a private mountain guide can be hired for around £190 a day (both rates apply for up to two clients).

Sea Kayaking
The sheltered coves and sea lochs around the coast of Skye provide water lovers with magnificent sea-kayaking opportunities. The centres listed here can provide kayaking instruction, guiding and equipment hire for both beginners and experts. It costs around £35 for a half-day kayak hire with instruction.

Whitewave Outdoor Centre SEA KAYAKING
(☎01470-542414; www.white-wave.co.uk; 19 Linicro; ◷Mar-Oct) Provides kayaking instruction, guiding and equipment hire for both beginners and experts.

Skyak Adventures SEA KAYAKING
(☎01471-820002; www.skyakadventures.com; 29 Lower Breakish) Expeditions and courses for beginners to experienced paddlers, to take you to places inaccessible any other way.

☞ Tours
There are several operators who offer guided tours of Skye, covering history, culture and wildlife. Rates are from £140 for a six-hour tour for up to six people.

Red Deer Travel GUIDED TOURS
(☎01478-612142) Historical and cultural tours by minibus.

Isle of Skye Tour Guide Co GUIDED TOURS
(☎01471-844440; www.isle-of-skye-tour-guide.co.uk) Geology, history and wildlife by car.

❶ Information
Portree and Broadford are the main population centres on Skye.

Internet Access
Columba 1400 Community Centre (Staffin; per hr £1; ◷10.30am-8pm Mon-Sat Apr-Oct)
Seamus's Bar (Sligachan Hotel, Sligachan; per 15min £1; ◷11am-11pm)
Portree tourist office (☎01478-612137; Bayfield Rd, Portree; internet per 20min £1; ◷9am-6pm Mon-Sat, 10am-4pm Sun Jun-Aug, 9am-5pm Mon-Fri, 10am-4pm Sat Apr, May & Sep, limited opening hours Oct-Mar)
South Skye Computers (Old Corrie Industrial Estate, Broadford; per 15min £1.25; ◷10am-5pm Mon-Fri, to 1pm Sat)

Medical Services
Portree Community Hospital (☎01478-613200; Fancyhill) There's a casualty department and dental surgery here.

Money
Only Portree and Broadford have banks with ATMs, and Portree's tourist office has a currency exchange desk.

Tourist Information
Broadford tourist office (☎01471-822361; Car Park; ◷9.30am-5pm Mon-Sat, 10am-4pm Sun Apr-Oct)
Dunvegan tourist office (☎01470-521581; 2 Lochside; ◷10am-5pm Mon-Sat Jun-Oct, 10am-4pm Sun Jul & Aug, 10am-5pm Mon-Fri Apr & May, limited opening hours Nov-Mar)
Portree tourist office (☎01478-612137; Bayfield Rd; ◷9am-6pm Mon-Sat, 10am-4pm Sun Jun-Aug, 9am-5pm Mon-Fri, 10am-4pm Sat Apr, May & Sep, limited opening hours Oct-Mar; @)

❶ Getting There & Away
Boat
Despite there being a bridge, there are still a couple of ferry links between Skye and the mainland. Ferries also operate from Uig on Skye to the Outer Hebrides.
CalMac (www.calmac.co.uk; driver or passenger/car £3.85/20.30) Operates the Mallaig to Armadale ferry (30 minutes, eight daily Monday to Saturday, five to seven on Sunday). It's very popular in July and August, so book ahead if you're travelling by car.
Skye Ferry (www.skyeferry.co.uk; car with up to four passengers £12) Runs a tiny vessel (six cars only) on the short Kylerhea to Glenelg crossing (five minutes, every 20 minutes). The ferry operates from 10am to 6pm daily from Easter to October only, till 7pm from June to August.

SKYE & THE WESTERN ISLES

Bus

Scottish Citylink runs buses from Glasgow to Portree (£38, seven hours, four daily) and Uig via Crianlarich, Fort William and Kyle of Lochalsh on the mainland. Buses also run from Inverness to Portree (£17, 3½ hours, five daily).

Car & Motorcycle

The Isle of Skye became permanently tethered to the Scottish mainland when the Skye Bridge opened in 1995. The controversial bridge tolls were abolished in 2004 and the crossing is now free.

There are petrol stations at Broadford (☉ 24 hours), Armadale, Portree, Dunvegan and Uig.

ℹ Getting Around

Getting around the island by public transport can be a pain, especially if you want to explore away from the main Kyleakin–Portree–Uig road. Here, as in much of the Highlands, there are only a few buses on Saturdays, and only one Sunday service (between Kyle of Lochalsh and Portree).

Bus

Stagecoach operates the main bus routes on the island, linking all the main villages and towns. Its Skye Dayrider ticket gives unlimited bus travel for one day for £6.70. For timetable info, call **Traveline** (☎0871 200 22 33).

Taxi

Kyle Taxi Company (☎01599-534323) You can order a taxi or hire a car from Kyle Taxi Company. Car hire costs from around £38 a day, and you can arrange for the car to be waiting at Kyle of Lochalsh train station.

Kyleakin (Caol Acain)

POP 100

Poor wee Kyleakin had the carpet pulled from under it when the Skye Bridge opened – it went from being the gateway to the island to a backwater bypassed by the main road. It's now a pleasant, peaceful little place, with a harbour used by yachts and fishing boats.

The community-run **Bright Water Visitor Centre** (☎01599-530040; www.eileanban. org) serves as a base for tours of **Eilean Ban** – the island used as a stepping stone by the Skye Bridge – where Gavin Maxwell (author of *Ring of Bright Water*) spent the last 18 months of his life in 1968–69, living in the lighthouse keeper's cottage. The island is now a nature reserve and tours operate at 11am and 2pm daily in summer. The visitor centre also houses an exhibition on Maxwell, the lighthouse and the island's wildlife.

Opening times were uncertain at the time of research – best call ahead to check.

Kyleakin is something of a backpacker ghetto, with four hostels in close proximity. The homely **Dun Caan Independent Hostel** (☎01599-534087; www.skyerover.co.uk; Castle View; dm from £15), in a fine, old, pine-panelled house overlooking the harbour, has the most attractive location.

About 3 miles southwest of Kyleakin, a minor road leads southwards to **Kylerhea**, where there's a 1½-hour nature trail to a shorefront **otter hide**, where you stand a good chance of seeing these elusive creatures. A little farther on is the jetty for the car ferry to Glenelg on the mainland.

A shuttle bus runs half-hourly between Kyle of Lochalsh and Kyleakin (five minutes), and there are eight to 10 buses daily (except Sunday) to Broadford and Portree.

Broadford (An T-Ath Leathann)

POP 1050

Broadford is a service centre for the scattered communities of southern Skye. The long, straggling village has a tourist office, a 24-hour petrol station, a large **Co-op supermarket** (☉8am-10pm Mon-Sat, 9am-6pm Sun), a laundrette and a bank with an ATM.

There are lots of B&Bs in and around Broadford and the village is well placed for exploring southern Skye by car.

🛏 Sleeping & Eating

Broadford Hotel   HOTEL ££

(☎01471-822204; www.broadfordhotel.co.uk; Torrin Rd; s/d from £115/128; P❀) The old Broadford Hotel has been revamped into a glamourous and stylish retreat with luxury fabrics and designer colour schemes. There's a formal restaurant and the more democratic **Gabbro Bar** (mains £7-9, ☉ noon-9pm) where you can enjoy a bar meal of smoked haddock chowder or steak pie washed down with Isle of Skye Brewery ale.

Berabhaigh   B&B ££

(☎01471-822372; berabhaigh@iselofskye.net; 3 Lime Park; r per person £34; ☉Mar-Oct; P) This is a lovely old croft house with bay views. It is located just off the main road, near Creelers.

Luib House   B&B ££

(☎01471-820334; www.luibhouse.co.uk; r per person £30; P🚡) This is a large, comfortable and well-appointed house 6 miles north of Broadford.

Creelers

SEAFOOD **££**

(☎01471-822281; www.skye-seafood-restaurant.co.uk; Lower Harrapool; mains £12-18; ☺noon-9.30pm Mon-Sat) Broadford has several places to eat but one really stands out: Creelers is a small, bustling, no-frills restaurant that serves some of the best seafood on Skye; the house speciality is a rich, spicy seafood gumbo. Best to book ahead.

If you can't get a table then nip around to the back door, where you'll find **Ma Doyle's Takeaway**, for fish and chips (£5) to go.

Sleat

If you cross over the sea to Skye on the ferry from Mallaig you arrive in Armadale, at the southern end of the long, low-lying peninsula known as Sleat (pronounced 'slate'). The landscape of Sleat itself is not exceptional, but it provides a grandstand for ogling the magnificent scenery on either side – take the steep and twisting minor road that loops through **Tarskavaig** and **Tokavaig** for stunning views of the Isle of Rum, the Cuillin Hills and Bla Bheinn.

ARMADALE

POP 150

Armadale, where the ferry from Mallaig arrives, is little more than a store, a post office and a couple of houses. There are six or seven buses a day (Monday to Saturday) from Armadale to Broadford and Portree.

◉ Sights & Activities

Museum of the Isles

MUSEUM

(☎01471-844305; www.clandonald.com; adult/child £6.95/4.95; ☺9.30am-5.30pm Easter-Oct) Just along the road from the ferry is the part-ruined **Armadale Castle**, former seat of Lord Macdonald of Sleat. The neighbouring museum will tell you all you ever wanted to know about Clan Donald, as well as providing an easily digestible history of the Lordship of the Isles.

Prize exhibits include rare portraits of clan chiefs, and a wine glass that was once used by Bonnie Prince Charlie. The ticket also gives admission to the lovely **castle gardens**.

FREE Aird Old Church Gallery

ART GALLERY

(☎01471-844291; www.skyewatercolours.co.uk; ☺10am-5pm Mon-Sat Easter-Sep) At the end of the narrow road that leads southwest from Armadale through Ardvasar village, this small gallery exhibits the powerful landscape paintings of Peter McDermott.

Sea.fari

BOAT TRIP

(☎01471-844787, 01471-833316; www.seafari.co.uk) Sea.fari runs one- to three-hour boat trips (£27/37 per person) in high-speed RIBs. These trips have a high success rate for spotting minke whales in summer (an average of 180 sightings a year), with rarer sightings of bottlenose dolphins and basking sharks – even a humpback whale and two killer whales have been spotted in recent years.

🛏 Sleeping & Eating

Flora MacDonald Hostel

HOSTEL **£**

(☎01471-844272; www.skye-hostel.co.uk; The Glebe, Kilmore; dm/tw/q £14/36/65; ☐) On a farm 3 miles north of Mallaig–Armadale ferry, with Highland cattle and Eriskay ponies.

Pasta Shed

SEAFOOD **££**

(☎01471-844264; The Pier; mains £6-12; ☺9am-6pm) A cute little conservatory with some outdoor tables; serves good seafood dishes, pizzas, fish and chips, crab salads and coffees – you can sit in or take away.

ISLEORNSAY

This pretty harbour, 8 miles north of Armadale, is opposite Sandaig Bay on the mainland, where Gavin Maxwell lived and wrote his much-loved memoir *Ring of Bright Water*. **Gallery An Talla Dearg** (admission free; ☺10am-6pm Mon-Fri, to 4pm Sat & Sun Apr-Oct) exhibits the works of artists who were inspired by Scottish landscapes and culture.

🛏 Sleeping & Eating

TOP CHOICE Toravaig House Hotel

HOTEL **£££**

(☎01471-820200; www.skyehotel.co.uk; Toravaig; r from £169; ☐🛜) This hotel, 3 miles south of Isleornsay, is one of those places where the owners know a thing or two about hospitality – as soon as you arrive you'll feel right at home, whether relaxing on the sofas by the log fire in the lounge or admiring the view across the Sound of Sleat from the lawn chairs in the garden.

The spacious bedrooms – ask for room 1 (Eriskay), with its enormous sleigh bed – are luxuriously equipped, from the rich and heavy bed linen to the huge, high-pressure shower heads. The elegant **Iona restaurant** serves the best of local fish, game and lamb. After dinner you can retire to the lounge with a single malt and flick through the yachting magazines – you can even arrange a day trip aboard the owners' 42ft sailing yacht.

Hotel Eilean Iarmain HOTEL **£££**
(☏01471-833266; www.eilean-iarmain.co.uk; s/d from £100/160; 🅿) A charming old Victorian hotel with log fires, an excellent restaurant and 12 luxurious rooms, many with sea views. The hotel's cosy, wood-panelled **An Praban Bar** (mains £7-10) serves delicious, gourmet-style bar meals – try the haddock in beer batter, venison burger or vegetarian lasagne.

Elgol (Ealaghol)

On a clear day, the journey along the road from Broadford to Elgol is one of the most scenic on Skye. It takes in two classic post-card panoramas – the view of Bla Bheinn across **Loch Slapin** (near Torrin), and the superb view of the entire Cuillin range from **Elgol pier**.

Just west of Elgol is the **Spar Cave**, famously visited by Sir Walter Scott in 1814 and mentioned in his poem *Lord of the Isles*. The 80m-deep cave is wild and remote, and filled with beautiful flowstone formations. It is a short walk from the village of **Glasnakille**, but the approach is over seaweed-covered boulders and is only accessible for one hour either side of low water. Check tide times and route information at Broadford tourist office, or ask at the tearoom in Elgol.

Bus 49 runs from Broadford to Elgol (40 minutes, three daily Monday to Friday, two Saturday).

🏃 Activities

Bella Jane CRUISE
(☏0800 731 3089; www.bellajane.co.uk; ⊙Easter–mid-Oct) Bella Jane offers a three-hour cruise (adult/child £20/8) from Elgol harbour to the remote Loch na Cuilce, an impressive inlet surrounded by soaring peaks. On a calm day, you can clamber ashore here to make the short walk to Loch Coruisk in the heart of the Cuillin Hills. You get 1½ hours ashore and visit a seal colony en route.

Aquaxplore BOAT TOURS
(☏0800 731 3089; www.aquaxplore.co.uk; ⊙Easter–mid-Oct) Runs 1½-hour high-speed boat trips from Elgol to an abandoned shark-hunting station on the island of **Soay** (adult/child £20/15), once owned by *Ring of Bright Water* author Gavin Maxwell. There are longer trips (adult/child £45/32, four hours) to Rum, Canna and Sanday to visit breeding colonies of puffins, with the chance of seeing minke whales on the way.

Misty Isle CRUISE
(☏01471-866288; www.mistyisleboattrips.co.uk; adult/child £18/7.50; ⊙Apr-Oct) The pretty, traditional wooden launch *Misty Isle* offers cruises to Loch Coruisk with 1½ hours ashore (no Sunday service).

Cuillin Hills

The Cuillin Hills are Britain's most spectacular mountain range (the name comes from the Old Norse *kjöllen,* meaning 'keel-shaped'). Though small in stature (**Sgurr Alasdair**, the highest summit, is only 993m), the peaks are near-alpine in character, with knife-edge ridges, jagged pinnacles, scree-filled gullies and acres of naked rock. While they are a paradise for experienced mountaineers, the higher reaches of the Cuillin are off limits to the majority of walkers.

The good news is that there are also plenty of good low-level hikes within the ability of most walkers. One of the best (on a fine day) is the steep climb from Glenbrittle camping ground to **Coire Lagan** (6 miles round trip; allow at least three hours). The impressive upper corrie contains a lochan for bathing (for the hardy!), and the surrounding cliffs are a playground for rock climbers – bring along your binoculars.

Even more spectacular, but much harder to reach, is **Loch Coruisk** (from the Gaelic *Coir'Uisg,* the Water Corrie), a remote loch ringed by the highest peaks of the Cuillin. Accessible by boat trip from Elgol (p188), or via an arduous 5.5-mile hike from Kilmarie, Coruisk was popularised by Sir Walter Scott in his 1815 poem *Lord of the Isles*. Crowds of Victorian tourists and landscape artists followed in Scott's footsteps, including JMW Turner, whose watercolours were used to illustrate Scott's works.

There are two main bases for exploring the Cuillin – **Sligachan** to the north, and **Glenbrittle** to the south.

🛏 Sleeping & Eating

Sligachan Hotel HOTEL **£££**
(☏01478-650204; www.sligachan.co.uk; per person from £59; 🅿@🛜) The Slig, as it has been known to generations of climbers, is a near village in itself, encompassing a luxurious hotel, a microbrewery, self-catering cottages, a bunkhouse, a campsite, a big barn of a bar and an adventure playground.

Sligachan Bunkhouse HOSTEL £
(☎01478-650204; www.sligachan.co.uk; Sligachan Hotel; per person £15) Comfortable and modern bunkhouse opposite the Sligachan hotel.

Sligachan Campsite CAMPGROUND £
(Sligachan Hotel; sites per person £5; ⏲Apr-Oct) Across the road from the Sligachan hotel is this basic campsite; be warned – this spot is a midge magnet. No bookings.

Glenbrittle SYHA HOSTEL £
(☎01478-640278; www.syha.org.uk; dm £15; ⏲Apr-Sep) Scandinavian-style timber hostel, quickly fills up with climbers on holiday weekends.

Glenbrittle Campsite CAMPGROUND £
(☎01478-640404; sites per adult/child £5.50/3.50) Excellent site, close to mountains and sea; the midges can be diabolical, though.

Seamus's Bar PUB GRUB £
(Sligachan Hotel; mains £8-10; ⏲food served 11am-11pm; @🛜👪) This place dishes up decent bar meals, including haggis, neeps and tatties, steak and ale pie, and fish pie, and serves real ales from its own microbrewery. It also has a range of 200 malt whiskies in serried ranks above the bar. As well as the adventure playground outside, there are games, toys and a play area indoors.

ℹ Getting There & Away

Sligachan, on the main Kyle of Lochalsh–Portree road, is easily accessible by bus; Glenbrittle is harder to reach. Bus 53 runs five times a day Monday to Friday (once on Saturday) from Portree to Carbost via Sligachan (50 minutes); from there, you'll have to hitch or walk the remaining 8 miles to Glenbrittle (this can be slow, especially late in the day).

Minginish

Loch Harport, to the north of the Cuillin, divides the Minginish Peninsula from the rest of Skye. On its southern shore lies the village of Carbost, home to the smooth, sweet and smoky Talisker malt whisky, produced at **Talisker Distillery** (☎01478-614308; www.discovering-distilleries.com; guided

CORUISK VIA THE BAD STEP

The hike from Kilmarie to Coruisk via the Bad Step is one of the most spectacular and challenging of Skye's low-level walks (11 miles round trip; allow at least six hours). The route begins at a parking area just south of Kilmarie, on the Broadford to Elgol road (signpost for Camasunary and Sligachan), and leads over a hill pass to the bay of Camasunary, following a stony track that was built by the army in the 1960s to provide better access for mountain rescue teams.

Camasunary (Camas Fhionnairigh) is a beautiful and remote bay with grand views to the hills of Rum and Eigg. At its far end is a comfortable **bothy** where you can spend the night for free (four rooms, two fireplaces, no other facilities), and plenty of space for **wild camping**. From here you can hike north through a glen to Sligachan (7 miles), or south along the coast to Elgol (4.5 miles).

The route to Coruisk continues on the far side of the Camasunary River – at low tide you can cross the stream dryshod on stepping stones, but if the tide is high you'll have to remove your boots and splash across further upstream. The path gets rougher as it climbs the hillside and curves around the lower slopes of Sgurr na Stri. The notorious **Bad Step** is opposite the north end of the little island in the loch, just past the only trees on the route. Stay high as you approach, descending to the shore only after you have passed the trees.

The 'step' is a rock slab that drops straight into the sea, where an overhang forces you to scramble out onto a shelf and along a rising crack. The secret is to drop down leftward when you reach a niche in the crack, rather than continuing along it (which looks the obvious way to go). There are no further obstacles, and 15 minutes beyond the Bad Step you arrive at Loch Coruisk.

This is one of the wildest and most remote spots in Scotland. All around the lochshore are jagged peaks of naked rock, with the River Scavaig tumbling over slabby waterfalls into the sea. The only signs of habitation are a climbers' hut, which was built in the 1950s, and the little pier where boats from Elgol put ashore. The easiest way out is back the way you came.

tour £5; ⏱9.30am-5pm Mon-Sat Easter-Oct, plus from noon Sun Jul & Aug, from 10am Mon-Fri Nov-Easter). This is the only distillery on Skye; the guided tour includes a free dram. Magnificent **Talisker Bay**, 5 miles west of Carbost, has a sandy beach, sea stack and waterfall.

🛏 Sleeping & Eating

Old Inn   B&B, HOSTEL **££**
(☎01478-640205; www.carbost.f9.co.uk; Carbost; s/d £42/74; P) The Old Inn is an atmospheric wee pub, offering accommodation in bright B&B bedrooms and an appealing chalet-style bunkhouse (from £14 per person). The bar is a favourite with walkers and climbers from Glenbrittle, and serves excellent pub grub (£8 to £12, noon to 10pm), from fresh oysters to haddock and chips.

There's an outdoor patio at the back with great views over Loch Harport.

Skyewalker Independent Hostel   HOSTEL **£**
(☎01478-640250; www.skyewalkerhostel.com; Fiskavaig Rd, Portnalong; dm £13.50; @) Three miles northwest of Carbost, this hostel is housed in the old village school.

❶ Getting There & Away

There are five buses a day on weekdays (one on Saturday) from Portree to Carbost via Sligachan.

Portree (Port Righ)

Portree is Skye's largest and liveliest town. It has a pretty harbour lined with brightly painted houses, and there are great views of the surrounding hills. Its name (from the Gaelic for King's Harbour) commemorates James V, who came here in 1540 to pacify the local clans.

◉ Sights & Activities

Aros Experience   VISITOR CENTRE
(☎01478-613649; www.aros.co.uk; Viewfield Rd; adult/child £3/£2; ⏱9am-5.30pm; ♿) On the southern edge of Portree, the Aros Experience is a combined visitor centre, book and gift shop, restaurant, theatre and cinema. The visitor centre offers a look at some fascinating, live CCTV images from local sea-eagle and heron nests, and a wide-screen video of Skye's impressive scenery (it's worth waiting for the aerial shots of the Cuillin).

The centre is a useful rainy-day retreat, with an indoor, soft play area for children.

MV Stardust   BOAT TOUR
(☎07798-743858; www.skyeboat-trips.co.uk; Portree Harbour) MV *Stardust* offers one- to two-hour boat trips to the Sound of Raasay (£12 to £15 per person), with the chance to see seals, porpoises and – if you're lucky – white-tailed sea eagles. On Saturday there are longer cruises to the Isle of Rona (£25).

You can also arrange to be dropped off for a hike on the Isle of Raasay and picked up again later.

✳ Festivals & Events

Isle of Skye Highland Games   HIGHLAND GAMES
(www.skye-highland-games.co.uk) These annual games are held in Portree in early August.

🛏 Sleeping

Portree is well supplied with B&Bs, but many of them are in bland, modern bungalows that, though comfortable, often lack character. Accommodation fills up fast in July and August so be sure to book ahead.

TOP CHOICE / Ben Tianavaig B&B   B&B **££**
(☎01478-612152; www.ben-tianavaig.co.uk; 5 Bosville Tce; r £65-75; P🐾) A warm welcome awaits from the Aussie–Brit couple who run this appealing B&B bang in the centre of town. All four bedrooms have a view across the harbour to the hill that gives the house its name and breakfasts include free-range eggs and vegetables grown in the garden.

Bosville Hotel   HOTEL **£££**
(☎01478-612846; www.bosvillehotel.co.uk; 9-11 Bosville Tce; s/d from £120/128; 🛜) The Bosville brings a little bit of metropolitan style to Portree with its designer fabrics and furniture, flatscreen TVs, fluffy bathrobes and bright, spacious bathrooms. It's worth splashing out a bit for the 'premier' rooms, with leather recliner chairs from which you can lap up the view over the town and harbour.

Peinmore House   B&B **££**
(☎01478-612574; www.peinmorehouse.co.uk; r per person £55; P) Signposted off the main road about 2 miles south of Portree, this former manse has recently been cleverly converted into a stylish and comfortable guesthouse with a spectacular oak-floored lounge, enormous bedrooms, excellent breakfasts and panoramic views.

Rosedale Hotel   HOTEL **££**
(☎01478-613131; www.rosedalehotelskye.co.uk; Beaumont Cres; s/d from £60/90; ⏱Mar-Nov)

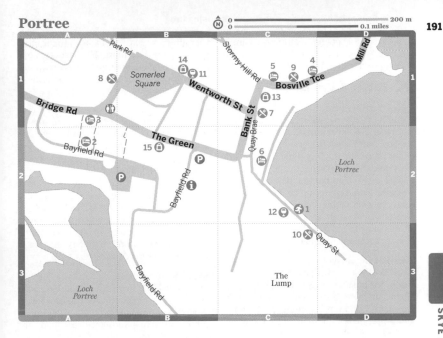

The Rosedale is a cosy, old-fashioned hotel – you'll be welcomed with a glass of whisky or sherry when you check in – delightfully situated down by the waterfront. Its three converted fishermen's cottages are linked by a maze of narrow stairs and corridors, and the excellent restaurant has a view of the harbour.

Woodlands   B&B ££

(☏01478-612980; www.woodlands-portree.co.uk; Viewfield Rd; r per person £32-34; P) The great location with views across the bay and unstinting hospitality make this modern B&B, half a mile south of the town centre, a good choice.

Bayfield Backpackers   HOSTEL £

(☏01478-612231; www.skyehostel.co.uk; Bayfield; dm £13; @🛜) Clean, central and modern, this hostel provides the best backpacker accommodation in town. The owner really makes you feel welcome, and is a fount of advice on what to do and where to go in Skye.

Bayview House   B&B £

(☏01478-613340; www.bayviewhouse.co.uk; Bayfield; r per person from £20; P🛜) This is a modern house with spartan but sparklingly clean rooms, some with sea and mountain views, and bathrooms with power showers. At this price and location, it's a bargain.

Portree

⊙ Activities, Courses & Tours
1 MV *Stardust* C2

⊝ Sleeping
2 Bayfield Backpackers..........................A2
3 Bayview House A1
4 Ben Tianavaig B&B.............................C1
5 Bosville Hotel C1
6 Rosedale Hotel....................................C2

⊗ Eating
Bistro at the Bosville ....(see 5)
7 Café Arriba C1
8 Granary Bakery....................................A1
9 Harbour View Seafood
   Restaurant C1
10 Sea Breezes C3

⊙ Drinking
11 Isles Inn B1
12 Pier Hotel..C2

⊙ Shopping
13 Carmina Gadelica C1
14 Isle of Skye Soap Co...........................B1
15 Skye Batiks B2

Torvaig Campsite CAMPGROUND £
(☏01478-612209; www.portreecampsite.co.uk; sites per person £5; ☺Apr-Oct) An attractive, family-run camping ground located 1.5 miles north of Portree on the road to Staffin.

Eating & Drinking

TOP CHOICE **Café Arriba** CAFE £
(☏01478-611830; www.cafearriba.co.uk; Quay Brae; light meals £5-8, dinner mains £10-13; ☺7am-10pm May-Sep, 8am-5.30pm Oct-Apr; ✐) Arriba is a funky little cafe, brightly decked out in primary colours and offering the best choice of vegetarian grub on the island, ranging from a veggie breakfast fry-up to Indian-spiced bean cakes with mint yoghurt, as well as carnivorous treats such as slow-cooked haunch of venison with red wine and beetroot gravy. Also serves excellent coffee.

Bistro at the Bosville SCOTTISH ££
(☏01478-612846; www.bosvillehotel.co.uk; 7 Bosville Tce; mains £9-20; ☺noon-2.30pm & 5.30-10pm) This hotel bistro sports a relaxed atmosphere, an award-winning chef and a menu that makes the most of Skye-sourced produce – including lamb, game, seafood, cheese, organic vegetables and berries – and adds an original twist to traditional dishes.

Harbour View Seafood Restaurant SEAFOOD ££
(☏01478-612069; www.harbourviewskye.co.uk; 7 Bosville Tce; mains £10-19; ☺noon-2.30pm & 5.30-10pm) The Harbour View is Portree's most congenial place to eat. It has a homely dining room with a log fire in winter, books on the mantelpiece and bric-a-brac on the shelves. And on the table, superb Scottish seafood, such as fresh Skye oysters, seafood chowder, king scallops, langoustines and lobster.

Sea Breezes SEAFOOD ££
(☏01478-612016; 2 Marine Buildings, Quay St; mains £10-20; ☺noon-2.30pm & 5.30-10pm Tue-Sun, closed Nov, Jan & Feb) A good choice for seafood, Sea Breezes is an informal, no-frills restaurant specialising in local fish and shellfish fresh from the boat – try the impressive seafood platter, a small mountain of langoustines, crab, oysters and lobster. Book early, as it's often hard to get a table.

Granary Bakery CAFE £
(Somerled Sq; light mains £5-8; ☺8am-5pm Mon-Sat) Most of Portree seems to congregate at the Granary's cosy coffee shop to snack on tasty sandwiches, filled rolls, pies, cakes and pastries.

Isles Inn PUB
(☏01478-612129; Somerled Sq) Portree's pubs are nothing special, but the Isles Inn is more atmospheric than most. The Jacobean bar, with its flagstone floor and open fires, pulls in a lively mix of young locals, backpackers and tourists.

Pier Hotel PUB
(☏01478-612094; Quay St) You can almost guarantee a weekend sing-song at this nautical-themed waterfront bar.

Shopping

Skye Batiks GIFTS
(www.skyebatiks.com; The Green; ☺9am-6pm May, Jun & Sep, to 9pm Jul & Aug, to 5pm Mon-Sat Oct-Apr) Skye Batiks is a cut above your average gift shop, selling a range of interesting crafts such as carved wood, jewellery and batik fabrics with Celtic designs.

Isle of Skye Soap Co BEAUTY
(☏01478-611350; www.skye-soap.co.uk; Somerled Sq; ☺9am-5.30pm Mon-Fri, to 5pm Sat) A sweet-smelling gift shop that specialises in handmade soaps and cosmetics made using natural ingredients and aromatherapy oils.

Carmina Gadelica MUSIC
(☏01478-612585; Bank St; ☺9am-5.30pm Mon-Sat, to 9pm Jul & Aug) Browse the shelves here for CDs of Gaelic music and books on local subjects.

Getting There & Around

BUS The main bus stop is in Somerled Sq. There are seven Scottish Citylink buses a day, including Sundays, from Kyle of Lochalsh to Portree (£13, one hour) and on to Uig.

Stagecoach services (Monday to Saturday only) run from Portree to Broadford (40 minutes, at least hourly) via Sligachan (15 minutes); to Armadale (1¼ hours, connecting with the ferries to Mallaig); to Carbost (40 minutes, four daily); to Uig (30 minutes, six daily) and to Dunvegan Castle (40 minutes, five daily Monday to Friday, three on Saturday). There are also five or six buses a day on a circular route around Trotternish (in both directions) taking in Flodigarry (20 minutes), Kilmuir (1¼ hours) and Uig (30 minutes). Buses from the mainland also come through Portree.

BIKE Island Cycles (☏01478-613121; The Green; ☺9am-5pm Mon-Sat) You can hire bikes here for £10/15 per half-/full day.

Dunvegan (Dun Bheagain)

Skye's most famous historic building, and one of its most popular tourist attractions, is **Dunvegan Castle** (☎01470-521206; www. dunvegancastle.com; adult/child £8/4; ☺10am-5pm Easter-Oct, 11am-4pm Nov-Easter), seat of the chief of Clan MacLeod. It has played host to Samuel Johnson, Sir Walter Scott and, most famously, Flora MacDonald. The oldest parts are the 14th-century keep and dungeon but most of it dates from the 17th to 19th centuries.

In addition to the usual castle stuff – swords, silver and family portraits – there are some interesting artefacts, most famous being the Fairy Flag, a diaphanous silk banner that dates from some time between the 4th and 7th centuries. Bonnie Prince Charlie's waistcoat and a lock of his hair, donated by Flora MacDonald's granddaughter, share a room with Rory Mor's Drinking Horn, a beautiful 16th-century vessel of Celtic design that could hold half a gallon of claret. Upholding the family tradition, in 1956, John MacLeod – the 29th chief, who died in 2007 – downed the contents in one minute and 57 seconds 'without setting down or falling down'.

From the end of the minor road beyond Dunvegan Castle entrance, an easy walk of one mile leads to the **Coral Beaches** – a pair of blindingly white beaches composed of the bleached exoskeletons of coralline algae known as *maerl*.

On the way to Dunvegan from Portree you'll pass **Edinbane Pottery** (☎0147 0-582234; www.edinbane-pottery.co.uk; ☺9am-6pm daily Easter-Oct, closed Sat & Sun Nov-Easter), one of the island's original craft workshops, established in 1971, where you can watch potters at work creating beautiful and colourful stoneware.

Duirinish & Waternish

The Duirinish peninsula to the west of Dunvegan, and Waternish to the north, boast some of Skye's most atmospheric hotels and restaurants, plus an eclectic range of artists' studios and crafts workshops. Portree tourist office provides a free booklet listing them all.

◉ Sights & Activities

The sparsely populated Duirinish peninsula is dominated by the distinctive flat-topped peaks of Helabhal Mhor (469m) and Helabhal Bheag (488m), known locally as **MacLeod's Tables**. There are some fine walks from Orbost, including the summit of Helabhal Bheag (allow 3½ hours return) and the 5-mile trail from Orbost to **MacLeod's Maidens**, a series of pointed sea-stacks at the southern tip of the peninsula.

It's worth making the long drive beyond Dunvegan to the west side of the Duirinish Peninsula to see the spectacular sea cliffs of **Waterstein Head**, and to walk down to **Neist Point lighthouse** with its views to the Outer Hebrides.

Trumpan Church   HISTORIC BUILDING
At the Waternish road-end, 4 miles beyond Stein, is the ruin of Trumpan Church, which was set alight by the MacDonalds of Uist in

FLORA MACDONALD

Flora MacDonald, who became famous for helping Bonnie Prince Charlie escape after his defeat at the Battle of Culloden, was born in 1722 at Milton in South Uist, where a memorial cairn marks the site of one of her early childhood homes.

In 1746 she helped Bonnie Prince Charlie make his way from Benbecula to Skye disguised as her Irish maidservant. With a price on the prince's head, their little boat was fired on, but they managed to land safely and Flora escorted the prince to Portree where he gave her a gold locket containing his portrait before setting sail for Raasay.

Waylaid on the way home, the boatmen admitted everything. Flora was arrested and imprisoned in the Tower of London. She never saw or heard from the prince again.

In 1747 she returned to Skye; she married Allan MacDonald and had nine children. Dr Samuel Johnson stayed with her in 1773 during his trip to the Western Isles. Later poverty forced her family to emigrate to North Carolina, where her husband was captured by rebels. Flora returned to Kingsburgh on Skye where she died in 1790. She was buried in Kilmuir Cemetery (behind the Skye Museum of Island Life; p195), wrapped in the sheet on which both Bonnie Prince Charlie and Dr Johnson had slept.

1578, burning alive an entire congregation of MacLeods. MacLeod forces marched from Dunvegan under their famous **Fairy Flag**, massacring the MacDonalds as they tried to flee to their galleys. Ghostly singing is said to be heard here on the anniversary of the battle.

Among the graves is the ancient **Trial Stone**, a squat stone pillar with a hole that the accused had to put their finger into whilst blindfolded; failure was taken as instant proof of guilt.

Shopping

Dandelion Designs   ARTS & CRAFTS
(www.dandelion-designs.co.uk; Captain's House, Stein; ⊙11am-5pm Easter-Oct) At Stein on the Waternish Peninsula, Dandelion Designs is an interesting little gallery with a good range of colour and monochrome landscape photography, lino prints by Liz Myhill, and a range of handmade arts and crafts.

Shilasdair Yarns   KNITWEAR
(www.shilasdair-yarns.co.uk; Carnach; ⊙10am-6pm Apr-Oct) A few miles north of Stein you'll find Shilasdair Yarns. The couple who run this place moved to Skye in 1971 and now raise sheep, hand-spin woollen yarn, and hand-dye a range of wools and silks using natural dyes. You can see the dyeing process in the workshop behind the studio, which sells finished knitwear as well as yarns.

Sleeping & Eating

TOP CHOICE **Three Chimneys**   RESTAURANT, LODGE £££
(☎01470-511258; www.threechimneys.co.uk; Colbost; 3-course lunch/dinner £35/55; ⊙lunch & dinner Mon-Sat Mar-Oct, dinner Nov-Feb) In Colbost, halfway between Dunvegan and Waterstein, the Three Chimneys is a superb romantic retreat combining a gourmet restaurant in a candlelit crofter's cottage with sumptuous five-star rooms (double £285, dinner/B&B per couple £405) in the modern house next door. Book well in advance, and note that there's a 'no children' policy in the restaurant in the evenings.

Stein Inn   PUB GRUB £
(☎01470-592362; www.steininn.co.uk; Stein; bar meals £7-10; ⊙food noon-4pm & 6-9.30pm Mon-Sat, 12.30-4pm & 6.30-9pm Sun Easter-Oct) This old country inn dates from 1790 and has a handful of bedrooms (per person £34 to £50) all with sea views, a lively little bar and a delightful beer garden – a real sun-trap on warm summer afternoons – beside the loch. The bar serves real ales from the Isle of Skye Brewery and does an excellent crab sandwich.

Lochbay Seafood Restaurant   SEAFOOD £££
(☎01470-592235; www.lochbay-seafood-restaurant.co.uk; Stein; mains £13-22, lobster £28-40; ⊙lunch & dinner Tue-Fri) Just along the road from the Stein Inn is one of Skye's most romantic restaurants, a cosy farmhouse kitchen with terracotta tiles and a wood-burning stove, and a menu that includes most things that either swim in the sea or live in a shell. Best to book ahead.

Trotternish

The Trotternish Peninsula to the north of Portree has some of Skye's most beautiful – and bizarre – scenery. Experience some of it on the Quiraing Walk (p215).

Sights & Activities

East Coast

Old Man of Storr   ROCK FORMATION
The 50m-high, potbellied pinnacle of crumbling basalt known as the Old Man of Storr is prominent above the road 6 miles north of Portree. Walk up to its foot from the car park in the woods at the northern end of Loch Leathan (round trip 2 miles). This seemingly unclimbable pinnacle was first scaled in 1955 by English mountaineer Don Whillans, a feat that has been repeated only a handful of times since.

Quiraing   ROCK FORMATION
Staffin Bay is dominated by the dramatic basalt escarpment of the Quiraing: its impressive land-slipped cliffs and pinnacles constitute one of Skye's most remarkable landscapes. From a parking area at the highest point of the minor road between Staffin and Uig you can walk north to the Quiraing in half an hour.

Duntulm Castle   CASTLE
Right at the tip of the Trotternish peninsula is the ruined MacDonald fortress of Duntulm Castle, which was abandoned in 1739, reputedly because it was haunted. The most famous spirit is the gibbering phantom of Hugh MacDonald, a local noble who was imprisoned in the dungeon for trying to seize Trotternish.

As punishment, he was deprived of water by his jailers and fed salted beef until he went insane, starving to death in the cells below the castle. You might also see the ghost of a nursemaid who accidentally dropped the baby of a MacDonald chieftain from the battlements and was executed by the grief-stricken chief.

West Coast
Whichever way you arrive at **Uig** (oo-ig), the picture-perfect bay ringed by steep hills rarely fails to impress.

Skye Museum of Island Life   MUSEUM
(📞01470-552206; www.skyemuseum.co.uk; Kilmuir; adult/child £2.50/50p; ☺9.30am-5pm Mon-Sat Easter-Oct) The peat-reek of crofting life in the 18th and 19th centuries is preserved in the thatched cottages of the Skye Museum of Island Life.

Behind the museum is **Kilmuir Cemetery**, where a tall Celtic cross marks the **grave of Flora MacDonald**; the cross was erected in 1955 to replace the original, of which 'every fragment was removed by tourists'.

Fairy Glen   NATURAL FORMATION
Just south of Uig, a minor road (signposted 'Sheader and Balnaknock') leads in a mile or so to the Fairy Glen, a strange and enchanting natural landscape of miniature conical hills, rocky towers, ruined cottages and a tiny roadside lochan.

🛏 Sleeping & Eating
East Coast
Flodigarry Country House Hotel   HOTEL **£££**
(📞01470-552203; www.flodigarry.co.uk; s/d from £90/120) Flora MacDonald lived in a farmhouse cottage at Flodigarry in northeast Trotternish from 1751 to 1759. The cottage and its pretty garden are now part of this delightful hotel – you can stay in the cottage (there are seven bedrooms), or in the more spacious rooms in the hotel itself.

The bright, modern **bistro** has great views over the Inner Sound, and serves lunch and dinner featuring local produce such as langoustines, lobster, lamb and venison.

Dun Flodigarry Hostel   HOSTEL **£**
(📞01470-552212; www.hostelflodigarry.co.uk; dm/tw £13/30) Shares the same superb views as the nearby Flodigarry Country House Hotel, but at a lesser cost, and you can still visit the hotel bar for afternoon tea. You can also **camp** (per person £6.50) nearby and use the hostel facilities.

West Coast
There's a cluster of B&Bs in Uig.

Uig SYHA   HOSTEL **£**
(📞01470-542746; www.syha.org.uk; dm £15; ☺late Apr-Sep) Sociable hostel with fantastic sunset views over Uig Bay. You have to vacate the place between 10.30am and 5pm, even when it's raining!

Uig Hotel   HOTEL **££**
(📞01470-542205; www.uighotel.com; s/d from £60/110; P) A lovely old coaching inn.

🛍 Shopping
Isle of Skye Brewery   FOOD & DRINK
(📞01470-542477; www.skyebrewery.co.uk; The Pier, Uig; ☺9am-5pm Mon-Fri) If you've time to kill while waiting for a ferry to the Outer Hebrides, the Isle of Skye Brewery shop sells locally brewed ales by the bottle, as well as gifts and souvenirs.

Isle of Raasay
POP 160

Raasay is the rugged, 10-mile-long island that lies off Skye's east coast. There are several good walks here, including one to the flat-topped conical hill of **Dun Caan** (443m). Forest Enterprise publishes a free leaflet (available from the tourist offices in Portree and Kyle of Lochalsh) with suggested walks and forest trails.

The extraordinary ruin of **Brochel Castle**, on a pinnacle at the northern end of Raasay, was home to Calum Garbh MacLeod, an early-16th-century pirate. At the Battle of Culloden in 1746 Raasay supplied Bonnie Prince Charlie with 100 fighting men and 26 pipers, but the people paid dearly for their Jacobite sympathies when government forces arrived and proceeded to murder, rape and pillage their way across the island.

Set in a rustic cottage high on the hill overlooking Skye, **Raasay Youth Hostel** (📞01478-660240; www.syha.org.uk; Creachan Cottage; dm £16; ☺May-Sep) is a fair walk from the ferry pier (2.5 miles) but is a good base for exploring the island.

See www.raasay.com for a full listing of accommodation.

A CalMac ferry (passenger/car £3.10/11.90) runs from Sconser, on the road from Portree to Broadford, to the southern end of Raasay (15 minutes, hourly Monday to Saturday, twice daily Sunday). There are no petrol stations on the island.

SMALL ISLES

The scattered jewels of the Small Isles – Rum, Eigg, Muck and Canna – lie strewn across the silvery-blue cloth of the Cuillin Sound to the south of the Isle of Skye. Their distinctive outlines enliven the glorious views from the beaches of Arisaig and Morar.

Rum is the biggest and boldest of the four, a miniature Skye of pointed peaks and dramatic sunset silhouettes. Eigg is the most pastoral and populous, dominated by the miniature sugarloaf mountain of the Sgurr. Muck is a botanist's delight with its wildflowers and unusual alpine plants, and Canna is a craggy bird sanctuary made of magnetic rocks.

If your time is limited and you can only visit one island, choose Eigg; it has the most to offer on a day trip.

ℹ️ Getting There & Away

CalMac (www.calmac.co.uk) Operates the passenger-only ferry from Mallaig to Eigg (£11 return, 1¼ hours, five a week), to Muck (£17 return, 1½ hours, four a week), Rum (£16 return, 1¼ hours, five a week) and Canna (£20 return, two hours, four a week). Bicycles are carried for free.

You can also hop between the islands without returning to Mallaig, but the timetable is complicated and it requires a bit of planning – you would need at least five days to visit all four.

Arisaig Marine (☎01687-450224; www. arisaig.co.uk; ⊗May-Sep) Operates day cruises from Arisaig harbour to Eigg (£18 return, one hour, six a week), Rum (£24 return, 2½ hours, two or three a week) and Muck (£19 return, two hours, three a week). The trips include whalewatching, with up to an hour for close viewing.

Sailing times allow four or five hours ashore on Eigg, two or three hours on Muck or Rum.

Isle of Rum

POP 30

The Isle of Rum – the biggest and most spectacular of the Small Isles – was once known as the Forbidden Island. Cleared of its crofters in the early 19th century to make way for sheep, from 1888 to 1957 it was the private sporting estate of the Bulloughs, a nouveauriche Lancashire family who made their fortune in the textile industry. Curious outsiders who ventured too close to the island were liable to find themselves staring down the wrong end of a gamekeeper's shotgun.

The island was sold to the Nature Conservancy in 1957 and has since been a reserve noted for its deer, wild goats, ponies, golden and white-tailed sea eagles, and a 120,000-strong nesting colony of Manx shearwaters. Its dramatic, rocky mountains, known as the Rum Cuillin for their similarity to the peaks on neighbouring Skye, draw hillwalkers and climbers.

⊙ Sights & Activities

Kinloch Castle CASTLE
(☎01687-462037; www.isleofrum.com; adult/child £6/3; ⊙guided tours Mon-Sat, to coincide with ferry times) When George Bullough – a dashing, Harrow-educated cavalry officer – inherited Rum along with half his father's fortune in 1891, he became one of the wealthiest bachelors in Britain. Bullough blew half his inheritance on building his dream bachelor pad – the ostentatious Kinloch Castle.

The bachelor shipped in pink sandstone from Dumfriesshire and 250,000 tonnes of Ayrshire topsoil for the gardens, and paid his workers a shilling extra a day to wear tweed kilts – just so they'd look more picturesque. Hummingbirds were kept in the greenhouses and alligators in the garden, and guests were entertained with an orchestrion, the Edwardian equivalent of a Bose hi-fi system. Since the Bulloughs left, the castle has survived as a perfect time capsule of upper-class Edwardian eccentricity. The guided tour should not be missed.

Bullough Mausoleum BURIAL SITE
The only part of the island that still belongs to the Bullough family is this mausoleum in Glen Harris. It's a miniature Greek temple that wouldn't look out of place on the Acropolis. Lady Bullough was laid to rest here, alongside her husband and father-in-law, in 1967, having died at the age of 98.

Nature Trails WALKING
There's some great coastal and mountain walking on the island, including a couple of easy, waymarked nature trails in the woods around Kinloch. **Glen Harris** is a 10-mile round trip from Kinloch, on a rough 4WD track – allow four to five hours' walking.

The climb to the island's highest point, **Askival** (812m), is a strenuous hike and involves a bit of rock scrambling (allow six hours for the round trip from Kinloch).

🛏 Sleeping & Eating

Accommodation on Rum is strictly limited, and if you want to stay overnight on the island you have to contact the **reserve office** (📞01687-462026) in advance. There are also two bothies (unlocked cottages with no facilities, for the use of hikers) on the island.

Kinloch Castle Hostel HOSTEL **£**
(📞01687-462037; www.isleofrum.com; dm £15, d £40-50; ⊗Mar-Oct) The castle has 45 hostel beds and four double bedrooms in its rear wing. There's a communal self-catering kitchen, and also a small restaurant offering a cooked breakfast (£7.50) and dinner (£15.50) to guests and nonguests alike.

Kinloch Campsite CAMPGROUND **£**
(www.isleofrum.com; tent sites per person £5) Situated near Kinloch castle, this basic campground has toilets, water supply and hot showers, but there's not much in the way of level ground! Book in advance with the reserve office (p197).

ℹ Information

Kinloch, where the ferry lands, is the island's only settlement; it has a small **grocery shop** (⊙5-7.30pm), post office and public telephone, and a **visitor centre** (⊙8.30am-5pm) near the pier where you can get information and leaflets on walking and wildlife.

There's a **tearoom** (⊙10am-4pm Apr-Sep; @) in the village hall, with internet access. The hall itself is open at all times for people to shelter from the rain (or the midges!). For more information see www.isleofrum.com.

Isle of Eigg

POP 70

The Isle of Eigg made history in 1997 when it became the first Highland estate to be bought out by its inhabitants. The island is now owned and managed by the **Isle of Eigg Heritage Trust** (www.isleofeigg.org), a partnership among the islanders, Highland Council and the Scottish Wildlife Trust.

🏃 Activities

Sgurr of Eigg Walk

The island takes its name from the Old Norse *egg* (edge), a reference to the Sgurr of Eigg (393m), an impressive minimountain that towers over Galmisdale, Eigg's main village. Ringed by vertical cliffs on three sides, it's composed of pitchstone lava with columnar jointing similar to that seen on the

Isle of Staffa and at the Giant's Causeway in Northern Ireland.

The climb to the summit (4.5 miles round trip; allow three to four hours) begins on the stony road leading up from the pier. From the pier, the road continues uphill through the woods to a red-roofed cottage. Go through the gate to the right of the cottage and turn left; just 20m along the road a cairn on the right marks the start of a boggy footpath that leads over the eastern shoulder of the Sgurr, then traverses beneath the northern cliffs until it makes its way up onto the summit ridge.

On a fine day the views from the top are magnificent – Rum and Skye to the north, Muck and Coll to the south, Ardnamurchan Lighthouse to the southeast and Ben Nevis shouldering above the eastern horizon. Take binoculars – on a calm summer's day there's a good chance of seeing minke whales feeding down below in the Sound of Muck.

UAMH FRAING WALK

A shorter walk (2 miles; allow 1½ hours round trip, and bring a torch) leads west from the pier to the spooky and claustrophobic Uamh Fraing (Massacre Cave). Start as for the Sgurr of Eigg, but 800m from the pier turn left through a gate and into a field. Follow the 4WD track and fork left before a white cottage to pass below it. A footpath continues across the fields to reach a small gate in a fence; go through it and descend a ridge towards the shore.

The cave entrance is tucked inconspicuously down to the left of the ridge. The entrance is tiny – almost a hands-and-knees job – but the cave opens out inside and runs a long way back. Go right to the back, turn off your torch, and imagine the cave packed shoulder to shoulder with terrified men, women and children. Then imagine the panic as your enemies start piling firewood into the entrance. Almost the entire population of Eigg – around 400 people – sought refuge in this cave when the MacLeods of Skye raided the island in 1577. But the raiders lit a fire in the narrow entrance and everyone inside died of asphyxiation. There are more than a few ghosts floating around in here.

GRUILIN & LAIG BEACH WALKS

Other good walks on the island are to the deserted crofts of **Gruilin** on the southwest coast (5 miles, two hours round trip), and north to **Laig Beach** (8 miles, three hours return) with its famous singing sands – the sand makes a squeaking noise when you walk on it. You can get more information on island walks from the craft shop in An Laimhrig.

🛏 Sleeping & Eating

All accommodation should be booked in advance. For a full listing of self-catering accommodation, see www.iseleofeigg.org.

Lageorna B&B ££
(☎01687-482405; www.lageorna.com; Cleadale; per person £60; 🛜) This converted croft house and lodge in the island's northwest is Eigg's most luxurious accommodation. Rooms are fitted with beautiful, locally made, 'driftwood-style' timber beds, and even have iPod docks (but no mobile-phone reception). Evening meals are part of the package, with the menu heavy on locally grown vegetables, seafood and venison.

Sandavore Bothy BOTHY £
(☎01687-482480; suehollands@talk21.com; Sandavore; per night £30) This tiny, one-room bothy, a 15-minute walk from the pier, has space for four people in one double bed and two bunk beds. It's a real Hebridean experience – accessible only on foot, no electricity (just gaslight and candles), cold running water only and an outside toilet.

Glebe Barn HOSTEL £
(☎01687-482417; www.glebebarn.co.uk; Galmisdale; dm/tw £15/36) Excellent bunkhouse accommodation, with a smart, maple-floored lounge with central fireplace, modern kitchen, laundry, drying room, and bright, clean dorms and bedrooms.

Sue Holland's Croft CAMPGROUND £
(☎01687-482480; suehollands@talk21.com; Cleadale; per tent £4) You can camp at this organic croft in the north of the island; basic facilities.

An Laimhrig Tearoom CAFE £
(Galmisdale; ⊙10am-5pm May-Sep) There's a good cafe here by the ferry pier. Winter opening hours coincide with ferry arrivals and departures.

ℹ Information

The ferry landing is at Galmisdale in the south. **An Laimhrig** (www.isleofeiggshop.co.uk; Galmisdale; ⊙10am-5pm Mon-Wed & Fri, 11am-3pm Thu, 11am-5pm Sat, noon-1pm Sun May-Sep, shorter hours in winter) The building above the pier houses a grocery store, post office, craft shop and tearoom. You can hire bikes here, too.

Isle of Muck

pop 30
The tiny island of Muck (www.isleofmuck.com), measuring just 2 miles by 1 mile, has exceptionally fertile soil, and the island is carpeted with wildflowers in spring and early summer. It takes its name from the Gaelic *muc* (pig), and pigs are still raised here.

Ferries call at the southern settlement of Port Mor. There's a **tearoom and craft shop** (⊙11am-4pm Jun-Aug, shorter hours May & Sep) above the pier, which also acts as an information centre.

It's an easy 15-minute walk along the island's only road from the pier to the sandy beach at **Gallanach** on the northern side of the island. A longer and rougher hike (1½ hours round trip) goes to the top of **Beinn Airein** (137m) for the best views. Puffins nest on the cliffs at the western end of Camas Mor, the bay to the south of the hill.

The cosy six-bed **Isle of Muck Bunkhouse** (☎01687-462042; dm £12), with its oil-fired Rayburn stove, is just above the pier, as is the welcoming eight-room **Port Mor House Hotel** (☎01687-462365; hotel@isleofmuck.com; per person £50); rates include evening meals, which are also available to nonguests (£16, book in advance).

You can camp on the island for free, but ask at the craft shop first. For a full accommodation listing see www.isleofmuck.com.

Isle of Canna

pop 19
The roadless island of Canna is a moorland plateau of black basalt rock, just 5 miles long and 1.25 miles wide. **Compass Hill** (143m), at the northeastern corner, contains enough magnetite (an iron oxide mineral) to deflect the navigation compasses in passing yachts.

The ferry arrives at the hamlet of **A'Chill** at the eastern end of the island, where tourists have left extensive graffiti on the rock face south of the harbour. There's a tearoom and craft shop by the harbour, and a tiny post office in a hut. There is no mobile-phone reception.

You can walk to **An Coroghon**, just east of the ferry pier, a medieval stone tower perched atop a sea cliff, and continue to Compass Hill, or take a longer hike along the southern shore past a **Celtic cross** and the remains of the 7th-century **St Columba's Chapel**.

Accommodation is very limited. **Tighard** (☎01687-462474; www.peaceofcanna.co.uk; per person £35-50) is the only B&B (evening meals £25 to £30), and cafe-restaurant **Gille Brighde** (www.cannarestaurant.com; mains £7-17; ⊙11am-3pm & 6-9pm Tue-Fri, 10am-9pm Sat) the only eating place. Search www.ntsholidays.com for self-catering accommodation.

Canna Camping Holidays (☎01687-460166; www.cannafolk.co.uk; £80 for two nights) offers luxury camping in pre-pitched bell tents (£80 for two nights, up to five people).

WESTERN ISLES

POP 26,500

A professor of Spanish and a professor of Gaelic met at a conference and began discussing the relative merits of their respective languages. 'Tell me, ' said the Spanish professor, 'do you have a Gaelic equivalent for the Spanish phrase *mañana, mañana*?' The Hebridean professor thought for a while, then replied, 'No, I do not think that we have in the Gaelic a word that conveys such a pressing sense of urgency'.

An old joke perhaps, but one that hints at the slower pace of life you can expect to find in the Gaelic-speaking communities of the Western Isles, a place where the morning papers arrive in the afternoon and almost everything – in Lewis and Harris at least – closes down on Sundays.

The Western Isles, or Na h-Eileanan an Iar in Gaelic – also known as the Outer Hebrides – are a 130 mile-long string of islands lying off the northwest coast of Scotland. There are 119 islands in total, of which the five main inhabited islands are: Lewis and Harris (two parts of a single island, although often described as if they are separate islands), North Uist, Benbecula, South Uist and Barra. The middle three (often referred to simply as 'the Uists') are connected by road-bearing causeways.

The ferry crossing from Ullapool or Uig to the Western Isles marks an important cultural divide – more than a third of Scotland's registered crofts are in the Outer Hebrides, and no less than 60% of the population are Gaelic speakers. The rigours of life in the old island blackhouses are still within living memory.

Religion still plays a prominent part in public and private life, especially in the Protestant north where shops and pubs close their doors on Sundays and some accommodation providers prefer guests not to arrive or depart on the Sabbath. The Roman Catholic south is a little more relaxed about these things.

The name Hebrides is not Gaelic, and is probably a corruption of Ebudae, the Roman name for the islands. But the alternative derivation from the Norse *havbredey* –'isles at the edge of the sea' – has a much more poetic ring, alluding to the broad vistas of sky and sea that characterise the islands' often bleak and treeless landscapes. But there is beauty here too, in the machair (grassy, wildflower-speckled dunes) and dazzling white-sand beaches, majesty in the rugged hills and sprawling lochs, and mystery in the islands' fascinating past. It's a past evidenced by neolithic standing stones, Viking place names, deserted crofts and folk memories of the Clearances.

If your time is limited, head straight for the west coast of Lewis with its prehistoric sites, preserved blackhouses and beautiful beaches. As with Skye, the islands are dotted with arts and crafts studios – the tourist offices can provide a list.

❶ Information

Internet Access
Community Library (☎01871-810471; Community School, Castlebay; ⊙9am-4.30pm Mon & Wed, 9am-4.30pm & 6-8pm Tue & Thu, 9am-3.30pm Fri, 10am-12.30pm Sat) Free internet access.

Stornoway Public Library (☎01851-708631; 19 Cromwell St, Stornoway; ⊙10am-5pm Mon-Wed & Sat, to 6pm Thu & Fri) Free internet access

Taigh Chearsabhagh (Lochmaddy; per 20min 50p; ⊙10am-5pm Mon-Sat Feb-Jun & Sep-Dec, 10am-5pm Mon-Thu & Sat, to 8pm Fri Jul & Aug)

Internet Resources
CalMac (www.calmac.co.uk) Ferry timetables.
Visit Hebrides (www.visithebrides.com)

Medical Services
Uist & Barra Hospital (☎01870-603603; Balivanich)

Money
There are banks with ATMs in Stornoway (Lewis), Tarbert (Harris), Lochmaddy (North Uist), Balivanich (Benbecula), Lochboisdale (South Uist) and Castlebay (Barra). Elsewhere, some hotels and shops offer cashback facilities.

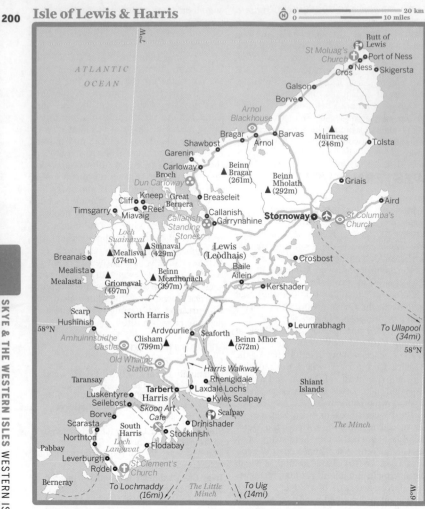

Tourist Information

Castlebay tourist office (☏01871-810336; Main St, Castlebay; ⊘9am-1pm & 2-5pm Mon-Sat, noon-4pm Sun Apr-Oct)

Lochboisdale tourist office (☏01878-700286; Pier Rd, Lochboisdale; ⊘9am-1pm & 2-5pm Fri-Mon & Wed, 9am-9.30pm Tue & Thu Apr-Oct)

Stornoway tourist office (☏01851-703088; 26 Cromwell St, Stornoway; ⊘9am-6pm & 8-9pm Mon, Tue & Thu, 9am-8pm Wed & Fri, 9am-5.30pm & 8-9pm Sat year-round)

Tarbert tourist office (☏01859-502011; Pier Rd, Tarbert; ⊘9am-5pm Mon-Sat, plus 8-9pm Tue, Thu & Sat Apr-Oct)

ⓘ Getting There & Away

Air

There are airports at Stornoway (Lewis), and on Benbecula and Barra. There are flights to Stornoway from Edinburgh, Inverness, Glasgow and Aberdeen. There are also two flights a day (weekdays only) between Stornoway and Benbecula.

There are daily flights from Glasgow to Barra and Benbecula. At Barra, the planes land on the hard-sand beach at low tide, so the timetable depends on the tides.

FlyBe/Loganair (☏01857-873457; www.loganair.co.uk)

Eastern Airways (☎0870 366 9100; www.easternairways.com)

Highland Airways (☎0845 450 2245; www.highlandairways.co.uk)

Boat

CalMac (www.calmac.co.uk) Runs car ferries from Ullapool to Stornoway (Lewis); from Uig (Isle of Skye) to Lochmaddy (North Uist) and Tarbert (Harris) and from Oban to Castlebay (Barra) and Lochboisdale (South Uist). CalMac has 12 different Island Hopscotch tickets for set routes in the Outer Hebrides, offering a saving of around 10% (tickets are valid for one month). See (p201) and the website for details.

Standard one-way fares:

CROSSING	DURATION (HOURS)	CAR	DRIVER/ PASSENGER
Ullapool–Stornoway	2¾	£38	£7.55
Uig–Lochmaddy	1¾	£24	£5.15
Uig–Tarbet	1½	£24	£5.15
Oban–Castlebay	4¾	£51	£11.40
Oban–Lochboisdale	6¾	£51	£11.40

From Monday to Saturday there are two or three ferries a day to Stornoway, one or two a day to Tarbert and Lochmaddy, and one a day to Castlebay and Lochboisdale; on Sundays there are ferries (same frequency) to Castlebay, Lochboisdale and Lochmaddy, but none to Tarbert and Stornoway. You can also take the ferry from Lochboisdale to Castlebay (car/passenger £20/6.50, 1½ hours, one daily Monday, Tuesday and Thursday) and from Castlebay to Lochboisdale (one daily Wednesday, Friday and Sunday).

Advance booking for cars is essential in July and August; foot and bicycle passengers should have no problems. Bicycles are carried for free.

ⓘ Getting Around

Despite their separate names, Lewis and Harris are actually one island. Berneray, North Uist, Benbecula, South Uist and Eriskay are all linked by road bridges and causeways. There are car ferries between Leverburgh (Harris) and Berneray; Tarbert (Harris) and Lochmaddy (North Uist); Eriskay and Castlebay (Barra); and Lochboisdale (South Uist) and Castlebay (Barra).

The local council publishes two booklets of timetables (one covering Lewis and Harris, the other the Uists and Barra) that list all bus, ferry and air services in the Outer Hebrides. Timetables can also be found online at www.cne-siar.gov.uk/travel.

Bicycle

Many visiting cyclists plan to cycle the length of the archipelago, but if you're one of them, remember that the wind is often strong (you may hear stories of people pedalling downhill and freewheeling uphill), and the prevailing direction is from the southwest – so south to north is usually the easier direction. There are few serious hills, except for a stiff climb on the main road just north of Tarbert.

Bikes can be hired for around £10 a day or £45 a week in Stornoway (Lewis), Leverburgh (Harris), Howmore (South Uist) and Castlebay (Barra). **Rothan Cycles** (www.rothan.com) offers a delivery and pick-up service at various points between Eriskay and Stornoway.

Bus

The bus network covers almost every village in the islands, with around four to six buses a day on all the main routes; however, there are no buses at all on Sundays. You can pick up timetables from the tourist offices, or call **Stornoway bus station** (☎01851-704327) for information.

Car & Motorcycle

Apart from the fast, two-lane road between Tarbert and Stornoway, most roads are single-track. The main hazard is posed by sheep wandering about or sleeping on the road. Petrol stations are far apart (almost all of those on Lewis and Harris are closed on Sunday), and fuel is about 10% more expensive than on the mainland.

There are petrol stations at Stornoway, Barvas, Borve, Uig, Breacleit (Great Bernera), Ness, Tarbert and Leverburgh on Lewis and Harris; Lochmaddy and Cladach on North Uist; Balivanich on Benbecula; Howmore, Lochboisdale and Daliburgh on South Uist; and Castlebay on Barra.

Cars can be hired from around £30 per day.

Arnol Motors (☎018510-710548; www.arnolmotors.com; Arnol; ☻Closed Sun)

Lewis Car Rentals (☎01851-703760; www.lewis-car-rental.co.uk; 52 Bayhead St; ☻Closed Sun)

Lewis (Leodhais)

POP 18,600

The northern part of Lewis is dominated by the desolate expanse of the Black Moor, a vast, undulating peat bog dimpled with glittering lochans, seen clearly from the Stornoway–Barvas road. But Lewis' finest scenery is on the west coast, from Barvas southwest to Mealista, where the rugged landscape of hill, loch and sandy strand is reminiscent of the northwestern Highlands. The Outer Hebrides' most evocative historic sites – Callanish Standing Stones, Dun Carloway, and Arnol Blackhouse Museum – are also to be found here.

The old blackhouses of this region may have been abandoned, but an increasing number are being restored as holiday homes. Most crofts still follow a traditional pattern dating back to medieval times, with narrow strips of land, designed to give all an equal share of good and bad soil, running from the foreshore (with its valuable seaweed, used as fertiliser), across the machair (the grassy sand dunes that provide the best arable land) to the poorer sheep-grazing land on hill or moor. Today few crofts are economically viable, so most islanders supplement their income with fishing, tweed-weaving and work on oil rigs and fish farms.

Accommodation and restaurants are concentrated in and around Stornoway, but there's a scattering of B&Bs and eateries even in the more remote parts of Lewis. However, it's best to book ahead if you're planning to overnight in the wilds.

STORNOWAY (STEORNABHAGH)
POP 6000

Stornoway is the bustling 'capital' of the Outer Hebrides and the only real town in the whole archipelago. It's a surprisingly busy little place, with cars and people swamping the centre on weekdays. Though set on a beautiful natural harbour, the town isn't going to win any prizes for beauty or atmosphere, but it's a pleasant enough introduction to this remote corner of the country.

Stornoway is the Outer Hebrides' administrative and commercial centre, home to the Western Isles Council (Comhairle nan Eilean Siar) and the islands' Gaelic TV and radio stations. It's a bit of a ghost town on Sundays, especially from 11am to 12.30pm, when almost everyone is at church.

⊙ Sights

FREE **An Lanntair Art Centre** ARTS CENTRE
(☏01851-703307; www.lanntair.com; Kenneth St; ☺10am-9pm Mon-Wed, to 10pm Thu, to midnight Fri & Sat; ☏) The modern, purpose-built An Lanntair Art Centre, complete with art gallery, theatre, cinema and restaurant, is the centre of the town's cultural life; it hosts changing exhibitions of contemporary art and is a good source of information on cultural events.

Museum nan Eilean MUSEUM
(☏01851-703773; Francis St; ☺10am-5.30pm Mon-Sat, shorter hours in winter) This museum strings together a loose history of the Outer Hebrides from the earliest human settlements some 9000 years ago to the 20th century, exploring traditional island life and the changes inflicted by progress and technology.

Lews Castle CASTLE
The Baronial mansion across the harbour from Stornoway town centre was built in the 1840s for the Matheson family, then owners of Lewis. The beautiful grounds are open to the public and host the Hebridean Celtic Festival.

The castle was gifted to the community by Lord Leverhulme in 1923 and was home to the local college for 40 years, but has lain empty since 1997 (the college now occupies modern buildings in the castle grounds); it is now slated for development as a museum and hotel.

THE BLACKHOUSES OF LEWIS

Until the second half of the 19th century, the 'blackhouse' was the main form of habitation in the Outer Hebrides. Built to a design that may go back 1000 years, blackhouses have very thick walls of uncut stone (an outer and inner layer, filled with turf in the middle), roofs thatched with turf and straw, and floors of beaten earth. Long and narrow, one end served as a byre for the cattle, the other for human habitation. There was no chimney; the smoke from the peat fire found its way out through the thatch.

After 1850, there was a trend towards building new houses for the islanders, to separate human and animal accommodation. These new houses, with their whitewashed walls of mortared stone, were called 'white houses'; in contrast, the old habitations became known as black houses.

Life in the old blackhouses was hard – there was no sanitation, no running water and no mains electricity. Nevertheless, widespread poverty in the islands in the first half of the 20th century saw many remain inhabited until after WWII – the last was vacated in the mid-1970s.

Stornoway

Lewis Loom Centre EXHIBITION
(☑01851 704500; 3 Bayhead; adult/child £1/50p;
⊙9am-5.30pm Mon-Sat) This centre houses
an exhibition on the history of Harris
Tweed; the 40-minute guided tour (£2.50
extra) includes spinning and weaving
demonstrations.

FREE **St Columba's Church** HISTORIC BUILDING
(⊙24hr) The roofless ruin of the 14th-century
St Columba's Church, 4 miles east of Stornoway on the Eye peninsula, features the grave
slabs of Roderick McLeod, 7th clan chief (c
1498), and his daughter (1503).

Hourly buses (Monday to Saturday) to
Point pass the turn-off to the church, where
there's a stone monument in the form of a
cairn torn asunder, a reminder of the Aignish Farm Raiders, who stormed Matheson's
farm at Aignish in 1888 to protest against
the Clearances.

Religion still plays a major role in island life, especially on predominantly Protestant Lewis and Harris where the Sabbath is still widely observed by members of the 'free churches'.

The Calvinist Free Church of Scotland (known as the 'Wee Frees'), and the even more fundamentalist Free Presbyterian Church of Scotland (the 'Wee Wee Frees'), which split from the established Church of Scotland in 1843 and 1893 respectively, are deeply conservative, permitting no ornaments, organ music or choirs in church. Their ministers deliver uncompromising sermons (usually in Gaelic) from central pulpits and precentors lead the congregation in unaccompanied but fervent psalm singing. Visitors are welcome to attend services, but due respect is essential.

The Protestants of the Outer Hebrides have succeeded in maintaining a distinctive fundamentalist approach to their religion, with Sunday being devoted largely to religious services, prayer and Bible reading. On Lewis and Harris, the last bastion of Sabbath observance in the UK, almost everything closes down on a Sunday. In fact, Stornoway must be the only place in the UK to suffer a Sunday rush hour as people drive to church around 10.30am; it's then a ghost town for an hour and a half until the services are over. But a few cracks have begun to appear.

There was outrage when British Airways/Loganair introduced Sunday flights from Edinburgh and Inverness to Stornoway in 2002, with members of the Lord's Day Observance Society spluttering that this was the thin end of the wedge. They were probably right – in 2003 a Stornoway petrol station began to open on a Sunday, and now does a roaring trade in Sunday papers and takeaway booze. Then in 2006 the CalMac ferry from Berneray to Leverburgh in Harris started a Sunday service, despite strong opposition from the residents of Harris (ironically, they were unable to protest at the ferry's arrival, as that would have meant breaking the Sabbath).

✵ Festivals

Hebridean Celtic Festival MUSIC
(www.hebceltfest.com) A four-day extravaganza of folk/rock/Celtic music held in the second half of July.

⌨ Sleeping

Braighe House B&B ££
(☎01851-705287; www.braighehouse.co.uk; 20 Braighe Rd; r per person from £45; P) This spacious and comfortable guesthouse, 3 miles east of the town centre on the A866, has stylish, modern bedrooms and a great seafront location. Good bathrooms with powerful showers, hearty breakfasts and genuinely hospitable owners round off the perfect package.

Park Guest House B&B ££
(☎01851-702485; www.theparkguesthouse.co.uk; 30 James St; s/d from £58/86; P) A charming Victorian villa with a conservatory and eight luxurious rooms (mostly en suite), the Park Guest House is comfortable and central and has the advantage of an excellent restaurant. The restaurant specialises in Scottish seafood, beef and game (plus one or two vegetarian dishes). Rooms overlooking the main road can be noisy on weekday mornings.

Royal Hotel HOTEL ££
(☎01851-702109; www.royalstornoway.co.uk; Cromwell St; s/d £79/109; P📶) The 19th-century Royal is the most appealing of Stornoway's hotels – the rooms at the front retain period features such as wood panelling, and enjoy a view across the harbour to Lews Castle. Ask to see your room first, though, as some are a bit cramped.

Cabarfeidh Hotel HOTEL £££
(☎01851-702604; www.cabarfeidh-hotel.co.uk; Manor Park; s/d £125/165; P📶) Owned by the same company as the Royal, the Cabarfeidh is big and luxurious and is handy for the golf course, but lacks the Royal's old-fashioned character.

Thorlee B&B £
(☎01851-705466, 01851-706300; www.thorlee.com; 1-3 Cromwell St; d from £45; P) The family-oriented Thorlee has bright and cheerful rooms and a great central location with views over the harbour – an absolute bargain. If there's no answer at the guesthouse, ask at the Stag Bakery next door.

Laxdale Holiday Park CAMPGROUND £
(☎01851-703234; www.laxdaleholidaypark.com; 6 Laxdale Lane; site £7-9, plus per person £3;

⊗Apr-Oct; 🐾) This camping ground, 1.5 miles north of town off the A857, has a sheltered woodland setting, though the tent area is mostly on a slope – get there early for a level pitch. There's also a bunkhouse (£15 per person) that stays open year-round.

Heb Hostel   HOSTEL **£**
(📞01851-709889; www.hebhostel.co.uk; 25 Kenneth St; dm £15; @🐾) The Heb is a friendly, easygoing hostel close to the ferry, with comfy wooden bunks, a convivial living room with peat fire and a welcoming owner who can provide all kinds of advice on what to do and where to go.

🍴 Eating

TOP CHOICE **Digby Chick**   RESTAURANT **£££**
(📞01851-700026; 5 Bank St; mains £18-23; ⊗noon-10pm Mon-Sat) A modern restaurant that dishes up bistro cuisine such as haddock and chips, sesame-glazed pork belly or garlic-roasted mushroom with duck-egg salad at lunchtime, the Digby Chick metamorphoses into a candlelit gourmet restaurant in the evening, serving dishes such as grilled langoustines, seared scallops, roast lamb and steak.

You can get a two-course lunch for £10 (11.30am to 2pm), and a three-course dinner for £20 (5.30pm to 6.30pm only).

Thai Café   THAI **£**
(📞01851-701811; 27 Church St; mains £5-7; ⊗noon-2.30pm & 5.30-11pm Mon-Sat) Here's a surprise – authentic, inexpensive Thai food in the heart of Stornoway. This spick-and-span little restaurant has a genuine Thai chef, and serves some of the most delicious, best-value Asian food in the Hebrides. If you can't get a table, it does takeaway too.

An Lanntair Art Centre Café   CAFE **££**
(Kenneth St; snacks £3-6, mains £10-16; ⊗cafe 10am-late, restaurant lunch & dinner Mon-Sat; 🐾) The stylish and family-friendly restaurant at the art centre serves a broad range of freshly prepared dishes, from tasty bacon rolls at breakfast, to burgers, baguettes or mince and tatties for lunch, and substantial Thai curry, beef-and-Guinness pie or nut roast for dinner.

Park Guest House Restaurant   SCOTTISH **££**
(📞01851-702485; www.theparkguesthouse.co.uk; 30 James St; mains £15-23; ⊗5-8.45pm Tue-Sat) The restaurant at the Park Guest House specialises in Scottish seafood, beef and game (plus one or two vegetarian dishes), simply

---

Most restaurants in Stornoway are closed Sundays. The few options for a sit-down meal include:

» **HS-1 Cafe-Bar** (📞01851-702109; Cromwell St; mains £8-11; ⊗noon-4pm & 5-9pm)

» **Stornoway Balti House** (📞01851-706116; 24 South Beach; mains £8-13; ⊗noon-2.30pm & 6-11pm)

---

prepared, allowing the flavour of the food to speak for itself. It offers a good-value, three-course dinner for £16.50 between 5pm and 6.30pm.

ℹ Information
Baltic Bookshop (📞01851-702802; 8-10 Cromwell St; ⊗9am-5.30pm Mon-Sat) Good for local history books and maps.

Sandwick Rd Petrol Station (📞01851-702304; Sandwick Rd) The only shop in town that's open on a Sunday (from 10am to 4pm); the Sunday papers arrive around 2pm.

ℹ Getting There & Around
BUS The bus station is on the waterfront, next to the ferry terminal. Bus W10 runs from Stornoway to Tarbert (one hour, four or five daily Monday to Saturday) and Leverburgh (two hours).

The Westside Circular bus W2 runs a circular route from Stornoway through Callanish, Carloway, Garenin and Arnol; the timetable means you can visit one or two of the sites in a day.

BIKE Alex Dan's Cycle Centre (📞01851 704025; www.hebrideancycles.co.uk; 67 Kenneth St; ⊗9am-6pm Mon-Sat) Hires out bikes.

BUTT OF LEWIS (RUBHA ROBHANAIS)
The Butt of Lewis (no snickering, please) – the extreme northern tip of the Hebrides – is windswept and rugged, with a very imposing lighthouse, pounding surf and large colonies of nesting fulmars on the high cliffs. There's a bleak sense of isolation here, with nothing but the grey Atlantic between you and Canada.

Just before the turn-off to the Butt at Eoropie (Eoropaidh), you'll find **St Moluag's Church** (Teampull Mholuidh), an austere, barnlike structure believed to date from the 12th century but still used by the Episcopal Church. The main settlement here is **Port of Ness** (Port Nis), which has an attractive harbour. To the west of the village is the sandy beach of **Traigh**, which is popular with surfers and has a kids adventure playground nearby.

FOR PEAT'S SAKE

In the Outer Hebrides, where trees are few and far between and coal is absent, peat has been the main source of domestic fuel for many centuries. Although oil-fired central heating is now the norm, many houses have held on to their peat fires for nostalgia's sake.

Peat in its raw state is extremely wet and can take a couple of months to dry out. It is cut from roadside bogs, where the cuttings are at least a metre deep. Rectangular blocks of peat are cut using a long-handled tool called a *tairsgeir* (peat-iron); this is extremely hard work and can cause blisters even on hands that are used to manual labour.

The peat blocks are carefully assembled into a *cruach-mhonach* (peat stack), each balanced on top of the other in a grid pattern, thus creating maximum air space. Once the peat has dried out it is stored in a shed.

Peat burns much more slowly than wood or coal and produces a not-unpleasant smell, but in the old blackhouses (which had no chimney) it permeated every corner of the dwelling, not to mention the inhabitants' clothes and hair, hence the expression 'peat-reek' – the ever-present smell of peat smoke that was long associated with island life.

ARNOL

One of Scotland's most evocative historic buildings, the **Arnol Blackhouse** (HS; ☎01851-710395; adult/child £2.50/1.50; ⊙9.30am-5.30pm Mon-Sat Apr-Sep, to 4.30pm Mon-Sat Oct-Mar, last admission 30min before closing) is not so much a museum as a perfectly preserved fragment of a lost world. Built in 1885, this traditional blackhouse – a combined byre, barn and home – was inhabited until 1964 and has not been changed since the last inhabitant moved out. The staff faithfully rekindle the central peat fire every morning so you can experience the distinctive peat-reek; there's no chimney, and the smoke finds its own way out through the turf roof, windows and door – spend too long inside and you might feel like you've been kippered! The museum is just off the A858, about 3 miles west of Barvas.

At nearby **Bragar**, a pair of whalebones form an arch by the road, with the rusting harpoon that killed the whale dangling from the centre.

GARENIN (NA GEARRANNAN)

The picturesque and fascinating **Gearrannan Blackhouse Village** is a cluster of nine restored thatch-roofed blackhouses perched above the exposed Atlantic coast. One of the cottages is home to the **Blackhouse Museum** (☎01851-643416; www.gearrannan.com; adult/child £2.20/1; ⊙9.30am-5.30pm Mon-Sat Apr-Sep), a traditional 1955 blackhouse with displays on the village's history, while another houses the **Taigh an Chocair Cafe** (mains £3-6; ⊙9.30am-5.30pm Mon-Sat).

Garenin Crofters' Hostel (www.gatliff.org.uk; dm adult/child £10/6) occupies another of the village blackhouses, and is one of the most atmospheric hostels in Scotland (or anywhere else for that matter).

The other houses in the village are let out as self-catering **holiday cottages** (☎01851-643416; www.gearrannan.co.uk; per week for 2 people £273-385) offering the chance to stay in a unique and luxurious modernised blackhouse with attached kitchen and lounge. There's a minimum five-night let from June to August.

CARLOWAY (CARLABAGH)

Dun Carloway (Dun Charlabhaigh) is a 2000-year-old, dry-stone broch, perched defiantly above a beautiful loch with views to the mountains of North Harris. The site is clearly signposted along a minor road off the A858, a mile southwest of Carloway village. One of the best-preserved brochs in Scotland, its double walls (with internal staircase) still stand to a height of 9m and testify to the engineering skills of its Iron Age architects.

The tiny, turf-roofed **Doune Broch Centre** (☎01851-643338; admission free; ⊙10am-5pm Mon-Sat Apr-Sep) nearby has interpretative displays and exhibitions about the history of the broch and the life of the people who lived there.

CALLANISH (CALANAIS)

The **Callanish Standing Stones**, 15 miles west of Stornoway on the A858 road, form one of the most complete stone circles in Britain. It is one of the most atmospheric prehistoric sites anywhere; its ageless mystery, impressive scale and undeniable beauty leave a lasting impression. Sited on a wild and secluded promontory overlooking Loch Roag, 13 large stones of beautifully banded gneiss are arranged, as if in worship, around a 4.5m-tall central monolith. Some 40 smaller stones radiate from the circle in the shape of a cross, with the remains of a chambered tomb at the centre. Dating from 3800 to 5000 years ago, the stones are roughly contemporary with the pyramids of Egypt.

The nearby **Calanais Visitor Centre** (☎01851-621422; www.callanishvisitorcentre.co.uk; admission free, exhibition £2; ⊙10am-9pm Mon-Sat Apr-Sep, to 4pm Wed-Sat Oct-Mar; **P**) is a tour de force of discreet design. Inside is a small exhibition that speculates on the origins and purpose of the stones, and an excellent **cafe** (snacks £2-5).

If you plan to stay the night, you have a choice of **Eshcol Guest House** (☎01851-621357; www.eshcol.com; 21 Breasclete; r per person £43; **P**) and neighbouring **Loch Roag Guest House** (☎01851-621357; www.lochroag.com; 22a Breasclete; r per person £40-55; **P**), half a mile north of Callanish. Both are modern bungalows with the same friendly owner, who is very knowledgeable about the local area.

GREAT BERNERA

This rocky island is connected to Lewis by a bridge built by the local council in 1953 – the islanders had originally planned to destroy a small hill with explosives and use the material to build their own causeway. On a sunny day, it's worth making the long detour to the island's northern tip for a picnic at the perfect little sandy beach of **Bosta** (Bostadh).

In 1996 archaeologists excavated an entire Iron Age village at the head of the beach. Afterwards, the village was reburied for protection, but a reconstruction of an **Iron Age house** (☎01851-612331; adult/child £2/50p; ⊙noon-4pm Mon-Fri May-Sep) now sits nearby. Stand around the peat fire, above which strips of mutton are being smoked, while the custodian explains the domestic arrangements – truly fascinating, and well worth the trip.

There are five buses a day between Stornoway and the hamlet of Breacleit (one hour, Monday to Saturday) on Great Bernera; two or three a day will continue to Bosta on request. Alternatively, there's a signposted 5-mile **coastal walk** from Breacleit to Bosta.

The B8011 road (signposted Uig, on the A858 Stornoway–Callanish road) from Garrynahine to Timsgarry (Timsgearraidh) meanders through scenic wilderness to some of Scotland's most stunning beaches. At **Miavaig**, a loop road detours north through the Bhaltos Estate to the pretty, mile-long white strand of **Reef Beach**; there's a basic **camping ground** (per person £2) in the machair behind the beach.

From April to September, **Sea Trek** (☎01851-672469; www.seatrek.co.uk; Miavaig Pier) runs two-hour boat trips (adult/child £35/25; Monday to Saturday) to spot seals and nesting seabirds. In June and July it also runs more adventurous, all-day trips (£90 per person; two per month) in a high-speed RIB to the **Flannan Isles**, a remote group of tiny, uninhabited islands 25 miles northwest of Lewis. Puffins, seals and a ruined 7th-century chapel are the main attractions, but the isles are most famous for the mystery of the three lighthouse keepers who disappeared without trace in December 1900. There's also a 12-hour round trip to remote **St Kilda** (£180, once or twice weekly, May to September, weather permitting).

From Miavaig the road continues west through a rocky defile to Timsgarry and the vast, sandy expanse of **Traigh Uige** (Uig Sands). The famous 12th-century Lewis chess pieces made of walrus ivory were discovered in the sand dunes here in 1831. Of the 78 pieces, 67 are in the British Museum in London, with 11 in Edinburgh's Museum of Scotland; you can buy replicas at various outlets on the isle of Lewis. There's a very basic campsite (per person £2) on the south side of the bay (signposted 'Ardroil Beach'; toilet only, no showers).

The minor road that continues south from Timsgarry to **Mealista** passes a few smaller, but still spectacular, white-sand beaches; beware, though – the surf can make swimming treacherous.

Harris (Na Hearadh)

POP 2000

Harris, to the south of Lewis, is the scenic jewel in the necklace of islands that comprise the Outer Hebrides. It has a spectacular blend of rugged mountains, pristine beaches, flower-speckled machair and barren rocky landscapes. The isthmus at Tarbert splits Harris neatly in two: North Harris is dominated by mountains that rise forbiddingly above the peat moors to the south of Stornoway – Clisham (799m) is the highest point; South Harris is lower-lying, fringed by beautiful white-sand beaches on the west and a convoluted rocky coastline to the east.

The Gaelic name for Harris, Na Hearadh, is derived from the Viking word for 'high island'. The boundary between Harris and Lewis was originally a clan division. The territory to the north belonged to the MacLeods of Lewis, descended from the Norse noble Torquil; while Harris belonged to the MacLeods of Harris and Skye, who were descended from Torquil's brother Tormod. Needless to say, relations between the two brothers – and subsequently the two clans – were less than amicable.

Harris is famous for Harris Tweed, a high-quality woollen cloth still hand-woven in islanders' homes. The industry employs around 400 weavers; staff at Tarbert tourist office can tell you about weavers and workshops that you can visit.

TARBERT (AN TAIRBEART)
POP 480

Tarbert is a harbour village with a spectacular location, tucked into the narrow neck of land that links North and South Harris. It has ferry connections to Uig on Skye.

Village facilities include a petrol station, bank with an ATM and two general stores. The **Harris Tweed Shop** (☑01880-502493; www.isleofharristweedshop.co.uk; Main St; ⊙9.15am-5.30pm May-Sep) stocks a wide range of books on the Hebrides and sells gifts, crafts and the famous cloth itself.

🛏 Sleeping & Eating

Hotel Hebrides HOTEL ££
(☑01859-502364; www.hotel-hebrides.com; Pier Rd; per person £65-80; ☎) The location and setting don't look promising – a drab newbuild squeezed between ferry pier and car park (you won't find any photos of the hotel exterior on the website) – but this new establishment brings a dash of urban design to Harris, with flashy fabrics and wall coverings, luxurious towels and toiletries, and a stylish restaurant and lounge bar.

Harris Hotel HOTEL ££
(☑01859-502154; www.harrishotel.com; s/d from £55/90; ℗☎) Run since 1903 by four generations of the Cameron family, Harris Hotel is a 19th-century sporting hotel, originally built for deer-stalkers visiting the North Harris Estates. It has spacious, comfy rooms and a good restaurant; look out for JM Barrie's initials scratched on the dining-room window (the author of *Peter Pan* visited in the 1920s).

The hotel is on the way out of the village, on the road north towards Stornoway.

Rockview Bunkhouse HOSTEL £
(☑01859-502081; imacaskill@aol.com; Main St; dm £10) This hostel on the street above the har-

---

HARRIS TWEED

The favourite fabric of the English upper classes, warm and durable Harris Tweed is still hand-woven by industrious islanders in their own homes. Known as *clo mhor* (the great cloth) in Gaelic, genuine Harris Tweed must be hand-woven in Lewis, Harris, Barra or the Uists, and must bear the distinctive 'orb' logo of the Harris Tweed Authority (www.harris tweed.org).

The process of making tweed dates back 2500 years; the wool is washed and scoured, then dyed using natural vegetable dyes (including lichen and heather flowers), before being spun and woven on hand-operated looms. It then undergoes the waulking process, to thicken and soften the fabric and set the dyes; this involves soaking the cloth in a mild ammonia solution and pounding it.

Today this process in mechanised, but in the old days the cloth was soaked in urine (both human and sheep) and beaten by hand against a table. This was women's work, and a waulking party would see a dozen or so women sat around a long table or board, rhythmically pounding a 70-yard length of tweed in time to traditional waulking songs. These songs have become an important part of Hebridean culture, and can be heard in many museums.

Today there are about 400 weavers in the Western Isles, working with locally produced wool in their own croft-house workshops. Harris Tweed still has a somewhat exclusive (some would say stuffy) image, but a number of British fashion designers, including John Galliano and Vivienne Westwood, have found radical new uses for the fabric.

bour is a bit cell-like with its cramped dorms and air of neglect, but it's close to the ferry.

Firstfruits CAFE
(☏01880-502439; Pier Rd; mains £3-10; ☺10am-4.30pm Mon-Sat Apr-Sep, 7-9pm Tue-Sat May-Aug) This is a cosy little cottage tearoom near the tourist office – handy while you wait for a ferry.

NORTH HARRIS

Magnificent North Harris is the most mountainous region of the Outer Hebrides. There are few roads here, but many opportunities for climbing, walking and birdwatching.

Clisham (799m), the highest summit in the Western Isles, can be reached from the high point of the Stornoway to Tarbert road; the round trip takes about four hours and offers wonderful views. Another good walk is the **Harris Walkway**, a waymarked network of old pony tracks and coffin roads that runs for 20 miles from Scaladale (on the Stornoway road, 12 miles north of Tarbert) to Seilebost (near Luskentyre in South Harris) via Laxdale Lochs, Tarbert, Grosebay and Stockinish. Ask for a leaflet at the Tarbert tourist office.

The B887 leads west, from a point three miles north of Tarbert, to **Hushinish**, where there's a lovely silver-sand beach. The road passes an **old whaling station**, one of Lord Leverhulme's failed development schemes, and the impressive shooting lodge of **Amhuinnsuidhe Castle**, now an exclusive hotel. Just northwest of Hushinish is the uninhabited island of **Scarp**, the scene of bizarre attempts to send mail by rocket in 1934, a story that was recounted in the movie *The Rocket Post* (2001), shot in Harris.

Rhenigidale Crofters' Hostel (www.gatliff.org.uk; dm adult/child £10/6) can be reached on foot from Tarbert (6 miles, allow three hours). It's an excellent walk, but take all the necessary supplies for a mountain hike (map, compass, protective clothing etc). Take the road towards Kyles Scalpay for 2 miles and, at a bend in the road just beyond Laxdale Lochs, veer off to the left on a signposted track across the hills (marked on Ordnance Survey maps). The hostel is a small white cottage standing above the road on the eastern side of the glen; the warden lives in the house closest to the shore.

The remote hamlet of Rhenigidale can also be reached by road; bus W11 (request service) takes you there from Tarbert (30 minutes, two a day Monday to Saturday), book in advance (☏01859-502871).

SOUTH HARRIS

The west coast of South Harris has some of the most beautiful beaches in Scotland. The blinding white sands and turquoise waters of **Luskentyre** and **Scarasta** would be major holiday resorts if they were in a warm climate; as it is, they're usually deserted.

The east coast is a complete contrast to the west – a strange, rocky moonscape of naked gneiss pocked with tiny lochans, the bleakness lightened by the occasional splash of green around the few crofting communities. Film buffs will know that the psychedelic sequences of the surface of Jupiter in *2001: A Space Odyssey* were shot from an aircraft flying low over the east coast of Harris.

The narrow, twisting road that winds its way along this coast is known locally as the **Golden Road**, because of the vast amount of money it cost per mile. It was built in the 1930s to link all the tiny communities known as 'The Bays'.

⊙ Sights & Activities

Seallam! Visitor Centre VISITOR CENTRE
(www.seallam.com; Northton; adult/child £2.50/2; ☺10am-5pm Mon-Sat) The culture and landscape of the Hebrides are celebrated in the fascinating exhibition at Seallam! Visitor Centre. *Seallam* is Gaelic for 'Let me show you'. The centre, which is in Northton, just south of Scarasta, also has a genealogical research centre for people who want to trace their Hebridean ancestry.

FREE **St Clement's Church** HISTORIC BUILDING
(Rodel) At the southernmost tip of the eastern coastline is the impressive 16th century St Clement's Church, built by Alexander MacLeod of Dunvegan between the 1520s and 1550s, but abandoned after the Reformation. The fortified construction shows it was built in troubled times.

The fine **tombs** inside the echoing stone hall, including the cenotaph of Alexander MacLeod, carved with hunting scenes, a castle, a birlinn (the traditional longboat of the islands) and various saints, including St Clement clutching a skull. There are interesting carved tomb-slabs featuring swords and Celtic knotwork. You can climb the tower for good views of the coast. On your way out look out for the carved sheila-na-gig – a pagan fertility symbol – on the tower.

Leverburgh
VILLAGE

(An t-Ob; www.leverburgh.co.uk) The village of Leverburgh is named after Lord Leverhulme. He had grand plans for Obbe, as Leverburgh was then known – it was to be a major fishing port with a population of 10,000 – but the plans died with him and the village reverted to a sleepy backwater.

There is a post office with an ATM, a general store and a petrol station.

MV Lady Catherine
WILDLIFE CRUISE

(☑01859-530310; www.scenic-cruises.co.uk; Flodabay; adult/child £15/7; ☺May-Sep) The *MV Lady Catherine*, based at Flodabay harbour halfway down the east coast, offers three-hour wildlife cruises.

🛏 Sleeping & Eating

Carminish Guest House
B&B ££

(☑01859-520400; www.carminish.com; 1a Strond, Leverburgh; s/d £50/68; ℗🛜) One of the few B&Bs in Harris that is open all year, the welcoming Carminish is a modern house with three comfy bedrooms. There's a view of the ferry from the dining room, and lots of nice touches such as handmade soaps, a tin of biscuits in the bedroom and the weather forecast posted on the breakfast table.

Sorrel Cottage
B&B ££

(☑01859-520319; www.sorrelcottage.co.uk; 2 Glen, Leverburgh; r per person from £30) Sorrel Cottage is a pretty crofter's house, about 1.5 miles west of the ferry at Leverburgh. Evening meals can be provided (£16 a head), and

vegetarians and vegans are happily catered for. Bike hire available.

Rodel Hotel
INN ££

(☑01859-520210; www.rodelhotel.co.uk; Rodel; s/d from £76/115; ℗) Don't be put off by the rather grey and grim exterior of this remote hotel – the interior has been refurbished to a high standard and offers four large, luxurious bedrooms; the one called Iona has the best view, across the little harbour.

The hotel **restaurant** (mains £14-18; ☺5.30-9.30pm) serves delicious local seafood and game, with dishes such as local scallops with Stornoway black pudding and Hollandaise sauce.

Am Bothan
HOSTEL £

(☑01859-520251; www.ambothan.com; Leverburgh; dm £17.50; ℗🛜) An attractive, chalet-style hostel, Am Bothan has small, neat dorms and a great porch where you can enjoy morning coffee with views over the creek. The hostel offers bike hire and can arrange wildlife-watching boat trips.

Skoon Art Café
CAFE, GALLERY £

(☑01859-530268; www.skoon.com; Geocrab; mains £4-7; ☺10am-4.30pm Tue-Sat Mar-Oct, noon-4pm Wed-Sat Nov-22 Dec, lunch served 11am-4pm) Halfway along the Golden Road, this neat little art gallery doubles as an excellent cafe serving delicious homemade soups (broccoli and roast almond, and carrot and fennel are favourites), sandwiches, cakes and desserts (try the marmalade and ginger cake).

LORD LEVERHULME

William Hesketh Lever (1851–1925), better known as Lord Leverhulme, was an industrialist and philanthropist who established world-famous soap brands such as Sunlight, Lux and Lifebuoy, and his empire formed the basis of present-day industrial giant Unilever.

Leverhulme purchased the Isle of Lewis in 1918 (followed by Harris in 1919), with the intention of transforming a depressed rural region with a population of 30,000 into a thriving industrial economy of 200,000 souls, based on fishing, fish processing and textile manufacture. His plans included the development of Stornoway as a fishing harbour and fish cannery; the building of new roads and harbours; even a railway and gasworks. Although this boost to the local economy was initially welcomed by the islanders, they soon realised their paternalistic landlord had no understanding of crofters and their relationship to the land, wanting them to submit totally to his industrialised vision of their future.

Faced with dwindling support in Lewis, he shifted his development efforts to Harris, but following his death in 1925 all projects were cancelled and the island sold off piecemeal as sporting estates. Relics of Leverhulme's grandiose plans include Stornoway's regular grid of streets, the abanoned whaling station in Harris, the harbour (and village name) at Leverburgh, and the Bridge to Nowhere at Tolsta, 13 miles north of Stornoway – part of a proposed road from Stornoway to Ness that was never built.

Getting There & Around

A CalMac car ferry zigzags through the reefs of the Sound of Harris from Leverburgh to Berneray (pedestrian/car £6.25/28.50, 1¼ hours, three or four daily Monday to Saturday). You can hire bicycles from Sorrel Cottage for £10 a day.

Berneray (Bearnaraigh)

POP 140

Berneray was linked to North Uist by a causeway in October 1998, but that hasn't altered the peace and beauty of the island. The beaches on its west coast are some of the most beautiful and unspoilt in Britain, and seals and otters can be seen in Bays Loch on the east coast.

Basic but atmospheric **Gatliff Hostel** (www.gatliff.org.uk; camping per person £5, dm adult/child £10/6), housed in a pair of restored blackhouses right by the sea, is the place to stay. You can camp outside, or on the grass above the gorgeous white-sand beach just to the north.

In summer snacks are available at the **Lobster Pot** (⊙9am-5.30pm Mon-Sat), the tearoom attached to Ardmarree Stores (a grocery shop near the causeway). The **Nurses Cottage** (www.isleofberneray.com; ⊙11am-3pm Mon-Fri Jun-Aug) provides tourist information.

Bus W19 runs from Berneray (Gatliff Hostel and Harris ferry) to Lochmaddy (30 minutes, six daily Monday to Saturday). There are ferries to Leverburgh (Harris).

North Uist (Uibhist A Tuath)

POP 1550

North Uist, an island half drowned by lochs, is famed for its fishing but also has magnificent beaches on its north and west coasts. For birdwatchers this is an earthly paradise, with regular sightings of waders and wildfowl ranging from redshank to red-throated diver to red-necked phalarope. For walkers there's the Eaval Walk (p216). The landscape is less wild and mountainous than Harris but it has a sleepy, subtle appeal.

Little Lochmaddy is the first village you hit after arriving on the ferry from Skye. There's a **tourist office** (☏01876-500321; Pier Rd; ⊙9am-1pm & 2-5pm Mon-Fri, 9.30am-1pm & 2-5.30pm Sat, plus 8-9pm Mon, Wed & Fri Apr-Oct), a couple of stores, a bank with an ATM, a petrol station, a post office and a pub.

Sights

211

Balranald Nature Reserve   WILDLIFE RESERVE

Birdwatchers flock to this Royal Society for the Protection of Birds (RSPB) nature reserve, 18 miles west of Lochmaddy, in the hope of spotting the rare red-necked phalarope or hearing the distinctive call of the corncrake. There's a **visitors centre** (☏01876-510372; ⊙Apr-Sep) with a resident warden who offers 1½-hour guided walks (£5, depart visitor centre 10am on Tuesdays, May to August).

Taigh Chearsabhagh   ARTS CENTRE, MUSEUM

(☏01876-500293; admission free, museum £1; ⊙10am-5pm Mon-Sat Feb-Jun & Sep-Dec, 10am-5pm Mon-Thu & Sat, to 8pm Fri Jul & Aug; @) Taigh Chearsabhagh is a museum and arts centre that preserves and displays the history and culture of the Uists, and is also a thriving community centre, post office and meeting place. The centre's lively **cafe** (mains £3-6) dishes up lovely homemade soups, sandwiches and cakes.

Bharpa Langass & Pobull Fhinn   PREHISTORIC SITES

A waymarked circular path beside the Langass Lodge Hotel (just off the A867, 6 miles southwest of Lochmaddy) leads to the chambered Neolithic burial tomb of **Bharpa Langass** and the stone circle of **Pobull Fhinn** (Finn's People); both are reckoned to be around 5000 years old. There are lovely views over the loch, where you may be able to spot seals and otters.

Sleeping & Eating

Tigh Dearg Hotel   HOTEL £££

(☏01876-500700; www.tighdearghotel.co.uk; s/d £99/139; P🐾) It looks a little like a hostel from the outside but the 'Red House' (as the name means) is actually Lochmaddy's most luxurious accommodation, with nine designer bedrooms, a lounge with leather sofas around an open fire, a gym and even a sauna. There's a good restaurant too, with sea views from the terrace.

Old Courthouse   B&B ££

(☏01876-500358; oldcourthouse@tiscali.co.uk; r per person from £30; P) This charming, Georgian-style villa has four guest rooms and is within walking distance of the ferry, on the road that leads to Uist Outdoor Centre. Excellent porridge for breakfast, and kippers are on the menu too.

Langass Lodge Hotel HOTEL **££**
(☑01876-580285; www.langasslodge.co.uk; Lo-cheport; s/d from £65/99; P🛜) The delightful Langass Lodge Hotel is a former shooting lodge set in splendid isolation overlooking Loch Langais. Refurbished and extended, it now offers a dozen appealing rooms, many with sea views, and one of the Hebrides' best **restaurants** (2-/3-course dinner £28/34), noted for its fine seafood and game.

Lochmaddy Hotel HOTEL **££**
(☑01876-500331; www.lochmaddyhotel.co.uk; s/d from £55/95; P🛜) The Lochmaddy is a tra-ditional anglers' hotel (you can buy fishing permits here) with comfy, recently refur-bished rooms, many with harbour views. The lively hotel **bar** (mains £9-13) pulls in anglers, locals and tourists, and serves ex-cellent pub grub including seafood, venison and king-size steaks.

Uist Outdoor Centre HOSTEL **£**
(☑01876-500480; www.uistoutdoorcentre.co.uk; Cearn Dusgaidh; dm £15; ⊙Mar–mid-Dec; P@🛜) This shore-side activity centre has a smart bunkhouse with four-bed dorms and offers a range of activities including sea kayaking, rock climbing and diving.

ℹ Getting There & Around

Buses from Lochmaddy to Berneray, Langass, Clachan na Luib, Benbecula and Lochboisdale run five or six times a day Monday to Saturday.

Benbecula (Beinn Na Faoghla)

POP 1200

Benbecula is a low-lying island whose flat, lochan-studded landscape is best appreci-ated from the summit of **Rueval** (124m), the island's highest point. There's a path around the south side of the hill (signposted from the main road; park beside the landfill site) that is said to be the route taken to the coast by Bonnie Prince Charlie and Flora Mac-Donald during the prince's escape in 1746.

The control centre for the British army's Hebrides Missile Range (located on the northwestern tip of South Uist) is the is-land's main source of employment, and **Balivanich** (Baile a'Mhanaich) – looking like a corner of a Glasgow housing estate planted incongruously on the machair – is the commercial centre serving the troops and their families. The village has a bank with an ATM, a post office, a large **Co-op** super-market (⊙8am-8pm Mon-Sat, 11am-6pm Sun) and a petrol station (open on Sundays).

South Uist (Uibhist A Deas)

POP 1900

South Uist is the second-largest island in the Outer Hebrides and saves its choicest corners for those who explore away from the main north–south road. The low-lying west coast is an almost unbroken stretch of white-sand beach and flower-flecked ma-chair – a new waymarked hiking trail, the **Machair Way**, follows the coast – while the multitude of inland lochs provide excellent trout fishing. The east coast, riven by four large sea lochs, is hilly and remote, with spectacular **Beinn Mhor** (620m) the high-est point.

Driving south from Benbecula you cross from the predominantly Protestant northern half of the Outer Hebrides into the mostly Roman Catholic south, a religious transition marked by the granite statue of **Our Lady of the Isles** on the slopes of Rueval (the hill with the military radomes on its summit), and the presence of many roadside shrines.

The ferry port of Lochboisdale is the is-land's largest settlement, with a tourist of-fice, a bank with an ATM, a grocery store and a petrol station. There's a **Co-op super-market** (⊙8am-8pm Mon-Sat, 12.30-6pm Sun) at Daliburgh, 3 miles west of the village.

◉ Sights & Activities

Loch Druidibeg National Nature Reserve WILDLIFE RESERVE
The northern part of the island is mostly occupied by the watery expanses of Loch Bee and Loch Druidibeg. Loch Druidibeg National Nature Reserve is an important breeding ground for birds such as dunlin, redshank, ringed plover, greylag goose and corncrake; you can take a 5-mile self-guided walk through the reserve.

Pick up a leaflet from the Scottish Natural Heritage office on the main road beside the loch.

Kildonan Museum MUSEUM
(☑01878-710343; adult/child £1.50/free; ⊙10am-5pm Mon-Sat, 2-5pm Sun Apr-Oct) Six miles south of Howmore, Kildonan Museum ex-plores the lives of local crofters through its collection of artefacts – an absorbing exhi-bition of black-and-white photography and many first-hand accounts of harsh Hebrid-ean conditions.

There's also an excellent **tearoom** (mains £3-8; ⊘11am-4pm Mon-Sat, 1-4pm Sun Apr-Oct) and craft shop.

Flora MacDonald's Birthplace   HISTORIC SITE
Amid Milton's ruined blackhouses, half a mile south of the museum, a cairn marks the site of Flora MacDonald's birthplace.

Howmore   VILLAGE
Two miles south of Loch Druidibeg, the attractive hamlet of Howmore (Tobha Mor) has several restored thatched blackhouses. One houses the **Tobha Mor Crofters' Hostel** (www.gatliff.org.uk; dm adult/child £10/6).

Askernish Golf Course   GOLF
(www.askernishgolfclub.com) Askernish Golf Course, originally laid out by the legendary Tom Morris in 1891, was recently rediscovered among the dunes on South Uist. It has been restored and this classic, old-fashioned links course is once again open for play.

Rothan Cycles   BICYCLE RENTAL
(☏01870-620283; www.rothan.com; per day/week from £10/43) Where the road to Tobha Mor Crofter's Hostel leaves the main road; also offers a delivery and pick-up service at various points between Eriskay and Stornoway.

🛏 Sleeping & Eating

[TOP CHOICE] **Polochar Inn**   INN **££**
(☏01878-700215; www.polocharinn.com; s/d from £60/90; P) Run by local sisters Morag McKinnon and Margaret Campbell, this 18th-century inn has been transformed into a stylish, welcoming hotel with a stunning location looking out across the sea to Barra. The excellent restaurant and bar menu (mains £9 to £19) includes fish chowder, haddock and chips, local salmon and Uist lamb.
Polochar is 7 miles southwest of Lochboisdale, on the way to Eriskay.

Lochboisdale Hotel   HOTEL **££**
(☏01878-700332; www.lochboisdale.com; s/d from £55/100; P) This old-fashioned huntin'-and-fishin' hotel has spacious, modernised rooms, many of which have stunning views across the Minch. The homely lounge bar has a roaring fire in winter, and hosts regular traditional music sessions; it also serves decent bar meals (£9 to £14).

Lochside Cottage   B&B **££**
(☏01878-700472; www.lochside-cottage.co.uk; r per person from £25; P) A friendly B&B, 1.5

miles west of the ferry. Its rooms have views and a sun lounge barely a fishing-rod's length from its own trout loch.

ℹ Getting There & Around
Ferries operate from Lochboisdale to Oban.

Eriskay (Eiriosgaigh)
POP 170
In 1745 Bonnie Prince Charlie first set foot in Scotland on the west coast of Eriskay, on the sandy beach (immediately north of the ferry terminal) still known as **Prince's Strand** (Coilleag a'Phrionnsa).

The SS *Politician* sank just off the island in 1941. Islanders salvaged much of its cargo of around 250,000 bottles of whisky and, after a binge of dramatic proportions, the police landed a number of the islanders in jail. The story was immortalised by Sir Compton Mackenzie in his comic novel *Whisky Galore*, made into a famous film.

A CalMac car ferry links Eriskay with Ardmhor at the northern end of Barra (pedestrian/car £6.70/19.55, 40 minutes, four or five daily).

Barra (Barraigh)
POP 1150
With its beautiful beaches, wildflower-clad dunes, rugged little hills and strong sense of community, diminutive Barra – just 14 miles in circumference – is the Outer Hebrides in miniature. For a great view of the island, walk up to the top of **Heaval** (383m), a mile northeast of Castlebay.

Castlebay (Bagh a'Chaisteil), in the south, is the largest village. There's a tourist office (p200), a bank with an ATM, post office and two grocery stores.

⊙ Sights & Activities
Kisimul Castle   CASTLE
(HS; ☏01871-810313; Castlebay; adult/child incl ferry £4.70/2.80; ⊘9.30am-5.30pm Apr-Sep) Castlebay takes its name from the island fortress of Kisimul Castle, first built by the MacNeil clan in the 11th century. A short boat trip (weather permitting) takes you out to the island, where you can explore the fortifications and soak up the view from the battlements.

The castle was restored in the 20th century by American architect Robert MacNeil, who became the 45th clan chief; he gifted the castle to Historic Scotland in 2000 for an annual rent of £1 and a bottle of whisky (Talisker single malt, if you're interested).

Barra Heritage Centre
HERITAGE CENTRE

(☎01871-810413; www.barraheritage.com; Castlebay; adult/child £2/1; ☺10.30am-4.30pm Mon-Sat May-Aug, 10.30am-4.30pm Mon, Wed & Fri Mar, Apr & Sep) This heritage centre has Gaelic-themed displays about the island, local art exhibitions and a tearoom. It also manages a restored 19th-century thatched cottage, the Black Shieling (adult/child £2/75p; ☺1-4pm Mon-Fri May-Sep), 3 miles north of Castlebay on the west side of the island.

Traigh Mor
BEACH

This vast expanse of firm golden sand (the name means 'Big Strand') serves as Barra's airport (a mile across at low tide, and big enough for three 'runways'), the only beach airport in the world that handles scheduled flights. Watching the little Twin Otter aircraft come and go is a popular spectator sport.

In between flights, locals gather cockles, a local seafood speciality, from the sands.

🛏 Sleeping & Eating

Accommodation on Barra is limited, so make a reservation before committing to a night on the island. Wild camping (on foot or by bike) is allowed almost anywhere; from 2010, campervans and car campers

---

THE EVEN-FURTHER-OUTER HEBRIDES

St Kilda (www.kilda.org.uk) is a collection of spectacular sea stacks and cliff-bound islands about 45 miles west of North Uist. The largest island, Hirta, measures only 2 miles by 1 mile, with huge cliffs along most of its coastline. Owned by National Trust for Scotland (NTS), the islands are a Unesco World Heritage Site and are the biggest seabird nesting site in the North Atlantic. They are home to more than a million birds.

History

Hirta was inhabited by a Gaelic-speaking population of around 200 until the 19th century when the arrival of church missionaries and tourists began the gradual breakdown of St Kilda's traditional way of life. By the 1920s disease and emigration had seen the islands' economy collapse, and the 35 remaining islanders were evacuated, at their own request, in 1930. The people had survived here by keeping sheep, fishing, growing a few basic crops such as barley, and climbing the cliffs barefoot to catch seabirds and collect their eggs. Over the centuries this resulted in a genetic peculiarity – St Kilda men had unusually long big toes.

Visiting St Kilda

The only way to spend more than a couple of hours in the islands is to join one of the two-week NTS work parties that visit St Kilda from mid-May to August. The NTS takes volunteers to do archaeological and conservation work in and around the village ruins – you have to be physically fit and prepared to work up to 36 hours per week. And you have to pay for the privilege – around £750 per person (including transport from Oban in a converted lifeboat and full board in dorm accommodation). To get an application form, send a stamped, self-addressed envelope to St Kilda Work Parties, NTS, Balnain House, 40 Huntly St, Inverness IV3 5HR. The closing date for applications each year is 31 January.

Boat tours to St Kilda are a major undertaking – day trips are 12-hour affairs, involving a minimum three-hour crossing each way, often in rough seas. For a full listing of tour operators, check out the website www.kilda.org.uk. Booking ahead is essential.

Sea Trek
BOAT TOUR

(☎01851-672469; www.seatrek.co.uk; Miavaig Pier) Runs a 12-hour day trip to St Kilda (£180 per person) once or twice weekly, May to September, weather permitting.

Kilda Cruises
BOAT TOUR

(☎01859-502060; www.kildacruises.co.uk) Operates frequent day trips to St Kilda (£180 per person) in summer, as well as customised cruises.

are restricted to official sites – check www.
isleofbarra.com for details.

Castlebay Hotel
HOTEL **££**

(☑01871-810223; www.castlebayhotel.com;
Castlebay; s/d from £60/95; **P**) The recently
refurbished Castlebay Hotel offers spacious
bedrooms decorated with a subtle tartan
motif – it's worth paying a bit extra for a sea
view – and there's a comfy lounge and conservatory with grand views across the harbour to the islands south of Barra.

The hotel bar is the hub of island social
life, with regular sessions of traditional music, and the restaurant specialises in local seafood and game (rabbit is often on the menu).

Dunard Hostel
HOSTEL **£**

(☑01871-810443; www.dunardhostel.co.uk; Castlebay; dm/d from £15/38; **P**) Dunard is a friendly,
family-run hostel just five minutes' walk from
the ferry terminal. The owners organise sea-
kayaking tours for £30/55 a half-/full day.

Faire Mhaoldonaich
B&B **££**

(☑01871-810511; www.fairemhaoldonaich.com;
Nasg; r per person £28-33; ☺Mar-Oct; **P**) This
B&B is a modern house with spacious, com-
fortable rooms and great views over Bagh
Beag to the isle of Mhaoldonaich; it's a mile
west of Castlebay on the road to Vatersay.

ⓘ Getting There & Around

Boat
CalMac offers ferries from Castlebay to Oban
and Lochboisdale (South Uist), and there also
daily flights from Glasgow. A ferry runs from Ardmhor, at the northern end of Barra, to Eriskay.

Bicycle
You can hire bikes from **Island Adventures**
(☑01871-810284; 29 St Brendan's Rd).

Bus
Bus W32 makes a regular circuit of the island
and also connects with flights at the airport.

Pabbay (Pabaidh), Mingulay (Miughalaigh) & Berneray (Bearnaraigh)

These uninhabited islands, gifted to the National Trust for Scotland (NTS) in 2000, are
important breeding sites for seabird species
such as fulmar, black guillemot, common
and Arctic tern, great skua, puffin and storm
petrel. There are boat trips to the islands
from Castlebay, Barra, in settled weather

for around £20 per person; ask at the Barra
tourist office for details. The puffin season
lasts from June to early August.

WALKING IN SKYE & THE WESTERN ISLES

The Quiraing Walk

The landslipped cliffs and pinnacles of the
Quiraing (meaning 'pillared enclosure') are
a compact and easily explored example of
the dramatic landscape features that make
the Trotternish peninsula unique. Generally easy paths give access to the summit of
Meall na Suiramach (543m) with fine views

ⓘ THE QUIRAING WALK

- » **Duration** 2–3 hours
- » **Distance** 3.5 miles (5.6km)
- » **Difficulty** Moderate
- » **Start/Finish** Quiraing road car park
- » **Summary** Explore the weird and
  wonderful pinnacles, crags and bluffs
  at the northern end of the Trotternish
  ridge.

The Quiraing Walk

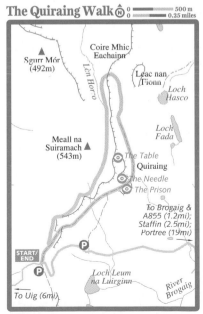

of the surrounding islands, the Applecross hills on the mainland and the towering Trotternish escarpment itself.

The walk starts at a car park at the summit of the Staffin to Uig road (not suitable for caravans or large vehicles), 1.8 miles west of its junction with the A855 at Brogaig, which is about 1 mile northwest of Staffin.

THE WALK

Set out along the well-worn path, signposted to Flodigarry. Follow it for 200 metres to the first **burn crossing** then strike up north and northeast across country to a grassed stone wall. Follow the wall northeast for a few hundred metres until it disappears, then zigzag up the steep slope to find a clear path leading northeast across the hillside. Wet in places, it leads into a wide, shallow and grassy **glen**; go through a gate in the fence here (35 minutes from the start).

Continue northeast up the slope. About 10 minutes further on, the path swings north to parallel the cliff edge. From the nearby rim there's a fantastic view down into the heart of the Quiraing and a series of flat-topped grassy plateaus between the cliff and a row of massive bluffs (the largest of these is the Table, which you can only reach from below, described later).

Continue past a cairn (the summit of Meall na Suiramach is further west) with fine views of the many offshore islands and the distant Western Isles. Keeping close to the edge, start to descend (15 minutes from the gate) and you'll soon reach a **large cairn**. A clear path descends north near the edge of the outer cliff line, down to a small saddle and a break in the cliffs.

Climb a stile and go down a steep, sunken zigzag path to begin the passage back south through the Quiraing, with towering black cliffs on the one hand and a jumble of crags and pinnacles on the other. Cross a stone wall and suddenly there's nothing but space on your left! Soon though there's solid ground close by as the path leads up the glen, past a lochan and up to a small saddle. Here, flat-topped Dun Caan on Raasay, and the Trotternish ridge come into view.

Descend steeply into the heart of the Quiraing. To your left is the **Prison**, a jumble of towers, blocks and pinnacles. High up to the right is the **Needle**, a huge, lopsided pinnacle. The adventurous (and sure-footed) can scramble up to the left of the Needle, and along a deep gully to find a

hidden, grass-topped plateau, known as the **Table**. Legend has it that stolen cattle were once hidden here, and a shinty match was played on the level turf to celebrate the end of WWI.

Retrace your steps to the main path, pass a large cairn and make your way carefully down a scree slope. The well-used path, subject to rock falls and even partial collapse in places, demands respect. Cross a **small gully**, where you need to use your hands, and continue on to the car park (40 minutes from the large cairn).

Eaval Walk

Eaval (347m) – the highest point on North Uist – was sometimes featured on the route of the Hebridean Challenge, an annual team marathon from Barra to Lewis, involving running, cycling and kayaking, that ran from 2001 to 2009. Consequently, there's a clear, if often muddy, path all the way from the end of the Locheport road at Drim Sidinish (Druim Saighdinis) to the top. It might not be particularly high, but the summit affords outstanding views both near and far. The unavoidable causeway not far from the start should be dry except after heavy rain and at very high tide. The walk described here involves 350m of ascent and is a simple out-and-back route.

The name Eaval, from two Norse words *ey fjall,* meaning 'island fell' or 'hill', accurately describes its situation. With the waters of Loch Obisary (Obasaraigh) and several smaller lochs on three sides, and Loch Eport (Euphort) and the open sea nearby, Eaval is almost surrounded by water. Rising steeply on all sides, it dominates the southeastern corner of North Uist.

With suitable transport arrangements, a through walk is possible, descending south-

---

ℹ️ EAVAL WALK

» **Duration** 3½–4 hours

» **Distance** 8 miles (13km)

» **Difficulty** Moderate

» **Start/Finish** Drim Sidinish

» **Summary** The highest peak in North Uist gives a superb panoramic view of the maze of lochans and land that comprise the Uists, and as far south as the Isle of Rum.

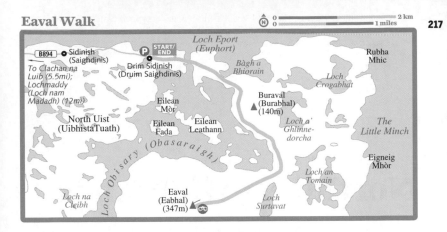

west from the summit to the shore of the narrow strait between North Uist and Grimsay. You can then work your way around the long, deep inlet of Oban nam Muca-mara and finally head cross-country to the end of a minor road at Cladach Chairinis, which is about a mile from the A865.

PLANNING

The walk starts from a parking area at the end of the B894, which branches off the A867 0.5 miles northeast of the A867/A865 junction at Clachan na Luib, or 6.7 miles southwest along the A867 from its junction with the A865 near Lochmaddy. The road end is 5 miles from the A867.

Eaval is on the OS Landranger 1:50,000 map No 22 *Benbecula & South Uist;* the adjoining map to the north, No 18 *Sound of Harris & St Kilda,* is useful for orientation and identification of local landmarks. Alternatively, use OS Explorer 1:25,000 map No 454 *North Uist & Benbecula.*

THE WALK

From the car park go through a gate beside the nearby cottage. Cross a field, through another gate then follow an old track leading down to a **small cove** with an old stone pier on Loch Eport. Head east on a grass track to a larger cove, with a ruined cottage on the far shore, and on to a **boulder causeway**. From here continue southeast towards the prominent bulk of Buraval (Burabhal). A path, easy to follow most of the way, leads above the very convoluted shores of Loch Obisary and across the lowermost slopes of Buraval.

Cross the boggy ground between the northern end of Loch Surtavat and the corner of Loch Obisary to the foot of Eaval's northeast ridge. Broad ribs of rock make for a surprisingly easy, although consistently steep, climb. About two hours from the start you should reach the trig point on the **summit of Eaval**. The panoramic vista takes in an extraordinary range of features – the north Harris 'hills', the Cuillin Hills on Skye and an incredible mosaic of rock, grass, water and scattered houses.

On the return it's much easier to pick the best route than it was on the way up; continue around Loch Obisary and back to the start (about 1½ hours from the summit).

SKYE & THE WESTERN ISLES EAVAL WALK

Northwest Highlands

Best Places to Eat

» The Albannach (p249)
» Captain's Galley (p238)
» Plockton Shores (p263)
» Badachro Inn (p259)
» Shorehouse Seafood
Restaurant (p247)

Best Places to Stay

» Mackays (p242)
» The Torridon (p261)
» Summer Isles Hotel (p253)
» Ceilidh Place (p255)
» Applecross Inn (p262)

Why Go?

Scotland's vast and melancholy soul is here: an epic land whose stark beauty leaves an indelible imprint on the hearts of those who journey through. Mist and mountains, rock and heather, and long, sun-blessed summer evenings are the payoff for so many days of horizontal rain. It is magical.

Stone tells stories throughout. The chambered cairns of Caithness and the brochs of Suthlerland are testament to the skills of prehistoric builders; cragtop castles and the broken walls of abandoned crofts tell of the Highlands' turbulent history.

Outdoors is the place to be, whatever the weather; there's nothing like comparing windburn or mud-ruined boots over a well-deserved dram by the crackling fire of a Highland pub. The landscape lends itself to activity, from woodland strolls to thrilling mountain-bike descents, from sea-kayaking to Munro-bagging, from beachcombing to birdwatching. Best are the locals, big-hearted and straight-talking; make it your business to get to know them.

When to Go
Ullapool

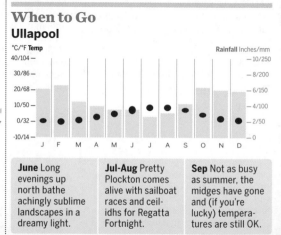

June Long evenings up north bathe achingly sublime landscapes in a dreamy light.

Jul-Aug Pretty Plockton comes alive with sailboat races and ceilidhs for Regatta Fortnight.

Sep Not as busy as summer, the midges have gone and (if you're lucky) temperatures are still OK.

EAST COAST

In both landscape and character, the east coast of the old counties of Ross and Sutherland is where the real wilderness of the Highlands begins to unfold. A mounting splendour and a feeling of escapism mark the route along the twisting A9, as it heads north for the last of Scotland's far-flung, mainland population outposts. With only a few exceptions the tourism frenzy is left behind once the road traverses Cromarty Firth and begins to snake its way along the wild and pristine coastline.

While the interior is dominated by the mournful moor-and-mountain landscapes of Sutherland, along the coast great heather-covered hills heave themselves out of the wild North Sea. Rolling farmland drops suddenly into the icy waters, and small, historic towns are moored precariously on the coast's edge.

Black Isle

The Black Isle – a peninsula rather than an island – is linked to Inverness by the Kessock Bridge. The villages of Avoch, Fortrose and Rosemarkie run along the peninsula's southern side.

The pretty village of Cromarty (pop 720) at the northeastern tip of the Black Isle has lots of 18th-century red-sandstone houses, and a lovely green park beside the sea for picnics and games. An excellent walk, known as the 100 Steps, leads from the north end of the village to the headland viewpoint of South Sutor (4 miles round trip).

⊙ Sights & Activities

Black Isle Wildlife Park   WILDLIFE PARK
(☏01463 731656; www.blackislewildlifepark.co.uk; North Kessock; adult/child £7.50/5.50; ⊙10am-6pm daily Apr-Oct; 🛈) Just north of the Kessock Bridge, this landscaped wildlife park has families of zebra, lemurs, and everybody's favourite – meerkats. There are also goat kids, lambs, baby rabbits and other animals you can pet.

Black Isle Brewery   BREWERY
(☏01463-811871; www.blackislebrewery.com; Old Allangrange, Munlochy; admission free; ⊙10am-6pm Mon-Sat, 11.30am-5pm Sun Apr-Sep) One of Britain's best artisan breweries, which has won many awards for its organically produced ales. Try a glass of Yellowhammer, a light, hoppy and refreshing bitter, or the strong, flowery Heather Honey Beer. Just north of the Kessock Bridge.

Clootie Well   SHRINE
Not far from the A9, on the road to Fortrose near Munlochy, the Clootie Well is an ancient shrine to St Boniface. Local people still come here to tie a cloot (piece of cloth) to the nearby tree and make a wish.

CROMARTY

Cromarty Courthouse   MUSEUM
(☏01381-600418; www.cromarty-courthouse.org.uk; Church St, Cromarty; adult/child £2/free; ⊙11am-4pm Apr-Sep) This 18th-century courthouse is now a museum chronicling the town's history using contemporary references. Kids will love the talking mannequins.

Hugh Miller's Cottage & Museum   MUSEUM
(Church St, Cromarty; adult/child £5.50/4.50; ⊙1-5pm Sun-Wed May-Sep) Hugh Miller's Cottage is the thatch-roofed birthplace of Hugh Miller (1802–56), a local stonemason and amateur geologist who later moved to Edinburgh and became a famous journalist and newspaper editor. The Georgian villa next door is home to a museum celebrating his life and achievements.

Ecoventures   WILDLIFE CRUISES
(☏01381-600323; www.ecoventures.co.uk; Cromarty Harbour, Cromarty; adult/child £22/16) Ecoventures runs 2½-hour boat trips from Cromarty harbour into the Moray Firth to see bottlenose dolphins and other wildlife.

FORTROSE & ROSEMARKIE

Fortrose Cathedral   HISTORIC SITE
At Fortrose Cathedral you'll find the vaulted crypt of a 13th-century chapter house and sacristy, and the ruinous 14th-century south aisle and chapel.

Dolphin Trips Avoch   WILDLIFE CRUISES
(www.dolphintripsavoch.co.uk; Avoch; adult/child £12/8) Chanonry Point, 1.5 miles east of Fortrose, is a favourite dolphin-spotting vantage point. One-hour dolphin-watching cruises depart from the harbour at Avoch (pronounced 'auch'), 3 miles southwest of Fortrose.

Groam House Museum   MUSEUM
(☏01381-620961; www.groamhouse.org.uk; High St, Rosemarkie; admission by donation; ⊙10am-5pm Mon-Sat, 2-4.30pm Sun May-Oct, 2-4pm Sat & Sun Apr & Nov) This museum in Rosemarkie has a superb collection of Pictish stones engraved with designs similar to those on Celtic Irish stones.

Northwest Highlands Highlights

1 Gorge on succulent seafood in the picture postcard village of **Plockton** (p262)

2 On a road trip from Durness to Ullapool, marvel at the epic **mountain scenery** (p244)

3 Venture out to, Britain's gloriously remote northwestern shoulder, **Cape Wrath** (p243)

4 Pack a picnic and hike to the remote and beautiful beach at **Sandwood Bay** (p264)

5 Make the long but rewarding climb to the magnificently isolated summit of **Suilven** (p249)

6 Wander the opulent halls of the Duke of Sutherland's **Dunrobin Castle** (p229)

7 Cast a fly on one of Assynt and Coigach's countless **trout lochs** (p248)

8 Take a boat trip to the bird-haunted seacliffs and stacks of **Handa Island** (p247)

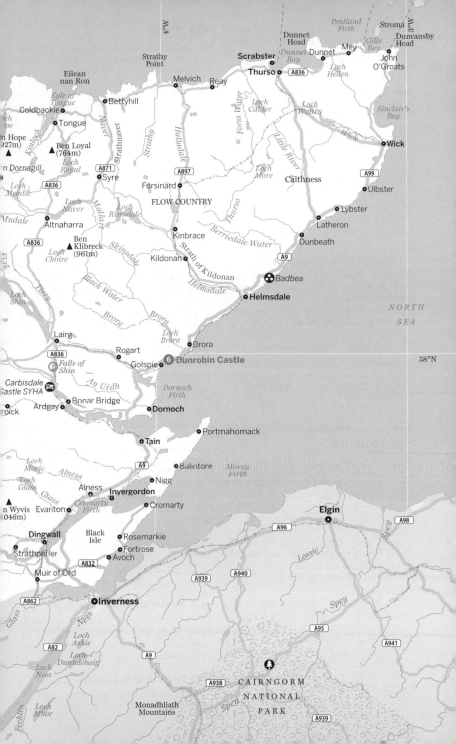

Fairy Glen

WALKING

(Rosemarkie) From the northern end of Rosemarkie's High St, a short but pleasant signposted walk leads you through the gorges and waterfalls of the Fairy Glen.

✗ Eating & Drinking

For something lighter, there's delicious filled rolls and savoury pies at the **Cromarty Bakery** (8 Bank St, Cromarty; ⊙9am-5pm Mon-Sat).

Sutor Creek

SEAFOOD, PIZZA ££

(✆01381-600855; www.sutorcreek.co.uk; 21 Bank St, Cromarty; mains £10-15; ⊙11am-9pm Wed-Sun) This is an excellent little cafe-restaurant serving wood-fired pizzas and fresh local seafood – we can recommend the Cromarty langoustines with garlic and chilli butter.

Anderson Hotel

PUB

(✆01381-620236; www.theanderson.co.uk; Union St, Fortrose) Once you've worked up a thirst, retire to the bar at the Anderson Hotel to sample its range of real ales (including Belgian beers and Somerset cider) and more than 200 single-malt whiskies.

ℹ Getting There & Away

Stagecoach (www.stagecoachbus.com) Buses 26 and 26A run from Inverness to Fortrose and Rosemarkie (30 to 40 minutes, twice hourly Monday to Saturday); half of them continue to Cromarty (one hour).

Strathpeffer

POP 918

Strathpeffer is a charming old Highland spa town, its creaking pavilions and grandiose hotels dripping with faded grandeur. The spa rose to prominence during Victorian times, when fashion-conscious gentlemen and ladies flocked here in huge numbers to bathe in, wash with and drink the sulphurous waters from the Morrison Well. The influx of tourists led to the construction of some grand Victorian buildings and architectural follies.

The 'Harrogate of the North' slipped into genteel decay after WWII, and the old spa baths were demolished in 1950. But in the last decade or so there's been a revival of interest in the spa's history and architecture, with the original Pump Room open to the public and the spa pavilion renovated as a tearoom and restaurant.

◉ Sights

The **Eagle Stone** (follow the signs from the main drag) is well worth a look when you're in town. It's a pre-7th-century Pictish stone connected to a figure from local history – the Brahan Seer, who predicted many future events.

Highland Museum of Childhood

MUSEUM

(✆01997-421031; www.highlandmuseumofchildhood .org.uk; Old Train Station; adult/child £2.50/1.50; ⊙10am-5pm Mon-Sat, 2-5pm Sun Apr-Oct) Strathpeffer's former Victorian train station houses a wide range of social-history displays about childhood in the Highlands, and also has activities for children, including a dressing-up box and a toy train. There's a good gift shop if you're after a present for a little somebody, and a peaceful cafe.

Pump Room

HEALTH RESORT

(✆01997-421415; Golf Course Rd; ⊙10am-5pm Tue-Sat, Jun-Sep) The renovated Pump Room has some splendid displays showing the bizarre lengths Victorians went to in the quest for a healthy glow. If you dare, you can sample the waters yourself; the chalybeate (iron-rich) spring water is delicious, but the sulphurous Morrison Well water is for strong stomachs only.

🏃 Activities

There are many good **walking trails** around Strathpeffer, a legacy of the days when brisk exercise was prescribed as part of the treatment for spa patients. One of the best follows the old carriage drive up to the remains of an Iron-Age fort on Knock Farrel (4½ miles, two hours). On the way back you can detour to the **Touchstone Maze**, a modern construction of 81 stones representing the various types of rock found in Scotland.

Golfers should head to the 18-hole **Strathpeffer Spa Golf Club** (✆01997-421219; www .strathpeffergolf.co.uk/visitors; green fees £20-30) on the hill above town; there are grand views from here to Ben Wyvis (1046m).

🎊 Festivals & Events

The **Strathpeffer & District Pipe Band** plays in the town square every Saturday from 8pm, May to September. There's also Highland dancing and a festive air.

🛏 Sleeping & Eating

There are a couple of large hotels in town geared to coach tours but no hostel.

Craigvar

B&B ££

(📞01997-421622; www.craigvar.com; The Square; s/d £50/80; P🛜) Luxury living with a refined touch is what you'll find in this delightful Georgian townhouse. All the little extras that mark out a classy place are here, such as a welcome drink, bathrobes and fresh fruit. Couples should go for the 'Blue Room' with its sensational four-poster bed – you'll need to collapse back into it after the gourmet breakfast.

Coul House Hotel

HOTEL £££

(📞01997-421487; www.coulhousehotel.com; s/d £85/155; P🛜) At Contin, south of Strathpeffer on the A835, Coul House is a fine country mansion dating from 1821. Set in its own private wilderness, this charming country hotel with blazing log fire will entice you to linger. Luxury rooms enjoy mountain views and four-poster beds. Its restaurant is open for dinner and serves eclectic, modern fusion cuisine; everything's delicious.

Maya

CAFE £

(📞01997-420008; www.mayachocolates.co.uk; Main St; box of chocolates from £2.50; ⏰10am-5pm Tue-Sat) Ohhh, this place is dangerous. Bringing Belgian chocolates to the Highlands, Maya is the ultimate in sweet indulgence. It also serves up hot drinks, including hot chocolate...which goes perfectly with a box of chocolates.

Red Poppy

INTERNATIONAL ££

(📞01997-423332; www.redpoppyrestaurant.co.uk; The Pavilion; mains £8-13; ⏰noon-8pm Tue-Sat, lunch Sun) In the restored historical Victorian spa pavilion is a much-needed dining option in town. There's a large selection of meals, including game dishes such as wild-boar steaks, and the dining is in elegant surrounds. It's a little cheaper at lunchtime.

ℹ️ Information

The self-service **tourist office** (📞01997-421415; Golf Course Rd; ⏰10am-5pm Tue-Sat Jun-Sep) is in the Pump Room and has limited info. The bike shop on the square is good for information, too.

ℹ️ Getting There & Around

BUS Stagecoach operates buses from Inverness to Strathpeffer (45 minutes, at least hourly Monday to Saturday, four on Sunday). The Inverness to Gairloch and Durness buses, plus some Inverness to Ullapool buses, also run via Strathpeffer.

BICYCLE Square Wheels Cycles (📞01997-421000; www.squarewheels.bizcom; The Square; ⏰10am-6pm Thu-Mon) Hires out mountain bikes for £10/15 per half-/full day; prices decrease with multiday hire. Staff can help with route information.

Ben Wyvis & Around

The easily accessible Munro of Ben Wyvis (1046m) looms to the northwest of Strathpeffer (the name Wyvis derives from a Gaelic word meaning 'enormous'). The mountain's eastern corries hold snow for much of the year, fortunately for the ancient Munro clan of Foulis Castle – their lands were granted on the condition that they paid the king the rent of one snowball in midsummer.

The peak is usually climbed from Garbat, to the west of Strathpeffer on the A835 to Ullapool. The hike to the summit is straightforward in summer, and takes about five hours return from Garbat; use OS map No 20 and carry plenty of food and drinking water (there's no ground-water on the hill). Stout footwear is essential as some of the tracks through the forestry can be extremely wet.

🛏️ Sleeping & Eating

Inchbae Lodge Guesthouse

B&B ££

(📞01997-455269; www.inchbae.co.uk; Garve; s/d £42/67) Just a mile from the start of the Ben Wyvis trail, the Inchbae Lodge Guesthouse offers cosy B&B accommodation (including one bedroom with a four-poster bed), as well as a residents lounge with leather sofas and an open fire, and a bar that serves real ale and excellent bar meals.

Aultguish Inn

B&B ££

(📞01997-455254; www.aultguish.co.uk; Aultguish; s/d from £50/85, bunkhouse per person £18; P) Located on the road to Ullapool just below the Glascarnoch dam, the friendly and recently renovated Aultguish Inn offers a choice between comfortable, modern pine-panelled bedrooms, or more basic hikers' accommodation in the adjacent bunkhouse.

ℹ️ Getting There & Away

Trains from Inverness to Kyle of Lochalsh stop at Garve (4 miles south of Garbat), while buses between Inverness and Ullapool can drop you at Garbat.

Dingwall

Dingwall is an unremarkable small Highland town, dominated by a hilltop **monument** to the impressively named Major-General Sir Hector Archibald MacDonald (better known as 'Fighting Mac'). Fighting Mac was the son of a local crofter who rose through the ranks of the British Army to become a hero of the Boer War. Macbeth is believed to have been born at **Dingwall Castle**, but little of the building remains today except a doocot (dove-cote) on Castle St, built from scavenged stones.

Lovers of pop music trivia might like to know that the Beatles played Dingwall Town Hall in January 1963 – to an audience of 19 (everyone had gone to hear local band, the Melotones, at Strathpeffer).

The displays at **Dingwall Museum** (☎01349-865366; www.dingwallmuseum.co.uk; Town House, High St; admission free; ☷10am-4.30pm Mon-Fri & to 4pm Sat mid-May–Sep) include reconstructions of a local blacksmith's workshop and an Edwardian kitchen, and there's an exhibit celebrating the military career of Fighting Mac.

The town has plenty of shops and services, including a **farmers market** held in the pedestrianised High St (second Saturday of each month).

Cromarty Firth

North of Dingwall the A9 follows the northern shore of the Cromarty Firth, a long narrow inlet of the sea fringed by maritime villages. Its sheltered waters provide safe haven for North Sea oil drilling rigs, whose towering derricks often dominate the view from the road – Nigg, near the entrance to the firth, is a major oil-rig repair yard.

Surrounded by towering hills, the tiny village of **Evanton** is the starting point for an excellent walk to the **Black Rock of Novar**, a very deep and narrow gorge leading up to Loch Glass. The mile-long chasm, which was cut by glacial melt waters at the end of the last Ice Age, is rarely more than 3.5m wide, but in places is more than 30m deep; a local man is said to have leapt it in a single bound (which would make for one of the longest standing jumps in history!). An information board in the village car park describes the

THE BRAHAN SEER

Còinneach Odhar, better known as the Brahan Seer, was Scotland's answer to Nostradamus. Legend has it that he gained his mystical powers after falling asleep in an enchanted glade, and was able to see the future by peering through a hole in a magical stone. His origins – and even whether he existed at all – are hotly debated, but he is said to have lived near Loch Ussie (between Strathpeffer and Dingwall) in the 17th century, working as a labourer on the Brahan Castle estate.

Like Nostradamus, the Brahan Seer is credited with a string of seemingly accurate predictions about the future. Amongst other things, he foresaw the Highland Clearances ('the clans will flee their native country before an army of sheep'), steam railways ('great black, bridleless horses, belching fire and steam, drawing lines of carriages through the glens'), the construction of the Caledonian Canal ('ships will sail round the back of Tomnahurich Hill') and North Sea oil ('a black rain will bring riches to Aberdeen'). His claim that a terrible disaster would befall the world when the River Ness could be crossed 'dryshod' in five places came true when the fifth bridge across the river was completed just days before the outbreak of WWII.

In 1660, the Countess of Seaforth summoned the Seer to her seat at Brahan Castle in order to discover what her husband, the earl, was up to while 'on business' in France. She flew into a rage on being informed that the earl had another woman on his lap and, accusing the Seer of slander, ordered him to be burned alive in a barrel of tar at Chanonry Point near Fortrose. A stone slab by the lighthouse there marks the spot.

The Seer left a parting prophecy of doom upon the Seaforth clan, predicting that the reign of the Seaforths at Brahan Castle would end with a 'deaf and dumb' chief who would follow his four heirs to the grave. The prophesy came true in 1793, when the Seaforth title passed to Francis Humberston MacKenzie, who lost both hearing and speech after contracting scarlet fever as a child – and who survived the deaths of his four sons.

route to the gorge (2.5 miles round trip), where a footbridge allows you to peer down into its dank and moss-draped depths.

Near the start of the walk, **Black Rock Caravan Park** (☑01349-830917; www.blackrock scotland.co.uk; tent site £8-12, dm £12-14; ☺Apr-Oct) offers backpacker accommodation in a 17-bed bunkhouse, as well as tent and caravan pitches in an attractive riverside setting.

A couple of miles north of Evanton is **Alness**, where you'll find the friendly little **Dalmore Distillery** (☑01349-882362; www .thedalmore.com; ☺11am-5pm Mon-Fri Apr-Oct, to 3pm Nov-Mar), which can arrange free tours if you book in advance. Dalmore is famous for possessing some of the oldest malt whiskies in the world, including 40- and 64-year-old malts, and stocks of spirits that were distilled more than a hundred years ago.

On a hilltop just west of Alness, the Scottish military hero Sir Hector Munro commemorated his most notable victory – the capture of the Indian town of Negapatam from the Dutch in 1781 – by erecting the **Fyrish Monument**. This curious triple arch, thought to be a representation of the Negapatam city gate, is reached by a steep footpath through the woods. If you're coming by car, turn towards Boath off the B9176 just west of Alness.

Tain & Around

POP 3511

Scotland's oldest royal burgh, Tain is a proud sandstone town that rose to prominence as pilgrims descended to venerate the relics of St Duthac, who is commemorated by the 12th-century ruins of **St Duthac's Chapel**, and St Duthus Church.

Collectively known as the **Seaboard Villages**, the tiny settlements of Balintore, Shandwick and Hilton of Cadboll to the east of Tain have a rich Pictish heritage, including a fine standing **Pictish stone** at Shandwick village. The stone is covered by a glass conservatory to protect the carvings, which include some fearsome depictions of mythical beasts.

A few miles farther south is the tiny village of **Nigg**, overlooking sandy Nigg Bay. The old parish church here contains another intricately carved **Pictish cross-slab**, featuring carvings of St Anthony and St Paul in the desert.

◉ Sights

Tain Through Time   HERITAGE CENTRE
(☑01862-894089; www.tainmuseum.org.uk; Tower St; adult/child £3.50/2.50; ☺10am-5pm Mon-Sat Apr-Oct) Set in the grounds of St Duthus Church is Tain Through Time, an entertaining heritage centre with a colourful and educational display on St Duthac, King James IV and key moments in Scottish history. Another building focuses on the town's fine silversmithing tradition. Admission includes an audio-guided walk around town.

Glenmorangie Distillery   DISTILLERY
(www.glenmorangie.com; tours £2.50; ☺9am-5pm Mon-Fri, plus 10am-4pm Sat & Sun Jun-Aug) Located on Tain's northern outskirts, the friendly distillery Glenmorangie (emphasis on the second syllable) produces a fine light malt, which is subjected to a number of different cask finishes for variation. The tour is less in-depth than some but finishes with a free dram.

🛏 Sleeping & Eating

Royal Hotel   HOTEL ££
(☑01862-892013; www.royalhoteltain.co.uk; High St; s/d £50/85; ☻) So much the heart of town that the main street has to detour around it, the Royal Hotel has undergone a refurbishment that has left its good-sized rooms looking very spruce. For only a tenner more, you get a four-poster room in the old part of the hotel; these have a choice of colour schemes, and are well worth the upgrade.

The **restaurant** is the best in town and bar meals are also decent.

Golf View House   B&B ££
(☑01862-892856; www.golf-view.co.uk; 13 Knockbreck Rd; s £35-50, d £54-72; ℗) Elegant B&B is available at Golf View House, set in an old manse in a secluded location. Rooms are bright, and a couple have views of the sea. Breakfast is delicious, and hospitality excellent.

❶ Getting There & Away

BUS Scottish Citylink (p156) and Stagecoach (p367) buses from Inverness to Thurso pass through Tain several times daily (£8.50, 50 minutes to 1¼ hours, five daily).

TRAIN There are up to three trains daily to Inverness (£11.20, one hour) and Thurso (£13.70, 2½ hours).

PICTISH SYMBOL STONES

The mysterious carved stones that dot the landscape of northeastern Scotland are the legacy of the warrior tribes who inhabited these lands 2000 years ago. The Romans occupied the southern half of Britain from AD 43 to 410, but the region to the north of the firths of Forth and Clyde – known as Caledonia – was abandoned as being too dangerous, sealed off behind the ramparts of the Antonine Wall and Hadrian's Wall.

Caledonia was the homeland of the Picts, a collection of tribes named by the Romans for their habit of painting or tattooing their bodies. In the 9th century they were culturally absorbed by the Scots, leaving behind only a few archaeological remains, a scattering of Pictish place names beginning with 'Pit', and hundreds of mysterious carved stones decorated with intricate symbols, mainly in northeast Scotland. The capital of the ancient Southern Pictish kingdom is said to have been at Forteviot in Strathearn, but Pictish symbol stones are to be found all the way up the eastern coast of Scotland into Easter Ross, Sutherland and Caithness.

It's thought that the stones were set up to record Pictish lineages and alliances, but no one is sure exactly how the system worked. They dramatically show the demise of pagan worship in Scotland. The earliest stones, known as Class I (6th to 8th century AD), are rough-hewn blocks carved with pagan symbols of snakes, fish, boar and mythical beasts, and the strange abstract symbols known as Z-rods (lightning bolt?), circles (the sun?), double discs (hand mirror?) and fantastical creatures, as well as figures of warriors on horseback and hunting scenes.

During the 8th century, coinciding with the cultural dominance of the Dalriada kings, Class II stones (8th to 9th century) began to appear, featuring both pagan symbols and Celtic Christian crosses. Some later had their pagan symbols savagely defaced. By the close of the 8th century, the pagan symbols had vanished, and the neat slabs of Class III (9th century) stones feature just carved Celtic crosses and human figures, backed by distinctive Celtic knotwork.

There are Pictish stones right across northeastern and northern Scotland, including many in their original locations in Caithness, Sutherland and the Black Isle. There are also several impressive stones on display in Inverness Museum (p149), Tain Through Time (p225) and Tarbat Discovery Centre (p226).

Portmahomack

POP 650

Portmahomack is a former fishing village in a flawless spot – right off the beaten track and gazing across the water at snowcapped peaks. The best place to enjoy the town is the grassy foreshore at the far end of Main St, near the little harbour.

The intriguing **Tarbat Discovery Centre** (☑01862-871351; www.tarbat-discovery.co.uk; Tarbatness Rd; adult/child £3.50/1; ☺10am-5pm May-Sep, 2-5pm Apr & Oct) has some excellent carved Pictish stones. When 'crop circles' appeared in aerial photos a few years ago, the foundations of an Iron Age settlement were discovered around the village church; ongoing investigation revealed a Pictish monastery and evidence of production of illuminated manuscripts. The exhibition is excellent and includes the church's spooky crypt. Ask staff to pinpoint other Pictish sites in the region on a map for you.

There are good coastal walks at **Tarbat Ness**, 3 miles northeast of the village; the headland is marked by a tall, red-and-white-striped lighthouse.

Seafood aficionados shouldn't miss the bright and cheerful **Oystercatcher Restaurant** (☑01862-871560; www.the-oystercatcher .co.uk; Main St; lunch mains £8-14, dinner mains £15-20; ☺lunch Wed-Sun, dinner Wed-Sat Apr-Oct). There's a bistro menu at lunchtime, where you can choose your serving size, and a classy brasserie evening menu with lots of lobster available among other delights. It also offers three cosy **rooms** (s/d £43/98). The rate includes what has to be the most amazing breakfast in Scotland, with numerous gourmet options – you can book it even if you're not staying there overnight (£20).

Stagecoach Inverness (p367) runs from Tain to Portmahomack (25 minutes, four to five Monday to Friday).

Bonar Bridge & Around

The A9 crosses the Dornoch Firth, on a bridge and causeway, near Tain. An alternative route goes around the firth via the tiny settlements of Ardgay, where you'll find a train station, shop and hotel, and Bonar Bridge, where the A836 to Lairg branches west.

◎ Sights & Activities

Croick   HISTORIC SITE
From Ardgay, a single-track road leads 10 miles up Strathcarron to Croick, the scene of notorious evictions during the 1845 Clearances. You can still see the evocative messages scratched by refugee crofters from Glencalvie on the eastern windows of **Croick Church**.

Kyle of Sutherland Trails   MOUNTAIN BIKING
(☎01408 634063; www.forestry.gov.uk/cyclenorth highland) Mountain bikers will find two networks of forest trails around Bonar Bridge. From the car park below the Carbisdale Castle hostel, there's a red and a blue trail (suitable for intermediate riders) with great views. At Balblair, a mile from Bonar Bridge off the Lairg road, 7 miles of black track will test expert bikers.

⌸ Sleeping

Carbisdale Castle SYHA   HOSTEL £
(☎01549-421232; www.syha.org.uk; dm/s/d £20/25/50; ☺mid-Mar–Oct; P@☎⚗) If a youth hostel could attract a five star rat-

ing, Carbisdale Castle would score six. The castle, 10 minutes' walk north of Culrain train station, was built in 1914 for the dowager duchess of Sutherland, but is now Scotland's biggest and most luxurious hostel, its halls studded with statues and dripping with opulence (advance bookings are highly recommended).

Kick back in the super-elegant library room or cook up a feast in the kitchen; catered meals (£11.50 for a three-course dinner) are also available. Mountain bikers coming off the trails can shower here for a small fee.

❶ Getting There & Away

Trains running from Inverness to Thurso stop at Culrain (£13.50, 1½ hours, two to three daily), half a mile from Carbisdale Castle.

Lairg

POP 900
Lairg is an attractive village, although the tranquillity can be rudely interrupted by the sound of military jets roaring overhead (the Loch Shin valley is frequently used by the RAF for low-flying exercises). Located at the southern end of Loch Shin, it's the gateway to the remote mountains and loch-speckled bogs of central Sutherland.

In **Ferrycroft Visitor Centre** (☎01549-402160; www.highland.gov.uk/ferrycroft; ☺10am-4pm Apr-Oct; @), across the river from the town centre, you'll find displays on local history, and a tourist information desk. The

---

THE HIGHLANDS' JURASSIC PARK

In a pristine spot near Croick a revolutionary project is changing the concept of wildlife conservation in Scotland. **Alladale Wilderness Lodge & Reserve** (☎01863-755338; www.alladale.com), home to the country's most northerly tuft of ancient Scots pine forest, is releasing species once extinct in Britain to roam on its vast estate. Wildlife on the reserve now includes elk, red deer, roe deer, wild boar, wild ponies and golden eagles. Longer-term plans include European bison and former predators, once abundant in Scotland, such as grey wolves, European brown bears and Eurasian lynx. There's plenty of local controversy over the project, with questions of public access and zoo licences being raised.

You can stay in the lodge, but it's for entire hire only, so you'd want a group of 10 or more. Smaller buildings accommodate up to four – rates start at around £600 per night, including full board. Call the lodge or see the website for details. Though broader public access for activities like pony trekking and wildlife tours of the enclosed estate is planned, at time of research there was public access only on a few fixed dates throughout the summer: check the website for details.

Alladale is off the Croick road beyond Ardgay, where you can drop into **Alladale Country Stores** (☎01863-766323; ☺9am-5pm Mon-Sat, 10am-4pm Sun) for information.

Ord Hut Circles & Chambered Cairns, a collection of prehistoric cairns and round-houses, lie a short walk west of the visitor centre.

Scenic drives that begin from Lairg (all on singletrack roads) include the lonely A836 to Tongue via Altnaharra, passing the isolated Munro of **Ben Klibreck** (961m) and the beautiful miniature mountain range of **Ben Loyal** (764m); and the A838 to Laxford Bridge along the shores of Loch Shin and the truly remote lochs Merkland and More (good fishing for brown trout and Arctic char). The A837 to Ledmore Junction climbs across the bleak moors at the head of Strath Oykel, but rewards you with a stunning view of the Matterhorn-like eastern peak of Suilven.

Rooms are surprisingly modern and very good value at the solid **Lairg Highland Hotel** (☎01549-402243; www.highland-hotel.co.uk; Main St; s/d £39/78; ᴘ⬚). The decor is bright, en suites are sparkling and the inn caters for solo travellers. The restaurant is open for lunch and dinner (£10 to £14) and bar meals are also available (£7 to £9).

Trains from Inverness to Thurso stop at Lairg (£13.50, 1¾ hours) two or three times daily in each direction. There are no direct buses from Inverness; change at Tain.

Dornoch

POP 1206

On the north shore of the Dornoch Firth, about 2 miles from the A9, this attractive old market town is one of the most pleasant settlements on the east coast. Dornoch is best known for its championship **golf course**, but there are some fine old buildings, including Dornoch Cathedral. Among other historical oddities, the last witch to be executed in Scotland was boiled alive in hot tar in Dornoch in 1722.

◉ Sights

If you've struck Dornoch on a sunny day make sure you have a walk along its golden sand **beach**, which stretches for miles. South of Dornoch, **seals** are often visible on the sand bars of Dornoch Firth.

FREE **Dornoch Cathedral**   CATHEDRAL
(www.dornoch-cathedral.com; St Gilbert St; ⊙10am-7pm or later) Consecrated in the 13th century, Dornoch Cathedral is an elegant Gothic edifice with an interior softly illuminated through modern stained-glass windows. It was restored in the late 1830s thanks to the generosity of Elizabeth, duchess-countess of Sutherland, whose husband – the controversial first duke of Sutherland – lies in a sealed burial vault beneath the chancel.

By the western door is the sarcophagus of Sir Richard de Moravia, who died fighting the Danes at the battle of Embo in the 1260s. Until he met his maker, the battle had been going rather well for him; he'd managed to slay the Danish commander with the unattached leg of a horse that was to hand.

Historylinks   MUSEUM
(www.historylinks.org.uk; The Meadows; adult/child £2/free; ⊙10am-4pm daily Jun-Sep, Mon-Fri Apr, May & Oct, Wed-Thu only Nov-Mar) Historylinks

---

WORTH A TRIP

FALLS OF SHIN

Four miles south of Lairg, in Achany Glen, the River Shin tumbles over the picturesque and powerful Falls of Shin. From June to September, this is one of the best places in the Highlands to see Atlantic salmon leaping the falls on their way upstream to spawn.

A short and easy footpath leads from the **Falls of Shin Visitor Centre** (☎01549-402231; www.fallsofshin.co.uk; ⊙9.30am-5pm year-round, to 7.30pm Jul & Aug; ⬚) to a viewing terrace overlooking the waterfall. The visitor centre has a display that explains the life cycle of the salmon, and a CCTV feed beams live images of the falls straight into the centre's coffee shop. There are waymarked forest trails here, as well as a geocaching trail, an adventure playground and miniature golf.

However, this is not your run-of-the-mill visitor centre. As you enter, you are greeted by a kilted waxwork of **Mohamed Al Fayed**, the owner of Harrods (the upmarket London department store). Mr Al Fayed purchased the surrounding Balnagown Estate in 1972, and the visitor centre contains an outpost of Harrods, complete with shelves of cashmere knitwear, smoked salmon, expensive wine, and Harrods-branded teddy bears.

is a child-friendly museum with displays on local history. It's located a block south of Dornoch Castle Hotel.

🛏 Sleeping & Eating

Dornoch Castle Hotel   HOTEL **£££**
(☑01862-810216; www.dornochcastlehotel.com; Castle St; garden s/d £71/118, superior/deluxe d £175/223; P🛜❄) This 16th-century former bishop's palace makes a wonderful place to stay, particularly if you upgrade to one of the superior rooms, which have views, space, malt whisky and chocolates on the welcome tray, and, in some cases, four-poster beds; the deluxe rooms are unforgettable. Cheaper rooms (s/d £51/66) are also available in adjoining buildings.

In the evening, toast your toes in the cosy bar before dining in style at the first-rate **restaurant** (3-course dinner £30) tucking into dishes featuring plenty of game and seasonal produce. The restaurant's open for lunch and dinner; bar meals are also available during the day.

2 Quail   B&B **£££**
(☑01862-811811; www.2quail.com; Castle St; s/d £110/130; 🛜) Intimate and upmarket, 2 Quail offers a warm welcome on the main street. The tasteful chambers are full of old-world comfort, with sturdy metal bedframes, plenty of books and plump duvets; the downstairs guest lounge is an absolute delight.

Trevose Guest House   B&B **££**
(☑01862-810269; jamackenzie@tiscali.co.uk; Cathedral Sq; s/d £35/60; ⊙Mar–Sep; 🛜) First impressions deceive at Trevose Guest House, a lovely stone cottage right by the cathedral. It looks compact but actually boasts very spacious rooms with significant comfort and well-loved old wooden furnishings. Character oozes from every pore of the place and a benevolent welcome is a given.

Rosslyn Villa   ROOMS **£**
(☑01862-810237; Castle St; r per person £22) The best accommodation comes with simplicity and a smile. No breakfast.

Eagle Hotel   PUB GRUB **£**
(☑01862-810008; www.eagledornoch.co.uk; Castle St; bar meals £8-10; ⊙lunch & dinner) Chow down at this top little boozer complete with eccentric ornamentation and simple bar food that comes in hefty portions and with a cheery smile.

THE RIGHT SIDE OF THE TRACKS

Scotland has some unusual hostels and **Sleeperzzz.com** (☑01408-641343; www.sleeperzzz.com; dm £14; ⊙Mar–mid-Nov; P) is one of them. Set in three caringly converted railway carriages parked up in a siding by **Rogart** station, it has cute two-person bedrooms, kitchenettes and tiny lounges. The owners make an effort to run the hostel on sustainable lines, and there's a hearty local pub that does food, as well as beautifully lonely Highland scenery in the vicinity. It's on the A839, 10 miles east of Lairg but is also easily reached by train on the Inverness–Wick line (10% discount if you arrive this way).

ℹ Information

The **tourist office** (☑01862-255121; Castle St; ⊙9am-12.30pm & 1.30-5pm Mon-Fri, also Sat & Sun Jun-Aug) is in the Highland Council Building next to Dornoch Castle Hotel.

ℹ Getting There & Away

Scottish Citylink has four to five daily services to/from Inverness (£9, one hour) and Thurso (£14, 2¼ hours), which stop in the square at Dornoch.

Golspie
POP 1400

Golspie is a pretty little village that has benefited over the centuries from the proximity of Dunrobin Castle. There are good facilities, including a couple of grocery stores, a bank and a post office, and a pleasant beach just back from the main street. It's a congenial place to spend a day or two, particularly if you feel like pulling on the walking boots, getting out the mountain bike, or exploring the northern Highlands' most opulent castle.

⊙ Sights

Dunrobin Castle   CASTLE
(☑01408-633177; www.dunrobincastle.co.uk; adult/child £8.50/5; ⊙10.30am-4.30pm Mon-Sat, noon-4.30pm Sun Apr, May & Sep–mid-Oct, 10.30am-5.30pm Jun-Aug) One mile north of Golspie is magnificent Dunrobin Castle, the largest house in the Highlands. Although it dates

back to 1275, most of what you see today was built in French style between 1845 and 1850. One of the homes of the earls and dukes of Sutherland, it's richly furnished and offers an intriguing insight into the aristocratic lifestyle.

This classic fairytale castle is adorned with towers and turrets, but only 22 of its 187 rooms are on display, with hunting trophies much to the fore. The exhibits also include innumerable gifts from farm tenants (probably grateful that they weren't victims of the Clearances). The castle is reputedly haunted by the ghost of a green lady known as the Ell-maid of Dunstuffnage.

Beautiful formal gardens extend from the castle down to the sea, where impressive falconry displays take place two to three times a day. Also found in the gardens is the house's museum, which offers an eclectic mix of archaeological finds, natural-history exhibits, more non-PC animal remains and an excellent collection of Pictish stones found in Sutherland, including the fine pre-Christian Dunrobin Stone.

In spite of its beauty, Dunrobin inspires mixed feelings among local people; the castle was once the seat of the first duke of Sutherland, notorious for his part in some of the cruellest episodes of the Highland Clearances. The duke's estate was once the largest privately owned area of land in Europe, covering 1.5 million acres, and around 15,000 people were evicted from their homes to make way for sheep.

Duke of Sutherland Monument MONUMENT
From its perch on top of Ben Bhraggie, the colossal monument to the the first duke of Sutherland dominates the skyline above Golspie, just as the man himself once dominated the surrounding country. Completed in 1837, the 9m-tall statue of the duke stands atop a 24m-tall plinth, creating a towering monument that is visible for many miles in all directions.

George Granville Leveson-Gower (1758–1833), the 2nd marquess of Stafford, became Britain's biggest landowner when he married Elizabeth, countess of Sutherland in 1785. He was created first duke of Sutherland in 1833, just six months before he died; he is buried in Dornoch Cathedral. Later known as 'the great improver', he opened up Sutherland by building roads, bridges and harbours, but became notorious for overseeing the eviction of thousands of tenant farmers to make way for more profitable sheep farms.

Although local people contributed money and labour to the building of the monument – those who escaped the misery of eviction considered the duke a successful improver – and the inscription reads 'of loved, revered and cherished memory, erected by his tenantry and friends', the statue remains controversial. Many locals now see it as a symbol of aristocratic power, oppression and greed, and there have been repeated campaigns for its demolition; it is occasionally vandalised or sprayed with grafitti.

Orcadian Stone Company MUSEUM
(☎01408-633483; www.orcadianstone.co.uk; Main St; adult/child £5/free; ⊙9am-5.30pm Mon-Sat Easter-Oct) The largest independent geological collection in the country is on display here, with thousands of fascinating specimens of rocks, fossils and minerals from all over the world, but with a focus on the geology of the northern Highlands. The neighbouring shop sells semiprecious stones, mineral specimens, and gold and silver jewellery made in Orkney.

🏃 Activities

Golspie is the starting point for some good walks. The classic local hike climbs steeply above the village to the summit of **Ben Bhraggie** (394m), which is crowned by the massive monument to the duke of Sutherland.

Highland Wildcat MOUNTAIN BIKING
(www.highlandwildcat.com; Big Burn Car Park; car parking £5; ⊙dawn-dusk) The experts-only black trail at Highland Wildcat is famous among UK mountain bikers for having the highest singletrack descent in the country (390m drop over 7km from the top of Ben Bhraggie almost to sea level). There's plenty for beginners and families too, with a scenic blue trail and some easy forest routes. No bike hire or other facilities.

🛏 Sleeping & Eating

Blar Mhor B&B ££
(☎01408-633609; www.blarmhor.co.uk; Drummuie Rd; s/d/f £30/50/70; 🛜) On the approach into Golspie from Dornoch is this excellent guesthouse with large, beautifully kept rooms (our fave is the double opposite the lounge) in a towering Victorian mansion. There are landscaped gardens and the lounge offers a chance to relax in the evening and socialise with other guests.

Granite Villa B&B ££

(📞01408-633146; www.granite-villa.co.uk; Fountain Rd; s/d £45/70; P🛜🐕) Set right in the middle of the village, this handsome Victorian villa provides a warm welcome, with bright and airy bedrooms and a comfortable residents lounge complete with open fire and a 200-strong DVD library. Breakfasts offer a choice of fresh fruit, cereal and home-produced honey, or a full Scottish fry-up (including haggis, if you so desire).

Coffee Bothy CAFE £

(Fountain Rd; mains £3-7; ⏱9am-5pm Tue-Fri, from 10am Mon & Sat) This little cafe on the village's central car park serves the best coffee on the east coast, accompanied by freshly made sandwiches, a beautifully crafted ploughman's lunch, and extremely more-ish homebaked cakes – the lemon drizzle cake is perfect for reloading with carbs after a hike or bike up Ben Bhraggie.

ℹ️ Getting There & Away

Buses between Inverness and Thurso stop in Golspie. There are also trains from Inverness (£15, two hours, two or three daily) to Golspie and to Dunrobin Castle.

Brora

POP 1150

Located at the mouth of a river famed for its salmon, the village of Brora once made its living from its modest coal mines, salt pans, brickworks and textile factory. Today, the main industries are whisky and tourism, and the village is a peaceful place with a pretty harbour and a fine beach. There are two small supermarkets, a bank and a post office.

👁 Sights & Activities

FREE **Brora Heritage Centre** HERITAGE CENTRE

(📞01408-622024; Coal Pit Rd; ⏱10.30am-4.30pm Mon-Fri May-Sep, Mon-Sat Jul & Aug; P🐕) The history of Brora is celebrated in this heritage centre, about a half mile inland from the main road. Pick up a copy of the *Brora Village Trail* booklet for a self-guided walking tour of the village.

Clynelish Distillery DISTILLERY

(📞01408-623000; www.discovering-distilleries .com/clynelish; guided tour £5; ⏱10am-5pm Mon-Fri year-round, plus Sat Jun-Sep) On the north edge of Brora is Clynelish Distillery, built in 1968 on the site of a much older distillery dating from 1819. Though modern, Clynel-

ish uses traditional copper stills to produce a distinctive, slightly sweet and smoky 14-year-old single malt – you can sample a dram of the stuff at the end of the guided tour.

Brora Golf Club GOLF

(📞01408-621417; www.broragolf.co.uk; Golf Rd; green fees £55/60 weekdays/weekends) Brora Golf Club flanks the beach on the north side of the River Brora, and is a classic Scottish links course where natural hazards include prickly gorse bushes and wandering sheep.

Walking

A path leads south for 6 miles from Brora to Golspie, providing an easy and enjoyable **coastal walk** that passes the Iron Age broch of **Carn Liath** (about 4 miles from Brora) and Dunrobin Castle (p229).

Fishing

The River Brora and Loch Brora offer some of the best sea trout, brown trout and salmon fishing in Sutherland. Permits for the loch (£25 per day) and the tidal stretch of the river can be obtained from **Cunningham's Newsagent** (📞01408-621204; South Brae) in the village centre.

🛏 Sleeping & Eating

Royal Marine Hotel HOTEL £££

(📞01408-621252; www.royalmarinebrora.com; Golf Rd; s/d from £95/140; P🛜🐕) Set in a country house built for a top Scottish architect in the early 1900s, the Royal Marine is the cream of Brora's accommodation options. Log fires, leather sofas and a luxurious spa are complemented by spacious bedrooms with classic styling and a choice of three excellent restaurants, all just a few minutes walk from the beach and golf course.

Sutherland Inn B&B ££

(📞0844 855 3238; www.sutherlandinn.co.uk; Fountain Sq; s/d £40/65) The local village pub offers basic B&B in the upstairs bedrooms – try to get one of the two rooms that overlook the river at the back of the building. The lively bar serves a range of real ales and single malts, as well as decent bar meals.

Dalchalm Caravan Site CAMPGROUND £

(📞01408-621479; www.caravanclub.co.uk; sites £12 plus per adult £6; ⏱Apr-Sep) Located just over a mile north of Brora, and a short stroll from the beach, Dalchalm is a peaceful, well sheltered and beautifully landscaped site that welcomes tents as well as caravans. Best to book during school holidays.

Helmsdale

POP 900

Surrounded by hills with gorse that explodes mad yellow in springtime, this sheltered fishing town, like many other spots on this coast, was a major emigration point during the Clearances and also a booming herring port. It's surrounded by stunning, undulating coastline.

In the centre of town, the **Timespan Heritage Centre** (www.timespan.org.uk; Dunrobin St; ⊙10am-5pm Mon-Sat, noon-5pm Sun Apr-Oct, 11am-4pm Sat & Sun, 2-5pm Tue Nov-Mar) has an impressive display covering local history (including the 1869 gold rush) and Barbara Cartland, late queen of romance novels, who was a Helmsdale regular. There are also local art exhibitions, a geology garden and a cafe.

The River Helmsdale offers some of the best **salmon fishing** in the Highlands. Permits, tackle and advice can be obtained from the **Helmsdale Tackle Company** (☑01431-821372; www.helmsdalecompany.com; 15-17 Dunrobin St; ⊙9am-5pm Mon, Tue, Thu & Fri, to 12.45pm Wed & Sat).

🛏 Sleeping & Eating

Bridge Hotel HOTEL ££

(☑01431-821100; www.bridgehotel.net; Dunrobin St; s/d £65/105; 🛜) Ideally located, this early-19th-century lodging is the smartest place to stay and the best place to eat in town. Proud of its Highland heritage, it displays a phalanx of antlers, even on the key fobs. But the rooms don't have the expected patina of age; they have wonderfully plush fabrics and a smart contemporary feel.

The downstairs bar and restaurant hum with good cheer and relaxed hospitality; check out the replica of Britain's biggest landed salmon.

Helmsdale Hostel HOSTEL £

(☑01431-821636; www.helmsdalehostel.co.uk; Stafford St; dm/tw/f £15/40/60; ⊙Apr-Sep; 🛜) This caringly run hostel is in very good nick and makes a cheerful, comfortable budget base for exploring Caithness. The dorm berths are mostly cosy single beds rather than bunks, and the en suite rooms are great for families. The lofty kitchen-lounge space has a wood stove and good kitchen.

La Mirage CAFE £

(☑01431-821615; www.lamirage.org; 7 Dunrobin St; mains £8-10; ⊙noon-8.30pm) Created in homage to Barbara Cartland by the larger-than-life late owner, this minor legend is a medley of pink flamboyance, faded celebrity photos and show tunes. The meals aren't gourmet – think chicken Kiev – but the fish and chips (also available to take away: eat 'em down on the pretty harbour) are really tasty.

❶ Getting There & Away

Buses from Inverness and Thurso stop in Helmsdale, as do trains (from Thurso £13.50, 1¼ hours, four daily).

CAITHNESS

Once you pass Helmsdale, you are entering Caithness, a place of jagged gorse-and-grass-topped cliffs hiding tiny fishing harbours. This top corner of Scotland was once Viking territory, historically more connected to Orkney and Shetland than to the rest of the mainland. It's a magical and mystical land with an ancient aura, peopled by wise folk with long memories who are fiercely proud of their Norse heritage.

The region is bristling with ancient cairns and monuments, as well as Pictish and Viking remains. Most of the settlements you see today, however, are crofting villages set up when the Highland Clearances forced people to the coast. With the herring boom, these little fishing ports flourished, and the region's chief town, Wick, became a harbour of international importance. In classic boom-and-bust style, the fish dried up, and these places lapsed into painful decline: it's only in recent years that there's been some recovery. Inland, the vast and lonely peat bogs of the Flow country, straddling the Caithness and Sutherland border, provides a haven for bird life.

Caithness is the main gateway to Orkney, but make sure you spend some time getting to know this intriguing and isolated corner of the country before taking the ferry.

Helmsdale to Lybster

About 7 miles north of Helmsdale is **Badbea**, an abandoned crofting village. It was established during the Highland Clearances in the early 19th century, when people were evicted from their homes in the nearby glens. The ruined cottages and rough fields strung along the clifftops provide a graphic illustration of the hardship endured by the people

The A897 from Helmsdale to Melvich – singletrack all the way – climbs along the Strath of Kildonan up to the bleak bogs of the Flow Country. On the way, at a bridge over the Kildonan Burn, it passes the site of the Scottish Gold Rush of 1869.

Robert Gilchrist, a local man recently returned from 17 years prospecting for gold in Australia, applied his panning skills to his home territory and in late 1868 discovered significant amounts of the precious metal in the Suisgill and Kildonan burns, tributaries of the Helmsdale River.

The news spread like wildfire and was eventually reported in the national newspapers. By March 1869 a shanty town of wooden huts and tents had sprung up at 'Baile an Or' (Gaelic for 'gold town'), where the Kildonan Burn meets the road, and around 600 hopeful prospectors from all over Britain (plus a few from America and Australia) were frantically staking claims and panning the river gravels.

The duke of Sutherland, who owned the land and the mineral rights, took his cut – a prospecting licence cost £1 a month (equivalent to £75 today) – and also claimed a 10% royalty payment on any gold found. However, at the height of the rush, a single prospector could expect to pan around £1 worth of gold in two or three days.

By the autumn of 1869 returns began to diminish as the easier deposits were depleted, and the less successful prospectors drifted off to find work in the farms or the herring fishery. By the end of the year all licences were revoked and the Kildonan gold rush was over. Nothing remains of all that activity except the name Baile an Or on the map.

But there is still gold to be found in them thar hills. Recreational gold panners are allowed to prospect for free in the Kildonan Burn, provided they follow the rules posted at the parking area (see www.helmsdale.org/gold-panning.html). A team of volunteers from the Timespan Heritage Centre in Helmsdale recently recovered 12g (almost half an ounce) of Kildonan gold, and are hopeful that it might be used to plate one of the medals for the 2014 Commonwealth Games in Glasgow.

who lived here (it was finally abandoned in 1911). The site is a 10-minute walk east of a parking area on the A9 (signposted).

The **Berriedale Braes**, 2.5 miles beyond the Badbea parking area, is a difficult section of the A9, with steep gradients and hairpin bends. On the south edge of the valley is a small crenellated folly tower with grand views; there are also nice walks along the valley, passing **Langwell House**, a private mansion with attractive gardens.

The village of **Dunbeath** has a spectacular setting in a deep glen – it makes a good stop on the way to the northern towns. There are a couple of shops and a **Heritage Centre** (☎01593-731233; www.dunbeath -heritage.org.uk; The Old School; adult/child £2/ free; ☺10am-5pm Sun-Fri Apr-Sep, 11am-3pm Mon-Fri Oct-Mar), which has a stone carved with runic graffiti, and a display on the work of Neil Gunn, whose wonderful novels evoke the Caithness of his boyhood.

Two miles north of Dunbeath is the **Laidhay Croft Museum** (☎0756 370 2321; www .laidhay.co.uk; adult/child £3.50/2.50; ☺10am-5pm Mon-Sat May-Sep), which recreates crofting life from the mid-1800s to WWII. It is

housed in an 18th-century Caithness longhouse with stable and byre at either end, thatched with local rushes; the nearby barn has its original wooden cruck roof. The museum's **tearoom** serves good soup and home baking.

At the **Clan Gunn Heritage Centre & Museum** (☎01593-741700; adult/child £2.50/ 50p; ☺11am-1pm & 2-4pm Mon-Sat Jun-Sep) in Latheron, a mile past Laidhay, you'll learn that a Scot, not Christopher Columbus, discovered America – but you might take this claim with a pinch of salt! Even if you don't want to go in, it's worth pulling into the car park on a fine day to admire the stunning views.

Lybster & Around

Lybster is a purpose-built fishing village dating from 1810, with a stunning harbour area surrounded by grassy cliffs. In its heyday, it was Scotland's third busiest port; things have changed – now there are only a couple of boats – but there are several interesting prehistoric sites in the area.

◉ Sights & Activities

Waterlines Visitor Centre VISITOR CENTRE
(☑01593-721520; The Harbour; adult/child
£2.50/50p; ☉11am-5pm May-Sep) Down at the
harbour is the Waterlines Visitor Centre,
with an exhibition on the fishing heritage
of Lybster and a popular downstairs cafe.
In summer it operates a smokehouse (giving
visitors a whiff of the kippering process).

Whaligoe Steps HISTORIC SITE
At **Ulbster**, 5 miles north of Lybster on the
A99, this spectacular staircase cut into the
cliff face provides access to a tiny natural
harbour ringed by vertical cliffs and echoing
with the cackle of nesting fulmars. The path
begins at the end of the minor road beside
the telephone box, opposite the road signposted
'Cairn of Get'.

Cairn o'Get PREHISTORIC SITE
The Cairn o'Get, a prehistoric burial cairn,
is a mile northwest of Ulbster. From the car
park cross the stile and follow the black-and-white
marker poles for approximately 1 mile.
Wear decent shoes as the ground is boggy.

Achavanich Standing Stones PREHISTORIC SITE
Five miles to the northwest of Lybster, on
the minor road to Achavanich, just south of
Loch Stemster, are the unsigned 30 Achavanich
Standing Stones. In a desolate setting,
these crumbling monuments of the
distant past still capture the imagination
with their evocative location. It's all about
colours: blue skies, a steely grey loch and the
soft browns and greens of the land.

The setting, and absence of modern tourism,
makes this place special.

Grey Cairns of Camster PREHISTORIC SITE
Dating from between 4000 BC and 2500 BC,
the Grey Cairns of Camster are burial chambers
hidden in long, low mounds rising from
an evocatively desolate stretch of moor. The
Long Cairn measures 60m by 21m. You can
enter the main chamber, but must first crawl
into the well-preserved Round Cairn, which
has a corbelled ceiling.

From a turn-off a mile east of Lybster on
the A99, the cairns are 4 miles north. From
the site you can then continue 7 miles north
on this remote road to approach Wick on
the A882.

Hill o'Many Stanes PREHISTORIC SITE
The Hill o'Many Stanes, 2 miles beyond the
Camster turn-off on the A99, is a curious,
fan-shaped arrangement of 22 rows of small
stones that probably date from around 2000
BC. Staggeringly, there were 600 in the original
pattern. On a sunny day, the views from
this hill are stunning.

ⓘ Getting There & Away

Stagecoach buses between Thurso and Inverness
run via Lybster (one hour, up to four
daily) and Dunbeath. There's also a coastal
service from Wick to Helmsdale stopping at
these places.

Wick

POP 7333
More gritty than pretty, Wick has been down
on its luck since the collapse of the herring
industry. It was once the world's largest fish
port for the 'silver darlings', but when the
market dropped off after WWII, job losses
were huge and the town hasn't totally recovered.
These days Wick is an important
local service centre and transport terminus.
It's well worth a look, particularly for its excellent
museum, which puts everything in
context.

◉ Sights & Activities

A path leads a mile south from town to the
ruins of 12th-century **Old Wick Castle**, with
the spectacular cliffs of the **Brough** and
the **Brig**, as well as **Gote o'Trams**, a little
further south. In good weather, it's a fine
coastal walk to the castle, but take care on
the final approach. Three miles northeast
of Wick is the magnificently located clifftop
ruin of **Castle Sinclair**.

TOP CHOICE Wick Heritage Centre MUSEUM
(☑01955-605393; www.wickheritage.org; 20 Bank
Row; adult/child £3/50p; ☉10am-5pm Mon-Sat
Apr-Oct, last entry 3.45pm) Tracking the rise
and fall of the herring industry, this great
town museum displays everything from
fishing equipment to complete herring fishing
boats. It's a fantastic museum – without
doubt one of the best in the country – and
is absolutely huge inside, crammed with
memorabilia and extensive displays describing
Wick's heyday in the mid-19th century.

The Johnston photographic collection
is the museum's star exhibit. From 1863 to
1977, three generations of Johnstons photographed
everything that happened around
Wick, and the 70,000 photographs are an
amazing portrait of the town's life. Prints of
the early photos are for sale.

Old Pulteney Distillery DISTILLERY
(☏01955-602371; www.oldpulteney.com; Huddart St; tours £4; ☺10am-1pm & 2-4pm Mon-Fri) Old Pulteney is the most northerly distillery on mainland Scotland and runs excellent tours twice a day. Old Pulteney whisky has a light, earthy character with a hint of sea air and sherry.

Caithness Seacoast BOAT TOUR
(☏01955-609200; www.caithness-seacoast.co.uk) Wick's a boat town, and this outfit will take you out to sea to inspect the rugged coastline of the northeast. There are various options, from a half-hour jaunt (adult/child £15/10) to a three-hour trip down to Lybster and back (adult/child £40/30).

🛏 Sleeping & Eating

Quayside B&B ££
(☏01955-603229; www.quaysidewick.co.uk; 25 Harbour Quay; s/d/f without breakfast £30/50/75; P🛜) Quayside should be your first port of call for accommodation.The owners couldn't be more helpful – they've been in the business for many years and know what they're doing. Right by the harbour, it's handy for everything worth seeing in town. Spruce rooms – including a family room with kitchenette – can be taken at B&B or bed-only rates.

There are self-catering flats available too, plus good facilities for cyclists and motorcyclists. Book ahead.

Mackays Hotel HOTEL ££
(☏01955-602323; www.mackayshotel.co.uk; Union St; s/d £89/119; @🛜) The renovated Mackays is Wick's best hotel. Rooms vary in layout and size, so ask to see a few; prices drop if you're staying more than one night, and walk-up prices are usually quite a bit lower than the rack rates we list here. The onsite **No 1 Bistro** (Union St; mains £10-13) is a fine-dining option for lunch or dinner.

The 2.75m-long Ebenezer Pl, the shortest street in Britain, runs past one end of the hotel.

Bord de L'Eau FRENCH ££
(☏01955-604400; 2 Market St; mains £14-21; ☺lunch Tue-Sat, dinner Tue-Sun) This serene, up-market French restaurant is the best place to eat in Wick. It overlooks the river and serves a changing menu of mostly meat French classics. The conservatory dining room overlooking the river is lovely on a sunny evening. It also opens for 'morning coffee'

before lunch, when you can down tasty pastries with your cafe au lait.

ℹ Information

Wick tourist office (66 High St; ☺9am-5.30pm Mon-Sat) Good selection of information; upstairs in McAllans Clothing Store.

Wick Carnegie Library (☏01955 602864; Sinclair Tce; ☺Mon-Sat; @) Free internet access.

ℹ Getting There & Away

AIR Wick is a transport gateway to the surrounding area. **Flybe** (☏0871 700 2000; www.flybe.com) flies between Edinburgh and Wick airport once daily except Saturday. **Eastern Airways** (☏01652-680600; www.easternairways.com) flies to Aberdeen (three Monday to Friday).

BUS Stagecoach (p367) and Citylink (p269) operate buses to/from Inverness (£17.50, three hours, five daily) and Thurso (30 minutes, five daily) and also to John O'Groats (45 minutes, up to five daily).

There's also connecting service to John O'Groats (40 minutes, five or six per day, Monday to Saturday) for the passenger ferry to Burwick, Orkney, and to the Gills Bay ferry to St Margaret's Hope, Orkney.

TRAIN Trains service Wick from Inverness (£16.10, four hours, four daily).

John O'Groats

POP 500

A car park surrounded by tourist shops, John O'Groats offers little to the visitor beyond a means to get across to Orkney; even the pub has been shut for a while now (though there are a couple of cafes). Though it's not the northernmost point of the British mainland (that's Dunnet Head), it still serves as the end-point of the 874-mile trek from Land's End in Cornwall, a popular if arduous route for cyclists and walkers, many of whom raise money for charitable causes.

👁 Sights & Activities

North Coast Marine Adventures WILDLIFE CRUISES
(☏01955-611797; www.northcoast-marine-adventures.co.uk; The Harbour; adult/child £25/15) North Coast Marine Adventures runs scenic wildlife trips every couple of hours. Seals, whales, dolphins and seabirds can all be spotted. There's also a half-hour 'white water' thrill-seeking option (£20), which will get you soaked as you take on the turbulent waters of the Pentland Firth.

Duncansby Head LOOKOUT

Two miles east, Duncansby Head provides a more solemn end-of-Britain moment with a small lighthouse and 60m cliffs sheltering nesting fulmars. A 15-minute walk from here through a sheep paddock yields spectacular views of the sea-surrounded monoliths known as **Duncansby Stacks**.

Caithness Broch Centre MUSEUM

(www.caithnessbrochcentre.co.uk; admission free; ⊘noon-4pm Tue-Sat) Six miles south of John O'Groats, in Auckengill on the Wick road, the Caithness Broch Centre has a small archaeological exhibition based on finds from these imposing ancient monuments. There is a broch, as well as Viking ruins, nearby.

🛏 Sleeping & Eating

There's a campsite and a few B&Bs in and around John O'Groats, as well as an SYHA hostel not far away, but it's not a great place to stay. For accommodation try Wick, Mey or Thurso – all nearby.

ℹ Information

John O'Groats tourist office (☑01955-611373; ⊘10am-5pm Apr-Oct) This tourist office is the best thing about John O'Groats, with its fine selection of local novels and books about Caithness and the Highland Clearances.

ℹ Getting There & Away

BOAT From May to September, a passenger ferry shuttles across to Burwick in Orkney. Ninety-minute wildlife cruises to the island of Stroma or Duncansby Head cost £15 (late June to August).

BUS Stagecoach runs buses between John O'Groats and Wick (40 minutes, four to seven Monday to Saturday). There are also three to eight services Monday to Saturday to/from Thurso.

Castle of Mey

The **Castle of Mey** (www.castleofmey.org.uk; adult/child £9.50/4; ⊘10.30am-4pm May-mid-Oct), a big crowd-puller for its Queen Mother connections, is about 6 miles west of John O'Groats, off the A836 to Thurso. The exterior may seem grand but inside it feels domestic and everything is imbued with the character of the late Queen Mum: from a surprisingly casual lounge area with TV showing her favourite show (*Dad's Army*, since you asked) to a photo of the king in 1943 that's lovingly inscribed 'Bertie' (her name for King George). All the in-jokes are explained by staff who once worked for her.

Elizabeth Bowes-Lyon (1900–2002), daughter of Scottish aristocrat Lord Glamis, was queen-consort to King George VI and mother of Queen Elizabeth II (she was played by Helena Bonham Carter in the 2011 film *The King's Speech*). Legend has it that other members of the Royal Family sneered at her origins, dismissing her as 'that common little Scottish girl', but she was easily the most popular royal among the British public. She purchased the semi-derelict Castle of Mey after her husband's death in 1952, and it served as her summer holiday home for the rest of her life.

Outside in the castle grounds there's an unusual walled garden that's worth a stroll and there are lovely views over the Pentland Firth. The castle closes for a couple of weeks at the end of July.

The nearby **Castle Arms Hotel** (☑01847-851992; www.castlearms.co.uk; s/d £40/70; P), a former 19th-century coaching inn, has a friendly bar downstairs and simple but comfortable rooms upstairs. Or try **Hawthorns** (☑01847-851710; www.thehawthornsmey.co.uk; s/d £35/60; P🖘), where rooms are huge and the owner's cheery smile is just as big.

Dunnet Head

Eight miles east of Thurso a minor road leads to dramatic Dunnet Head, the **most northerly point on the British mainland**, which beats John O'Groats hands down. There are majestic cliffs dropping into the turbulent Pentland Firth, inspiring views of the Orkney islands, basking seals and nesting seabirds below, and a lighthouse built by Robert Louis Stevenson's granddad. On the road to the headland, you can stay at **Dunnet Head B&B** (☑01847-851774; www.dunnethead.iberacal.com; s/d from £27/44; 🖘), which offers simple, comfortable rooms in the former post office.

Just west, **Dunnet Bay** offers you one of Scotland's finest beaches, backed by high dunes, as well as **Seadrift** (☑01847-821531; ⊘2-5pm Sun-Wed & Fri May-Sep) – a small wildlife display and the base for local rangers, who organise walks in summer – and a caravan-dominated **campground** (☑01847-821319; www.caravanclub.co.uk; members pitch £13.80; ⊘Apr-Sep; P) backing the beach. At the southern end of Dunnet Bay lies the tiny harbour of **Castlehill**. Here a heritage trail explains the evolution of the local flagstone industry.

Thurso & Scrabster

POP 7737

Britain's most northerly mainland town, Thurso makes a handy overnight stop if you're heading west or across to Orkney. There's a pretty town beach, riverbank strolls and a good new museum. Thurso, which gets its name from the Norse for 'Thor's river', is also an unlikely surfing centre, with the choppy Pentland Firth raising some very respectable waves. Ferries cross from Scrabster, 2.5 miles west of Thurso, to Orkney.

Tiny Scrabster, little more than a collection of BP oil storage containers, revolves around its port, where there are a couple of good eating options.

◎ Sights

FREE Caithness Horizons   MUSEUM
(www.caithnesshorizons.co.uk; High St, Thurso; ⊙10am-6pm Mon-Sat, 11am-4pm Sun) This museum brings much of the history and lore of Caithness to life through its excellent displays. A couple of fine Pictish cross-slabs greet the visitor downstairs; the main exhibition is a wide-ranging look at local history using plenty of audiovisuals – check out the wistful account of the now-abandoned island of Stroma for an emotional slice of social history.

There's also a gallery space, an exhibition on the Dounreay nuclear reactor and a cafe.

✸ Activities

Thurso is an unlikely surfing centre but the nearby coast has arguably the best and most regular surf on mainland Britain. There's an excellent right-hand reef break on the eastern side of town, directly in front of Lord Thurso's castle (closed to the public), and another shallow reef break 5 miles west at **Brimms Ness**. Pack a drysuit: this is no Hawaii.

Thurso's idyllic country **Riverside Walk** (Riverside) will make you feel miles away from town. Access is near Waterside House and you can walk upstream, retracing your footsteps to come back (there was a bridge you could once cross to come back on the other side, but it's been washed out). It's a beautiful walk, taking about 45 minutes at a stroll, and is a very popular local pursuit in decent weather. You can also walk all the way to Scrabster (40 minutes) along cliffs for brilliant views. Take care in windy weather.

⊨ Sleeping

Forss House Hotel   HOTEL £££
(☏01847-861201; www.forsshousehotel.co.uk; Forss; s/d £95/125, superior s/d/ste £110/160/230; ℗⊚) Tucked into a thicket of trees 4 miles west of Thurso is an old Georgian mansion offering elegant accommodation that has both character and style. Sumptuous upstairs rooms are preferable to basement rooms as they have lovely views of the garden. There are also separate, beautifully appointed suites in the garden itself, which provide both privacy and a sense of tranquillity.

Thoughtful extras like a selection of CDs and books in every room add appeal. It's right alongside a beautiful salmon river – the hotel can sort out permits and equipment – and if you've had a chilly day in the waders, some 300 malt whiskies await in the hotel bar.

Sandra's Hostel   HOSTEL £
(☏01847-894575; www.sandras-backpackers.co.uk; 24 Princes St, Thurso; dm/d/f £14/34/50; ℗@⊚) A byword for backpacker excellence, Sandra's was awash with free facilities back when some hostels still had you scrubbing floors before checkout. Sporting an excellent kitchen, it offers free internet and wi-fi, a help-yourself continental breakfast, laundry and downstairs chip shop. Dorms, mostly four-berthers, are en suite and spotless.

Murray House   B&B ££
(☏0184/-895759; www.murrayhousebb.com; 1 Campbell St, Thurso; s/d £35/70; ⊚) A solid 19th-century town house on a central corner, Murray House gives a good first impression with a genuine welcome. It continues with new carpets, smart rooms with solid wooden furniture, an appealing lounge space and the option of an evening meal, all at very friendly prices. No credit cards.

Pentland Hotel   HOTEL ££
(☏01847-893202; www.pentlandhotel.co.uk; Princes St, Thurso; s/d £40/70) The business-style rooms in this place are great value. They're big enough to have a couch and a separate nook with a desk. It's a stylish place and surprisingly tranquil inside, given its central location. There are plenty of open areas for lounging around while you wait for the ferry to Orkney.

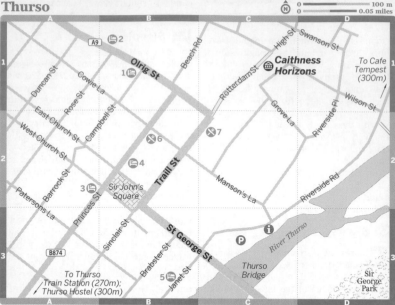

Waterside House   B&B £

(☎01847-894751; www.watersidehouse.org; 3 Janet St, Thurso; s £25, d £35-50; ℗) This straight-up guesthouse is easy to find (turn left just after the bridge coming into town), and has parking outside and comfortable beds in well-priced rooms. There's a range of them, from double en suites to cheaper attic rooms that share a spotless bathroom. Breakfast choices include egg-and-bacon rolls or takeaway if you've got an early ferry. No credit cards.

Thurso Hostel   HOSTEL £

(Ormlie Lodge; ☎01847-896888; ormlielodge@ btconnect.com; Ormlie Rd, Thurso; s/d £15/25; ℗)

This scruffy hostel is a students' hall of residence a few minutes' walk from the train station. It has a decent, if slightly ragged, range of budget accommodation. It's the place to go if you want a single room at a low price.

Orcadia Guest House   B&B £

(☎01847-894395; 27 Olrig St, Thurso; s/d £22/44) This old and central budget favourite has been doing no-frills, value-packed B&B for decades, with simple and comfortable rooms that share bathrooms.

✕ Eating

Captain's Galley   SEAFOOD £££

(☎01847-894999; www.captainsgalley.co.uk; Scrabster; 3-course dinner £46; ⊙dinner Tue-Sat) Right by the ferry terminal in Scrabster, Captain's Galley is a classy but friendly place offering a short, seafood-based menu that features local and sustainably sourced produce prepared in relatively simple ways, letting the natural flavours shine through. Most rate it the best eatery in Caithness.

Cafe Tempest   CAFE £

(☎01847-892500; The Harbour, Thurso; mains £4-8; ⊙10am-5pm daily May-Sep, shorter hours low season) A blue shed by the harbour houses this cool wee cafe, with its comfy armchairs and sofas, beachcomber bric-a-brac and chilled surfing vibe. The coffee is brewed just right, and the menu ranges from breakfast dishes to homebaked cakes and filled panini.

Holborn SEAFOOD, PUB GRUB **££**
(🖉01847-892771; www.holbornhotel.co.uk; 16 Princes St, Thurso; mains £13-18) A trendy, comfortable place decked out in light wood, the Holborn contrasts starkly with more traditional Thurso watering holes. Quality seafood – including delicious home-smoked salmon – is the mainstay of a short but solid menu at its **Red Pepper restaurant**, where desserts are excellent too.

Its bar, **Bar 16**, is a modern space with couches and comfy chairs where bar meals (£7 to £10) are uncomplicated but decent.

Ferry Inn STEAKHOUSE, SEAFOOD **££**
(www.ferryinnscrabster.co.uk; Scrabster; mains £11-19; ⊗food breakfast, lunch & dinner) Near the ferry dock in Scrabster, this traditional stone pub has rather ugly extensions, but these house the busy restaurant. It specialises in steaks – pick your size – and local haddock; we reckon it's a tad overpriced but the evening view over the harbour is great. Cheaper bar meals (£8 to £11) are downstairs, along with a pool table.

Le Bistro INTERNATIONAL **££**
(🖉01847-893737; 2 Traill St, Thurso; lunch £5-8, dinner mains £10-15; ⊗lunch & dinner Tue-Sat) Less sophisticated than when it was Thurso's main gourmet option, this eatery buzzes with chatter on weekend evenings as locals of all ages chow down on its simple meat and carb creations. What it does, it does well: the respectably sized steaks come on a sizzling platter and service has a smile.

ℹ️ Information

Dunbar Hospital (🖉01847-893263; Ormlie Rd, Thurso) Located 0.75 miles southwest of the town centre.

Laundrette (Riverside Pl, Thurso; ⊗9am-6pm Mon-Fri, 10am-5.30pm Sat)

Thurso Library (🖉01847-893237; Davidson's Lane, Thurso; ⊗10am-6pm Mon & Wed, to 8pm Tue & Fri, to 1pm Thu & Sat; @) Free internet.

Thurso tourist office (🖉01847-893155; thurso@visitscotland.com; Riverside Rd, Thurso; ⊗Mon-Sat Apr-May & Sep-Oct, daily Jun-Aug)

ℹ️ Getting There & Around

It's a 2-mile walk from Thurso train station to the ferry port at Scrabster or there are buses from Olrig St.

BUS From Inverness, Stagecoach/Citylink run via Wick to Thurso/Scrabster (£17.50, 3½ hours, five daily) and also head to John O'Groats (one hour, three to eight Monday to Saturday).

TRAIN There are two or three daily train services from Inverness in summer (£16.10, 3¾ hours). Space for bicycles is limited, so book ahead.

NORTH & WEST COASTS

Quintessential Highland country such as this, marked by single-track roads, breathtaking emptiness and a wild, fragile beauty, is a rarity on the modern, crowded, highly urbanised island of Britain. You could get lost up here for weeks – and that still wouldn't be enough time.

Thurso to Durness

It's 80 winding – and often spectacular – coastal miles from Thurso to Durness.

DOUNREAY & MELVICH

Ten miles west of Thurso is the **Dounreay nuclear power station**, which was the first in the world to supply mains electricity and is currently being decommissioned. The clean-up is planned to be finished by 2025; it's still a major employment source for the region.

Just beyond Dounreay, **Reay** has a shop and an interesting little harbour dating from 1830. **Melvich** overlooks a fine beach and there are great views from **Strathy Point** (a 2-mile drive from the coast road, then a 15-minute walk).

BETTYHILL
POP 550

The panorama of a sweeping, sandy beach backed by velvety green hills with bulbous, rocky outcrops makes a sharp contrast to the sad history of this area. Bettyhill is a crofting community of resettled tenant farmers kicked off their land during the Clearances. Just west of town, an enormous stretch of white sand flanks the River Naver as it meets the sea.

The **Strathnaver Museum** (🖉01641-521418; www.strathnavermuseum.org.uk; adult/child £2/50p; ⊗10am-5pm Mon-Sat Apr-Oct), housed in an old church, tells the sad story of the Strathnaver Clearances through post-

THE FLOW COUNTRY

Just east of Melvich, the singletrack A897 runs south along Strath Halladale to the bleak and exposed moors of the Flow Country (pronounced to rhyme with cow; from the Norse *floi* meaning 'marshy ground'). At 1500 sq miles, this area of moorland on the border between Caithness and Sutherland is the biggest expanse of blanket bog in Europe, and possibly the world – it makes up 13% of the world's total surviving blanket bog environment.

Blanket bog develops in areas with high rainfall, mild to low temperatures and poor drainage, where peat can accumulate across large expanses of rolling land, and not just in wet, boggy hollows. Peat is produced by the slow decomposition of plant remains (mainly sphagnum moss) in waterlogged acid soils, and builds up at a rate of around 1mm a year. The peat of the Flow Country has been formed over a period of around 6000 years, and the landscape has barely changed its appearance in all that time.

This ancient habitat is home to numerous rare Highland plants, including the insect-eating sundew, and insects such as water boatmen, dragonflies and damselflies. The flat, sparse heathland dotted with tiny lochans (small inland lochs) is a prime nesting site for birds such as golden plover, greenshank and red-throated diver, and also provides a perfect hunting ground for birds of prey, including short-eared owl, hen harrier, merlin and golden eagle.

In the 1970s and 80s, parts of the Flow Country were damaged by the widespread cutting of drainage ditches and the planting of nonnative conifers by private forestry companies. In response, the RSPB secured the purchase of 8398 hectares of peatland around Forsinard Station, which is protected as a nature reserve. In 2011 the Flow Country was placed on the shortlist for consideration as a UNESCO World Heritage Site.

The **Forsinard Flows Visitor Centre** (www.rspb.org.uk; admission free; ⊙9am-5.30pm Apr-Oct) at Forsinard Station has maps and exhibits detailing the natural history of the Flow Country, info on local walks, and up-to-date reports on the most recent wildlife sightings. The most popular walk is the **Dubh Lochan trail** (1 mile), which begins opposite the station and passes several lochans with plentiful bird and insect life. Four miles north of the visitor centre is the four-mile **Forsinain trail**, crossing golden plover and dunlin nesting grounds. There are also ranger-led walks starting from the centre; call for details.

South of Forsinard, the road passes through epic, lonely moorscapes that stir the heart with their desolate beauty. Take a right turn at the hamlet of **Kinbrace** onto the B871, which covers more jaw-dropping scenery before bringing you to the village of Syre. Turn right here to follow the **Strathnaver** valley back to the north coast near Bettyhill, or left to reach the lonely outpost of **Altnaharra**.

Trains from Inverness to Thurso stop right by the visitor centre at Forsinard station (£17 from Inverness, 3¼ hours, four a day Monday to Saturday, one on Sunday).

ers written by local kids. The museum contains memorabilia of Clan Mackay, various items of crofting equipment and a 'St Kilda mailboat', a small wooden boat-shaped container bearing a letter that was used by St Kildans to send messages to the mainland. Outside the back door of the church is the **Farr Stone**, a fine carved Pictish cross-slab.

Bettyhill Hotel (☑01641-521352; www.betty hill.info; s/d from £25/50; mains £10; ⊙lunch & dinner) is a friendly place, with a range of rooms: some are distinctly more modern than others. There are rip-roaring views from some (such as No 2) over the sandy beach fringing Torrisdale Bay.

Bettyhill **tourist office** (☑01641-521244; ⊙10.15am-5pm Mon-Sat Apr-Oct) has limited information on the area, but if you're after a bite to eat, the **Cafe at Bettyhill** (☑01641-521244; Old Police Station; mains £5-8; ⊙11am-4pm Mon-Sat, 5-7.30pm Fri & Sat) here serves coffee, tea and home baking, plus baked potatoes, filled baguettes, prawn salads, and fish and chips.

COLDBACKIE & TONGUE
POP 450

Coldbackie has outstanding views over sandy beaches, turquoise waters and offshore islands. If you haven't seen that magical Scottish light at work yet, there's a good chance you'll see it here – park the car for a few minutes and watch.

Only 2 miles further on is Tongue, with the evocative 14th-century ruins of **Castle Varrich**, once a Mackay stronghold. To get to the castle, take the trail next to the Royal Bank of Scotland, near Ben Loyal Hotel – it's an easy stroll. Tongue has a shop, post office, bank and petrol station.

🛏 Sleeping & Eating

Cloisters   B&B **££**
(☎01847-601286; www.cloistertal.demon.co.uk; Talmine; s/d £32.50/55; P) Vying for the position of best-located B&B in Scotland, Cloisters has three en suite twin rooms with brilliant views over the Kyle of Tongue and offshore islands. Breakfast is in the artistically converted church alongside. To get here from Tongue, cross the causeway and take the first turning on the right to Melness; Cloisters is a couple of miles down this road.

Tongue SYHA   HOSTEL **£**
(☎01847-611789; www.syha.org.uk; Tongue; dm/tw £16.25/39; ☉Apr-Oct; P) In a wonderful spot right by the causeway across the Kyle of Tongue, a mile west of town, Tongue SYHA is the top budget option in the area, with clean, comfortably refitted dorms – some with views – a decent kitchen and cosy lounge. The helpful warden has plenty of local advice and turns her hand to delicious home baking.

Tongue Hotel   HOTEL, PUB **££**
(☎01847-611206; www.tonguehotel.co.uk; Tongue; s/d £65/100, superior s/d £75/120; P🛰🛜) Tongue Hotel is a welcoming spot that offers cosy, recently renovated rooms in a former hunting lodge. It has upmarket Highland restaurant fare (mains £16 to £18) in the evenings and great-value bar meals (£6, open lunch and dinner) in the snug Brass Tap bar in the basement, a good spot to chat with locals or shelter from the weather.

Tigh-nan-Ubhal   B&B **££**
(☎01847-611281; www.tigh-nan-ubhal.com; Main St, Tongue; d £65; P🛜) There are snug, loft-style rooms with plenty of natural light here, but the basement double with spa is the pick of the bunch – it's the biggest en suite we've seen in northern Scotland.

Craggan Hotel   SCOTTISH, PUB GRUB **££**
(☎01847-601278; www.thecraggan.co.uk; Melness; mains £8-16; ☉breakfast, lunch & dinner) On the side road to Melness, across the causeway from Tongue village, the Craggan Hotel doesn't look much from outside, but go in and you'll find smart, formal service and a menu ranging from exquisite burgers (£6.50) to classy game and seafood dishes, presented beautifully. The wine list's not bad for a pub either.

THE STRATHNAVER TRAIL

The broad valley of Strathnaver runs south from Bettyhill to the remote hamlet of Altnaharra. In 1814 this tranquil glen was the scene of some of the cruellest episodes of the Highland Clearances, overseen by the Duke of Sutherland's factor (property manager), the notorious Patrick Sellar. Strathnaver Museum (p239) has lots of information on the clearances, and on Sellar (who was later tried for murder, but acquitted). You can pick up a booklet on the **Strathnaver Trail**, an interpretive guide to 29 marked historical sites between Bettyhill and Altnaharra.

These include **Rosal Township**, a 200-year-old crofting village abandoned during the Clearances; a series of informative panels tells the tragic story. You can see where some of the houses were, and there are traces of small ploughed fields. On the opposite side of the river, beside the road, is a monument to **Donald MacLeod**, a stonemason who was evicted from Rosal and later emigrated to Canada, where he published *Gloomy Memories*, a first-hand account of the Strathnaver Clearances.

On the shores of lovely Loch Naver, with the bulk of Ben Klibreck looming in the distance, is **Grummore Township**, another evocative abandoned village; nearby, next to the Grummore Caravan Site, are the remains of a 2000-year-old **broch**.

The atmospheric, 180-year-old **Altnaharra Hotel** (☎01549-411222; www.altnaharra.com) provides luxury accommodation, and offers salmon and trout fishing in nearby lochs, and deerstalking in the surrounding hills. The hotel's Ghillie Bar serves excellent meals at lunch and dinner, including steak, fish and chips, and local venison.

TONGUE TO DURNESS

From Tongue it's 37 miles to Durness – the main road follows a causeway directly across the **Kyle of Tongue**, while the old road goes around the head of the kyle, with beautiful views of **Ben Loyal**. Continuing west, the road crosses a desolate moor past **Moine House** (a ruin built as a shelter for travellers in 1830) to the northern end of freshwater **Loch Hope**.

Here a scenic minor road leads south along the lochside beneath the menacing profile of **Ben Hope** (927m), Scotland's most northerly Munro, to reach the Tongue–Lairg road at Altnaharra. After 10 miles you reach **Dun Dornaigil**, a well-preserved broch on the bank of a fast-flowing burn. If you'd like to climb Ben Hope, it's a 4.5-mile, four-hour round trip from a car park 2 miles north of the broch, near a large barn. It's a relatively easy walk but often cold and windy at the exposed summit.

Beyond Loch Hope, as the main road descends towards the sea, there are stunning views over **Loch Eriboll**.

Durness

POP 350

The scattered village of Durness (www.durness .org) is strung out along cliffs, which rise from a series of pristine beaches. It has one of the finest locations in Scotland. When the sun shines the effects of blinding white sand, the cry of seabirds and the lime-coloured seas combine in a magical way.

There are shops, an ATM, petrol and plenty of accommodation options in Durness.

◉ Sights & Activities

Walking around the sensational sandy coastline is a highlight here, as is a visit to Cape Wrath. Durness' beautiful **beaches** include Rispond to the east, Sargo Sands below town and Balnakeil to the west; the sea offers scuba-diving sites complete with wrecks, caves, seals and whales. At **Balnakeil**, less than a mile beyond Durness, a craft village occupies what was once an early-warning radar station. A walk along the beach to the north leads to **Faraid Head**, where you can see puffin colonies in early summer.

John Lennon's Holiday Cottage
HISTORIC BUILDING

As a boy, John Lennon spent many summer holidays at Durness, staying on a croft with his aunt (whose husband's family owned the cottage). He returned in 1969 with wife Yoko Ono and son Julian to revisit old times. To find it, walk southwest along the main road from the tourist office and you'll see a transmitter on a hill; the croft is on the road below it.

There's a blue **memorial plaque** on the whitewashed cottage. Lennon's aunt, Elizabeth Parkes, is buried in the cemetery at Balnakeil.

Smoo Cave
CAVE

A mile east of the village centre is a path, near the SYHA hostel, down to Smoo Cave. The vast cave entrance stands at the end of an inlet, or geo, and a river cascades through its roof into a flooded cavern, then flows out to sea. From the vast main chamber, you can head through to a smaller flooded cavern where a waterfall sometimes cascades from the roof.

There's evidence the cave was inhabited about 6000 years ago. You can also take a **boat trip** (adult/child £3/2; ⊙Apr-Sep) to explore a little further into the interior.

🛏 Sleeping & Eating

TOP CHOICE Mackays
HOTEL ££

(☏01971-511202; www.visitmackays.com; d standard/deluxe £110/125; ⊙Apr-Nov; 🛜) You really feel you're at the furthest corner of Scotland here, where the road turns through 90 degrees. But whether you're heading south or east, you'll go far before you find a better place to stay than this haven of Highland hospitality. With big beds and soft fabrics it's a romantic spot, but what impresses most is the warm-hearted personal service.

The restaurant (mains £11-17) presents local seafood and robust meat dishes.

Lazy Crofter Bunkhouse
HOSTEL £

(☏01971-511202; www.durnesshostel.com; dm £15) Lazy Crofter Bunkhouse is Durness' best budget accommodation. A bothy vibe gives it a Highland feel. The inviting dorms have plenty of room and lockers, and there's also a sociable shared table for meals and board games, and a great wooden deck with sea views, perfect for midge-free evenings.

Loch Croispol Bookshop
CAFE £

(www.scottish-books.net;lightmeals£4-8;⊙10.30am-5pm) At this place you can feed your body and your mind. Set among books featuring all things Scottish are a few tables where you can enjoy an all-day breakfast, sandwiches and

Between Tongue and Durness, the A838 skirts the edge of the curiously named Loch Eriboll (from the Old Norse, meaning 'the farm by the beach'). This sheltered sea loch has long served as a deepwater anchorage for the Royal Navy, and in WWII it was used for marshalling Arctic convoys; British servicemen stationed here used to call it 'Loch 'Orrible', because of the bad weather. More than 30 U-boats of the German Atlantic fleet surrendered here in May 1945.

In 1937 HMS *Hood*, then the world's largest warship, anchored in Loch Eriboll. During her stay, crewmen climbed the hillside above Portnancon on the loch's western shore and spelled out the ship's name in stones. Four years later, in the 1941, the *Hood* was sunk during the Battle of Denmark Strait, with the loss of 1400 lives. The **Hood Stones** are still there, and have recently been repainted with whitewash. They can be seen (best with binoculars) from the the main road at Heilam on the east side of the loch, and are even visible with Google Earth (coordinates 58.507N, 4.724W).

other scrumptious fare at lunch, such as fresh Achiltibuie salmon.

Glengolly B&B   B&B ££
(☎01971-511255; www.glengolly.com; r per person £28-33; P) This B&B has quaint, cottage-style rooms in a working croft. The helpful owners have numerous dogs, both ceramic and real. Breakfast is excellent.

Sango Sands Oasis   CAMPGROUND £
(☎01971-511222; www.sangosands.com; sites per adult/child £5.75/3.50; P) You couldn't imagine a better location for a campground: great grassy areas on the edge of cliffs descend to two lovely sandy beaches. Facilities are good and very clean and there's a pub next door.

Smoo Cave Hotel   PUB GRUB ££
(www.smoocavehotel.co.uk; mains £8-13) Signposted off the main road at the eastern end of town, this no-frills local offers the top corner's best bar food in hefty portions. Haddock or daily specials are an obvious and worthwhile choice; there's also a restaurant area with clifftop views.

Cocoa Mountain   CAFE
(☎01971-511233; hot choc £2.50, 9 truffles £6.50; ☻9am-6pm high season, 10am-5pm low season) Handmade chocolates include a chilli, lemongrass and coconut white-chocolate truffle and many more unique flavours. Tasty espresso and – of course – hot chocolate warm the cockles on those blowy horizontal-drizzle days.

ⓘ Information
Durness Community Building (1 Bard Tce; per 30min £1; @) Coin-op internet access, opposite Mackays.

Durness Health Centre (☎01971-511273)
Durness tourist office (☎01971-511368; durness@visitscotland.com; ☻10am-5pm Mon-Sat Apr-Oct, plus Sun Apr-Aug) Organises guided walks in summer. Closes for an hour for lunch.

Cape Wrath

Though its name actually comes from the Norse word *hvarf* (meaning 'turning point'), there is something daunting and primal about Cape Wrath, the northwesternmost point of the British mainland.

The hazards involved in navigating the often stormy seas around here were long recognised and led to the building of the **lighthouse** at the cape by Robert Stevenson and Alan Stevenson in 1828. The last keepers had left by 1997, when people were replaced by automatic equipment. (There's a **cafe** at the lighthouse serving soup and sandwiches.) Three miles to the east are the seabird colonies of **Clo Mor**, the British mainland's highest vertical sea cliffs (195m).

Part of the Balnakeil Estate on the moorland east of the cape is owned by the Ministry of Defence and has served for decades as a **bombing range** where live ammunition is used. The island of An Garbh-Eilean, 5 miles east of the cape, has the misfortune to be around the same size as an aircraft carrier and is regularly ripped up by RAF bombs and missiles. (There is no public access when the range is in use – the times are displayed at Durness post office, and on the Cape Wrath Minibus website.)

Activities

A **bothy** at Kearvaig, just over halfway between the ferry and Cape Wrath, offers free accommodation (no facilities), and it's possible to continue hiking south from the cape to **Sandwood Bay** and on to Kinlochbervie.

An increasingly popular walking route is the **Cape Wrath Trail** (p264; www.capewrathtrail.co.uk), which runs from Fort William to the cape (200 miles). It's unmarked, so you may want to do it guided – **C-n-Do** (☎01786-445703; www.cndoscotland.com) is one of the operators – or buy *North to the Cape* by Dennis Brook and Phil Hinchcliffe (www.cicerone.co.uk).

Getting There & Away

Getting to Cape Wrath involves taking the **Cape Wrath Ferry** (☎01971-511246; return adult/child £5.50/3, bicycle £2; May-Sep) – passengers and bikes only – across the Kyle of Durness and connecting with the (optional) **Cape Wrath Minibus** (☎0774 267 0196, 01971-511284; www.capewrath.org.uk; return £10; May-Sep), which covers the 12 miles to the cape (40 minutes). This is a friendly but eccentric and sometimes shambolic service, with limited capacity, so plan on waiting in high season, and ring before setting out to make sure the ferry is running. The ferry leaves from Keoldale pier, about 1.5 miles southwest of Durness, and runs two or more times daily from May to September.

Durness to Ullapool

Perhaps Scotland's most spectacular road trip, the 69 miles from Durness to Ullapool is a smorgasbord of dramatic scenery, almost too much to take in. From Durness to Rhiconich the road is nearly all singletrack, passing through a broad heathered valley with the looming grey bulk of Foinaven and Arkle to the southeast. Heather gives way to a rockier landscape of Lewisian gneiss with hundreds of small lochans, and gorse-covered hills prefacing the magnificent Torridonian sandstone mountains of Assynt and Coigach, including ziggurat-like Quinag, the distinctive sugarloaf of Suilven and pinnacled Stac Pollaidh. No wonder the area is dubbed the **Northwest Highlands Geopark** (www.northwest-highlands-geopark.co.uk).

KINLOCHBERVIE & AROUND

The road from Durness meets the sea again at Rhiconich, at the head of Loch Inchard. Here, a minor road leads west to **Kinlochbervie**, which is one of Scotland's premier fish-landing ports, much used by east-coast boats to land their catch, and increasingly by Faroese boats too. The harbour was modernised in the late 1980s, when KLB (as it is known locally) was the third-busiest fish-landing port in Britain – it is close to the superb fishing grounds to the north and west of Cape Wrath. Although its importance has since declined, it is still a hive of activity when the **fishmarket** is in full swing, with refrigerated trucks taking fresh Scottish seafood away to grace the fishmongers slabs and restaurant tables of France, Spain and Portugal.

The minor road continues beyond Kinloch-bervie to the crofting settlement of **Oldshoremore**, which has a lovely sandy beach, and **Blairmore**, the starting point for the walk to Sandwood Bay, one of Scotland's best and most isolated beaches, guarded at one end by the spectacular rock pinnacle Am Buachaille. The road ends at **Sheigra**, where a track leads past the cemetery and down to an idyllic little beach where **wild camping** is allowed (no facilities); cars must be left at the cemetery, a five-minute walk from the beach.

Sights & Activities

Reay Forest Estate HUNTING ESTATE

Stretching inland from Loch Laxford, and covering a vast 96,000 acres, is the Reay Forest Estate belonging to the Duke of Westminster. This privately owned hunting estate is dominated by the vast hills of Foinaven (911m) and Arkle (787m), both of which have had famous racehorses (owned by the Duchess of Westminster) named after them.

Ridgway Adventure OUTDOOR ACTIVITIES

(☎01971-521006; www.ridgway-adventure.co.uk) Loch Laxford is home to this outfit run by Rebecca Ridgway, the first woman to kayak around Cape Horn (daughter of John Ridgway, who was, with Chay Blyth, the first man to row across the Atlantic). As well as outdoor activity courses, the centre offers introductory sea kayak days (adult/child £65/45) for adults and children aged eight and over.

Foinaven HILL WALKING

Falling just short of the magical height of 3000ft (914.4m) means Foinaven escapes the crowds of Munro-baggers heading for Ben Hope, but it is still a challenging and spectacular mountain with a shapely summit ridge, dramatic northern corries, and acres of bare rock and scree. The shortest route to the summit begins at a parking area near a waterfall on the A838, 2.25 miles north of Rhiconich.

The going is pathless and rough. Strike out across the moor, skirting some lochans, aiming straight towards the northwest ridge of Ceann Garbh, where steep grass slopes lead to the top, then follow the main ridge south to Ganu Mor, the highest point of Foinaven. Returning the way you came makes for a round trip of 8 miles (allow five or six hours). Foinaven is an anglicisation of the Gaelic *fionne bheinn* (white mountain), so named for its glittering white screes of Cambrian quartzite.

Sleeping & Eating

Kinlochbervie Hotel HOTEL ££

(☎01971-521275; www.kinlochberviehotel.com; s/d £55/95; P) The outlook from the Kinlochbervie Hotel combines the muscular fishing boats of the commercial harbour with dreamy bay vistas. Traditionally furnished, rooms 1 and 2 are the best, with simply magnificent water views. Meals are available (mains £9 to £10).

Old School B&B ££

(☎01971-521383; www.oldschoolklb.co.uk; s/d £50/75; P) Two miles short of Kinlochbervie, in Inshegra, the Old School is a most welcoming B&B with a variety of rooms, as well as cheaper ones in a bungalow alongside, and good-value evening meals (mains £10 to £12).

KYLESKU & LOCH GLENCOUL

Hidden from the main road on the shores of Loch Glencoul, the hamlet of Kylesku served as a ferry crossing on the route north from the beginning of the 19th century until it was made redundant by the **Kylesku Bridge** in 1984. Designed by Ove Arup, best known for their work on the Sydney Opera House, this elegantly curved bridge is often described as one of the most beautiful in Britain (there's a good view from above the parking area on the north side).

Kylesku marks a geological dividing line between mountain scenery dominated by the reddish-brown Torridonian sandstone of Coigach and Assynt to the south, and the silvery grey quartzite hills of the Foinaven and Arkle ranges to the north. The final flourish of the Torridonian sandstone is the magnificent forked ridge of **Quinag** (808m; from the Gaelic *cuinneag*, meaning 'milking churn', a reference to its barrel-shaped northern buttress), which rises to the south of Kylesku. The easiest route to the summit starts from a parking area near the highest point of the road between Kylesku and Skiag Bridge, and follows a good path to the north side of Lochan Bealach Cornaidh then directly up to the saddle to the west of the highest point.

There isn't much at Kylesku – just a few houses and a pub – but it's a good base for walks and there are several places to stay.

Sights & Activities

Eas a'Chuil Aluinn WATERFALL

Five miles southeast of Kylesku, in wild and remote country beyond the head of Loch Glencoul, lies the 213m-high Eas a'Chuil Aluinn, Britain's highest waterfall. You can hike to the top of the falls from a parking area at a sharp bend in the main road 3 miles south of Kylesku.

The path leads along the north side of Loch na Gainmhich and is clearly marked on OS 1:50,000 map sheet No 15 *Loch Assynt,* but the going is rough and can be very boggy after rain (6 miles round trip, allow five hours).

MV Statesman BOAT TRIP

(☎01971-502345; adult/child £15/5; ⏲Apr-Sep) In summer the *MV Statesman* runs two-hour trips twice daily from Kylesku pier to see the Eas a'Chual Aluinn waterfall and local seal colonies.

Sleeping & Eating

Kylesku Hotel SEAFOOD ££

(☎01971-502231; www.kyleskuhotel.co.uk; bar meals £9-13, mains £13-17; ⏲noon-9pm; wi-fi) You can toast your toes by a log fire, enjoy a pint (decent ales on tap) and tuck into a superb all-day bar meal at the Kylesku Hotel overlooking the Kylesku pier. Seafood is the speciality including local mussels and fish cakes. There's also a restaurant open for even tastier fishy delights at dinner time.

If you fancy bunkering down for the night, a variety of rooms (single/double from £55/80) are available – the separate, motel-style ones with views are the best.

SCOURIE & AROUND

Scourie (www.scourie.co.uk) is a pretty crofting community conveniently located halfway between Durness and Ullapool, with a grocery store and post office, petrol pump and several B&Bs. The surrounding country is pockmarked with countless lochans large and small, providing some of Scotland's best **trout fishing** territory; around 300 lochans

NORTHWEST HIGHLANDS GEOLOGY: A BEGINNER'S GUIDE

It's impossible to explore the northwest Highlands of Scotland without wondering about the subject of geology. There's a lot of naked rock exposed in this harsh but beautiful landscape, and since the 19th-century geologists have learned a great deal about the history of the earth from mapping the area and attempting to understand its intricate details. Despite areas of great complexity, the geology of much of the region is fairly simple, and even a basic knowledge can add to your appreciation of the scenery.

The oldest and most fundamental rock type is **Lewisean gneiss** (3 billion years old), a banded grey and/or pink crystalline rock that underlies much of Scotland's northwest coast and all of the Outer Hebrides (it's named after the Isle of Lewis). Formed deep in the earth's crust, it creates poorly drained, acid soils that support meagre vegetation, and produces a distinctive 'cnoc-and-lochan' landscape (from the Gaelic for 'small hill' and 'small loch'), well seen in Assynt and to the east of Scourie.

Overlying the gneiss is a great thickness of reddish-brown **Torridonian sandstone** (1 billion years old), which is itself topped by a layer of glittering white **Cambrian quartzite** (540 million years old). These rocks were carved and sculpted by the glaciers of the last Ice Age into the fantastically shaped hills of the northwest, with the Torridonian forming steep, stratified cliffs and the quartzite shattering into silvery grey scree. Mountains such as Liathach and Beinn Eighe in Torridon, and Canisp and Quinag in Assynt, display lower slopes of layered sandstone rising above foothills of hummocky gneiss, topped with summit caps of silvery quartzite.

These rock layers slope gently towards the east, so that as you travel from west to east you pass upwards throught the geological succession. On top of the quartzite and outcropping along a narrow band that roughly follows a line between Ullapool and Loch Eriboll, lies the **Durness limestone** (500 million years old). This layered, grey rock – rare in the Highlands – produces a fertile, lime-rich soil that has created oases of lush green pasture among the more typical bog and heather of the region. Easily dissolved by rainwater, it is also responsible for the creation of subterranean rivers and caves such as Smoo Cave (p242) and the caves of Inchnadamph.

Finally, there are the **Moine schists**, which began life as siltstones and sandstones deposited far to the southeast around the same time as the Cambrian quartzite. Then, around 420 million years ago, a continental collision – of the type that created the Alps and the Himalayas – folded and heated the Moine rocks (metamorphosing them into crystalline schists) and shunted them tens of miles to the northwest, sliding over the Cambrian, Torridonian and Lewisian rocks on a near-horizontal fault plane known as the **Moine Thrust**.

As you travel from west to east, the line of the Moine Thrust – which runs roughly from Kinlochewe via Inchnadamph to the eastern shore of Loch Erinboll, and is famously exposed at Knockan Crag (p251) – marks a transition from the dramatic and varied landscape of the northwest Highlands to the rounded, heather-clad hills typical of the Moine schists (which make up most of the eastern and central Highlands).

If you're interested in learning more, the Assynt Visitor Centre (p250) has a geological model of the northwest Highlands, and sells *Exploring the Landscape of Assynt,* a simplified geological map of the region accompanied by a guidebook detailing ten geological walks.

are managed by the Scourie Hotel (permits £25 a week, free to hotel guests, boat hire £10 a day).

At Laxford Bridge, 6.5 miles north of Scourie, the A839 leads southeast towards Loch Shin and Lairg. A few miles from the junction rises the magnificent minimountain of **Ben Stack** (720m), which appears perfectly conical when seen from the road between Scourie and Laxford Bridge. It can be climbed easily via a stalker's path which begins about 500m northwest of the turnoff to Lochstack Lodge, near a parking area at a small stone building; when you reach Loch na Seilge, turn left and follow the fence towards the summit, which is approached via an exhilaratingly narrow ridge.

Activities

Scourie Wildlife Cruises WILDLIFE WATCHING
(☎0777 562 2890; www.scouriewildlifecruises
.co.uk; 2hr cruise adult/child £25/15; ◷10am-4pm
Mon-Sat Apr-Sep) Runs speedboat trips (on demand, minimum four persons) south to the
Badcall Islands and Eddrachilles Bay to spot
seals, basking sharks, dolphins and whales,
and north to Handa Island to see the spectacular seacliffs and seabird colonies.

Sleeping

Scourie Hotel HOTEL, PUB ££
(☎01971-502396; www.scouriehotel.co.uk; s/d
£54/102; ℗) The Scourie Hotel is very much
an angler's hotel, adorned with stuffed
trout in glass cases and a lounge full of
blokes telling tales about the one that got
away. The rooms are determinedly old-
fashioned – 'definitely no televisions' says
the brochure – and the wonderful, wood-
panelled bar is famous for its selection of
cask ales and malt whiskies.

Scourie Lodge B&B ££
(☎01971-502248; s/d £50/75; ℗) If you're looking to spoil yourself, Scourie Lodge, in a
gorgeous building overlooking the bay, has
old-style comfort and hospitality in a lovely
setting; the garden's palm trees are proof
of the Gulf Stream's good works. Dinner is
available (£25). Cards aren't taken.

Scourie Camp Site CAMPGROUND £
(☎01971-502060; Harbour Rd; sites £6-10; ◷Apr-
Sep) Basic facilities but a beautiful setting,
and the added advantage of an onsite pub. No
bookings taken, so turn up early if you want
to grab a prime location overlooking the bay.

ASSYNT

With its otherworldly scenery of isolated
peaks rising above a sea of crumpled, lo-
chan-spattered gneiss, Assynt epitomises
the wild magnificence of the northwest
Highlands. The poorly drained bedrock of
Lewisian gneiss has created a wilderness
of bog, lochan and bare rock outcrops (the
name Assynt comes from the Old Norse *ass,*
meaning 'rocky'), while the glaciers of the
last Ice Age have sculpted the hills of Suilven
(731m), Canisp (846m), Quinag (808m) and
Ben More Assynt (998m) into strange and
wonderful silhouettes.

The crofters of Assynt made history in
1993 when they engineered a community
buyout of the land they lived on. The **North
Assynt Estate**, including the townships of
Achmelvich, Clachtoll, Stoer and Drumbeg,
is now owned and managed by the Assynt
Crofters' Trust (www.assyntcrofters.co.uk)
on behalf of the inhabitants. They were
followed in 2005 by the Assynt Foundation (www.assyntfoundation.org), which
purchased the Glencanisp and Drumrunie
estates, so that most of the region's glorious
scenery is now in community ownership.
The foundation's stated objective is 'to man-
age community land and associated assets
for the benefit of the Community and the
public in general as an important part of the
protection and sustainable development of
Scotland's natural environment'.

WORTH A TRIP

HANDA ISLAND

A few miles north of Scourie Bay lies **Handa Island** (www.swt.org.uk), a nature reserve
run by the Scottish Wildlife Trust. The island's western sea cliffs of stratified Torridonian
sandstone rise to over 100m and provide nesting sites for important breeding populations of great skuas, arctic skuas, puffins, kittiwakes, razorbills and guillemots. There's a
nice beach near the ferry landing, from which a rough path leads for a mile or so across
the centre of the island to the clifftops where you can admire the **Great Stack of Handa**,
a 110m-tall sea stack first climbed in 1969, and fantastic views south to the Old Man of
Stoer on the far side of Eddrachillis Bay. From here, you can follow a rough path westward
around the coast to return to the ferry.

The **ferry** (☎07775-625890; adult/child £10/5; ◷9am-2pm Mon-Sat Apr-early Sep) to
Handa (just a small motor boat) leaves from Tarbet Pier, 5.5 miles north of Scourie. At
Tarbet you'll find the **Shorehouse** (☎01971-502251; Tigh-na-Mara; mains £9-18; ◷noon-7pm
Mon-Sat), a restaurant and cafe in a lovely setting, looking across the sound to the sandy
beach on Handa Island. There's a conservatory and outdoor terrace that make the most
of the view, and a menu that concentrates on local seafood including crab and prawn
salads and Achiltibuie smoked salmon.

Lochinver is the main settlement in the Assynt region, a busy little fishing port that's a popular port of call for tourists, with its laid-back atmosphere, good facilities, striking scenery and range of accommodation.

◎ Sights

The Lochinver–Lairg road (A837) runs along the northern shore of wild and moody **Loch Assynt**, and meets the Durness road (A894) at Skiag Bridge, about 10 miles east of Lochinver. Perched on an island at the edge of the loch, half a mile south of here, are the romantic ruins of **Ardvreck Castle**, a 15th-century stronghold of the MacLeods of Assynt. There are rumoured to be several ghosts at Ardvreck, including the daughter of a MacLeod chieftain who was sold in marriage to the devil by her father. Nearby are the ruins of a barrack house built by the MacKenzies in the 1720s. There are wonderful summer sunsets over the castle and the loch.

At the eastern end of Loch Assynt is the tiny hamlet of **Inchnadamph**, a favourite haunt of geology students and speleologists, sitting as it does near the Moine Thrust and a large area of cave-riddled Durness limestone.

Heading south from Kylesku to Lochinver, an alternative to the main road is the scenic B869 loop via Drumbeg and Stoer, 27 miles of steep and twisting singletrack that offers majestic vistas of sea and mountain. It passes through **Drumbeg**, a picturesque hamlet perched above Loch Drumbeg, a superb loch for trout fishing. Drumberg is the centre for the 200 or so **trout lochs** managed by the North Assynt Estate; permits (per day adult/child £5/free) can be purchased at Drumbeg Stores, the Drumbeg Hotel and the Assynt Visitor Centre.

Five miles west of Drumbeg the road passes the fine sandy bay of **Clashnessie beach** before cutting across the headland to the hamlet of Stoer. On the way, a minor road cuts north to **Stoer Head lighthouse** – from the car park below the lighthouse, a rough path (signposted) leads 2.5 miles along the clifftops to the **Old Man of Stoer**, a spectacular 60m-tall seastack. If you're lucky, there will be rock climbers scaling the stack – to get there they have to swim the chilly waters of the channel between the stack and the mainland.

Just a few miles short of Lochinver, a side road leads to **Achmelvich**. It's no more than a hamlet with a campsite and youth hostel, but it sits close to some fine sandy beaches. If the main bay is too crowded for your tastes, you can walk north about 250m to the next sandy cove, or continue along the coastal path for a mile to the so-called **Secret Beach** of Port Alltan na Bradhan. At low tide this is a perfectly sheltered swimming cove fringed with sand and shingle; on the stream nearby is the ruin of an ancient **barley mill**, complete with discarded millstones. You can also reach this spot from a small parking area on the B869 (at grid reference 055263 on the OS 1:50,000 map sheet 15 *Loch Assynt*), where a rough path (signposted 'Mill') leads to the beach in just 300m.

🏃 Activities

The limestone hills around Inchnadamph are famous for their caves. The Assynt Visitor Centre (p250) in Lochinver has plenty of information on walking and other activities.

Traligill Caves   WALKING

From the car park near the Inchnadamph Hotel you can follow an unsurfaced road and footpath along the north side of the River Traligill to the Traligill Caves, a series of sinkholes and caverns in the valley floor where the river disappears and resurges (4.5 miles return, allow 2.5 hours).

First you arrive at the impressive Uamh an Uisge (Water Cave), a deep diagonal rift with the stream foaming along in the depths; a short distance on (to the left) is the arched opening of Uamh an Tartair (the Cave of Roaring); you can hear the roar of the underground stream from the entrance.

Bone Caves   WALKING

A car park about 2 miles south of Inchnadamph is the starting point for a walk along the Allt nan Uamh (Stream of the Cave) to the so-called Bone Caves (3 miles round trip, allow two hours). In 1889, geologists excavated the bones of bears, wolves, reindeer and lynx from the floors of these caves; more recently, the bones of four human beings, dating back to 4500 years ago, have been discovered.

Ben More Assynt   HILL-WALKING

The principal attraction for Munro baggers around Assynt is Ben More Assynt (998m), reached by a 10.5-mile (allow eight hours) round-trip hike via Gleann Dubh and the northern ridge of Conival (988m), starting along the Traligill Caves path from the Inchnadamph Hotel parking area. Check at the hotel regarding access during the deer-stalking season, from August to October.

The shapely peak of Suilven (731m) is one of the most distinctive of all Scottish mountains – it appears as a sugarloaf when seen from the west, a shapely pointed peak from the east, and a long, serrated ridge from north or south. No keen walker can resist its allure but, despite its modest height, the hill's remote setting makes it a challenging objective.

There are three possible starting points – **Loch Cam** near Ledmore Junction; **Glencanisp Lodge**, 1.5 miles east of Lochinver; and **Inverkirkaig**, 3 miles south of Lochinver. All involve a 12- to 14-mile round trip; the Glencanisp Lodge route is marginally the shortest, but the Inverkirkaig approach is the most scenic and is described here.

Starting from the car park at the bridge over the River Kirkaig (4 miles south of Lochinver), follow a good path southeast along the north side of the river. After 2.25 miles you reach the spectacular **Falls of Kirkaig** (worth visiting in their own right as the objective of a shorter walk), and a half-mile beyond that (at a cairn) fork left to cut across a neck of land to the **Fionn Loch**. There are superb views of Suilven ahead as the path weaves around the head of the loch and along its boggy northern shore.

When almost level with the **Bealach Mor** (the low point in the middle of Suilven's ridge), a fainter path strikes north across moorland towards the mountain itself. The path climbs steeply up boulders, turf and scree, becoming badly eroded in its upper part, to reach the bealach. Turn left for an airy ridgewalk to the flat-topped summit, passing through a gap in a beautifully made but mysterious drystane dyke (no one seems to know who built it, or why). At the summit – weather permitting – you will be rewarded with incredible panoramas of mountain, moorland, loch and sea. Return the way you came (14 miles, allow seven to nine hours).

🛏 Sleeping

TOP CHOICE **Albannach**   HOTEL £££
(☏01571-844407; www.thealbannach.co.uk; Baddidarroch; s/d/ste with dinner from £200/260/340; ⊙Mar-Dec; P🛜) The Albannach is sheer indulgence, on a grand scale. You'll discover roaring fireplaces, furniture found only in antique shops and a demure, sophisticated atmosphere. Roomy lodgings decorated with elegant flair, spacious grounds with fruit trees, and inspiring panoramas combine to make it a special spot. The **restaurant** (☏01571-844407; www.thealbannach.co.uk; Baddidarroch; 5-course dinner £58) conjures up wonderful dinners using organic ingredients and well-selected local produce.

Ruddyglow Park   B&B £££
(☏01571-822216; www.ruddyglowpark.co.uk; Loch Assynt; d £120-160; P🛜) Set in 4 acres of private grounds on the shores of Loch Assynt, Ruddyglow (named after a racehorse) is a gorgeous boutique guesthouse offering five-star luxury in a relaxed and homely setting. Choose among three indulgent bedrooms (with Egyptian cotton sheets and silk-covered goosedown duvets) or the privacy of a wooden chalet in the garden.

Veyatie   B&B ££
(☏015/1-844424; www.veyatie-scotland.co.uk; Baddidarroch; s/d £48/76; ⊙Jan-Nov; P🛜) Overseen by a personable Belgian shepherd (dog), this choice at the end of the road across the bay has perhaps the best views of all, as well as sweet rooms, a little conservatory and a grassy garden.

Lochinver Mission Bunkhouse   HOSTEL £
(☏01571-855313; www.lochinvermission.org.uk; Culag Park; dm £17; P) There was no hostel accommodation available in Lochinver at the time of research, but a new community-run hostel housed in the former fishermen's mission down by the harbour opened while this book was in production.

Inchnadamph Hotel   HOTEL ££
(☏01571-822202; www.inchnadamphhotel.com; Inchnadamph; per person £44; ⊙closed Nov-Feb; P🛜) This 200-year-old coaching inn is as comfortable and worn as a pair of old hiking boots. It's a haven of peace (no TVs or mobile phone reception) in the middle of nowhere. A favourite haunt of hillwakers, anglers, cavers and geologists, it's a bit musty and lived-in, but the owners are friendly and welcoming and very knowledgable about the local area.

Inchnadamph Lodge
HOSTEL, B&B £

(☎01571-822218; www.inch-lodge.co.uk; Inchnadamph; dm/d £17.25/51; P@☎) Situated by the Lochinver–Lairg road, this place is a friendly 50-bed lodge with lots of rustic accommodation. Most rooms are spacious and clean and there's a separate music/TV lounge for late partying. The facilities are excellent and it's very popular with groups.

Shore Caravan Site
CAMPGROUND £

(☎01571-844393; shorecaravansite.yolasite.com; Achmelvich; tent site £5-12, campervan £8-12; ☺Apr-Sep) Grassy site in an attractive setting next to Achmelvich's gorgeous sandy beach. Onsite shop open 8am to 8pm from May to August. First-come first-served (no bookings), and no dogs allowed.

✗ Eating

Lochinver Larder & Riverside Bistro
SCOTTISH, SEAFOOD ££

(☎01571-844356; www.lochinverlarder.co.uk; 3 Main St, Lochinver; pies £6, mains £10-16; ☺10am-8.30pm) Serving as coffee shop, bistro and takeaway, the Larder offers an outstanding menu of inventive food made with local produce. The bistro turns out delicious seafood dishes in the evening, while the takeaway counter (open till 7pm) sells delicious Lochinver pies with a wide range of gourmet fillings: try the smoked haddock, or wild boar and apricot – very tasty.

Caberfeidh
PUB GRUB ££

(☎01571-844321; www.thecaberfeidh.co.uk; Main St, Lochinver; mains £10-17; ☺lunch & dinner, closed Mon & Tue winter) Providing some stiff competition for the Lochinver Larder, this convivial pub (with a riverside beer garden) serves a range of real ales and some excellent pub grub. As well as catch of the day, the menu offers steaks, burgers, scallops, mussels and haddock and chips, and a couple of vegetarian dishes.

🛍 Shopping

Highland Stoneware
ARTS & CRAFTS

(www.highlandstoneware.com; Lochinver; ☺Mon-Fri, plus Sat Easter-Oct) Using local landscapes as inspiration, Highland Stoneware ensures that you can relive the majesty of the northwest every time you look into the bottom of your teacup. Even better are the mosaics outside, especially the car.

Achins Bookshop
BOOKS

(☎01571-844262; www.scotbooks.freeuk.com; Inverkirkaig; ☺10am-6pm May-Sep) Probably Scotland's most remote bookshop, this snug literary haven is a short walk uphill from the car park at Inverkirkaig bridge. It has been around for 35 years and is well stocked with titles on local history, wildlife and Scottish interest. It also has an excellent coffee shop (closes at 5pm).

🛈 Information

There's a supermarket in town, as well as a post office, bank (with an ATM) and petrol station.

Assynt Visitor Centre (☎01571-844654; www.assynt.info; Main St; ☺10am-5pm Mon-Sat Easter-Oct, also 10am-4pm Sun Jun-Aug) Has leaflets on hill walks in the area and a display on the story of Assynt, from wildlife and geology to clans, conflict and controversy.

COIGACH

The region to the south of Assynt, bounded on the east by the main A835 road from Ullapool to Ledmore Junction, is known as Coigach (www.coigach.com). A lone, single-track road penetrates this wilderness, leading through gloriously wild scenery to the remote settlements of Altandhu, Achiltibuie and Achininver. At the western end of Loch Lurgainn, a branch leads north to Lochinver, a scenic backroad so narrow and twisting that caravans are prohibited, and locals refer to it as the **Wee Mad Road**.

Coigach is a wonderland for walkers and wildlife enthusiasts, with a patchwork of sinuous silver lochs dominated by the isolated peaks of Cul Mor (849m), Cul Beag (769m), Ben More Coigach (743m) and Stac Pollaidh (613m). Ordnance Survey map sheet 15, *Loch Assynt,* charts this magical landscape in all its glory.

The area was designated as Inverpolly National Nature Reserve from 1962 until 2004, when a conflict with one of the estate owners over land management led SNH to abandon the reserve. The area is still designated as a Site of Special Scientific Interest, and falls within the Coigach-Assynt National Scenic Area; the region south of Loch Lurgainn is managed by the Scottish Wildlife Trust as the **Ben More Coigach Nature Reserve**. Otters and black-throated divers can be seen on the freshwater lochs, and golden eagles are a common sight overhead.

ACHILTIBUIE

The main settlement in Coigach is the straggling township of **Achiltibuie**, 15 miles from the main road. With sheep nibbling the grassy roadside verges, the gorgeous Summer Isles moored just off the coast and the silhouettes of mountains skirting the bay, this village epitomises idyllic Scottish beauty – the perfect place for some serious relaxation.

Achiltibuie has a **general store** (☎01854-622496; www.achiltibuiestores.com; ⊙9am-5.30pm Mon-Sat, to 6pm May-Sep) with petrol pump, and a craft shop and hotel. To its southeast is the hamlet of Achininver, and along the coast to the northwest lie the crofting settlements of Polbain, Altandhu and Reiff.

SUMMER ISLES

The dozen islands scattered in the sea to the west of Achiltibuie are known as the **Summer Isles**. There's a superb view of the islands, with the hills of Wester Ross in the background, from the minor road between Altandhu and Achnahaird – look out for a layby with a bench and a signpost, where a short path leads to the viewpoint.

In the late 19th century the Summer Isles were home to 120 people working at the herring fishery, but now the permanent population is only half a dozen, augmented by up to 30 holiday visitors. The largest island, **Tanera Mor** (☎01854-622252; www.summer-isles.com), has five self-catering holiday cottages to rent, and offers arts and crafts courses and a summer sailing school (see website for details). It also has a cafe (p253) and a privately run **post office** (⊙10am-5pm Mon-Sat May-Sep) that produces its own (highly collectable) stamps.

◉ Sights

Knockan Crag   NATURE RESERVE
(www.knockan-crag.co.uk; Knockan; admisson free; ⊙24hrs) Discovered by Victorian scientists, and visited by generations of British geology students, Knockan Crag is an outcrop of rock that revolutionised earth science. Info boards and interactive displays keep the kids amused and explain the significance of the site, while a sculpture trail leads up to the geological anomaly that inspired all this – an exposure of the **Moine Thrust**.

It was here that geologists first recognised the existence of thrust faults – low angle shear zones where continental collisions have forced older rocks to slide up and over younger ones for distances of many miles. Here, the older Moine schist rests on top of the younger Durness limestone, a conundrum that puzzled geologists for almost a century. Knockan lies on the main A835 road, 13 miles north of Ullapool.

ℹ SUILVEN PHOTO OPS

If you're hoping to bag some classic images of Suilven, here are three viewpoints that are easily reached by car; all are at their best late in the day, when the setting sun tinges the peaks with gold.

» **Baddidarrach**: the minor road that leads along the north shore of the loch from Lochinver village (and the footpath beyond the road end) provides a grandstand view of the classic profile that gave Suilven its name (Pillar Mountain) – from here it looms over the village like a giant sugarloaf, seemingly inaccessible.

» **Loch Culag**: about a mile south of Lochinver, on the road to Inverkirkaig (park at the cattle grid, not in a passing place), this spot offers another picture-postcard classic of Suilven's massive, blunt summit reflected in the lily-dappled waters of the loch (best with a telephoto lens).

» **Clachtoll Road**: there's a parking area and viewpoint on the B869 road (signposted Achmelvich, Clachtoll and Stoer), about 4 miles northwest of Lochinver. From here, the view is broad and expansive, taking in not only Suilven but also Canisp and Cul Mor, and provides a breathtaking impression of the wildness and isolation of the Assynt hills.

Hydroponicum   GARDEN
(Achiltibuie Garden; ☎01854-622202; www.thehydroponicum.com; Achiltibuie; admission £1; ⊙11am-4pm Mon-Fri Easter-Oct) The Hydroponicum is a demonstration garden based in a couple of large greenhouses opposite the Summer Isles Hotel. It shows how tropical fruit, vegetables and flowers can be grown without the need for soil by feeding their roots with nutrient-rich water. A shop sells all you need to dabble in hydroponics yourself, from window basket starter kits to full greenhouse equipment.

The Hydroponicum was originally established in the 1980s by Robert Irvine, the then owner of the Summer Isles Hotel (and father of Lucy Irvine, author of bestselling memoir *Castaway*), to provide the hotel kitchen with fresh fruit and veg. It is now run by three local businesswomen; at the time of research a new visitor centre was under construction.

Achiltibuie Smokehouse   SMOKEHOUSE
(☎01854-622353; www.summerislesfoods.co.uk; Altandhu; ☺9am-5pm Mon-Fri) This small-scale family-run smokehouse specialises in producing organic smoked salmon, but also turns out kippers, smoked venison and smoked cheese. Visitors get an explanation of the smoking process, and a chance to sample the produce.

Isle Martin   ISLAND
(www.islemartin.co.uk; Ardmair; ferry return £6; ☺Jun-Sep) Until WWII this island, just 4 miles northwest of Ullapool, had a population of 30; now it is deserted. It's run as a nature reserve by the local community of Ardmair, and visitors can explore the old herring curing station and the remains of an early Christian monastery, go birdwatching or just climb to the summit of the island for a view of the Summer Isles.

🏃 Activities
There are several short, easy **coastal walks** beginning at Achininver Youth Hostel, and around the lovely sandy beach at **Achnahaird Bay**. A more strenuous, pathless hike with superb coastal views goes from the road-end at Reiff to **Rubha Coigeach** (5 miles round trip).

Loch an Doire Dhuibh   WALKING
One of the best low-level walks in the northwest starts from the minor road along Loch Lurgainn, at a small wood 1.5 miles east of the Stac Pollaidh car park. A path leads over the pass between Stac Pollaidh and Cul Beag, to reach a fork above Loch an Doire Dhuibh; take the righthand branch to descend through birchwoods and around the east end of the loch. Cross the stream beyond the loch and follow it northwestwards, downstream past a gamekeeper's hut and a smaller loch, then cross back via a footbridge. From here another path leads back to the original fork and thence back to the road (4 miles, allow two to three hours).

Postie's Path   WALKING
For a more challenging walk, try the 'Postie's Path', a 6-mile scramble along the southern slopes of Ben More Coigach between Strath Kanaird (8 miles north of Ullapool) and Achininver. Although the path has been maintained and keeps to a low altitude, it demands respect – a sign at the beginning warns, 'You are entering remote, sparsely populated, potentially dangerous mountain country. Please ensure that you are adequately experienced and equipped to complete your journey without assistance'. If you find the going tough, just think that from Victorian times until the 1960s, when a tarmac road finally connected the village to the outside world, the Achiltibuie postman walked this route to Ullapool and back twice every week, carrying the mail.

Stac Pollaidh   WALKING
Despite its diminutive size, Stac Pollaidh (613m) provides one of the most exciting hill walks in the Highlands with some good scrambling on its narrow sandstone crest. Begin at the car park overlooking Loch Lurgainn, 5 miles west of the A835, and follow a clearly marked and well-made footpath around the eastern end of the hill to ascend from the far side; return by the same route (3 miles round trip, allow two to four hours).

Loch Sionascaig   CANOEING, FISHING
The convoluted Loch Sionascaig, and its neighbours to the north Loch Veyatie and Fionn Loch, provide some of the most spectacular wilderness canoeing in Scotland, through remote and uninhabited country. This is challenging terrain, involving portages and long paddling sessions, but the rewards include superb mountain scenery, camping on deserted islands, and unparalleled tranquillity.

Loch Sionascaig is also one of the best **trout lochs** in the northwest Highlands, packed with small but feisty brownies and the occasional large ferox. Permits and information on hiring boats can be obtained from the **Inverpolly Estate Office** (☎01854-622452; www.inverpolly.com).

Wilderness Scotland   OUTDOOR ACTIVITIES
(☎0131 625 6635; www.wildernessscotland.com; per person £695) Runs six-day, guided canoeing-and-hiking trips into the Loch Sionascaig area, for reasonably fit people with no previous experience of canoeing.

NorWest Sea Kayaking   SEA KAYAKING
(☎01571-844281; www.norwestseakayaking.com; 6 Inver Tce) This outfit offers three-day introductory sea kayaking courses based on the island of Tanera Beg in the Summer Isles (£300 per person including equipment hire, accommodation and food). It also runs guided kayaking tours around the Summer Isles and in the Lochinver and Ullapool area.

Summer Isles Cruises

BOAT TOURS

(☎01854-622200; www.summer-isles-cruises
.co.uk; adult/child £22/11; ⊗Mon-Sat May-Sep)
Operates boat trips to the Summer Isles
where you'll see some magnificent island
scenery. Three-hour trips include one hour
ashore on Tanera Mor, where the post office
issues its own stamps.

🛏 Sleeping & Eating

Accommodation is limited to the coastal
villages of Achiltibuie (hotel), Achininver
(youth hostel), Polbain (a couple of B&Bs)
and Altandhu (campground); best to book
ahead. Self-catering accommodation is listed at www.coigach.com. Wild camping is
possible in many places.

TOP CHOICE Summer Isles Hotel

HOTEL £££

(☎01854-622282; www.summerisleshotel.co.uk; s
£115-175, d £145-210; ⊗Easter-Oct; P) The Summer Isles Hotel is a special place indeed,
with wonderfully snug rooms – some are
suites in separate cottages sleeping two to
six – plus cracking views and a snug bar
with convivial outdoor seating. It's the perfect spot for a romantic getaway or some
quality time off life's treadmill.

Achininver SYHA

HOSTEL £

(☎01854-622482; www.syha.org.uk; Achininver;
dm £15; ⊗mid-May-Aug) The rudimentary 20-
bed Achininver hostel is designed for walkers and outdoor enthusiasts – you have to
walk half a mile off the main road to reach
it. Its remote, serene location has to be one
of the best in the country.

Port A'Bhalgh Campsite

CAMPGROUND £

(☎01854-622339; www.portabhaigh.co.uk; Altand-
hu; sites £8-12, plus per adult/child £2/1 ; ⊗Easter-
Sep; 🖰) An excellent new campground below
Am Fuaran Bar, with an outlook across Isle
Ristol towards summer sunsets.

TOP CHOICE Summer Isles Hotel

SEAFOOD £££

(www.summerisleshotel.co.uk; 5-course dinner £56;
⊗lunch & dinner) Until 2011 the restaurant at
the Summer Isles Hotel sported a Michelin
star, but while the accolade has gone the
chef remains the same and the quality of the
food – especially the local seafood – is still
superb. You can also enjoy excellent food in
the hotel bar (served noon to 8.30pm), but
for half the price.

Summer Isles Cafe

CAFE £

(Summer Isles; mains £3-7; ⊗10am-4pm Mon-Sat
May-Sep) Serves homemade scones, cakes,
and vegetarian sandwiches, using organic,
fair trade and local produce as much as
possible.

Am Fuaran Bar

PUB GRUB, SEAFOOD ££

(☎01854-622339; www.amfuaran.co.uk; Altandhu; mains £9-18; ⊗lunch & dinner; 🖰🖰) A snug
little watering hole with a cosy, rustic atmosphere, Am Fuaran (the name is Gaelic for
'The Well' – there's one near the entrance)
has a menu of homemade soup, smoked
salmon and steaks, but the main attraction
is chalked on the blackboard – the day's
selection of fresh local seafood, including
plump langoustines and lobster.

ℹ Getting There & Around

BOAT Tanera Mor Ferry (☎01854-622252;
www.summer-isles.com; return £15)

BUS There are buses operating Monday to Saturday from Ullapool to Reiff, Badenscallie (half a
mile from Achininver Youth Hostel) and Achiltibuie (1½ hours, two daily Monday to Friday, one
Saturday).

Ullapool

POP 1308

The pretty port of Ullapool, on the shores
of Loch Broom, is the largest settlement
in Wester Ross and one of the most alluring spots in the Highlands, a wonderful
destination in itself as well as a gateway to
the Western Isles. Offering a row of whitewashed cottages arrayed along the harbour
and special views of the loch and its flank-
ing hills, the town has a very distinctive
appeal.

Ullapool takes its name from a Viking
noble; the old Norse name, Ulla-Bolsadr,
means 'Ulla's farmstead'. The village was
planned by the rather important-sounding
British Society for Extending the Fisheries
and Improving the Sea Coasts of the Kingdom of Great Britain, which laid out the
grid pattern of streets in 1788. The land
originally belonged to the MacLeods and
MacKenzies of Easter Ross but was ceded
to the crown after the 1745 Rebellion. The
harbour also served as an emigration point
during the Clearances, with thousands
of Scots watching the loch recede behind
them as the diaspora cast them across the
world.

At the height of the herring boom, hundreds of 'dipping luggers' plied the waters
around Loch Broom, but the 'silver darlings'
eventually vanished from the loch after

Ullapool

Ullapool

WWII. Ullapool found a new lease of life as a mackerel-fishing station, attracting dozens of Eastern Bloc factory ships until the collapse of the Soviet Union. Today there are only a dozen or so local boats, fishing mostly for prawns, lobsters and scallops.

Although it's a popular stop on the tourist circuit, Ullapool still has heaps of charm and is an excellent base for exploring the west coast. There are good walks in the area, plus some excellent places to stay and regular transport links to other parts of the Highlands. Ferries sail daily from Ullapool to Stornoway on the Isle of Lewis.

◉ Sights & Activities

Ullapool is a great centre for **walking**. Good walking books sold at the tourist office include *Walks in Wester Ross* (£2.95), or you can pick up a copy of the freebie guide to local woodland walks.

If you're just after a stroll, try the low-level track beside the Ullapool River to **Loch Achall** (two hours return), starting from the sign at the end of Mill St. The path is well marked and offers grand views of **An Teallach** (1062m) on the far side of Loch Broom.

For something slightly longer, there's a pleasant hill walk along the **Ullapool River** to East Rhidorroch Lodge, a return trip of 16 miles (seven hours). The **Postie's Path** (p252) to Achiltibuie is a challenging 6-mile walk beneath Ben More Coigach, starting at Strath Kanaird (8 miles north of Ullapool).

Serious hill-walkers come to Ullapool to bag the nearby Munro of **Beinn Dearg** (1084m), northeast of Braemore, reached by a good path from the Inverlael forest, at the inner end of Loch Broom. Another way of approaching this rough and wild mountain is from the south, from the top of Loch Glascarnoch (no path). The walk will take about eight hours, whichever your route. Make sure that you're well equipped, and remember to carry OS map No 20. The regular buses to Inverness on the A835 can be used to reach either trailhead.

In summer the ferry company CalMac (p199) runs **day trips** to Lewis and Harris.

Ullapool Museum
MUSEUM

(www.ullapoolmuseum.co.uk; 7 West Argyle St; adult/child £3/50p; ☺10am-5pm Mon-Sat Apr-Oct) Housed in a converted Telford Parliamentary church, this museum relates the prehistoric, natural and social history of the town and Lochbroom area, with a particular focus on the emigration to Nova Scotia and other places. There's also a genealogy section if you want to trace your Scottish roots.

FREE An Talla Solais
ART GALLERY

(Ullapool Visual Arts; ☎01854-612310; www.antallasolais.org; Market St; admission free; ☺2-5pm daily) An Talla Solais is a community-run gallery that stages changing exhibitions of works by Highlands artists, from paintings and photography to ceramics and textiles. Opening hours can vary, so check the website or local flyers for the latest exhibition dates and times.

FREE Rhue Studio
GALLERY

(☎01854-612460; www.rhueart.co.uk; admission free; ☺Mon-Sat Apr-Sep) This studio, 2.5 miles northwest of Ullapool, displays and sells the excellent art of contemporary landscape painter James Hawkins. The vivid and reflective works take a moment to adjust to but they are wonderful interpretations – his work on the Outer Hebrides is breathtaking. Call for winter opening hours.

Seascape
ISLANDS TOUR

(☎01854-633708; www.sea-scape.co.uk; adult/child £28.50/20) Runs two-hour tours out to the Summer Isles in an orange rigid inflatable boat (RIB).

Summer Queen
ISLANDS TOUR

(☎07713 257219; www.summerqueen.co.uk; ☺Mon-Sat May-Sep) The stately *Summer Queen* takes you out (weather permitting) around **Isle Martin** (£20/10 per adult/child, two hours) or to the **Summer Isles** (£30/15, four hours), with a stop on Tanera Mor.

🛏 Sleeping

Note that during summer Ullapool is very busy and finding accommodation can be tricky – book ahead.

TOP CHOICE Ceilidh Place
HOTEL ££

(☎01854-612103; www.theceilidhplace.com; 14 West Argyle St; d £100-146; P ☺) The Ceilidh Place is one of the more unusual and delightful places to stay in the Highlands. Rooms go for character rather than modern conveniences, and come with a selection of books chosen by Scottish literati, eclectic artwork and nice little touches like hot-water bottles. Best of all is the sumptuous lounge, with sofas, chaises longues and an honesty bar.

The hotel is also a celebration of Scottish culture, with a capital C – we're talking literature and traditional music, not tartan and Nessie dolls.

West House
B&B ££

(☎01854-613126; www.accommodationullapool.net; West Argyle St; d £70; ☺) Slap bang in the centre of Ullapool, this solid white house that was once a manse offers excellent rooms with contemporary style and great bathrooms. Breakfast is continental style: rooms come with a fridge stocked with fresh fruit salad and juice so you can eat at your leisure in your own chamber. Hires out bikes to explore the surrounding area.

Woodlands
B&B £

(☎01854-612701; www.ullapoolbandb.com; 1a Pulteney St; d £50; ☺May-Sep; P ☺) With just two comfortable rooms sharing a bathroom, this place should be booked ahead; the effervescent hosts make it a great bet. The breakfast is memorable: they make marmalade, jams and bread and smoke their own fish out the back.

Ullapool SYHA
HOSTEL £

(☎01854-612254; www.syha.org.uk; Shore St; dm/tw £17.25/38; ☺Mar-Oct) You've got to hand it to the SYHA; it has chosen some very sweet locations for its hostels. This is as close to the water as it is to the town's best pub: about four seconds' walk. The front rooms have harbour views but the busy dining area and little lounge are also good spots for contemplating the water.

Point Cottage
B&B ££

(☎01854-612494; www.pointcottage.co.uk; 22 West Shore St; d £70; ☺Mar-Oct; P) A haven of good taste, the courteous and welcoming Point Cottage has a great headland location – even the back rooms have water views. It's one of those shorefront cottages you've already admired if you arrived by ferry, and it'll feel comfy for both hedonists – smoked fish for breakfast – and walkers, with plenty of maps and advice.

Ceilidh Clubhouse
HOSTEL £

(☎01854-612103; West Lane; r per person £18-20; P) Opposite the Ceilidh Place (p256), and under the same management, this annex offers no-frills accommodation for walkers, journey-people and staff. A big building, it has hostel-style rooms with sturdy bunks and basins. Though showers and toilets are a little institutional, the big bonus is that rooms are private: if you're woken by snores, at least they'll be familiar ones.

Old Surgery
B&B ££

(☎01854-612520; www.oldsurgery.co.uk; 3 West Tce; d £62) It's worth paying the extra few pounds to bag rooms No 1 or 2 (£70), which have big bay windows with super water vistas, tables to sit at and contemplate them from, extra berths for kids and a shared balcony.

Broomfield Holiday Park
CAMPGROUND £

(☎01854-612664; www.broomfieldhp.com; West Lane; one/two person tent site £8/12, plus £4 for car; ☉May-Oct) Great grassy headland location very close to centre. Midge-busting machines in action.

🍴 Eating & Drinking

Ferry Boat Inn
PUB GRUB ££

(☎01854-612366; www.ferryboat-inn.com; Shore St; mains £9-12) Known as the FBI, this inn is to Ullapool what the castle is to Edinburgh. The pub's a little less traditional-looking these days with its bleached wood and non-stained carpet, but it's still the place where locals and visitors mingle. Some dishes on the menu are a little bland, but a well-run dining room, quality ingredients and great presentation compensate.

Arch Inn
SCOTTISH, FRENCH ££

(☎01854-612454; www.thearchinn.co.uk; West Shore St; bar meals £7-9, mains £14-18; 🐾) There's plenty to like about this waterfront inn, from its cosy bar (with pool table) serving comfort food like bangers and mash, to its classy upstairs restaurant with glorious loch views and smart creations using Scottish produce with a regional French twist. The outdoor tables right beside the lapping water are a top spot for a pint.

Ceilidh Place
SCOTTISH ££

(☎01854-612103; 14 West Argyle St; mains £11-16; ☉breakfast, lunch & dinner) The restaurant at the Ceilidh Place serves up inventive dishes catering for most palates. It was a little disappointing last time we visited but the bar is still a great place, with a cosy atmosphere, outdoor seating, good wines by the glass and regular live music and events.

Frigate Café
ITALIAN, PIZZA £

(www.ullapoolcatering.co.uk; Shore St; mains £7-9; ☉noon-9pm) This waterfront cafe is a popular venue for coffee, tea and ice cream; it also sells a very tasty local smoked cheese. But you can also sit down and graze the Italian-influenced menu of salads, pizzas and pastas, or just drop by for a glass of wine or a beer.

Tea Store
CAFE £

(☎01854-612995; Argyle St; mains £3-7; ☉8am-5pm Mon-Sat, 10am-4pm Sun) Billed as 'the cafe the locals use', this trad tearoom with chunky pine tables serves fried breakfasts, filled rolls, soup, baked potatoes and home-bakes, plus the house speciality – venison burgers. There's also OS maps and walking information for hikers to consult over coffee and cake.

Seaforth
PUB GRUB, £

(www.theseaforth.com; Quay St; bar meals £7-11; ☉food noon-10pm; 🐾) Family-friendly and always packed, this big establishment in the heart of town does good-value bar meals and takeaway fish and chips downstairs, and pricier but more peaceful bistro fare upstairs, with serene harbour views.

❶ Information

Ullapool Bookshop (☎01854-612918; Quay St; ☉daily; @) Lots of books on Scottish topics and maps of the area. Internet access available at £1 per 15 minutes.

Ullapool Laundry (☎01854-613123; 7a Latheron Centre; ☉Mon-Sat) Service washes for muddied walkers.

Ullapool Library (☎01854-612543; Mill St; ☉9am-5pm Mon-Fri plus 6-8pm Tue & Thu, closed Mon & Wed during holidays; @) Free internet access.

Ullapool tourist office (☎01854-612486; ullapool@visitscotland.com; Argyle St; ☉daily Jun-Sep, Mon-Sat Apr-May & Oct, Mon-Fri Nov-Mar)

❶ Getting There & Around

Citylink has three daily buses, Monday to Saturday and one on Sunday, from Inverness to Ullapool (£12, 1½ hours), connecting with the Lewis ferry.

Ullapool to Plockton

Although it's less than 50 miles as the crow flies from Ullapool to Plockton, it's more like 150 miles along the circuitous coastal road – but don't let that put you off. It's a deliciously remote region and there are fine views of beaches and bays backed by mountains all the way along.

If you're in a hurry to get to Skye, head inland on the A835 (towards Inverness) and catch up with the A832 further south, near Garve.

BRAEMORE & AROUND

Twelve miles southeast of Ullapool at Braemore, near the head of Loch Broom, the A832 doubles back towards the coast as it heads for Gairloch (the A835 continues southeast across the wild **Dirrie More** pass to Garve and Inverness, sometimes closed by snow in winter).

Just west of the junction, a car park gives access to the **Falls of Measach** ('ugly' in Gaelic), which spill 45m into the spectacularly deep and narrow **Corrieshalloch Gorge**. You can cross to the far side of the gorge on a swaying suspension bridge, built in 1874 by Sir John Fowler of Braemore (codesigner of the Forth Rail Bridge), and walk west for 250m to a viewing platform that juts out dizzyingly above a sheer drop. The thundering falls and misty vapours rising from the gorge are very impressive.

Ridge-walking in the **Fannichs** – the range of hills directly south of Braemore – is relatively straightforward (though the routes can be long and tiring), with numerous paths to the 10 Munro summits. The tourist office in Ullapool can supply you with all the information and maps you need.

Two miles northwest of Corrieshalloch is **Braemore Square** (☑01854-655357; www.braemoresquare.com; s/d £55/70; ℙ🖤), a charming, three-bedroomed B&B housed in a delightful stone gatehouse and staging post, built for Sir John Fowler's Victorian hunting estate in 1840; the stables were used to rest and change horses before the climb over the Dirrie More pass towards Inverness. Self-catering accommodation is also available.

Citylink buses running between Inverness and Ullapool will drop you at Corrieshalloch or Braemore.

DUNDONNELL & AROUND
POP 200

The beautifully wooded valley of the Dundonnell River comes as a pleasant surprise after the bleak moorland pass to the northwest of Corrieshalloch Gorge. Dundonnell is a private hunting estate belonging to Tim Rice (the lyricist of popular musicals such as *Evita*), but the hotel here has long been a base for hillwalkers bound for the peaks of An Teallach.

An Teallach (1062m) is a magnificent mountain, with rocky pinnacles soaring above a lochan-filled corrie. The highest summit can be reached by a path starting less than 500m southeast of the Dundonnell Hotel (six hours return). Traversing the ridge to Sail Liath is a more serious proposition, with lots of scrambling in precarious places and difficult route-finding. Carry OS 1:50,000 map sheet No 19 *Gairloch*, food, water and waterproofs – it's amazing how quickly the weather can turn foul here.

🛏 Sleeping & Eating

Badrallach   CAMPGROUND, B&B £
(☑01854-633281; www.badrallach.com; Badrallach; bothy per person £6, camp sites per 2 people £8, r per person £35; ℙ) Badrallach, 7 miles from the A832, has a range of accommodation, including camping, a bothy, a self-catering cottage, and B&B in a classic Airstream caravan, as well as boats and bikes for hire. It's the perfect place to get away from it all and enjoy the rural beauty of this region. There's an extra charge of £1.50 per car.

Dundonnell Hotel   HOTEL ££
(☑01854-633204; www.dundonnellhotel.com; Dundonnell; s/d £65/110) This hotel has elegant, traditionally furnished rooms; the loch- and mountain-facing premier rooms have great views. Tempting food and friendly staff round out the experience.

Maggie's Tearoom   CAFE £
(☑01854-633326; www.camusnagaul.com; Camusnagaul; mains £4-8; ☺10am-4.30pm Mon-Sat Apr-Sep; 🖤) This is a cracker of a cafe, with lunch specials of local seafood complementing the homebaked cakes and tarts. There's an outdoor terrace overlooking the loch, and a garden filled with toys where young children can play in safety. It's at Camusnagual, 2 miles west of Dundonnell.

POOLEWE

The pretty village of Poolewe sits at the mouth of the River Ewe, at a bridge over a deep salmon pool. There's an attractive **walk** along the east side of the River Ewe to nearby Loch Kernsary, offering excellent views of Slioch and other lofty peaks (three hours). From a parking area a mile south of Poolewe on the road to Gairloch, the **Tollie Path** leads to Slattadale on Loch Maree.

◉ Sights & Activities

Poolewe Tuesday Market   MARKET
(www.poolewetuesdaymarket.co.uk; Poolewe Village Hall; ⊙10am-2.30pm Tue; ⛱) Every Tuesday Poolewe's village hall is crammed with stalls selling local arts and crafts, photography, secondhand books, freerange eggs, homemade cakes, jams, marmalades and chutneys. There's also a kids' play area and a cafe corner.

Inverewe Garden   GARDEN
(NTS; www.nts.org.uk; adult/concession £8.50/5.50; ⊙10am-4pm Apr-Oct, to 3pm Nov-Mar) About a mile north of Poolewe, this splendid garden is a welcome splash of colour on an otherwise bleak stretch of coast. The climate here is warmed by the waters of the Gulf Stream, which allowed Osgood MacKenzie, a son of the laird of Gairloch, to create this exotic woodland garden in 1862.

MacKenzie gathered plants from as far afield as Australia, South Africa, Chile and China; after his death, his wife gifted the garden and estate to the National Trust. There are free guided tours on weekdays at 1.30pm (March to October). The cafe provides a pleasant pit stop and has great cakes.

🛏 Sleeping & Eating

TOP CHOICE **Pool House**   BOUTIQUE HOTEL **£££**
(☎01445-781272; www.pool-house.co.uk; ste £250-500; ⊙closed Mon; ℗) An unexpected delight in this tiny, far-flung village, the Pool House is one of the Highlands' most romantic retreats, with five sumptuous themed suites draped with rich fabrics, crammed with antiques and curios, and glowing with gilt mirrors and polished wood. There are open fires, four-poster beds and Victorian rolltop baths, and a restaurant with a soaring reputation (guests only).

The hotel has a fascinating history – it was a former home of Osgood MacKenzie, creator of Inverewe Garden, and served as a Royal Navy headquarters during WWII.

Bridge Cottage Coffee Shop   CAFE **£**
(☎01445-781335; mains £3-7; ⊙10.30am-4.30pm Thu-Tue Easter-Oct; ⛱) The social hub of the village, this friendly cafe offers excellent homemade soups, salads and cakes, and serves as a gallery exhibiting the works of local artists. It's also the place to go to buy the Sunday papers.

GAIRLOCH & AROUND
POP 1100

Gairloch is a group of villages (comprising Achtercairn, Strath and Charlestown) around the inner end of a loch of the same name. The surrounding area has beautiful sandy beaches, good trout-fishing and birdwatching. Hill walkers also use Gairloch as a base for the Torridon hills and An Teallach.

◉ Sights & Activities

The B8056 road runs along the southern shore of Loch Gairloch, past the cute little harbour of **Badachro**, to end at the gorgeous pink-sand beach of **Red Point** – a perfect picnic spot. As the road crests the hill before reaching the parking area, there's a **Victorian letter box** cut into the solid rock at the side of the road – a rare survival, still in use after more than 100 years. Nearby is a **viewpoint** with a magnificent panorama that ranges from the Trotternish peninsula and the Cuillin Hills of Skye to the mountains of Torridon.

From the parking area at Red Point, a walk of just over a mile south past Redpoint Farm leads to another glorious beach, with a deserted salmon-fishing station at the far end. The coastal path continues southeast for 6 miles to Diabaig on Loch Torridon, passing the remote house of **Craig**, formerly a youth hostel but now a bothy open to all (shelter, but no facilities).

Another coastal road leads north from Gairloch for 10 miles to the settlement of **Melvaig**. From here a private road (open to walkers and cyclists) continues for 3 miles to **Rua Reidh Lighthouse**.

Gairloch Heritage Museum   MUSEUM
(www.gairlochheritagemuseum.org; Achtercairn; adult/child £4/1; ⊙10am-5pm Mon-Sat Apr-Oct) This museum has all sorts of interesting displays on life in the West Highlands from Pictish times to the present, including locally built fishing boats and a faithful re-creation of a crofter's cottage.

FREE **Gairloch Marine Wildlife Centre**   WILDLIFE CENTRE
(☎01445-712636; www.porpoise-gairloch.co.uk; Pier Rd, Charlestown; admission free; ⊙10am-4pm Easter-Oct) The Gairloch Marine Wildlife

Centre has audiovisual and interactive displays, lots of charts and photos, and knowledgeable staff. Cruises (adult/child £20/10) run from the centre and sail up to three times daily (weather permitting); during the two-hour trips you may see basking sharks, porpoises and minke whales.

The crew collect data on water temperature and conditions, and monitor cetacean populations, so your fare is subsidising an important research project.

FREE Rua Reidh Lighthouse   VISITOR CENTRE
(☎01445-771263; www.ruareidh.co.uk; Melvaig; admission free; ☺9am-6pm year-round) The visitor centre here has information on local wildlife and the history of the lighthouse, plus a viewing platform with telescope and binoculars so you can keep a weather eye open for whales and porpoises.

Gairloch Trekking Centre   HORSE RIDING
(☎01445-712652; www.gairlochtrekkingcentre.co.uk; Flowerdale Mains, Gairloch; ☺Fri-Wed Mar-Oct) Offers riding lessons, pony trekking and guided treks in the ample grounds of the local Gailoch Estate.

🛏 Sleeping & Eating

Old Inn   INN, PUB ££
(☎01445-712006; www.theoldinn.net; Charlestown; s/d £57/99; **P** 🗟) This rustic classic has a range of excellent snug rooms, some (such as room No 4) with four-poster beds. Downstairs, the pub is an atmospheric nook-and-cranny affair, with the best pint of ale in town, and serves recommended bar meals (£7 to £14) of the delectable seafood variety. It's just opposite Gairloch Pier.

Gairloch View Guest House   B&B ££
(☎01445-712666; www.gairlochview.com; Achtercairn; s/d £50/75; **P** 🗟) The unique selling point of this unassuming modern house is a patio with a stunning view over the sea to Skye – a view that you can enjoy from your breakfast table. The three bedrooms are comfortably furnished in classic country style, and the residents lounge has satellite TV and a small library of books and games.

Rua Reidh Lighthouse Hostel   HOSTEL £
(☎01445-771263; www.ruareidh.co.uk; Melvaig; dm/d £10.50/28; **P**) Beyond Melvaig, 13 miles north of Gairloch (at the end of the road), this is an excellent hostel and will give you a taste of a lighthouse-keeper's life. Buses from Gairloch run as far as Melvaig, then it's a 3-mile walk along the road to the light-

house. En suite twins and doubles (£35 to £42) and family rooms are also available.

Wayside Guest House   B&B ££
(☎01445-712008; issmith@msn.com; Strath; s/d £35/60) If you're looking for a place to hole up for the night in town, Wayside has water views from two cosy rooms, which share a bathroom. Another double and family room have no view but are en suite. It's right next to Strath Stores.

TOP CHOICE Badachro Inn   SEAFOOD ££
(☎01445-741255; www.badachroinn.com; Badachro; mains £10-15; ☺food noon-3pm & 6-9pm) Set in an enchanting location overlooking a sheltered yacht harbour, this old Highland inn serves real ales from the An Teallach brewery on Loch Broom, and platters of fresh local seafood: crab, scallops and langoustines, some landed at the pier right beside the inn. The bar staff will recommend the potato wedges as a side dish – say yes!

Mountain Coffee Company   CAFE £
(Strath; light meals £3-6; ☺9am-5pm, shorter hours in winter) Not the sort of cafe you expect in a Highland village, this offbeat and cosy spot is a shrine to all things mountaineering, with a lazy, chilled-out vibe. It sells hearty food for walkers, best consumed in the conservatory, and a range of decadent coffees and hot chocolates stuffed with sugary things. The attached **Hillbillies Bookshop** is worth a browse.

❶ Information
Gairloch tourist office (☎01445-712071; ☺daily May-Sep) Found at the car park in Achtercairn, where a road branches off to the main centre at Strath.

LOCH MAREE & AROUND
Stretching for 12 miles between Poolewe and Kinlochewe, **Loch Maree** is one of the most beautiful lochs in Scotland. Named after the 7th century Celtic missionary St Maelrubha, who built a cell on one of its islands, it has shores cloaked in Scots pine, birch, oak and heather, and is overlooked by the towering Munro of **Slioch** (980m).

The broad central part of the loch contains a scatter of islands large and small – the **Loch Maree Islands Nature Reserve** – where some of the last surviving untouched native woodland in Britain can be found. **Isle Maree**, where St Maelrubha built his cell, has been a sacred place since pre-Christian times, and as well as an ancient burial ground has a pagan **wishing tree** (now dead) festooned with coins – pilgrims would hammer a coin into its trunk, or tie a rag of clothing to a branch and make a wish. There are no boat trips to the islands, so the only visitors are canoeists and anglers who have their own boats.

Queen Victoria visited the island in 1877 during a tour of the Highlands, and also went to **Victoria Falls** (named after her visit), which tumble down to the loch through forestry land between Slattadale and Talladale. The falls are easily reached via a 150m walk from the Forestry Commission car park; unfortunately, a storm in 2005 brought down most of the trees surrounding the falls, and the setting is not as picturesque as it once was.

A better bet for scenery is the nearby **Slattadale** car park, reached via 300m of rough road from a turning just to the west of Victoria Falls. Here there are lochside picnic tables with picture-postcard views of Slioch, and a 1-mile forest walk to a **viewpoint** looking out over the Loch Maree Islands. This walk continues north as the **Tollie Path**, which runs for 5 miles to Poolewe.

At the southern end of the loch, tiny **Kinlochewe** makes a good base for outdoor activities. Here you'll find an outdoor-equipment shop, a petrol station with a tearoom and a shop/post office that runs a cafe in summer. The **Beinn Eighe Visitor Centre** (☎01445-760254; www.nnr-scotland.org.uk/beinn-eighe; admission free; ☉10am-5pm Easter-Oct; ♿), a mile north of Kinlochewe, has interactive displays (good for kids, too) on local geography, ecology, flora and fauna, and provides information on local walking routes including the **Beinn Eighe Mountain Trail** (263).

Kinlochewe Hotel (☎01445-760253; www.kinlochewehotel.co.uk; dm/s £12.50/45, d £70-90; P🐕) is a welcoming place that's very walker-friendly. As well as comfortable rooms with prices dependent on facilities, there are nice features like a handsome lounge well stocked with books, a great bar with several real ales on tap and a thoughtful menu of locally sourced food. There's also a bunkhouse with one no-frills 12-bed dorm, a decent kitchen and clean bathrooms.

East of Kinlochewe, the single-track A832 continues up Glen Docherty to Achnasheen, where there's a train station. The parking area at the top of the pass offers a splendid view back along the length of Loch Maree.

TORRIDON & AROUND

The road southwest from Kinlochewe passes through **Glen Torridon**, amid some of the most beautiful scenery in Britain (the Torridon estate was gifted to the National Trust for Scotland in 1967). Carved by ice from massive layers of the ancient sandstone that takes its name from the region, the mountains here are steep, shapely and imposing, whether flirting with autumn mists, draped in dazzling winter snows, or reflected in the calm blue waters of Loch Torridon on a summer's day.

The road through the glen reaches the sea at **Torridon village**, from where a single-track road heads west along the north side of Loch Torridon, climbing steeply through a landscape of knobbly crags to the village of **Diabaig**, which clings perilously to the hillside above a small beach. There's a popular walking trail from here to the beach at Red Point.

The A896 continues westwards to lovely **Shieldaig**, which boasts an attractive main street of whitewashed houses right on the water, before turning south to Applecross, Lochcarron and Kyle of Lochalsh.

◉ Sights & Activities

The Torridon Munros – **Liathach** (1054m; pronounced '*lee*-agakh', Gaelic for 'the Grey One'), **Beinn Eighe** (1010m; 'ben *ay*', 'the File') and **Beinn Alligin** (986m; 'the Jewelled Mountain') – are big, serious mountains for experienced hillwalkers only. Though not technically difficult, their ascents are long and committing, often over rough and rocky terrain. Information is available at the NTS Countryside Centre (p261) in Torridon; the NTS rangers also offer **guided mountain walks** (£25 per person; weekdays only, advance booking necessary) in July and August.

If Munro-bagging is not to your taste, there are a couple of valley walks that should not be missed. Beginning from a parking area on the A896 near the road to Coulin Lodge (signposted Public Footpath to Glen Carron by the Coulin Pass), a 4WD track leads south along the eastern shore of **Loch Clair**. In good weather, this path provides one of the classic Scottish mountain views, reproduced countless times in postcards and paintings – Liathach reflected in the waters of Loch Clair. The track continues to Coulin Lodge, allowing you to make a circuit of Loch Coulin, with stunning views of Beinn Eighe (5.5 miles round trip, allow three hours).

The trek to **Coire Mhic Fhearchair** (corrie vik *err*-ekher) is harder going, but follows a good stalker's path all the way (9 miles round trip, allow five hours). Your reward is some of the most impressive mountain scenery in Scotland, with the soaring Triple Buttress – half sandstone, half quartzite – rising above the crystal waters of Loch Coire Mhic Fhearchair.

Torridon Countryside Centre VISITOR CENTRE
(NTS; ✆01445-791221; www.nts.org.uk; Torridon Village; adult/child £3.50/2.50; ⊙10am-5pm Sun-Fri Apr-Sep) Offers information on wildlife, geology and walks in the area. The NTS rangers also offer guided mountain walks (£25 per person; weekdays only, advance booking necessary) in July and August.

FREE **Deer Museum** MUSEUM
(Torridon Village; admission free; ⊙daylight hours year-round) The unstaffed Deer Museum contains a collection of photos and odds and ends put together by a previous ranger.

🛏 Sleeping & Eating

The Torridon BOUTIQUE HOTEL £££
(✆01445-791242; www.thetorridon.com; Annat; s £180, d standard/superior/master £295/345/505; P@🛜) If you prefer the lap of luxury to the sound of rain beating on your tent, head for The Torridon, a lavish Victorian shooting lodge with a romantic lochside location. Rooms are gradually being converted from a classic look to a more contemporary one; the standard rooms are swish, but the enormous master rooms will make you feel gloriously decadent.

Dinners are sumptuous affairs, also open to non-residents (£45). Friendly staff can organise any number of activities on land or water. Part of the same set-up, the adjacent **Torridon Inn** (Annat; d £87) offers motel-style rooms and a welcoming bar serving meals.

Ferroch D&D ££
(✆01445-791451; www.ferroch.co.uk; Annat; s/d £68/84; P) Ferroch, just southwest of Torridon village, is a guesthouse with a spacious garden in a fabulous position. Once you've woken up to the views, you'll never want to leave. It does top evening meals, too.

Torridon SYHA HOSTEL £
(✆01445-791284; www.syha.org.uk; Torridon Village; dm/tw £16.25/40; ⊙Mar-Oct; P@) The modern, boxy-looking Torridon hostel is in a magnificent location surrounded by spec-

tacular mountains. It's a very popular walking base, so book ahead in summer.

Torridon Campsite CAMPGROUND
(✆01445-791368; Torridon Village; sites free) This free campsite is tents-only (no bookings). There are good showers and toilets, but possible downsides include midges and boggy ground – after heavy rain it can be impossible to find a dry place to pitch.

TOP CHOICE **Tigh an Eilean Hotel** SEAFOOD ££
(✆01520-755251; www.tighaneilean.co.uk; Shieldaig; bar & bistro mains £8-13, 3-course dinner £45; ⊙lunch & dinner) The Tigh an Eilean Hotel is famous for its seafood, and offers the choice of eating in the formal hotel restaurant or the more laidback Shieldaig Bar and Coastal Kitchen bistro. The latter has an outdoor roof terrace, and serves unusual dishes such as a wood-fired pizza topped with crayfish, shrimps, squid and a plump langoustine in the shell.

APPLECROSS
POP 200

A long side trip abandons the A890 at Shieldaig to follow the coast road for 25 winding miles to the delightfully remote seaside village of **Applecross**. (This road was built in 1975 to provide relief for the remote settlements here that were regularly cut off in winter.) Applecross feels more like an island retreat due to its isolation and the magnificent views of Raasay and the hills of Skye that set the pulse racing, particularly at sunset. On a clear day it's an unforgettable place, though the tranquil atmosphere isn't quite the same when the campsite and pub fill to the brim in school holidays.

Alternatively, you can continue a bit further down the A896 to one of the best drives for remote and incredibly rugged scenery in the country. Until the coast road was opened, the only road into Applecross was over the **Bealach na Ba** (626m; Pass of the Cattle), the third-highest motor road in the UK, and the longest continuous climb. Originally built in 1822, it climbs steeply and hair-raisingly via a couple of hairpin bends perched over sheer drops, with gradients up to 25%, then drops dramatically to the village with views ahead to Skye.

Back on the main road, the A896 runs south from Shieldaig to **Kishorn**, where there's a general store and post office – as well as spectacular views westwards to the steep, sandstone Applecross hills.

Sleeping & Eating

TOP CHOICE Applescross Inn
INN ££

(☎01520-744262; www.applecross.uk.com; Shore St; s/d £70/100; mains £9-17; ⊙food noon-9pm; P) The hub of the spread-out community here is the Applecross Inn, the perfect shoreside location for a sunset pint. The inn is famous for its food, mostly daily blackboard specials that concentrate on local seafood and venison, and sports half a dozen snug bedrooms, all with a view of the Skye hills and the sea.

Applecross Campsite
CAMPGROUND £

(☎01520-744268; www.applecross.uk.com; sites per person £7, 2-person hut £30; P) You can pitch your tent at the Applecross Campsite, which offers green grassy plots, cute little wooden cabins and a good cafe.

LOCHCARRON
POP 950

The appealing, whitewashed village of Lochcarron is a veritable metropolis in these parts, with two supermarkets, a bank (with an ATM), post office and petrol station. A long shoreline footpath at the loch's edge provides the perfect opportunity for a stroll to walk off breakfast.

Old Manse
GUESTHOUSE ££

(☎01520-722208; www.theoldmanselochcarron .com; Church St; s/d £35/60, tw with loch view £65; P) is a top-notch Scottish guesthouse, in a prime lochside position. Rooms are gorgeous and the twin overlooking the water is larger and well worth the extra fiver. Breakfast is great and this place would really suit couples: it's made for snuggling.

Rockvilla Hotel
GUESTHOUSE ££

(☎01520-722379; www.rockvilla-hotel.co.uk; Main St; r £70-79) Choose rooms No 1 or 2 at this small, quiet place. They're cheaper, have private facilities and dreamy views. Open for lunch and dinner (mains £8 to £13), the hotel kitchen serves some wonderful fresh seafood and is renowned for its scallops.

PLOCKTON
POP 450

Idyllic little **Plockton** (www.plockton.com), with its perfect cottages lining a perfect bay, looks like it was designed as a film set. And in fact it *was* designed – it was built around 1800 as a planned fishing and crofting village by Sir Hugh Innes for the tenants of his estate. And it has indeed served as a film set – scenes from *The Wicker Man* (1973) were filmed here, and the village became famous as the location for the 1990s TV series *Hamish Macbeth*.

With all this picture-postcard perfection, it's hardly surprising that Plockton is a tourist hotspot, crammed with daytrippers and holidaymakers in summer. But there's no denying its appeal, with 'palm trees' (actually hardy New Zealand cabbage palms) lining the waterfront, a thriving small-boat sailing scene, and several good places to stay, eat and drink. The big event of the year is the **Plockton Regatta** (www.plockton-sailing.com), a fortnight of boat races that culminates in a concert and ceilidh.

Shops in the village sell a booklet called *Walks Around Plockton* detailing around 20 local **walks**. These include an easy walk of about 1.5 miles west from the village to the sheltered **swimming** spots of Camas Dubhaird and the enchanting Coral Beach.

🏃 Activities

Plockton Boat Hire
CANOEING

(www.plocktonboathire.co.uk; single/double canoe per hr £9/12; ⊙Apr-Oct) If you fancy exploring the bay and seeing the village from the water, you can rent one- and two-person canoes and rowing boats from this operator on the Plockton waterfront. Lifejackets are supplied; no previous experience is necessary.

Calum's Seal Trips
WILDLIFE CRUISES

(☎01599-544306; www.calums-sealtrips.com; cruises adult/child £8/5; ⊙Apr-Oct) Calum's Seal Trips runs seal-watching cruises – there are swarms of the slippery fellas just outside the harbour and the trip comes with an excellent commentary. Trips leave daily at 10am, noon, 2pm and 4pm. You may even spot otters or dolphins.

Sleeping & Eating

The village has some excellent places to stay, but it's popular. Best to book ahead, especially if you plan to be here during regatta fortnight.

📝 Plockton Hotel
HOTEL ££

(☎01599-544274; www.plocktonhotel.co.uk; 41 Harbour St; s/d £85/120, cottage s/d £55/80; mains £8-13; ⊙lunch & dinner; 🛜) The black-painted Plockton Hotel is one of those classic Highland spots that manages to make everyone happy, whether it's thirst, hunger or fatigue that brings you knocking. The assiduously tended rooms are a delight, with excellent facilities and thoughtful touches like bathrobes. Those without a water view are consoled with more space and a balcony with rock-garden perspectives.

Just down the way, the cottage offers simpler comfort. The cosy bar, or wonderful beer garden on a sunny day, are memorable places for a pint, and food ranges from sound-value bar meals to seafood platters and local langoustines brought in on the afternoon boat.

Plockton Station Bunkhouse HOSTEL £
(☎01599-544235; gillcoe@btlnternet.com; dm £13; P❓) Airily set in the former train station (it's now opposite), Plockton Station Bunkhouse has cosy four-bed dorms, a garden and kitchen-lounge with plenty of light and good perspectives over the frenetic comings and goings (OK, that last bit's a lie) of the platforms below. The owners also do good-value B&B (single/double £25/45) next door in the inaccurately named 'Nessun Dorma'.

Shieling B&B ££
(☎01599-544282; www.lochalsh.net/shieling; d £60; ⏰Easter-Oct) Slap-bang by the sea, characterful Shieling is surrounded by an expertly trimmed garden and has two carpeted rooms with views and big beds. Next door is a historic thatched blackhouse (a low-walled stone cottage with a turf roof and earthen floor).

Duncraig Castle B&B ££
(☎01599-544295; www.duncraigcastle.co.uk; d standard/superior £109/119; P) Duncraig Castle offers luxurious, offbeat hospitality, as long as stuffed animals don't offend you. It needs a bit of work still – the curiously ugly school building alongside is thankfully destined for removal – but ongoing improvements are in progress. It's very close to Plockton but has its own train station.

[TOP CHOICE] **Plockton Shores** SCOTTISH, SEAFOOD ££
(☎01599-544263; 30 Harbour St; mains lunch £9-18, dinner £11-22; ⏰cafe 9.30-5pm Mon-Sat, noon-5pm Sun; restaurant lunch daily, dinner Tue-Sun; 🖊) This cafe-cum-restaurant sports a tempting menu of local seafood, including hand-dived scallops with lemon-and-basil dressing, squat lobster tails cooked in white wine and garlic, and a splendid platter of langoustines with paprika and garlic butter. There are also steaks, haggis and saddle of venison, and a small selection of tasty vegetarian dishes that are more than an afterthought.

Beinn Eighe Mountain Trail Walk

Beinn Eighe National Nature Reserve was established in 1951, the first such reserve in Britain. It was created to help safeguard the largest remnant of ancient Caledonian pine forest in the western Highlands, and covers 4750 hectares between the shore of Loch Maree and the mountain massif of Beinn Eighe (pronounced 'ben *ay*', probably meaning 'File Mountain', for its long, slender ridge).

There are actually two walking trails and both of them explore the most interesting parts of the area's habitats. The **Woodland Trail** is only 1 mile long and explores the Caledonian woodland bordering Loch Maree; the **Mountain Trail** is longer and ventures higher up the slopes of Beinn Eighe for some great views. Both trails are well marked by stone cairns with 'indicator points' showing features of interest that are fully explained in the trail guidebooks (available from the visitor centre).

The trails are open during the short stalking season, when signs will request walkers to keep strictly to the defined path.

The Mountain Trail may be relatively short and clearly waymarked, but don't underestimate it, the terrain is steep and you will need to use your hands to steady yourself on occasional rocky sections. It offers an ideal introduction to mountain walking, and is an informative and exciting place to bring older children.

ℹ️ BENN EIGHE MOUNTAIN TRAIL WALK

» **Duration** 2½–3½ hours

» **Distance** 2.5 miles (4km)

» **Difficulty** Easy to moderate

» **Start/Finish** Glas Leitir car park

» **Summary** A short, steep walk that explores the beautiful woodland and wild mountain terrain of the Beinn Eighe National Nature Reserve.

PLANNING

Beinn Eighe Visitor Centre (p260) is 0.75 miles north of Kinlochewe, housing displays about the nature reserve's habitats and selling maps and natural-history guides. These include two of SNH's own publications: *Beinn Eighe: Britain's First National Nature Reserve* (£9.95), a beautiful coffee-table volume with photos by Scotland's best-known outdoor photographer, Colin Baxter; and *Beinn Eighe: First Among Equals* (£2.50), which is more down-to-earth and provides a comprehensive introduction to the area.

The walk is covered by the OS Landranger 1:50,000 map No 19 *Gairloch & Ullapool*. For more detail use the OS Explorer 1:25,000 map No 433 *Torridon – Beinn Eighe & Liathach*.

THE WALK

From the information board at the Glas Leitir parking area, about 2.5 miles north of Kinlochewe, pass under the road on a walkway beside the river. Keep left at the trail junction just after the tunnel, following the direction of the mountain symbol on a marker post. The stony path follows the banks of Allt na h-Airidhe for a short time, then veers away through a silver birch grove densely carpeted with bracken. The trail begins its ascent almost immediately, although the gradient is easy at first, and the silver birch gives way to Scots pine.

The path joins a tumbling burn and climbs more steeply up its banks on stone steps, then crosses a wooden footbridge. The steps become more continuous as the trees dwindle in size and the path emerges onto open slopes. Views of Loch Maree and Slioch open up to the north. The rock steps gradually give way to natural slab and loose stone and the terrain becomes wilder. Just beyond the 305m marker cairn you'll need to use your hands to haul yourself up a couple of rock ledges as you climb a very steep section of the trail.

With the steepest section over, views of the Beinn Eighe massif open up ahead as the path weaves among craggy outcrops and finally reaches the Conservation Cairn. At 550m this is the high point of the trail, and there's a real feeling of being in the heart of the mountains. The 360-degree panorama takes in the precipitous Torridon peaks, clustered to the southwest, and the lofty landscape of the Letterewe mountains spread out to the north. In good visibility a total of 31 Munros (mountains over 914m) can be seen from this vantage point.

The trail drops down to the west and threads its way among several beautiful lochans. An t-Allt is crossed on stepping stones and the path turns north to follow the burn and begin the descent. The terrain is more gently graded than it was on the climb up. The burn soon disappears into a gorge to your right and, as you descend further, there are impressive views into the deep, sheer-sided chasm.

After a right bend and small rise the path leads to the rim of the gorge; take care here. Continue into the forest below where the path joins the Woodland Trail and turns left, soon reaching a wooden conservation cabin and a trig point. It leads on through silver birch woodland, across a boardwalk over marshy ground and back to the road. Cross the road and pass through trees to a beautiful pebble beach on the shore of Loch Maree. Turn right and walk along the top of the beach back to the car park.

Sandwood Bay to Cape Wrath Walk

Sandwood Bay, the most beautiful beach in Scotland, and the long stretch of magnificent, unspoiled coastline to its north, are the highlights of this finest of coastal walks. This is lonely and remote country – not a soul lives anywhere near the route, except at its southern extremity in the crofting settlement of Blairmore.

Along the coast, the cliffs, deep inlets (geos) and the offshore stacks and islets are predominantly sandstone, mixed with ancient gneiss, the most widespread rock type.

ⓘ SANDWOOD BAY TO CAPE WRATH WALK

» **Duration** 6½–7 hours
» **Distance** 14 miles
» **Difficulty** Moderate
» **Start** Blairmore
» **Finish** Cape Wrath
» **Summary** An outstanding coastal walk, from an incomparable beach to the northwestern tip of the country, through a remote and uninhabited area of great beauty and wildness.

At Cape Wrath the red gneiss cliffs soar to a height of about 120m. A few miles east, at Kervaig, are the highest vertical coastal cliffs in mainland Britain, at 195m. Glaciers and ice sheets left their mark in sculpting the river valleys; large gneiss boulders perched on sandstone platforms were left behind by retreating glaciers.

An extensive area around Sandwood Bay and nearby Sandwood Loch is owned and managed by the John Muir Trust in partnership with the local community. The peatlands, sand dunes and machair (coastal grasslands) from Sandwood to Sheigra, and the dunes and machair between Sheigra and Oldshoremore, are protected in two Sites of Special Scientific Interest. The machair, found along the west coast and in the Western Isles, comes alive between late June and August with carpets of globeflower, bell flower, vetch, knapweed and orchid.

The walk can be done in either direction. From south to north, as described here, you'll have to check the times of the minibus and ferry service to get from Cape Wrath to Durness (see Planning), or plan to spend a night at Kearvaig bothy before hiking out to the ferry the next day.

Camping at Sandwood Bay offers the chance of being lulled to sleep by the soothing music of the waves, and of spreading a return walk over a leisurely three days: one into Sandwood, another to the cape and back, and a third back to Blairmore. Choose your pitch with care, steering well clear of the fragile dunes. If there's enough driftwood to make a good fire, light it on bare sand.

In midsummer, and transport permitting, it's possible to walk from Cape Wrath to Sandwood and back in a day from a base in Durness on the north coast; the round-trip distance is 19.5 miles with 300m of ascent.

PLANNING

Although Cape Wrath marks the end of the walk, it's still a long way from civilisation. To get to Durness, you'll need to link up with the Cape Wrath Minibus (p244) service that covers the 12 miles from the cape to the Kyle of Durness, where a small passenger ferry (p244) takes you to Keoldale pier, about 1.5 miles south of Durness village.

Note that the area around Cape Wrath is used as a military bombing range. Details of when the range is closed to the public can be obtained from Durness tourist office (p243), and the Cape Wrath minibus website.

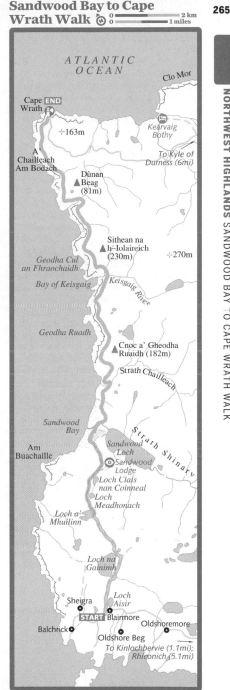

If you're planning to camp at Sandwood Bay, a fuel stove is an absolute must, as are a trowel (there are no toilets) and a bag to carry out all your rubbish. Water containers will be handy; some potential camp sites are close to the limited supplies of freshwater but they're midge havens in summer.

The walk is covered by the OS Explorer 1:25,000 map No 446 *Durness & Cape Wrath,* and the OS Landranger 1:50,000 map No 9 *Cape Wrath.*

THE WALK

From the car park at Blairmore, a hamlet 3.5 miles west of Kinlochbervie, set out along the unsealed road signposted to Sandwood. This road, used by crofters tending their sheep, leads across rather featureless moorland, which is enlivened by several nearby lochs; it deteriorates into a footpath at Loch a' Mhuilinn. Little more than 1 mile further on, the path (much of it repaired and built by John Muir Trust volunteers) curves round a steep-sided hill on the left and starts to descend, affording the first glimpse of the beach at Sandwood Bay.

A flat, grassed area with old, stone-walled enclosures is a possible camp site. Water should be available from the small burn near the roofless cottage about 200m to the south; otherwise you'll have to go right down to peat-dark Sandwood Loch, although it may be slightly brackish. The shore of Sandwood Loch may seem like an idyllic camp site but beware the midges.

The path leads down through marram-grassed dunes to the beach at Sandwood Bay, a superb sweep of pinkish-cream sand (about 1¾ hours from the start). The towering rock stack of Am Buachaille stands guard close to the cliffs that extend southwest from the sands.

Walk north along the beach, cross the outlet from Sandwood Loch on stepping stones and go up the steep, sandy slope ahead, through a gap in the low cliffs. Cross a patch of grass and make your way through the jumble of rock slabs and boulders down to a shallow valley, then along the cliff edge to Strath Chailleach.

Cross the stream at the top of the cascades and follow the spur leading northeast for about 0.3 miles, then turn generally north to skirt the steep-sided Cnoc a' Gheodha Ruaidh on its seaward side. Keep close to the cliff edge, across a dip above Geodha Ruadh and up past the next hill.

At the top of the long slope down to the Keisgaig River, there's a good view of a remarkable rock stack on the northern side of the bay, its profile resembling a rather sullen face. Just above the river is a low, turf-roofed stone shelter, somewhat the worse for wear (2¼ hours from Sandwood Bay). There's space for a tent or two nearby if you want to camp.

Cross the river just above the cascade coursing down onto the shingle beach and climb up the very steep slope. Steer a course west of Sithean na h-Iolaireich to overlook the superb vertical, dark-pink cliffs in Geodha Cul an Fhraochaidh.

Continue along the cliff tops, mainly across bare, stony ground for 1 mile or so, to the top of the next descent to the unnamed burn immediately south of Dùnan Beag. Detour inland (northeast) around the cliffs lining the seaward reaches of the burn to a small stream junction; cross over and head back towards the cliffs.

There's a potential camp site at the next stream crossing (north of Dùnan Beag), a short distance inland. A bit further on, the two remarkable rock stacks A' Chailleach and Am Bodach (the 'old woman' and 'old man') dictate a photo stop. If you look back (south) from here on a clear day, you'll be able to see Sandwood Bay.

Continue across a small burn towards the lighthouse, keeping close to the cliffs. Skirt the walled enclosure around the buildings, which are now forlornly deserted, to reach the courtyard in front of the lighthouse and the end of the walk (about 2½ hours from the Keisgaig River).

Orkney Islands

Includes »

Best Places to Eat

» The Creel (p285)

» Hamnavoe
Restaurant (p272)

» Kirkwall Hotel (p281)

» Julia's Cafe & Bistro (p272)

» Haff Yok Cafe (p296)

Best Places to Stay

» West Manse (p296)

» Woodwick House (p276)

» Links House (p276)

» Bis Geos (p296)

Why Go?

There's a magic to the Orkney Islands that you begin to feel as soon as the Scottish mainland slips astern. Only a few short miles of ocean separate Stromness from Scrabster, but the Pentland Firth is one of Europe's most dangerous waterways, a graveyard of ships that adds an extra mystique to these islands shimmering in the sea mists.

An archipelago of mostly flat, green-topped islands stripped bare of trees by Atlantic gales and ringed with red sandstone cliffs, its heritage dates back to the Vikings – it's recorded in the *Orkneyinga Saga* – whose influence is still strong today. Famed for its ancient standing stones and prehistoric villages, for sublime sandy beaches and spectacular coastal scenery, this is a region whose ports tell of lives shared with the blessings and rough moods of the sea, and a destination where seekers can find melancholy wrecks of warships and the salty clamour of remote seabird colonies.

When to Go
Kirkwall

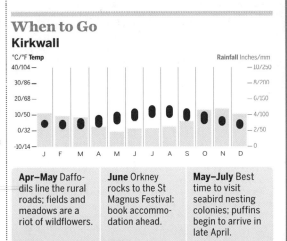

Apr–May Daffodils line the rural roads; fields and meadows are a riot of wildflowers.

June Orkney rocks to the St Magnus Festival: book accommodation ahead.

May–July Best time to visit seabird nesting colonies; puffins begin to arrive in late April.

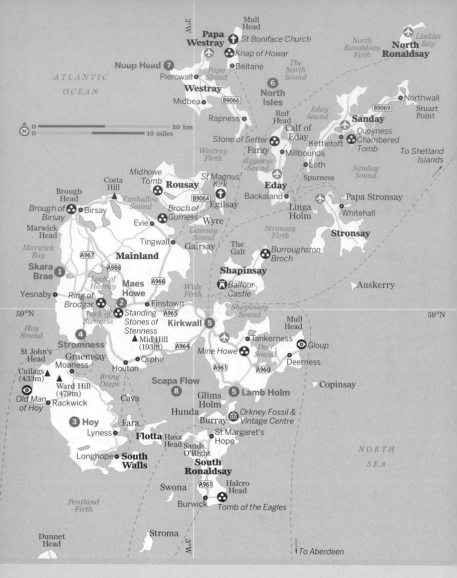

Orkney Islands Highlights

1 Travel back in time at **Skara Brae** (p272), a village of prehistoric perfection that pre-dates the pyramids

2 Plunge down the passageway into spooky **Maes Howe** (p274), a vast Stone Age tomb with bawdy Viking graffiti

3 Soak up glorious scenery on a hike to spectacular **Old Man of Hoy** (p299)

4 Learn about Orcadian history at the fascinating **Stromness Museum** (p271)

5 Admire magnificent **St Magnus Cathedral** (p277) at Kirkwall and humble **Italian Chapel** (p283) at Lamb Holm

6 Island-hop the magical **North Isles** (p288), where crystal waters lap against glittering white-sand beaches

7 Take in the raucous sound and sheer spectacle of nesting seabirds at **Noup Head** (p294)

8 Dive the sunken WWI warships of **Scapa Flow** (283)

☞ Tours

Orkney Island Holidays ACTIVITY HOLIDAY
(☏01856-711373; www.orkneyislandholidays.com)
Based on Shapinsay, with guided tours of archaeological sites, birdwatching and wildlife trips and excursions to other islands. One-week, all-inclusive packages cost £1095.

Discover Orkney WALKING TOURS
(☏01856-872865; www.discoverorkney.com) Offers guided tours and walks throughout the islands in the company of a qualified guide. Specific tours are tailored to your interests.

Orkney Archaeology Tours GUIDED TOURS
(☏01856-721217; www.orkneyarchaeologytours.co
.uk) Runs private half- (£160 for up to four) and full-day (£240) tours with an archaeologist guide.

Wildabout Orkney GUIDED TOURS
(☏01856-877737; www.wildaboutorkney.com) Operates tours covering Orkney's history, ecology, folklore and wildlife. Day trips operate year-round and cost £49, with pick-ups in Stromness and Kirkwall.

John O'Groats Ferries BUS TOUR
(☏01955-611353; www.jogferry.co.uk) If you're in a hurry, this operator runs a one-day tour of the main sites for £46, including the ferry from John O'Groats. You can do the whole thing as a long day trip from Inverness.

Dawn Star Boat Trips BOAT TOUR
(☏01856-876743; www.orkneyboattrips.co.uk;
☺May-Sep) Runs boat trips on Scapa Flow.

❶ Getting There & Away

Air
Flybe (☏0871 700 2000; www.flybe.com) flies daily from Kirkwall to Aberdeen, Edinburgh, Glasgow, Inverness and Sumburgh (Shetland). In summer it also serves Bergen (Norway).

Boat
During summer, book ahead for car spaces. Fares vary according to season (low to peak fares are quoted).

FROM SCRABSTER, SHETLANDS & ABERDEEN Northlink Ferries (☏0845 6000 449; www.northlinkferries.co.uk) operates ferries from Scrabster to Stromness (passenger £14 to £17, car £45 to £50, 1½ hours, three daily Monday to Friday, two on weekends) and from Aberdeen to Kirkwall (passenger £17 to £26, car £69 to £94, six hours, three or four weekly). It also sails from Kirkwall to Lerwick (passenger one way £15 to £22, car one way £55 to £90, 6 to 8 hours, three a week) on the Shetland Islands.

FROM GILLS BAY Pentland Ferries (☏01856-831226; www.pentlandferries.co.uk) offers a shorter, cheaper car-ferry crossing. Boats leave from Gills Bay, about 3 miles west of John O'Groats, and head to St Margaret's Hope on South Ronaldsay (passenger/car £13/30, one hour). There are three to four crossings daily.

FROM JOHN O'GROATS From May to September, **John O'Groats Ferries** (☏01955-611353; www.jogferry.co.uk) operates a passenger-only service from John O'Groats to Burwick, on the southern tip of South Ronaldsay (one way/return £18/28). A bus to Kirkwall meets the ferry (all-included return from John O'Groats to Kirkwall is £30). There are four departures daily (two in May and September).

Bus
Citylink (☏0871 266 33 33; www.citylink.co.uk) runs daily from Inverness to Scrabster, connecting with the Stromness ferries.

John O'Groats Ferries (p269) operates the summer-only Orkney bus service from Inverness to Kirkwall. Tickets (one way/return £34/46, five hours) include bus-ferry-bus travel from Inverness to Kirkwall. There are two buses daily from June to early September.

❶ Getting Around

The *Orkney Transport Guide,* a detailed schedule of bus, ferry and air services around and to/from Orkney, is available free from tourist offices.

The largest island, Mainland, is joined by causeways to Burray and South Ronaldsay. The other islands can be reached by air and ferry services.

Air
Loganair (☏01856-873457; www.loganair.co
.uk) operates interisland flights from Kirkwall to North Ronaldsay, Westray, Papa Westray, Stronsay, Sanday and Eday. See each island's entry in this chapter for details.

Bicycle
Various locations on Mainland hire bikes, including **Cycle Orkney** (☏01856-875777; www.cycle orkney.com; Tankerness Lane; per day £15; ☺Mon-Sat; ♿) and **Orkney Cycle Hire** (☏01856-850255; www.orkneycyclehire.co.uk; 54 Dundas St; per day £7.50-10).

Boat
Orkney Ferries (☏01856-872044; www
.orkneyferries.co.uk) operates car ferries from Mainland to the islands. See each island's entry in this chapter for details.

Bus
Stagecoach (☏01856-878014; www.stage coachbus.com) Runs bus services on Mainland and South Ronaldsay. Most buses don't operate on Sunday. Dayrider (£7.25) and 7-Day Megarider (£16.25) tickets allow unlimited travel.

Car

There are several car-hire companies on Mainland. Small-car rates begin at around £32/165 per day/week, although there are specials for as low as £28 per day.

Drive Orkney (☑01856-872044; www.drive orkney.com; Garrison Rd, Kirkwall)

Norman Brass Car Hire (☑01856-850850; www.stromnesscarhire.co.uk; North End Rd, Stromness) At the Blue Star Garage.

Orkney Campers (☑07919-103115; www .orkneycampers.com; Beesbrick, Orphir; per week peak season £45) Rents out sturdy old VW campervans, complete with all camping equipment and advice on where to go.

Orkney Car Hire (☑01856-872 866; www .orkneycarhire.co.uk; Junction Rd, Kirkwall) Mainland car-hire companies include Orkney Car Hire. Its small-car rates begin at around £34/164 per day/week, although its specials can go as low as £25 per day.

WR Tullock (☑01856-875500; www.orkney carrental.co.uk; Castle St, Kirkwall)

STROMNESS

POP 1600

The appealing grey-stone port of Stromness is the very image of an island town, with a narrow, flagstone-paved main street and tiny alleys leading down to the waterfront between tall stone houses. The town has changed little since its heyday in the 18th century, when it was a busy staging post for ships avoiding the troublesome English Channel during the European wars. In the 19th century, Stromness became an important herring and whaling port and was used as a depot by the Hudson's Bay Company of Canada, which employed many local men.

Vikings had sheltered in the natural harbour of Hamnavoe (Norse for 'safe harbour') since the 12th century, but Stromness wasn't formally founded until the 1620s, when the bishop of Orkney established a series of *feus* (feudal plots) on the bay. When the *Discovery* and *Resolution* stopped here on their return from Captain Cook's fatal voyage to the South Seas, they found a busy village of at least 200 residents.

Stromness became a Royal Burgh in its own right in 1817. It's the main arrival point for ferries from the Scottish mainland, but it still has the atmosphere of a working fishing village, with locals stopping to chat in the narrow streets and a handful of family-run general merchants,

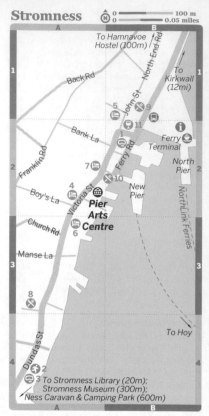

Stromness

◎ **Top Sights**
   Pier Arts Centre A2

◉ ❍ **Activities, Courses & Tours**
  1 Diving Cellar...B2
  2 Orkney Cycle Hire A4
  3 Scapa Scuba...A4

▭ **Sleeping**
  4 Brown's Hostel...A2
  5 Miller's House..B1
  6 Orca Hotel...A3
  7 Stromness Hotel......................................A2

❌ **Eating**
  8 Hamnavoe Restaurant A3
  9 Julia's Café & Bistro B1
  10 Stromness Cafe-Bar B2

❑ **Drinking**
  11 Ferry Inn..B2

butchers and grocery shops. Stromness is also ideally located for trips to Skara Brae, Maes Howe, the Ring of Brodgar and the island of Hoy.

◎ Sights

The main recreation in Stromness is simply strolling up and down the narrow, atmospheric main street.

FREE **Pier Arts Centre**   GALLERY
(☎01856-850209; www.pierartscentre.com; 30 Victoria St; ◎10.30am-5pm Mon-Sat) Resplendently redesigned, this gallery has really rejuvenated the Orkney modern-art scene with its sleek lines and upbeat attitude. It's worth a look as much for the architecture as its high-quality collection of 20th-century British art and the changing exhibitions.

Stromness Museum   MUSEUM
(☎01856-850025; www.orkneyheritage.com; 52 Alfred St; adult/child £3.50/1; ◎10am-5pm Apr-Sep, 11am-3.30pm Mon-Sat Oct-Mar) Crammed with fascinating artefacts from maritime and natural-history collections covering whaling, the Hudson's Bay Company and the sunken German fleet in Scapa Flow, this is a superb museum where you can easily lose a couple of hours nosing around the display cases.

Among the more unusual exhibits are South Sea Islander artefacts left here by the survivors of Captain Cook's final expedition to the Pacific in 1776–79, and the tiny inflatable boat used by Dr John Rae in his Arctic explorations.

Across the street from the museum is the house where local poet and novelist **George Mackay Brown** lived from 1968 until his death in 1996. Further south on the main street is **Login's Well**, where famous ships such as the *Discovery* and *Resolution* stopped to take on water.

✸ Festivals & Events

Orkney Folk Festival   MUSIC
(☎01856-851331; www.orkneyfolkfestival.com) A four-day event based in Stromness in the third week of May, with a program of folk concerts, *ceilidhs* (evenings of traditional Scottish entertainment including music, song and dance) and casual pub sessions. The town packs out, and late-night buses from Kirkwall are laid on. Book ahead for event tickets and accommodation.

🛏 Sleeping

Orca Hotel   HOTEL ££
(☎01856-850447; www.orcahotel.moonfruit.com; 76 Victoria St; s/d £40/54) Warm and homelike, this small hotel right in the heart of things is likeably out of the ordinary, and features cosy rooms with narrow, comfortable beds; rates vary slightly depending on the room you choose. In winter you can use the hotel's kitchen.

Miller's House   B&B ££
(☎01856-851969; www.millershouseorkney.com; 13 John St; s/d £50/70; ◎Easter-Oct) Miller's House is a historic Stromness residence – check out the wonderful 1716 stone doorway. There are two delightful en suite bedrooms where you can smell the cleanliness, and there's plenty of light and an optimistic feel. Showers hit the spot, and there's a laundry for guest use. Exceptional breakfasts include vegetarian options and daily baked bread.

Hamnavoe Hostel   HOSTEL £
(☎01856-851202; www.hamnavoehostel.co.uk; 10a North End Rd; dm £16-18; ☎) This well-equipped hostel lacks a bit of character but makes up for that with excellent facilities, including a fine kitchen and a lounge room with great perspectives over the water. The dorms are very commodious, with duvets and reading lamps, and the showers are good.

Brown's Hostel   HOSTEL £
(☎01856-850661; www.brownshostel.co.uk; 45 Victoria St; dm £14-15; @☎) On the main street, this handy, sociable place has cramped but cosy and homelike dorms (the upstairs ones are a pound more but have more space) as well as small private rooms. Life centres on its inviting common area, where you can browse the internet for free or swap pasta recipes in the open kitchen. There are overflow rooms in a house up the street.

Stromness Hotel   HOTEL ££
(☎01856-850298; www.stromnesshotel.com; Victoria St; s/d £55/98; ☎) Proudly overlooking the main street and surveying the harbour, this lofty Victorian hotel is a reminder of the way things used to be, with its posh revolving door and imposing facade. The pink-hued rooms are spacious, but sadly the yielding beds have seen better days and the claustrophobic lift means your suitcase will have to find its own way up.

Ness Caravan & Camping Park CAMPGROUND £
(☑01856-873535; Ness Rd; 1-person/2-person/family tents £5.80/9/11; ⊛Apr-Sep; P) This breezy, fenced-in campground overlooks the bay at the southern end of town and is as neat as a pin.

✖ Eating & Drinking

Hamnavoe Restaurant SEAFOOD ££
(☑01856-850606; 35 Graham Pl; mains £13-19; ⊛dinner Tue-Sun Apr-Oct) Tucked away off the main street, this Stromness favourite specialises in excellent local seafood backed up by professional service. There's always something good off the boats, and the chef prides himself on his lobster. Booking is a must. From November to March, it's only open Saturday and Sunday for dinner; in summer it also opens for lobster lunches on Saturday.

Stromness Hotel SEAFOOD ££
(☑01856-850298; www.stromnesshotel.com; 15 Victoria St; restaurant mains £8-15; ⊛lunch & dinner) This central hotel does excellent seafood dishes fused with tastes of the Orient, and there are vegetarian options. There's a lounge bar with harbour views, or the earthier, convivial Flattie Bar downstairs.

Julia's Café & Bistro CAFE £
(☑01856-850904; 20 Ferry Rd; mains £5-8; ⊛9am-5pm Sep-May, plus dinner Wed-Sun Jun-Aug; @🛜) This cafe with a conservatory, opposite the port, keeps all-comers happy, with massive fry-ups offset on the cardiac-karma scale by the wraps, salads and tempting vegetarian dishes such as nut roast or couscous. In summer it opens for dinner with elaborate fare (£10 to £13) on offer.

Stromness Cafe-Bar CAFE £
(☑01856-850551; 22 Victoria St; light meals £3-7; ⊛breakfast, lunch & dinner) This quirky little space, with attached shop, is good for a snack or even something more substantial. Orkney beer is available and best enjoyed on the back terrace overlooking the water.

Ferry Inn PUB £
(☑01856-850280; www.ferryinn.com; 10 John St; mains £7-11; ⊛breakfast, lunch & dinner) Every port has its pub, and in Stromness it's the Ferry. Convivial and central, it warms the cockles with folk music, local beers and characters, and pub food that's unsophisticated but generously proportioned and good value.

ℹ Information

Stromness Library (☑01856-850907; Alfred St; ⊛2-7pm Mon-Thu, to 5pm Fri, 10am-5pm Sat; @) Free internet access.

Stromness tourist office (☑01856-850716; Ferry Rd; ⊛10am-4pm Mon-Sat Apr-Oct) In the ferry terminal. Also open on Sunday in summer.

ℹ Getting There & Around

BOAT Northlink Ferries (p269) runs services from Stromness to Scrabster on the mainland.
BUS Bus 1 runs regularly to Kirkwall (40 minutes) and on to St Margaret's Hope.

WEST MAINLAND

This part of the island, to the west of Kirkwall, is sprinkled with outstanding prehistoric monuments: the journey up to Orkney is worth it for these alone. It would take the best part of a day to see all of them – if pushed for time, visit Skara Brae and then Maes Howe, but be sure to book your visit to the latter in advance.

Heading east to Kirkwall, there are two roads from Stromness: the A964, which runs along the south coast via Houton; and the more direct A965, which passes several of Orkney's most famous archaeological sites, including the Standing Stones of Stenness, the Ring of Brodgar and Maes Howe. The A967, for Skara Brae, branches north off A965 a mile north of Stromness, while the A964 branches south at Loch of Stenness.

Heart of Neolithic Orkney

In 1999 Unesco designated the Heart of Neolithic Orkney as a World Heritage Site for being 'an outstanding example of a type of architectural ensemble and archaeological landscape which illustrates a significant stage of human history, during which the first large ceremonial monuments were built'. The neolithic village of Skara Brae, the chambered tomb of Maes Howe, the stone circles of Stenness and the Ring of Brodgar are among the finest examples of their kind on the planet.

SKARA BRAE & SKAILL HOUSE

A visit to extraordinary **Skara Brae** (HS; www.historic-scotland.gov.uk; joint ticket with Skaill House adult/child £6.70/4; ⊛9.30am-5.30pm Apr-Sep, to 4.30pm Oct-Mar), northern Europe's best-preserved neolithic village and one of the world's most evocative prehistoric sites, offers the unique opportunity to take

One of Orkney's most famous sons is the inimitable Dr John Rae (1813–93), the Arctic explorer who is credited with discovering the final link in the Northwest Passage between the Atlantic and the Pacific. Born in the Hall of Clestrain (now sadly derelict), near Orphir, Rae became a surgeon and explorer for the Hudson's Bay Company. In the 1840s he mapped hundreds of miles of Canada's Arctic coast, often travelling alone and hunting or trading with the native Inuit for food.

He was unique among Victorian explorers in adopting the skills and equipment of the native people of the Arctic, rather than assuming the superiority of Western technology. He became a superb hunter and a prodigious walker, on one occasion hiking 1200 miles in two months on snowshoes. He thus became a leading expert on cold-climate travel and survival, but back in Britain he was shunned by polite society for having 'gone native'.

With such a track record, it was inevitable that Rae was enlisted in the search for the missing Franklin Expedition. Led by Sir John Franklin, this lavishly funded Royal Navy expedition had set off from London to chart the Northwest Passage in 1845, but within a year its two ships, *Erebus* and *Terror*, had vanished without a trace north of Baffin Island. Several rescue missions and search parties were dispatched in the succeeding years, including Rae's attempt in 1848, but all were in vain.

Then in 1854 Dr Rae returned to England with 'melancholy tidings'; he had spoken with Inuit hunters who had discovered the bodies of around 30 sailors from the doomed expedition, frozen solid. He wrote, 'From the mutilated state of many of the bodies and the contents of the kettles, it is evident that our wretched Countrymen had been driven to the last dread alternative – cannibalism – as a means of prolonging existence.'

This was too much for the 'civilised' English to contemplate. Dr Rae's reputation was shot down by Lady Franklin and other establishment figures – including Charles Dickens – who refused to believe that such high-ranking socialites as Sir John could have fallen so low as to eat the bodies of their fallen comrades. Franklin was posthumously credited with the discovery of the Northwest Passage, and Dr Rae was marginalised, working quietly as a physician in London until his death in 1893. Only long after his death were his incredible achievements given the recognition they deserved.

There's a fine memorial to Dr John Rae in St Magnus Cathedral (p277) in Kirkwall, and an informative exhibit on him in Stromness Museum (p271).

a glimpse into everyday Stone Age life. Built around 3500 BC, and predating Stonehenge and the pyramids of Giza, Skara Brae is idyllically situated by a sandy bay 8 miles north of Stromness.

This remarkable site was hidden under the sand dunes until 1850, when waves whipped up by a severe storm eroded the sand and grass above the beach, exposing the stone huts beneath. The local laird discovered the complex, which sits just half a mile from his mansion at Skaill, and made excavating the ruins his personal project for the next 18 years.

The stylish visitor centre includes a museum, a good cafe, and a re-creation of House No 1 as it may have looked when it was inhabited. An excellent interactive exhibit and short video arms visitors with facts and theory that will enhance the impact of the site. The official guidebook, available from the visitor centre, includes a good self-guided tour.

The houses are in an incredible state of preservation. Even the stone furniture – beds, boxes and dressers – has survived the 5000 years since a community lived here. Within the buildings archaeologists discovered carved ceremonial stones, stone tools, bone pots and even tokens and primitive dice from ancient games. (You can walk around on the banks between the huts and look down into their interiors, but walking inside the huts is forbidden.)

The joint ticket will also get you into **Skaill House** (HS; joint ticket with Skara Brae adult/child £6.70/4; ☺Apr-Sep), an early-17th-century mansion built for the local bishop, and the former home of the laird of Breckness, William Watt, who discovered Skara Brae. There are fine displays of period furniture and memorabilia including Captain Cook's dinner service (donated to the laird, who entertained the officers of Cook's ship on its way home after the captain's death in Hawaii in 1779). It's a bit anticlimactic, catapulting you straight from the neolithic to the 1950s decor, but you can see a clever hidden compartment in the library as well as the bishop's original 17th-century four-poster bed.

Three miles south of Skara Brae, a minor road leads to the coast at Yesnaby, where the west coast rises into a truly dramatic series of cliffs and exposed sea stacks. You can walk south from the Yesnaby parking area (or even from Skara Brae; total 9 miles) all the way to Stromness, via a clifftop path that takes you past spectacular **Yesnaby Castle** (about 0.75 miles south of the Yesnaby parking area), a precarious-looking sea stack that is pierced by a natural arch at its base. Take care on the cliffs in high winds, and in early summer watch out for nesting seabirds, which may dive-bomb you to scare you away from their nests.

Buses run to Skara Brae from Kirkwall and Stromness (Monday, Thursday and Saturday May to September only).

MAES HOWE

Egypt has its pyramids, Scotland has **Maes Howe** (HS; ☎01856-761606; www.historic -scotland.gov.uk; adult/child £5.20/3.10; ☉tours hourly 10am-3pm Oct-Mar, also 4pm Apr-Sep). Constructed about 5000 years ago, it's the finest chambered tomb in Western Europe, an extraordinary structure built from enormous sandstone blocks, some of which weigh many tons and were brought from several miles away. From the outside, the grass-covered mound looks nothing special, but once you start crawling along the long stone passageway to the main chamber, over 6.7m high and 3.5m wide, you begin to sense the indescribable gulf of years that separate us from the architects of this mysterious place.

No remains were found when the tomb was excavated in the 19th century, so it's not known how many people were originally buried here or whether they were buried with any of their worldly goods. What is known is that Vikings returning from the Crusades broke into the tomb in the 12th century, searching for treasure. They found none, but left a wonderfully earthy collection of graffiti, carved in runes on the walls of the tomb. These include such profundities as 'Thorni bedded Helgi' and several 12th-century tags of the 'Ottarfila-was-here' variety – some things never change. There are some more artistic engravings too, including a crusader cross, a wonderful dragon-like lion, a walrus and a knotted serpent.

By chance or design, for a few weeks around the winter solstice the setting sun shines along the entrance passage and strikes the back wall of the tomb in a spooky alignment. If you can't be there to see it in person, check the webcams on www.mae showe.co.uk.

Maes Howe is about 10 minutes' walk east of the Stenness crossroads. Buy your ticket at Tormiston Mill, across the road from the tomb, where there's a cafe serving snacks and light meals, a gift shop, a small exhibition and a 15-minute video about Orkney's prehistoric sites. Be sure to reserve your tour-slot in advance by phone.

Entry is by 45-minute guided tours that leave on the hour. On site, a guide will take you through the history of Maes Howe and pinpoint the various bits of graffiti with a torch. The official guide is worth buying: it contains all the runes, mapped to the walls of the tomb.

RING OF BRODGAR

Situated about a mile north of Stenness, along the road towards Skara Brae, is this wide circle of **standing stones** (HS; www .historic-scotland.gov.uk; admission free; ☉24hr), some over 5m tall. The last of the three Stenness monuments to be built (2500–2000 BC), it remains a most atmospheric location. Twenty-one of the original 60 stones still stand among the heather. These mysterious giants, their curious shapes mutilated by years of climatic onslaught, fire the imagination – what were they for? On a grey day with dark clouds thudding low across the sky, the stones look secretive and seem to be almost sneering at the jostling summer crowds. Free guided tours leave from the carpark at 1pm from June to August.

STANDING STONES OF STENNESS

Within sight of Maes Howe, four mighty **stones** (HS; www.historic-scotland.gov.uk; admission free; ☉24hr) remain of what was once a circle of 12. Recent research suggests they were perhaps erected as long ago as 3300 BC, and they impose by their sheer size; the tallest measures 5.7m in height. On the narrow strip of land they're on, the Ness of Brodgar, separates the Harray and Stenness lochs and was the site of a large settlement, inhabited throughout the Neolithic period (3500–1800 BC).

A short walk to the east are the excavated remains of **Barnhouse Neolithic Village**, thought to have been inhabited by the builders of Maes Howe. Don't skip this: it brings the area to life.

☆ Entertainment

Orkney Folklore & Storytelling Visitor Centre   FOLKLORE
(☏01856-841207; www.orkneyattractions.com) Located between Brodgar and Skara Brae, this offbeat centre focuses on the islands' folkloric tradition. The best way to experience it is on one of their atmospheric storytelling evenings (Sunday, Tuesday and Friday at 8.30pm March to October, adult/child £10/6) where local legends are told around a peat fire.

🛏 Sleeping & Eating

Ashleigh B&B   B&B ££
(☏01856-771378; www.ashleigh-orkney.com; Howaback Rd, Dounby; s/d £35/78; P☎) This large, modern house with big, modern bedrooms enjoys a superb setting in the heart of West Mainland, looking out across the Loch of Harray to the hills of Hoy. There's a sun lounge where you can soak up the view, and the breakfast goes beyond the usual offerings to include smoked haddock with poached egg.

Appie's Tea Room   CAFE £
(☏01856-841562; www.pamfarmer.co.uk; Sandwick; mains £4-8; ☉11.30am-4.30pm Sun-Fri Apr-Oct; ☎) Decked out all in white, this bright and welcoming cafe commands superb views – with an outdoor deck for sunny days – and offers a menu of fresh, inventive salads, and vegetarian and wholefood dishes such as puy lentil and cumin patties. It's located at the end of a farm road off the A967, 2 miles east of Skara Brae.

Gerri's Ice Cream Parlour   ICE CREAM £
(☏01856-850668; Stenness; snacks £2-6; ☉10.30am-7pm Mon-Fri, 10.30am-5pm Sat, 11am-6pm Sun) Housed in an ordinary looking bungalow opposite the petrol station, Gerri's is a good old-fashioned ice-cream parlour decorated in bubblegum pink, with jars of boiled sweets ranged along the shelves. It serves cappuccinos and herbal teas, gorgeous homebaked fairy cakes and a range of locally made ice creams. Their speciality is the Stenness Monster Cone – six scoops!

ⓘ ORKNEY EXPLORER PASS

Orkney contains an amazing concentration of prehistoric monuments, many of them in the care of Historic Scotland (HS), which charges a small admission fee to help fund their skilled conservation work. All the sites are well worth a visit and you can save money with an **Orkney Explorer Pass**, which covers all HS sites in Orkney, including big ticket items such as Maes Howe, Skara Brae, the Broch of Gurness, the Brough of Birsay and the Bishop's Palace and Earl's Palace in Kirkwall; it costs £17 per person from April to September (not available October to March, as many sites are closed then).

Birsay

The small village of Birsay is 6 miles north of Skara Brae. Between the two, about 1.5 miles south of Birsay you can walk along the cliffs to Marwick Head, where the dramatically located **Kitchener Memorial** looks out to sea. It's dedicated to Lord Kitchener of Khartoum, who drowned (along with 600 crewmen) when the HMS *Hampshire* was sunk by a German mine off this headland in 1916.

⊙ Sights & Activities

FREE **Earl's Palace**   RUINS
(☉24hr) The ruins of this palace, built in the 16th century by the despotic Robert Stewart, earl of Orkney, dominate the village of Birsay. Today it's a mass of half walls and crumbling columns that look like dilapidated chimney stacks. Nevertheless, the size of the palace is impressive, matching the reputed ego and tyranny of its former inhabitant.

Brough of Birsay   PREHISTORIC SITE
(HS; www.historic-scotland.gov.uk; adult/child £3.20/1.90; ☉9.30am-5.30pm mid-Jun–Sep) At low tide – check tide times at the shop in Earl's Palace (p275) – you can walk out to the Brough of Birsay, about 0.75 miles northwest of the Earl's Palace. This windswept island is the site of extensive Norse ruins, including a number of longhouses and the 12th-century **St Peter's Church**.

There's also a replica of a Pictish stone which was found here, carved with an eagle and human figures. St Magnus was buried here after his murder on Egilsay in 1117, and the island was a place of pilgrimage until a few centuries ago. You can continue across the headland to the attractive lighthouse, built in 1925, which has fantastic views along the coast.

FREE **Barony Mills**   HISTORIC BUILDING
([☎]01856-721439; ⊙10am-1pm & 2pm-5pm May-Sep) Located 600m east of the Earl's Palace (p275), at the northeastern end of Loch of Boardhouse, this is the last working water-powered bere (barley) mill in Orkney. You can watch the miller at work, and buy 1.5kg bags of bere meal to take home to bake your own traditional Orkney bere bannocks with (recipes supplied).

🛏 Sleeping

Birsay Hostel   HOSTEL, CAMPGROUND £
([☎]01856-873535; www.hostelsorkney.co.uk; 4-person tents £5-10, dm £14.50; ⊙May-Oct; [P]) Birsay makes a lovely, peaceful place to stay amid the Orkney countryside. Birsay Hostel is a former activity centre and school that now has dorms that vary substantially in spaciousness – go for one of the four-bedded ones. There's a big kitchen and a grassy camping area.

Links House   B&B ££
([☎]01856-721221; www.ewaf.co.uk; s/d £49/78; [P]) One of Orkney's most charming B&Bs, this is a welcoming stone house near the sea. The beautiful rooms – one with comforting sloping ceiling, one with a toilet that has wonderful vistas – are complemented by a little gazebo where you can contemplate the scenery, or browse the books and maps kept here (along with a wee decanter of sherry).

Breakfast here is a treat – pancakes with blueberries and crème fraiche, anyone?

Evie

On an exposed headland at Aikerness, a 1.5-mile walk northeast from the straggling village of Evie, you'll find the **Broch of Gurness** (HS; www.historic-scotland.gov.uk; adult/child £4.70/2.80; ⊙9.30am-5.30pm Apr-Sep), a fine example of the drystone fortified towers that were both status symbol for powerful farmers and useful protection from raiders some 2200 years ago. The imposing entranceway and sturdy stone walls –

originally 10m high – are impressive; inside you can see the hearth and where a mezzanine floor would have fitted. Around the broch are a number of well-preserved outbuildings, including a curious shamrock-shaped house. The visitor centre has some interesting displays on the culture that built these remarkable fortifications.

Woodwick House   HOTEL ££
([☎]01856-751330; www.woodwickhouse.co.uk; s/d £65/100, with shared bathroom £45/70; [P][☎]) A mansion of understated elegance in a lovely setting down a turning about a mile west of the Tingwall ferry turnoff. The sizeable, commodious rooms are in harmony with the relaxed rural atmosphere, as are the cosy lounges with a fire and books; the courteous hosts do fine three-course dinners (£26; open to nonguests) and put on the odd cultural event. If you've been on Orkney for a while, you may not recognise those wooden things around the house – trees.

Eviedale Campsite   CAMPGROUND £
([☎]01856-751270; www.creviedale.orknet.co.uk; sites £5-9; ⊙Apr-Sep; [P][☎]) Set at the northern end of the village, Eviedale has a good grassed area for tents, with picnic tables. It would suit people looking to avoid the larger municipal sites. Self-catering accommodation is available next door at three excellent, renovated farm cottages with wi-fi (per week £320-350).

South Coast

With its gently rolling landscape, South Mainland may not have the archaeological treasures of the north, but it does have its share of the island's history.

◉ Sights & Activities

There are a few things to see at **Orphir**, a scattered community with no shop, about 9 miles west of Kirkwall. The **Orkneyinga Saga Centre** (admission free; ⊙9am-5pm) has displays relating to the *Orkneyinga Saga*, and an interesting video depicting some of the saga's deeds.

Just behind the centre is **Earl's Bu** (admission free; ⊙24hr), the foundations of a 12th-century manor house belonging to the Norse earls of Orkney. There are also the remains of **St Nicholas' Church**, a unique circular building that was originally 9m in diameter. Built before 1136 and modelled on the rotunda of the Church of the Holy Sepulchre in Jerusalem, it was popular with pilgrims after the capture of the Holy Land during the First Crusade.

If it's sunny and you're thinking about a picnic, head to **Waulkmill Bay**, between Kirkwall and Orphir. The huge sandy beach is perfect for strolling and there is bench seating with impressive views.

🛏 Sleeping

Foinhaven B&B **££**
(📞01856-811249; www.foinhaven.co.uk; Germiston Rd, Orphir; s/d £40/60; 🅿) For a farmstay, old-fashioned hospitality and one of the best breakfasts around, try the solitude at this place, 1.5 miles from Orphir, overlooking Waulkmill Bay. Rooms are traditional and bathrooms modern – a speck of dirt would feel lonely in here. The rate comes down if you stay more than one night.

Houton Bay Lodge HOTEL **££**
(📞01856-811320; www.houtonbaylodge.com; Houton; d/ste £75/95; 🅿@🛜) Particularly good for families or business folk, this old seaplane base has been extensively refurbished, and the stylish rooms decked out with pine furniture are top-notch (room 5 is a fave). Slick leather chairs, comfy beds and en suites complete the happy picture, as does a bar, a proper snooker table and other indoor games. The lodge is right behind the Houton ferry terminal.

ℹ Getting There & Away

BOAT A car ferry runs daily from Houton to Hoy and Flotta (285).

BUS Bus 2 runs from Kirkwall to Houton (20 minutes, three to five daily Monday to Saturday) via Orphir. An extra bus, the Hoy Hopper, runs Wednesday to Friday in summer.

KIRKWALL

POP 6200

The capital of Orkney is a bustling market town, set back from a wide bay. Although Stromness is a prettier base from which to explore the island, Kirkwall's long, wind-

ing, paved main street and twisting wynds (lanes) are still very atmospheric, and the town is home to a handful of must-see attractions, including the Highland Park Distillery, the magnificent St Magnus Cathedral, and the ruins of the Bishop's Palace and the Earl's Palace, where so many of the power struggles between the church and the oppressive Stewart rulers of Orkney took place.

Founded in the early 11th century, when Earl Rognvald Brusson established his kingdom here, the original part of Kirkwall is one of the best examples of an ancient Norse town. (The name is derived from *kirkjuvagar,* meaning 'church bay'.) It was established as a royal burgh in 1486 by James III.

👁 Sights

St Magnus Cathedral CATHEDRAL
(📞01856-874894; www.stmagnus.org; Broad St; tours per person £6; ⏰9am-6pm Mon-Sat, 1-6pm Sun Apr-Sep, 9am-1pm & 2-5pm Mon-Sat Oct-Mar) Founded in 1137 and built out of local red sandstone and yellow Eday stone, fabulous St Magnus Cathedral is Kirkwall's centrepiece. The powerful atmosphere of an ancient faith pervades the impressive interior. During summer, 40-minute tours of the cathedral's upper levels start at 11am and 2pm on Tuesday and Thursday and cost £6 per person.

Earl Rognvald Brusason commissioned the cathedral in the name of his martyred uncle, Magnus Erlendsson, who was killed by Earl Hakon Paulsson on Egilsay in 1117. Work began in 1137, but the building is actually the result of 300 years of construction and alteration. The bones of St Magnus and St Rognvald are interred in the rectangular pillars in the middle of the cathedral.

At the far end of the south aisle is a splendid monument to **Dr John Rae**, the Arctic explorer, depicting him carelessly sprawled in sleep, wrapped in animal furs and wearing native moccasins, a book and shotgun by his side. There's also a memorial to **William Balfour Baikie**, a missionary who explored much of the Congo River, and the bell from

---

ORKNEYINGA SAGA

Written around 1200, this saga is a rich tale of sorcery, political intrigue, and cunning and unscrupulous acts among the Viking earls of Orkney. Part myth and part historical fact, it begins with the capture of the islands by the king of Norway and then recounts the next tumultuous centuries until they become part of Scotland. It's a wonderful piece of medieval literature. Head to the Orkneyinga Saga Centre (p276) for more background.

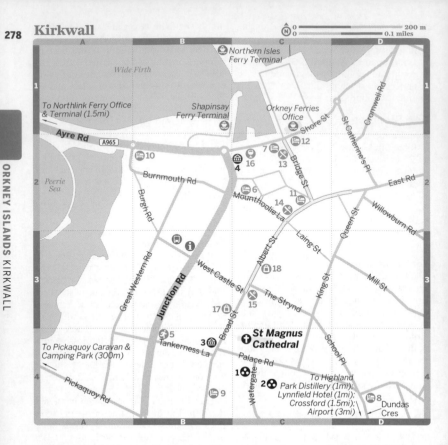

the *HMS Royal Oak*, torpedoed and sunk in Scapa Flow during WWII with the loss of 833 crewmembers.

Between the knave and the apse, the cathedral walls are lined with medieval gravestones carved with hourglasses, coffins, skulls and crossbones, and other poignant symbols of mortality (the stones have never been exposed to the elements and are probably the best-preserved medieval slabs in Scotland). Hanging in the northern aisle is a sinister 17th-century **Mort Brod**, a wooden grave marker bearing an image of the Grim Reaper.

Bishop's Palace RUINS
(HS; ☎01856-871918; www.historic-scotland .gov.uk; Watergate; incl Earl's Palace adult/child £4.50/2.70; ⊙9.30am-6.30pm Apr-Sep) The Bishop's Palace was built in the mid-12th century to provide comfortable lodgings for Bishop William the Old. The floors have collapsed but the outer walls are remarkably

intact, and you can climb Bishop Reid's Tower, added in the 16th century, for wonderful views of the cathedral. On the outside of the tower is a small statue of Earl Rognvald.

Earl's Palace RUINS
(HS; www.historic-scotland.gov.uk; Watergate; incl Bishop's Palace adult/child £4.50/2.70; ⊙9.30am-6.30pm Apr-Sep) Across the road from the Bishop's Palace is the ruin of the Earl's Palace, built by the tyrant Earl Patrick Stewart in 1600 (though the earl ran out of money and the palace was never completed). It's said to be the finest example of French-Renaissance architecture in Scotland.

Both palaces were repossessed by Bishop James Law in 1615 and the earl and his son were publicly executed. Remarkably, the despotic Patrick was found to be so ignorant that he was unable to recite even the Lord's Prayer; his execution had to be delayed by a day while priests taught him the words.

Kirkwall

FREE **Orkney Museum**   MUSEUM
(📞01856-873191; www.orkney.gov.uk; Broad St; ⊙10.30am-5pm Mon-Sat May-Sep, 10.30am-12.30pm & 1.30-5pm Mon-Sat Oct-Apr) Opposite St Magnus Cathedral, in a former merchant's house, is this labyrinthine display. It has an overview of Orcadian history and prehistory, including Pictish carvings and a display on the Ba'. Most engaging are the last rooms, covering 19th- and 20th-century social history; the earlier sections could do with a bit of a facelift (but then again, it's free).

Highland Park Distillery   DISTILLERY
(📞01856 874619; www.highlandpark.co.uk; Holm Rd; tour £6; ⊙daily May-Aug, Mon-Fri Sep-Apr) Among Scotland's more respected whiskymakers, this distillery, where they malt their own barley, is great to visit. You can see the barley and the peat kiln used to dry it on the excellent, well-informed hour-long tour (hourly when open, and weekdays at 2pm in winter).

The standard 12-year-old is a soft, balanced malt, great for whisky novices and aficionados alike; the 18-year-old is among the world's finest drams. These and others can be tasted on more specialised tours (£15), which you can prearrange.

Orkney Wireless Museum   MUSEUM
(📞01856-871400; www.orkneywirelessmuseum.org.uk; 1 Junction Rd; adult/child £2/1; ⊙10am-4.30pm Mon-Sat & 2pm-4.30pm Sun Apr-Sep) This museum houses a collection of more than 100 wireless and transistor radio sets from the earliest Phillips radios to the 1960s, plus a fascinating jumble of communications equipment dating from around 1930 onwards, much of it relating to the Scapa Flow naval base.

✪ Festivals & Events

St Magnus Festival   ARTS, MUSIC
(📞01856-871445; www.stmagnusfestival.com) A colourful celebration of music and the arts; takes place in June.

🛏 Sleeping

Narvik   B&B ££
(📞01856-879049; carolevansnarvik@hotmail.co.uk; Weyland Tce; s/d £40/60; P) Dodge the B&B fascists who sweep you out of bed with a stiff-bristled broom for your 7am breakfast by staying at this charmingly peaceful spot. Accommodation is in a beautifully decorated separate flat, with a tiled floor, a wooden double bed, DVDs and a grassy garden.

You'll have your own kitchenette, which your genial hosts stock with eggs, bacon, croissants and juices, so your morning meal is wholly at your own pace. Head east on East Rd, bear left when you reach Berstane Rd, and Weyland Terrace is first on the left.

Orcades Hostel   HOSTEL £
(📞01856-873745; www.orcadeshostel.com; Muddisdale Rd; dm/d £17/50; P🛜) Book ahead to get a bed in this cracking new hostel near the campground on the western edge of town. It's a guesthouse conversion so there's a very smart kitchen and lounge area, and great-value doubles. Comfortable dorms with just four bunks make for sound sleeping, and young, enthusiastic owners give the place plenty of spark.

Mrs Muir   B&B ££
(📞01856-874805; www.twodundas.co.uk; 2 Dundas Cres; s/d £35/70; P) This former manse is a magnificent building that has four enormous rooms blessed with large windows

and sizeable beds. There are plenty of period features, but the en suite bathrooms are not among them: they're sparklingly new, and one has a free-standing bathtub. Both the welcome and the breakfast will leave you more than satisfied.

Lynnfield Hotel HOTEL ££
(☎01856-872505; www.lynnfieldhotel.co.uk; Holm Rd; s/d £80/110; ▣☎) Within whiffing distance of the Highland Park distillery, this recently refitted hotel is run with a professional, yet warmly personal, touch. With individual rooms featuring four-poster beds, a jacuzzi or antique writing desk, and a cosy dark-wood drawing room, it's an intimate place, and also boasts a good restaurant.

Crossford B&B ££
(☎01856-876142; heatherandbobbo@yahoo.co.uk; Heatherly Loan; s/d £60/76; ▣) Situated just up the road from Highland Park Distillery, this excellent little B&B has just one double en suite room (with a lovely outlook), a small dining and sitting area and lots of privacy. It's very convenient to Kirkwall, but with a rural setting, you get the best of both worlds.

Pomona B&B B&B £
(☎01856-872325; www.pomonacatering.co.uk; 9 Albert St; s/d £24/48) We rubbed our hands with glee when we found this old-fashioned B&B at the back of the cafe with the same name. With six en suite rooms it's not the roomiest lodging in Orkney, but it is a bargain and possibly the best located, just off the main drag in the heart of town.

Albert Hotel HOTEL ££
(☎01856-876000; www.alberthotel.co.uk; Mounthoolie Lane; s/d £110/128; ☎) Stylishly refurbished, this central but peaceful hotel is just about Kirkwall's finest address. Comfortable contemporary rooms in a variety of categories sport super-inviting beds and smart bathrooms. A great Orkney base, but you may end up spending more time in the excellent Bothy Bar downstairs.

Kirkwall Hotel HOTEL ££
(☎01856-872232; www.kirkwallhotel.com; Harbour St; s/d from £70/100; ☎) A grand old bastion of Orcadian hospitality, this hotel sits in a prime location gazing proudly over the harbour. Superior and superior-plus rooms are a little pricier, but are substantially grander and better value than the standards. They also face the front, with views of the harbour, from where you can watch the lifeboat drills.

Peedie Hostel HOSTEL £
(☎01856-875477; kirkwallpeediehostel@talk21.com; Ayre Rd; dm £15) Nestling into a corner at the end of the Kirkwall waterfront, this cute hostel squeezes in all the necessary features for a comfortable stay in a small space. The dorms actually have plenty of room – it's only in the tiny kitchen that territorial squabbles might break out.

Orkney Hotel HOTEL ££
(☎01856-873477; www.orkneyhotel.co.uk; 40 Victoria St; s/d £85/109; ▣@☎) This historic hotel has been revitalised, with walls the colour of shiraz and smartly refurbished rooms; some with disabled access are across the street. The best bed is a four-poster with cathedral views. Prices are usually £10 lower than the rack rates quoted here.

Kirkwall SYHA HOSTEL £
(☎01856-872243; www.syha.org.uk; Old Scapa Rd; dm/s/tw £16/19/34; ⏾mid-Mar–Oct; ▣@) This functional hostel is a 15-minute walk from the centre, set in a prefabricated former naval barracks. Never meant to last beyond the war, it now shows its age: long walks to the institutional showers, lockout till 5pm, midnight curfew and no power points in the rooms. However, the big, sociable lounge and kitchen and large capacity are plus points.

Pickaquoy Caravan & Camping Park CAMPGROUND £
(☎01856-879900; www.pickaquoy.co.uk; Pickaquoy Rd; sites 1 person £6.50, 2-3 people £10.50; ⏾Apr-Sep; ▣) No view, but plenty of grass and excellent modern facilities. If the office is unattended, check in at the nearby Pickaquoy leisure centre.

Lerona B&B ££
(☎01856-874538; Cromwell Cres; s/d £30/60, without bathroom £25/50; ▣) Guests come first here, but the wee folk – a battalion of garden gnomes and clans of dolls with lifelike stares – are close behind.

Shore HOTEL ££
(☎01856-872200; www.theshore.co.uk; 6 Shore St; s/d £58/85; ☎) Smart contemporary rooms with a light Scandinavian touch above a lively harbourfront bar and restaurant. Those at the front are larger and (slightly) costlier. Breakfast extra.

Eating & Drinking

Reel
CAFE £

(Albert St; sandwiches £3; ⊙9am-6pm) Part music shop and part cafe, Kirkwall's best coffee-stop sits alongside St Magnus Cathedral, and bravely puts tables outside at the slightest threat of sunshine. It's a relaxed spot that's good for morning-after debriefing, as well as lunchtime panini and musically named sandwiches (along with their cheese one: Skara Brie). It's a centre for local folk musicians, with regular evening sessions.

Kirkwall Hotel
SCOTTISH ££

(☑01856-872232; www.kirkwallhotel.com; Harbour St; mains £9-15; ⊙lunch & dinner) This grand old hotel on the waterfront is one of Kirkwall's best places to dine. The elegant bar and eating area packs out; it's a favourite spot for an evening out with the clan. There's a fairly standard pub-food list that's complemented by a seasonal menu featuring local seafood and meat – the lamb is delicious.

Dil Se
INDIAN, BANGLADESHI £

(☑01856-875242; 7 Bridge St; mains £8-11; ⊙4-11pm) Upbeat and inventive, this main-street subcontinental choice tries to steer Orcadians away from the clichéd curry classics in favour of baltis – the spinach one is fabulous – and other creations. The late opening means you can enjoy those long summer evenings outdoors and not go hungry at the end of them.

Shore
SCOTTISH, SEAFOOD ££

(www.theshore.co.uk; 6 Shore St; restaurant mains £8-15; ⊙food 8am-9pm) This popular harbourside eatery brings the gastropub concept to Kirkwall, offering bar meals combined with more adventurous fare in the restaurant section. It's a little hit-and-miss, but the local chefs are assured when it comes to the sea – monkfish is always a good bet.

Peppermill Deli
DELI £

(☑01856-878878; 21 Albert St; lunch £3; ⊙8.30am-6pm Mon-Fri, 9am-5.30pm Sat, 11am-4pm Sun) The best place in town to grab a takeaway lunch: the selection of fillings for paninis, baguettes, wraps and toasties is almost limitless. It's also numero uno for coffee and you can grab smoked seafoods and cheeses here for picnics.

Bothy Bar
PUB

(☑01856-876000; www.alberthotel.co.uk; Mounthoolie Lane; mains £7-10; ⊙lunch & dinner) In the Albert Hotel, the Bothy looks very smart these days with its modish floor and black-and-white photos of old-time Orcadian farming, but its low tables provide the customary cheer and sustaining food: think sausages, haddock and stews – good pub grub.

Helgi's
PUB

(www.helgis.co.uk; 14 Harbour St) There's a traditional cosiness about this place, but the decor has moved beyond the time-honoured beer-soaked carpet to a comfortable contemporary slate floor and quotes from the *Orkneyinga Saga* plastering the walls. It's more find-a-table than jostle-at-the-bar and serves cheerful comfort food. Take your pint upstairs for quiet harbour contemplation.

Shopping

Kirkwall has some gorgeous jewellery and crafts along Albert St. Try the **Longship** (www.olagoriejewellery.com; 7 Broad St) for Orkney-made crafts and gifts and exquisite designer jewellery. **Orcadian Bookshop** (www.orcadian.co.uk; 50 Albert St) has a great selection of local books and newspapers.

❶ Information

Balfour Hospital (☑01856-888000; New Scapa Rd)

Launderama (☑01856-872982; 47 Albert St; ⊙Mon-Sat) Service washes for £9.

Orkney Library (☑01856-873166; 44 Junction Rd; ⊙Mon-Sat; @) Fast free internet access (one-hour maximum).

Support Training (☑01856-873582; cnr Junction Rd & West Tankerness Lane; per hr £4; ⊙Mon-Sat; @🛜) Internet access.

Kirkwall tourist office (☑01856-872856; www.visitorkney.com; W Castle St; ⊙9am-6pm daily summer, 9am-5pm Mon-Fri & 10am-4pm Sat winter) Has a good range of publications on Orkney.

❶ Getting There & Away

AIR Flybe (p269) and Loganair (p269) services use **Kirkwall Airport** (www.hial.co.uk), located 2.5 miles east of town.

BOAT Ferries to the North Isles depart from the town harbour; however, Northlink Ferries to Aberdeen and Shetland use the Hatston terminal, 1 mile northwest of Kirkwall. For details of flights and ferries from Kirkwall to the islands, see the individual island sections.

BUS Bus 1 runs direct from Kirkwall to Stromness (40 minutes, hourly, four to six Sunday); bus 2 runs to Orphir and Houton (20 minutes, four or five Monday to Saturday); bus 6 runs from Kirkwall to Evie (30 minutes, three to five daily Monday to Saturday) and to Tingwall to connect with the ferry to Rousay.

THE BA'

Every Christmas Day and New Year's Day, Kirkwall holds a staggering spectacle: a crazy ball game known as The Ba'. Two enormous teams – the 'Uppies', families from Up-the-Gates (ie north of the cathedral), and the 'Doonies', who live Doon-the-Gates (ie south of it) – fight their way, no holds barred, through the streets, trying to get a cork-filled leather ball (the ba') to a goal at the other end of town.

At the stroke of 1pm, the ball is thrown into the crowd from the Mercat Cross in front of the cathedral and the mad melee begins. The Uppies' goal is a wall at the southern end of town, while the Doonies aim to get the ball into the harbour at the northern end of town. All the shops barricade their doors and windows and the streets become a single heaving mass of people, striking this way and that as the ba' moves through the throng. It's not unknown for teams to take short cuts through shops and houses, or even across the rooftops, in their determination to get the ball to goal. Violence, skulduggery and other stunts are common and the event, fuelled by plenty of strong drink, can last for hours.

The origins of The Ba' lie in the age-old battle between church and state. In the 14th century, Kirkwall was divided into two departments: the Burgh, controlled by Earl Henry St Clair, and the Laverock, controlled by the bishop of Orkney. The boundary between the two was the kirkyard around St Magnus, and the original game grew from the rivalry between the Church's men (Uppies) and the King's men (Doonies). The Ba' is an incredible spectacle, but if you venture into the streets be prepared to be jostled by the crowd.

EAST MAINLAND TO SOUTH RONALDSAY

East Mainland and the string of islands to the east of Scapa Flow are linked together by causeways, so it's possible to drive all the way to Burwick without a single ferry crossing.

Since 1914, the narrow passages between Mainland and the islands of Burray and South Ronaldsay had been blocked by anti-submarine nets and a series of deliberately scuttled shipwrecks (known as 'blockships'). But in 1939 a German U-boat was still able to squeeze between the blockships in Holm Sound into Scapa Flow and torpedo the battleship HMS *Royal Oak*, killing 833 seamen.

After the disaster, Winston Churchill set Italian POWs to work erecting vast causeways of concrete blocks across the channels on the eastern side of Scapa Flow, linking Mainland to the islands of Lamb Holm, Glims Holm, Burray and South Ronaldsay. The **Churchill Barriers**, as they became known, flanked by the rusting wrecks of the blockships, now support the main road from Kirkwall to Burwick.

There are good **sandy beaches** by Barriers No 3 and 4. Several diving companies offer training and beach dives on the blockships.

ⓘ Getting There & Away

Bus 3 from Kirkwall runs to Deerness in East Mainland (30 minutes, three to five Monday to Saturday), with some buses calling at Tankerness. There are buses from Kirkwall to South Ronaldsay's St Margaret's Hope (30 minutes, almost hourly Monday to Saturday).

East Mainland

The land to the southeast of Kirkwall is mainly agricultural. The A961 heads south to the Churchill Barriers, while the A960 cuts east past Kirkwall airport towards Deerness.

On a farm at **Tankerness** is the mysterious Iron Age site of **Mine Howe** (☎01865-861234; adult/child £2.50/1.50; ☺10am-4pm daily Jun-Aug, 11am-3pm Tue & Fri Sep & May), an eerie underground chamber, the function of which is unknown. In the centre of an earthen mound ringed by a ditch, a flight of narrow steps descends steeply to a stone-lined room about 1.5m in diameter and 4m high. Archaeologists from the TV series *Time Team* carried out a dig here in 2000 and concluded that it may have had some ritual significance, perhaps as an oracle or shrine. More recently, three Iron Age human burials were found just outside the circular ditch.

Beyond Tankerness, the road crosses a narrow isthmus (with a large sandy beach) to reach the peninsula of Deerness, and ends at a car park for the **Mull Head Nature Reserve**. From here, a five-minute walk brings you to the **Gloup**, a spectacular natural arch and narrow channel.

You can continue walking north along the coast for 0.75 miles to the **Broch of Deerness**, an isolated, cliffbound promontory reached via a narrow neck of land with stonecut steps and a chain for a handrail (not for those afraid of heights). On top of the headland are the roofless remains of a tiny **12th-century chapel**; abandoned in the 16th century, it remained a place of pilgrimage until the middle of the 19th century.

Lamb Holm

On the tiny island of Lamb Holm, the **Italian Chapel** (☑01865-781268; admission free; ☉9am-dusk) is all that remains of a POW camp that housed the Italian soldiers who worked on the Churchill Barriers. They built the chapel in their spare time, using two Nissen huts, scrap metal and their considerable artistic and decorative skills. In 1960, one of the original artists responsible for the exquisite trompe l'oeil painting, Domenico Chiocchetti, returned to restore the chapel to its original glory. It's an extraordinary monument to human ingenuity and definitely worth seeing.

Alongside is the enthusiastic little shop of the **Orkney Wine Company** (☑01856-878700; www.orkneywine.co.uk; ☉Feb-Dec), which produces handmade wines made from berries, flowers and vegetables, all naturally fermented. Get stuck into some strawberry-rhubarb wine or carrot-and-malt-whisky liqueur – unusual flavours but surprisingly addictive.

Burray

The small island of Burray is linked to Mainland and South Ronaldsay by the Churchill Barriers and has a fine beach at Northtown on the east coast, where you may see seals. Burray village, on the southern side of the island, has a general store with petrol, a post office and a hotel.

◉ Sights

Orkney Fossil & Vintage Centre   MUSEUM
(☑01865-731255; www.orkneyfossilcentre.co.uk; adult/child £3.50/2; ☉10am-5pm Apr-Sep) The Orkney Fossil & Vintage Centre has a quirky collection of household and farming relics, 360-million-year-old Devonian fish fossils found in the local rocks and galleries devoted to the world wars. There's an excellent coffee shop here. Located on the A961 at Echnaloch Bay.

⊟ Sleeping & Eating

Ankersted   B&B ££
(☑01856-731217; www.ankersted.co.uk; r per person £24; ℗) Ankersted is a great place to stay, with fine rooms, all with private bathroom. The upstairs lounge and balcony area, overlooking Watersound Bay and Churchill Barrier 4, are exclusively for guests' use. Stay a week and you get a free night.

DIVING SCAPA FLOW

One of the world's largest natural harbours, Scapa Flow has been in near-constant use by various fleets from the Vikings onwards. After WWI, 74 German ships were interned in Scapa; when the terms of the armistice were agreed upon on 6 May 1919, with the announcement of a severely reduced German navy, Admiral von Reuter, who was in charge of the fleet, decided to take matters into his own hands. On 21 June, a secret signal was passed from ship to ship and the British watched incredulously as every German ship began to sink. Fifty-two of them went to the bottom, with the rest left aground in shallow water.

Most of the ships were salvaged, but seven vessels remain to attract divers. There are three battleships – the *König*, the *Kronprinz Wilhelm* and the *Markgraf* – all of which weigh over 25,000 tonnes. The first two were subjected to blasting for scrap metal, but the *Markgraf* is undamaged and considered one of the best dives in the area.

As well as the German wrecks, numerous other ships rest on the sea bed in Scapa Flow. HMS *Royal Oak*, which was sunk by a German U-boat in October 1939 with the loss of 833 crew, is an official war grave – diving here is prohibited.

Recommended diving operators:

» **Diving Cellar** (☑01856-850055; www.divescapaflow.co.uk; 4 Victoria St)

» **Scapa Scuba** (☑01856-851218; www.scapascuba.co.uk; Dundas St)

Sands Hotel
HOTEL **££**

(☎01856-731298; www.thesandshotel.co.uk; s/d/ste £80/100/155; **P**🛜) This is a spiffy, refurbished 19th-century herring station, right on the pier. Very modern rooms have stylish furnishings, and all have great water views. Families and groups should consider a suite: two-level self-contained flats that sleep four and have a kitchen.

Watersound Restaurant
RESTAURANT **££**

(☎01856-731298; www.thesandshotel.co.uk; Sands Hotel; mains £15, bar meals £8; ☉lunch & dinner) Has a genteel, nautical feel, and dishes out decent nosh. Tables in the sunlit conservatory migrate outside in sunny weather.

South Ronaldsay

This large, flat island is covered with a patchwork of fields and feels surprisingly remote, even though it's only 6 miles from the Scottish mainland. Most people come here to see the remarkable and thoroughly entertaining Tomb of the Eagles at the southern tip of the island. It's also worth detouring across to the immaculately white **Sands O'Right** on the road to Hoxa Head.

The pristine village of **St Margaret's Hope** is the largest settlement on South Ronaldsay. The village was named after Margaret, the Maid of Norway, who died here in 1290 on the way from her homeland to marry Edward II of England (strictly a political affair: Margaret was only seven years old when she died). This is where the car ferry from Gills Bay on mainland Scotland docks.

◉ Sights

Tomb of the Eagles
PREHISTORIC SITE

(☎01865-831339; www.tomboftheeagles.co.uk; Liddel; adult/child £6.50/3; ☉9.30am-5.30pm Apr-Oct, 10am-noon Mar, by arrangement Nov-Feb) Set in a spectacular clifftop position, this 5000-year-old chambered tomb was discovered by local farmers who now run it privately as a visitor attraction. It's as interesting for their entertaining and informative guided tour and for the unusual access (lying prone on a trolley, you wheel yourself into the low entrance tunnel) as for the tomb itself.

Before taking the mile's airy walk out to the site, an excellent personal explanation is given to you at the visitor centre; you meet a few spooky skulls and get to handle some of the artefacts found in the tomb, including some sea-eagle talons.

On the way you visit a circular Bronze Age stone building with a firepit, indoor well and plenty of seating; orthodox theory suggests it was a communal cooking site (but we reckon it's the original Orkney pub). Next to it is a 'burnt mound', the shattered remains of stones that were heated in the fire and then used to heat water (whether for cooking or washing is unknown).

The neolithic tomb itself is an elaborate stone construction that once held the remains of up to 340 people, along with the bones of at least 14 sea eagles. It's possible that sky burials took place here, with the dead placed on top of wooden platforms outside the tomb entrance for eagles and carrion birds to pick clean.

The visitor centre is a 20-minute walk east from Burwick, and you can continue the walk around the headland to a **gloup** (seacliff blowhole), less than a mile away, at Halcro Head.

Orkney Marine Life Aquarium
AQUARIUM

(☎01856-831700; www.orkneymarinelife.co.uk; Grimness; adult/child £6/4.25; ☉10am-6pm Easter-Oct) This aquarium showcases the fascinating collection of marine animals found in Scapa Flow and Orcadian coastal waters. Giant shellfish such as lobsters are a feature, and there's a rock pool that allows up-close-and-personal inspections of local creatures – great for everyone, especially kids. Injured seals that have been nursed back to health can be viewed in open-air pools.

✹ Festivals & Events

Festival of the Horse
CULTURAL

On the third Saturday in August, St Margaret's Hope hosts this unusual festival; dating back to the early 19th century, it's the only survivor of a tradition that once took place all over Orkney. Village boys compete to make the most perfect plough tracks on the Sands O'Right using exquisite miniature ploughs, while young girls dress up in elaborate copies of plough-horse harnesses.

🛏 Sleeping & Eating

Bankburn House
B&B **££**

(☎08444 142310; www.bankburnhouse.co.uk; St Margaret's Hope; s/d £48/65, with shared bathroom £38/55; **P@**🛜) This place has four smashing upstairs rooms in a large rustic house. Two rooms have en suite bathrooms, all are a brilliant size, and a lot of thought has been put into guests' comfort. There's also a huge stretch of lawn out the front, which overlooks the town and bay – perfect for sunbathing on those shimmering Orkney summer days.

There's a substantial discount if you stay more than one night. It's on the A961, just outside the village.

Murray Arms Hotel   B&B **££**
(☑01856-831205; www.murrayarmshotel.com; St Margaret's Hope; s/d £40/80; ☜) This friendly local has small but very cosy and well-kitted-out rooms. Semi-skylight windows mean you can see what the weather's doing without getting out of bed. The **bar** (mains £7-9) is popular with locals and a great spot to have a chinwag with some Orcadians.

St Margaret's Hope Backpackers   HOSTEL **£**
(☑01856-831225; www.orkneybackpackers.com; St Margaret's Hope; dm £13; ⓟ) Just a short walk from the ferry, this hostel is a lovely stone cottage offering small, simple rooms with up to four berths – great for families. There's a lounge, kitchen, laundry and good, hot showers. It's an excellent set-up, particularly as you can use the wi-fi in the adjacent cafe. Make enquiries at the Trading Post shop next door.

🍽**Creel**   SEAFOOD RESTAURANT **£££**
(☑01856-831311; www.thecreel.co.uk; Front Rd, St Margaret's Hope; 2/3-course dinner £32/38; ☻dinner Tue-Sun) On the waterfront in an unassuming house, on unpretentious wooden tables, some of Scotland's best seafood has been served up for well over 20 years. Upstairs and next door, three spacious, comfortable **rooms** (single/double £75/110) face the spectacular sunset over the water. It was up for sale at the time of research, so fingers crossed.

SOUTH ISLES

The South Isles – Hoy, South Walls, Graemsay and Flotta – guard the southern and western sides of Scapa Flow, and encompass both the wildest parts of the Orkney archipelago (the hills of Hoy) and the most industrialised (the oil terminal on Flotta).

❶ Getting There & Away

Orkney Ferries (☑01856-850624; www .orkneyferries.co.uk; adult/bicycle one way

£3.75/1) runs a passenger ferry (adult/bicycle one way £3.75/1, 30 minutes, two to five daily) between Stromness harbour and Moaness Pier at the north end of Hoy, calling at Graemsay on the way there (or the way back, depending on the tide).

There's also a frequent **car ferry** (☑01856-811397; www.orkneyferries.co.uk; passenger/car £3.75/11.95, 40 minutes, up to seven daily Monday to Friday, two or three Saturday and Sunday) to Lyness (on Hoy) from Houton on Mainland; cars must be booked in advance. The Sunday service runs only from May to September. This ferry also calls at Flotta (same fares).

Hoy & South Walls

Orkney's second-largest island, **Hoy** (meaning 'High Island'), got the lion's share of the archipelago's scenic beauty. Shallow turquoise bays lace the east coast and massive seacliffs guard the west, while peat and moorland cover Orkney's highest hills; the highest point is Ward Hill (479m), in the north. Much of the northern part of the island is a Royal Society for the Protection of Birds (RSPB) reserve, with breeding guillemots, kittiwakes, fulmars, puffins and great skuas. Note that the ferry service from Mainland gets very busy over summer – book ahead.

Across a narrow causeway at the southern end of Hoy is **South Walls**, originally a separate island. The village of Longhope here is the largest settlement on the two islands, with a bustling population of around 40. In 1969, South Walls was the scene of one of Britain's worst lifeboat disasters. Called out in a Force-9 gale to a freighter in distress in the Pentland Firth, the Longhope lifeboat capsized in a storm and all eight of the crew were lost, including the coxwain and his two sons, as well as the second coxwain and his two sons. In a community this small, the effect was devastating, and the event is still remembered to this day.

◉ Sights & Activities

Old Man of Hoy   ROCK FORMATION
Hoy's best-known sight is this spectacular 137m-high rock stack that juts improbably from the ocean off the tip of an eroded headland. It was first scaled in 1966 by mountaineers Sir Chris Bonington, Tom Patey and Rusty Baillie; the climb was repeated the next year for the BBC's first-ever televised rock-climb.

There are walks to the Old Man of Hoy from Moaness or Rackwick (see p298), but if you don't have time to visit, you can see him/it as you pass on the Scrabster–Stromness ferry.

St John's Head
SEA CLIFFS

The northwest coast of Hoy has the highest sea cliffs in Britain, rising sheer from the ocean to reach 346m. Like the Old Man of Hoy, it's been the scene of extreme rock-climbing adventures, from its first ascent in 1970 (a seven-day epic) to the first free ascent by Scotland's leading climber, Dave MacLeod, in 2011.

Hoy Walks
WALKING

There are pleasant walks along the low cliffs at **Cantick Head** at the island's east end, where there's a Stevenson lighthouse and a poignant memorial to the crew of the Longhope lifeboat; and at the **Hill of White Hamars** nature reserve, on the south coast.

Scapa Flow Visitor Centre
MUSEUM

(☑01856-791300; www.orkney.gov.uk; Lyness; admission by donation; ⊗9am-4.30pm Mon-Fri Mar-Oct, Sat May-Oct & Sun May-Sep) Lyness, on the eastern side of Hoy, was an important naval base during both world wars, when the British Grand Fleet was based in Scapa Flow. It isn't a pretty place, but this fascinating museum and photographic display, located in an old pumphouse that once fed fuel to the ships, is a must-see for anyone interested in Orkney's military history.

Take your time to browse the exhibits about WWI and WWII, and have a look at the folders of supplementary information: the letters home from a seaman lost when the HMS *Royal Oak* was torpedoed are particularly moving. You'll find the story of the first-ever landing of an aircraft on a moving ship in 1917, and the construction of the Churchill Barriers in the 1940.

The museum features a fine collection of armaments, including a torpedo, plus photographs of and artefacts retrieved from the wrecks of various historic vessels which sailed from or sank in Scapa Flow. Included in the admission price is an evocative audiovisual show in a vast oil tank behind the centre, which also houses various boats, a Bofors anti-aircraft gun and a DUKW amphibian landing craft.

FREE Dwarfie Stane
PREHISTORIC SITE

(Rackwick Glen; ⊗24hr) The 5000-year-old Dwarfie Stane is the only example of a neo-lithic rock-cut tomb in Britain, hollowed out of a huge sandstone boulder dropped here by a glacier during the last Ice Age. It lies a 10-minute walk east of the road through Rackwick Glen (signposted from a parking area), beneath cliffs that are loud with nesting fulmars in summer.

An opening in the west side, a metre square, gives access to two small, rounded burial chambers; a large block of stone that once sealed the entrance sits just outside. A concrete repair on the roof (dating from the 1950s) marks where the tomb was plundered at some unknown time in the distant past.

The stone is associated with Viking legends of dwarves and trolls, and was a popular sight for Victorian tourists, including Sir Walter Scott, who gave it a mention in his novel *The Pirate*. There's some interesting grafitti carved on its south side (away from the road), left by the eccentric British spy and amateur archaeologist Major William Mounsey, who camped here in 1850. First is the year and his name in Latin, spelt backwards: YESNVOM SUMLEILVG AD 1850; beneath is a line of Persian script that translates as 'I have sat two nights and so learned patience'.

Lyness Naval Cemetery
MILITARY CEMETERY

(Lyness; ⊗dawn-dusk) Established in 1915, this beautifully maintained cemetery contains the graves of more than 650 WWI and WWII servicemen, including sailors lost on the *Vanguard*, the *Hampshire* and the *Royal Oak*, as well as 14 sailors of the German High Seas Fleet that surrendered in Scapa Flow in 1918.

Hackness Martello Tower
HISTORIC BUILDING

(HS; ☑01856-701727; South Walls; adult/child £4.50/2/70; ⊗9.30am-5.30pm Apr-Oct) On the south headland of Longhope Bay stands a Martello tower, built in 1814 to protect convoys heading for the Baltic during the Napoleonic Wars (there's another, less well preserved, on the bay's northern headland). The tower and its adjacent gun battery have been extensively restored, and house exhibits detailing 19th-century barrack-room life.

Longhope Lifeboat Museum
MUSEUM

(☑caretaker 01856-701332; www.longhopelifeboat .org.uk; Aith Hope) At the southern tip of Hoy, near the causeway to South Walls, Longhope's former lifeboat station houses a small museum centred on one of the old boats itself (the modern lifeboat is moored afloat off Longhope village). If it's not open, call the caretaker to have a look.

Betty Corrigall's Grave HISTORIC SITE

(Scad Head) Betty Corrigall was a local girl who was made pregnant and then abandoned by a visiting sailor in the late 18th century. Shamed and ostracised by the tight-knit community, she hanged herself – but as a suicide, she was denied a burial in hallowed ground. So poor Betty was interred on the high moors near the parish boundary.

Her resting place lay forgotten until the coffin was accidentally unearthed by peat cutters in 1933. Beside the main road, halfway between Moaness and Lyness, it is now marked by a simple white headstone and planted with flowers, the loneliest and most poignant grave in Scotland.

🛏 Sleeping & Eating

Uppersettir B&B £

(☎01856-791234; uppersettir@freeuk.com; Uppersettir; r per person £23; P) If you can snag a bed in this spectacularly situated hilltop farm 2.5 miles south of the Lyness ferry, count yourself fortunate. It's like staying at a friend's house: a comfortable room, a make-yourself-at-home attitude and hosts who couldn't be more welcoming – an out-of-the-ordinary B&B experience. Book in advance; two-night minimum stay.

Hoy Centre HOSTEL £

(☎office hrs only 01856 873535 ext 2415; www .hostelsorkney.co.uk; Moaness; dm adult/child £16/12, f £38; P) This clean, bright hostel has an enviable location, around 15 minutes' walk from Moaness Pier, at the base of the rugged Cuilags. Rooms come with twin beds and a bunk bed, or there are family rooms, all with en suite bathrooms.

Quoydale B&B £

(☎01856-791315; www.orkneyaccommodation.co .uk; Quoydale Farm; s/d £25/42) This welcoming B&B is nestled at the base of Ward Hill, on a working farm 1 mile south of the ferry terminal. It has spectacular views over Scapa Flow and offers tours and a taxi service.

Stromabank Hotel HOTEL, PUB ££

(☎01856-701494; www.stromabank.co.uk; Longhope; s/d £42/64; ☺lunch Sat & Sun, dinner Fri-Wed) Perched on the hill above Longhope, the small and atmospheric Stromabank has very acceptable, refurbished en suite rooms,

as well as an attractive **bar** (lunch Sun, dinner Fri-Wed), whose small menu offers tasty home-cooked meals (£6 to £10) using lots of local produce. Limited opening hours in winter.

Rackwick Outdoor
Centre HOSTEL, CAMPGROUND £

(☎office hrs only 01856-873535 ext 2415; www .hostelsorkney.co.uk; Rackwick; dm adult/child £13/11, f £33; ☺Apr-Sep; P) Newly refurbished, this cosy spot, 6 miles from the ferry at Moaness, is a snug, clean place, popular with walkers, with two four-bed dorm rooms. You can also camp outside and use the facilities (per night adult/child £4.50/3).

Wild Heather B&B £

(☎01856-791098; www.wildheatherbandb.co.uk; Lyness; s/d £32/50; P) Turn right from the ferry to reach this great place right on the bay. Plenty of thoughtful extras add value, and evening meals are available.

Pump House Cafe CAFE £

(Lyness; mains £2-4; ☺9am-4.30pm Mon-Fri Mar-Oct, Sat May-Oct & Sun May-Sep) Housed in the Scapa Flow Visitor Centre, this wartime-style canteen serves hearty homemade soups, homebaked cakes and tea and coffee (don't expect an espresso machine, though).

❶ Getting Around

BUS Hoy Hopper (£17/8.50 adult/child; ☺Wed-Fri, mid-May–mid-Sep) Hoy's only public transport is this summertime bus service (information available from the Kirkwall tourist office). It departs from Kirkwall, crosses to Hoy on the Houton–Lyness ferry, then shuttles around the island between Lyness, Longhope and Moaness (but not Rackwick), allowing you to hop on and off at will, before returning to Kirkwall in the evening.

TAXI There's no public transport to Rackwick Bay, so if you don't feel like walking call **Rendall's** (☎01856-791262) or **North Hoy Transport** (☎01856-791315) for a minibus taxi service.

Graemsay

This tiny, low-lying agricultural island between Hoy and Stromness once supported a healthy population of crofting families (more than 200 people in 1841), but today is home to only a couple of farms. You can stop here on the way to or from Hoy and walk around the island – there's a fine **sandy beach** on the north side, a short walk from the ferry landing.

The island has two Stevenson-designed lighthouses dating from 1851: **Hoy Low** at the southern tip of the island, and the rather fine **Hoy High** in the north, a brilliant-white 33m-high tower with a balcony supported by Gothic arches. The keepers' houses were built in the Stevensons' distinctive 'Egyptian temple' style.

Flotta

The most distinctive feature of this small, flat island - in fact, the name comes from the Norse for 'flat island' – is the 68m-tall **flare stack** that rises from the oil terminal in the north of the island like a medieval beacon (inevitably christened the Old Man of Flotta). As a result of the oil industry Flotta is fairly industrialised – since 1976 the island has been one of the pipeline terminals for bringing North Sea oil ashore – but there are many wartime remains dotted around the island, and some pleasantly rural corners.

As the island commands the main entrance channel into Scapa Flow, it was heavily fortified during the two world wars. Major relics include a sprawling WWII **rocket battery** on the northern peninsula, and the Buchanan and NEB **coastal defence batteries** in the south. The **Peerie Museum** (admission free; ⊙9am-12.30pm & 1.30-5.30pm Mon-Wed & Fri, 9am-1pm Thu & Sat), next to the island's post office (and only shop), houses a jumble of military memorabilia collected from the island over the years. The museum building – known as the Silent Shed – once housed the hydrophone operators who listened out for enemy submarines.

The most attractive part of the island is at **Cletts**, near the southeastern tip, where there are some picturesque sea stacks. The *Islands of Hoy* brochure, available free from the Stromness and Kirkwall tourist offices, lists all the points of interest on Flotta.

NORTH ISLES

The group of windswept islands north of Mainland provides a refuge for migrating birds and a nesting ground for seabirds; there are several RSPB reserves here. Some of the islands are also rich in archaeological sites, but it's the beautiful scenery, with wonderful white-sand beaches and azure seas, that's the main attraction. Most islands are home to traditional Orcadian communities that give a real sense of what Orkney was like before the modern world infringed upon island life.

The tourist offices in Kirkwall and Stromness have the useful *Islands of Orkney* brochure with maps and details of these islands. Note that the 'ay' at the end of each island name (from the Old Norse for 'island') is pronounced 'ee' (Shapinsay is pronounced *'shap-in-see'*).

❶ Getting There & Away

Orkney Ferries (☏01856-872044; www.orkney ferries.co.uk) and **Loganair** (☏01857-873457; www.loganair.co.uk) enable you to make day trips to many of the islands from Kirkwall on most days of the week (North Ronaldsay services run only on Friday). That said, it's really best to stay a few days and soak up the slow, easy pace of life.

LOCAL KNOWLEDGE

JOHN BAIN: INTERISLAND PILOT

Best time to visit? The summer, but it's the busiest. Not a lot of visitors like the climate in winter, and a lot of places close down. Ferries are less frequent; you don't have the same chances to move around. But you do get some beautiful winter days.

Ferry or plane? If you've got time, experience both. I'm biased but I would say that from the aircraft you see more, and you can fit more into your trip. You can see nearly all the main islands in a few days.

Most beautiful island? Oh, no, I'd get hung, drawn, and quartered if I picked just one! I live up on North Mainland and look out on the islet of Eynhallow [near Evie] every morning. The stories say that's where strange folk, the Finmen, lived. That's one of the great things about Orkney, the storytelling. Go to a storytelling night, you'll be hooked.

On a rainy day? You can go round to the craft shops in Kirkwall. And the island's got some good pubs, like Helgi's, for a quiet drink.

Favourite out-of-the-way spot? The Brough of Birsay. Go up there for a picnic.

Local Words? Peedie – it means little. It's a very common word on the islands.

Shapinsay

Just 20 minutes by ferry from Kirkwall, Shapinsay is a low-lying, intensively cultivated island with a fine castle and good beaches along its western edge. The ferry trip passes tiny **Thieves Holm**, formerly a prison for thieves and witches, and the lighthouse on Helliar Holm.

The main settlement of **Balfour village** is made up of the former workers' cottages for Balfour Castle, overlooking Elwick Bay, where King Haakon's fleet sheltered before setting off for the Battle of Largs in 1263. There's a general store, a couple of craft shops and a post office; the island is only 6 miles long, making it easy to explore on foot (p289).

◎ Sights & Activities

Balfour Castle   CASTLE
(www.balfourcastle.com; Balfour Village; tours £20) Completed in 1848 in the turreted Scottish Baronial style, Balfour Castle dominates the southern end of the island. Guided tours (2.15pm Sunday from May to September) must be booked in advance; the price includes the ferry, admission to the castle and afternoon tea. It's also available as a private hotel that can be hired for shooting parties.

The castle was built by the Balfours, who made their fortune in the British Raj in India, and was owned by the Polish Zawadski family from 1961 till 2009. Examples of the Balfours' civic projects include the neat line of cottages in the main village, the ornate **Gatehouse** (which now serves as the village pub), a sea-flushed public toilet near the jetty and the **Gasometer**, a castle-like folly which once provided the island with electricity. South of the ferry pier is the interesting **Dishan Tower** (known locally as 'the douche') housing a saltwater shower topped by a doocot (dove-cote).

FREE **Burroughston Broch**   PREHISTORIC SITE
(⊙24hr) About 4 miles from the pier, at the far northeastern corner of Shapinsay island, is the Iron Age Burroughston Broch, one of the best-preserved brochs (defensive towers) in Orkney.

FREE **Shapinsay Heritage Centre**   HERITAGE CENTRE
(The Smithy, Balfour Village; ⊙10am-4pm Mon-Sat May-Sep) Housed in the former blacksmith's forge, the heritage centre documents the island's history with photographs and artefacts.

⌑ Sleeping & Eating

Hilton Farmhouse   B&B ££
(☑01856-711239; www.hiltonorkneyfarmhouse .co.uk; Hilton; s/d £50/70; 🅿🛜) Less than a mile east of the ferry pier, this appealing farmhouse B&B also houses the island's main restaurant (p289).

Conservatory Restaurant   SCOTTISH ££
(☑01856-711239; Hilton Farmhouse; 2-course dinner £15; ⊙lunch & dinner Fri-Sun; 🛜) Housed, as the name suggests, in a sunny farmhouse conservatory, this restaurant specialises in fresh local produce, from Orkney beef to locally caught seafood.

Smithy Restaurant   SEAFOOD £
(☑01856-711722; The Smithy, Balfour Village; snacks £2-6; 2-/3-course dinner £15/20; ⊙noon-4.30pm Mon-Thu, to 8pm Fri & Sat, to 7pm Sun) Housed in the old Smithy alongside the island's heritage centre, this snug, stone-walled cottage restaurant serves coffees, teas and homemade treats during the day, but offers a more sophisticated seafood-based menu at lunch and dinner time. They also do takeaway fish and chips from 5pm to 7.30pm Friday and Saturday.

❶ Getting There & Away

Orkney Ferries (p269) operates a ferry from Kirkwall (passenger/car £3.60/11.50, 25 minutes). Services are limited in winter.

Rousay

Just off the north coast of Mainland, and connected by regular ferry from Tingwall, Rousay makes a great little day trip, but you may well feel the desire to stay longer. This hilly island is famous for its numerous archaeological sites, earning it the nickname 'Egypt of the North' (though that might be pushing it a *bit* too far).

◎ Sights & Activities

Most of the island is classed as a Site of Special Scientific Interest (SSSI), and it also hosts the RSPB's **Trumland Reserve**, covering much of the heath-filled interior. You can walk through the reserve to **Blotchnie Fiold** (250m), the highest point on the island, a good place to spot hen harrier, merlin and short-eared owl. The lochs of Muckle Loch and Peerie Water are good for **trout fishing**.

Quandale, at the western end of Rousay, was the only place in Orkney to suffer from the Highland Clearances (the full story is told at the heritage centre). From the **Quandale viewpoint**, a half-mile north of the Midhowe car park, you can look out across an abandoned agricultural landscape, with tumbled cottages, field dykes and the ridge-and-furrow outlines of run rig cultivation still clearly visible.

You can **hire a bike** at Trumland Farm and take on the winding, hilly 14-mile circuit of the island. Rousay's informal **heritage centre** – a series of posters and displays in the ferry waiting room – includes a map describing the cycling circuit.

It's also possible to **walk** from the ferry pier to Midhowe Broch, taking in the Westness Walk and all the main historic sites (12 miles return, allow six hours).

Westness Walk
WALKING

The south shore of Rousay from Midhowe Tomb to Westness Farm has been described as the richest archaeological mile in Britain, recording 5000 years of Orkney history. Here you can see the remains of human habitation ranging from the neolithic through the Iron Age to Viking and Pictish burial sites, medieval farms and the 12th-century **St Mary's Church**.

The coast here is a good place for watching seals and otters, looking out across the turbulent tidal waters of Eynhallow Sound to the Broch of Gurness. The little island of **Eynhallow**, now uninhabited, was once a sacred place, and houses the ruins of an early Celtic chapel (the name is Old Norse for 'holy island').

Tourist offices on Mainland can provide a *Westness Walk* leaflet detailing this mile-long hike.

FREE Midhowe Tomb
PREHISTORIC SITE

(⊘24hr) Dating from back around 3500 BC, the 30m-long Midhowe Tomb that's been dubbed the 'Great Ship of Death' is the longest chambered cairn in Orkney. The vast stone tomb has been covered by a modern stone building that has a suspended walkway allowing you to walk above the main passage where you can see the 24 stone 'stalls' in which the bones of 25 people were discovered.

As well as human remains, many bird and animal bones were found in the cave, perhaps meant as food for the deceased. The cairn is 5.5 miles west of the pier and a steep 550m walk down from the road.

FREE Midhowe Broch
PREHISTORIC SITE

(⊘24hr) Next to the Midhowe Tomb is Midhowe Broch, the sturdy stone lines of which echo the stratifications of the rocky shoreline. The best example of a broch in Orkney, it's a muscular, Iron Age fortified compound with a central partition fashioned out of stone slabs, with two hearths, water tanks, quern stones and lots of Skara Brae–style stonebuilt storage shelves.

Dating from around 100 BC, it has a cluster of well-preserved outbuldings, including dwelling houses (you can see the holes for the hinge pins of wooden doors) and a forge for smelting iron.

FREE Taversoe Tuick
PREHISTORIC SITE

(HS; ⊘24hr) Taversoe Tuick is an intriguing burial cairn constructed on two levels, with separate entrances – perhaps a joint tomb for different families, a semi-detached solution to a shortage of afterlife housing. You can squeeze into the cairn and descend a steel ladder to explore both levels, but there's not much space.

FREE Blackhammer Cairn
PREHISTORIC SITE

(⊘24hr) Blackhammer, 1.5 miles west of the ferry pier, is a chambered cairn that served as the burial place for a farming community around 2500 BC. Only two sets of human remains were found here, but there were animal bones and fragments of neolithic pottery.

FREE Knowe of Yarso
PREHISTORIC SITE

(HS; ⊘24hr) A boggy half-mile walk from the road leads you to the Knowe of Yarso, a stalled cairn; it contained the remains of 29 adults, and was in use from 2900 BC to 1900 BC.

Trumland House
GARDEN

(gardens £1.50; ⊘10am-5pm Mon-Fri May-Oct) Undergoing extensive restoration at the time of research, this is probably the largest private house in Orkney. The grounds, with their thicket of native trees, are worth a stroll – you enter the walled garden through a medieval gate.

🛏 Sleeping & Eating

Trumland Farm Hostel HOSTEL **£**
(☑01856-821252; trumland@btopenworld.com; sites £5, dm £10, bedding £2; **P**) An easy stroll from the ferry, this organic farm has a wee hostel with rather cramped six-bed dorms and a pretty little kitchen and common area. You can pitch tents outside and use the facilities; there's a well-equipped self-catering cottage that sleeps three (£60 to 100).

Taversoe Hotel HOTEL **££**
(☑01856-821325; www.taversoehotel.co.uk; s/d £45/75; **P**) About 2 miles west from the pier, the island's only hotel is a low-key place, with neat, simple doubles with water vistas that share a bathroom and a twin with en suite bathroom but no view. The best views, however, are from the dining room, which serves good-value meals. The friendly owners will pick you up from the ferry.

Pier Restaurant CAFE **£**
(☑01856-821359; meals £5-7; ⊙11am 11pm, closes 6.30pm Wed & Sun; **@**) Just above the ferry, this simple place does burgers and standard bar meals, and is good for a coffee or a whisky while waiting for the boat, or a chat and a game of pool after a long day's walking. There's also internet access and a list of local residents who offer B&B.

ⓘ Information

Marion's Shop (☑01856-821365; ⊙2-5.30pm Wed-Sat, 2-4pm Sun, noon 1pm Mon, 11am-1pm Thu), Rousay's only grocery store, and the **post office** are at the eastern end of the island, 2.5 miles north of the ferry pier.

ⓘ Getting There & Around

BOAT A small **car ferry** (☑01856-751360; www.orkneyferries.co.uk) connects Tingwall on Mainland with Rousay (passenger/bicycle/car return £7.50/2/23.90, 30 minutes, up to six daily) and the nearby islands of Egilsay and Wyre. You can buy tickets and make vehicle bookings (compulsory) at the office at Tingwall pier.

BUS Stagecoach (p269) buses connect Kirkwall to Tingwall at times that connect with the ferries (Monday to Saturday only).

BICYLE Bikes can be hired for £7 per day from Trumland Farm (p291).

TAXI Rousay Tours & Taxis (☑01856-821234; www.rousaytours.co.uk; tours adult/child £16.50/5; ⊙daily, year-round) offers guided taxi tours of the island, including wildlife-spotting (seals and otters) and visits to the prehistoric sites. They also provide general taxi service.

Egilsay & Wyre

These two small islands lie east of Rousay, and are served by the Tingwall–Rousay ferry (p291). Unfortunately, the ferry timings make it difficult to spend time on more than one of the three islands in one day.

Much of **Egilsay**, the larger of the two, is an RSPB reserve; listen for the corncrakes at the southern end of the island. A cenotaph erected in 1938 marks the spot where Earl Magnus was murdered in 1116 on the orders of Earl Haakon Paulsson. A few years later, Magnus' nephew Rognvald Kali seized the earldom and made his uncle into a saint, building the dramatic St Magnus Cathedral in Kirkwall in his honour. Pilgrims soon flocking to Egilsay seeking miracle cures and **St Magnus Kirk** was built, one of only two surviving Viking round-towered churches in Britain. There's a small shop and post office near the jetty.

Wyre was the domain of the Viking Baron Kolbein Hruga (known as 'Cubbie Roo'); the substantial ruins of **Cubbie Roo's Castle**, built around 1145, stand dramatically above the northern shore. Either Cubbie Roo or his son Bjarni, bishop of Orkney, built **St Mary's Chapel**, which is still remarkably intact. From the jetty, you can walk south to a small **heritage centre** displaying photos of life in Wyre, passing the **Bu**, the former home of Scottish poet Edwin Muir. Continuing to the far western tip of the island, there's a small beach at the **Taing**, where you're almost guaranteed to see seals.

Stronsay

Shaped like a bent crucifix, Stronsay attracts walkers and cyclists for its lack of serious inclines and the beautiful landscapes of its four curving bays. You can spot wildlife here: chubby seals basking on the rocks, puffins and other seabirds.

In the 18th century, the major industry here was the collection and burning of kelp (a kind of seaweed) to produce potash and soda, which were exported for use in the production of glass, iodine and soap. At its height, some 3000 Orcadians were employed in the seaweed business.

In the 19th century, herring fishing whipped Stronsay into a frenzy; it was said that you could walk from Whitehall village to the island of Papa Stronsay on the decks of the herring boats. However, the industry faded away after the collapse of the fisheries; these days Stronsay is a friendly, relaxed little island, with a patchwork of pastures and some good beaches.

◉ Sights & Activities

The heyday of Stronsay's herring industry is recalled in the old **Stronsay Fish Mart** (admission free; ⊙daily May-Sep), which houses an interpretation centre, a hostel and a cafe.

There's a fine beach at **St Catherine's Bay** on the west coast, where you may see locals collecting 'spoots' (razor shells), an island delicacy. There's another good beach at **Rothiesholm Sand** on the southwestern peninsula. The heath-covered headland here was the source of the island's peat and is home to numerous seabirds.

Over on the east coast is a small bird reserve at **Mill Bay** run by the bird artist John Holloway, while the rugged southeast coast has some unusual rock formations, including the **Vat o'Kirbuster**, the best example of a gloup in Orkney. It's a dramatic spot, with a deep cauldron eroded by the ocean on the landward-side of the arch. A nature trail leads from a car park to the Vat; you can also walk the 10-mile round trip along the coast from Whitehall. There are pleasant beaches around Holland Farm, which has a **seal-watching hide** down on the shore, and you may see otters around nearby **Loch Lea-shun**.

Just across the harbour from Whitehall is the small island of **Papa Stronsay**, where Earl Rognvald Brusason was murdered in 1046. There's lots of wildlife and seals to be seen on the shore. In 1999 the island was purchased by the Transalpine Redemptorists, a breakaway sect from the Catholic Church, who built a new monastery here, continuing a tradition going back all the way to the 5th century. The monks are regularly seen on the main island and you can take **boat trips** (✆01856-616389) to the monastery by prior arrangement.

🛏 Sleeping & Eating

Stronsay Hotel   HOTEL, PUB **££**
(✆01857-616213; www.stronsayhotelorkney.co.uk; Whitehall; s/d £38/76; 🛜) The island's watering hole has immaculate refurbished rooms. There's also recommended pub grub (meals from £7; open lunch and dinner) in the bar, with excellent seafood (including paella and lobster) in particular. There are good deals for multinight stays.

Stronsay Fish Mart   HOSTEL **£**
(✆01857-616386; Whitehall; dm £14) Part of the island's former herring station has been converted into a 10-bed hostel with shower and kitchen. It's clean and well run, and the neighbouring cafe serves takeaways, snacks and meals all day.

❶ Information

Whitehall, where the ferry arrives, is the main village; here you'll find a **general store** (✆01857-616339; ⊙8.30am-6.30pm Mon-Sat) (with bike hire), post office and hotel.

❶ Getting There & Away

AIR Loganair (p288) flies from Kirkwall to Stronsay (£35 one way, 20 minutes, two daily Monday to Saturday).

BOAT A **car ferry** (✆01856-872044; www .orkneyferries.co.uk) links Kirkwall with Stronsay (passenger/car £7.35/17.40, 1½ hours, two to three daily) and Eday.

Eday

This slender island was extensively cut for peat to supply the surrounding islands, and many of the farms here still use peat fires. The interior is hilly and covered in peat bog, while the coast and the north of the island are mostly low-lying and green.

There's no real village on Eday, but most of the population is concentrated in the north near **Millbounds** (5 miles from the ferry pier), where you'll find **Eday Community Enterprises** (✆01857-622283; ⊙9am-noon & 2-4pm Mon, Wed, Thu & Sat, 9am-1pm Tue, 2-5.30pm Fri year-round, 2-4pm Sun summer), the island's only shop, and the Eday Heritage & Visitor Centre.

Across the fast-flowing waters of Carrick Bay is the little island of **Calf of Eday**, with a 17th-century saltworks, two chambered cairns, one stalled cairn and numerous seabirds and seals, particularly around Grey Head in the north. Boat trips can be arranged to the Calf through local B&Bs for around £15 return.

◉ Sights & Activities

Eday Heritage Walk   WALKING
It's worth getting hold of the *Eday Heritage Walk* leaflet from the Kirkwall tourist office, which details this interesting four-hour hike from the Community Enterprises shop up to the cliffs of **Red Head** in the north of the island, where much of the

stone for St Magnus Cathedral in Kirkwall was quarried.

The walk skirts the edge of brilliant blue **Mill Loch**, an RSPB reserve with a bird-hide and a large population of red-throated divers, before cutting across the side of Vinquoy Hill at the distinctive **Stone of Setter**, Orkney's largest standing stone. The path is marked by stakes and it crosses the fields to **Braeside Chambered Cairn**, which is open to the sky, and **Huntersquoy Chambered Cairn**, which has two chambers reached by separate passages (you can wriggle into one of the chambers along a damp passage if you have a torch).

More impressive is **Vinsquoy Chambered Cairn** on the hill top, with a beehive-shaped corbelled roof, reached through a narrow but dry tunnel. The path continues to the end of the headland, passing several ruined farm buildings and a small offshore lighthouse. You can also start the walk near the early-17th-century Carrick House.

Carrick House HISTORIC BUILDING
(☎01857-622260; Eday; adult/child £3/1; ⊘by appointment) This early-17th-century house was the site of a failed pirate raid in 1725, leading to the arrest of John Gow, the inspiration for Sir Walter Scott's novel *The Pirate* – there's even still a bloodstain on the drawing-room floor. The pirates were later executed in London. It's worth a visit; tours of the house run in summer with advance notice.

FREE **Eday Heritage & Visitor Centre** HERITAGE CENTRE
(☎01857-622283; www.visiteday.com; Millbounds; ⊘9am-5.30pm daily summer, 10am-5pm Sun only winter) Has a range of local history exhibits, as well as an audiovisual about tidal energy initiatives.

Eday Minibus Tour GUIDED TOUR
(☎01857-622206; tours adult/child £12/8) Offers 2¼-hour guided tours from the ferry pier on Monday, Wednesday and Friday from May to August. It also operates as a taxi service.

🛌 Sleeping & Eating

Eday SYHA HOSTEL £
(☎07973-716278; www.syha.org.uk; dm £15; P@) Four miles north of the ferry pier, this recently renovated, community-run hostel is an excellent place to stay.

Blett B&B B&B £
(☎01857-622248; Blett; B&B incl dinner per person £30, croft house per person £25) Mrs Popplewell has a charming cottage opposite the Calf of Eday islet with one double and one single room. There's also a couple of fully equipped, self-catering croft houses nearby, sleeping three people each. Mrs Popplewell bakes fresh bread daily, and she serves snacks and meals at her craft shop.

Red House CAFE £
(☎01857-622217; light meals £4-8; ⊘10am-5pm Tue-Fri Jun-Sep & by arrangement) Drop into this group of 19th-century croft buildings for home-cooked lunches, evening meals, local history and a chat.

❶ Getting There & Around

AIR There are two flights from Kirkwall (one way £35, 30 minutes) to London airport – that's London, Eday – on Wednesday only.

BOAT Ferries sail from Kirkwall, usually via Stronsay (passenger/car £7.35/17.40, two hours, two to three daily). There's also a link between Sanday and Eday (20 minutes).

Sanday

Aptly named, blissfully quiet Sanday is ringed by Orkney's best beaches – with dazzling-white sand of the sort you'd expect in the Caribbean. The island is almost entirely flat apart from a colossal sand dune and the cliffs at Spurness; the island is 12 miles long and growing, due to sand build-up.

There's a fine sand beach at **Backaskaill**, across a small headland to the west of Kettletoft. At the tip of the headland to the east of the village is the **Quoyness chambered tomb**, similar to Maes Howe and dating from the 3rd millennium BC. It has triple walls, a main chamber and six smaller cells.

Continuing northeast, there is a vast dramatic **beach walk** along the eastern coast from the Bay of Newark to the Bay of Lopness and around to the tip of the island, where a low-tide causeway leads over to the islet of **Start Point**, with its distinctive black-and-white lighthouse, built by the Stevenson brothers in 1802.

Beyond the loch at the northeastern tip of Sanday is **Tofts Ness**, a largely unexcavated funerary complex with some 500 prehistoric burial mounds and the remains of an Iron Age roundhouse; when the area is finally excavated, it may radically alter the island's tourism potential.

THE LIGHTHOUSE STEVENSONS

Robert Louis Stevenson (1850–94) is famous as a novelist, the author of timeless classics such as *Treasure Island*, *Kidnapped!* and *The Strange Case of Dr Jekyll and Mr Hyde*. But when he entered Edinburgh University in 1867, he went to study not literature, but engineering. Why? It was the family business.

Robert belonged to one of Scotland's foremost engineering dynasties, known as the 'Lighthouse Stevensons'. From 1790 to 1940, four generations of the Stevenson family dominated the field of lighthouse design and construction, building no fewer than 97 lighthouses around the Scottish coast. Many, such as the Bell Rock and Skerryvore, were remarkable feats of engineering, built on remote rocks far out to sea, awash at high tide and frequently battered by storms.

But the Stevensons' lighthouses were not mere safety beacons – they were objects of architectural beauty, designed with an aesthete's eye. Inspired by the legend of Pharos, the lighthouse at Alexandria in ancient Egypt (one of the seven wonders of the ancient world), many of their buildings adopted a style influenced by ancient Egyptian temples, including those at Hoy High (p287), Ardnamurchan Point (p174) and Cape Wrath (p244).

🛌 Sleeping & Eating

Kettletoft Hotel   HOTEL, PUB ££
(☎01857-600217; www.kettletofthotel.co.uk; Kettletoft; s/d £35/70; ℗) The welcoming and family-friendly Kettletoft is a refurbished elderly statesman near the centre of the island. The pub here serves tasty bar meals for around £9, leaning towards the seaward side of things, with even lobster scuttling onto some dishes.

Ayre's Rock Hostel & Campsite   HOSTEL, CAMPGROUND £
(☎01857-600410; www.ayres-rock-sanday-orkney.co.uk; 1-/2-person tents £5/7, dm/s £13.50/18; ℗@) Cosy hostel sleeping eight in the outbuildings of a farm. There's a craft shop and chip shop on site, breakfasts and dinners are available, and you can also pitch a tent. It's on the west coast, 6 miles north of the ferry pier.

Belsair   B&B, PUB £
(☎01857-600206; www.belsairsanday.co.uk; Kettletoft; r per person £30) Overlooks the harbour with tidy en suite rooms that are good value. Bar meals and evening dinner feature Orcadian produce.

ℹ Information

Ferries arrive at Loth, at the very southern tip of Sanday, a good 7.5 miles from from the main settlement of Kettletoft, which is home to two hotels, a post office and **Kettletoft Stores** (☎01857-600255; ⊙9am-noon & 1-5pm Mon-Sat, 7-9pm Mon, Thu & Sat), the biggest of four grocery shops on the island. Almost everything of interest is in the north of the island.

ℹ Getting There & Around

AIR There are flights from Kirkwall to Sanday (one way £35, 20 minutes, twice daily Monday to Saturday).

BOAT Ferries run from Kirkwall (passenger/car £7.05/16.75, 1½ hours), with a link to Eday.

BICYLE Bikes can be hired from Ayre's Rock Hostel (p294).

BUS Sanday Bus (☎01857-600344) From May to September, this bus meets the ferry at Loth and takes passengers to any destination on the island (advance booking advised). On Wednesdays in summer, the same outfit runs guided bus tours of Sanday (adult/child £30/20 including afternoon tea), picking up and dropping off at the ferry pier.

Westray

If you've time to visit only one of Orkney's northern islands, make Westray the one. The largest of the group, it has rolling farmland, handsome sandy beaches, great coastal walks and several appealing places to stay. The islanders have also been very proactive in promoting tourism with an ecological bent.

Most of the island is agricultural, but there's also a busy fishing industry landing monkfish, haddock, crab and lobster, all of which are locally processed.

⊙ Sights & Activities

FREE **Noup Head**   NATURE RESERVE
The RSPB reserve at Noup Head, at the northwestern tip Westray, is a dramatic area of sea cliffs which attracts vast numbers of

breeding seabirds from April to July. There are big puffin colonies, plus fulmars, skuas and other familiar species, and you can often see dozens of seals hauled out on the sloping skerries to the north of the headland.

You can walk to Noup Head along the clifftops from a parking area near Bis Geos hostel, passing the impressive chasm of Ramni Geo, and return via the lighthouse access road (4 miles, allow two to three hours).

West Coast Walk   WALKING
One of the best coastal walks in Orkney begins at Kirbest farm car park and leads north for 5.5 miles to Noup Head through increasingly dramatic sea-cliff scenery (allow three hours one way). Pick up a copy of the *Westray Walking Guide* leaflet from Kirkwall tourist office (p281) or the Haff Yok Cafe (p296).

Castle O'Burrian   BIRDWATCHING
Just 1.5 miles north of the ferry pier, a cute little wooden signpost marked 'puffins' points the way to Castle O'Burrian, the most accessible puffin-watching spot in Orkney. A 10-minute walk from the road leads to a cliff-top view of the puffin colony on the sea stack's grassy summit; the birds are in residence from late April to August.

Westray Heritage Centre   HERITAGE CENTRE
(☎01857-677414; www.westrayheritage.co.uk; adult/child £2.50/50p; ◎11.30am-5pm Mon, 10am-noon & 2-5pm Tue-Sat, 1.30-5.30pm Sun May-Sep) This heritage centre has displays on local history and interesting nature dioramas, as well as archaeological finds, including the famous 5000-year-old 'Westray Wife'. Also known as the 'Orkney Venus', this 4cm-tall sandstone figurine was found during a dig at the nearby Links of Noltland; it's the oldest depiction of the human form yet found in Scotland, and possibly in Britain.

The Links of Noltland, between Grobust beach and Noltland Castle, has recently emerged as one of the most important prehistoric sites in Scotland. Like Skara Brae, it's a neolithic village buried in the sand, and threatened by erosion. Archaeological excavations will continue for several years – in 2010 a second figurine, made of clay, was discovered.

FREE Noltland Castle   CASTLE
A half-mile west of Pierowall stand the ruins of this tower house, built by Gilbert Balfour,

an aide to Mary, Queen of Scots. The castle bristles with no fewer than 61 shot holes, part of the defences of the deceitful Balfour, who plotted to murder Cardinal Beaton and, after being exiled, the king of Sweden.

Head upstairs and look out for the bread oven in the kitchen and the secret compartments in the windowsills. If the castle is locked, you can ask for the key at the farmhouse across the road.

FREE Wheeling Steen Gallery   GALLERY
(☎01857-677292; www.wheeling-steen.co.uk; ◎11am-5pm Mon-Sat May-Sep, shorter hrs winter) Situated about 2 miles north of Pierowall near the airfield, this appealing gallery showcases the photographs and paintings of local farmer-turned artist Edwin Randall, and crafts created by his daughter. There's a cafe too, serving tea, coffee, hot chocolate and cakes.

Westraak   GUIDED TOUR
(☎01857-677777; www.westraak.co.uk; Quarry Rd) Runs informative and engaging trips around the island, covering everything from Viking history to puffin mating habits.

🛏 Sleeping & Eating

Cleaton House Hotel   HOTEL ££
(☎01857-677508; www.cleatonhouse.co.uk; Westray; s/d from £65/95; @🎧) This delightful hotel is a relaxed slice of island life, situated as it is in a quiet enclave on the east side of Westray about 5 miles from the ferry pier. With only 5 spacious rooms and a comfortable suite, it's proof that getting away from it all doesn't necessarily mean losing the luxuries.

There are plenty of indulgences in this hotel, from the drawing room – complete with stereo and a few good books to while away rainy days – to the pleasant pub out the back with several local ales for sampling and idyllic views of the bay. All the rooms have en suites, but our pick is the Bis Geos suite overlooking the sea. Voldigarth is a two-room suite with a view to the lighthouse of North Ronaldsay, winking every 10 seconds at night. All rooms come with digital TV and have wi-fi internet available as well as dial-up. Facilities like this mean that corporate retreats are not uncommon here, though it's more popular with holidaymakers who can always enjoy the excellent bar when the weather is dubious.

West Manse B&B, SELF-CATERING £
(☎01857-677482; www.millwestray.com; Westside; r £30-35 per person; P🐾) No timetables reign at this imposing house with arcing coastal vistas; make your own breakfast when you feel like it. Your welcoming hosts have introduced a raft of green solutions for heating, fuel and more. Kids will love this unconventional place while art exhibitions, cooking classes, comfortable furniture and clean air are drawcards for parents.

The Barn HOSTEL, CAMPGROUND £
(☎01857-677214; www.thebarnwestray.co.uk; Pierowall; sites £5 plus per person £1.50, dm £16; P) This excellent, intimate, modern 13-bed hostel is an Orcadian gem. It's heated throughout and has an inviting lounge, complete with DVD collection for when the weather turns foul. The price includes bed linen, shower and pristine kitchen facilities; local advice comes free. There's also a campground on site complete with laundry and campers' kitchen.

No 1 Broughton B&B ££
(☎01857-677726; www.no1broughton.co.uk; Pierowall; s/d £35/60; P) This solid pinkish house sits right on Pierowall Bay and offers a very comfortable B&B with unusual extras, such as original artworks on the walls and a sauna. There are three spacious rooms and a conservatory breakfast room, where you can feel the sun but not that nasty wind.

Bis Geos SELF-CATERING £
(☎01857-677420; www.bisgeos.co.uk; Bis Geos; per week from £292; P) Stunning views at this spectacular self-catering option between Pierowall and Noup Head.

Haff Yok Cafe CAFE £
(☎01857-677777; Quarry Rd, Pierowall; mains £3-5; ⏱10.30am-5pm Tue-Sat, 12.30-5pm Sun & Mon late Apr–Sep) Pierowall's only cafe is the village's social hub and information centre, offering a selection of homebaked cakes, decadent Westray tablet (Scottish candy made with sugar and butter) and cups of tea served in granny's best china. There's soup and sandwiches for lunch, and a selection of cards, gifts, books and maps for sale. ('Haff yok' is local slang for a labourer's tea break.)

Pierowall Hotel PUB GRUB £
(☎01857-677472; www.pierowallhotel.co.uk; Pierowall; mains £8-10; ⏱lunch & dinner) The heart of this island community, the local pub is famous throughout Orkney for its popular fish and chips – the fish is caught fresh by the hotel's boats and whatever has turned up in the day's catch is displayed on the blackboard. There are also tasty curries available, but the sea is the way to go here.

❶ Information

The ferry docks at Rapness in the south of the island but Pierowall, 7 miles to the north, is the main village, spread around one of the best natural harbours in Orkney; it was once a strategic Viking base. There are several well-stocked food shops here, including **Tulloch's** (☎01857-677373; ⏱9am-9pm Mon-Sat year-round, plus 2-4.30pm Sun May-Sep), which houses the post office, and a bakery.

Tourist info is provided at the Haff Yok Cafe.

❶ Getting There & Around

AIR There are flights from Kirkwall to Westray (one way £35, 20 minutes, one or two daily Monday to Saturday).

BOAT A ferry (p269) links Kirkwall with Rapness (passenger/car £7.05/16.75, 1½ hours, daily).

BICYCLE You can hire bikes from Westraak (p295).

BUS The **Westray Bus** (☎01857-677758) carries passengers between the ferry at Rapness and Pierowall village; from May to September it meets the ferry, and picks up at Pierowall Hotel car park for the return journey. In winter, service is on request only, with advance booking necessary.

Papa Westray

Known locally as Papay (*pa-pee*), this exquisitely peaceful, tiny island (4 miles long by a mile wide) attracts superlatives. It is home to Europe's oldest domestic building, the **Knap of Howar** (built about 5500 years ago), and to Europe's largest colony of arctic terns (about 6000 birds) at North Hill. Even the two-minute hop from Westray airfield is featured in *Guinness World Records* as the world's shortest scheduled air service. The island was also the cradle of Christianity in Orkney – **St Boniface's Church** was founded in the 8th century, though most of the recently restored structure is from the 12th century.

Beyond the church, the entire northern end of the island, centred on the appropriately named North Hill, is a **nature reserve** with a huge breeding colony of Arctic terns from May to August, and plentiful guillemots, kittiwakes, razorbills and puffins. The reserve was established too late to save one species – the very last great auk was killed here in 1813.

From May to September, **Jim Davidson** (☎01857-644259; per person £5) runs boat trips to the **Holm of Papay**, a small island about a half-mile east of Papa Westray, for £5 per person. The main reason for a visit is to see the huge **chambered cairn**, with 16 beehive cells, and wall carvings. You enter through the roof – there's a torch so you can light the way as you crawl around in the gloomy interior.

🛏 Sleeping & Eating

Beltane Guest House &
Hostel   GUESTHOUSE, HOSTEL **£**
(☎01857-644224; www.papawestray.co.uk; dm/s/d £15/24/35; ☺lunch & dinner; P) Owned by the local community co-op, this is the best place to stay on the island. It comprises a 20-bed hostel and a guesthouse with four simple and immaculate rooms with en suite and self-catering kitchen access. It's just over a mile north of the ferry.

School Place   B&B **£**
(☎01857-644268; www.papawestray.co.uk; r per person £20) B&B and tasty evening meals (dinner £17) are available at warm, welcoming School Place. The conservatory is good for quiet reflection and the owners are *the* people to speak to about life in their beloved island community.

ℹ Getting There & Away

AIR There are daily flights to Papa Westray (£17, 15 minutes) from Kirkwall, Monday to Saturday; there's an excellent £20 return offer.

BOAT A passenger-only ferry runs from Pierowall to Papa Westray (£3.55, 25 minutes, three to six daily in summer); the crossing is free if you travel direct from the Rapness ferry from Westray. From October to April the boat sails by arrangement (☎01857-677216).

North Ronaldsay

Three miles long and almost completely flat, North Ronaldsay is a real outpost surrounded by rolling seas and big skies. The delicious peace and quiet and excellent birdwatching – fulmars, oystercatchers and terns are particularly numerous – lures all sorts of visitors here: the island is home to cormorant and seal colonies and is an important stopover for migratory birds.

There are enough of Ronaldsay's unique breed of semi-feral sheep here to seize power, but a 13-mile drystone wall running around the flat island keeps them off the grass; they have to make do with seaweed, and that's what gives their meat a unique flavour.

At the north end of the island are two **lighthouses** – the old one was one of Scotland's earliest, while the new one is a Stevenson family special.

⊙ Sights & Activities

North Ronaldsay Tour   GUIDED TOUR
(☎07703 112224; adult/child £4/2) Offers excellent tours of one of North Ronaldsay's lighthouses and the Woollen Mill.

Woollen Mill   HISTORIC BUILDING
(adult/child £4/2, combined ticket £6/3) This mill offers real insight into both the history and current lifestyle of the island.

New Kirk   CHURCH
(☺24hr) In the centre of the island, the New Kirk holds an interesting exhibition of black-and-white photos that document various aspects of North Ronaldsay life.

🛏 Sleeping

🦜Observatory Guest
House   HOSTEL, CAMPGROUND **££**
(☎01857-633200; www.nrbo.co.uk; sites £4.50, dm/s/d £15/35/70; P@☎) Powered by wind and solar energy, this is a great spot next to the ferry pier, and offers first-rate accommodation and ornithological activities. There's a cafe-bar with lovely coastal views and convivial communal dinners (£12.50) in a sun-kissed (sometimes) conservatory; if you're lucky, local lamb might be on the menu. You can also camp here.

Garso Guest House   B&B **£**
(☎01857-633244; muir886@htinternet.com; B&B per person £35, cottage per person per night £30; P) A comfortable B&B and self-catering cottage sleeping five, with an open fire and all your mod cons. It's at the northern end of the island, about 3 miles from the pier. A taxi and minibus service is also available.

ℹ Getting There & Away

AIR There are two or three daily flights to North Ronaldsay (£17, 20 minutes) from Kirkwall. The £20 return offer is great value.

BOAT A weekly ferry runs from Kirkwall on Friday (passenger/car £7.05/16.75, 2½ hours).

WALKING IN THE ORKNEY ISLANDS

Old Man of Hoy Walk

The Old Man of Hoy, all 137m of him, is the tallest sea stack in Europe, built of thin slabs of sandstone standing close to colourful, near-vertical cliffs that are 200m or more high.

This walk is described as an out-and-back jaunt from Hoy's Moaness pier, where the ferry from Stromness arrives; an ascent of Ward Hill is suggested as a side trip. Should you prefer a shorter walk, you can start and finish at Rackwick, a settlement on Hoy's south coast, directly accessible by car, or by minibus from Moaness. Allow 2½ to three hours for this 5-mile walk.

If you're prepared to arrive at Rackwick with enough food and gear to stay over-night, you can sleep at the SYHA Rackwick Outdoor Centre (p287) there; it's possible to

camp nearby and use hostel facilities, or stay at the Burnmouth Cottage bothy.

PLANNING

Use either OS Explorer 1:25,000 map No 462 *Hoy* or OS Landranger 1:50,000 map No 7 *Orkney – Southern Isles*.

THE WALK

From **Moaness pier** walk up the single track road leading generally west. Follow it for 1.5 miles, ignoring left and right turns, climbing gently at first then more steeply past a church. At the top of the hill (40 minutes from the start) the road turns right and a good track continues straight on to-wards the gap between Cuilags on the right and Ward Hill on the left. Follow the track to **Sandy Loch**, where it deteriorates to a rough, wide path. This gains height steadily through the impressive glen, eventually reaching the watershed, from where it drops purposefully past the small glen to the west; known as **Berrie Dale**, it shelters hardy

Old Man Of Hoy Walk

OLD MAN OF HOY WALK

Duration 5½–6 hours
Distance 13.6 miles
Start/Finish Moaness pier, Hoy
Summary A close encounter with Orkney's famous landmark, impressively high sea cliffs and the chance to climb Hoy's highest hill.

dwarf birches, the most northerly native woodland in Scotland. The path improves as you descend and there are bridges across the burn. An hour from Sandy Loch turn right at a minor road then shortly afterwards right again to reach the **youth hostel**.

The signposted path to the Old Man starts on the south side of the hostel; go through a gateway and continue up past a small cottage on the right. Turn left beside a fence then right briefly. Turn left to cross a burn, pass behind a cottage and within 50m bear right uphill. The path angles up the slope, below another cottage, to a gate, giving onto moorland. The path, clear now, curves round the hillside. Turning north, you'll see the head of the Old Man peeking above the cliffs – if you didn't know what was there, you'd wonder what on earth this isolated block of rock was. A wide path, rocky in places, leads north across moorland and on to the cliff-top **viewpoint for the Old Man** and adjacent cliffs.

Retrace your steps to **Rackwick**, where you have a choice of returning to Moaness pier by the same route (with the possibility of the side trip described next), or walking along the minor road to the south of Ward Hill, visiting the Dwarfie Stane on the way.

SIDE TRIP: WARD HILL
» **Duration** 2 hours
» **Distance** 3.1 miles
» **Ascent** 330m

Ward Hill (479m), the highest point in all of Orkney, rises sharply from Hoy's north-eastern coastal fringe, and gives superb views across the isles and south to the mainland. The west ridge of the hill, rising from the junction of the Moaness path and the Rackwick road, is covered with fairly deep heather. An easier approach is from a large cairn beside the path, just south of the Burn of Redglen. It's simply a matter of climbing steeply up to the ridge, then heading east and northeast along the undulating ridge to the summit of Ward Hill, topped by a cairn and a survey pillar inside a low, circular stone shelter. On a clear day you can see virtually all of Orkney, and the Scottish mainland in the general vicinity of Duncansby and Dunnet Heads. From the first bump with a cairn south from the summit descend northwest, regaining the path a short distance south of Sandy Loch.

Shetland Islands

Best Places to Eat

» Hay's Dock (p306)

» Peerie Shop Cafe (p306)

» Mill Cafe (p310)

» Frankie's Fish & Chips (p315)

» Burrastow House (p310)

Best Places to Stay

» Burrastow House (p310)

» Busta House Hotel (p315)

» Almara B&B (p316)

» Gardiesfauld Hostel (p319)

» Nesbister Camping Böd (p310)

Why Go?

Adrift in the North Sea and close enough to Norway geographically and historically to make nationality an ambiguous concept here, the Shetland Islands are Britain's most northerly outpost. There's a distinct Scandinavian lilt to the local accent, and walking down streets named King Haakon or St Olaf recalls the fact that Shetland was under Norse rule until 1469, when it was gifted to Scotland in lieu of the dowry of a Danish princess. The setting of this archipelago of mighty, wind-ravaged clumps of brown and green earth rising from the frigid waters of the North Sea is still uniquely Scottish though, with deep, naked glens flanked by steep hills, twinkling, sky-blue lochs and (of course) sheep on the roads.

One of the great attractions of Shetland is the birdlife; it's definitely worth packing binoculars even if you're not fanatical about it.

When to Go
Lerwick

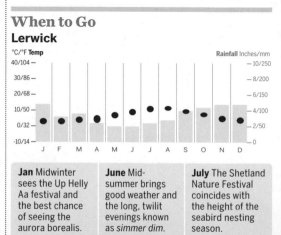

Jan Midwinter sees the Up Helly Aa festival and the best chance of seeing the aurora borealis.

June Midsummer brings good weather and the long, twilit evenings known as *simmer dim*.

July The Shetland Nature Festival coincides with the height of the seabird nesting season.

Shetland Islands Highlights

① Discover your inner Viking at Shetland's **Up Helly Aa** (p303) festival

② Pose with puffins and dodge dive-bombing skuas at the birdwatching honeypot of **Hermaness** (p318)

③ Blow away the cobwebs amid the remote and beautiful landscapes of **Foula** (p311)

④ Check out 5000 years of history at the absorbing **Shetland Museum** (p303)

⑤ Watch the wild Shetland weather pummel the spectacular seacliffs of **Eshaness** (p316)

⑥ Delve into the islands' fascinating archaeology at the ancient sites of **Jarlshof** (p313) and **Old Scatness** (p314)

⑦ Take advantage of offbeat accommodation in a no-frills camping **böd** or a romantic **lighthouse cottage** (p307)

⑧ Explore Shetland's countless creeks and remote islands by **sea kayak** (p313)

ⓘ Getting There & Away

Air

The oil industry ensures that air connections are good. The main **airport** (☏01950-460345; www.hial.co.uk) is at Sumburgh, 25 miles south of Lerwick. **Flybe** (☏0871 700 2000; www.flybe .com) runs daily services to Aberdeen, Kirkwall, Inverness, Edinburgh and Glasgow, and also to Bergen (Norway) in summer.

Boat

Northlink Ferries (☏0845 600 0449; www .northlinkferries.co.uk) runs car ferries between Lerwick and Kirkwall in Orkney.

Northlink also runs overnight car ferries from Aberdeen to Lerwick (passenger £23 to £35, car £92 to £124, 12 to 14 hours, daily), leaving Aberdeen at 5pm or 7pm.

ⓘ Getting Around

Public transport within and between the islands of Shetland is managed by **ZetTrans** (www .zettrans.org.uk). Timetable information for all air, bus and ferry services can be obtained from the ZetTrans website and Lerwick's **Viking bus station** (☏01595-694100; Commercial Rd; ⊙9am-5.15pm Mon-Sat), or you can pick up a free *Directory of Shetland's Transport* booklet from the Lerwick tourist office (p307).

Air

Interisland flights are operated by **DirectFlight** (☏01595-840246; www.directflight.co.uk), and depart from Tingwall airport, 6.5 miles north-west of Lerwick. See individual island sections for details of flights.

Boat

There are a dozen ferry services linking Mainland to the various inhabited islands, all run by **Shetland Islands Council** (☏01806-244200; www.shetland.gov.uk/ferries) – except for the Foula ferry, which is operated by **Atlantic Ferries** (☏07881-823732; www.atlanticferries .co.uk). See individual island sections for interisland ferry details.

Bicycle

If it's fine, cycling on the islands' excellent roads can be an exhilarating way to experience the stark beauty of Shetland. It can be very windy, however, and there are few spots to shelter. You can hire bikes from several places, including **Grantfield Garage** (☏01595-692709; www .grantfieldgarage.co.uk; North Rd; per day/week £7.50/40) in Lerwick and the Sumburgh Hotel (p314), near the airport.

Bus

Shetland has an extensive network of bus services radiating from Lerwick's Viking bus station (p302) to all corners of Mainland, and on (via ferry) to the islands of Yell and Unst. Fares range from £1 to £5.

However, bus times are scheduled to serve the needs of local shoppers and commuters, generally arriving in Lerwick in the morning and departing in the evening, so are no use for day trips from the capital to the outlying areas.

Car & Motorcycle

Shetland's broad, well-made roads (think 'oil money') seem more like motorways after Orkney's tiny, winding lanes. There are three car-hire outfits that process rentals with little fuss.

Bolts Car Hire (☏01595-693636; www.bolts carhire.co.uk; 26 North Rd, Lerwick; ⊙9am-5.30pm Mon-Fri, to 1pm Sat) Rates for small cars start from £39/177 per day/week. Also has an office at Sumburgh airport.

Shetland Motorhomes (☏01595-810328; www.shetlandmotorhomes.com) Rents out 4-berth motorhomes for £270/600 per three days/week in peak season (June to August).

Star Rent-a-Car (☏01595-692075; www .starrentacar.co.uk; 22 Commercial Rd, Lerwick) Opposite the bus station; from £36/164 per day/week. Has an office at Sumburgh airport.

LERWICK

POP 6830

This busy but surprisingly attractive town is built almost entirely of grey stone, straddling a narrow neck of land overlooking a superb natural harbour. Although it's full of atmosphere, Lerwick wasn't founded until the 17th century, making it almost a new town by Shetland standards. The original capital was on the west coast at Scalloway, which was better located for Shetland's narrow agricultural belt, but the arrival of Dutch herring fleets in the 17th century prompted a shift to the protected harbour at *leir vik* (from the Viking for 'muddy bay'). Lerwick's claim to capital status was confirmed when Fort Charlotte was built here in 1665 to keep a safe eye on British ships during the Anglo-Dutch wars.

At the height of the herring industry, in the late 19th century, Lerwick was the largest herring port in northern Europe, but the collapse of the Eastern European herring market during WWI led to a sharp decline in Lerwick's fortunes. The islands became something of a backwater until the discovery of oil offshore in the 1970s.

Today Lerwick is home to about a third of the islands' population and has a solid maritime; aquiline oil-boats compete for harbour space with the dwindling fishing fleet. The water's clear blue tones makes wandering along atmospheric Commercial St a delightful stroll, and the town's excellent new museum provides all the cultural background you could desire.

⊙ Sights

FREE **Shetland Museum**   MUSEUM
(☑01595-695057; www.shetland-museum.org.uk; Hay's Dock; ☺10am-5pm Mon-Sat, noon-5pm Sun) This modern museum is an impressive recollection of 5000 years' worth of culture, people and their interaction with this ancient landscape. Comprehensive but never dull, the display covers everything from the archipelago's geology to its fishing industry, via a great section on local mythology – find out about the scary *nyuggles* (ghostly horses), or use the patented machine for detecting *trows* (fairies).

The Pictish carvings and replica jewellery are among the finest pieces here; the museum also includes a working lighthouse mechanism, small art gallery, and – what great smells! – a boatbuilding workshop, where you can watch carpenters at work restoring and re-creating traditional Shetland fishing vessels.

FREE **Böd of Gremista**   HISTORIC BUILDING
(☑01595-695057; ☺10am-1pm & 2-5pm Tue-Sat May–mid-Sep) This house was once the headquarters of a fish-curing station, and was also the birthplace of Arthur Anderson, who went on to found P&O Ferries. The friendly custodian is a delight, and will show you around two rooms restored to how they were 200 years ago, as well as an exhibit on the history of the whitefish industry.

The building also houses the **Shetland Textile Working Museum**, with displays on the knitted and woven textiles and patterns that take their name from the islands. The

böd is a mile north of the town centre, overlooking the small-boat harbour.

FREE **Clickimin Broch**   PREHISTORIC SITE
(☺24hr) This fortified site, just under a mile southwest of the town centre, was occupied from the 7th century BC to the 6th century AD. It's impressively large, and its setting on a small loch gives it a feeling of being removed from the present day – quite unusual given the surrounding urban encroachment.

FREE **Fort Charlotte**   HISTORIC BUILDING
(Charlotte St; ☺9.30am-sunset) Fort Charlotte, built in 1781 during a time of war with France and Spain, occupies the site of an earlier fortification built in 1665 to protect the harbour from the Dutch navy. The five-sided fortress never saw action, but today houses the local Territorial Army (volunteer units) and provides excellent views over the harbour.

Up Helly Aa Exhibition   EXHIBITION
(www.uphellyaa.org; St Sunniva St; adult/child £3/1; ☺2-4pm & 7-9pm Tue, 7-9pm Fri, 2-4pm Sat mid-May–mid-Sep) This exhibition provides the background to Shetland's bizarre, annual Viking fire festival, with photos and videos documenting the event, and displays of the galleys and costumes from the last 10 years.

✯✯ Festivals & Events

Shetland Folk Festival   MUSIC
(www.shetlandfolkfestival.com) Held during the last week of April.

Johnsmas Foy   CULTURE
(www.johnsmasfoy.com) Midsummer festival; runs for four weeks in June.

Fiddle & Accordion Festival   MUSIC
(www.shetlandaccordionandfiddle.com) Held in mid-October.

UP HELLY AA!!

The long Viking history of the Shetlands has rubbed off in more ways than just street names and square-shouldered locals. Most villages have their own fire festival, a continuation of the old Viking midwinter celebrations of the rebirth of the sun. The most spectacular one happens in Lerwick.

Up Helly Aa (www.uphellyaa.org) takes place on the last Tuesday in January. Squads of *guizers* (disguised men with blackened faces) dress in Viking costume and march through the streets with blazing torches, dragging a replica longship, which they then surround and burn, bellowing out Viking songs from behind bushy beards.

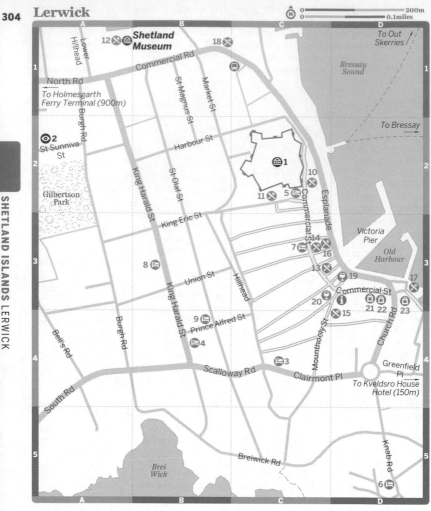

SHETLAND ISLANDS LERWICK

🛏 Sleeping

Fort Charlotte Guesthouse   B&B ££
(📞01595-692140; www.fortcharlotte.co.uk; 1 Charlotte St; s £25-30, d £60; 🛜) Sheltering under the walls of the fortress, this friendly place offers summery en suite rooms, including great singles. Views down the pedestrian street are on offer in some; sloping ceilings and oriental touches add charm to others. There's a bike shed and local salmon for breakfast. It's a very popular spot so you need to book ahead to avoid disappointment.

Woosung   B&B £
(📞01595-693687; sandraconroy43@btinternet. com; 43 St Olaf St; s/d £25/44) A budget gem in the heart of Lerwick B&B-land, this has a wise and welcoming host, and comfortable, clean, good-value rooms which share a bathroom. The solid stone house dates from the 19th century, built by a clipper captain who traded tea out of the Chinese port it's named after.

Lerwick SYHA   HOSTEL £
(Isleburgh House; 📞01595-745100; www.syha .org.uk; King Harald St, Lerwick; dm/f £16.50/50; ⌚Apr-Sep; 🅿@🛜🛗) This typically grand

Lerwick

Lerwick mansion houses an excellent hostel, with comfortable dorms, a shop, a laundry, a cafe and an industrial kitchen. Electronic keys offer excellent security and no curfew. It's wise to book ahead, and it's worth asking about winter availability as it sometimes opens for groups.

Kveldsro House Hotel   HOTEL **££**
(☑01595-692195; www.shetlandhotels.com; Greenfield Pl; s/d £98/120; P☎) Shetland's most luxurious hotel overlooks the harbour. It's a dignified small hotel that will appeal to older visitors or couples looking for a treat. Rooms 415 and 417 are doubles with striking views over the harbour; if after a twin, try room 413, which has two walls of windows and Shetland views.

Clickimin Caravan & Camp Site   CAMPGROUND **£**
(☑01595-741000; www.srt.org.uk; Lochside; sites per small/large tent £8/11; ☺May-Sep; P☎⛟) By the loch on the western edge of town, Clickimin is a small and tidy park with good grassy sites overlooking a small loch. There's a laundry and shower block, and you've got a leisure centre with pool and more as part of the complex.

Carradale Guest House   B&B **££**
(☑01595-692251; carradale@btinternet.com; 36 King Harald St; s/d £35/60; ☎) It's very amicable at Carradale and perpetually busy. The rooms, although a mix of old and new, are large and well furnished and provide a concoction of comforts for visitors. Couples should ask for the huge family room, which is traditionally decked out and has a private bathroom.

Grand Hotel   HOTEL **££**
(☑01595-692826; www.kgqhotels.co.uk; Commercial St; s/d £77/100; P☎) Once the hub of town, this stately hotel isn't what it was when Victoria reigned, but ongoing modernisation is slowly bringing the rooms into the 21st century. Those on the top floors offer harbour views. Couples should go straight for No 330, which is an enormous room (refurbished with a four-poster bed) with dazzling harbour views.

Alderlodge Guest House   B&B **££**
(☑01595-695705; www.alder-lodge.co.uk; 6 Clairmont Pl; s/d £40/60; ☎) This large stone building, a former bank, is a delightful place to stay. Imbued with a sense of space and light, common in these gracious old buildings, the rooms are large and, in this particular case, well furnished. The cordial hosts, who are flexible with checking-out and breakfast times, make the place special.

Eddlewood Guest House   B&B **££**
(☑01595-692772; catherinemarshall@live.co.uk; 8 Clairmont Pl; s/d £39/62) Run by a cheery soul, this sound selection has spacious, very well-kept rooms, some with limited sea views. The beds offer plenty of space to stretch out in, and these showers might just be Shetland's finest.

Glen Orchy House   HOTEL **££**
(☑01595-692031; www.guesthouselerwick.com; 20 Knab Rd, Breiwick Bay; s/d £60/85; P☎) In a great spot close to the centre but also within a stone's throw of coastal walks, this huge

place, once a convent, has spruce rooms and a large conservatory, complete with stunning coastal views. The friendly hospitality is complemented by good Thai food, among other choices.

✗ Eating

TOP CHOICE Hay's Dock SCOTTISH ££
(☎01595-741569; www.haysdock.co.uk; Hay's Dock; mains lunch £5-10, dinner £13-21; ◷lunch daily, dinner Fri & Sat) The upstairs cafe-restaurant in the Shetland Museum sports a wall of picture windows and a fairweather balcony that overlooks the harbour. Its clean lines and pale wood recall Scandinavia, but the menu relies on carefully selected local and Scottish produce. Lunch dishes range from smoked-salmon sandwiches to seafood chowder, while the evening menu concentrates on seafood and steak.

Peerie Shop Cafe CAFE £
(☎01595-692816; www.peerieshopcafe.com; Esplanade; mains £2-5; ◷9am-6pm Mon-Sat) If you've been craving proper espresso since leaving the mainland, head to this gem of a spot, with art exhibitions, wire-mounted halogens and industrial-gantry chic. Newspapers, scrumptious cakes and sandwiches, hot chocolate that you deserve after that blasting wind outside, and – more rarely – outdoor seating give everyone a reason to be here.

Monty's Bistro INTERNATIONAL ££
(☎01595-696555; www.montys-shetland.co.uk; 5 Mounthooly St; mains lunch £8-9, dinner £13-20; ◷lunch Tue-Sat, dinner Mon-Sat) Though well hidden away behind the tourist office, Monty's is far from a secret and Shetlanders descend on its wee wooden tables with alacrity. The happily orange upstairs dining room is fragrant with aromas of Gressingham duck and local mussels from the short, quality menu, and the wine list has some welcome old friends.

Queen's Hotel SEAFOOD ££
(☎01595-692826; Commercial St; mains £12-19; ◷lunch & dinner) The dining room in this slightly run-down hotel wins marks for its harbour views – book one of the window tables. While some of the roast-pork-with-fish combo platters are a bit strange, the seafood here is pretty good – the catch of the day is reliable, and the Queen's stew is a feast of molluscs and crustaceans. Portions are generous, too.

La Piazza ITALIAN ££
(☎01595-696005; www.oslas.co.uk; 88 Commercial St; mains £7.50-15; ◷lunch & dinner Mon-Sat, lunch Sun) Upstairs from Osla's Cafe, La Piazza is where you'll discover the joys of Italian cooking. Authentic, thin-crust pizzas are just like Papa used to make...well, almost.

Havly Cafe CAFE £
(☎01595-692100; 9 Charlotte St; mains £4-9; ◷10am-4pm Mon-Sat; 🛜👶) Offers cappuccino and carrot cake, and lunch dishes based on quality Shetland produce such as seafood, lamb and homebaked bread. Has a children's play area.

Karibuni CAFE £
(☎01595-690606; Harrison Sq; mains £3-5; ◷9am-4pm Mon-Sat) Best spot in town for freshly roasted coffee. It also does paninis, bagels, tasty pitta breads and wraps with a variety of fillings.

Raba Indian Restaurant INDIAN £
(☎01595-695585; 26 Commercial Rd; mains £5-8; ◷lunch & dinner) Highly recommended curry house; Sunday buffet is a bargain at £9.50.

Fort Café CAFE £
(☎01595-693125; 2 Commercial St; fish & chips £5-6; ◷10am-8pm) Lerwick's salty air often creates fish-and-chip cravings. Eat in, or munch down on the pier if you don't mind the seagulls' envious stares.

🍷 Drinking & Entertainment

The **Shetland Fiddlers Society** plays at a number of locations around town, and it's worth attending a session – enquire at the tourist office. Look out for **Mareel**, a new arts venue scheduled to open on the waterfront near the museum in early 2012.

Captain Flint's PUB
(2 Commercial St; ◷11am-1am) This lively bar – by some distance Lerwick's best – throbs with happy conversation and has a distinctly nautical, creaky-wooden feel. There's a cross-section of young 'uns, tourists, boat folk and older locals. There's live music some nights and a pool table upstairs.

Lounge PUB
(☎01595 692231; 4 Mounthooly St) A hospitable local bar patrolled by Andy Capp characters during the day, Lounge features a variety of live music performances several nights a week, including informal jam sessions.

Shopping

Best buys are the woollen jerseys, cardigans and sweaters for which Shetland is world famous. Plus it's the perfect climate for stepping out in your new clothes.

Spiders Web   KNITWEAR
(☎01595-695246; www.shetland-handknits.co.uk; 51 Commercial St) It's worth dropping in here as much for a chat as for the store's excellent array of hand-knitted garments, which are very high quality.

Jamieson's Knitwear   KNITWEAR
(☎01595-693114; 93 Commercial St) You'll find real Fair Isle sweaters with the distinctive OXOXO pattern here.

Shetland Times Bookshop   BOOKS
(☎01595-693622; www.shetland-times.co.uk; 71 Commercial St; ⊙Mon-Sat) Has every book you could possibly want to read about the Shetlands.

❶ Information

Gilbert Bain Hospital (☎01595-743000; South Rd)

Shetland Library (☎01595-693868; Lower Hillhead; ⊙10am-7pm Mon, Wed & Fri, to 5pm Tue, Thu & Sat; @) Free internet.

Support Training (☎01595-695026; 6a Mounthooly St; ⊙9am-5pm Mon-Fri) Free internet.

Lerwick tourist office (☎01595-693434; www.visitshetland.com; Market Cross; ⊙9am-5pm summer, 10am-4pm Mon-Sat winter) Helpful, with a good range of books and maps and a comprehensive brochure selection.

❶ Getting There & Around

AIR Flybe (p269) operates regular flights to Sumburgh airport. From Sumburgh airport, **Leask's** (☎01595-693162; www.leaskstravel .co.uk) runs regular buses that meet flights.

BOAT Northlink Ferries (p302) services dock at **Holmsgarth terminal**, a 15-minute walk from the town centre.

TAXI **Allied Taxis** (☎01595-690069; www .alliedtaxis.co.uk)

Bressay & Noss
POP 350

These two islands lie across Bressay Sound immediately to the east of Lerwick. The 34-sq-km island of **Bressay** (*bress*-ah), just a seven-minute ferry crossing from Lerwick, has some interesting walks, especially along the cliffs and up **Ward Hill** (226m), which has good views of the islands.

The much smaller **Isle of Noss**, to the east of Bressay, is a nature reserve.

⊙ Sights & Activities

Isle of Noss   NATURE RESERVE
(☎01595-693345; www.nnr-scotland.org.uk/noss; ferry adult/child £3/1.50; ⊙11am-5pm Tue, Wed & Fri-Sun late May–Aug) The little Isle of Noss, barely 1.5 miles wide, lies just east of Bressay, across the 150m-wide Noss Sound. The seacliffs on its east coast rise to 180m, providing nesting sites for more than 100,000 pairs of breeding seabirds, including gannets, guillemots, kittiwakes and puffins, while the inland heath supports 400 pairs of great skua.

It takes around three hours to make a complete walking circuit of Noss. Going anticlockwise makes for an easier hike, and provides better views of the cliffs.

Noss is managed as a national nature reserve, and can be visited only from late May to August (closed Monday and Thursday). During this period, **Scottish Natural Heritage** (SNH; ☎0800 107 7818; www.snh.gov.uk) operates a small visitor centre at Gungstie, near the landing place. The three-minute boat crossing from Bressay is weather-dependent – a red flag on Noss means it's not running.

OFFBEAT ACCOMMODATION

Shetland offers intriguing options for getting off the beaten accommodation track. There's a great network of böds – simple rustic cottages or huts with peat fires, which might mean bringing a sleeping bag, coins for the meter, or even a campstove. Contact and book via **Shetland Amenity Trust** (☎01595-694688; www.camping-bods.com).

The same organisation runs three **Lighthouse Cottages** (☎01595-694688; www. shetlandlighthouse.com), all commanding dramatic views of rugged coastline: one near the airport at Sumburgh, one on the island of Bressay near Lerwick, and one in Mainland's northwest at Eshaness. Sleeping six to seven, the cottages cost from £190 to £230 for a three-night booking in high season.

FREE Bressay Heritage
Centre   HERITAGE CENTRE
(📞01595-820368;www.shorewatch.co.uk/cruester;
⏱10am-4pm Tue, Wed, Fri & Sat, 11am-5pm Sun
May-Sep) The heritage centre by the ferry
pier on Bressay has an exhibition on island
life and history, local artwork and an unusual marine display. For birdwatchers, there's
photos of birds to be found on Bressay and
Noss.

Alongside the centre is a Bronze Age
archaeological site that has been rescued
from an eroding coastal location. The Cru-
ester Burnt Mound is now the focus of an
experimental archaeology project to unlock
the secrets of prehistoric burnt mounds in
general.

Seabirds & Seals   WILDLIFE CRUISE
(📞07595-540224; www.seabirds-and-seals.com;
adult/child £40/25) Runs three-hour wildlife
cruises (10am and 2pm) around Bressay
and Noss, departing from Victoria Pier in
the centre of Lerwick. The trip includes an
underwater viewing session, where you get
to see live images of marine life via a re-
motely operated submarine camera. Trips
run year-round, weather permitting; you
can book by phone or at the Lerwick tourist office.

🛏 Sleeping & Eating

Maryfield Hotel   B&B ££
(📞01595-820207; Bressay; s/d £40/65; P)
Pause for an ale or excellent shellfish meal
(mains £7-15) at Maryfield Hotel, which
offers secluded accommodation near the
ferry.

Northern Lights Holistic Spa   B&B ££
(📞01595-820257; www.shetlandspa.com; Up-
house, Bressay; d £100; P🛜) This modern
guesthouse offers colourful, relaxing en
suite accommodation and various mas-
sage and spa treatments. Use of the sauna
and steam room is included in the room
rate, and it serves very smart meals.

❶ Getting There & Away

Daily ferries (passenger/car return £3.60/8.40,
seven minutes, frequent) link Lerwick and
Bressay. It's then a 2.5-mile walk or bike ride
across the island (some people bring hired bikes
from Lerwick) to reach the crossing point to
Noss. The boat doesn't operate in bad weather,
though, so if in doubt check with SNH (p32)
before leaving Lerwick.

CENTRAL & WEST MAINLAND

Scalloway
POP 812

Surrounded by bare, rolling hills, Scalloway
(*scall*-o-wah) – the former capital of Shetland – is now a busy fishing and yachting
harbour with a thriving seafood-processing
industry. It lies on the west coast 6 miles
from Lerwick.

There are some pretty beaches and pleasant walks on the islands of Tronda and East
and West Burra, just south of Scalloway (the
islands are linked to each other and to the
mainland by bridges). The **Sands of Meal**,
south of the pretty village of Hamnavoe on
West Burra, is one of Shetland's best sandy
beaches, and a popular local picnic spot.

◉ Sights & Activities

FREE Scalloway Castle   CASTLE
(HS; www.historic-scotland.co.uk) The town's
most prominent landmark is Scalloway Castle, built around 1600 by Earl Patrick Stewart, of the Earl's Palace (p278) in Kirkwall,
Orkney. The turreted and corbelled tower
house is fairly well preserved – there's an
intertpretive display in a vaulted storeroom
on the ground floor. If the gateway is locked,
the keys can be obtained from the Scalloway
Hotel.

Shetland Bus Memorial   MONUMENT
(Main St) During WWII a fleet of small boats –
known as the Shetland Bus – shuttled from
Scalloway to occupied Norway, carrying
agents, wireless operators and military supplies for the resistance movement, and returning with refugees, recruits for the Free
Norwegian forces and Christmas trees for
treeless Shetland. The memorial is a moving
tribute, built of stones from both countries.

Cycharters   BOAT TOURS, WILDLIFE CRUISES
(📞01595-696598; www.cycharters.co.uk) As well
as running day trips to Foula from Scalloway
harbour, this outfit also offers fishing, sightseeing and wildlife-watching cruises around
the islands of Papa, Oxna, Hildasay and
North Havra, just to the west of Scalloway.

🛏 Sleeping & Eating

Scalloway Hotel   HOTEL ££
(📞01595-880444; www.scallowayhotel.com; Main
St; s/d £65/90; P) Close to the waterfront, the

Scalloway Hotel has modern, spotless rooms with small en suites; some rooms have good views over the harbour. There's also some really tasty, creative bar food here, as well as more upmarket fare in the restaurant.

Da Haaf Restaurant SEAFOOD ££
(☎01595-880747; www.nafc.ac.uk; Port Arthur; mains £9-14; ☺lunch Wed-Fri, dinner Thu-Fri) Being part of the North Atlantic Fisheries College, it's no surprise that Da Haaf Restaurant specialises in seafood – and excellent local seafood at that. It's solid value, but ring ahead to check if it's open.

❶ Getting There & Away

Buses run from Lerwick (25 minutes, roughly hourly Monday to Saturday) to Scalloway.

Tingwall & Around

North of Scalloway, the B9074 follows the western shore of **Loch of Tingwall** through the fertile Tingwall Valley. The two lochs here – Loch of Asta and Loch of Tingwall – are good for trout fishing; contact the **Shetland Anglers Association** (☎01595-696025; www.shetlandtrout.co.uk) for information and permits.

Just south of Veensgarth village, near a parking area at the northern end of Loch of Tingwall, is the site of **Law Ting Holm**, where Shetland's annual Norse parliament, the *althing*, was held in the 13th century. Criminals being tried here could gain amnesty if they managed to run through the crowd of spectators and touch nearby **St Magnus Kirk** without being caught. **Tingwall Church**, on the same site, is more recent than St Magnus, but there's a burial vault from the original medieval kirk in the kirkyard, which is full of carved medieval graveslabs.

At the north end of the valley is Tingwall airport – little more than an airfield – which handles flights within Shetland.

Weisdale & Around

Amid the bleak moorland that characterises much of the Shetland landscape, the parallel valleys of Weisdale and Petta Dale in central Mainland are unusually green and pleasant. They mark the outcrop of thick beds of limestone, which weathers down to produce a rich and fertile soil.

Surrounding 19th-century **Kergord House**, in the middle of Weisdale, is something even more unusual for Shetland – trees. There are around 8 acres of mixed woodland here, planted from 1910 to 1920 by the local landowner; it's famous as Shetland's only 'forest'. The house was built in 1850 for the local laird, and served during WWII as the headquarters for the Shetland Bus.

On the western shore of Weisdale Voe, south of the mill, are the ruins of the house where John Clunies-Ross (1786–1853) – better known as the King of the Cocos – was born. In 1827 this Shetland seafarer and adventurer settled in the Indian Ocean's Cocos Islands, then uninhabited, where he proclaimed himself king. Queen Victoria granted the islands to him and his descendants in 1886, and they remained a feudal possession until Clunies-Ross's great-great-grandson was forced to sell up to the Australian government in 1978.

❂ Sights & Activities

FREE **Bonhoga Gallery** GALLERY
(☎01595-830444; www.shetlandarts.org/venues/bonhoga-gallery; Weisdale Mill; admission free; ☺10.30am-4.30pm Tue-Sat, noon-4.30pm Sun) Housed in restored 19th-century Weisdale Mill – once one of Shetland's largest corn mills – this gallery has monthly, changing exhibitions; everything you see – jewellery, crafts and paintings – is on sale. It's an excellent place to visit, and you're likely to meet some resident artists. There's also an excellent cafe (p310).

Shetland Jewellery JEWELLERY
(☎01595-830275; www.shetlandjewellery.co.uk; Soundside; ☺9am-5pm Mon-Thu & 9am-4pm Fri year-round, 10am-5pm Sat & 2-5pm Sun Jun-Aug) Nestled on the shore of the Loch of Hellister, 2 miles south of Weisdale, this workshop turns out handmade gold and silver jewellery based on Nordic, Celtic and traditional Shetland motifs, as well as pieces inspired by nature. Visitors can watch the jewellers at work, and there's a cafe corner serving tea and coffee.

⌂ Sleeping & Eating

Westings Inn B&B ££
(☎01595-840242; www.originart.eu/westings; Whiteness; s/d £45/80; P�) Perched high on Wormadale Hill, 8 miles west of Lerwick and 4 miles south of Weisdale, the Westings Inn offers you one of the finest vistas in

Shetland. The bedrooms are neat and functional, and all share that magnificent view. The hotel bar has a good reputation for real ale, serving Valhalla beers as well as guest ales from all over Britain.

Nesbister Camping Böd
BOTHY £

(☏01595-694688; www.camping-bods.com; Nesbister; dm £8; ☺Mar-Oct) This original fisherman's shack has the most picturesque setting of all Shetland's böds, poised on a rocky point only a couple of metres from the high-water mark (in rough weather the waves wash over the approach). It's for connoisseurs of roughing it, offering 4 bunk beds in one tiny room, no electricity, and a 'bucket-and-bury-it' toilet.

TOP CHOICE Mill Cafe
CAFE £

(☏01595-830444; Wesidale Mill; mains £3-6; ☺10.30am-4.30pm Tue-Sat, noon-4.30pm Sun; ☏🖃) Set in a sunny conservatory downstairs from Bonhoga Gallery (p309), this cafe serves superb homemade soups, sandwiches and cakes, with a local twist provided by dishes such as bannock and salt beef, dill herrings and oatcakes, and delicious smoked salmon from Scalloway. There's a kids' menu (and toys for them to play with), and an outdoor terrace overlooking the mill stream.

West Side

The western part of Mainland (known locally as 'the West Side') is notable for its varied scenery: bleak moors, sheer cliffs, rolling green hills and numerous cobalt-blue lochs and inlets. Its quiet backroads and secluded bays are ideal for walking, cycling and fishing. The main settlement out here is Walls, which has basic services, B&Bs and a böd, but doesn't really entice.

The West Side begins where the A971 road from Weisdale crests the hill at Scord of Sound. About a mile beyond Bixter, the B9071 strikes south towards Skeld, a remote harbour village in the midst of striking coastal scenery. A few miles west of Skeld, the old telephone box at **Culswick** marks the beginning of the West Side's best coastal walk: from the phone box, follow a peat track west for 1.5 miles, past a Methodist chapel and the Loch of Sotersta, to the **Broch of Culswick**, which commands a superb panorama of islands, seacliffs, stacks and caves.

Four miles north of Skeld, a side road leads to **Sand**, where you'll find **Da Gairdins i Sand** (www.gairdins.org.uk; admission free;

☺dawn-dusk), a brave attempt to create a colourful woodland garden amid the bleak moors of western Shetland. Various environs, including grassland, wildflower meadows, rhododendron walks and wildlife ponds, have been created in the lee of conifer shelter belts; pick up a leaflet at the entrance for a description of the various walks.

From Bixter the A971 snakes west through a remote moonscape of rocky bluffs and lochans. At Bridge of Walls a left fork leads to the village of **Walls** (pronounced 'waas'), overlooking Vaila Sound. **Stanydale Temple**, a huge Neolithic roundhouse thought to have been used for ceremonial purposes, is a half-mile walk from the minor road beisde the Loch of Gruting – turn south off the A971 just before Bridge of Walls. The **Scord of Brewster**, a prehistoric farm, is on the hillside above Bridge of Walls, near the turn-off to Walls. The countryside here is dotted with tiny abandoned crofts, though it's hard to believe whole families lived in these miniature dwellings.

The right-hand fork here strikes across desolate moorland, emerging at the small crofting community of **Sandness**, which faces the island of Papa Stour. The village is home to the **Jamieson's Spinning** (☏01595-870285; www.jamiesonsofshetland.co.uk; ☺8am-5pm Mon-Fri) woollen mill, which specialises in producing yarn from native Shetland sheep. As well as seeing the mill at work, you can buy yarn for knitting, or purchase machine-knitted Shetland and Fair Isle pattern garments at factory prices

A mile west of Sandness are the **Huxter Mills**, a series of three traditional Norse-style watermills (with horizontal water wheels), set in a row; one remained in use until WWII and is being restored. From here, the **Sandness Coastal Walkway** leads east for 4km along the shoreline, with grand views of Papa Stour.

🛏 Sleeping & Eating

There are grocery stores and petrol pumps at Bixter, Aith and Walls, and camping böds (p307) at Walls and Skeld. Wild camping is possible almost anywhere (with the local landowner's permission). The only places to eat are at Walls: a tearoom, and Burrastow House.

TOP CHOICE Burrastow House
B&B ££

(☏01595-809307; www.burrastowhouse.co.uk; Walls; B&B per person £50, incl dinner £85; ☺Apr-Oct; 🖃) This fine old *haa* – the 18th-century seat of the local laird – sits on the shore of Vaila

Sound, about 2 miles southwest of Walls. Of the six bedrooms, four are in the modern extension; the Laird's Room in the old house is the one to go for, with a grand half-tester bed and views across to Vaila Island.

The restaurant serves fresh local seafood and lamb, and the breakfast table groans with homebaked bread and croissants, porridge, kippers and local smoked salmon. Children aged 3 to 14 are charged half the adult rate; under-threes stay for free.

Skeld Caravan & Camping Site
CAMPGROUND £

(☑01595-860287; Skeld; tents £6.50-8.50, campervans £12; ☺year-round) This cute little campsite is right on the harbour – you can watch seals and otters playing in the water, and buy shellfish straight off the fishing boats.

Papa Stour

Visible about a mile offshore from Sandness is the island of Papa Stour, home to huge colonies of auks, terns and skuas. The buckled volcanic strata have been wonderfully eroded by the sea to produce dramatic caves, arches, stacks and underground passages. Probably the most impressive is **Kirstan's Hole**, a partially collapsed gloup (blowhole) on the southwest coast.

There are fine views from **Virda Field** (87m), the island's highest point, in the northwest, and several wrecks offshore that attract divers. The island was once a 'leper colony', though the poor souls who were banished here were actually suffering from a noninfectious, hereditary skin disease caused by malnutrition.

Right beside the island's only road, about 200m north of the church, are the partly reconstructed remains of a 13th-century **Viking stofa** (a single-roomed house). It's thought to have belonged to Duke Hakon Hakonsson of Norway, and is mentioned in Shetland's oldest surviving document, which dates from 1299 (on display in the Shetland Museum (p303) in Lerwick).

There's no shop or pub on the island, and the only accommodation is the **Hurdiback Backpackers Bunkhouse** (☑01595-873227; www.hurdibackhostel.co.uk; dm £20).

❶ Getting There & Away

AIR There are Tuesday-only flights (p302) from Tingwall airport (return £37.50), with a day return possible.

BOAT Access to the island is by ferry (☑01595-745804; www.shetland.gov.uk/ferries/) from West Burrafirth (passenger return £6.80, car/driver return £8.40, 40 minutes, daily except Tuesday and Thursday), which is reached via a minor road leading north from the A971 between Bixter and Bridge of Walls.

Foula

POP 30

Out in the Atlantic Ocean, about 15 miles southwest of Walls, stands the remote, windswept, island of Foula (Bird Island). Seen from Mainland it has a distinctive outline, rising to a series of peaks – the highest point is **Da Sneug** (418m) – then dropping dramatically to the sea at the cliffs of **Da Kame** (376m). It competes with Fair Isle for the title of Britain's most isolated community, with just 30 human inhabitants, a handful of Shetland ponies and 1500 sheep, plus 500,000 seabirds, including the rare Leach's petrel and Manx shearwater, and the world's largest colony of great skuas.

The islanders live on a narrow strip of low-lying land on the east coast; the population declined to its present level from around 270 at the end of the 19th century. In the 1960s Foula's infrastructure was sorely neglected by the authorities, who thought the island would soon be abandoned, but the islanders were so determined to stay that they built their own airstrip in 1976.

Foula remained under the medieval Norse *udal* law until the 16th century, and the Norse dialect known as Norn was spoken here until the 1920s. Island culture clings to the old Julian calendar, celebrating Auld Yule (Christmas) on 6 January, and Newerday (New Year's Day) on 13 January. The classic 1937 movie *The Edge of the World* (directed by Michael Powell), a dramatisation of the evacuation of St Kilda, was filmed on Foula.

Walking and **birdwatching** are the main reasons to visit. There are superb hikes to the summit of Da Kame and Da Sneug, and spectacular coastal scenery at Gaada Stack in the north and Da Noup in the south. At the north end of Da Noup is the intriguingly named **Sneck Ida Smaalie**, a spectacular cleft – 30m deep and barely 2m wide – that splits the sea cliffs. The **Foula Ranger Service** (☑01595-753233) can provide route information and arrange guided walks.

SHETLAND BIRD NAMES

Many birds in Shetland have distinctive names in the local dialect. Here are a few to listen out for.

Common Name	Shetland Name
Arctic skua	Skootie alan
Arctic tern	Tirrick
Black guillemot	Tystie
Black-headed gull	Hoodie maa
Cormorant, shag	Skarf
Eider duck	Dunter
Fulmar	Maalie
Gannet	Solan
Greater black-backed gull	Swaabie
Great skua	Bonxie
Guillemot	Loom, longvie
Kittiwake	Maa, waeg
Lesser black-backed gull	Peerie swaabie
Oystercatcher	Shalder
Puffin	Tammy norie
Razorbill	Sea craa
Storm petrel	Aalamootie

Sleeping & Eating

There is a post office, a school and a church on the island, but no shop, so bring all you need in the way of supplies. Accommodation is very limited and must be booked in advance – the centrally located **Leraback** (☎01595-753226; B&B incl dinner per person £35; P) offers B&B and evening meals.

Getting There & Away

AIR DirectFlight (p302) flies from Tingwall airport on Monday, Tuesday, Wednesday and Friday. From March to mid-October there are two flights a day on Wednesday and Friday, allowing you to make a day trip, with six to seven hours spent on the island.

BOAT Atlantic Ferries (p302) runs two passenger ferries per week (on Tuesday and Thursday) year-round, departing from Walls; bookings are essential. From May to September there's an additional ferry from Walls every Saturday, plus a service from Scalloway every second Thursday. None of the ferries allows for a day trip. Note that the ferry crossing is exposed to the full might of the Atlantic, and is very weather-sensitive.

You can also visit Foula on a day trip from Scalloway harbour with Cycharters (p308) (Wednesdays only). The trip allows 2½ hours ashore, and includes a cruise around the island to view the seacliffs.

SOUTH MAINLAND

From Lerwick, the main road south winds 25 miles down the eastern side of this long, narrow, hilly tail of land to Sumburgh Head. The waters lapping against the cliffs are an inviting turquoise in many places – if it weren't for the raging Arctic gales, you might almost be tempted to have a quick dip.

Sandwick & Around

Opposite the scattered village of Sandwick, where you cross the 60-degree latitude line, is the small isle of **Mousa**, an RSPB reserve protecting some 7000 breeding pairs of storm petrels. Mousa is also home to rock-basking seals as well as impressive **Mousa Broch**, the best preserved of these northern fortifications. Rising to 13m, it's an imposing structure, typically double-walled, and with a spiral staircase to access a 2nd floor. It features in two Viking sagas as a hideout for eloping couples; these days petrels favour it as a nesting spot.

Sights & Activities

Mousa Boat Trips BOAT TOURS, WILDLIFE CRUISES (☎01950-431367; www.mousaboattrips.co.uk) From April to mid-September, this operator runs daily boat trips to Mousa (adult/child £13/6.50, 25 minutes) out of Leebitton harbour in Sandwick, allowing visitors to spend two hours ashore on the island. It also offers night trips if you want to view the petrels.

FREE **Hoswick Visitor Centre** VISITOR CENTRE (☎01950-431406; ⊙10am-5pm Mon-Sat, 11am-5pm Sun May-Sep; @) Hoswick Visitor Centre has a great collection of old wirelesses, as well as displays on fishing, whaling, various types of weaving and peat casting; there's a cafe here, too.

Sleeping

Orca Country Inn B&B ££ (☎01950-431226; www.orcacountryinn.co.uk; Hoswick; s/d/f £43/65/73; P🐾) There's plenty of comfort at the Orca Country Inn, which of-

DON'T MISS

SEA KAYAKING IN SHETLAND

Paddling is a top way to explore Shetland's tortuous coastline, and allows you to get up close to seals and bird life without the roar of the motor scaring them away. **Sea Kayak Shetland** (☑01595-840272; www.seakayakshetland .co.uk) is a reliable and professional operator that caters for beginner and expert alike, offering guided kayaking trips from various points around Shetland.

fers great views from its lounge area and its cosy chambers, all named after birds. Rooms are decorated with great photos taken by one of the owners, who also runs photography courses here.

Solbrekke   B&B £

(☑01950-431410; Park Rd, Sandwick; s/d £25/50; P) Solbrekke is a welcoming spot that overlooks the isle of Mousa from its hilltop vantage point.

❶ Getting There & Away

There are buses between Lerwick and Sandwick (25 minutes, three to seven daily).

Bigton & Around

Buses from Lerwick stop twice daily (Monday to Saturday) in Bigton on the west coast, but it's another couple of miles to the **tombolo** (a narrow isthmus) that connects Mainland with St Ninian's Isle. This geologically important site is the largest shell-and-sand tombolo in Britain and is a Site of Special Scientific Interest (SSSI).

Walk across the tombolo to beautiful, emerald-capped **St Ninian's Isle**, where you'll find the ruins of a 12th-century church, beneath which are traces of an earlier Pictish church. During excavations in 1958, Pictish treasure, consisting of 27 silver objects that probably dated from AD 800, was found beneath a broken sandstone slab. They're now kept in the Museum of Scotland in Edinburgh, though there are replicas in Lerwick's Shetland Museum.

Boddam & Scousburgh

From small Boddam a side road leads to the **Shetland Crofthouse Museum** (☑01950-460557; www.shetlandheritageassociation.com; admission free; ☉10am-1pm & 2-5pm mid-Apr–Sep) (donations welcomed). The years drop away when you enter as you step back into a primitive existence. Built in 1870, this former dwelling has been restored, thatched and furnished with 19th-century furniture and utensils. The Lerwick–Sumburgh bus stops right outside.

West of Boddam, Scousburgh sits placidly above Shetland's best beach, the gloriously white **Scousburgh Sands**. Near Scousburgh is the **Spiggie Hotel** (☑01950-460409; www.thespiggiehotel.co.uk; s/d £55/100; P🛜), with compact rooms and good seafood (lunch Wednesday to Sunday, dinner daily). The rooms and dining room boast great views down over the local loch, which offers fishing and birdwatching opportunities.

Quendale

South of Boddam, a minor road runs southwest to Quendale. Here you'll find the small but excellent, restored and fully operational 19th-century **Quendale Watermill** (☑01950-460969; www.quendalemill.co.uk; adult/child £2/50p; ☉10am-5pm mid-Apr–mid-Oct), the last of Shetland's watermills. There's also a cafe here.

The village overlooks a long, sandy beach to the south in the Bay of Quendale. West of the bay there's dramatic **cliff scenery** and **diving** in the waters between Garth's Ness and Fitful Head, and to the wreck of the oil tanker *Braer,* off Garth's Ness.

From Lerwick there are two buses daily to Quendale, from Monday to Saturday.

Sumburgh

With its sea cliffs, and grassy headlands jutting out into sparkling blue waters, Sumburgh is one of the most scenic places to stay on the island. There's a tourist office open daily at Sumburgh airport, with internet access.

◉ Sights

Jarlshof   HISTORIC SITE

(HS; ☑01950-460112; www.historic-scotland.gov .uk; adult/child £4.70/2.80, 20% discount with Old

Scatness ticket; ⏱9.30am-5.30pm Apr-Sep) Old and new collide here, as Sumburgh airport lies only a few metres from this picturesque and instructive archaeological site. Various periods of occupation from 2500 BC to AD 1500 can be seen, and the complete change that occurred upon the Vikings' arrival is obvious: their rectangular longhouses present a marked contrast to the brochs, roundhouses, and wheelhouses that preceded them.

Atop the site is the Old House of Sumburgh, built in the 16th century and named 'Jarlshof' in a novel by Sir Walter Scott. There's an informative audio tour included with admission.

Old Scatness
PREHISTORIC SITE

(☎01950-461869; www.shetland-heritage.co.uk/scatness; adult/child £4/3, 20% discount with Jarlshof ticket; ⏱10am-5pm Sun-Thu May-Oct) This archaeological dig brings Shetland's prehistoric past vividly and entertainingly to life; it's a must-see for archaeology buffs, but fun for kids, too. Clued-up guides in Iron Age clothes show you around the site, which is still being excavated – it has provided important clues on the Viking takeover specifically, and the dating of these northern Scottish sites in general.

Discovered during the construction of an airport access road, the site has revealed an impressive broch from around 300 BC, roundhouses and, later, wheelhouses. Best of all is the reconstruction of one of these, complete with smoky peat fire and working loom.

Sumburgh Head
BIRDWATCHING

(www.rspb.org.uk) Near Jarlshof, the spectacular cliffs of Sumburgh Head offer a good chance to get up close and personal with puffins, and also to see huge nesting colonies of fulmars, guillemots and razorbills. If you're lucky, you might spot dolphins or orcas; the car-park noticeboard advises on the most recent sightings.

🛏 Sleeping & Eating

Another option is the atmospheric Sumburgh Lighthouse cottage (p307).

Betty Mouat's Camping Böd
BOTHY £

(☎01595-694688; www.camping-bods.com; Dunrossness; dm £8; ⏱Apr-Sep; P) Just behind Old Scatness, this is a simple and comfortable hostel run by the Shetland Amenity Trust, with peat fire (£5 a bag), power and decent

hot-water bathrooms. You can also book at Old Scatness.

Sumburgh Hotel
HOTEL ££

(☎01950-460201; www.sumburghhotel.com; s/d £65/80; P@☎) Next to Jarlshof is this upmarket, country-style hotel with a high standard of accommodation. There are fine views for birdwatchers, prehistorians and plane-spotters alike, comfortable pinkish rooms, and excellent restaurant and bar meals. Larger sea-view rooms cost more (singles/doubles £80/100).

❶ Getting There & Away

To get to Sumburgh from Lerwick, take the airport bus (45 minutes, four to six daily).

NORTH MAINLAND

The north of Mainland is very photogenic – jumbles of cracked, peaty brown hills, blending with grassy pastureland, extend like bony fingers of land into numerous lochs and out into the wider, icy, grey waters of the North Sea. Different shades of light give it a variety of characters. Around Hillswick, there's stunning scenery and several good places to stay; this makes one of the best bases in the Shetlands.

Voe

Lower Voe is a pretty collection of buildings beside a tranquil bay on the southern shore of Olna Firth.

In previous incarnations, **Sail Loft** (☎01806-588327; www.camping-bods.co.uk; dm £9), by the pier, was a fishing shed and knitwear factory, but it's now a camping böd, with coin-operated showers and fuel for sale. Opposite, try the excellent seafood, including local salmon, in the appealing, wood-panelled **Pierhead Restaurant & Bar** (☎01806-588332; Lower Voe; mains £10-16; ⏱lunch & dinner). Eat in the upstairs restaurant or go for the cheaper bar meals downstairs.

There are buses from Lerwick to Voe (35 minutes, up to six daily Monday to Saturday).

Whalsay & Out Skerries

South of Voe, the B9071 branches east to Laxo, the ferry terminal for the island of **Whalsay**. This is one of the most prosperous islands, due to its large fishing fleet based at the modern harbour of **Symbister**.

Whalsay is popular for **sea angling**, and for **trout fishing** in its lochs. There are also **scenic walks** past colonies of breeding seabirds, where you may catch sight of seals.

Northeast of Whalsay, another thriving fishing community occupies the tiny **Out Skerries**, made up of the three main islands of Housay, Bruray (these two are connected by a road bridge) and Grunay, plus a number of islets. Their rugged cliffs teem with birdlife.

🛌 Sleeping & Eating

Grieve House Camping Böd   BOTHY **£**
(☑01595-694688; www.camping-bods.com; dm £8) The former home of poet Hugh Mac-Diarmid is now a camping böd. There's no electricity or shower, but there is fuel for sale. Heading out of Symbister towards Isbister, it's on the left about half a mile from town.

Oot Ower   CABINS, CAMPGROUND **£**
(☑01806-566658) Not far out of Symbister, the Oot Ower offers self-catering bungalows, a weekend-only bar (11am to 1am Friday to Sunday) and Chinese restaurant (1-10pm Saturday). You can camp here, too.

❶ Getting There & Away

Inter-Island Ferry Service (☑01806-566259; www.shetland.gov.uk/ferries) Regular ferries link Laxo (Mainland) and Symbister on Whalsay (car/passenger return £3.60/8.40, 30 minutes, daily).

Out Skerries Ferry (☑01806-515226; www.shetland.gov.uk/ferries) There are ferries between Out Skerries and Lerwick on Tuesday and Thursday (passenger/car and driver return £5.60/8, 2½ hours), and Friday to Monday to Vidlin in North Mainland, 3 miles northeast of Laxo (passenger/car and driver return £6.80/8.40, 1½ hours), which only sails if it's booked.

Brae & Around

Accommodation is the reason to stop in the township of Brae; there are several guesthouses. However, you should book in advance, as they mainly cater to oil workers.

There's fine **walking** on the peninsula west of Brae, and to the south on the red-granite island of **Muckle Roe** (p312), which

is connected to the peninsula by a bridge. Muckle Roe also offers good **diving** off its west and north coasts.

🛌 Sleeping & Eating

The Busta offers the best dining in the area, but there are a couple of pubs, a chippie and an Indian takeaway in Brae, so you won't be lacking for a cheaper bite. There's a supermarket at the road junction in the centre of town.

TOP CHOICE / Busta House Hotel   HOTEL **££**
(☑01806-522506; www.bustahouse.com; Busta; s/d £90/110; P🅿🛜) Genteel Busta House is perhaps Shetland's most characterful hotel, with a long, sad history and inevitable rumours of a (friendly) ghost. Built in the late 18th century (though the oldest part dates from 1588), its refurbished rooms – all individually decorated and named after islands in Shetland – retain a classy but homely charm. Rooms with sea views and/or four-poster bed cost a bit more.

Busta Lounge   SCOTTISH, SEAFOOD **££**
(☑01806-522506; Busta; mains £10-13; ⊙lunch & dinner) The lounge bar-restaurant at the Busta House Hotel (p315) is famed for its dedication to local produce – not only the seafood and lamb, but all dairy produce is from Shetland, and the beef is from Orkney. The more formal Pitcairn Room serves dinner only (£35 per person).

Frankie's Fish & Chips   FISH & CHIPS **£**
(☑01806-522700; www.frankiesfishandchips.com; Brae; mains £4-7; ⊙9.30am-8pm Mon-Sat, 1-8pm Sun) This award-winning chippie uses only locally sourced and sustainable seafood. As well as the usual chip-shop standards, the menu ranges from breakfast rolls and fry-ups (till 11.30am) to *moules marinières*, pizza and lasagne.

❶ Getting There & Away

Buses from Lerwick to Eshaness and North Roe stop in Brae (35 minutes, up to seven daily Monday to Saturday).

Northmavine Peninsula

The remote and beautiful Northmavine peninsula is almost a separate island, joined to Mainland by the tiny isthmus of **Mavis Grind**. Barely 100m wide, this narrow neck of land was a Viking portage, where boats could be dragged across (the name comes from the Old Norse for 'gateway of the portage') – it's said you can throw a stone from the North Sea to the Atlantic here.

Six miles north of Mavis Grind the road forks; the westerly branch leads to **Hillswick**, a former fishing station and the main settlement in Northmavine, while the easterly branch continues to the remote outpost of **North Roe**.

◎ Sights & Activities

From Hillswick, an excellent coastal walk makes a clockwise circuit of the **Ness of Hillswick** (4.5 miles, allow three hours). The going is rough and pathless but the views are breathtaking; otters are a common sight on the east side, while on the west you can see the shapely pinnacle of **Gordi Stack**, with the cluster of granite stacks known as **The Drongs** rising far out to sea.

Six miles west of Hillswick the road ends at the black, purple and orange lava cliffs of **Eshaness**, which form some of the most impressive and wild coastal scenery in Shetland. Howling Atlantic gales whip the ocean into a white-cap frenzy before it crashes into the base of the cliffs. When the wind subsides there is superb walking and panoramic views from the **lighthouse** on the headland (closed to the public, but available to rent as self-catering accommodation (p307)).

The most spectacular feature here is the **Holes of Scraada**, a mile's walk north from the lighthouse. This tortured fissure, floored by a black-sand beach, lies well inland but is linked to the sea by a 100m-long tunnel. The chasm was originally a cave, but the roof collapsed in 1873 when a local man rode across on his horse. If you follow the burn inland, you'll find three ancient watermills, and the ruins of a broch in Loch Houlland.

North again is the **Grind o da Navir** (Gate of the Borer), an impressive rock formation where the sea has carved an opening between two 30m-high cliffs. The winter storms here are so fierce that huge blocks of rock – up to 3m long – have been piled high above the waterline by the force of the waves.

Just south of Eshaness is the ruined settlement of **Stenness**, a former herring fishing station that once supported a fleet of 72 fishing boats. There are just a few ruined stone buildings here now, but it's worth walking to the end of the headland for views of **Dore Holm**, a sea stack with a perilously thin arch that looks like a drinking horse.

A mile east of Eshaness, a side road leads south to the **Tangwick Haa Museum** (☎01806-503389; admission free; ◎11am-5pm mid-Apr–Sep), housed in a restored 17th-century house. The wonderful collection of ancient B&W photos capture the sense of community in this area.

Beyond the turn off to Hillswick and Eshaness, the A970 continues north to the village of North Roe, passing **Ronas Hill** (499m), the highest point in Shetland. The haunting cloud-shrouded peak can be climbed from the end of the dirt road to Collafirth Hill (near the turn off to Ollaberry). Allow about two hours for the 4-mile round trip.

⊨ Sleeping & Eating

Places to stay and eat are concentrated in and around Hillswick and Eshaness.

TOP CHOICE Almara B&B   B&B ££
(☎01806-503261; www.almara.shetland.co.uk; Urafirth; s/d £30/60; Ⓟ⌂) Follow the puffin signpost a mile short of Hillswick to find the most wonderful welcome in Shetland. With sweeping views over the bay, this house has a great lounge, a few unusual features in the excellent rooms and bathrooms, and a good eye on the environment. You'll feel completely at home and appreciated; this is B&B at its best.

St Magnus Bay Hotel   HOTEL ££
(☎01806-503372; www.stmagnusbayhotel.co.uk; Hillswick; s/d £65/95; Ⓟ⌂) St Magnus Bay Hotel occupies a wonderful wooden mansion built in 1896. Enthusiastic new owners have invested some much-needed attention and are renovating it beautifully. The rooms vary in size, shape, and views – grab one of the corner ones for a stunning double vista over the bay – but all are very appealing. There's a sauna for guest use, and a lounge bar serving food.

Johnnie Notions Camping Böd   BOTHY £
(☎01595-694688; www.camping-bods.co.uk; Hamnavoe; dm £8; ◎Apr-Sep) There are four spacious berths in this cute wee stone bothy (cottage) with its challengingly low door. It's very basic; there are no showers or electricity. This was the birthplace of Johnnie

'Notions' Williamson, an 18th-century black-smith who inoculated several thousand people against smallpox using a serum and method he had devised himself. The böd is 3.5 miles east of Eshaness.

Braewick Cafe & Caravan Park
CAMPGROUND £

(☎01806-503345; www.eshaness.shetland.co.uk; Braewick; sites/wigwams £7/33; ☺10am-5pm Mar-Oct) Decent tent pitches and tasty light meals served in a cafe with stunning views over St Magnus Bay, and its weird and wonderful rock formations, are on offer here. It also has 'wigwams' – wooden huts with fridge and kettle that sleep four (or six at a pinch).

Da Böd
VEGETARIAN

(☎01806-503348; www.shetlandwildlifesanctuary.com; Hillswick; suggested donation per dish £3-8; ☺noon-6pm Jun-Sep; ☑) Down on the quay, Da Böd serves vegetarian food in a hippie crofters' house, which is actually a 300-year-old former Hanseatic trading-post house and one of Shetland's oldest buildings. All proceeds go to the local wildlife sanctuary. Opening hours are flexible, so call ahead if you want to be sure it's open.

❶ Information

The main grocery store is the **Hillswick Shop** (☎01806-503767; ☺9am-7pm Mon-Thu & Sat, 7.30am-7pm Fri, noon-5pm Sun), which also has a part-time post office counter (10am to 12.30pm Monday and 3pm to 5.30pm Thursday) and an ATM. There's another shop and post office, and the area's only petrol pump, at **Ollaberry**.

❶ Getting There & Away

Buses from Lerwick (once daily Monday to Saturday, evening departure) run to Hillswick (£3, 1¼ hours), Eshaness (1½ hours) and North Roe (1½ hours).

THE NORTH ISLES

Yell, Unst and Fetlar make up the North Isles, all connected to each other by ferry.

Yell

Yell if you like but nobody will hear; the desolate peat moors here are typical Shetland scenery, though the bleak landscape has an undeniable appeal. Yell is all about colours: the browns and vivid, lush greens of the bogland, grey clouds scudding across the sky and the steely blue waters of the North Atlantic, which are never far away. The peat makes the ground look cracked and parched, although it is totally sodden most of the year.

◉ Sights & Activities

Though many folk fire on through to Unst, Yell offers several good hill walks, especially around the **Herra peninsula**, about halfway up the west coast.

Across Whale Firth from the peninsula is **Lumbister RSPB Reserve**, where red-throated divers (called rain geese in Shetland), merlins, skuas and other bird species breed. The area is home to a large otter population, too, best viewed around Whale Firth, where you may also spot common and grey seals.

WILDLIFE-WATCHING IN SHETLAND

For birdwatchers, Shetland is a paradise – a stopover for migrating Arctic species, it hosts vast seabird breeding colonies, too.

Of the 24 seabird species that nest in the British Isles, 21 are found here. June is the height of the breeding season. The **Royal Society for the Protection of Birds** (RSPB; ☎01950-460800; www.rspb.org.uk) maintains several reserves on south Mainland and on the island of Fetlar. There are National Nature Reserves at **Hermaness** (where you can't fail to be entertained by the clownish antics of the almost tame puffins), **Keen of Hamar** and on the **Isle of Noss**. **Fair Isle** also supports large seabird populations.

But keep an eye on the sea itself: killer whales are regularly sighted (as are other cetaceans), as well as sea otters. A useful website for all species is www.nature-shetland.co.uk, which details latest sightings.

Held over a week in early July, the **Shetland Nature Festival** (www.shetlandnaturefestival.co.uk) is a series of guided walks, talks, boat trips, open days and art and photography workshops celebrating the wildlife and geology of Shetland.

South of Lumbister, on the hill side above the main road, stand the reputedly haunted ruins of **Windhouse**, dating from 1707. About a mile east of here is **Mid Yell**, the island's largest village. The road north to Gutcher passes **Basta Voe**, where many otters inhabit the shores. In the north, around **Cullivoe**, there's more good walking along the attractive coastline.

FREE Old Haa Museum   MUSEUM

(☑01957-702431; ⊙10am-4pm Tue-Thu & Sat, 2-5pm Sun Apr-Sep) The Old Haa Museum has a medley of curious objects (pipes, a piano, a doll-in-cradle, tiny bibles, ships in bottles and a sperm-whale jaw) as well as an archive of local history, and a tearoom. It's in Burravoe, 4 miles east of the southern ferry terminal in Ulsta.

🛏 Sleeping & Eating

After a couple of closures, sleeping options are limited to say the least. But there are lots of excellent self-catering cottages dotted around the island; check www.visitshetland.com for options.

Windhouse Lodge Camping Böd   BOTHY £

(☑01957-702475; www.camping-bods.co.uk; Mid Yell; dm £9) Below the haunted ruins of Windhouse you'll find this well-kept, clean, snug camping böd with a pot-belly stove to toast your toes by.

Wind Dog Café   CAFE £

(☑01957-744321; www.winddogcafe.co.uk; Gutcher; mains £2-5; ⊙9am-5pm Mon-Fri, 10am-5pm Sat & Sun, dinner Jun-Aug; ◎) This eclectic little cafe wins no prizes for decor – think Portakabin-meets-charity shop – but makes up for it with a warm atmosphere and good-value homemade nosh: burgers, the house speciality, are particularly good. Soup, panini and breakfast fry-ups are also on the menu. There's a small library too; an ideal spot if the rain is pelting down outside.

❶ Getting There & Away

BOAT Yell is connected with Mainland by the **Inter-Island Ferry Service** (☑01595-745804; www.shetland.gov.uk/ferries) between Toft and Ulsta (passenger return £3.60, car and driver return £8.40, 20 minutes, frequent). Although you don't need to book, it's wise to do so in the summer months.

BUS There are two buses Monday to Saturday from Lerwick to Yell and Unst, and a further one

to Toft ferry pier (one hour). Connecting buses at Ulsta serve other parts of the island.

Unst

POP 1100

You're fast running out of Scotland once you cross to Unst, a rugged island of ponies and seabirds. Britain's most northerly inhabited island is prettier than Yell, with bare, velvety-smooth hills and clusters of settlements that cling to their waterside locations, fiercely resisting the buffeting winds; it also feels less isolated and has more of a community.

Unst's unusual geology includes a large outcrop of serpentine and gabbro in the east, a fragment of oceanic crust that has been thrust to the surface. This rock – which weathers to a distinctive rusty orange, and can be seen on the road between Baltasound and Haroldswick – was once mined for chromite (used as a bright yellow pigment in paint).

◉ Sights & Activities

Unst's main attraction is the marvellous RSPB reserve at **Hermaness**, where a 4.5-mile round-trip walk from the parking area at the end of the road beyond Haroldswick takes you to cliffs where gannets, fulmars and guillemots nest and numerous puffins frolic. The outward path is easy going, mostly on duckboards, over heathland haunted by skylark and golden plover, and guarded by a small army of great skuas. Be aware that they nest in the nearby heather, and dive-bomb at will if they feel threatened.

Once you reach the coast, you can return by the same path or else follow the clifftops north, past a puffin colony and the spectacular gannetries of **Humla Stack** and **Vesta Skerry** to the headland of Hermaness itself. Here, a sloping greensward makes a perfect picnic spot and viewpoint for Britain's most northerly point, the rocks of **Out Stack**, and the guano-spattered island of **Muckle Flugga**, with its lighthouse built by Robert Louis Stevenson's uncle. From here, a line of wooden stakes marks the return path over the top of Hermaness Hill, with views across to the radar domes of the abandoned, Cold War–era listening station **RAF Saxa Vord**.

For more tips on wildlife-watching duck into the **Hermaness Visitor Centre** (☑01595-711278; Burrafirth; admission free; ⊙9am-5pm Apr–mid-Sep), on the right just before the car park; it has an entertaining seabird exhibit with lots of seabird noises. Guided walks are offered in season (call for details), and you can also book **boat trips** (🖂01806-522447; www.muckleflugga.co.uk; Burrafirth; ☺Tue, Thu, Sat Jun-Sep) to Muckle Flugga from here.

Unst Heritage Centre   HERITAGE CENTRE
(🖂01957-711528; Haroldswick; adult/child £3/2, joint ticket with Unst Boat Haven £5; ☺11am-5pm May-Sep) This heritage centre houses a modern museum with a history of the Shetland pony, a re-creation of a croft house complete with box bed and – for the weather-obsessed – a summary of the last 170 years of Shetland weather.

Unst Boat Haven   MUSEUM
(🖂01957-711528; Haroldswick; adult/child £3/2, joint ticket with Unst Heritage Centre £5; ☺11am-5pm May-Sep) This large shed is a boaty's delight, housing a collection of Shetland rowing and sailing boats, photographs of more boats, and maritime artefacts.

FREE Skidbladner Longship   MUSEUM
(🖂01595-694688; www.vikingshetland.com; Haroldswick) Unst has the highest concentration of Viking longhouse sites in the country. The Viking Unst project manages three excavation sites, and has as its centrepiece this Viking longship, a replica of the 9th-century Gokstad ship on display in Oslo. A re-creation of a Viking longhouse is being constructed alongside the ship.

Unst Bus Shelter   LANDMARK
(www.unstbusshelter.shetland.co.uk; Baltasound) Just east of Baltasound stands what must be the most unusual bus stop in Britain. A surreal project, begun by a local schoolboy in 1998, has seen the bus shelter lavishly decorated and equipped with a sofa, flowers, an old telly and a visitors' book. The decor is changed regularly, and is now complemented by the adjacent John Peel Memorial Traffic Island.

FREE Hagdale Horse Mill   HISTORIC BUILDING
(Hagdale; ☺24hr) At Hagdale you can see Britain's only surviving horse mill, where chromite ore from a nearby quarry was ground to a coarse gravel. The building has been restored, but the mill wheel – driven by a horse walking in circles – is original. You can still find samples of chromite ore lying around: look for black-and-white speckled rock.

Valhalla Brewery   BREWERY
(🖂01957-711658; www.valhallabrewery.co.uk; Baltasound; tours £3.50; ☺9am-5pm Mon-Fri) Valhalla brews the most northerly-made beer in Britain, including its Island Bere, a throwback to original ale made with an indigenous variety of barley.

🛏 Sleeping & Eating

The only restaurants are at the Baltasound Hotel and Saxa Vord. There are cafes at Saxa Vord, the Final Checkout, and Skibhoul Stores.

Self-caterers can stock up at **Skibhoul Stores** (🖂01957-711304; Baltasound; ☺9.30am-5.30pm Mon-Wed & Fri, 9am-6pm Thu, 9am-5pm Sat), which has a bakery and cafe, and the **Final Checkout** (🖂01957-711666; Hagdale; ☺8am-6pm Mon-Sat, 11am-6pm Sun) between Baltasound and Haroldswick. Known locally as 'the garage', the Final Checkout has an ATM, and sells petrol and diesel.

Gardiesfauld Hostel   HOSTEL, CAMPGROUND £
(🖂01957-755279; www.gardiesfauld.shetland.co.uk; Uyeasound; 2-person tent £6, dm £12; ☺Apr-Sep; ℗) This 35-bed hostel is very clean and offers spacious dorms with lockers, family rooms, a garden, an elegant lounge and a wee conservatory dining area with great bay views. You can camp here, too. Nonresidents are welcome to use common areas. The bus stops right outside. Bring 20p pieces for the shower.

Belmont House   SELF-CATERING ££
(🖂01957-744394; www.belmontunst.org.uk; Belmont; per week £1400; ℗📶) This historic 18th-century Georgian country house, on the left as you leave Unst's southern ferry terminal, has been restored to provide luxurious self-catering accommodation for eight to twelve people. Features include an elegant drawing room, a Venetian-style writing room, extensive gardens and glorious sea views.

Saxa Vord   HOSTEL, SELF-CATERING £
(🖂01957-711711; www.saxavord.com; Haroldswick; s/d £18.50/37; ℗📶) This former Royal Air Force base is something of a white elephant these days, but various plans are afoot. It's not the most atmospheric lodging, but the barracks-style rooms offer great value and there's something nice about watching the rain squalls through the window and skylight.

The **restaurant** (open mid-May to September) dishes out reasonable local food, and there's a bar – Britain's northernmost,

SHETLAND ISLANDS FAIR ISLE

by our reckoning – and a friendly, helpful atmosphere. The self-catering holiday houses (£485 per week) here are good for families.

Prestegaard B&B ££
(☎01957-755234; Uyeasound; s/d £28/50; ℗) This solid old manse near the water makes a great base. Rooms are spacious and comfy, with sea views and separate (but private) bathroom – we particularly like the upstairs one. The breakfast room with Up Helly Aa shields and axes on the wall will bring out the Viking in you, and the kindly owner will make your stay a delightful one.

Baltasound Hotel HOTEL, PUB ££
(☎01957-711334; www.baltasound-hotel.shetland.co.uk; Baltasound; s/d £49/78; ℗) The cottage-style rooms inside this solid place are good. It's also a decent watering hole with a lovely country outlook, and does adequate bar meals in a dining room dappled by the evening sun.

❶ Information

There's no tourist office on the island; for general information see www.unst.org.uk.
Baltasound Post Office (☎01957-711655; ☺9am-5.30pm Mon, Tue & Fri, 9am-4.30pm Wed, 9am-1pm Thu & Sat) Baltasound's post office offers the chance to send postcards (for sale here) and letters stamped with a special postmark that includes a pair of puffins and the legend 'Britain's most northerly post office'.

❶ Getting There & Around

BOAT Unst is connected with Yell by a small ferry (p318) between Gutcher and Belmont (free, 10 minutes, frequent).
BUS There are two buses a day Monday to Saturday from Lerwick to Yell and Unst (£5, 2.5 hours).
CAR & BICYCLE You can hire cars and bikes from the Final Checkout (p319), or bikes from **P & T Coaches** (☎01957-711666).

Fetlar

POP 90

At just 5 miles by 2 miles, Fetlar is the smallest but most fertile of the North Isles. Its name is derived from the Viking term for 'fat land'. Much of the island is given over to pasture, but on the higher ground you'll see numerous *planticrues*, walled enclosures covered by fishing nets and used for growing cabbages.

☉ Sights & Activities

There's great birdwatching – Fetlar is home to three-quarters of Britain's breeding population of red-necked phalaropes, which nest around the **Loch of Funzie** (pronounced 'finnie') in the east. From April to October, you can view them from an RSPB hide in the nearby marshes.

There are several scenic walks around the island, including the hike around the Lamb Hoga headland, beginning at **Tresta Beach**, about a mile west of Houbie. You may see Shetland ponies, a diminutive breed used for carrying seaweed, roaming on the hills here. On the coast about a mile from the ferry port at Oddsta is **Brough Lodge**, a bizarre assembly of arches, buttresses and towers, built for the Nicolson family in the 1820s; there's an interesting folly on the hillock behind the lodge.

Fetlar Interpretive Centre VISITOR CENTRE
(☎01957-733206; www.fetlar.com; Houbie; adult/child £2/free; ☺11am-3pm Mon-Fri, 1-4pm Sat & Sun May-Sep) The excellent Fetlar Interpretive Centre has photos, audio recordings and videos on the island and its history.

🛏 Sleeping

The **Garths Campsite** (☎01957-733227; Gord; sites £5-9; ☺May-Sep), 2.5 miles from the ferry, overlooks the beach at Tresta and has great facilities. Run by the same people is friendly **Gord B&B** (☎01957-733227; nicboxall@btinternet.com; Gord; s/d/tw £35/50/70, dinner £15; ℗), with terrific sea views and two twin rooms and one double, all with en suite. There's also a camping böd (p307) on the island.

❶ Information

There's no petrol on Fetlar, but there's a part-time shop in Houbie, the main village.

❶ Getting There & Away

Four to seven daily free ferries (p318) connect Fetlar with Gutcher on Yell and Belmont on Unst.

FAIR ISLE

POP 70

It's a stomach-churning ferry ride to Fair Isle, but it's worth it for the stunning cliff scenery, isolation and hordes of winged creatures. About halfway to Orkney, Fair Isle is one of Scotland's most remote inhabited islands. It's only 3 miles by 1.5 miles in size

Shetland lies 60 degrees north of the equator, putting it at a similar latitude to Anchorage, Alaska; Hudson's Bay, Canada; and the southern tip of Greenland. This makes it the best place in Britain for seeing the Northern Lights (aurora borealis), known in local dialect as the 'mirrie dancers'. Midwinter is the best time for viewing, though the phenomenon is notoriously unpredictable. Lancaster University's **AuroraWatchUK** (aurorawatch. lancs.ac.uk) monitors geomagnetic activity and provides free SMS alerts when the aurora is likely to be visible.

Shetland's high latitude also produces the effect known as the 'simmer dim'. Around midsummer (21 June) the sun doesn't set until 10.30pm, and rises again five hours later. Between sunset and sunrise it doesn't get properly dark, there's just a modest twilight. Not quite the midnight sun, but close.

A third natural phenomenon will be familiar to sailors, but if you haven't seen it before, the mareel is just magical. 'Mareel' is local dialect for phosphorescence, a natural light emitted by plankton in seawater when they are agitated by an oar or a propellor. Only visible on dark nights (the effect peaks in August), this ghostly greenish glow in the wake of a moving boat is a strange and wonderful sight.

and is probably best known for its patterned knitwear, still produced in the island's cooperative, Fair Isle Crafts.

It's also a paradise for birdwatchers, who form the bulk of the island's visitors. Fair Isle is in the flight path of many migrating birds, and thousands breed here. They're monitored by the **Fair Isle Bird Observatory**, which collects and analyses information year-round; visitors are welcome to participate.

Small **George Waterston Memorial Centre** (☎01595 760244; donations welcome; ⏰2-4pm Mon, 10.30am-noon Wed, 2-4pm Fri May-Sep) has photos and exhibits on the island's natural history, crofting, fishing, archaeology and knitwear.

The smart new **Fair Isle Lodge & Bird Observatory** (☎01595-760258; www.fairisle birdobs.co.uk; s/d with full board £55/100; ⏰May-Oct; P@🛜⚓) offers good en suite rooms. Rates are full board, and there are free guided walks and other bird-related displays and activities.

❶ Getting There & Away

AIR From Tingwall, DirectFlight (p302) operates flights to Fair Isle (£60 return, 25 minutes, twice on Monday, Wednesday and Friday year-round and on Saturday May to September). A day-return ticket allows about seven hours on the island.

BOAT Ferries (☎01595-760363; www.fairisle .org.uk) sail from Grutness (near Sumburgh) with the odd one from Lerwick to Fair Isle (one-way per person/car and driver £3.40/15.80, three hours), running on Tuesday and Saturday year-round plus Thursday from May to early October.

You can also book a boat charter with Cycharters (p308).

WALKING IN THE SHETLAND ISLANDS

Muckle Roe Walk

Muckle Roe is an island, though a bridge has long since replaced the original stepping stones that connected it to the west coast of Mainland. It's a wonderfully rugged area of craggy red and green hills, lochans and magnificent coast.

The route of this walk invites further exploration and variation by venturing out onto each and every headland, climbing the several small hills and lingering at the secluded coves and beaches; you could easily spend the whole day here.

PLANNING
Use either OS Explorer 1:25,000 map No 469 *Shetland – North West* or OS Landranger 1:50,000 map No 3 *Shetland – North Mainland*.

THE WALK
The walk starts and finishes at a small roadside parking area at Little Ayre, 4.5 miles southwest of Brae, at the end of a quiet, single-track road signposted to Muckle Roe.

Go through a gate near the parking area where signposts point to 'Lighthouse' and

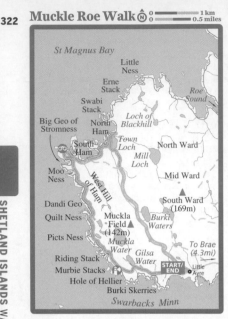

St Magnus Bay

Little
Ness

Erne
Stack

Roe
Sound

Swabi
Stack

Loch of
Blackhill

Big Geo of
Stromness

North
Ham

Town
Loch

North Ward

South
Ham

Mill
Loch

Moo
Ness

Mid Ward

West Hill of Ham

South Ward
(169m)

Dandi Geo

Quilt Ness

Muckla
Field
(142m)

Burki
Waters

Picts Ness

Muckla
Water

Gilsa
Water

To Brae
(4.3mi)

Riding Stack

Murbie Stacks

START/
END

Little
Ayre

Hole of Hellier

Burki Skerries

Swarbacks Minn

MUCKLE ROE WALK

Duration 3¼–3½ hours
Distance 7.5 miles
Start/Finish Little Ayre
Summary An exceptionally scenic walk along a rugged and intricately indented coast, with wide-ranging views along the central west coast of Mainland.

Continue south up the slope from the stile and along the cliff top, past deep, colourful geos, then down, from near a ruined stone building, to **South Ham**. From the further shingle beach, follow a track up to a gate then swing left (more or less west) uphill to a roofless stone cottage. Climb to the crest to overlook the **Big Geo of Stromness**, where there's a stack in the making on the southern cliff line. Cross a stile over a fence in a slight dip, then go up to the elongated ridge that is **West Hill of Ham**.

From a large cairn (45 minutes from North Ham) drop down to the head of **Dandi Geo**. The route continues in undulating fashion, past a lochan and on until the beacon above **Murbie Stacks** comes into view. Follow the ridge crest to a wide glen and walk across to the beacon, a lovely spot for a spell (40 minutes from the cairn). Head north and northeast up the glen; keep east of a cairn on the crest and follow a path across the slope above **Gilsa Water** to its outlet. From here a clear path leads east, keeping below the high ground to the north, past a nameless beach, across moorland then steeply down to another strand. Follow a path on the seaward side of a low hill, through a gate; the car park is nearby (50 minutes from the beacon).

'Hams'; shortly, follow a track to the right towards Hams. It leads northwest up the wide glen, across a broad saddle, then gradually down past **Burki Waters** and on to a wider, more fertile glen. At a junction near a stream crossing, continue straight on, over a stile beside a large green shed, through a gateway and on, beside a small burn. Soon you'll reach a stile next to a gate at the northern end of **Town Loch** (one hour from the start). Below, the sheltered inlet of **North Ham** allows for a break on green grass beside bleached shingle and deep-blue water reflecting brick-red and black cliffs and stacks.

Understand Scotland's
› Highlands & Islands

Scotland's Highlands & Islands Today

Renewable Energy

The Scottish National Party (SNP), which had led a minority government in Edinburgh since 2007, surprised the nation in the 2011 elections with a landslide victory to the Scottish parliament, winning 69 out of 129 seats. The Highlands and Islands voted overwhelmingly for the SNP (except for Orkney and Shetland, which returned Liberal Democrat MSPs).

One of the central planks of the SNP's vision for an independent Scotland is its energy policy. The party leader, Alex Salmond, has said that he wants the country to be the 'Saudi Arabia of renewable energy' – becoming self-sufficient in energy by 2020, and a net exporter of 'clean' electricity.

The Highlands and Islands are central to this plan. In the first half of the 20th century it was one the first regions in the world to develop hydroelectric power on a large scale, and in the last decade, wind turbines have sprung up all over the place. By 2009, renewables provided 27% of Scotland's energy consumption; government targets are for this to rise to 31% in 2011 and 100% by 2020.

But the future of Scotland's energy industry lies not on land, but in the sea: Scotland has access to 25% of Europe's available tidal energy, and 10% of its wave power. The Highlands and Islands are at the leading edge of developing wave, tidal and offshore wind power: a £4 billion project was launched in 2010 to test marine generating systems in the waters around Orkney, including the Pelamis 'sea snake' wave generator and SeaGen tidal turbines.

» Highest point: Ben Nevis (1344m)

» Annual whisky export: 1 billion bottles

» Number of Scottish islands: 790

» Number of Munros (peaks of 3000ft and over): 283

Development vs Conservation

In 2010 the Scottish government gave the go-ahead to a 135-mile, high-voltage overhead power line from Beauly (near Inverness) to Denny in

Books

Raw Spirit (Iain Banks) A jaunt around the Highlands and Islands to find the perfect whisky.
Mountaineering in Scotland (WH Murray) Climbing in the Highlands in the 1930s, when getting to Glen Coe was an adventure in itself.

The Poor Had No Lawyers (Andy Wightman) A penetrating, and fascinating, analysis of who owns the land in the Highlands, and how they got it.
The Scottish Islands (Hamish Haswell-Smith) A beautifully illustrated guide to 162 islands.

Movies

Local Hero 1983 film that caused a tourist stampede to the Highlands in search of Ben's Beach.
Whisky Galore! Classic 1949 comedy – islanders plunder a shipwrecked cargo of whisky under the nose of authorities.

belief systems
(% of population)

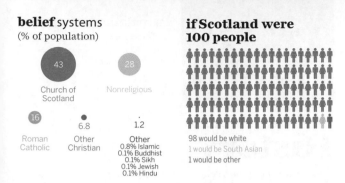

43 Church of Scotland

28 Nonreligious

16 Roman Catholic

6.8 Other Christian

1.2 Other
0.8% Islamic
0.1% Buddhist
0.1% Sikh
0.1% Jewish
0.1% Hindu

if Scotland were 100 people

98 would be white
1 would be South Asian
1 would be other

Stirlingshire, to connect wind- and marine-generated electricity from the north to the heart of the national grid. It will be carried on 600 giant pylons marching through some of the Highlands' most scenic areas, including Strathglass, Fort Augustus and Bridge of Tummel.

Supporters like to point out that the scheme also involves the removal of almost 60 miles of low-voltage pylons from the Cairngorms National Park; opponents claim that a seabed cable, while more expensive, would be a better alternative. The debate reflects a larger tension that exists across the Highlands and Islands – between those keen to develop the region's resources and conservationists who want to keep the area unspoiled.

Land Reform

Crofting and land ownership are important issues in the Gaelic-speaking areas of northwest Scotland, especially since a headline-grabbing clause in the *Land Reform (Scotland) Act (2003)* allowed crofting communities to buy out the land that they live on (with the aid of taxpayers' money as some are quick to mention), in the hope of reversing the gradual depopulation of the Highlands.

Several estates have followed Eigg, Gigha, Knoydart and North Harris into community ownership; in 2006 South Uist saw the biggest community buy out yet. The latest case to make the headlines is the Pairc estate on Lewis, where a Warwickshire-based accountant, whose family has owned the estate since 1920, has leased the land to a power company who plan to erect a £200 million wind farm. The locals voted in favour of a community buy out (which was approved by the government), but the landowner has challenged the legality of the Land Reform Act and is appealing the government's decision.

Along with Wales and England, Scotland is part of Great Britain. Throw in Northern Ireland and you have the United Kingdom. It's OK to talk about Scotland's inhabitants as Scottish or British – but *never* English!

Myths

The Jacobite rebellion of 1745 led by the Bonnie Prince wasn't Scotland vs England (there were English Jacobites, and lowland Scots were anti-Jacobite), nor Highland vs Lowland. It was an attempt to reclaim the throne of Britain for the Stuart dynasty.

Media

» *West Highland Free Press* (www.whfp.com)
» *Press & Journal* (www.pressandjournal.co.uk)
» *The Orcadian* (www.orcadian.co.uk)
» *Shetland Times* (www.shetlandtimes.co.uk)

Radio

BBC Radio nan Gaidheal (www.bbc.co.uk/radionan gaidheal) News, current affairs, culture and music presented in Gaelic.

History

From the decline of the Vikings onwards, Scottish history has been predictably and often violently bound to that of its southern neighbour. Battles and border raids were commonplace until shared kingship, then political union, drew the two together. However, there has often been as much – if not more – of a cultural divide between Highland and Lowland Scotland than ever between Lowland Scotland and England.

Scotland's misty prehistory has left outstanding monuments, particularly in the northern and western islands, but the first outside reference to northern Britain's inhabitants comes from the Romans, whose struggles with the Picts caused the construction of two massive walls to keep them out.

If the Roman presence pushed formerly disparate tribes into union, the Vikings did the same. Their incursions led the Gaelic kingdom of Dalriada and the Pictish kingdom to unite, creating for the first time a Kingdom of Scotland.

Once Viking power was broken, a familiar story of strong and weak monarchs, political intrigues and dynastic struggles played out over the centuries. The Wars of Independence freed Scotland from English interference and set up William Wallace and Robert the Bruce as heroes.

Political union in the early 18th century was born of pragmatism but widely resented. This, and the ousting of the Catholic King James in favour of his Protestant son-in-law led to widespread anger – the Jacobite rebellions of the 18th century attempted to wrest power back by putting James's son, and then his grandson (Bonnie Prince Charlie), on the throne.

The Battle of Culloden in 1746 marks one of the great dividing lines in Highland history, tolling the death-knell of the clan system. The Highlands had been ruled as a 'nation apart' by clan chiefs who, stripped of power but possessed of vast lands, evicted their crofters in favour of large-scale sheep farming. This brutal period, the Clearances, left the

TIMELINE	4000–2200 BC	2200–750 BC	750 BC–AD 500
	Neolithic farmers move to Scotland from mainland Europe; stone circles and tombs from these ancient times dot the Highlands and Islands; the best are concentrated in Orkney.	The Bronze Age produces swords and shields, and the construction of hill forts, crannogs and burnt mounds.	Impressive stone towers known as brochs are built during the Iron Age.

Highlands an empty wilderness and forced hundreds of thousands to emigrate.

Those that sought the cities were the fuel for the Industrial Revolution, building a spine of heavy industry across southern Scotland that lasted through to the late 20th century.

Stories in Stone

The human history of the Highlands and Islands began to unfold as the glaciers retreated in the wake of the last Ice Age, around 10,000 BC. Tribes of hunters and gatherers came north in waves from the European continents, taking advantage of the unoccupied land. These Mesolithic peoples left behind the remains of their encampments: discarded seafood shells and animal bones provide signs of the earliest human habitation in Scotland.

Only limited evidence of this early culture remains, but Scotland's Neolithic period (3200 to 2200 BC) has left behind an astonishing record of human development, most impressively at Skara Brae in Orkney and Jarlshof in Shetland – some of the world's best-preserved prehistoric villages – but also in the cairns and stone circles of Lewis, Caithness and Kilmartin. All aspects of early life are represented, from primitive field systems and houses to ceremonial structures such as standing stones, tombs and tribal halls.

Crannogs (artificial islands built on stilts or heaped stones) were a favoured form of defensible dwelling through the Bronze Age (2200 BC to 750 BC), but the signature structure of this period is the mysterious 'burnt mound'. Found all over Scotland, but particularly prevalent in the northern isles, these are heaps of stones that have been cracked and splintered through exposure to heat. They are always associated with crude stone basins, and it is thought the stones were heated in a fire, and then placed in the basin to heat water – whether for cooking, washing or some ritual practice is unknown.

The Iron Age (750 BC to AD 500) saw the construction of a remarkable series of defence-minded structures of a different sort: the drystone defensive towers known as brochs, which are unique to Scotland. This was a time of great uncertainty, with frequent raids by marauding European tribes, and villages pooled their resources to build these mighty lookouts, which reached 10m or 12m in height. Beneath the towers were individual houses and networks of tunnels known as souterrains, used to store food (or as a last line of defence). The best preserved examples are Mousa in Shetland, Dun Carloway in Lewis and Dun Telve in Glenelg.

Top Prehistoric Sights

» Jarlshof, Shetland

» Skara Brae, Orkney

» Maes Howe, Orkney

» Kilmartin Glen, Argyll

» Callanish, Lewis

» Tomb of the Eagles, Orkney

» Scottish Crannog Centre, Kenmore

AD 43	AD 84	AD 122	AD 142
Claudius begins the Roman conquest of Britain, almost a century after Julius Caesar first invaded. By AD 80 a string of forts is built from the Clyde to the Forth.	Romans have trouble with the people they call the Picts, clashing at the Battle of Mons Graupius near modern-day Inverness. Score: Romans 1, Picts 0.	Romans retreat, and the 74-mile-long Hadrian's Wall is begun, designed to keep Picts in their place. Score: Romans 1, Picts 1.	Building of Antonine Wall marks northern limit of Roman Empire; it's patrolled for about 40 years until the Romans decide the Highlands too difficult to conquer. Final score: Romans 1, Picts 2.

Romans & Picts

The origins of the people known as the Picts is a mystery, but they may have emerged as a confederation of northern Celtic tribes in reaction to the Roman invasion of Scotland in AD 80. Their territory (Pictland, or Pictavia) extended north through the Highlands and northeastern Scotland, from the Forth and Clyde estuaries to Orkney and the Western Isles.

Resistance to the Romans by lowland British tribes collapsed quickly, but the northern province, which the Romans named Caledonia (after the Caledones tribe), proved a tougher nut to crack. Eventually, the Roman general Agricola was able to advance along the eastern edge of the Highlands, supported from the sea by Roman galleys, defeating a vast army of Picts at the decisive Battle of Mons Graupius in AD 84 (thought to be near modern-day Inverness). Agricola went on to sail around the Orkney Islands, establishing for the first time that Britain was an island. However, the Romans were unable to press home their military advantage, and later retreated south of Hadrian's Wall.

Much of what we know about the Picts comes from the Romans, including their name (from the Latin pictus, meaning 'painted', or possibly 'tattooed'). The main material evidence of their culture is their fabulous carved symbol stones, found in many parts of northern and eastern Scotland, but whatever language they spoke has been lost.

The 7th century was a golden age for Pictish culture, when the disparate tribes were unified under the northern king Bridei mac Máelchú; most of the carved stones date from this time. However, Pictish unity only served to postpone the inevitable. The Picts held out against Irish and Anglian invaders until the end of the 8th century, but in 793 Viking marauders from Scandinavia began to raid the north and west coasts.

In the following decades, the northern Picts were decimated, and Caithness, the Western Isles, Orkney and Shetland were all absorbed into the Viking empire. The southern Picts retreated to Fife, before slowly being assimilated into the Gaelic kingdom of Dalriada. By the 9th century, Gaelic was the dominant language of the Highlands and the Celtic cross had replaced pagan symbols on the Pictish stones.

The Saltire – a diagonal white cross on a blue ground – is one of the oldest national flags in the world. According to legend, white clouds in the form of a cross appeared in a blue sky during a battle between Scots and Anglo-Saxons, urging the Scots to victory.

The Kingdom of Dalriada

When the Romans fled Britain in the 5th century there were at least two indigenous peoples in the region that is now Scotland: the Picts in the north and east, and the Britons in the southwest. By AD 500 another Celtic tribe, the Scots (from Scotti, a derogatory name given to them by the Romans), had begun to colonise western Scotland from northern Ireland, establishing a kingdom called Dalriada. From their ceremonial

5th century	Early 500s	6th century	685
Roman soldiers stationed in Britain are recalled to Rome as the Empire faces attack from barbarian tribes. The last Romans depart and Emperor Honorius tells Britons to fend for themselves.	A Celtic tribe, known as the Scots, cross the sea from northern Ireland and establish a kingdom in Argyll called Dalriada.	St Columba establishes a Christian mission on Iona. By the late 8th century the mission is responsible for the conversion of most of pagan Scotland.	The Pictish king Bridei defeats the Northumbrians at Nechtansmere in Angus, an against-the-odds victory that sets the foundations for Scotland as a separate entity.

headquarters at the hill fort of Dunadd, these seafaring Celts conquered a territory that stretched from Kintyre and the Antrim coast of Ireland to the Isle of Skye and Wester Ross.

Their influence lives on in the districts of Lorn and Cowal, which take their names from Dalriadan chiefs, and the county name of Argyll (from *earra gael*, meaning 'the seaboard of the Gael') – and of course, they eventually gave their name to the kingdom of Scotland. But perhaps their most important legacy is that they brought the Gaelic language to the western highlands and islands of Scotland.

After centuries of tribal war between the Scots and the Picts, it was the Norsemen who finally tipped the balance in favour of the Gaels. The destruction of the northern Picts created a power vacuum, which the kings of Dalriada quickly exploited. Given the choice between forming an alliance with the Scots or dying at the hands of the Norsemen, many Pictish tribes willingly capitulated to the Gaelic kings.

In 843 the Dalriadan king Kenneth MacAlpin, who was the son of a Pictish princess, used the Pictish custom of matrilineal succession to take over the Pictish throne, uniting Scotland north of the Firth of Forth into a single kingdom. Thereafter the Scots – bringing with them Gaelic and Christianity – gained complete cultural and political ascendancy. By AD 900 Dalriada and Pictland had become the Kingdom of Alba.

Viking Invaders

The first Viking longboats were spotted off the shores of Orkney in the 780s, and must have inspired terror in those who saw them. The marauders struck without warning, ransacking entire villages, butchering the occupants and carting anything of value back to Norway. For the next 500 years, the Norsemen pillaged the Scottish coast and islands, eventually taking control of Orkney, Shetland, the Outer Hebrides and all the islands off the west coast of Scotland from Skye to Arran, plus the mainland districts of Cowal and Kintyre.

The Viking reputation for brutality may have been deserved, but they were probably no more bloodthirsty than the Romans, Picts or Scots; however, they made the fatal public relations error of repeatedly attacking the monasteries, and it was the monks who wrote all the history books from that period. In reality, rather than wiping out the indigenous people, a combination of placename and DNA evidence suggests that the Norse takeover was a more gradual process of intermarriage, integration and assimilation.

Eventually the Viking colonies returned to Scottish rule, but they always retained a distinctively Scandinavian-tinged culture, especially Orkney and Shetland, which – unlike the Western Isles – were taken over

Admonan (627–704) succeeded St Columba as the abbot of Iona. His book, *Vita Columbae* (Life of Columba), is one of our most important sources of information on the Picts and the kingdom of Dalriada.

A well-presented and easily absorbed introduction to Scottish history is at www.bbc.co.uk/scotland/history. The accompanying videos help to bring the past to life.

HISTORY

7th century	780	848
Golden age of Pictish culutre sees the creation of hundreds of carved stones, decorated with beautiful but mysterious symbols.	Norsemen in longboats from Scandinavia begin to pillage the Scottish coast and islands, eventually taking control of Orkney, Shetland and the Western Isles.	Kenneth MacAlpin unites the Scottish and Pictish thrones, thus uniting Scotland north of the Firth of Forth into a single kingdom.

» Pictish standing stone

by nobles from the lowlands and ended up speaking a mixture of Scots and Norn (an ancient Viking dialect), rather than Gaelic.

The west coast was returned to the Scottish king Alexander III after the Battle of Largs in 1263. Three years later the Western Isles were ceded to Scotland by the Treaty of Perth, in exchange for an annual rent to the King of Norway. Orkney and Shetland remained Norwegian possessions until 1468 and 1469 respectively, when they were mortgaged to King James III of Scotland in lieu of a dowry for his bride, Margaret, daughter of the king of Denmark.

Clan vs Crown

The dynasty founded by Kenneth MacAlpin tightened its grip on the Highland mainland during the 10th century, but it wasn't until the reign of Malcolm II (1005–18) that the Scots extended their control south of the Forth–Clyde line, creating a single Scottish kingdom extending as far as the River Tweed. This was the beginning of a drift that saw the centre of royal power move southward from Scone to Stirling and Dunfermline, and then to Edinburgh, which eventually emerged as the capital of Scotland by the early 16th century.

However, the cultural and linguistic divide between Highlands and Lowlands had its origins at the other end of Britain, in the Norman invasion of 1066. Malcolm II's great-grandson Malcolm Canmore (1058–93) took a Saxon queen. His youngest son David I (1124–53) had been raised in England, and introduced the Anglo-Norman feudal system to Scotland, granting lands and titles (mostly in the south and east) to English-speaking Norman noblemen.

But in the remote Highland glens the Gaelic language and the clan system still held sway: loyalty and military service were based on ties of blood rather than feudal superiority. The clan was led by a chief who was granted his position through the ancient Dalriadan system of tanistry, in which the heir to the chief was nominated from a pool of eligible candidates whose great-grandfathers had been chiefs before them. This ensured that a chief never died without a potential heir, but resulted in many bloody feuds and murders instigated by those who felt their claim to the title had been denied.

The history of the Highlands from the 12th to the 16th centuries was volatile and violent. Robert the Bruce's struggle to win the Scottish crown involved not only fighting the English, but also vanquishing his foes in the Highlands. In 1306 Bruce famously murdered John Comyn, his main rival as king, making Bruce a blood enemy of the powerful Macdougalls of Lorne, whose chief Alexander was related to Comyn by marriage. The Macdougalls harried Bruce mercilessly until the king-to-be finally routed them at the Battle of the Pass of Brander in 1309.

ORKNEY

The main source for the history of Orkney during the Viking period is the *Orkneyinga Saga*, compiled in Iceland sometime around 1200. A rip-roaring tale of battle, murder and political intrigue, it blends historical fact with oral tradition (and no small amount of poetic licence).

872	1263	1314	1320
The King of Norway creates an earldom in Orkney, also governing Shetland; these island groups become a vital Viking base for raids and colonisation down the west of Scotland.	Norse power controls the entire western seaboard but is broken at the Battle of Largs, marking the retreat of Viking influence and eventual handing back of the western isles to Scotland.	Robert the Bruce wins a famous victory over the English at the Battle of Bannockburn, turning the tide in favour of the Scots for the next 400 years.	The Declaration of Arbroath asserts Scotland's status as an independent kingdom in submission to the pope.

Even after Bruce had defeated the English at Bannockburn in 1314 and guaranteed Scottish independence, the wrangling for power between (and among) the Highland clans and the Scottish crown raged on for several centuries. Clan Campbell, supporters of Bruce, were rewarded for their continuing loyalty to the king with grants of land and titles, earning the bitter enmity of their rivals the MacDougalls and the MacDonalds. By the beginning of the 18th century, the chief of Clan Campbell had become the Duke of Argyll, owning most of the southwestern Highlands and capable of putting 5000 men into battle.

Much of the fighting that disrupted the Highlands during this period was between rival clans. The longest-running feud was between the Camerons and the MacKintoshs: following a battle over disputed land in 1337, the two clans remained sworn enemies for more than 300 years. The Battle of Mulroy (near Roy Bridge) in 1688, between Camerons and MacDonalds on one side and MacKintoshs on the other, turned out to be the last inter-clan battle before the Jacobite rebellions changed the Highlands forever.

Although Orkney and Shetland became Scottish possessions in 1469, the old Norse legal system of Udal law still pertains in the islands, especially in relation to land ownership and inheritance. This has resulted in many court battles over the right to build, notably on the foreshore and the seabed.

The Jacobite Rebellions

The 'Glorious Revolution' of 1688 saw the Catholic king James II (of England)/VII (of Scotland) deposed from the British throne, and replaced by his Protestant son-in-law William of Orange. From then until 1746 much of Highland history was dominated by the Jacobite rebellions that sought to restore a Catholic Stuart king to the British throne. Indeed, one of England's motivations for union with Scotland was fear of Jacobite sympathies in the Highlands being exploited by its enemies, the French.

A major manifestation of this fear was the building of government garrisons throughout the Highlands, notably Fort William, Fort Augustus and Fort George, and the driving of new military roads through the glens by General Wade and his successors. This wariness was justified – there were Jacobite uprisings in 1689, 1708 and 1715.

By no means all of the Highland clans were Jacobite supporters, though. From his seat at Inveraray Castle, the Duke of Argyll, chief of Clan Campbell, served as the British government's political manager in Scotland for the first half of the 18th century. In fact, many of the clans that joined in the rebellions did so more out of hatred towards the Campbells than support for the exiled Stuart king. Following the 1689 uprising, King William demanded that all Highland chieftains swear an oath of allegiance or suffer violent reprisals; it was Campbell soldiers who were charged with making an example of the Macdonalds with the infamous Massacre of Glencoe (see p 173).

In 1745 Charles Edward Stuart (better known as Bonnie Prince Charlie) landed in Scotland to claim the British crown for his father.

Jacobite, a term derived from the Latin for 'James', is used to describe the political movement committed to the return of the Stuart kings to the thrones of England and Scotland.

1328	1468–69	1488–1513	1560
Continuing raids on northern England force Edward II to sue for peace; the Treaty of Northampton gives Scotland its independence, with Robert I, the Bruce, as king.	Orkney and then Shetland are mortgaged to Scotland as part of a dowry from Danish King Christian I, whose daughter is to marry the future King James III of Scotland.	The Scottish Renaissance produces an intellectual climate that encourages Protestantism, a reaction against the perceived wealth and corruption of the medieval Roman Catholic Church.	As a result of the Reformation, the Scottish parliament creates a Protestant Church independent of Rome and the monarchy. The Latin Mass is abolished and the pope's authority denied.

Bonnie Prince Charlie's flight after Culloden is legendary. He lived in hiding in the remote Highlands and Islands for months before being rescued by a French frigate. His narrow escape from Uist to Skye, dressed as Flora MacDonald's maid, is the subject of the 'Skye Boat Song'.

Supported by an army of Highlanders, he marched southwards and captured Edinburgh in September 1745. He got as far south as Derby in England, but success was short-lived; a Hanoverian army led by the Duke of Cumberland pushed him all the way back to the Highlands, where Jacobite dreams were finally extinguished at the Battle of Culloden in 1746. Many wounded Highlanders were executed by 'Butcher' Cumberland following the battle, but Charles escaped and fled to France via Skye, aided by Flora MacDonald; he later died in exile.

The Highland Clearances

In the aftermath of the Jacobite rebellions, the government outlawed the wearing of Highland dress and the playing of the bagpipes. The Highlands were put under military control and private armies were banned. The ties of kinship and duty that once marked the relationship between Highland laird and clansman gradually transformed into the merely economic relationship of landlord and tenant. Lands that had been confis-

THE LORDS OF THE ISLES

In medieval times, when overland travel through the Scottish Highlands was slow, difficult and dangerous, the sea lochs, kyles (narrow sea channels) and sounds of the west coast were the motorways of their time. Cut off from the rest of Scotland, but united by these sea roads, the west coast and islands were a world – and a kingdom – unto themselves. Dominated by Viking invaders for almost five centuries, the region later formed the heartland of the Lords of the Isles.

Descended from the legendary Somerled (a half-Gaelic, half-Norse warrior of the 12th century) the chiefs of Clan Donald claimed sovereignty over this watery kingdom. It was John Macdonald of Islay who first styled himself Dominus Insularum (Lord of the Isles) in 1353. He and his descendants ruled this vast territory from their headquarters at Finlaggan in Islay, backed up by fleets of swift birlinns and nyvaigs (Hebridean galleys), an intimate knowledge of the sea routes of the west, and a network of coastal castles that included Skipness, Dunstaffnage, Duart, Stalker, Dunvegan and Kisimul.

Clan Donald held sway over the isles, often in defiance of the Scottish king, from 1350 to 1493. At its greatest extent, in the second half of the 15th century, the Lordship of the Isles included all the islands on the west coast of Scotland, the west-coast mainland from Kintyre to Ross-shire, and the Antrim coast of northern Ireland. But in challenging the Scottish king for territory, and siding with the English king against him, Clan Donald finally pushed its luck too far.

Following a failed rebellion in 1493, the Lordship was forfeited to King James IV of Scotland, and the title has remained in possession of the Scottish, and later British, royal family ever since. 'Lord of the Isles' is one of the many titles held today by Prince Charles, heir to the British throne.

1603

James VI of Scotland inherits the English throne in the so-called Union of the Crowns, becoming James I of Great Britain.

1689

First Jacobite uprising, led by John Graham of Claverhouse ('Bonnie Dundee'); a rebel victory at Killiecrankie is soon followed by defeat, but rebellion prompts building of a government garrison at Fort William.

PATRICK HORTON/LONELY PLANET IMAGES ©

» Jacobite Steam Train (p166)

cated after 1745 were returned to their owners in the 1780s, but by then the chiefs had tasted the aristocratic high life and were tempted by the easy profits to be made from sheep farming.

So began the Highland Clearances, one of the most shameful episodes in Scottish history. By no means all of the people who left their homes in the late 18th and 19th centuries were forcibly evicted; in the Hebridean islands, for example, a combination of poverty, overcrowding and lack of suitable land led many to choose emigration. But some of the forced clearances, especially in Sutherland, were so brutal that newspaper reporting of the events caused a national scandal.

Under the pretext of agricultural 'improvement', the peasant farmers, no longer of any use as soldiers and uneconomical as tenants, were evicted from their homes and farms to make way for flocks of hardy Cheviot sheep – in the Highlands the year 1792 (when Cheviots were first introduced) was known for decades afterwards as *Bliadhna nan Caorach* (the Year of the Sheep). The most notorious events took place in Strathnaver, where Patrick Sellar – the factor (land agent) of the Duke of Sutherland – cleared people from their homes using dogs, and set fire to cottages while possessions were still inside. He was later charged with arson and culpable homicide, but was acquitted.

After the evictions a few cottars stayed behind to work the sheep farms, but most were relocated to desperate crofts on poor coastal land or fled to the cities in search of work. Many th   ousands emigrated – some willingly, some under duress – to the developing colonies of North America, Australia and New Zealand. All over the Highlands today, only a ruckle of stones among the bracken remains where once there were whole villages. The Mull of Oa on Islay, for example, once supported a population of 4000 – today there are barely 40 people there.

Although the Clearances took place two centuries ago, they remain an emotive subject in the Highlands today. They marked the final nail in the coffin of the old clan system, and the beginning of the depopulation of the Highlands, a process that is still going on. But it was rarely a straightforward story, and recent scholarship has challenged the popular image of poor tenants versus greedy landlords, claiming that in many cases the population pressure on marginal land had become unsustainable – something had to give. In bookshops from Oban to Inverness you'll find plenty of accounts of the Highland Clearances that offer food for thought.

Most clan tartans are in fact a 19th-century invention (long after the demise of the clan system), inspired partly by the writings of Sir Walter Scott.

Tartanry, Tourism & Deer-stalking

The pacification of the Highlands in the wake of the Jacobite rebellions led to a wave of adventurous travellers venturing north in search of the wild and the picturesque. The most famous of these were Samuel

1692	1707	1745–46	Late 1700s
The Massacre of Glencoe causes further rifts between those clans loyal to the crown and those loyal to the old ways.	Despite popular opposition, the Act of Union, which brings England and Scotland under one parliament, one sovereign and one flag, takes effect on 1 May.	The culmination of the Jacobite rebellions: Bonnie Prince Charlie lands in Scotland, gathers an army and marches south. He gains English territory but is eventually defeated at the Battle of Culloden.	Lowland Scotland flourishes during the Industrial Revolution, but the Highlands suffer the misery of the Clearances and mass emigration.

Johnson (compiler of the first *Dictionary of the English Language*) and his biographer James Boswell, who travelled to Inverness, Skye, Mull and Oban in 1773 and wrote separate accounts of their journey – both were bestsellers.

Tales of this 'primitive' and 'unspoilt' region proved irresistible to the emerging Romantic movement in art and literature. Poets and artists toured the Highlands in search of the sublime, including William Wordsworth and Samuel Taylor Coleridge in 1803, and artist JMW Turner in 1831, the latter in the company of Sir Walter Scott. Scott himself penned a series of hugely popular historical novels – notably *Waverley, Rob Roy* and *The Pirate* – and the epic poems *The Lady of the Lake* and *The Lord of the Isles,* all of which were set in the Highlands.

In fact, it was Scott who pretty much single-handedly invented the romantic, tartan-clad image of the Highlands. In 1822, Scott engineered a state visit to Edinburgh by King George IV – the first time a reigning British monarch had been to Scotland since 1650 – where the king was greeted by a stage-managed parade of Highlanders in traditional tartan costume. The king himself was persuaded to wear a kilt for the occasion, triggering a wave of tartan-mania amongst the English fashionable classes.

George's successor, Queen Victoria, fell utterly in love with the Highlands. Her consort Prince Albert purchased the Balmoral estate in 1852, and the royal couple spent their summer holidays there (a tradition maintained by the royal family to this day). After Albert's death in 1861, Victoria spent up to four months a year at Balmoral, often sneaking around the Highlands incognito in the company of her Scottish ghillie (attendant), John Brown.

All this provoked enormous interest in the Highlands among the British upper and middle classes, sparking a wave of tourism assisted by the spread of the railways, which reached Inverness by the 1850s, Wick and Thurso in 1874, Kyle of Lochalsh in 1897 and Mallaig in 1901. The trains linked to a dense network of steamer services that plied the coastal waters and islands from Glasgow all the way around the west and north coasts as far as Thurso.

In the second half of the 19th century a decline in the profitability of sheep farming combined with the emergence of a wealthy nouveau-riche class in England led to a new phenomenon: the rise of the Highland sporting estate. Struggling Highland chiefs sold off their ancient lands to rich merchants from the south, who ran them as private fiefdoms of salmon-fishing, grouse-shooting and deer-stalking. Today, more than 50% of the land area of the Highlands and Islands is occupied by around 340 private sporting estates, two-thirds of them owned by absentee landlords.

John Prebble's classic *The Highland Clearances* (1963) is an emotive account of this controversial period of history. Eric Richards' book of the same name from 2007 takes a more balanced look at the factual events.

1850–1900	1886	1914–1932	1919
The spread of the railways opens up the Highlands to tourism; wealthy southerners buy up huge tracts of land as sporting estates.	Rent strikes and land raids lead to the Crofters Holdings (Scotland) Act, which grants security of tenure to crofters for the first time.	Scottish industry slumps during WWI and collapses in its aftermath in the face of new Eastern production and the Great Depression. About 400,000 Scots emigrate between 1921 and 1931.	The surrendered German High Seas fleet, anchored in Orkney's Scapa Flow, is scuttled in a final act of defiance: 74 ships deliberately sunk.

Crofting

Up until the 19th century the most common form of farming settlement in the Highlands and Islands was the *baile,* a township consisting of a dozen or so families who farmed the land granted to them by the local chieftain in return for military service and a portion of the harvest. The arable land was divided into strips called rigs, which were allocated to different families by annual ballot so that each took turns at getting the poorer soils; this system was known as runrig. The families worked the land communally and their cattle shared the grazing land.

During the mass upheaval of the Highland Clearances, those who chose not to emigrate or move to the cities were forced to eke a living from narrow plots of marginal agricultural land, often close to the coast. This was a form of smallholding that became known as crofting. The small patch of land was not enough to produce a living on is own, and had to be supplemented by other work such as fishing and

The effects of the Clearances were exacerbated by the potato famine of the 1840s. Between 1841 and 1861 the western Highlands and Islands lost one third of its population, mostly through emigration.

POWER FROM THE GLENS

The high rainfall and rushing rivers of the Scottish Highlands led to the region being a world pioneer in the development of hydroelectric power. In 1896 the Foyers generating station on Loch Ness was the first large-scale hydroelectric scheme in Britain, powering one of the world's first electric aluminium smelters. Its success led the British Aluminium Company to build a much larger scheme based on the Blackwater Dam north of Glen Coe – in fact, it built a whole town at Kinlochleven to house workers from the smelter and the power station. By 1911, the Highlands of Scotland were producing one-third of the world's aluminium.

A vision of bringing investment, employment and electricity to the economically depressed Highlands spurred the government into creating the North of Scotland Hydro-Electric Board (motto: 'Power from the Glens'). Over the next few decades the Hydro Board masterminded a series of vast civil engineering projects from Loch Awe to Glen Affric: by 1965, 78 dams had been built, with 54 power stations providing a total generating capacity of over 1000 megawatts.

Conscious of criticism that these developments would be detrimental to areas of great scenic beauty, the board decreed that the power stations be designed by architects in Modernist and International styles using local stone, and some were concealed underground. Many sites are now tourist attractions, including the Cruachan power station at Loch Awe, and the salmon ladder beside the dam at Pitlochry power station.

With today's emphasis on renewable energy sources, hydro power is back in fashion, and has the potential to supply up to one quarter of Scotland's homes. The country's biggest recent civil engineering project is the Glendoe Dam, hidden in the hills to the east of Fort Augustus, which came online in 2009.

1939–45	1970s	1999–2005	2003
WWII sees the sea lochs of the Highlands used as marshalling areas for Arctic and Atlantic convoys. In Shetland, the Shetland Bus operation ferries agents and supplies to occupied Norway.	The discovery of oil and gas in the North Sea brings new prosperity to Aberdeen and the surrounding area, and also to the Orkney and Shetland Islands.	Scottish parliament is convened for the first time on 12 May 1999. Among the first policies to be enacted are the reform of land laws, and the recognition of Gaelic as an official language.	Land Reform Act establishes the right of responsible access to private land, and the right of communities to buy the land they live on.

kelp-gathering. Tenure was always precarious, as tenancies were granted on a year-by-year basis, and there was no guarantee of benefiting from any improvements made – on a whim of the landlord, a crofter could be evicted and lose not only the farm but also the house they'd built on it.

The economic depression of the late 19th century meant that many crofters couldn't pay their rent. This time, however, the people resisted eviction, creating instead the Highland Land League and their own political movement, the Crofters Party. Several of their demands were met by the government in the Crofters' Holdings Act of 1886, including security of tenure and fair rents.

But it failed to address the issue of the lack of land for new crofts. More rent strikes and land raids (occupations) followed, most famously in the Isle of Lewis, where a monument recalls the Pairc Deer Raid of 1887, when several hundred crofters killed a large number of deer in protest at their landlord's clearing of crofts to make way for deer-stalking. Police and troops were sent to quell this 'riot', an over-reaction that only generated more public sympathy for the crofters.

Further legislation improved the situation, but it wasn't until 1976 that crofters won the right to purchase their own land and become owner-occupiers. Today in the Highlands and Islands there are around 18,000 crofts (smallholdings) averaging 5 hectares in area, supporting a crofting population of around 33,000 people.

2010

Links of Noltland emerges as one of the most important archaeological sites in Scotland, with the discovery of a second clay figurine to match the famous 5000-year-old 'Westray Wife'.

2011

These days, around 340 private sporting estates occupy more than 50% of the land in Scotland's Highlands and Islands. Most of these estates are owned by absentee landlords.

» Arkle looks over Loch Stack and its valley of heather

Highland Culture

Literature
Gaelic Poetry

Little has survived of early Gaelic literature, although the monks of Iona and other Scottish monasteries are known to have written in their native language as well as in Latin. But as descendants of the Celts, the Gaels had a strong bardic tradition, with songs, poems, stories and stirring tales of historic events passed down from generation to generation by word of mouth.

Alexander Macdonald (Alasdair Mac Mhaighstir Alasdair; 1695–1770), a schoolmaster from Moidart, is widely regarded as one of the finest of Gaelic poets, and was a genuine bard of the Clanranald Macdonalds. An ardent Jacobite, he gathered with the clans at Glenfinnan in 1745, and fought at Culloden the following year. His poetry ranged from minute descriptions of nature and wildlife to satirical and political verse, as well as songs in praise of Bonnie Prince Charlie.

Another bard who fought in the Jacobite wars was Duncan Ban Mac-Intyre (Donnchadh Bàn Mac an t-Saoir; 1724–1812) of Glen Orchy. But 'Fair Duncan', as he was known, fought on the Hanoverian side under the Duke of Argyll. He was also illiterate, and his beautiful nature poems were composed and stored in his memory before being dictated for someone else to write down. A prominent monument to him stands on a hilltop above Dalmally.

The greatest Gaelic poet of modern times was Sorley MacLean (Somhairle MacGill-Eain; 1911–96) from the Isle of Raasay. He was a teacher who wrote powerfully about the Highland Clearances, the Spanish Civil War and WWII, but who also produced some of the 20th century's most moving and delicate love poetry.

MacLean's contemporary, Lewis-born Iain Crichton Smith (1928–98) was one of the most prolific writers of Gaelic poetry (though he also wrote widely in English). Notable collections include *Burn is Aran* (*Water and Bread*) and *Na Guthan* (*Voices*); his *Towards the Human* is a fine collection of essays and poems on Gaelic life.

No mention of Gaelic literature would be complete without a word about the poet and politican James Macpherson (1736–96), from Ruthven (near Kingussie), who caused a huge stir in 1761 with the publication of *Fingal, an Ancient Epic Poem in Six Books*. An avid collector of Gaelic poetry, Macpherson claimed to have discovered the works of Ossian, a 3rd-century Gaelic bard. *Fingal* and two subsequent volumes of Ossian's poetry were denounced as fake – Macpherson never produced the original Gaelic manuscripts – but nevertheless proved enormously popular. The epic poems were translated into several European languages, and strongly influenced the emerging Romantic movement. (The poems were also responsible for the naming of Fingal's Cave on the Isle of Staffa.)

An Leabhar Mor: The Great Book of Gaelic is a collection of 100 Gaelic poems (with English translations) dating from AD 600 to the present day, accompanied by specially commissioned artworks. Described as a '21st-century Book of Kells', it can be viewed online at www .leabharmor.net.

GAELIC POETRY

20th-century Highland Writers

The poet and storyteller George Mackay Brown (1921–96) was born in Stromness (in the Orkney Islands), and lived there almost all his life. Although his poems and novels are rooted in Orkney, his work transcends local and national boundaries. His novel *Greenvoe* (1972) is a warm, witty and poetic evocation of everyday life in an Orkney community; his last novel, *Beside the Ocean of Time* (1994), is a wonderfully elegiac account of remote island life. His poetry has been published in collections such as *Travellers* (2001) and *Collected Poems: 1954–1992* (2005).

Another Orcadian worth looking out for is poet Edwin Muir (1887–1959), who wrote longingly about Orkney from his later life in Glasgow, and wrote the interesting travelogue *Highland Journey* in 1935.

Norman McCaig (1910–96) was born in Edinburgh but came from a Harris family and is widely regarded as the finest Scottish poet of his generation. He wrote eloquently about the Highlands and Islands – his poem 'Climbing Suilven' is a superb description of what it feels like to climb a mountain, its images instantly recognisable to any hillwalker. *Selected Poems* is probably the best collection of his work.

The hugely popular writer Neil Munro (1863–1930), born in Inverarary (in Argyll), is responsible for some of the best-loved books about the region, including the humorous *Tales of Para Handy*, featuring a rascally skipper and his boat the *Vital Spark*, which have been repeatedly dramatised on television, radio and the stage.

Caithness writer Neil M Gunn (1891–1973), born in Dunbeath, is celebrated as the best Scottish novelist of the 20th century, penning such evocative tales as *Morning Tide* and *The Silver Darlings*, a book about the herring industry. Sir Compton MacKenzie (1883–1972) spent much

---

Five Essential Highland Novels

» *Waverley* (1814, Sir Walter Scott)

» *The Silver Darlings* (1941, Neil M Gunn)

» *Whisky Galore* (1947, Compton MacKenzie)

» *Consider the Lilies* (1968, Iain Crichton Smith)

» *Greenvoe* (1972, George Mackay Brown)

THE GAELIC LANGUAGE

Scottish Gaelic (*Gàidhlig* – pronounced 'gah-lic' in Scotland) is spoken by about 80,000 people in Scotland, mainly in the Highlands and Islands. It is a member of the Celtic branch of the Indo-European family of languages, which has given us Gaelic, Irish, Manx, Welsh, Cornish and Breton.

Although Scottish Gaelic is the Celtic language most closely associated with Scotland, it was quite a latecomer to these shores. Other Celtic languages, namely Pictish and Brittonic, had existed prior to the arrival and settlement by Gaelic-speaking Celts from Ireland around the 5th century AD. These Irish settlers, known to the Romans as *Scotti*, were eventually to give their name to the entire country. As their territorial influence extended so did their language, and from the 9th to the 11th centuries Gaelic was spoken throughout the country. For many centuries the language was the same as the language of Ireland; there is little evidence of much divergence before the 13th century. Even up to the 18th century the bards adhered to the strict literary standards of Old Irish.

Gaelic culture flourished in the Highlands until the 18th century and the Jacobite rebellions. After the Battle of Culloden in 1746 many Gaelic speakers were forced from their ancestral lands, and the use of Gaelic was discouraged in favour of English. Although still studied at academic level, the spoken language declined, being regarded as little more than a mere 'peasant' language of no modern significance.

It was only in the 1970s that Gaelic began to make a comeback with a new generation of young enthusiasts who were determined that it should not be allowed to die. After two centuries of decline, the language is now being encouraged through financial help from government agencies and the EU. Gaelic education is flourishing from playgroups to tertiary levels, flowing on into the fields of music, literature, cultural events and broadcasting; now people from all over Scotland, and even worldwide, are beginning to appreciate their Gaelic heritage.

of his life on the island of Barra, where he is buried; his famous comedy *Whisky Galore* (made into a successful film in 1949) is based on the true story of islanders rescuing a cargo of whisky from the wreck of a ship off the island of Eriskay.

Scott & Stevenson

Sir Walter Scott (1771–1832) was Scotland's greatest and most prolific novelist. Although he was the son of an Edinburgh lawyer, and very much a lowlander, Scott was a student of Highland history and legend, and many of his works are set north of the Highland line.

Scott's early works were rhyming ballads, such as *The Lady of the Lake* (set in the Trossachs, about a medieval war between Highland clans and lowland nobles) and *The Lord of the Isles* (about Robert the Bruce), both of which created a surge of tourism to their Highland settings.

His first historical novel – Scott effectively invented the genre – was *Waverley,* which recounted the adventures of Edward Waverley, a young English soldier who is sent north in 1745 to fight with the Hanoverian army against the Jacobites. It was published anonymously (in those days novels were considered a poor relation to poetry, and Scott wanted to be taken seriously as a poet), but was so successful that he could not refuse the demand for more. The so-called Waverley novels included more on a Highland theme, including *Rob Roy,* about the notorious MacGregor outlaw, and *The Pirate,* based on the life of John Gow, an Orkney adventurer.

Along with Scott, Robert Louis Stevenson (1850–94) ranks among Scotland's best-known novelists. Born in Edinburgh into a family of famous lighthouse engineers, Stevenson is known and loved around the world for classic tales that include *Kidnapped!,* set in the Highlands in the aftermath of Culloden, and *The Master of Ballantrae*, about a family torn in two by the Jacobite wars.

The website www .scottish-folk -music.com is a useful source for listings of folk sessions, gigs, venues and bands, as well as providing the lyrics for popular Scottish folk songs.

Music & Dance
Traditional Music

The Highlands and Islands have always had a strong folk tradition, and in the 1960s the roots revival provided a forum for the Gaelic songs of Cathy-Ann MacPhee from Barra and Margaret Stewart from Lewis. Initially, most of the performers came from outside the region, but the arrival of the Boys of the Lough, headed by Shetland fiddler Aly Bain, introduced the world to authentic Highland folk music. Aly was probably the most influential folk musician Scotland has seen. He brought pipes, concertinas, mandolins and other traditional instruments to a wide audience, recording with performers such as Tom Anderson and Phil Cunningham.

Other much-admired fiddlers include Scott Skinner, Willie Hunter and Catriona MacDonald, who studied under the same master fiddler as Aly Bain.

The traditional melodies of the Highlands and Islands reached a broader audience through the Gaelic compositions of Skye band Runrig, who transformed *ceilidh* music into stadium rock in the two decades following their formation in 1973. Other powerful ambassadors for Gaelic music included Capercaillie, Ossian and the Battlefield Band, which have both seen plenty of Highland and Island musicians in their line-ups.

In recent years there has been a revival in traditional music, often adapted and updated for the modern age. Bands such as Shooglenifty blend Scottish folk music with anything from indie rock to electronica, producing a hybrid that has been called 'acid croft'.

A *ceilidh* is an evening of traditional Scottish entertainment including music, song and dance. To find one, check the village noticeboard, or just ask at the local pub; visitors are always welcome to join in.

The Scots folk songs that you will often hear sung in pubs, at folk festivals and at *ceilidhs* draw on Scotland's rich history. A huge number of the songs relate to the Jacobite rebellions in the 18th century and, in particular, to Bonnie Prince Charlie – *Hey Johnnie Cope,* the *Skye Boat Song* and *Will Ye No Come Back Again,* for example – while others relate to themes of working the land, emigration and the Highland Clearances.

Bagpipes

Although no piece of film footage about Scotland is complete without the drone of the pipes, this curious instrument actually originated in ancient Egypt and was brought to Scotland by the Romans. Highland soldiers were traditionally accompanied into battle by the skirl of the pipes, and the Scottish Highland bagpipe is unique in being the only musical instrument ever to be classed as a weapon.

In 1747, the playing of the pipes was banned – under pain of death – by the British government in 1747 as part of a scheme to suppress Highland culture after the Jacobite uprising of 1745, but the pipes were revived when Highland regiments were drafted into the British army towards the end of the 18th century.

The bagpipe consists of a leather bag held under the arm, kept inflated by blowing through the blowstick; the piper forces air through the pipes by squeezing the bag with the forearm. Three of the pipes, known as drones, play a constant note (one bass, two tenor) in the background. The fourth pipe, the chanter, plays the melody.

Queen Victoria did much to repopularise the bagpipes with her patronage of all things Scottish. When staying at Balmoral she liked to be wakened by a piper playing outside her window. Competitive piping is still a popular pastime in the Highlands and Islands – the sound of duelling bagpipes is quite an experience.

Scotland's most famous instrument has been reinvented by bands like the Red Hot Chilli Pipers, who use pipes, drums, guitars and keyboards to create rock versions of traditional tunes that have been christened (tongue firmly in cheek) as 'Jock 'n' Roll'. They feature regularly at festivals throughout the country.

Highland Dancing

Another homespun art form that the Scots have made their own is dance. The most famous dances are the formal Highland Dances performed at Highland Games, which date back to the foundation of Scotland. There are four official dance disciplines: the Sword Dance, Seann Triubhas, the Reel of Tulloch and the Highland fling.

The Sword Dance, or *gillie callum*, dates back to the legend that Malcolm Canmore celebrated his victory over a Macbeth chieftain by dancing over a crucifix made from his own claymore (sword) and the sword of his rival. The Seann Triubhas is attributed to the desire of Highlanders to shake off the hated *triubhas* (trousers) they were forced to wear after the 1745 rebellion.

A chilly congregation who danced to keep warm are credited with inventing the Reel of Tulloch, while the famous Highland fling was invented in the 1790s to mimic the movements of a stag; clansmen reputedly danced the steps on their targes (leather-covered shields).

Sport
Highland Games

According to oral tradition, Highland games date back to the kingdom of Dalriada and were essentially war games, allowing clan leaders to

---

TARTAN

The original Scottish Highland dress was not the kilt but the plaid, a long length of tartan cloth wrapped around the body and over the shoulder. The modern kilt only appeared in the 18th century and was reputedly invented by Thomas Rawlinson, an Englishman!

This distinctive checked pattern, traditionally associated with the kilt, has become the definitive symbol of Scotland and the Highlands, inspiring skirts, scarves, blankets, ties, key-fobs and a thousand other saleable souvenirs. The pattern is thought to date back to at least the Roman period, though it has become romantically associated with the Gaels, who arrived from Ireland in the 6th century. What is certain is that a tartan plaid had become the standard uniform of Highlanders by the start of 18th century. Following the Battle of Culloden in 1746, the Disarming Act banned the wearing of Highland dress in an attempt to undermine the solidarity of the clans.

However, the ban was enforced only in the Highlands (it was repealed in 1782) and did not apply to the armed services, which in the second half of the 18th century included a large number of Highland regiments. The weaver William Wilson established a factory at Bannockburn to supply the army with tartan, experimenting with a wide range of new designs and colours. In 1778, the London Highland Society requested that clan chiefs submit a piece of their clan tartan to preserve the traditional designs, but most of the tartans recorded by the society were actually designed and woven by the Wilsons.

In the 19th century, tartan got caught up in the cult of so-called 'Balmorality' – Queen Victoria's patronage of Scottish culture – and many of the setts (tartan patterns) now associated with particular clans were created out of thin air by a pair of brothers known as the Sobieski Stuarts, who claimed descent from Bonnie Prince Charlie. The brothers' setts were based on a 'lost' document dating back to the 15th century and they published a hugely successful book of invented tartans, *The Costume of the Clans,* which became established as the genuine tartans of many Highland clans before their elaborate fraud was exposed. Today every clan, and indeed every football team, has one or more distinctive tartans, though few date back more than 150 years.

---

select their most skilled warriors for battle. In the 11th century, King Malcolm Canmore is believed to have staged a royal contest to find the fastest runners in the kingdom to carry his messages across the Highlands.

Historical evidence for a tradition of annual clan games is rather patchy but the games certainly took off in the 19th century with the creation of the first Highland Societies. In 1848 Queen Victoria patronised the Braemar Highland Games and the tradition was incorporated into Highland legend.

Most of the activities in the games are based on equipment readily available to the average Highlander in ages past. The hammer throw was derived from the traditional mell used to drive fence-posts, while steel-yard weights were thrown for distance and height. The caber (from the Gaelic for 'tree') was simply a tree trunk, and rounded river stones were used for putting the stone.

These days the traditional sporting events are accompanied by piping and dancing competitions, and attract both locals and tourists alike. Games are held all over Scotland from May to September, with the biggest events staged at Dunoon, Oban and Braemar. You can find the dates and details about Highland games at the website for VisitScotland (p358).

Shinty

Shinty (*camanachd* in Gaelic) is a fast and physical ball-and-stick sport similar to Ireland's hurling, with more than a little resemblance to clan warfare. It's an indigenous Scottish game played mainly in the Highlands, and the most prized trophy is the Camanachd Cup. The cup final, held in September, is a great Gaelic get-together. The Fort William team has dominated in recent times, winning the cup every year from 2007

While Scotland is the home of golf, it's more a lowland than a Highland game. Nevertheless, there are some top-notch courses in the Highlands, including Royal Dornoch, Brora, Tain and Nairn. The 1891 Askernish course in South Uist was restored in 2008 after lying unused and overgrown for decades.

to 2010. The venue for the final is announced annually in February (see www.shinty.com).

Each year in October there's an international match between Scotland and Ireland, played under composite shinty/hurling rules, and held alternately in Ireland and Scotland.

Curling

Curling, a winter sport which involves propelling a granite stone weighing 42lb (19kg) along the ice towards a target, was probably invented in Scotland in medieval times. Though traditionally Scottish, it was very much a minority sport until it got an enormous publicity boost when the British women's team (all Scots) won the gold medal in the 2002 Winter Olympics.

Scottish teams took gold in the men's world championship in 2006 and 2009, and silver in 2011; and silver in the women's world championship in 2010. For more information, see royalcaledoniancurlingclub.org.

Landscape & Wildlife

Scotland's wildlife is one of its big attractions, and the best way to see it is to get out there: pull on the boots, sling on the binoculars, go quietly and see what you can spot. Many species that have disappeared from or are rare in the rest of Britain survive here.

Of course, most animals you'll see will be in fields or getting in your way on single-track roads. Several indigenous sheep varieties are still around, smaller and stragglier than the purpose-bred supermodels we're used to. Other emblematic domestic animals include the Shetland pony and the gentle Highland cow, with its horns and shaggy reddish-brown coat and fringe.

The thistle is commonly used as a Scottish emblem, but the national flower is the Scottish bluebell (*Campanula rotundifolia*) which carpets woodland floors in spring. Loch Lomond is a good place to see them.

Geography & Geology

Scotland covers 30,414 sq miles, about half the size of England. It can be divided into three areas: Southern Uplands, Central Lowlands, and the Highlands and Islands.

South of a line joining Dunbar to Girvan lie the Southern Uplands, a range of rounded, heathery hills bordering England. The Central Lowlands comprise a broad slice from Edinburgh and Dundee in the east to Glasgow and Ayr in the west, home to the industrial belt and 80% of Scotland's population.

The Highland Boundary Fault, a geological feature, runs northeast from Helensburgh (west of Glasgow) to Stonehaven (south of Aberdeen) on the east coast. North of it lie the Highlands and Islands, a mountainous area that makes up roughly two-thirds of the country. However, the low-lying, fertile agricultural belt that runs along the northeast coast from Aberdeen to Fraserburgh is usually lumped together, geographically and culturally, with the lowlands.

The Highland hills – most summits reach the 900m to 1000m mark – were deeply dissected by glaciers during the last Ice Age, creating a series of deep, U-shaped valleys. The long, narrow sea lochs that today are such a feature of Highland scenery are, like Norway's fjords, glacial valleys that have been flooded by rising sea levels. Despite their pristine beauty, the wild, empty landscapes of the western and northern Highlands are artificial wildernesses. Before the Highland Clearances (p332) many of these empty corners of Scotland supported sizable rural populations.

Of Scotland's 790 islands, 130 are inhabited. To the west are the Inner Hebrides (from Islay to Skye) and the Outer Hebrides (Barra to Lewis). To the north are two other island groups, Orkney and Shetland, the northernmost outposts of the British Isles.

Moor & Mountain

Most of the Highland landscape consists of uncultivated heather moorland, peat bog and steep rocky mountains. Heather, whose tiny pink and purple flowers emerge on moor and mountain in August, is one of the symbols of Scotland, and also an excellent food source for the red grouse, an important game bird.

Peat bog – an endangered environment – covers large areas of the Highlands and Islands, most notably in the Flow Country of Caithness and Sutherland, where it provides a haven for unusual plant species, such as the insect-eating sundew, and a nesting ground for birds that include golden plover, hen harrier, and red-throated diver.

Britain's largest land animal, the red deer, is present in large numbers, managed as a sporting asset for hunting estates. You're bound to see them if you spend any time in the Highlands; in winter especially, some are quite content to wander down the village street in the evening and crop the roadside verges.

On the high mountain tops, and especially in the subarctic climate of the Cairngorm plateau, alpine plants thrive alongside bird species such as the snow bunting and the ptarmigan (a type of grouse). Seldom seen below 700m, the ptarmigan has feathered feet and is the only British bird that plays the Arctic trick of changing its plumage from mottled brown in summer to dazzling white in winter, the better to blend in with the snowfields. Another mountain resident that displays this feature is the blue mountain hare.

Perhaps the most majestic wildlife sight on moor and mountain is the golden eagle, which uses its 2m wingspan to soar on rising thermals. Almost all of the 400 or so pairs known to nest in the UK are to be found in the Scottish Highlands and Islands, preferring remote glens and open moorland well away from human habitation.

The grassland habitat of the once-common corncrake (a summer visitor from Africa) was almost completely wiped out by modern farming methods, but it still breeds in pockets of sedge and iris in the Hebrides, including nature reserves in Islay, Coll and the Uists. Listen for their distinctive *krek-krek-krek* call – like a thumbnail drawn along the teeth of a comb.

Scotland accounts for one third of the British mainland's surface area, but it has a massive 80% of Britain's coastline and only 10% of its population.

WINDING BACK THE CLOCK

Over the centuries many species have disappeared from Scotland, hunted into oblivion or left in the lurch after the destruction of their habitat or food supply. As a means of increasing biodiversity, there's a strong case for bringing some of them back. Though it has detractors, reintroduction of species has been implemented successfully in several instances. The red kite and the majestic white-tailed eagle, both absent from Britain since the 19th century, are now soaring in Scottish skies again. The former, distinguishable by their yellow beak and talons, are found along the west coast and in the Hebrides, particularly on Mull and Skye – visitors can watch a nesting site via TV cameras at Aros Experience on Skye.

The European beaver was released into the Scottish wilds in 2009, a move opposed by some campaigners, who felt beavers might negatively impact the forests or water quality; the situation is being carefully monitored. The first beaver kits (young) were spotted in an Argyll forest in the summer of 2010 (p70). But the mildly controversial beaver pales beside events at the Alladale estate: the owner has already shipped in elk (moose), and wants to go for wolves next (p227).

One of Scotland's most thrilling sights is the salmon's leap up a fast-flowing cascade, resolutely returning to the river of its birth several years before. The salmon's life begins in early spring, hatching in a gravel bed of a stream in some Scottish glen. Called 'fry' at this stage and only an inch long, they stay for a couple of years, growing through the 'parr' stage to become 'smolt', when they head out to sea.

Their destination could be anywhere in the North Atlantic, but eventually, sometimes after several years, they return home to reproduce – scientists think they may use the Earth's magnetic field to navigate on the journey. Arriving all through the year, but most commonly in late spring, they regain strength after the arduous journey and spawn in late autumn. That job done, the salmon dies and the cycle begins anew.

Forest & Woodland

Although much of the Highlands was originally covered by the Caledonian forest – vast swathes of Scots pine in the inland glens, with coastal woods of oak, silver birch, alder and rowan – deforestation has reduced this to a few small pockets of native woodland; barely 1% remains. Important remnants of native Scots pine can be found at Rothiemurchus, Glen Affric and Beinn Eighe.

Managed regeneration forests are slowly covering more of the landscape, especially in the Highlands. Some 5000 sq miles (1.3 million hectares) of tree cover – 17% of the land area – now exists: not a huge figure compared to a worldwide average of 30%, but an improvement on what it was. About a third of this is controlled by the government's Forestry Commission which, as well as conducting managed logging, dedicates large areas of it to sustainable recreational use. The vast majority of this tree cover is coniferous, and there's a plan to increase it to 25% of land area by 2050.

Scotland's woods are home to 75% of Britain's red squirrel population; they've been pushed out in most of the rest of the country by the dominant greys, native to North America. The greys often carry a virus that's lethal to the reds, so measures are in place to try to prevent their further encroachment.

Other forest mammals that were slaughtered to the point of extermination in the 19th century include pine martens, polecats and wildcats. Populations of these are small and remote, but are slowly recovering thanks to their protected status and greater awareness.

The capercaillie, a black, turkeylike member of the grouse family, and the largest native British bird, was hunted to extinction in 1785 – then reintroduced from Sweden in 1837. Though still rare, it still inhabits forests of native Scots pine, notably in Rothiemurchus.

River & Loch

It rains a real lot in Scotland – some parts of the western Highlands get over 4500mm of rain a year, making it the wettest place in Europe – so it's not surprising there's plenty of water about. Around 90% by volume of Britain's fresh water is in Scotland; Loch Ness alone contains more than double the volume of water in all of the lakes in England and Wales combined.

The most iconic of Scottish fish is the Atlantic salmon, which fights its way up Highland rivers to spawn. Salmon arrive in different rivers at different times of year between March and October, and are usually seen leaping waterfalls; good places to spot them include Pitlochry fish ladder and the Falls of Shin.

OTTERS

One of the best-loved pieces of Scottish wildlife writing is *Ring of Bright Water* by Gavin Maxwell, in which the author describes life on the remote Glenelg peninsula with his pet otters in the 1960s.

As much as the untamed wildness of Scotland lifts the spirit, another of the country's delights is a more managed beauty — its numerous gardens, which emerge from harsh winter with a riotous explosion of colour in spring and summer. In the 19th century, every castle and stately home worth its salt had a planned garden in the grounds; the milder parts of the country, particularly the Gulf Stream–warmed west coast, are absolutely studded with them.

From Benmore Botanic Garden in the south to Inverewe Garden in the north, there's a great deal more variety than anyone could reasonably expect at these latitudes. Among the most popular blooms with visitors are the colourful displays of rhododendrons and azaleas, introduced to Scotland from the Himalayas by 19th-century estate owners, which add a blaze of pink, purple, red and yellow to many a Highland hillside in May and June.

The National Trust for Scotland (p359) manages many of the finest gardens; its website is a good first stop to plan a route among the blooms.

The majestic osprey (a fish-eating bird of prey absent from Scotland for most of the 20th century) nests in Scotland from mid-March through to September, after migrating from West Africa. There are around 200 breeding pairs and you can see nesting sites throughout the country, notably at Loch Garten in the Cairngorms.

Coast & Islands

The waters off Scotland's north and west coasts are rich in marine mammals. Harbour porpoises are the most common sighting, though common and bottle-nosed dolphins are also seen. Minke whales are regular summer visitors, and orcas (killer whales) are regularly sighted around Shetland and Orkney.

Seals are widespread. Both the Atlantic grey seal (identified by its Roman nose) and the common seal (with a face shaped more like a dog's) are easily spotted along the coasts, especially in the islands.

Otters are widespread in the Highlands and Islands. They frequent both fresh and salt water, but are easiest to spot along the coast, where they time their foraging to coincide with an ebbing tide (river otters tend to be nocturnal). The best places to spot them are in the north and west, especially in Orkney, Shetland, Skye and the Outer Hebrides. The piers at Kyle of Lochalsh and Portree are otter 'hot spots', as the animals have learned to scavenge from fishing boats.

From May to August the sea cliffs of Orkney and Shetland and the north and west coasts of Scotland support some of the largest breeding colonies of seabirds in Europe, including 60% of the world's population of gannets and great skuas. Twenty-one of the British Isles' 24 breeding seabird species can be seen in Shetland, nesting in huge colonies: being entertained by the clownish antics of the puffins is a highlight for many visitors.

Scottish Environment LINK, the umbrella body for Scotland's voluntary environmental organisations, includes 36 bodies committed to environmental sustainability.

National Parks & Nature Reserves

Scotland has two national parks – Loch Lomond & the Trossachs National Park (p49) and the Cairngorms National Park (p127). But national parks are only part of the story. There's a huge range of protected areas with a bewildering array of 25 distinct classifications. Fifty-one National Nature Reserves span the country, and there are also marine areas under various levels of protection.

News on endangered Scottish birds has generally been positive in the last couple of decades. The Royal Society for the Protection of Birds (p317) is active here, with 34 reserves in the Highlands and Islands, and has overseen several success stories, including the reintroduction of the white-tailed eagle and the red kite.

Environmental Issues

Scotland's abundance of wind and water means the government hasn't had to look far for sources of renewable energy. The grand plan is to generate half of the country's energy needs from renewable sources by 2020, and things look to be well on track. Scotland has been a European leader in the development of wind technology; wind farms now dot the hills and firths (estuaries), and the near-constant breeze in some areas means record-breaking output from some turbines.

The problem is that although everyone agrees that wind power is clean and economical, there's a powerful NIMBY (Not In My Back Yard) element who don't want the windmills spoiling their view. And it's not just the whirring blades, of course. A remote Highland wind farm is one thing, but the power lines trailing all the way down to the south have a significant visual and environmental impact.

One of Scotland's major goals over the last decade or so has been to halt a worrying decline in biodiversity on land, in the air and in the sea. You can see progress reports on the Scottish Natural Heritage website, but a huge threat to existing species is, of course, climate change. A rise of a few degrees across the north would leave plenty of mountain plants and creatures with no place to go; it's already been speculated that the steady decline in Scotland's seabird population since the early '90s is partly caused by a temperature-induced decrease in certain plankton species.

The main cause of the worrying level of some fish stocks is clear: we've eaten them all. In 2010, the Marine (Scotland) Act was passed – it's a compromise solution that tries to both protect vulnerable marine areas and stocks and sustain the flagging fishing industry. But it may well be too little, too late.

Scottish Bird watching Top 10 List

» Golden Eagle
» White-tailed Eagle
» Osprey
» Capercaillie
» Ptarmigan
» Scottish Crossbill
» Crested Tit
» Corncrake
» Red-Necked Phalarope
» Great Skua

LANDSCAPE & WILDLIFE

The Scottish Larder

Traditional Scottish cookery is all about basic comfort food: solid, nourishing fare, often high in fat, that would keep you warm on a winter's day spent in the fields or out fishing, and sweet treats to come home to in the evening.

But a new culinary style known as Modern Scottish has emerged over the last two decades. It's a style that should be familiar to fans of Californian Cuisine and Mod Oz (Australian). Chefs take top-quality Scottish produce – from Highland venison, Aberdeen Angus beef and freshly landed seafood to root vegetables, raspberries and Scottish cheeses – and prepare it simply, in a way that enhances the natural flavours, often adding a French, Italian or Asian twist.

Scotland's traditional drinks – whisky and beer – have also found a new lease of life in recent years, with single malts being marketed like fine wines, and a new breed of microbreweries springing up all over the country.

A Caledonian Feast by Annette Hope is a fascinating and readable history of Scottish cuisine, providing a wealth of historical and sociological background.

Scottish Specialties

Mince & Tatties

Haggis may be the national dish that Scotland is most famous for, but when it comes to what Scottish people actually cook and eat most often, the hands-down winner has to be mince and tatties (potatoes). Minced beef, browned in the pan and then stewed slowly with onion, carrot and gravy, is served with mashed potatoes (with a splash of milk and a knob of butter added during the mashing) – it's tasty, warming and you don't even have to chew it.

The Full Scottish

Surprisingly not many Scots eat porridge for breakfast – these days a cappuccino and a croissant is just as likely – and even fewer eat it in the

FOOD COSTS

In this guide, eating choices are flagged with price indicators based on the cost of an average main course from the dinner menu:

» £ Budget: mains less than £9
» ££ Midrange: mains £9 to £18
» £££ Top end: mains more than £18

Lunch mains are often cheaper than dinner mains, however, and many places offer an 'early bird' special with lower prices (usually available between 5pm and 7pm). See the Directory chapter for restaurant opening hours.

Scotland's national dish is often ridiculed because of its ingredients, which admittedly don't sound promising – the finely chopped lungs, heart and liver of a sheep, mixed with oatmeal and onion and stuffed into a sheep's stomach bag. However, it actually tastes surprisingly good.

Haggis should be served with champit tatties and bashed neeps (mashed potatoes and turnips), with a generous dollop of butter and a good sprinkling of black pepper.

Although it's eaten year-round, haggis is central to the celebrations of 25 January, which honour Scotland's national poet, Robert Burns. Scots worldwide unite on Burns Night to revel in their Scottishness. A piper announces the arrival of the haggis and Burns' poem *Address to a Haggis* is recited to this 'Great chieftan o' the puddin-race'. The bulging haggis is then lanced with a dirk (dagger) to reveal the steaming offal within: 'warm, reekin, rich'.

Vegetarians (and quite a few carnivores, no doubt) will be relieved to know that veggie haggis is available in some restaurants.

traditional way: with salt to taste, but no sugar. The breakfast offered in a B&B or hotel usually consists of fruit juice and cereal or muesli, followed by a choice of bacon, sausage, black pudding (a type of sausage made from dried blood), grilled tomato, mushrooms and a fried egg or two. If you're lucky, there'll be tattie scones (fried potato bread) as well.

Fish for breakfast may sound strange, but was not unusual in crofting (smallholding) and fishing communities, where seafood was a staple; many hotels still offer grilled kippers (smoked herrings) for breakfast, or smoked haddock poached in milk and served with a poached egg – delicious with lots of buttered toast.

It's illegal to import haggis into the USA, as the US government has declared that sheep lungs are unfit for human consumption.

Broth, Skink & Bree

Scotch broth, made with mutton stock, barley, lentils and peas, is nutritious and tasty, while cock-a-leekie is a hearty soup made with chicken and leeks. Warming vegetable soups include leek and potato soup, and lentil soup (vegetarians beware: it's traditionally made using ham stock).

Seafood soups include the delicious Cullen skink, made with smoked haddock, potato, onion and milk, and *partan bree* (crab soup).

Surf & Turf

Steak eaters will enjoy a thick fillet of world-famous Aberdeen Angus beef, and beef from Highland cattle is also much sought after. Venison from red deer is leaner and appears on many menus. Both may be served with a wine-based or creamy whisky sauce. And of course there's haggis, Scotland's much-maligned national dish.

Scottish salmon is famous worldwide, but there's a big difference between the now-ubiquitous farmed salmon (even the certified organic farmed salmon) and the leaner, tastier and considerably more expensive wild fish. Also, there are concerns over the environmental impact of salmon farms on the marine environment. Smoked salmon is traditionally dressed with a squeeze of lemon juice and eaten with fresh brown bread and butter. Trout, the salmon's smaller cousin – whether wild, rod-caught brown trout or farmed rainbow trout – is delicious fried in oatmeal.

Popular Scottish TV chef Nick Nairn's book *Wild Harvest* contains over 100 recipes based on the use of fresh, seasonal Scottish produce.

As an alternative to kippers you may be offered Arbroath smokies (lightly smoked fresh haddock), traditionally eaten cold. Herring fillets fried in oatmeal are good, if you don't mind picking out a few bones. Mackerel pâté and smoked or peppered mackerel (both served cold) are also popular.

OAT CUISINE

'Oats: a grain, which in England is generally given to horses, but in Scotland appears to support the people.' – From *A Dictionary of the English Language* by Samuel Johnson (1709–84)

The most distinctive feature of traditional Scottish cookery is the abundant use of oatmeal. Oats grow well in the cool, wet climate of Scotland and have been cultivated here for at least two thousand years. Up to the 19th century, oatmeal was the main source of calories for the rural Scottish population. The crofter in his field, the cattle drover on the road to market, the soldier on the march – all would carry with them a bag of meal that could be mixed with water and baked on a girdle (a flat metal plate) or on hot stones beside a fire.

Long despised as an inferior foodstuff (see Johnson's sneering description above), oatmeal is enjoying a return to popularity as research has proved it to be highly nutritious (high in iron, calcium and B vitamins) and healthy (rich in soluble fibre, which helps to reduce cholesterol).

The best-known Scottish oatmeal dish is, of course, porridge, which is simply rolled oatmeal boiled with water. A lot of nonsense has been written about porridge and whether it should be eaten with salt or with sugar. It should be eaten however you like it – as a child in the 1850s, author Robert Louis Stevenson had his with golden syrup.

Oatcakes are another traditional dish that you'll certainly come across during a visit to Scotland, usually as an accompaniment to cheese at the end of a meal. A mealie pudding is a sausage-skin stuffed with oatmeal and onion and boiled for an hour or so. Add blood to the mixture and you have a black pudding.

Skirlie is chopped onions and oatmeal fried in beef dripping and seasoned with salt and pepper; it's usually served as a side dish. Trout and herring can be dipped in oatmeal before frying, and it can be added to soups and stews as a thickening agent. It's even used in desserts: toasted oatmeal is a vital flavouring in cranachan, a delicious mixture of whipped cream, whisky and raspberries.

Top 10 Seafood Restaurants

» Café Fish, Tobermory

» Waterfront Restaurant, Oban

» Lochleven Seafood Cafe, Kinlochleven

» Badachro Inn, Badachro

» Summer Isles Hotel, Achiltibuie

» Shorehouse Seafood Restaurant, Tarbet

» Plockton Shores, Plockton

» Tigh an Eilean Hotel, Shieldaig

» Lochbay Seafood Restaurant, Stein

» Fish Market Restaurant, Mallaig

Juicy langoustines (also known as Dublin Bay prawns), crabs, lobsters, oysters, mussels and scallops are also widely available.

Vegetarians & Vegans

Scotland has the same proportion of vegetarians as the rest of the UK – around 8% to 10% of the population. Vegetarianism has moved away from the hippie-student image of a few decades ago and is now firmly in the mainstream. Even the most remote Highland pub usually has at least one vegetarian dish on the menu, and there are many dedicated vegetarian restaurants in towns and cities. If you get stuck, there's almost always an Italian or Indian restaurant where you can get meat-free pizza, pasta or curry. Vegans, though, may find their options a bit limited outside of Edinburgh and Glasgow.

Eating with Kids

Sadly, restaurants in the UK have a reputation for not being all that welcoming to children. A survey of 8000 diners published in 2011 by the restaurant guide Harden's found that 92% of parents had struggled to find a child-friendly restaurant, and 31% had been turned away by a restaurant or cafe while looking for a place to eat with their young family.

This situation is changing, albeit slowly, especially in the cities and more popular tourist towns, where many restaurants and pubs now have family rooms and/or play areas. However, in many smaller towns and country areas toddlers and babies will occasionally get a frosty reception.

You should be aware that children under the age of 14 are not allowed into the majority of Scottish pubs, even those that serve bar meals. In family-friendly pubs (those in possession of a Children's Certificate), under-14s are only allowed in between 11am and 8pm, and must be accompanied by an adult aged 18 or over.

Cookery Courses

There are two principal places in the Highlands that offer courses in Scottish cookery. **Kinloch Lodge Hotel** (☎01471-833333; www.claire-mac donald.com; Sleat) on the Isle of Skye, offers cookery demonstrations using fresh, seasonal Scottish produce with Lady Claire Macdonald, author of *Scottish Highland Hospitality* and *Celebrations*. **Airds Hotel** (☎01631-730236; www.airds-hotel.com; Port Appin) in Argyll, runs three-night culinary weekends where you can learn how to prepare the perfect dinner menu using the best of Scottish produce.

What Are Ye Drinking?
A Pint...

Scottish breweries produce a wide range of beers. The market is dominated by multinational brewers such as Scottish & Newcastle, but smaller local breweries generally create tastier brews, some of them very strong. The aptly named Skull Splitter from Orkney is a good example, at 8.5% alcohol by volume.

Many Scottish beers use old-fashioned shilling categories to indicate strength (the number of shillings was originally the price per barrel; the stronger the beer, the higher the price). The usual range is from 60 to 80 shillings (written 80/-). You'll also see IPA, which stands for India Pale Ale, a strong, hoppy beer first brewed in the early 19th century for export to India (the extra alcohol meant that it kept better on the long sea voyage).

Draught beer is served in pints (usually costing from £2 to £3) or half-pints; alcoholic content generally ranges from 3% to 6%. What the English call bitter, Scots call heavy, or export.

Clootie dumpling is a rich pudding made with currants, raisins and other dried fruits; it is wrapped in a linen cloth (or *cloot*, in old Scots) and steamed. It can be served freshly cooked with custard, or sliced cold the day after and fried in butter.

THE SCOTTISH LARDER

The website www .scottishbrewing .com has a comprehensive list of Scottish breweries, both large and small.

SSSSMOKIN!

Scotland is famous for its smoked salmon, but there are many other varieties of smoked fish – plus smoked meats and cheeses – to enjoy. Smoking food to preserve it is an ancient art that has recently undergone a revival, but this time it's more about flavour than preservation.

There are two parts to the process – first the cure, which involves covering the fish in a mixture of salt and molasses sugar, or soaking it in brine; and then the smoke, which can be either cold smoking (at less than 34°C), which results in a raw product, or hot smoking (at more than 60°C), which cooks it. Cold-smoked products include traditional smoked salmon and kippers. Hot-smoked products include bradan rost ('flaky' smoked salmon) and Arbroath smokies (haddock).

Kippers (smoked herring) were invented in Northumberland, in northern England, in the mid-19th century, but Scotland soon picked up the technique, and both Loch Fyne and Mallaig were famous for their kippers.

There are dozens of modern smokehouses scattered all over Scotland, many of which offer a mail-order service as well as an onsite shop. We recommend:

» **Inverawe Smokehouse** (☎0844 8475 490; www.smokedsalmon.co.uk; Taynuilt) Delicate smoked salmon, plump juicy kippers.

» **Hebridean Smokehouse** (☎01876-580209; www.hebrideansmokehouse.com; Cladach) Peat-smoked salmon and sea trout.

» **Salar Smokehouse** (☎01870-610324; www.salar.co.uk; Lochcarnan) Famous for its flaky, hot-smoked salmon.

» **Achiltibuie Smokehouse** (p252) Organic smoked salmon, kippers, smoked venison.

SCOTTISH ALES

The increasing popularity of real ales and a backlash against the bland conformity of globalised multinational brewing conglomerates has seen a huge rise in the number of specialist brewers and microbreweries springing up all over Scotland. They take pride in using only natural ingredients, and many try to revive ancient recipes, such as heather- and seaweed-flavoured ales.

These beers are sold in pubs, off-licences and delicatessens. Here are a few of our favourites to look out for:

» **Black Isle Brewery** (p219) Has a range of organic beers.

» **Cairngorm Brewery** (☎01479-812222; www.cairngormbrewery.com; Dalfaber Industrial Estate) Creator of multi-award-winning Trade Winds ale.

» **Colonsay Brewery** (p89) Produces lager, 80/- and IPA.

» **Islay Ales** (p84) Refreshing and citrusy Saligo Ale.

» **Isle of Skye Brewery** (p195) Distinctive Hebridean Gold ale, brewed with porridge oats.

» **Orkney Brewery** (☎01667-404555; www.sinclairbreweries.co.uk; Quoyloo) Famous for its rich, chocolatey Dark Island ale, and the dangerously strong Skull Splitter.

» **Valhalla Brewery** (p319) Brews the most northerly beer in Britain.

» **Isle of Arran Brewery** (p61) Produces light and hoppy Arran Blonde, and the highly addictive Arran Dark.

Scotland's most famous soft drink is Barr's Irn-Bru: a sweet fizzy drink, radioactive orange in colour, that smells like bubble gum and almost strips the enamel from your teeth. Many Scots swear by its restorative effects as a cure for a hangover.

...Or a Wee Dram?

Scotch whisky (always spelt *without* an 'e' – 'whiskey' is Irish or American) is Scotland's best-known product and biggest export. The spirit has been distilled in Scotland at least since the 15th century.

As well as whiskies, there are whisky-based liqueurs, such as Drambuie. If you must mix your whisky with anything other than water, try

---

HOW TO BE A MALT WHISKY BUFF

'Love makes the world go round? Not at all! Whisky makes it go round twice as fast.' – From *Whisky Galore* by Compton Mackenzie (1883–1972)

Whisky-tasting today is almost as popular as wine-tasting was in the yuppie heyday of the late 1980s. Being able to tell your Ardbeg from your Edradour is de rigueur among the whisky-nosing set, so here are some pointers to help you impress your friends.

What's the difference between malt and grain whiskies? Malts are distilled from malted barley – that is, barley that has been soaked in water, then allowed to germinate for around 10 days until the starch has turned into sugar – while grain whiskies are distilled from other cereals, usually wheat, corn or unmalted barley.

So what is a single malt? A single malt is a whisky that has been distilled from malted barley and is the product of a single distillery. A pure (vatted) malt is a mixture of single malts from several distilleries, and a blended whisky is a mixture of various grain whiskies (about 60%) and malt whiskies (about 40%) from many different distilleries.

Why are single malts more desirable than blends? A single malt, like a fine wine's terroir, somehow captures the essence of the place where it was made and matured – a combination of the water, the barley, the peat smoke, the oak barrels in which it was aged, and (in the case of certain coastal distilleries) the sea air and salt spray. Each distillation varies from the one before, like different vintages from the same vineyard.

How should a single malt be drunk? Either neat, or preferably with a little water added. To appreciate the aroma and flavour to the utmost, a measure of malt whisky should be cut (diluted) with one-third to two-thirds as much spring water (bottled, still spring water will do). Ice, tap water and – heaven forbid – mixers are for philistines. Would you add lemonade or ice to a glass of Chablis?

a whisky-mac (whisky with ginger wine). After a long walk in the rain there's nothing better to put a warm glow in your belly.

At a bar, older Scots may order a 'half' or 'nip' of whisky as a chaser to a pint or half-pint of beer: a 'hauf and a hauf'. (Only tourists ask for 'Scotch' – what else would you be served in Scotland?) The standard measure in pubs is either 25mL or 35mL.

TOP 10 SINGLE MALT WHISKIES – OUR CHOICE

After a great deal of diligent research (and not a few sore heads), Lonely Planet's various Scotland authors have selected their 10 favourite single malts from across the country:

» **Ardbeg** (Islay) The 10-year-old from this noble Islay distillery is a byword for excellence. Peaty but well balanced. Hits the spot after a hill walk.

» **Bowmore** (Islay) Smoke, peat and salty sea air – a classic Islay malt. One of the few distilleries that still malts its own barley.

» **Bruichladdich** (Islay) A visitor-friendly distillery with a quirky, innovative approach – famous for very peaty special releases such as Moine Mhor.

» **Glendronach** (Speyside) Only sherry casks are used here, so the creamy, spicy result tastes like Grandma's Christmas trifle.

» **Highland Park** (Island) Full and rounded, with heather, honey, malt and peat. Has an award-winning distillery tour.

» **Isle of Arran** (Island) One of the newest of Scotland's distilleries, offering a lightish, flavoursome malt with flowery, fruity notes.

» **Macallan** (Speyside) The king of Speyside malts, with sherry and bourbon finishes. The distillery is set amid waving fields of Golden Promise barley.

» **Springbank** (Campbeltown) Complex flavours – sherry, citrus, pear-drops, peat – with a salty tang. Entire production process from malting to bottling takes place on site.

» **Talisker** (Island) Brooding, heavily peaty nose balanced by a satisfying sweetness from this lord of the isles. Great postdinner dram.

» **The Balvenie** (Speyside) Rich and honeyed, this Speysider is liquid gold for those with a sweet tooth.

The most expensive bottle of whisky ever sold? A Dalmore 64 Trinitas. Only three were made, with a blend of rare malts that had matured for up to 140 years. A US-based collector paid £100,000 for a bottle in 2010; today there's only one left...

Survival Guide

Directory A-Z

Accommodation

Scotland provides a comprehensive choice of accommodation to suit all visitors. In this book accommodation choices are flagged with price indicators, based on the cheapest accommodation for two people in high season:

£	up to £50
££	from £50 to £130
£££	£130 and over

For budget travel, the options are campsites, hostels and cheap B&Bs. In Highland areas you'll find bothies – simple walkers' hostels and shelters; in the Shetlands you'll find böds. Above this price level is a plethora of comfortable B&Bs and guesthouses (£25 to £40 per person per night). Midrange hotels are present in most places, while for high-end lodgings (£65-plus per person a night) there are some superb hotels, the most interesting being converted castles and mansions, or chic designer options in cities.

If you're travelling solo, expect to pay a supplement in hotels and B&Bs, meaning you'll often be forking over 75% of the price of a double for your single room.

Almost all B&Bs, guesthouses and hotels (and even some hostels) provide breakfast; if this is not the case, then it is mentioned in individual reviews throughout this book.

Prices increase over the peak tourist season (June to September) and are at their highest in July and August. Outside of these months, and particularly in winter, special deals are often available at guesthouses and hotels. Smaller establishments will often close from around November to March, particularly in more remote areas. If you're going to be in Edinburgh in the festival month of August or at Hogmanay (New Year), book as far ahead as you can – a year if possible – as the city will be packed.

Tourist offices have an accommodation booking service (£3 to £4, local and national), which can be handy over summer. However, note that they can only book the ever-decreasing number of places that are registered with **VisitScotland** (✆0845 225 5121; www.visitscotland .com). There are many other fine accommodation options which, mostly for the hefty registration fee, choose not to register with the tourist board. Registered places tend to be a little pricier than nonregistered ones. VisitScotland's star system is based on a rather stringent set of criteria, so don't set too much store by it.

B&Bs & Guesthouses

B&Bs are a Scottish institution. At the bottom end you get a bedroom in a private house, a shared bathroom and a fry-up (juice, coffee or tea, cereal and cooked breakfast – bacon, eggs, sausage, baked beans and toast). Midrange B&Bs have en suite bathrooms, TVs in each room and more variety (and healthier options) for breakfast. Almost all B&Bs provide hospitality trays (tea- and coffee-making facilities) in bedrooms. Also excellent are farm B&Bs, which offer traditional Scottish hospitality, huge breakfasts and a quiet rural setting – good for discharging urban grit. Pubs may also offer cheap (and sometimes noisy) B&B and can be good fun.

Guesthouses, often large converted private houses, are an extension of the B&B concept. They are normally larger and more upmarket than B&Bs, offering quality food and more luxurious accommodation.

Bothies, Barns & Bunkhouses

Bothies are simple shelters, often in remote places; many are maintained by the **Mountain Bothies Association** (www.mountainbothies.org.uk). They're not locked, there's no charge – usually no toilet – and you can't book. Take your own cooking equipment, sleeping bag and mat. Users should stay one night only, and leave it as they find it.

Walkers can stay in camping barns – usually converted farm buildings – for around £5 to £10 per night. Take your own cooking equipment, sleeping bag and mat. Bunkhouses, a grade or two up from camping barns, have stoves for heating and cooking and may supply utensils. They may have mattresses but you'll still need a sleeping bag. There will be toilets but probably no showers. Most charge from £10.

The **Shetland Amenity Trust** (☎01595-694688; www .camping-bods.com) has created a number of böds – converted croft houses or fishing huts with bunks and washing and cooking facilities, but often no electricity or heating – many in remote and dramatic locations. Beds cost £8 but you will need to prebook through the trust in Lerwick, who will give you the keys.

Camping & Caravan Parks

Free, so-called 'wild' camping became a legal right under the Land Reform Bill. However, campers are obliged to camp on unenclosed land, in small numbers and away from buildings and roads.

Commercial campgrounds are often geared to caravans and vary widely in quality. There are a lot of campgrounds covered in this book, but it is not possible to include every one in the much wider network. VisitScotland has a free map, available at tourist offices, showing a selection of caravan parks and campgrounds around Scotland.

Homestays & Hospitality Exchange

A convenient and increasingly popular holiday option is to join an international house-exchange organisation. You sign up for a year and place your home on a website giving details of what you're looking for, where and for how long. You organise the house swap yourself with people in other countries and arrange to swap homes, rent-

free, for an agreed period. Shop around, as registration costs vary between organisations. Check out **Home Base Holidays** (www.homebase-hols .com) and **Home Link International** (www.homelink.org .uk).

Organisations such as **Hospitality Club** (www .hospitalityclub.org) put people in contact for more informal free accommodation offers – a bit like blind-date couch-surfing. Even if you're not comfortable crashing in a stranger's house, these sites are a great way to meet locals just to go out for a pint or two.

Hostels

Hostels are widespread, offer cheap accommodation and are great centres for meeting fellow travellers. In Scotland the standard of facilities is generally very good: the more upmarket hostels have en suite bathrooms in their dorms, and all manner of luxuries giving them the feel of hotels (if it weren't for the bunk beds).

Hostels have facilities for self-catering, and many provide internet access and can usually arrange activities and tours.

From May to September and on public holidays, hostels – even the remote rural ones – can be booked out, sometimes by large groups, so phone in advance.

INDEPENDENT & STUDENT HOSTELS

There are a large number of independent hostels, most with prices around £10 to £16. Facilities vary considerably, but some of the best are listed in this book; because they're aimed at young backpackers, they can often be great places to party. The free *Independent Backpackers Hostels Scotland* guide (www.hostel -scotland.co.uk), available from tourist offices, lists over 100 hostels in Scotland, mostly in the north.

The **SYHA** (☎0845 293 7373; www.syha.org.uk) has a network of decent, reasonably priced hostels and produces a free booklet available from SYHA hostels and tourist offices. There are more than 60 to choose from around the country, ranging from basic walkers' digs to mansions and castles. You've got to be an SYHA or HI member to stay, but nonmembers can pay a £2 supplement per night that goes towards the £10 membership fee. Prices vary according to the month, but average around £16 to £18 per adult in high season.

Most SYHA hostels close from mid-October to early March but can be rented out by groups.

Hotels

There are some wonderfully luxurious places to stay in Scotland, including rustic countryhouse hotels in fabulous settings and castles complete with crenellated battlements, grand staircases and the obligatory rows of stag heads. Expect all the perks at these places, often including a gym, a sauna, a pool and first-class service. Even if you're on a budget, it's worth splashing out for a night at one of the classic Highland hotels, which function as community centres, including the local pub and restaurant.

Increasingly, hotels use an airline-style pricing system, so it's worth booking well ahead to take advantage of the cheapest rates. The website www.moneysaving expert.com has a good guide to finding cheap hotel rooms.

Try these online discount sites:

» www.hotels.com
» www.lastminute.com
» www.laterooms.com
» www.priceline.co.uk

Self-Catering Accommodation

Self-catering accommodation is very popular in Scotland, and staying in a cottage in the country gives you an opportunity to get a feel for a region and its community. The minimum stay is usually one week in the summer peak season, three days or less at other times.

We've only listed limited self-catering options in this guide. The best place to start looking for this kind of accommodation is the website of **VisitScotland** (www.visit scotland.com), which lists numerous self-catering options all over Scotland. These options also appear in the regional accommodation guides available from tourist offices.

Expect a week's rent for a two-bedroom cottage to cost from £160 in winter, and up to £280 during July to September.

The following are other places to search:

CKD Galbraith (☎0131-556 4422; www.ckdgalbraith .co.uk) Offers a wide range of self-catering accommodation, from cottages to castles.

Cottage Guide (www .cottageguide.co.uk) Lots of Scottish cottages to browse online.

Ecosse Unique (☎01835-822277; www.uniquescotland .com) Offers furnished holiday homes all over the country.

Landmark Trust (☎01628-825925; www.land marktrust.org.uk) A building preservation charity that restores historic buildings and lets them out as accommodation.

BOOK YOUR STAY ONLINE

For more reviews by Lonely Planet authors, check out hotels.lonelyplanet.com. You'll find independent reviews, as well as recommendations on the best places to stay. Best of all, you can book online.

Business Hours

Shops open from at least 9am to 5.30pm Monday to Friday, and most open Saturday too. A growing number are also open on Sunday, typically 11am to 5pm. It's common for there to be little or no public transport on Sundays, especially in the Western Isles.

In this guide, specific opening hours are only listed if they differ markedly from the following:

Banks 9.30am to 4pm Monday to Friday, plus some open 9.30am to 12.30pm Saturday.

Post offices 9am to 5.30pm Monday to Friday, 9am to 12.30pm Saturday.

Pubs & Bars 11am to 11pm Monday to Thursday, 11am to 1am Friday and Saturday, 12.30pm to 11pm Sunday; lunch is served noon to 2.30pm, dinner 6pm to 9pm daily.

Shops 9am to 5.30pm Monday to Saturday, 11am to 5pm Sunday.

Restaurants Lunch noon to 2.30pm, dinner 6pm to 9pm; in small towns and villages the chippy (fish-and-chip shop) is often the only place to buy cooked food after 8pm.

Children

Throughout this book we have listed child-friendly accommodation and recommended places and activities suitable for families. Reviews of accommodation and eating places that are especially child-friendly are indicated by the use of this icon: 🏠. It's well worth asking in tourist offices for local family-focused publications.

With the exception of many restaurants, children are well received around Scotland, and every area has some child-friendly attractions and B&Bs. Even somewhat-dry local museums usually make an effort with an activity sheet or child-focused information panels.

A lot of pubs are family-friendly and some have great beer gardens where kids can run around and exhaust themselves while you have a quiet pint. However, be aware that many Scottish pubs, even those that serve bar meals, are forbidden by law to admit children under 14; even in family-friendly pubs (ie those in possession of a Children's Certificate), under-14s are only admitted between 11am and 8pm, and only when accompanied by an adult.

Children under a certain age can often stay for free with their parents in hotels, but be prepared for hotels and B&Bs (normally upmarket ones) that won't accept children; call ahead to enquire. More hotels and guesthouses these days provide child-friendly facilities, including cots. Many restaurants (especially the larger ones) have high chairs and decent children's menus available.

The larger car-hire companies can provide safety seats for children, but they're worth booking well ahead.

See also Lonely Planet's *Travel with Children,* by Brigitte Barta et al.

Customs Regulations

Travellers arriving in the UK from other EU countries don't have to pay tax or duty on goods for personal use, and can bring back as much EU duty-paid alcohol and tobacco as they like. However, if you bring in more than the following, you'll probably be asked some questions:

» 3200 cigarettes, 400 cigarillos, 200 cigars, 3kg of smoking tobacco

» 10L of spirits, 20L of fortified wine (eg port or sherry), 90L of wine or 110L of beer.

Those under 17 years cannot import any alcohol or tobacco. There are also different allowances for tobacco products from the newer EU member countries (such as Estonia, Poland, Hungary, Latvia, Lithuania, Slovakia, the Czech Republic and Slovenia) – check the website of **HM Customs and Excise** (www.hmrc.gov.uk) for further details.

Travellers from outside the EU can bring in, duty-free:

» 200 cigarettes or 100 cigarillos or 50 cigars or 250g of tobacco

» 4L of still table wine

» 1L of spirits or 2L of fortified wine

» 60mL of perfume

» £300 worth of all other goods, including gifts and souvenirs.

Anything over this limit must be declared to customs officers on arrival.

For details of restrictions and quarantine regulations, see the customs website.

Discount Cards

Historic Sites

Membership of Historic Scotland (HS) and the National Trust for Scotland (NTS) is worth considering, especially if you're going to be in Scotland for a while. Both are nonprofit organisations that care for hundreds of sites of historical, architectural or environmental importance. Throughout this guide the abbreviations HS and NTS are used to indicate places that are under the care of these organisations. You can join up at any of their properties.

Historic Scotland (HS; ☑0131 668 8600; www.historic -scotland.gov.uk) A year's membership costs £40.50/76 per adult/family, and gives free entry to HS sites (half-price entry to sites in England and Wales).

Also offers short-term Explorer membership – three days out of five for £22, seven days out of 14 for £31.50.

National Trust for Scotland (☑0131 243 9300; www .nts.org.uk) A year's membership of the NTS, costing £46/76 for an adult/family, offers free access to all NTS and National Trust properties (in the rest of the UK).

Hostel Cards

If travelling on a budget, membership to the **Scottish Youth Hostels Association/Hostelling International** (SYHA; ☑0845 293 7373; www.syha.org.uk) is strongly recommended (annual membership over/ under 16 years is £10/free, life membership is £100).

Senior Cards

Discount cards for those over 60 years are available for train travel.

Student Youth Cards

The most useful card is the International Student Identity Card (ISIC), which displays your photo. This can perform wonders, including producing discounts on entry to attractions and on many forms of transport.

There's a global industry in fake student cards, and many places now stipulate a maximum age for student discounts or substitute a 'youth discount' for 'student discount'. If under 26 but not a student, you can apply for the Euro/26 card, which goes by various names in different countries, or an International Youth Travel Card (IYTC) issued by the **International Student Travel Confederation** (ISTC; www.istc.org). These cards are available through student unions, hostelling organisations or youth travel agencies.

PRACTICALITIES

» The Aberdeen-based daily newspaper Press & Journal covers the Highlands & Islands, as does the weekly Oban Times. The Daily Record is a popular Labour-supporting tabloid, while the Sunday Post offers up rose-tinted nostalgia.

» BBC Radio Scotland (AM 810kHz, FM 92.4-94.7MHz) provides a Scottish point of view.

» Watch BBC1 Scotland, BBC2 Scotland and STV for Scottish-specific programming. Channel Four and Five are nationwide channels with unchanged content for Scotland.

» Use the metric system for weights and measures, with the exception of road distances (in miles) and beer (in pints). The pint is 568mL, more than the US version.

» In Scotland you can't smoke in any public place with a roof that's at least half enclosed, which means pubs, bus shelters, restaurants and hotels (basically, anywhere you might want to).

Electricity

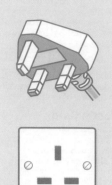

230V/50Hz

Embassies & Consulates

Be aware that the Australian consulate in Edinburgh does not provide notarial services; travellers in need of these should contact the **Australian High Commission** (☏020-7379 4334; www.uk .embassy.gov.au) in London instead.

Food

In this guide eating choices are flagged with price indicators based on the cost of an average main course from the dinner menu:

£	up to £9
££	from £9 to £18
£££	£18 and over

Note though that lunch mains are often cheaper than dinner mains, and many places offer an 'early bird' special with lower prices (usually available between 5pm and 7pm). See p358 for restaurant opening hours

and the Scottish Larder chapter (p348) for information about Scottish cuisine.

Gay & Lesbian Travellers

Although many Scots are fairly tolerant of homosexuality, overt displays of affection aren't wise if conducted away from acknowledged 'gay' venues or districts – hostility may be encountered.

The website www.gayscot land.com and the monthly magazine *Scotsgay* (www .scotsgay.com) keep gays, lesbians and bisexuals informed about local scenes.

Health

» If you're an EU citizen, a European Health Insurance Card (EHIC) – available from health centres or, in the UK, post offices – covers you for most medical care. An EHIC will not cover you for non-emergencies, or emergency repatriation.

» Citizens from non-EU countries should find out if there is a reciprocal arrangement for free medical care between their country and the UK.

» If you do need health insurance, make sure you get a policy that covers you for the worst possible case, such as an accident requiring an emergency flight home.

» No vaccinations are required to travel to Scotland.

» The most painful problems facing visitors to the Highlands and Islands are midges (see p33).

Insurance

» This not only covers you for medical expenses, theft or loss, but also for cancellation of, or delays in, any of your travel arrangements.

» Lots of bank accounts give their holders automatic

travel insurance – check if this is the case for you.

» Always read the small print carefully. Some policies specifically exclude 'dangerous activities', such as scuba diving, motorcycling, skiing, mountaineering and even trekking.

» There's a variety of policies and your travel agent can give recommendations. Make sure the policy includes health care and medication in the countries you may visit on your way to/from Scotland.

» You may prefer a policy that pays doctors or hospitals directly rather than forcing you to pay on the spot and claim the money back later. If you have to claim later, make sure you keep all documentation. Some policies ask you to call back (reverse charges) to a centre in your home country for an immediate assessment of your problem.

» Not all policies cover ambulances, helicopter rescue or emergency flights home. Most policies exclude cover for pre-existing illnesses.

» Worldwide travel insurance is available at www.lonely planet.com/travel_services. You can buy, extend and claim online anytime – even if you're already on the road.

Internet Access

» If you're travelling with a laptop, you'll find a wide range of places offering a wi-fi connection, from cafes and B&Bs to public spaces. We've indicated accommodation and eating and drinking options that have wi-fi with the 🛜 symbol in the text. Wi-fi is often free, but some places (typically, upmarket hotels) do charge.

» There are some increasingly good deals on pay-as-you-go mobile internet from mobile network providers.

» Places with internet terminals are indicated by the @ symbol.

Most foreign diplomatic missions are in London, but many countries also have consulates in Edinburgh:

Australia	0131-538 0582	www.uk.embassy.gov.au	5 Mitchell St
Canada	0131-473 6320	www.canadainternational.gc.ca	Festival Sq, 50 Lothian Rd
Denmark	0131-220 0300	www.amblondon.um.dk	48 Melville St
France	0131-225 7954	www.ambafrance-uk.org	11 Randolph Cres
Germany	0131-337 2323	www.edinburgh.diplo.de	16 Eglinton Cres
Ireland	0131-226 7711	www.irishconsulatescotland.co.uk	16 Randolph Cres
Japan	0131-225 4777	www.edinburgh.uk.emb-japan.go.jp	2 Melville Cres
Netherlands	0131-524 9436	www.dutchembassyuk.org	127 George St
New Zealand	0131-222 8109	www.nzembassy.com/united-kingdom	Rutland Sq
USA	0131-556 8315	www.usembassy.org.uk	3 Regent Tce

» If you don't have a laptop, the best places to check email and surf the internet are public libraries – almost every town and village in the country has at least a couple of computer terminals devoted to the internet; they're free to use, though there's often a time limit.

» Internet cafes also exist in the cities and larger towns and are generally good value, charging approximately £2 to £3 per hour.

» Many of the larger tourist offices across the country also have internet access.

Legal Matters

» The *1707 Act of Union* preserved the Scottish legal system as separate from the law in England and Wales.

» Police have the power to detain, for up to six hours, anyone suspected of having committed an offence punishable by imprisonment (including drugs offences). They can search you, take your photo and fingerprints, and question you. You are legally required to provide police with your correct name and address – not doing so,

or giving false details, is an offence – but you are not obliged to answer any other questions. After six hours, the police must either formally charge you or let you go.

» If you are detained and/or arrested, you have the right to inform a solicitor and one other person, though you have no right to actually see the solicitor or to make a telephone call. If you don't know a solicitor, the police will inform the duty solicitor for you.

» The government can now detain foreigners suspected of terrorist activities, without charge, for a period of 28 days.

» If you need legal assistance, contact the **Scottish Legal Aid Board** (0131-226 7061; www.slab.org.uk; 44 Drumsheugh Gardens).

» Possession of a small amount of cannabis is punishable by a fine, but possession of a larger amount of cannabis, or any amount of harder drugs, is much more serious, with a sentence of up to 14 years in prison. Police have the right to search anyone they suspect of possessing drugs.

» The maximum blood-alcohol level allowable when driving is 35mg/100mL.

» Traffic offences (illegal parking, speeding etc) usually incur a fine, to be paid within 30 to 60 days. In Glasgow and Edinburgh the parking inspectors are numerous and without mercy – never leave your car around the city centres without a valid parking ticket or you risk a hefty fine.

» The legal minimum age in Scotland for drinking alcohol and smoking is 18; for driving, it's 17.

Maps

If you're planning to walk more than a few hundred yards from the road, you'll require maps with far greater detail than the maps in this guide, or the ones supplied by tourist offices. The Ordnance Survey (OS) caters to walkers, with a wide variety of maps at 1:50,000 and 1:25,000 scales. Alternatively, look out for the excellent walkers' maps published by Harveys; they're at scales of 1:40,000 and 1:25,000.

Money

The British currency is the pound sterling (£), with 100 pence (p) to a pound. 'Quid' is the slang term for 'pound'.

Three Scottish banks issue their own banknotes, meaning there's quite a variety of different notes in circulation. They are legal currency in England too, but you'll occasionally run into problems changing them. They're also harder to exchange once you get outside the UK.

Euros are accepted in Scotland only at some major tourist attractions and a few upmarket hotels – it's always better to have sterling cash. For exchange rates see the inside front cover of this book.

ATMs

» ATMs (called cashpoints in Scotland) are widespread and you'll usually find at least one in small towns and villages. You can use Visa, MasterCard, American Express (Amex), Cirrus, Plus and Maestro to withdraw cash from ATMs belonging to most banks and building societies in Scotland.

» In small villages where there are no ATMs, you can often ask for 'cash back' – you pay for goods or services at a shop, pub or hotel using a debit card and ask for (eg) £20 cash back; your card is charged for the cost of the goods plus £20, and you get £20 cash in hand.

» Cash withdrawals from some ATMs may be subject to a small charge, but most are free.

Credit Cards

Visa, MasterCard, Amex and Diners Club cards are widely recognised, although some places will charge for accepting them (generally for small transactions). Charge cards such as Amex and Diners Club may not be accepted in smaller establishments. Credit and debit cards like Visa

and MasterCard are more widely accepted, but smaller B&Bs (and some restaurants) may not take cards.

Moneychangers

Be careful using bureaux de change; they may offer good exchange rates but frequently levy outrageous commissions and fees. The best-value place to change money in the UK is at post offices, but only those in larger towns and cities offer this service. Larger tourist offices also have exchange facilities.

Tipping

» Tip 10% in sit-down restaurants, but not if there's already a service charge on the bill. In very classy places they may expect closer to 15%.

» Service is at your discretion: even if the charge is added to the bill, you don't have to pay it if you feel that the service has been poor.

» Don't tip in pubs: if the service has been exceptional over the course of an evening, you can offer to pay for a drink for the bartender (say 'have one for yourself').

» Tip taxi drivers in cities around 10%, or else just round up.

Public Holidays

» Although bank holidays are general public holidays in the rest of the UK, in Scotland they only apply to banks and some other commercial offices.

» Scottish towns normally have four days of public holiday, which they allocate themselves; dates vary from year to year and from town to town. Most places celebrate St Andrew's Day (30 November) as a public holiday. General public holidays:
New Year 1 & 2 January
Good Friday March or April
Christmas Day
25 December
Boxing Day 26 December

Telephone

The famous red telephone boxes are a dying breed now, surviving mainly in conservation areas. You'll mainly see two types of phone booths in Scotland: one takes coins (and doesn't give change), while the other uses pre-paid phonecards and credit cards. Some phones accept both coins and cards. Payphone cards are widely available.

The cheapest way of calling internationally is to buy a discount phonecard; you'll see these in newsagents, along with tables of countries and the number of minutes you'll get for your money.

Mobile Phones

» Codes for mobile phones usually begin with ☑07. The UK uses the GSM 900/1800 network, which covers the rest of Europe, Australia and New Zealand, but isn't compatible with the North American GSM 1900 network. Most modern mobiles, however, can function on both networks – check before you leave home.

» Network coverage can be patchy or nonexistent in the more remote parts of the Highlands and Islands.

» International roaming charges can be prohibitively high, and you'll probably find it cheaper to get a UK number. This is easily done by buying a SIM card (around £10 including calling credit) and sticking it in your phone. Your phone may be locked to your home network, however, so you'll have to either get it unlocked, or buy a pay-as-you-go phone along with your SIM card (around £50).

» Pay-as-you-go phones can be recharged by buying vouchers from shops.

Phone Codes & Useful Numbers

» **Dialling the UK** Dial your country's international access code, then ☑44 (the UK country code), then the area code (dropping the first 0) followed by the telephone number.

» Dialling out of the UK
The international access code is ☑00; dial this, then add the country code and telephone number you wish to call.

» Making a reverse charge (collect) international call
Dial ☑155 for the operator. It's an expensive option, but not for the caller.

» Area codes in Scotland
These begin with ☑01xxx, eg Inverness ☑01463, Wick ☑01955.

» Directory Assistance
There are several numbers available; ☑118500 is one.

» Mobile phones Codes usually begin with ☑07.

» Free calls Numbers starting with ☑0800 are free; calls to ☑0845 numbers are charged at local rates.

Time

Scotland is on GMT/UTC. The clocks go forward one hour for 'summer time' at 2am Sunday on the last weekend in March, and go back on the last weekend in October. The 24-hour clock is used for transport timetables, but plenty of folk still struggle to get the hang of it.

Tourist Information

The Scottish Tourist Board, known as **VisitScotland** (☑0845 225 5121; www .visitscotland.com; 94 Ocean Dr, Edinburgh EH6 6HJ), deals with inquiries made by post, email and telephone. You can request, online and by phone, for regional brochures be posted out to you.

Most larger towns have tourist offices that open 9am or 10am to 5pm Monday to Friday, and on weekends in summer. In small places, particularly in the Highlands and Islands, tourist offices only open from Easter to September. Details of tourist offices can be found throughout the guide.

Travellers with Disabilities

Travellers with disabilities will find Scotland a strange mix of user-friendliness and unfriendliness. Most new buildings are accessible to wheelchair users, so modern hotels and tourist attractions are fine. However, most B&Bs and guesthouses are in hard-to-adapt older buildings, which means that travellers with mobility problems may pay more for accommodation. Things are constantly improving, though.

It's a similar story with public transport. Newer buses have steps that lower for easier access, as do trains, but it's wise to check before setting out. Tourist attractions usually reserve parking spaces near the entrance for drivers with disabilities.

Many places such as ticket offices and banks are fitted with hearing loops to assist the hearing-impaired; look for a posted symbol of a large ear.

A few tourist attractions have Braille guides or scented gardens for the visually impaired.

VisitScotland produces the guide *Accessible Scotland* for wheelchair travellers, and many tourist offices have leaflets with accessibility details for their area. Regional accommodation guides have a wheelchair-accessible criterion.

Many regions have organisations that hire out wheelchairs; contact the local tourist office for details. Many nature trails have been adapted for wheelchair use.

For more information:

Disabled Persons Railcard (www.disabledpersons railcard.co.uk) Discounted train travel.

Historic Scotland (HS; ☑0131 668 8600; www. historic-scotland.gov.uk) Has a free leaflet outlining access and facilities at HS properties, and also produces a large-print version of the HS promotional brochure.

Holiday Care Service (☑0845 124 9971; www .holidaycare.org.uk) Publishes regional information guides (£5) to Scotland and can offer general advice.

Royal Association for Disability & Rehabilitation (RADAR; ☑020-7250 3222; www.radar.org.uk; 12 City Forum, 250 City Rd) Excellent; publishes a guide (£10) on travel in the UK and has an accommodation website.

TIME DIFFERENCE BETWEEN SCOTLAND & WORLD CITIES

Paris, Berlin, Rome	1 hour ahead
New York	5 hours behind
Sydney	9 hours ahead Apr-Sep, 10 hours Oct, 11 hours Nov-Mar
Los Angeles	8 hours behind
Mumbai	5½ hours ahead, 4½ hours Mar-Oct
Tokyo	9 hours ahead, 8 hours Mar-Oct

Visas

» If you're a citizen of the EEA (European Economic Area) nations or Switzerland, you don't need a visa to enter or work in Britain – you can enter using your national identity card.

» Visa regulations are always subject to change, so it's essential to check with your local British embassy, high commission or consulate before leaving home. Currently, if you're a citizen of Australia, Canada, New Zealand, Japan, Israel, the USA and several other countries, you can stay for up to six months (no visa required), but are not allowed to work.

» Nationals of many countries, including South Africa, will need to obtain a visa: for more info, see www.ukvisas .gov.uk.

» The Youth Mobility Scheme, for Australian, Canadian, Japanese, and New Zealand citizens aged 18 to 31, allows working visits of up to two years, but must be applied for in advance.

» Commonwealth citizens with a UK-born parent may be eligible for a Certificate of Entitlement to the Right of Abode, which entitles them to live and work in the UK.

Commonwealth citizens with a UK-born grandparent could qualify for a UK Ancestry Employment Certificate, allowing them to work full time for up to five years in the UK.

» British immigration authorities have always been tough; dress neatly and carry proof that you have sufficient funds with which to support yourself. A credit card and/or an onward ticket will help.

Women Travellers

Women travelling alone are highly unlikely to have problems in Scotland, though there are still a few pubs where you'll turn heads if you walk in alone. Cosmopolitan city pubs and most rural pubs are fine – you'll get a pretty good idea as soon as you open the door.

The contraceptive pill is available only on prescription; however, the 'morning-after' pill (effective against conception for up to 72 hours after unprotected sexual intercourse) is available over the counter at chemists.

Work

» EU citizens don't need a permit to work in the UK, though citizens of some of

those countries may need to register before starting work.

» See Visas for details of the Youth Mobility Scheme working holiday visa.

» Students and recent graduates are eligible to apply through **BUNAC** (www .bunac.org) for an internship allowing them to work for six months in the UK.

» Whatever your skills, it's worth registering with a number of temporary employment agencies – there are plenty in the cities.

» Low-paid seasonal work is often available in the tourist industry, usually in restaurants and pubs. Once the domain of Australian, South African and New Zealand travellers, the enlargement of the EU has seen many Eastern Europeans also travel to Scotland for these jobs. At Highland pubs, rates usually include bed and board, so it can be a good way to save money.

» Hostel noticeboards sometimes advertise casual work. Without skills, it can be difficult to find a job that pays enough to save money. Pick up a free copy of *TNT* (www .tntmagazine.com), found in larger cities – it lists jobs and employment agencies aimed at travellers.

Transport

GETTING THERE & AWAY

Flights, tours and rail tickets can be booked online at lonelyplanet.com/bookings.

Air

There are direct flights to Scottish airports from England, Wales, Ireland, the USA, Canada, Scandinavia and several countries in western and central Europe. From elsewhere, you'll probably have to fly into a European hub and catch a connecting flight to a Scottish airport – London, Amsterdam, Frankfurt and Paris have the best connections. If flying from North America, it's worth looking at Icelandair, which often has good deals to Glasgow via Reykjavík.

Airports & Airlines

Scotland has four main international airports: Aberdeen, Edinburgh, Glasgow and Glasgow Prestwick. A few short-haul international flights land at Inverness and Sumburgh, while London is the main UK gateway for long-haul flights.

» **Aberdeen**
(ABZ; www.aberdeenairport.com)

» **Edinburgh** (EDI; www.edinburghairport.com)
» **Glasgow** (GLA; www.glasgowairport.com)
» **Glasgow Prestwick** (PIK; www.gpia.co.uk)
» **Inverness** (INV; www.hial.co.uk/inverness-airport)
» **London Gatwick** (LGW; www.gatwickairport.com)
» **London Heathrow** (LHR; www.heathrowairport.com)
» **Sumburgh** (LSI; www.hial.co.uk/sumburgh-airport).

There are many airlines serving Scottish airports.
» **Aer Arann** (RE; www.aerarann.com)
» **Aer Lingus** (EI; www.aerlingus.com)
» **Air France** (AF; www.airfrance.co.uk)
» **bmi** (BD; www.flybmi.com)
» **bmibaby** (WW; www.bmibaby.com)
» **British Airways** (BA; www.ba.com)
» **Canadian Affair** (www.canadianaffair.com)
» **Cimber Sterling** (QI; www.cimber.com)
» **Cityjet** (WX; www.cityjet.com)
» **Continental Airlines** (CO; www.continental.com)

» **Eastern Airways** (T3; www.easternairways.com)
» **easyJet** (U2; www.easyjet.com)
» **Falcontravel** (www.falcontravel.ch)
» **FlyBe** (BE; www.flybe.com)
» **Germanwings** (4U; www.germanwings.com)
» **Icelandair** (FI; www.icelandair.com)
» **Jet2.com** (LS; www.jet2.com)
» **KLM Cityhopper** (UK; www.klmuk.com)
» **Lufthansa** (LH; www.lufthansa.co.uk)
» **Norwegian** (DY; www.norwegian.com)
» **Ryanair** (FR; www.ryanair.com)
» **Scandinavian Airlines** (SK; www.flysas.com)
» **Spanair** (JKK; www.spanair.com)
» **US Airways** (US; www.usairways.com)
» **Wideroe** (WF; www.wideroe.no)

Land

Bus

» Buses are usually the cheapest way to get to Scotland from other parts of the UK.
» **Megabus** (☎0871 266 3333; www.megabus.com) One-way fares from London to Glasgow from as little as £5.50 if you book well in advance (up to eight weeks).
» **National Express** (☎0871 81 81 78; www.gobycoach.com) Regular services from London and other cities in England and Wales to Glasgow and Edinburgh.
» **Scottish Citylink** (☎0871 266 33 33; www.citylink.co.uk) Daily service between Belfast and Glasgow and Edinburgh via Stranraer ferry.

Car & Motorcycle

Drivers of EU-registered vehicles will find bringing a car or motorcycle into Scotland fairly easy. The

CLIMATE CHANGE & TRAVEL

Every form of transport that relies on carbon-based fuel generates CO_2, the main cause of human-induced climate change. Modern travel is dependent on aeroplanes, which might use less fuel per person than most cars but travel much greater distances. The altitude at which aircraft emit gases (including CO_2) and particles also contributes to their climate change impact. Many websites offer 'carbon calculators' that allow people to estimate the carbon emissions generated by their journey and, for those who wish to do so, to offset the impact of the greenhouse gases emitted with contributions to portfolios of climate-friendly initiatives throughout the world. Lonely Planet offsets the carbon footprint of all staff and author travel.

vehicle must have registration papers and a nationality plate, and you must have insurance. The International Insurance Certificate (Green Card) isn't compulsory, but it is excellent proof that you're covered. If driving from mainland Europe via the Channel Tunnel or ferry ports, head for London and follow the M25 orbital road to the M1 motorway, then follow the M1 and M6 north.

For rules of the road, such as speed limits, see p368.

Train

Travelling to Scotland by train is usually faster and more comfortable than the bus, but more expensive. Taking into account check-ins and travel time between city centre and airport, the train is a competitive alternative, time-wise, to air travel on the London to Edinburgh route.

East Coast (☑08457 225 111; www.eastcoast.co.uk) Trains between London Kings Cross and Edinburgh (four hours, every half-hour).

Eurostar (☑08432 186 186; www.eurostar.com) You can travel from Paris or Brussels to London in around two hours on the Eurostar service. From St Pancras it's a quick and easy change to Kings Cross or Euston for trains to Edinburgh or Glasgow. Total journey time from Paris to Edinburgh is about eight hours.

ScotRail (☑08457 55 00 33; www.scotrail.co.uk) Runs the *Caledonian Sleeper*, an overnight service connecting London Euston with Edinburgh, Glasgow, Stirling, Perth, Dundee, Aberdeen, Fort William and Inverness.

» National Rail Enquiry Service (☑08457 48 49 50; www.nationalrail.co.uk) Timetable and fares info for all UK trains.

» Virgin Trains (☑08719 774 222; www.virgintrains.co.uk) Trains between London Euston and Glasgow (4½ hours, hourly).

Sea

Car Ferry

Car-ferry links between Northern Ireland and Scotland are operated by **Stena Line** (☑08447 70 70 70; www.stenaline.co.uk) and **P&O Irish Sea** (☑08716 645 645; www.poirishsea.com). Stena Line travels the Belfast–Stranraer route and P&O Irish Sea the Larne–Troon (March to October only) and Larne–Cairnryan routes. There's a choice of standard and high-speed ferries on the Stranraer and Cairnryan routes, but high-speed only on the Troon route.

The prices in the table are for advance purchase one-way fares for a foot passenger/car with driver, in high season; fares vary with time and day of departure, and are often less than quoted here.

GETTING AROUND

Public transport in Scotland is generally good, but it can be costly compared with other European countries. Buses are usually the cheapest way to get around, but also the slowest. With a discount pass, trains can be competitive; they're also quicker and often take you through beautiful scenery.

» Traveline (☑0871 200 22 33; www.travelinescotland.com) provides timetable info for all public transport services in Scotland, but can't provide fare information or ticket bookings.

FERRIES TO/FROM NORTHERN IRELAND

CROSSING	DURATION	FREQUENCY	FARE (£)
Belfast–Stranraer	3¼hr	2–4 daily	25/89
Belfast–Stranraer	1¾hr	4 daily	25/99
Larne–Cairnryan	1¾hr	8 daily	24/69
Larne–Cairnryan	1hr	2 daily (Mar–Sep)	24/79
Larne–Troon	1¾hr	2 daily (Mar–Sep)	24/79

Air

Most domestic air services are geared to business needs, or are lifelines for remote island communities. Flying is a pricey way to cover relatively short distances, and only worth considering if you're short of time and want to visit the Hebrides, Orkney or Shetland.

Airlines in Scotland

» **Eastern Airways** (☎0870 366 9100; www.easternairways .com) Flies from Aberdeen to Stornoway and Wick.

» **Flybe/Loganair** (☎01857-873457; www.loganair.co.uk) The main domestic airline in Scotland, with flights from Glasgow to Barra, Benbecula, Campbeltown, Islay, Kirkwall, Sumburgh, Stornoway and Tiree; from Edinburgh to Inverness, Kirkwall, Sumburgh, Stornoway and Wick; from Aberdeen to Kirkwall and Sumburgh; and from Inverness to Kirkwall, Stornoway and Sumburgh. It also operates interisland flights in Orkney and Shetland, and from Barra to Benbecula.

» **Hebridean Air** (☎0845 805 7465; www.hebrideanair.co .uk) Flies from Connel airfield near Oban to the Islands of Coll, Tiree, Colonsay and Islay.

Bicycle

Scotland is a compact country, and travelling around by bicycle is a perfectly feasible proposition if you have the time. Indeed, for touring the islands a bicycle is both cheaper (in terms of ferry fares) and more suited to their small size and leisurely pace of life. For more information on cycling activities see p31.

Boat

The main car-ferry operators to Scotland's larger islands

are CalMac (west coast) and Northlink (Orkney and Shetland), but there are many other car and passenger-only ferries, often run by the local council, serving smaller islands and making short sea crossings.

Taking your car on a ferry, particularly to the farther-flung islands, can be expensive; you might save some money by hiring a car once you arrive there. Bicycles, on the other hand, travel free on most car ferries (there may be a small charge for bikes on passenger ferries).

It's recommended that you make reservations for ferry crossings if you're travelling by car, especially in summer; the Mallaig to Armadale (Skye) ferry in particular can get very busy, with long waits for those without bookings. Reservations are not needed for foot passengers and bicycles.

CalMac (www.calmac.co .uk) Serves the west coast and islands, a comprehensive timetable booklet is available from tourist offices. CalMac Island Hopscotch offers over two dozen tickets giving reduced fares for various combinations of crossings; these are listed on the website and in the CalMac timetables booklet.

CalMac Island Rover Ticket Allows unlimited travel on CalMac ferries; costs £48.50/70 for a foot passenger for eight/15 days, plus £232/348 for a car or £116/175 for a motorbike. Bicycles travel free with a foot passenger's ticket.

Northlink Ferries (☎0845 6000 449; www.north linkferries.co.uk) Runs ferries from Aberdeen and Scrabster (near Thurso) to Orkney, from Orkney to Shetland and from Aberdeen to Shetland.

Bus

Scotland is served by an extensive bus network that covers most of the country. In remote rural areas, however, services are more geared to the needs of locals (getting to school or the shops in the nearest large town) and may not be conveniently timed for visitors.

» **First** (☎0871 200 2233; www.firstgroup.com) Operates local bus routes in the Loch Lomond, the Trossachs and Stirlingshire area.

» **Royal Mail Postbus** (☎08457 740 740; www.postbus .royalmail.com) Minibuses, or sometimes four-seater cars, driven by postal workers delivering and collecting the mail – there are no official stops, and you can hail a postbus anywhere on its route. Although services have been cut severely in recent years, it's still the only public transport in some remote parts of Scotland.

» **Scottish Citylink** (☎0871 266 33 33; www.citylink.co.uk) National network of comfy, reliable buses serving all main towns. Away from main roads, you'll need to switch to local services.

» **Stagecoach** (www.stage coachbus.com) Operates local bus routes in many parts of Scotland.

ROAD EQUIVALENT TARIFF

In 2008 the Scottish Government introduced a scheme called the Road Equivalent Tariff (RET) on certain ferry crossings. This reduced the price of ferry transport to what it would cost to drive the same distance by road, in the hope of attracting more tourists and reducing business costs in the islands. The routes in the pilot scheme, which runs until spring 2012, are Ullapool to Stornoway, Uig (Skye) to Tarbert (Harris) and Lochmaddy (North Uist), Oban to Castlebay (Barra) and Lochboisdale (South Uist), and Oban to Coll and Tiree.

Fares on these crossings have been cut by around 40%, and initial signs are that the scheme has been successful, with tourist numbers up by 25%. It is hoped that RET will be extended to more routes after the pilot scheme ends, with Argyll and Clyde islands first in line.

Traveline (☑0871 200 22 33; www.travelinescotland.com) Offers up-to-date timetable information.

Bus Passes

Scottish Citylink offers discounts to students, SYHA members and holders of the **NEC Smartcard** (www .youngscot.org), which gives discounts all over Scotland and Europe. Holders of a National Entitlement Card, available to seniors and disabled people who are UK citizens, gives free bus travel throughout the country.

The **Scottish Citylink Explorer Pass** offers unlimited travel on Scottish Citylink services within Scotland for any three days out of five (£35), any five days out of 10 (£59) or any eight days out of 16 (£79). Also gives discounts on various regional bus services, on Northlink and CalMac ferries, and in SYHA hostels. Can be bought in the UK by both UK and overseas citizens. It is not valid on National Express coaches.

Car & Motorcycle

Scotland's roads are generally good and far less busy than in England, so driving is more enjoyable. However, cars are nearly always inconvenient in city centres.

Motorways (designated 'M') are toll-free dual carriageways, limited mainly to central Scotland. Main roads ('A') are dual or single carriageways and are sometimes clogged with slow-moving trucks or caravans; the A9 from Perth to Inverness is notoriously busy.

Life on the road is more relaxed and interesting on the secondary roads (designated 'B') and minor roads (undesignated), although in the Highlands and Islands there's the added hazard of suicidal sheep wandering onto the road (be particularly wary of lambs in spring), not to mention deer.

At around £1.36 per litre (equivalent to more than US$10 per US gallon), petrol is expensive by American or Australian standards; diesel is about 4p per litre more expensive. Prices tend to rise as you get further from the main centres and are more than 10% higher in the Outer Hebrides (around £1.50 a litre). In remote areas petrol stations are widely spaced and sometimes closed on Sunday.

Driving Licence

A non-EU licence is valid in Britain for up to 12 months from time of entry into the country. If bringing a car from Europe, make sure you're adequately insured.

Hire

Car hire is relatively costly here and it's often cheaper to arrange a fly/drive deal from home. The international hire companies charge from around £140 a week for a small car (eg Ford Fiesta, Peugeot 106); local companies, such as **Arnold Clark** (www.arnoldclarkrental.co.uk), start from £26 a day or £128 a week. Tourist offices have lists of local car-hire companies.

The main international hire companies:

» **Avis** (www.avis.co.uk)
» **Budget** (www.budget.co .uk)
» **Europcar** (www.europcar .co.uk)
» **Hertz** (www.hertz.co.uk)
» **Thrifty Car Rental** (www .thrifty.co.uk)

The minimum legal age for driving is 17 but to rent a car, drivers must usually be aged 23 to 65 – outside these limits special conditions or insurance requirements may apply.

If you're planning to visit the Outer Hebrides, Orkney or Shetland, it'll often prove cheaper to hire a car on the islands, rather than pay to take a hire car on the ferry.

Road Rules

The *Highway Code,* widely available in bookshops, details all UK road regulations. Vehicles drive on the left. Front seatbelts are compulsory; if the back seat has belts, they must be worn too. The speed limit is 30mph in built-up areas, 60mph on single carriageways and 70mph on dual carriageways. Give way to your right at roundabouts (traffic already on the roundabout has right of way). Motorcyclists must wear helmets.

It is a criminal offence to use a hand-held mobile

phone or similar device while driving; this includes while you are stopped at traffic lights, or stuck in traffic, when you can expect to be moving again at any moment.

The maximum permitted blood-alcohol level when driving is 35mg/100mL; to stay under this level, drink no more than one pint of beer or one glass of wine.

Traffic offences (illegal parking, speeding etc) usually incur a fine for which you're allowed 30 to 60 days to pay. In Glasgow and Edinburgh the parking inspectors are numerous and without mercy – never leave your car around the city centres without a valid parking ticket, or you risk a hefty fine.

Hitching

Hitching is never entirely safe in any country and we don't recommend it. Travellers who hitch take a small but potentially serious risk. However, many people choose to hitch, and the advice that follows should help to make their journeys as fast and safe as possible.

Hitching is fairly easy in Scotland, except around big cities and built-up areas, where you'll need to use public transport. Although the northwest is more difficult because there's less traffic, waits of over two hours are unusual (except on Sunday in 'Sabbath' areas). On some islands, where public transport is infrequent, hitching is so much a part

of getting around that local drivers may stop and offer you lifts without you asking.

It's against the law to hitch on motorways or their immediate slip roads; make a sign and use approach roads, nearby roundabouts or service stations.

Tours

There are lots of companies in Scotland offering all kinds of tours, including historical, activity-based and backpacker tours. It's a question of picking the tour that suits your requirements and budget. More companies are listed in destination chapters under Tours.

» **Haggis Adventures** (www.haggisadventures.com) Offers backpacker tours, with longer options taking in the Outer Hebrides or Orkney.

» **Heart of Scotland Tours** (www.heartofscotlandtours.co.uk) Specialises in mini-coach day tours of central Scotland and the Highlands, departing from Edinburgh.

» **Hebridean Princess** (www.hebridean.co.uk) Luxury cruises around the west coast of Scotland, the Outer Hebrides and the Orkney and Shetland islands (HM the Queen chartered this ship for her summer holiday in 2010).

» **Macbackpackers** (www.macbackpackers.com) Minibus tours for backpackers, using hostel accommodation, from Edinburgh to Loch Ness, Skye, Fort William, Glen Coe, Oban and Stirling.

» **Mountain Innovations** (www.scotmountain.co.uk) Guided activity holidays and courses in the Highlands; walking, mountain biking and winter mountaineering.

» **Rabbie's Trail Burners** (www.rabbies.com) One- to five-day tours of the Highlands in 16-seat minibuses with professional driver/guide.

» **Scot-Trek** (www.scot-trek.co.uk) Guided walks for all levels; ideal for solo travellers wanting to link up with others.

Train

Scotland's train network extends to all major cities and towns, but the railway map has a lot of large, blank areas in the Highlands where you'll need to switch to bus or car. The West Highland line from Glasgow to Fort William and Mallaig and the Inverness to Kyle of Lochalsh line offer two of the world's most scenic rail journeys.

» **National Rail Enquiry Service** (08457 48 49 50; www.nationalrail.co.uk) For info on train timetables.

» **ScotRail** (08457 55 00 33; www.scotrail.co.uk) Operates most train services in Scotland; website has downloadable timetables.

Costs & Reservations

Train travel is more expensive than the bus, but usually more comfortable: a standard return from Edinburgh to Inverness is about £55, compared with £26 on the bus.

Reservations are recommended for intercity trips, especially on Fridays and public holidays; for shorter journeys, just buy a ticket at the station before you go. On certain routes, and in places where there's no ticket office at the station (a frequent occurrence in the Highlands), you can buy tickets on the train.

SINGLE TRACK ROADS

In many parts of the Highlands and Islands you will find single track roads that are only wide enough for one vehicle. Passing places (usually marked with a white diamond sign, or a black-and-white striped pole) are used to allow oncoming traffic to pass. Passing places are also for overtaking – check your rear-view mirror often, and pull over to let faster vehicles pass if necessary. Be aware that it's illegal to park in passing places.

THE WEST HIGHLAND LINE

The West Highland Railway runs between Mallaig and Fort William through some of Scotland's wildest and most spectacular mountain scenery, and some of Britain's finest hiking terrain.

Stations such as Arrochar & Tarbet, Crianlarich, Bridge of Orchy and Spean Bridge allow you to set off on an endless array of wonderful mountain walks, direct from the platform. There are several opportunities for circular walks, or you can get off at one station, have yourself a jolly tramp, then jump on another train from another station. From Fort William Station it's only a few miles' walk to Britain's highest peak, Ben Nevis.

Possibly the most intriguing place to get off the train is at Corrour, which, at 408m, is Britain's highest and most remote station (there's no road access). It lies in the middle of Rannoch Moor (121), which was so soft and boggy that the line here had to be laid on a platform of earth, ashes and brushwood. It's a tribute to the railway's Victorian engineers that it has remained in place for over a century and nobody has ever managed (or wanted) to build a road up here. Film buffs will already know that Corrour is where Renton, Sick Boy, Spud and Tommy got back to nature in the film *Trainspotting*; unlike them, however, you won't be disappointed: from Corrour you can reach lonely peaks or wind your way through remote valleys that are out of reach to mere motorists.

Beyond Fort William the train runs through more glorious scenery and across the Glenfinnan Viaduct (of Harry Potter film fame) to Mallaig – the **Jacobite Steam Train** (☎0845 128 4681; www.steamtrain.info; day return adult/child £28/£16; ☉departs Fort William 10.20am and Mallaig 2.10pm Mon-Fri late May–early Oct, plus Sat & Sun Jul & Aug) also plies this section of the line – from where it's a short ferry ride to the Isle of Skye.

Children under five travel for free; kids aged five to 15 usually pay half-fare. On weekends on some intercity routes you can upgrade a standard-class ticket to 1st class for £3 to £5 per single journey – ask the conductor.

Bikes are carried free on all ScotRail trains but space is sometimes limited. Bike reservations are compulsory on certain train routes, including the Glasgow–Oban–Fort William–Mallaig line and the Inverness–Kyle of Lochalsh line; they are recommended on many others. You can make reservations for your bicycle from eight weeks to two hours in advance at main train stations, or when booking by phone.

There are several types of ticket; in general, the further ahead you can book the cheaper your ticket will be.

» **Advance Purchase** Book by 6pm on the day before travel; cheaper than Anytime.

» **Anytime** Buy and travel any time, with no restrictions.

» **Off-Peak** There are time restrictions (you're not usually allowed to travel on a train that leaves before 9.15am); relatively cheap.

Discount Cards

Discount **railcards** (☎0845 605 0525, textphone 0845 601 0132; www.railcard.co.uk) are available for people aged 60 and over, for people aged 16 to 25 (or mature full-time students), and for those with a disability. The **Senior Railcard** (£26), **Young Persons Railcard** (£26) and **Disabled Persons Railcard** (£18) are each valid for one year and give one-third off most train fares in Scotland, England and Wales. Fill in an application at any major train station. You'll need proof of age (birth certificate, passport or driving licence) for the Young Persons and Seniors railcards, proof of enrolment for mature-age students and proof of entitlement for the Disabled Persons Railcard.

Train Passes

ScotRail has a range of good-value passes for train travel. You can buy them at BritRail outlets in the USA, Canada and Europe; at the British Travel Centre in Regent St, London; at train stations throughout Britain; at certain UK travel agents and through **ScotRail Telesales** (☎08457 55 00 33; www .scotrail.co.uk). Note that Travelpass and Rover tickets are not valid for travel on certain (eg commuter) services before 9.15am weekdays.

Freedom of Scotland Travelpass Gives unlimited travel on all Scottish train services (some restrictions), all CalMac ferry services and on certain Scottish Citylink coach services (on routes not covered by rail). It's available for four days' travel out of eight (£114) or eight days out of 15 (£153).

Highland Rover Allows unlimited train travel from Glasgow to Oban, Fort William and Mallaig, and from Inverness to Kyle of Lochalsh, Aviemore, Aberdeen and Thurso; it also gives free travel on the Oban/Fort William to Inverness bus, on the Oban–Mull and Mallaig–Skye ferries, and on buses on Mull and Skye. It's valid for four days' travel out of eight (£74).

Glossary

For a glossary of Scottish place names, see the boxed text, p74.

bag – reach the top of (as in 'Munro bagging')
birlinn – Hebridean galley
blackhouse – low-walled stone cottage with thatch or turf roof and earth floors
böd – simple trading booths used by fishing communities, now used as basic accommodation
bothy – hut or mountain shelter
brae – hill
broch – defensive tower
burgh – town
burn – stream

cairn – pile of stones to mark a path or a peak
camanachd – Gaelic for *shinty*
ceilidh (*kay*-lay) – evening of traditional Scottish entertainment including music, song and dance
Celtic high cross – a large, elaborately carved stone cross decorated with biblical scenes and Celtic interlace designs dating from the 8th to 10th centuries
champit tatties – mashed potatoes

chippy – fish-and-chip shop
Clearances – eviction of Highland farmers from their land by lairds wanting to use it for grazing sheep
Clootie dumpling – rich steamed pudding filled with currants and raisins
close – entrance to an alley
corrie – circular hollow on a hillside
craig – exposed rock
crannog – an artificial island in a loch built for defensive purposes
crofting – smallholding in marginal agricultural areas following the Clearances
Cullen skink – soup made with smoked haddock, potato, onion and milk

dirk – dagger
dram – a measure of whisky

factor – land agent
firth – estuary

gloup – natural arch or blowhole
guizers – disguised men in Viking robes

Hogmanay – Scottish celebration of New Year's Eve
howff – pub or shelter
HS – Historic Scotland

kyle – narrow sea channel

laird – estate owner
linn – waterfall
loch – lake
lochan – small loch

machair – grass- and wildflower-covered dunes
Mercat Cross – a symbol of the trading rights of a market town or village, usually found in the centre of town and usually a focal point for the community
Munro – mountain of 3000ft (914m) or higher
Munro bagger – a hill walker who tries to climb all the Munros in Scotland

NNR – National Nature Reserve, managed by the SNH
NTS – National Trust for Scotland
nyuggle – ghostly horses
nyvaig – Hebridean galley

OS – Ordnance Survey

Picts – early inhabitants of north and east Scotland (from Latin *pictus,* or 'painted', after their body-paint decorations)

RIB – rigid inflatable boat
rood – an old Scots word for a cross
RSPB – Royal Society for the Protection of Birds

shinty – fast and physical ball-and-stick sport similar to Ireland's hurling
SMC – Scottish Mountaineering Club
SNH – Scottish Natural Heritage, a government organisation directly responsible for safeguarding and improving Scotland's natural heritage
SSSI – Site of Special Scientific Interest
SYHA – Scottish Youth Hostel Association

wynd – lane

behind the scenes

SEND US YOUR FEEDBACK

We love to hear from travellers – your comments keep us on our toes and help make our books better. Our well-travelled team reads every word on what you loved or loathed about this book. Although we cannot reply individually to postal submissions, we always guarantee that your feedback goes straight to the appropriate authors, in time for the next edition. Each person who sends us information is thanked in the next edition – and the most useful submissions are rewarded with a free book.

Visit **lonelyplanet.com/contact** to submit your updates and suggestions or to ask for help. Our award-winning website also features inspirational travel stories, news and discussions.

Note: We may edit, reproduce and incorporate your comments in Lonely Planet products such as guidebooks, websites and digital products, so let us know if you don't want your comments reproduced or your name acknowledged. For a copy of our privacy policy visit lonelyplanet.com/privacy.

AUTHOR THANKS

Neil Wilson

Many thanks to all the helpful and enthusiastic staff at tourist offices throughout the country, and to the many travellers I met on the road who chipped in with advice and recommendations. Thanks also to Carol Downie, and to Andy Symington, Andrew Henderson, Steven Fallon, Russell Leaper, Amy Hickman, Erlend Tait and Pamela Tait. Finally, thanks to the ever-helpful and patient editors and cartographers at Lonely Planet.

ACKNOWLEDGMENTS

Climate map data adapted from Peel MC, Finlayson BL & McMahon TA (2007) 'Updated World Map of the Köppen-Geiger Climate Classification', Hydrology and Earth System Sciences, 11, 163344.

Cover photograph:
The Old Man of Storm rock formation on the Isle of Skye. © Cheryl Forbes / Lonely Planet

Many of the images in this guide are available for licensing from Lonely Planet Images:
www.lonelyplanetimages.com.

THIS BOOK

The 2nd edition of *Scotland's Highlands & Islands* was researched and written by Neil Wilson. Joe Bindloss and Clay Lucas wrote the 1st edition. This guidebook was commissioned in Lonely Planet's London office, and produced by the following:

Commissioning Editor Dora Whitaker

Coordinating Editors Jocelyn Harewood, Ali Lemer

Coordinating Cartographers Anita Banh, Erin McManus

Coordinating Layout Designer Adrian Blackburn

Managing Editors Bruce Evans, Kirsten Rawlings

Senior Editor Angela Tinson

Managing Cartographers Adrian Persoglia, Amanda Sierp

Managing Layout Designer Jane Hart

Assisting Editors Beth Hall, Alan Murphy

Assisting Cartographer Alex Leung

Cover Research Rebecca Skinner

Internal Image Research Aude Vauconsant

Thanks to Chris Aitchison, Merlin Ananth, Sudha Ananth, Dan Austin, Karthick Balakrishnan, Gus Balbontin, Sasha Baskett, Anitha Bharanidharan, Nikki Buran, Sophia Cangan, David Carroll, Alan Castles, Lena Chan, Rebecca Chau, Gordon Christie, Helen Christinis, Daniel Corbett, Ryan Evans, Tobias Gattineau, Chris Girdler, Michelle Glynn, Satishna Gokuldas, Vasanthi Govindarajulu, Daniel Heath, Liz Heynes, David Hodges, Ken Hoetmer, Manju Krishnan, Sandeep Krishnan, Vijay Kumar, David Kunjumon, Anthony Langhorne, Ross Macaw, Ioomi Manners, Rowan McKinnon, Erin McManus, Darren O'Connell, Sunny Or, Krishnaprasad Palani, Jani Patokallio, Trent Paton, Martine Power, Suresh Ramani, Anthony Reinbach, Jon Ricketson, Averil Robertson, Luke Robins, Vaneesa Rowe, Wibowo Rusli, Fiona Siseman, Brent Snook, Satish Thayagu, Boopathi Vasan, Kavitha Velu, Sue Visic, Gerard Walker, Justin Wark

index

how to use this book

These symbols will help you find the listings you want:

👁	Sights	👉	Tours	🍷	Drinking
🏊	Beaches	🎉	Festivals & Events	☆	Entertainment
🏃	Activities	🛌	Sleeping	🛍	Shopping
🎓	Courses	🍴	Eating	ℹ	Information/Transport

These symbols give you the vital information for each listing:

📞	Telephone Numbers	📶	Wi-Fi Access	🚌	Bus
⏰	Opening Hours	🏊	Swimming Pool	⛴	Ferry
P	Parking	🥗	Vegetarian Selection	Ⓜ	Metro
⊖	Nonsmoking	🍽	English-Language Menu	Ⓢ	Subway
❄	Air-Conditioning	👪	Family-Friendly	⊖	London Tube
@	Internet Access	🐾	Pet-Friendly	🚊	Tram
				🚆	Train

Reviews are organised by author preference.

Look out for these icons:

TOP CHOICE — Our author's recommendation

FREE — No payment required

🌿 — A green or sustainable option

Our authors have nominated these places as demonstrating a strong commitment to sustainability – for example by supporting local communities and producers, operating in an environmentally friendly way, or supporting conservation projects.

Map Legend

Sights
- 🏖 Beach
- 🅰 Buddhist
- 🏰 Castle
- ✝ Christian
- 🕉 Hindu
- ☪ Islamic
- ✡ Jewish
- 🗽 Monument
- 🏛 Museum/Gallery
- 🏺 Ruin
- 🍷 Winery/Vineyard
- 🐾 Zoo
- ⦿ Other Sight

Activities, Courses & Tours
- 🤿 Diving/Snorkelling
- 🛶 Canoeing/Kayaking
- ⛷ Skiing
- 🏄 Surfing
- 🏊 Swimming/Pool
- 🚶 Walking
- 🏄 Windsurfing
- ➕ Other Activity/Course/Tour

Sleeping
- 🛏 Sleeping
- ⛺ Camping

Eating
- 🍴 Eating

Drinking
- ☕ Drinking
- ☕ Cafe

Entertainment
- ☆ Entertainment

Shopping
- 🛍 Shopping

Information
- 📮 Post Office
- ℹ Tourist Information

Transport
- ✈ Airport
- ⊗ Border Crossing
- 🚌 Bus
- 🚡 Cable Car/Funicular
- 🚲 Cycling
- ⛴ Ferry
- Ⓜ Metro
- 🚝 Monorail
- P Parking
- Ⓢ S-Bahn
- 🚕 Taxi
- 🚆 Train/Railway
- 🚊 Tram
- ⊖ Tube Station
- Ⓤ U-Bahn
- ● Other Transport

Routes
- Tollway
- Freeway
- Primary
- Secondary
- Tertiary
- Lane
- Unsealed Road
- Plaza/Mall
- Steps
- ⌇ Tunnel
- Pedestrian Overpass
- Walking Tour
- Walking Tour Detour
- Path

Boundaries
- International
- State/Province
- Disputed
- Regional/Suburb
- Marine Park
- Cliff
- Wall

Population
- ★ Capital (National)
- ◉ Capital (State/Province)
- ● City/Large Town
- ● Town/Village

Geographic
- 🏠 Hut/Shelter
- 🚨 Lighthouse
- 👁 Lookout
- ▲ Mountain/Volcano
- 🌴 Oasis
- 🌳 Park
-)(Pass
- 🏕 Picnic Area
- 💧 Waterfall

Hydrography
- River/Creek
- Intermittent River
- Swamp/Mangrove
- Reef
- Canal
- Water
- Dry/Salt/Intermittent Lake
- Glacier

Areas
- Beach/Desert
- + + + Cemetery (Christian)
- × × × Cemetery (Other)
- Park/Forest
- Sportsground
- Sight (Building)
- Top Sight (Building)

OUR STORY

A beat-up old car, a few dollars in the pocket and a sense of adventure. In 1972 that's all Tony and Maureen Wheeler needed for the trip of a lifetime – across Europe and Asia overland to Australia. It took several months, and at the end – broke but inspired – they sat at their kitchen table writing and stapling together their first travel guide, *Across Asia on the Cheap*. Within a week they'd sold 1500 copies. Lonely Planet was born.

Today, Lonely Planet has offices in Melbourne, London and Oakland, with more than 600 staff and writers. We share Tony's belief that 'a great guidebook should do three things: inform, educate and amuse'.

OUR WRITERS

Neil Wilson

Neil was born in Scotland and save for a few years spent abroad has lived there most of his life. A lifelong enthusiasm for the great outdoors has inspired hiking, biking and sailing expeditions to every corner of the country. While researching this book he fulfilled a long-held ambition to climb Suilven on a gloriously sunny spring day, sampled single malts at Highland Park Distillery and picnicked among the puffins at Hermaness. Neil has been a full-time author since 1988 and has written more than 50 guidebooks for various publishers, including Lonely Planet's guides to Scotland and his home town of Edinburgh.

Read more about Neil at:
lonelyplanet.com/members/neilwilson

Published by Lonely Planet Publications Pty Ltd
ABN 36 005 607 983
2nd edition – January 2012
ISBN 978 1 74059 537 7
© Lonely Planet 2012   Photographs © as indicated 2012
10 9 8 7 6 5 4 3 2 1
Printed in Singapore